BUG
the Backpackers Ultimate Guide

Britain & Ireland

BUG Britain & Ireland
First edition – May 2005

Published by:
BUG Backpackers Guide
ABN 47 801 693 475
Kilcunda, VIC 3995, Australia
www.backpackersultimateguide.com

Printed in China by Everbest Printing Co. Ltd.

National Library of Australia
Cataloguing in Publication data:

BUG Britain & Ireland

Includes index
ISBN 0 9581796 5 4

1. Backpacking – Great Britain - Guidebooks. 2. Backpacking – Ireland – Guidebooks. Great Britain – Guidebooks. 4. Ireland – Guidebooks. 5. Great Britain – Description ar travel. 6. Ireland – Description and travel.

914.10486

Cover photographs
Front cover: Rock of Cashel (Cashel, Co Tipperary, Ireland), Digital Vision
Back cover: River Thames from Waterloo Bridge with bus (London, England); www.britainc view.com; Big Ben (London, England), Ablestock; London Underground sign (London, En land), britainonview/Sheradon Dublin; Highland cow in front of a stone building (Duirinis Highland, Scotland), britainonview/Rod Edwards; Deacon Brodies pub on the Royal Mi (Edinburgh, Scotland); www.britainonview.com

copyright BUG Backpackers Guide © 2005

Maps are created using data and base maps supplied by Ordnance Survey (Great Britain), Ordnance Survey of Northern Ireland, Ordnance Survey Ireland and Graphi-Ogre/Geo-Atlas Public transport maps are supplied by CENTRO, GMPTE, SPT and Transport for London. Fu map acknowledgements are on page 435.

Disclaimer
This book is current at the time of writing and information may change after the publicatior date. Every effort has been made to make this book as complete and accurate as possible However, there may be mistakes, both typographical and in content. Furthermore this guid contains travel information that is current only up to the printing date.

There are many factors that may cause prices to change and establishments reviewed an listed in this book to close down or alter the services that they offer. Many hostels may also change their prices throughout the year to take advantage of variations in seasonal demand.

The reviews in this book are the opinion of the BUG researcher at the time of reviewing. This information is to be used as a general guide and readers should be aware that prices, opening hours, facilities and standards may change over time.

This book is not intended to be used as a sole source of information, but rather to complement existing sources of information such as word of mouth, travel brochures, timetables, travel magazines and other guidebooks. You are urged to read all the available material and talk to hostel staff and other travellers to learn as much as you can about you travel options.

Like anything in life, travel entails certain risks. BUG Backpackers Guide and the author shall have neither liability nor responsibility to any person or entity with respect to any loss or damage caused, or alleged to have been caused, directly or indirectly, by the informatior contained within this book.

If you do not wish to be bound by the above, you may return this book (as new) to the publisher for a refund.

BUG provides honest and independent travel advice. BUG Backpackers Guide does nc receive any payment in exchange for listing any establishment and BUG's researchers neve accept free accommodation in exchange for favourable reviews.

Contents

WELCOME — 11

ESSENTIALS — 14

GETTING AROUND — 29
Air 29
Bus 30
Train Travel 35
Driving 45
Hitchhiking 48

ENGLAND — 51

LONDON — 53

EAST ANGLIA — 97
Cambridgeshire 97
Cambridge 97
Ely 99
Norfolk 100
Kings Lynn 100
Castle Acre 101
North Norfolk Coast 101
Norwich 103
Great Yarmouth 104

SOUTHEAST ENGLAND — 106
Kent 106
Maidstone 106
Canterbury 107
Margate 109
Broadstairs 110
Dover 110
Deal 111
Sandwich 112
East Sussex 112
Rye 112
Hastings 113
Battle 114
Pevensey 115
Herstmonceux 115
Brighton 115
West Sussex 119
Arundel 119
Chichester 119
Hampshire 120
Portsmouth & Southsea 120
Southampton 125
Winchester 126

SOUTH WEST ENGLAND — 128
Wiltshire 128
Salisbury 128
Avebury 130
Dorset 131
Bournemouth & Poole 131
Devon 132
Exeter 132
Torbay (Torquay/Paignton/Brixham) .. 134
Plymouth 136
Ilfracombe 138
Bath, Bristol & Somerset 139
Bath 139
Bristol 143
Glastonbury 146
Wells 147
Cheddar 148
Cornwall 148
Fowey 148
Falmouth 149
Penzance 150
Lands End & the Penwith Peninsula .. 152
St Ives 153
Newquay 154
Tintagel 157
Bude 157

HEART OF ENGLAND — 158
Berkshire 158
Windsor & Eton 158
Oxfordshire 159
Henley-on-Thames 159
Oxford 160
Woodstock 162
Gloucestershire 163
Stow-on-the-Wold 163

4 Contents

Cheltenham 163	**Staffordshire** **179**
Gloucester....................................... 164	Stoke-on-Trent................................. 179
Warwickshire **165**	Lichfield... 180
Stratford-upon-Avon 165	**Leicestershire** **181**
Warwick... 167	Leicester 181
Kenilworth 168	**Lincolnshire**..................................**182**
Rugby.. 169	Lincoln 182
West Midlands **169**	**Nottinghamshire**...........................**183**
Birmingham 169	Nottingham...................................... 183
Coventry 175	Edwinstowe & Sherwood Forest........ 185
Shropshire.....................................**176**	**Derbyshire**....................................**186**
Ludlow 176	Derby 186
Shrewsbury...................................... 177	Peak District National Park............... 187
Ironbridge Gorge 177	

NORTH WEST ENGLAND 193

Manchester...................................**193**	Lancaster 206
Merseyside **199**	**Cumbria** **207**
Liverpool 199	Kendal 207
Cheshire **203**	Lake District National Park............... 208
Chester 203	Carlisle.. 213
Ellesmere Port 205	Dentdale 214
Lancashire **205**	
Blackpool 205	

YORKSHIRE 215

West Yorkshire..............................**215**	York 225
Leeds.. 215	Harrogate & Knareborough................ 228
Bradford 217	Ripon 229
Saltaire 218	North York Moors National Park........ 230
Haworth... 219	Helmsley 230
South Yorkshire.............................**220**	Pickering 231
Sheffield.. 220	Whitby... 231
Hull & East Riding of Yorkshire **223**	Robin Hoods Bay.............................. 232
Kingston-upon-Hull 223	Scarborough 233
Beverley 224	Yorkshire Dales National Park 234
North Yorkshire **225**	

NORTHUMBRIA 238

Tees Valley **238**	**Newcastle-upon-Tyne** **242**
Middlesbrough & Stockton-on-Tees ... 238	**Northumberland**............................**246**
Hartlepool.. 239	Alnwick.. 247
County Durham..............................**240**	Berwick-upon-Tweed 247
Barnard Castle................................. 240	Hadrian's Wall 248
Durham 240	Northumberland National Park.......... 249
Beamish 241	

WALES 251

Cardiff 253	Brecon (Aberhonddu) 263
Swansea 256	Abergavenny 264
Pembrokeshire Coast National Park.. 257	Blaenavon 264
Pembroke 259	Aberystwyth 265
St Davids 260	Snowdonia National Park 266
Fishguard 261	Porthmadog..................................... 269
Wye Valley....................................... 261	Harlech 270
Brecon Beacons National Park 262	Caernarfon 270

Conwy & Llandudno 271
Llangollen 272
Bangor 272
Isle of Anglesey (Ynys Môn) 272

SCOTLAND 275

SCOTTISH BORDERS 277
Jedburgh 277
Melrose 278

EDINBURGH 279

GLASGOW & STRATHCLYDE 291
Glasgow **291**
South Lanarkshire **300**
New Lanark 300
Ayrshire **300**
Ayr & Alloway 300
Isle of Arran 301

CENTRAL SCOTLAND 303
Argyll & Bute **303**
Loch Lomond 303
Inveraray 304
Oban 305
Stirling **306**
Stirling 306
The Trossachs 308
Fife **309**
St Andrews 309
Perthshire & Kinross **310**
Perth 310
Dunkeld & Birnam 311
Pitlochry 312
Aberdeen **313**

HIGHLAND 316
Fort William & Ben Nevis 316
Inverness & Loch Ness 319
Culrain & Carbisdale Castle 322
Drumnadrochit 322
Fort Augustus, Invermoriston
& Invergarry 323
Strathspey & the Cairngorms 324
Isle of Skye 328
Ullapool 333
Thurso 334
John O'Groats 334

WESTERN ISLES 337
Lewis 337
Harris 339
The Uists 340
Barra 342

ORKNEY & SHETLAND 343
Orkney Islands **343**
Shetland Islands **347**

NORTHERN IRELAND 349
County Derry **351**
Derry 351
Downhill 352
Portstewart 353
County Antrim **353**
Portrush 353
Bushmills & the Giant's Causeway ... 354
Ballintoy 354
Ballycastle 355
Cushendun 356
Belfast 356
Counties Down & Armagh **359**
Newcastle 359
Armagh 360

REPUBLIC OF IRELAND 361

LEINSTER 363
Co Dublin **363**
Dublin 363
Dún Laoghaire 376
Malahide 376
County Louth **377**
Drogheda 377
County Wicklow **378**
Wicklow 378
Wicklow Mountains National Park 378
County Wexford **379**

Enniscorthy (Inis Coirthaidth) 379
Wexford (Lough Garman) 380
Rosslare Harbour (Ros Láir) 380

MUNSTER
County Tipperary **383**
Tipperary 383
Cashel 384
County Waterford **385**
Waterford 385
County Cork **385**
Youghal 386
Cork 386
Cobh 388
Kinsale 389
Dunmanway 389
Clonakilty 390
Skibbereen 390
Baltimore 391
Cape Clear Island 391
Schull 391
Bantry 391

CONNAUGHT
County Galway **406**
Galway 406
Aran Islands 410
Clifden 411
Inishbofin 411
Letterfrack 412
Connemara National Park 412
Leenane 412

COUNTY DONEGAL
Donegal Town (Dún na nGall) 419
Slieve League Peninsula 420

INDEX

County Kilkenny **381**
Kilkenny (Cill Chainnigh) 381

383
Beara Peninsula 392
County Kerry **393**
Kenmare 393
Killarney 394
Killarney National Park 395
Ring of Kerry 396
Killorglin 397
Tralee 397
Dingle Peninsula 398
Tarbert 401
County Limerick **401**
Limerick 401
County Clare **402**
Ennis 402
Lahinch 404
Liscanor & the Cliffs of Moher 404
Doolin (Dubh Linn) 405

406
County Mayo **413**
Cong 413
Westport 414
Achill Island 415
Ballina 416
County Sligo **416**
Sligo 416

419
Letterkenny (Leitir Ceannain) 421
Inishowen Peninsula 421

423

Map Contents

BRITISH ISLES 8

ENGLAND 51

London
London Underground 60	Bristol 144
Bayswater & Paddington 72	Penzance... 151
Earls Court & Kensington................... 74	**Heart of England............................158**
Camden Town & Kings Cross 76	Oxford 161
West End.. 78	Birmingham 170
Victoria & Westminster 80	Birmingham Transport 172
The City & Southwark 82	**North West England.......................193**
South East England 106	Manchester 194
Canterbury....................................... 108	Manchester Metrolink Tram Network. 196
Brighton 116	Liverpool 199
Portsmouth...................................... 121	**Yorkshire 215**
South West England 128	Leeds.. 216
Salisbury 129	Sheffield.. 221
Exeter 133	York 226
Plymouth 137	**Northumbria 238**
Bath.. 140	Newcastle-upon-Tyne 243

WALES 251
Cardiff 254

SCOTLAND 275
Scottish Borders 277	**Highland 317**
Edinburgh......................................280	Cairngorms 324
Glasgow..294	Isle of Skye..................................... 329
Glasgow Transport 296	**Western Isles 337**
Central Scotland 303	**Orkney & Shetland Islands..............343**

NORTHERN IRELAND 349
Belfast 357

REPUBLIC OF IRELAND 361
Leinster 363	**Connaught 406**
Dublin 366	Galway 408
Munster 383	**Co Donegal 419**
Cork 387	

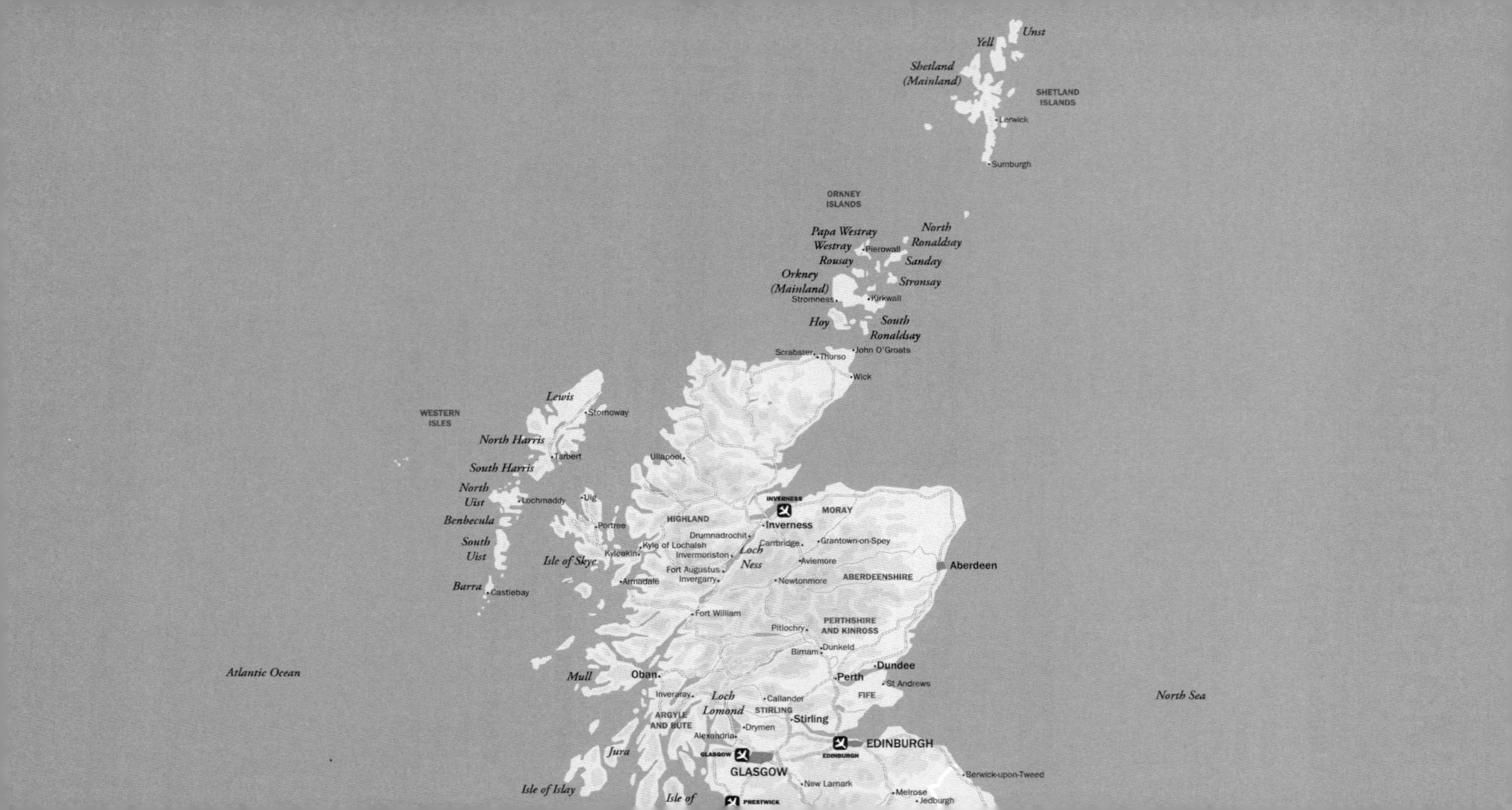
Unst
Yell
Shetland (Mainland)
SHETLAND ISLANDS
Lerwick
Sumburgh
ORKNEY ISLANDS
Papa Westray
Westray
Pierowall
North Ronaldsay
Sanday
Rousay
Orkney (Mainland)
Stronsay
Stromness
Kirkwall
Hoy
South Ronaldsay
Scrabster
Thurso
John O'Groats
Wick
WESTERN ISLES
Lewis
Stornoway
North Harris
Tarbert
South Harris
Ullapool
North Uist
Lochmaddy
Uig
Benbecula
Portree
South Uist
Isle of Skye
Kyleakin
Kyle of Lochalsh
Barra
Castlebay
Armadale
HIGHLAND
INVERNESS
Inverness
MORAY
Drumnadrochit
Invermoriston
Cairnbridge
Grantown-on-Spey
Loch Ness
Fort Augustus
Invergarry
Aviemore
Newtonmore
ABERDEENSHIRE
Aberdeen
Fort William
Pitlochry
PERTHSHIRE AND KINROSS
Birnam
Dunkeld
Atlantic Ocean
Mull
Oban
Dundee
Perth
St Andrews
FIFE
North Sea
Inveraray
Loch Lomond
Callander
STIRLING
Stirling
ARGYLE AND BUTE
Drymen
Alexandria
EDINBURGH
Jura
GLASGOW
GLASGOW
Berwick-upon-Tweed
Isle of Islay
New Lamark
Melrose
Jedburgh
Isle of
PRESTWICK

NEWCASTLE-UPON-TYNE
NORTHUMBERLAND
DUMFRIES AND GALLOWAY
TYNE AND WEAR
Carlisle
Durham
Hartlepool
CO DURHAM
TEES VALLEY
Middlesbrough
Whitby
Darlington
CUMBRIA
Kendal
Scarborough
NORTH YORKSHIRE
York
Lancaster
Harrogate
LEEDS
EAST RIDING OF YORKSHIRE
Kingston-upon-Hull
Blackpool
Blackburn
Bradford
Preston
Wakefield
MANCHESTER
LIVERPOOL
SHEFFIELD
Rotherham
LINCOLNSHIRE
Lincoln
Chester
Stoke-on-Trent
Derby
Nottingham
Shrewsbury
Telford
Leicester
BIRMINGHAM
Coventry
Rugby
Warwick
Stratford-upon-Avon
Worcester
Hereford
Cheltenham
Gloucester
Oxford
Milton Keynes
Cambridge
Kings Lynn
Norwich
Great Yarmouth
NORFOLK
SUFFOLK
ESSEX
Chelmsford
LONDON
Reading
Swindon
Bath
Bristol
Newport
Cardiff
Swansea
Caerphilly
Aberystwyth
Llandudno
Caernarfon
Margate
Canterbury
Dover
Maidstone
KENT
Hastings
Eastbourne
Brighton
Chichester
Winchester
Southampton
Portsmouth
Bournemouth
Salisbury
Dorchester
Exeter
Torquay
Plymouth
Barnstaple
Ilfracombe
Bude
Newquay
Fowey
Truro
Falmouth
Penzance
St Ives
Lands End
Isle of Man
Irish Sea
BELFAST
Ballycastle
Derry
Letterkenny
Donegal
Sligo
Armagh
Newry
Newcastle
Dundalk
Drogheda
DUBLIN
Dún Laoghaire
Wicklow
Ballina
Westport
Castlebar
Galway
Ennis
Limerick
Kilkenny
Enniscorthy
Wexford
Waterford
Tralee
Killarney
Kenmare
Cork
Achill Island
Clare Island
Inishbofin
Aran Islands
Valentia Island
Cape Clear Island
200km

Welcome

Welcome to BUG

BUG is the Backpackers' Ultimate Guide and we believe this is the best guidebook available for anyone backpacking around Great Britain and Ireland. We set out to publish a guidebook dedicated solely to backpackers (independent budget travellers). You won't find any information about fancy hotels in this book and because of this we can better concentrate on giving you honest and detailed information about hostels and budget travel options across Ireland and the UK. Compare us with other guides, you'll find that we have more details on more hostels for any given destination.

This is the first edition of BUG Britain & Ireland and it features BUG's unique hostel star rating system that has been tested in BUG's guidebooks to Australia and New Zealand.

How to use this book

The BUG team has travelled extensively and know what should be in a guidebook and what you can find out for yourself. We've kept this in mind when putting this book together to ensure that it's packed with loads of useful information and not weighed down with stuff you don't need.

This book won't bore you with the trivial details of history or politics. Instead of making you lug around an extra 100 or more pages we jump straight into the useful stuff.

The Essentials chapter has information on passports and visas, discount cards and money. Boring, but important things that you need to know before you arrive.

The next chapter is Getting Around – we don't tell you how to get to Britain or Ireland because that's what travel agents are for. The Getting Around chapter has the low-down on transport options in Great Britain and Ireland including details on bus and train passes, hitchhiking, flying and driving. Read this before you buy your ticket so you know whether you're getting a good deal when the travel agent tries to sell you a travel pass.

After these introductory chapters it's straight into the destination chapters. There are chapters for major regions within England, Wales, Scotland, Northern Ireland and the Republic of Ireland, which are organised geographically by county. The book starts in London and then covers southeastern and southwestern England before making its way north. The Northern Ireland chapter starts in Derry before making its way along the coast towards Belfast and the Ireland chapters start in Dublin and move clockwise around the country.

When you arrive in a new destination you generally want to find a place to stay, take your backpack off and start exploring. We have put details on local transport and accommodation at the start of each destination guide, so you can choose where you want to stay and find your way there.

Once you've checked into a hostel you'll find that the staff behind the front desk are experts on the local area and will be able to help you with any little questions such as where to do your laundry, check your email or grab a bite to eat. For this reason we cut out the crap such as restaurant reviews and shopping information to make room for much more comprehensive accommodation reviews.

We have organised the information on accommodation and attractions so that every listing is followed by the address, the closest underground stations and which bus routes stop nearby, telephone number, website address, prices and opening hours (reception hours for accommodation listings).

Some hostels give discounts to holders of VIP and Hostelling International hostel cards. When we list accommodation prices the discounted price is shown after the full price as follows: Dorm bed £14 (£13 HI/SYHA). Because An Óige, HINI, SYHA and YHA are all part of Hostelling International we list this as HI/An Óige, HI/YHA, etc. depending on which country you are travelling in. Just because a hostel offers a discount to someone holding a card from a particular hostel organisation is no indication that that hostel is affiliated with it. Where a price range is specified, for example: (Dorm bed €15-34), the low price is often the cheapest bed off-season and the high price the most expensive in the peak season. In a lot of hostels the cheapest beds are in the largest dormitories and the more expensive ones in the small dorms. In some cities – especially Dublin – prices can skyrocket during special events like rugby weekends and St Patrick's Day.

In BUG, we define a dormitory bed (or dorm bed) as any bed in a room that you share with other people with whom you are not travelling. In Great Britain and Ireland most dorms have four to six beds. We quote the price per person for a dorm bed and the price per room for single, double and twin rooms. We classify a double room as a private room with one double, queen or king-size bed in it. A twin room is a private room with two single beds.

Some small hostels don't keep regular reception hours, in this case we don't list any hours. If the reception is unattended there is often a phone number to call to contact the manager who usually isn't far away. If you're arriving late it's a good idea to call in advance to arrange a bed for the night, in many cases you may be able to check in after reception hours if this is arranged in advance.

Each hostel review includes symbols indicating that hostel's facilities. These symbols are:
- 🅿 Off street parking
- 🅿 Secure off street parking
- ♿ Wheelchair access
- 🔒 Lockers for each dormitory bed
- 📺 TV lounge
- 🍳 Kitchen
- 🧺 Laundry
- 🍺 Bar
- 🏊 Swimming pool
- 🎾 Tennis court
- 🚲 Free use of bicycles
- ⊗ Women only hostel (no male guests allowed)
- 🚫 No alcohol allowed
- 🔓 Not all dormitories can be locked

BUG's hostel ratings

We wanted to provide the most comprehensive resource that could quickly describe a hostel while also providing more in depth information on hostels than any other guidebook. To achieve this we set about creating our own star rating system that highlighted the maintenance and cleanliness, facilities, atmosphere and character and security of each hostel while also providing an overall rating.

BUG's hostel reviewers fill out a comprehensive form that collects information about various features, which are then rated to calculate that hostel's star rating. In addition to determining an objective star rating, the BUG hostel reviewer also writes a more subjective review of each hostel.

The individual ratings for particular characteristics are a handy way for travellers to choose a hostel based on what is important to them. For instance if a place with a great atmosphere is more important to you than cleanliness and maintenance, then you can just look at the atmosphere & character star rating rather than the other ratings.

When we set about creating our hostel rating system, we used what we believe are the best hostels as a benchmark for being awarded five stars. For instance we looked at the hostel we thought offered the most facilities to calculate our scoring system for this category. We did the same for security, cleanliness and atmosphere. It is very rare to find a hostel that excels in each area and because of this we have yet to award a full five stars to any hostel but any place with an overall score of four stars or higher can be considered outstanding.

The 'cleanliness and maintenance' rating shows how clean and well maintained the hostel is. A brand new purpose built place should score five stars and recently renovated hostels shouldn't be too far behind. The 'facilities' rating indicates the extent, but not necessarily the quality, of the facilities and amenities. The 'atmosphere and character' rating combines the charm of the building with the "fun factor" of staying at the hostel. The 'security' rating indicates the degree of security precautions that the hostel has taken for its guests.

The overall rating is calculated by averaging the other four ratings, weighted to give priority to the most important aspects of the hostel

There are other rating systems out there. Individual tourism organisations such as the English, Scottish and Welsh national tourist boards also produce a star rating system for hostels. The main differences between these and BUG's rating system are that we developed our rating system from the ground up as a hostel rating (rather than an adaptation of a hotel rating), we rate every hostel and the BUG score is broken into categories so you can see how the overall score is awarded. Unlike the score given by the tourism organisations, hostels don't choose to be rated and we certainly don't make them pay for a rating or give advance warning that we are coming so they can make their hostel look nice for us. Furthermore, while tourism boards have a vested interest in promoting tourism, we are concerned solely with providing honest, independent and unbiased advice.

We use the same criteria to rate hostels regardless of where they are in the world. No other hostel rating system has the same international consistency and you can be confident that a 3½ star hostel in Edinburgh will offer a similar standard of accommodation as a hostel in Sydney that has the same BUG rating.

Help keep us up-to-date

Although we update everything every year it is impossible to keep everything current for the entire life of this guide.

If you find something wrong please let us know so we can keep everyone up-to-date; you can email us at editor@bugeurope.com or fax us at +61 3 5678 7033 or (03) 5678 7033 from within Australia. If you think one of our hostel reviews is way off track, you can write your own review on our website (www.bugeurope.com).

We update our website with the correct details as soon as we know them. Check our website (www.bugeurope.com) for up-to-date facts.

Visit us on the Web

BUG started out in 1997 with a small website about budget travel in Europe and we have grown to become an extensive network of websites that can be accessed from our homepage *(www.bug.co.uk)*. This guide is online *(www.bugeurope.com)* and features interactive hostel reviews where you can write your own reviews of hostels all over Britain and Ireland (and also elsewhere in Europe, plus Australia, New Zealand and the Pacific islands). There are also forums where you can share travel tips with other travellers and a ride sharing service *(http://europe.bugride.com)* where you can organise a lift around the British Isles and also on the European continent.

Our network of websites extends beyond Britain, Ireland and Europe and includes budget travel information on Australia, New Zealand and the Pacific.

If you're also planning on visiting New Zealand and other Pacific islands such as Fiji or Hawaii; then take a look at BUG Pacific (www.bugpacific.com). BUG Australia (website www.bugaustralia.com is useful if you're planning to travel around Australia. During the course of 2005 BUG will launch websites for budget travel in the Americas (www.bugamerica.com) and Asia (www.bugasia.com).

Essentials

Tourism Offices

There are national tourism associations for England, Scotland, Wales, Northern Ireland and the Republic of Ireland as well as a tourism board covering the entire United Kingdom. Most tourism offices maintain information centres and also provide information online.

British Tourist Authority

The BTA encompasses the tourist organisations for England, Scotland, Wales and Northern Ireland. It runs the Visit Britain website, which is a good starting point for researching your trip to the UK.
Website www.visitbritain.com

Each country in the United Kingdom also operates its own national tourist board.

English Tourist Board
Website www.visitengland.com

Scottish Tourist Board
Website www.visitscotland.com

Welsh Tourist Board
Website www.visitwales.com

Northern Ireland Tourist Board
Website www.discovernorthernireland.com

Bord Fáilte (Irish Tourist Board)

The Irish Tourist Board has maintains a network of tourist information centres throughout the Republic of Ireland.
Website www.ireland.travel.ie

Tourism Ireland

Tourism Ireland is the tourism organisation that promotes the whole of Ireland (the Republic of Ireland plus Northern Ireland).
Website www.tourismireland.com

Entry Requirements

Everyone needs a valid passport to travel to Ireland and the United Kingdom and some travellers may need a visa to enter either country depending upon their nationality, length of stay or purpose of their visit.

Passports

It is essential that your passport does not expire within six months of entering the UK or Ireland or you will not be allowed into the country – even if you're only planning on staying a few days.

You should allow plenty of time to apply for a new passport, although some passport agencies will rush your application for an additional cost.

Most travellers apply for a passport at the passport agency in their home country, but people living outside their country of citizenship should apply through their nearest embassy or consulate.

Australia

You can get passport application forms and apply for a passport at one of 1700 Australia Post passport agencies.

You will need to make an appointment for an interview at a post office and bring along your completed application form and original documents confirming your citizenship and identity. Australian passports cost $150 for a 32-page passport or $226 for a 64-page passport. They are usually issued within 10 days.

Contact the Australian Passport Information Service (☎ *13 12 32; website* www.passports.gov.au) for further information.

Canada

To obtain a passport you will need the following: two identical passport photos; at least one document, such as a drivers' licence, to prove your identity; proof of Canadian citizenship; any previous Canadian passport, certificate of identity or refugee travel document issued to you in the last five years; a completed application form and the application fee. A Canadian passport costs CDN$85-90 and is usually issued within eight working days, although you should allow additional time for your passport to arrive through the mail.

You can either apply at your local passport office or by sending your application forms to the main passport office in Hull, Québec.
The Passport Office, Place du Centre Commercial, Level 2, 200 Promenade du Portage, Hull, Québec J8X 4B7
☎ *(819) 994 3500 or 1800 567 6868*
Website *www.ppt.gc.ca*

New Zealand
New Zealand passport application forms can be downloaded from the passport office website and are also available from most travel agencies. Completed application forms should be sent to the passport office in Wellington along with two passport photos and the NZ$71 application fee. If you were not born in New Zealand you may also need to send proof of citizenship and identity along with your passport application. In most cases passport applications are processed within 10 working days. New Zealand passports are valid for 10 years.
The Department of Internal Affairs, Passport Office, PO Box 10-526, Wellington
☎ *0800 22 50 50*
Website *www.passports.govt.nz*

South Africa
Passport application forms are available at all Department of Home Affairs offices in South Africa and South African consulates and embassies abroad. South African passports are valid for 10 years and cost R135. Passport applications take around six weeks.
Department of Home Affairs, Civitas Building, 242 Struben Street, Pretoria
☎ *(012) 314 8911*
Website *www.home-affairs.gov.za*

United States
US citizens can apply for a passport at over 6,000 public places that accept passport applications, which include courthouses, and many post offices. Applications can take longer than eight weeks to be processed but applications lodged at one of 13 passport offices are processed quicker – usually within five weeks. Passports cost US$55 plus a US$30 execution fee.

For more information, contact the US Passport office (☎ *(202) 647 0518;* ***website*** *http://travel.state.gov/passport_services.html*).

Tourist Visas
All travellers visiting Ireland and the United Kingdom require a valid passport. Citizens of European Union countries plus Australia, Canada, New Zealand, South Africa and the United States do not require a visa to visit Ireland or the United Kingdom. However visas may be required for longer visits or if you plan on working.

IRELAND
Travellers from European Union countries plus Australia, Canada, New Zealand, South Africa and the United States do not require a tourist visa for visits of up to 90 days. You should contact your nearest Irish embassy or consulate if you're from a country that requires a visa.

UNITED KINGDOM
Travellers from Switzerland, European Union countries and countries in the European Economic Area do not require a visa to visit the United Kingdom.

Travellers from Australia, Canada, Hong Kong SAR, Japan, Malaysia, New Zealand, Singapore, South Africa, South Korea and the USA do not require a visa for visits of up to six months. However you may be asked to show that you have an onward ticket plus enough money to support yourself while in the United Kingdom.

See the UK Visas website *(**website** www.ukvisas.gov.uk)* for more information.

Embassies, Consulates & High Commissions
BRITISH EMBASSIES, CONSULATES & HIGH COMMISSIONS
Australia
British High Commission (Canberra), Level 10, SAP House, Corner Akuna & Bunda Streets, Canberra
☎ *(02) 6270 6666*
Website *www.uk.emb.gov.au*
Open *Mon-Fri 9am-3pm*

British Consulate (Melbourne), 17th Floor, 90 Collins Street, Melbourne
☎ *(03) 9652 1600*
Open *Mon-Fri 9am-4.30pm*

British Consulate (Sydney), 16th Floor, 1 Macquarie Place, Sydney
☎ *(02) 9247 7521*
Open *Mon-Fri 9am-5pm*

Canada
British High Commission (Ottawa), 80 Elgin Street, Ottawa
☎ *(613) 237 1530*
Website *www.britainincanada.org*
Open *Mon-Fri 8.30am-4.30pm*

British Consulate-General (Montréal), Suite 4200, 1000 rue de la Gauchetière Ouest, Montréal
☎ *(514) 866 5863*
Website *www.britainincanada.org*
Open *Mon-Fri 8.30am-5pm*

British Consulate-General (Toronto), Suite 2800, 777 Bay Street, Toronto
☎ *(416) 593 1290*
Website *www.britainincanada.org*
Open *Mon-Fri 9am-4.30pm*

British Consulate-General (Vancouver), Suite 800, 1111 Melville Street, Vancouver
☎ *(604) 683 4421*
Website *www.britainincanada.org*
Open *Mon-Fri 8.30am-4.30pm*

Ireland
British Embassy (Dublin), 27 Merrion Road, Ballsbridge
☎ *(01) 205 3700*
Website *www.britishembassy.ie*
Open *Mon-Thu 9am-12.45pm & 2pm-5.15pm; Fri 9am-12.45pm & 2pm-5pm*

New Zealand
British High Commission (Wellington), 44 Hill Street, Wellington
☎ *(04) 924 7356*
Website *www.britain.org.nz*
Open *Mon-Fri 8.45am-5pm*

British Consulate-General (Auckland), 17th Floor, NZI House, 151 Queen Street, Auckland
☎ *(09) 303 2973*
Open *Mon-Fri 9am-5pm*

South Africa
British High Commission (Pretoria), 255 Hill Street, Arcadia 0002, Pretoria
☎ *(012) 421 7500*
Website *www.britishhighcommission.gov.uk*
Open *Mon-Thu 8am-5pm, Fri 8am-12.30pm*

British Consulate-General (Cape Town), 15th Floor, Southern Life Centre, 8 Riebeck Street, Cape Town
☎ *(021) 405 2400*
Website *www.britishhighcommission.gov.uk*
Open *Mon-Thu 9am-3pm, Fri 9am-12.30pm*

USA
British Embassy (Washington DC), 3100 Massachusetts Avenue NW, Washington DC 20008
☎ *(202) 588 7800*
Website *www.britainusa.com/embassy/*
Open *Mon-Fri 9am-5.30pm*

British Consulate-General (Atlanta), Georgia Pacific Centre, Suite 3400, 133 Peachtree Street NE, Atlanta GA 30303
☎ *(404) 954 7700*
Website *www.britainusa.com/consular/atlanta/*
Open *Mon-Fri 9am-noon & 2pm-4pm*

British Consulate-General (Boston), One Memorial Drive, Suite 1500, Cambridge MA 02142
☎ *(617) 245 4500*
Website *www.britainusa.com/boston/*
Open *Mon-Fri 8.30am-12.30pm & 1.30pm-5pm*

British Consulate-General (Chicago), 13th Floor, The Wrigley Building, 400 N Michigan Avenue, Chicago IL 60611
☎ *(312) 970 3800*
Website *www.britainusa.com/chicago/*
Open *Mon-Fri 9am-11am*

British Consulate-General (Dallas), 2911 Turtle Creek Boulevard, Suite 940, Dallas TX 75219
☎ *(214) 521 4090*
Website *www.britainusa.com/dallas/*
Open *Mon-Fri 9am-1pm*

British Consulate-General (Denver),
Suite 1030, World Trade Center, 1675
Broadway, Denver CO 80202
☎ *(303) 592 5200*
Website *hwww.britainusa.com/denver/*
Open *Mon-Fri 9am-1pm*

British Consulate-General (Houston),
Wells Fargo Plaza, 19th Floor, 1000
Louisiana, Suite 1900, Houston TX
77002
☎ *(713) 659 6270*
Website *www.britainusa.com/houston/*
Open *Mon-Fri 9am-5pm*

British Consulate-General (Los Angeles),
11766 Wilshire Boulevard, Suite 1200,
Los Angeles, CA 90025
☎ *(310) 481 0031*
Website *www.britainusa.com/la/*
Open *Mon-Fri 8.30am-noon & 2pm-4pm*

*British Consulate-General
(San Francisco), 1 Sansome Street,
Suite 850, San Francisco, CA 94104*
☎ *(415) 617 1300*
Website *www.britainusa.com/sf/*
Open *Mon-Fri 8.30am-5pm*

IRISH EMBASSIES & CONSULATES

Australia
Irish Embassy (Canberra),
20 Arkana Street, Yarralumba
☎ *(02) 6273 3022*
Open *Mon-Fri 9.30am-12.45pm & 2pm-4pm*

Irish Consulate-General (Sydney),
Level 30, 400 George Street, Sydney
☎ *(02) 9231 6999*

Canada
Irish Embassy (Ottawa),
Suite 1105, 130 Albert Street, Ottawa
☎ *(613) 233 6281*

Irish Honorary Consul (Calgary),
3808-8A Street SW, Calgary
☎ *(403) 243 2970*

Irish Honorary Consul (Montréal),
1590 Dr Penrose Avenue, Montréal
☎ *(514) 848 7389*

*Irish Honorary Consul (Toronto), Suite
1210, 20 Toronto Street, Toronto*
☎ *(416) 366 9300*

Irish Honorary Consul (Vancouver),
401-1385 West 8th Avenue, Vancouver
☎ *(604) 683 9233*

New Zealand
*Irish Honorary Consul (Auckland), 6th
Floor, 18 Shortland Street, Auckland*
☎ *(09) 977 2252*
Website *www.ireland.co.nz*

South Africa
*Irish Embassy (Pretoria), First Floor,
Southern Life Plaza, 1059 Schoeman
Street, Arcadia 0083, Pretoria*
☎ *(012) 342 5062*
Website *www.emassyireland.org.za*

United Kingdom
*Irish Embassy (London), 17 Grosvenor
Place, London*
☎ *(020) 7235 2171*

*Irish Consulate General (Cardiff), 2
Fitzalan Road, Cardiff*
☎ *(029) 2066 2000*

*Irish Consulate General (Edinburgh), 16
Randolph Crescent, Edinburgh*
☎ *(0131) 226 7711*

USA
Irish Embassy (Washington DC),
2234 Massachusetts Avenue NW, Washington DC
☎ *(202) 462 3939*
Website *www.irelandemb.org*
Open *Mon-Fri 9am-1pm & 2pm-4pm*

Irish Consulate-General (Boston),
535 Boylston Street, Boston
☎ *(617) 267 9330*
Open *Mon-Fri 10am-3pm*

Irish Consulate-General (Chicago),
400 N Michigan Avenue, Suite 911,
Chicago
☎ *(312) 337 1868*
Open *Mon-Fri 10am-noon*

*Irish Consulate-General (New York),
Ireland House, 17th Floor, 345 Park
Avenue, New York*

☎ *(212) 319 2555*
Open *Mon-Fri 10am-3pm*

Irish Consulate-General (San Francisco), 100 Pine Street, 33rd Floor, San Francisco
☎ *(415) 392 4214*
Open *Mon-Fri 10am-noon & 2pm-3.30pm*

Working

Because of the common language and availability of working holiday permits, both Ireland and the United Kingdom are popular spots for travellers to find work.

IRELAND

Ireland has a working holiday programme open to citizens of Australia, Canada and New Zealand and US citizens may work in Ireland through the CIEE work exchange programme.

Working Holidays for Australians

Australians aged between 18 and 30 may apply for a working holiday permit that allows them to work in Ireland for up to one year, although you may not work for any one employer for longer than three months. Applications to the Irish embassy in Canberra must include a bank draft for €60 and applicants under 25 years must provide a copy of their Year 12 Certificate, while applicants aged over 25 must provide qualifications, their CV and employment references. You should allow four to six weeks for your application to be processed.

Working Holidays for Canadians

Canadians wanting to apply for a working holiday authorisation must apply through the Student Work Abroad Programme *(SWAP; **website** www.swap.ca)*. The programme is open to full time tertiary students aged over 18 and to non-students aged 18 to 35. It allows you to work in Ireland for up to one year. The application fee is CDN$345 and you may be asked to show access to CDN$2000.

SWAP also has a Britain/Ireland combo working holiday programme that allows you to work in the UK for two years and in Ireland for one year. It is open to Canadians aged 18 to 30; the application fee is CDN$550 and you may be asked to show funds of CDN$2500.

Working Holidays for New Zealanders

New Zealand citzens aged between 18 and 30 may apply for a working holiday authorisation from the Honorary Consul in Auckland. Applicants must be resident in New Zealand at the time of application and they must have an onward ticket and provide evidence of access to at least NZ$2500.

CIEE Work Exchange Programmes for US Citizens

US Citizens can work in Ireland but they have to apply through the Council on International Educational Exchange *(CIEE;* ☎ *1 207 553 7600 from USA; **website** www.ciee.org)*. This programme allows you to work for up to four months.

The programme is open to students who are US citizens or permanent US residents. You must begin the programme within six months of your most recent full time study.

The exchange programme costs US$375 plus an additional US$40 per month insurance fee. You will need to allow up to four weeks for your application to be processed.

UNITED KINGDOM

There are several programmes that allow travellers to legally work in the UK.

Au Pairs

Citizens of Andorra, Bosnia-Herzegovina, Bulgaria, Croatia, Faroe Islands, Greenland, Macedonia, Monaco, Romania, San Marino and Turkey aged between 17 and 27 can come to the UK to study English under the au pair scheme.

Under this programme you can live for up to two years with an English-speaking family working in the home for up to five hours day in exchange for accommodation in your own room and a recommended weekly allowance of £55.

To qualify for this scheme you must show that you:
- are not married
- have no dependents
- will leave the UK within two years
- will not need help from public funds
- plan to leave the United Kingdom when you complete your stay as an au pair

The International Au Pair Association (*website* www.iapa.org) can refer you to an agency that can match you with a host family.

If you intend on coming to the United Kingdom under this scheme you must apply for entry clearance through a British embassy, consulate or high commission.

Gap Year Entrants

This immigration category allows non-EAA nationals to come to the United Kingdom to work in schools during their 'gap year' (between secondary and tertiary education).

To qualify as a gap year entrant you must:
- be 18 or 19 years old
- have completed secondary education less than 12 months ago
- have an offer of a place on a degree course outside the UK that will commence after you have left the UK
- have a written employment offer as a teacher or teaching assistant in a school in the UK for three consecutive academic terms
- intend to take this employment and not intend to take any other employment
- have the means to pay for your return or onward journey

You can stay in the United Kingdom for up to 12 months as a gap year entrant.

If you intend on coming to the United Kingdom under this scheme you must apply for entry clearance through a British embassy, consulate or high commission.

Working Holidaymaker Programme

The Working Holidaymaker scheme allows people from Commonwealth countries aged between 17 and 30 to come to the United Kingdom for up to two years, taking casual or temporary work as part of a working holiday.

You qualify as a working holidaymaker if you meet these conditions:
- you are a British Dependent Territories citizen, a British Overseas citizen or a citizen of a Commonwealth country
- you are aged 17 to 30
- you are either single or married to someone who also qualifies as a working holiday maker; if you are married you must both plan to take the working holiday together
- you have no dependent children who will reach five before returning home from your holiday
- you will not need help from public funds
- you have enough money to pay for your return or onward journey
- you plan to leave the United Kingdom at the end of your holiday

You must get an entry clearance as a working holidaymaker through a British embassy, consulate or high commission.

Refer to the Home Office website *(www.workingintheuk.gov.uk)* for more information.

Canadians can also apply for a working holiday visa through the Student Work Abroad Programme *(SWAP; website www.swap.ca)*. This is open to Canadian citizens aged 18 to 30 allowing you to work in the UK for up to two years. The application fee is CDN$315 and you have to show access to funds of CDN$2,500.

Tax

If you're working in Ireland or the UK you will have to pay tax on your income there.

IRELAND

If you're working in Ireland you will be taxed at a rate of 24% on the first €30,000 you earn each year.

You will need to get a Personal Public Service (PPS) number before you start working in Ireland. You can apply for a PPS number from a Social Welfare office *(website www.welfare.ie)*. Call (01) 878 6444 for the address of your nearest Social Welfare office and bring your passport with a work permit and proof of your address when you come in to apply for your number. The application process takes around two weeks.

Contact the Irish Revenue Commissioners *(website www.revenue.ie)* for more information on tax matters in Ireland.

UNITED KINGDOM

If you're working in the United Kingdom you will pay tax ranging from 10 to 40% depending on how much you earn.

You will need to get a National Insurance number before you start work in the United Kingdom. You will need to bring your passport, proof of your address and other identification to your local Department of Social Security (DSS) office. Expect to spend plenty of time waiting at the DSS office plus a further couple of months waiting for your National Insurance number to arrive in the mail. Call (020) 7712 2171 for details of your nearest DSS office.

If you don't work a full tax year or leave the UK before the end of the financial year (5 April) you will most likely be owed a tax refund.

There are plenty of tax refund agencies advertising in backpacker magazines like TNT at the end of each tax year, however doing your own tax return is a fairly simple process in the UK and it is a waste of money to pay someone else to do this for you.

Finding Work

Your best option for work is to register at temporary employment agencies. This fits within the scope of your working holiday permit and also lines you up with reasonably well paying work. You could try one of the following agencies:

IRELAND
Accounting Solutions
Accountancy, banking and finance
Merchants Hall, 25-26 Merchants Quay, Dublin
☎ *(01) 679 7990*
Website *www.accountancysolutions.ie*

Accreate
Accountancy, banking and finance
5 Fitzwilliam Square East, Dublin
☎ *(01) 661 2000*
Website *www.accreate.com*

Alliance Nurses Agency
Nursing
59 Merrion Square, Dublin
☎ *(01) 678 7333*
Website *www.alliancenurses.ie*

BrightWater Selection
Accounting, banking and finance
36 Merrion Square, Dublin
☎ *(01) 662 1000*
Website *www.brightwater.ie*

O'Neill & Brennan
Construction and engineering work
Unit 2, Ballymount Business Park, Lower Ballymount Road, Dublin
☎ *(01) 456 9899*
Website *www.oneillandbrennan.com*

Osborne
General office work including data entry, receptionists and secretarial
104 Lower Baggot Street, Dublin
☎ *(01) 638 4400*
Website *www.osborne.ie*

TMP/Hudson Global Resources
Accounting and finance, IT and sales and marketing
10 Lower Mount Street, Dublin
☎ *(01) 676 5000*
Website *http://ie.hudsonresourcing.com*

UNITED KINGDOM
A Star Teachers
Teaching
Unit 31, City North, Seven Sisters Road, Finsbury Park, London N4
🚇 *Finsbury Park*
☎ *(020) 7272 7070*
Website *www.astarteachers.co.uk*

Accountancy Additions
Accounting and finance
Devonshire House, 146 Bishopsgate, London EC2
🚇 *Liverpool Street*

☎ *(020) 7247 6414*
Website *www.accountancyadditions.com*

Anders Elite
Engineering
69 Old Broad Street, London EC2
⊖🚇 *Liverpool Street*
☎ *(020) 7256 5555*
Website *www.anderselite.com*

Badenoch & Clark
Accountancy and finance, legal, sales and marketing
16-18 New Bridge Street, London EC4
⊖🚇 *Blackfriars*
☎ *(020) 7583 0073*
Website *www.badenochandclark.com*

Banking Additions
Banking and finance
50 Cannon Street, London EC4
⊖🚇 *Cannon Street*
☎ *(020) 7269 1991*
Website *www.bankingadditions.com*

Capita Education Resourcing
Teaching
☎ *0800 731 6871*
Website *www.capitaers.co.uk*

Classroom Teachers
Teaching
☎ *(020) 7636 0600*
Website *www.classroomteachers.co.uk*

Elite Recruitment Specialists
Medical laboratory staff, occupational therapists, pharmacists, physiotherapists, social workers and speech therapists
11 Grosvenor Place, London SW1
🚇 *Hyde Park Corner*
☎ *0800 43 53 63*
Website *www.elitemedical.co.uk*

Finance Professionals
Accountancy and finance
26-28 Bedford Row, London WC1
🚇 *Chancery Lane, Holborn*
☎ *(020) 7845 4110*
Website *www.financeprofessionals.com*

Indigo Selection
Accountancy and finance, legal
7 Hanover Square, London W1
🚇 *Oxford Circus*
☎ *(020) 7930 9066*
Website *www.indigoselection.com*

Montagu Nurses
Nursing
18 Nottingham Place, London W1
🚇 *Baker Street*
☎ *(020) 7486 0818*
Website *www.montagugroup.co.uk*

Nigel Lynn Associates
Accountancy
1st Floor, 30-31 Furnival Street, London EC4
🚇 *Chancery Lane*
☎ *(020) 7269 5850*
Website *www.nigel-lynn.com*

Office Angels
General office work, receptionists
67-69 George Street, London W1
🚇 *Oxford Circus*
☎ *(020) 7935 7248*
Website *www.office-angels.com*

Verity Legal
Legal secretaries
10 South Molton Street, London W1
🚇 *Bond Street*
☎ *(020) 7493 0437*
Website *www.verityappointments.com*

You can also look at the job advertisements in free weekly newspapers and magazines including the backpacker-oriented TNT Magazine.

Health Cover

It is always a good idea to have travel insurance that covers medical emergencies while you're away from home, however citizens of Australia and European Economic Area countries are eligible for free medical treatment in the UK and emergency treatment in Ireland and visitors from New Zealand are eligible for free medical treatment in the UK but not Ireland. In addition both Ireland and the UK allow all travellers who are studying or who have a working holiday authorisation to receive free medical treatment.

IRELAND
Ireland has a reciprocal healthcare agreement with Australia, Switzerland

and all European Union and European Economic Area (EEA) countries. Basically this means that citizens of these countries get free emergency healthcare.

You are entitled to more extensive health benefits if you are a temporary resident in Ireland, this includes travellers studying in Ireland or working on a working holiday authorisation.

Refer to the following website for more details: www.oasis.gov.ie/health/health_services_in_ireland/health_services_and_visitors_to_ireland.html.

UNITED KINGDOM

Countries in the European Economic Area plus Australia, New Zealand and several other countries have bilateral healthcare agreements with the United Kingdom. If you are a citizen of one of these countries you are entitled to free medical care in the United Kingdom through the National Health Service *(NHS; website www.nhs.uk)*. If you visit a doctor at a GP practice you will need your passport as proof of your eligibility and will be asked to fill out the paperwork required to register you as a NHS patient. If you are not yet a NHS patient and are admitted to a hospital you will need to show your passport to prove your eligibility as an NHS patient.

If you are legally working in the United Kingdom, including working on a Working Holiday permit, you are entitled to free NHS treatment regardless of your nationality. It is a good idea to go to your local GP practice to register as an NHS patient as soon as you have arrived in the country.

Money

Both Ireland and the United Kingdom are very expensive countries to visit. The price of accommodation in Dublin and London will come as a shock to many people as will the cost of train tickets in Britain and fuel if you're driving. However there are some bargains like cheap clothes at some of the bigger supermarkets, brilliant £1 bus tickets in Great Britain and some good free museums. The cost of visiting Britain and Ireland is substantially cheaper once you leave London or Dublin.

Work out your daily budget by tripling your accommodation cost. Multiply this by the number of days you're planning on travelling, and add the cost of your airfare and bus/travel passes and you should get a pretty good idea of the costs of travelling around Great Britain and Ireland.

You should be able to save some money by cooking all your own meals and not drinking alcohol, however there are lots of easy ways to blow through a wad of cash such as a few big nights out on the town or by spending most of your time in the bigger cities.

Travellers' Cheques

Travellers' cheques used to be the best way to carry travel money, but they're not as common now that ATMs and credit cards are so widely accepted.

It is worthwhile taking some of your money as travellers' cheques since it is a great backup if you lose your wallet with all your credit cards or if you arrive to discover that your cash card won't work in the ATM.

The beauty of travellers' cheques is that they can be replaced if they're lost or stolen. It helps if you keep a record of your travellers' cheque numbers in a safe place, preferably a copy with you (but not with your cheques) and another copy at home (or somewhere where someone can fax them to you if you need to make a claim for lost cheques).

Many travellers buy travellers cheques in British pounds or euros, which lets you use them as an alternative to cash as long as you can find someone willing to accept them.

If you bring travellers' cheques with you, make sure that you sign them when you buy them, but do not countersign them until you are ready to cash them. You may also need to have identification such as your passport with you when you cash your cheques.

The most widely accepted brands of travellers' cheques are American Express, Thomas Cook and Visa. Don't travel with anything else as many people will not recognise or accept them.

ATMs & Credit Cards

Plastic has become the preferred way to access your cash while you're on the road and most cards are widely accepted throughout Ireland and the UK.

There are several types of cards, each with their advantages. Most travellers have at least one credit card, and also a card to draw cash from an ATM (either from an account at home or from a British or Irish bank account).

CREDIT CARDS

Credit cards are great for getting out of trouble and are often tied to a frequent flyer programme. One of the main advantages of credit cards is the favourable currency exchange rate as well the freedom to spend more money than you have. Of course this spending can get out of hand and you'll end up paying for it later on.

The most useful cards in Britain and Ireland are MasterCard and Visa, followed by Laser (in Ireland only), American Express and Diners Club. In tourist areas you may find some places that accept JCB card.

Most credit cards can be replaced quickly if they are lost or stolen. Call one of the following numbers if you need a new card:

American Express
☎ *0808 100 2255 (from UK)*
☎ *00 44 1273 696 933 (from Ireland)*
Website *www.americanexpress.com*

Diners Club
☎ *0800 460 800 (from UK)*
☎ *00 44 1252 513 500 (from Ireland)*
Website *www.dinersclub.com*

MasterCard
☎ *0800 964 767 (from UK)*
☎ *1800 557 378 (from Ireland)*
Website *www.mastercard.com*

Visa
☎ *0800 169 5189 (from UK)*
☎ *1800 509 042 (from Ireland)*
Website *www.visa.com*

ATM CARDS

ATM cards are a popular way to access your cash, particularly if your card is part of an international network allowing you to use Automatic Teller Machines (ATMs) in Britain and Ireland. If the bank that issued your card is part of the Plus, Cirrus or Visa networks you should find plenty of ATMs in the British Isles where you can withdraw money.

Despite the favourable exchange rate and the ease of drawing your money from a cash dispenser, there are sometimes problems using your cash card abroad. Before leaving home you should check with your bank whether it is possible to use your card in Ireland and the UK. In some cases you may need to change your PIN or even have a new card issued.

British Bank Accounts

If you're planning on working in the UK you'll need your own bank account.

The biggest banks in the UK are Barclays (**website** *www.barclays.co.uk*), HSBC (**website** *www.hsbc.co.uk*), Lloyds TSB (**website** *www.lloydstsb.co.uk*), NatWest (**website** *www.natwest.co.uk*) and the Royal Bank of Scotland (**website** *www.rbs.co.uk*).

It can be extremely difficult for travellers to open bank accounts in the UK, particularly in areas where lots of backpackers live such as London's Bayswater or Earl's Court neighbourhoods and some travellers take the tube to the East End or suburbs in south London to open an account where banks are less wary of giving accounts to temporary residents.

You may have more luck opening an account with smaller banks and building societies such as Abbey National (**website** *www.abbey.co.uk*) and Alliance Leicester (**website** *www.alliance-leicester.co.uk*) or with online banks like Egg (**website** *www.egg.co.uk*), First Direct (**website** *www.firstdirect.com*) and Smile (**website** *www.smile.co.uk*).

When you go to open your account you'll need loads of identification including your passport, a letter from your bank at home (not always necessary but very helpful), bank statements from home and proof of your address (such as utility bills with your address on them).

Irish Bank Accounts

You'll need an Irish bank account if you're planning on working there.

The biggest banks are Allied Irish Bank *(AIB; website www.aib.ie)*, Bank of Ireland *(website www.bankofireland.ie)*, National Irish Bank *(website www.nib.ie)* and Ulster Bank *(website www.ulsterbank.ie)*.

When you go to open your account you will need identification such as your passport plus bank statements and a letter from your bank at home to show your banking history.

VAT & the Retail Export Scheme

The United Kingdom has a 17.5% Value Added Tax (VAT), which is a sales tax imposed on most products and services except food, books and medicine. This tax is included in the price. Ireland also has VAT included in retail prices. In Ireland this tax is 21% although some items qualify for a lower rate of 13%.

In some instances travellers from outside the European Union can obtain a refund of the VAT of purchases of goods that are to be taken out of the European Union.

To be eligible you must:
- be resident outside the European Union;
- intend to leave Ireland or the UK for a destination outside the European Union with the goods within three months of purchasing them;
- remain outside the European Union for at least 12 months;
- produce the goods, their receipts and a completed VAT refund document to a Customs office when leaving the European Union.

If you want to reclaim VAT on items purchased in the UK you have to buy the goods from a shop that participates in the VAT refund scheme. You will need to show your passport when you purchase the goods and you will also have to fill in several customs forms. You will need to hold on to these forms until you are ready to leave the country.

There are several options if you want to reclaim VAT on items purchased in Ireland. In some cases the retailer will sell you the goods tax free (only if you pay by credit card), they may work with a VAT refunding agency that will eventually send you a refund or the shop may charge you the tax free price but send the goods directly to your home address.

Tipping & Bribery

Bribery in exchange for good service is common in restaurants across Britain and Ireland. You would normally tip around 15% but you don't have to tip where a restaurant includes a 'service charge' in the bill.

Tipping is common, but not always expected, in taxis. You would normally tip a taxi driver 10 to 15% although it's OK to round up the fare for a short trip.

You never have to tip in a bar or pub.

Discount Cards

If you're travelling on a budget you're crazy to pay full price if there is a cheaper option. Armed with a wallet full of discount cards you should be able to drastically cut the cost of travel.

Discount cards come in two varieties – hostel cards and student/youth cards. Both types of cards are worth taking, particularly if you're travelling for a while. Student cards are generally best for getting cut-price admission to museums and other attractions and often allow for cut-price transport; with hostel cards, the emphasis is on cheaper accommodation although these also give you excellent discounts on buses, trains and domestic airfares.

Student & Youth Cards

It's worth bringing along several student cards if you're a student, if you're not a student but are aged under 26 you can get a youth discount card that gives you similar discounts.

Most sightseeing attractions including museums, wildlife parks and zoos allow substantial discounts for students. Many attractions throughout the British Isles refer to the discounted price as the concession rate. Some hostels will also extend a discount to you if you have a student card. In many cases just flashing the card issued by your university will get you these discounts, however some attractions require an internationally recognised card such as the ISIC or ISE card. This is a good reason why you should have at least two student cards.

Both ISIC and ISE publish a list of available discounts, however virtually all establishments that offer discounts will grant the discount for either card even if it that establishment is not listed in the card's discount guide.

The concession rate on the public transport networks in most British and Irish cities is not available with these cards and in most cases it is restricted to students enrolled in local schools.

ISE

The International Student Exchange (ISE) card is a good option with loads of discounts. Although this card is not as established as the ISIC, many establishments that give discounts to the ISIC will also provide the same discounts to ISE cardholders. The ISE card costs US$25 and you can order it online. See the ISE website *(www.isecards.com)* for more information.

ISIC, IYTC & ITIC

The International Student Travel Confederation *(ISTC; **website** www.isiccard.com)* produces three discount cards that give discounts to students; teachers and travellers aged under 26. Some of these cards include basic travel insurance although this is dependant on where the card is issued. ISIC, IYTC and ITIC cards each cost US$22 or £7.

The International Student Identity Card (ISIC) is the most widely accepted of the student cards. Many travellers buy fake ISIC cards while they're travelling through Asia which means non-students can sometimes pick one up; because of this the cards aren't quite as good for big discounts as they used to be and you may sometimes be asked for a secondary identification such as your student ID from your university at home. This is yet another reason why you should have a couple of student ID cards.

The International Youth Travel Card (IYTC) is an alternative for travellers aged under 26 who do not qualify for an ISIC. There is a wide range of discounts, although it is not as good as a student card.

The International Teacher Identity Card (ITIC) is a good alternative if you are a full-time teacher. Like the IYTC this isn't quite as good as a student card but it's worthwhile if you don't qualify for anything else.

Hostel Cards

Cards issued by the different hostelling organisations offer excellent discounts, particularly for transport and accommodation. Many travellers take along two cards, a Hostelling International card and one issued by an independent hostelling organisation such as VIP Backpackers Resorts. There is more information about hostel cards in the following hostel section.

In our accommodation listings we list the price without a hostel card followed by the price charged if you have a card. Just because a hostel offers a discount to someone with a card from a particular hostel network does not mean that that hostel is part of the network.

Hostels

Hostels are a great cheap accommodation option, however they have much more to offer than a cheap bed. A good backpackers' hostel is also a place to party, meet new friends from around the world and get information on other cool places to go.

Hostels provide dormitory accommodation, along with shared shower and kitchen facilities. Generally there are four to six people sharing a room and there is somewhere like a TV room or bar where you can meet other travellers. Often the people running the hostel are backpackers themselves, and are a mine of information about places to see, things to do and transport and accommodation options elsewhere in Britain and Ireland.

Ireland and Scotland have some very good small hostels but hostels in Dublin and London aren't of such a high standard. However the backpacking industry in Britain and Ireland is getting more competitive and the quality is improving all the time.

The best hostels are usually either small hostels in historic buildings that are full of character or newer purpose-built places with first-class facilities. Hostels in rural areas like the Scottish Highlands and the Isle of Skye or in small Irish villages like Doolin are among the best, however hostels in bigger cities and less visited regional centres aren't as predictable.

A good hostel should provide a way for travellers to meet each other with common areas and a design that is conducive to meeting other people. This is one of the main features that distinguish hostels from hotels, which are designed to offer their guests privacy. For this reason, many hostels with self-contained facilities (usually those that are former hotels or apartment complexes) don't have as much atmosphere as your average backpackers hostel.

Hostels that are located above pubs are among the worst. In many of these places the bar downstairs is the main business and a lot less attention is paid to the accommodation.

Although we believe that the hostel reviews in this book are more comprehensive than any other guidebook, the reviews on our website *(www.bugeurope.com)* are even more detailed and allow you to write your own hostel reviews and read reviews submitted by other travellers.

A lot of the hostels reviewed on our website also allow online booking; where this is possible there will be a 'Book this Hostel' button next to the address on the review.

Hostel Chains

There are several hostel groups in the British Isles but only Hostelling International (called An Óige in Ireland, HINI in Northern Ireland, YHA in England and Wales and SYHA in Scotland) offers its own discount/membership card that gives discounts on accommodation and transport although the VIP card also offers discounts in some hostels.

HOSTELLING INTERNATIONAL

Like many European youth hostels, Hostelling International hostels in the British Isles are more institutional catering more to school groups and families rather than young independent travellers. Despite the school groups, the average age of travellers staying at HI hostels is higher than that in independent hostels.

An Óige

An Óige *(website www.anoige.ie)* is the Irish branch of Hostelling International. An Óige is a relatively small organisation with only 32 hostels throughout the Republic of Ireland. There are hostels in the major towns and quite a few in the Wicklow Mountains although An Óige doesn't have hostels in many popular backpacker spots. In general An Óige hostels feel a little drab and lack the atmosphere that you find in a lot of independent hostels.

It costs €20 to become a member of An Óige for one calendar year.

HINI

Hostelling International Northern Ireland *(HINI; website www.hini.org.uk)* has six hostels in Northern Ireland and most of them are of a very high standard.

HI members get a £1 discount off each night's accommodation. It costs £13 to join Hostelling International in Northern Ireland.

YHA

The Youth Hostel Association *(YHA; website www.yha.org.uk)* has 226 hostels throughout England and Wales. Most of the hostels are small rural properties that cater to families and older British hikers and there is a particularly high concentration of YHA hostels in areas with lots of walking tracks like the Lake District, the Peak District and the Pembrokeshire Coast. A lot of YHA hostels have a very old fashioned approach to hostelling with confusing opening times including lockouts and curfews and their focus on accommodating groups can make them feel unwelcoming to many independent travellers. The few YHA hostels in major cities, including flash new hostels in Bristol,

London, Manchester and Oxford, are more geared toward independent travellers but are also much more expensive than most other YHA hostels.

HI members get a £2 discount off each night's accommodation. It costs £14 to join the YHA in England and Wales or you can become a member by collecting seven stamps (one each time you pay the non-member rate).

SYHA

The Scottish Youth Hostel Association *(SYHA;* **website** *www.syha.org.uk)* operates over 70 hostels throughout Scotland. They range from small rustic places to opulent buildings like the Carbisdale Castle and Loch Lomond hostels.

HI members get a £1 discount off each night's accommodation. Scotland is the cheapest place to become a Hostelling International member, costing only £6 for a one year membership – less than half what it costs in England.

INDEPENDENT BACKPACKERS HOSTELS
Independent Backpackers Hostels Scotland

Independent Backpackers Hostels Scotland *(IBHS;* **website** *www.hostel-scotland.co.uk)* is a network of over 120 independently operated hostels. Hostels in IBHS are of a relatively high standard as each hostel is regularly inspected and must comply with a set of standards. Hostels in this network are listed in a blue brochure that is updated annually.

Independent Holiday Hostels of Ireland

Independent Holiday Hostels of Ireland *(IHH;* **website** *www.hostels-ireland.com)* is a group of over 100 hostels that

---

Don't let the bed bugs bite

Bed bugs are a serious problem encountered by travellers throughout the world. They can be found on buses, on trains, in cinemas, in hostels and even in five-star hotels.

Although they are blood-sucking parasites, bed bugs do not transmit any disease and for most people the bites are no more irritating that a flea, mosquito or sand fly bite. However some people do have serious reactions to bed bug bites.

There is quite a stigma surrounding bed bugs and travellers that have been bitten often feel dirty and are ashamed to tell people about them, or they assume that it is the hostel's fault and tell other travellers to avoid the hostel. However bed bugs can prefer cleaner environments and an isolated case of bed bugs is no indication of a bad hostel.

It is impossible for hostels to completely eliminate bed bugs but they can take steps to prevent bed bugs from becoming a serious problem. These include not having carpet, wallpaper and wooden furniture where bed bugs can hide and prohibiting guests from using their own sleeping bags. However one of the best things a hostel manager can do is to admit that the problem exists and react quickly whenever they hear of a case of bed bugs. Hostel managers that claim to never have bed bugs are living a lie and will inevitably be slow to act when bed bugs are found in their hostel.

There are a lot of misconceptions about bed bugs. A lot of people think that are so tiny that they are virtually invisible, however they are brown flat oval shaped insects that are around 5mm across and quite easy to spot on your bed.

It is quite easy to quickly inspect your room for bed bugs by checking for small dots of blood on the bed slats and around the seams of the mattresses, however blood spots could merely indicate a previous infestation that has been cleared up. Infested rooms may also have an unpleasant almond-like smell.

If you think you have bed bugs you should:
- Tell the hostel staff so they can treat your room
- Wash all your clothes and anything else that can be washed on the highest heat setting and dry in a clothes dryer for 20 minutes
- Have a hot shower
- Empty your backpack, clean it with boiling water and (if possible) dry in a clothes dryer for 20 minutes
- Visually check anything that can't be washed for signs of bed bugs

comprises Ireland's largest hostelling organisation. There is no membership card required to stay in these hostels although some of them will give you a discount if you show a VIP card. The quality is pretty good, as all hostels in the group have to be approved by the Irish or Northern Irish Tourist Board.

Every year IHH publish a guide listing its hostels, which is available from information centres and IHH hostels.

Independent Hostel Owners of Ireland

Independent Hostel Owners *(IHO;* **website** *www.holidayhound.com/ihi/)* also has over 100 hostels throughout Ireland and publishes an annual guide that looks very much like the one IHH brings out. Although there is the odd outstanding hostel in the IHO, the average IHO hostel does not quite compare with the standard of the hostels in IHH.

Getting Around

Air

Britain and Ireland are relatively small geographically so air travel is unnecessary but there are cheap airlines that can make flying a cost effective way to cover long distances.

Many travellers are familiar with cut-price airlines like bmi baby, easyJet, Flybe, Jet2, MyTravelLite, Ryanair and Thomson Fly that offer cheap fares to Europe. Many of these airlines also offer cheap flights between Ireland and Great Britain and there are also some affordable domestic fares within the UK and Ireland.

Long established carriers like Aer Arran, Aer Lingus, BMI and British Airways have to compete with the low price airlines and they sometimes have tickets available at similar prices to their budget rivals. In fact for online bookings, Aer Lingus often has airfares for around the same price as Ryanair.

Aer Arran

Aer Arann *(website www.aerarann.ie)* is Ireland's main domestic airline with flights from Dublin to Cork, Donegal, Galway, Kerry, Knock and Sligo plus flights between Ireland and Great Britain. Fares quoted on their website are one way inclusive of tax.

Aer Lingus

Aer Lingus *(website www.aerlingus.com)* is Ireland's main airline and it offers very good value fares for a full service airline. They have extensive flights in Europe including lots of flights connecting Ireland and Great Britain and they also have good value trans-Atlantic flights.

British Airways

British Airways *(website www.britishairways.com)* is the UK's biggest airline with an extensive network of domestic and international flights. BA have very good services to some of the more remote parts of the UK such as Scotland's Orkney, Shetland and Western Isles.

BMI

BMI *(website www.flybmi.com)* is the UK's second-largest full service airline. They are based at Heathrow and fly to a large range of destinations in the UK, Europe and North America. BMI's advertised prices are inclusive of taxes and they are part of the Star Alliance frequent flyer programme.

bmi baby

Bmi baby *(website www.bmibaby.com)* is BMI's budget subsidiary. It has flights from Birmingham, Cardiff, London (Gatwick), Manchester, Nottingham and Durham Tees Valley to lots of European destinations including flights to several cities in Ireland plus domestic UK flights that include Cardiff and Nottingham to Glasgow and Birmingham, Cardiff and Nottingham to Edinburgh. Their advertised prices include taxes and charges.

easyJet

EasyJet *(website www.easyjet.com)* is one of the longest running budget airlines and it has useful flights from London (Luton and Stansted) to Belfast and Scotland. EasyJet advertises fares exclusive of taxes and fees, which can add an extra £14 to the cost of each one-way flight.

Flybe

Flybe *(website www.flybe.com)* advertises their prices inclusive of taxes and charges. Flybe's main hubs are Exeter and Southampton in Southern England and they also have lots of flights from Belfast City, Birmingham and Bristol. They are useful for domestic flights from southern England to Edinburgh, Glasgow, Manchester and Newcastle. They also have very good value flights between Belfast (Belfast City Airport) and Great Britain.

Jet2

Jet2 *(website www.jet2.com)* is a Yorkshire-based airline with flights from Leeds-Bradford to European destinations. They offer cheap flights between

MyTravelLite
MyTravelLite (**website** www.mytravellite.com) fly from Birmingham to Spain and Portugal and they also have flights to Dublin and Knock in Ireland. Their advertised prices are inclusive of tax.

Ryanair
Ryanair (**website** www.ryanair.com) has the cheapest flights although their prices are quoted before taxes and charges, which can add an extra £14 to each one-way fare. They are particularly good for flights between Ireland and Great Britain with flights from Dublin to most regional British airports. Ryanair also has some very cheap domestic fares within the UK such as London Stansted to Blackpool and Newquay (Cornwall).

Thomson Fly
Thomson Fly (**website** www.thomsonfly.com) has flights from Coventry to destinations throughout Europe including Cork and Shannon in Ireland. The major drawback with Coventry Airport is the lack of public transport between the airport and the city centre. Their advertised price includes taxes and charges.

Bus

Bus travel is one of the most popular ways to get around Ireland and the UK. There are some good value travel passes available and buses travel to most destinations.

Great Britain

Considering the relatively short distances in the UK and the savings against train travel, most travellers choose buses as their main travel option.

National Express (**website** www.nationalexpress.com) is the most comprehensive bus operator with services to over 1200 destinations in England, Scotland and Wales. There are a number of other bus companies such as Arriva (**website** www.arrivabus.co.uk), First (**website** www.firstgroup.com), Green Line (**website** www.greenline.co.uk), Megabus (**website** www.megabus.com), Scottish Citylink (**website** www.citylink.co.uk) and Stagecoach (**website** www.stagecoachbus.co.uk) which provide comprehensive services in a specific region or along a particular route.

Arriva
Arriva (**website** www.arriva.com) operates local bus services throughout Great Britain. In most cases these are just town and city routes but there are some useful bus routes that connect towns and villages over a larger rural area.

Arriva buses cover the following areas: southeast England including London, Hastings, Reading, Oxford, Luton and Colchester; the Midlands including Birmingham, Derby, Leicester and Nottingham; North Wales; the Chester, Liverpool, Manchester, Preston area; Yorkshire including Leeds, Huddersfield, Sheffield, Wakefield and York; and northeast England including Durham, Middlesbrough, Newcastle and Berwick-upon-Tweed.

There are several bus passes available that give you unlimited travel within a specified area. These include:

DAY & WEEKLY TICKETS
There are day and weekly tickets for most towns and cities served by Arriva. However the day and weekly tickets that cover a wider area are the best deal for most travellers. These include the following tickets:

Kent, Surrey & Sussex
Day ticket £5.50

Midlands area
Day ticket £3.75
Weekly ticket £15

North East region
Day ticket £4.50
Weekly ticket £17

North West region
Day ticket £3.30

Wales & the North West
Day ticket £5
Weekly ticket £12.50

North Yorkshire
(except Dales and Lakes bus services)
Day ticket £3.80

West Yorkshire
(except Dales and Lakes bus services)
Day ticket £3.80

Yorkshire
(except Dales and Lakes bus services)
Day ticket £4.80

Arriva 'Go Anywhere' Ticket
This ticket costs £6.50 and gives you one day unlimited travel on all Arriva services (excluding buses in London and some park and ride services). Although it is impossible to travel across the whole country with this ticket because of the way the Arriva network is set up this ticket is still excellent value if you want to travel across more than one adjoining region (for example if you want to travel from Leicester to North Wales).

First
First *(website www.firstgroup.com)* operate local bus services in over 40 towns and cities across the UK. They also run buses in rural areas including connecting services between towns and cities. There are a number of regional passes that are a good value way to get around using First buses. These include:

FirstDay (South West)
One day unlimited travel on First buses in Bath, Bristol, Somerset, Cornwall, Devon, Dorset and Hampshire.
Cost £7

FirstDay Explorer (Dorset)
One day unlimited travel on most First bus services between Exeter and Maidenhead.
Cost £5

FirstDay (Pembrokeshire)
One day unlimited travel on First bus services around Haverfordwest and Pembrokeshire, Wales.
Cost £4

FirstDay (South & West Wales)
One day unlimited travel on First bus services in South Wales (except Shuttle services).
Cost £5.50

FirstDay (South Yorkshire)
One day unlimited travel on First bus services in South Yorkshire plus parts of north east Derbyshire, north Nottinghamshire, West Yorkshire, York and Greater Manchester.
Cost £2.90; £2.50 after 9am on weekdays and all day on weekends

First Bus & Rail Card (Bath-Bristol)
One day unlimited travel on First buses in Bath and Bristol plus First Great Western trains between Bath, Bristol and Weston-super-Mare.
Cost £7

First Bus & Rail Card (Devon)
One day unlimited travel on First buses in Devon plus travel on First Great Western Trains between Totnes and Penzance.

FirstTourist (East Anglia)
One day unlimited bus travel on First buses in the Eastern Counties.
Cost £7

FirstTourist (Herefordshire & Worcestershire)
One day unlimited bus travel on First buses in Herefordshire, Worcestershire and adjoining counties (excludes some night buses and park and ride services).

National Express
National Express *(website www.nationalexpress.com)* is the only real national bus network with services to over 1200 destinations in England, Scotland and Wales. They serve most towns and villages and have particularly good service between the major cities.

NX2 Card
The NX2 Card gives discounts of up to 30% off National Express bus travel in the UK. The card costs £10 and is available to anyone aged between 16 and 26.

Brit Xplorer Pass
The Brit Xplorer pass is good for unlimited travel on the National Express

network, but it is not available to British passport holders. The pass is valid for seven, 14 or 28 consecutive days of travel.

It is a simple pass to use, as you don't need to book your travel, you need to turn up at the coach terminal and show your pass to the driver. If there is space on the bus you can hop on board. This pass is only available to international travellers.

	Price
7 Days (Hobo)	£79
14 Days (Footloose)	£139
28 Days (Rolling Stone)	£219

Scottish Citylink

Scottish Citylink (☎ 08705 505050; *website www.citylink.co.uk*) provides an extensive bus network in Scotland with service to over 200 towns and cities.

Scottish Citylink Explorer Pass

This good value pass can be used for coach travel in Scotland on Scottish Citylink. This pass also gives you discounts on Caledonian Macbrayne and Northlink ferries allowing you to visit the Hebrides, Orkney and Shetland islands. It also gives you discounts at over 200 Scottish hostels.

	Price
3 consecutive days travel	£39
5 travel days in 10 days	£62
8 travel days in 16 days	£85

Stagecoach

Stagecoach (*website www.stagecoach bus.com*) operates a very extensive network of local buses although it can take a while to get around with a network comprised mostly of local routes.

Like Arriva and First buses, Stagecoach is best for exploring a specific geographic area. Stagecoach operates buses in the following regions: the southeast coast; Cheltenham, Oxford and the Cotswolds; northwest England including the Lake District; Ayrshire, Scotland and northeast Scotland.

DAY TICKETS

There is a day ticket for each of the the regions where Stagecoach operate. These are a very good value for exploring an area for a day or two.

Most towns and cities covered by Stagecoach offer day tickets but the best deal for travellers are day tickets that cover a larger area such as an entire county. These tickets are covered in detail under the Local Transport section of each destination.

Explorer Tickets

The Explorer ticket is brilliant value allowing travel on Stagecoach as well as some other local bus operators. Most Explorer tickets are valid for one day but some regions also have three, four and seven-day Explorer tickets.

These tickets are covered in detail under the Coming & Going and Local Transport sections of the relevant destination.

Goldrider

The Goldrider ticket gives you unlimited travel on Stagecoach buses outside London.

There are also Goldrider tickets that give unlimited travel on Stagecoach buses within a wide area (usually within a specified county). These tickets are covered in detail under the Coming & Going and Local Transport sections of the relevant destination.

£1 Bus Fares

EasyBus, Megabus and National Express all offer £1 bus fares to destinations throughout the UK, although this is mostly limited to excursions from London and for links between the larger cities. However it is a cheap way to get across the country or just for a day or weekend trip out of the capital.

These cheap fares are booked online like tickets for a budget airline. A set number of seats are available at the cheap price, with the prices increasing once all the cheap seats have been sold.

EasyBus

The same company that runs the easy Internetcafé chain and the easyJet budget airline runs easyBus (*website www.easybus.co.uk*). At the moment they only operate from London to Luton Airport and Milton Keynes so it's not much use unless you're catching an easyJet flight from Luton. Their bright orange minibuses leave from the bus stop outside Hendon Way Motors on Hendon Way in Hendon in London's northern suburbs (◉ *Hendon Central*).

Megabus

Megabus (*website www.megabus.com*) have an ever-improving network of cheap bus routes across the UK. Like easyBus and National Express, Megabus fares start at £1 although they are subject to a 50p booking fee.

They have big double decker buses from London to Birmingham, Bournemouth, Brighton, Bristol, Cardiff, Cheltenham, Chesterfield, Exeter, Glasgow, Gloucester, Leeds, Leicester, Manchester, Milton Keynes, Oxford, Plymouth, Portsmouth, Sheffield, Southampton and Swansea. Other services include Manchester to Leeds, London and Glasgow; Edinburgh to Dundee, Perth and St Andrews; Dundee to Aberdeen, Edinburgh, Glasgow and Perth and Inverness to Perth.

National Express

National Express's Fun Fares are limited seats available at just £1 on routes from London to the following 20 cities: Birmingham, Bournemouth, Brighton, Bristol, Cambridge, Canterbury, Cardiff, Exeter, Glasgow, Leeds, Leicester, Liverpool, Manchester, Newcastle, Norwich, Nottingham, Portsmouth, Sheffield, Southampton and Swansea. Fun Fares are also available on travel from Manchester to Birmingham, Liverpool and London.

Scottish Citylink

Scottish Citylink (☎ *08705 505050; website www.citylink.co.uk*) also offers £1 tickets, but only on the Glasgow-Edinburgh route. However they also have £2 fares on their Glasgow-Perth and Edinburgh-Perth routes and £3 fares on their Aberdeen-Dundee, Aberdeen-Edinburgh, Aberdeen-Glasgow, Aberdeen-Perth, Inverness-Edinburgh, Inverness-Glasgow and Inverness-Perth services.

Alternative/Backpacker Transport

There are several small bus companies catering specifically to the backpacker. Some of them run really good trips stopping directly at the hostel door rather than the central bus station. These can be a good way to get around and because they are minibuses filled with other backpackers they can be good fun. Some companies have got on the backpackers bandwagon but run structured tours rather than offer an independent travel option allowing you to hop-on and hop-off when you feel like it. There are some cases when this sort of travel option is the best way to get around especially in remote areas with poor public transport. However if you have the option of choosing a tour or the more independent hop-on hop-off option, choose the hop-on hop-off.

MacBackpackers

MacBackpackers (*website www.macbackpackers.com*) run a flexible hop on hop off bus service around Scotland. The itinerary varies according to the season but it covers the main spots in the Highlands and the jump off points are in places that make good bases for exploring places like the Isle of Skye (not included in the trip but an optional extra).
Fare £65
Departs Edinburgh
Overnight stops Pitlochry, Inverness, Kyleakin, Fort William

Road Trip

Road Trip (*website www.roadtrip.co.uk*) run trips through England and Wales departing from London. Road Trip also run tours of southern England with an emphasis on Cornwall, but only their five-day four-night Northern Exposure trip has a hop on hop off option. You have to spend a week in your destination between hopping off and on the bus. This trip includes Sherwood Forest, Newcastle, Edinburgh, the Lake District, Liverpool, Wales, Stratford-upon-Avon and Oxford – many of the main tourist spots but also bypassing some important places in northern and central England.

Fare £139
Departs London
Overnight stops York, Newcastle, Edinburgh, Liverpool, Stratford-upon-Avon

Shaggy Sheep
Shaggy Sheep *(website www.shaggysheep.com)* run hop on hop off trips around Wales. The trips visit the main spots in Wales including the Wye Valley, Brecon Beacons, Cardiff, the Pembrokeshire Coast, Aberystwyth, Snowdonia and Caernarfon.
Fare £79
Departs London
Overnight stops Cardiff, Carmarthen, Machynlleth

Ireland

Buses are the most convenient way to get around Ireland. The majority of buses in the Republic are operated by Bus Éireann *(website www.buseireann.ie)*, which has regular departures to most towns and cities. Buses in Northern Ireland are operated by Ulsterbus *(website www.ulsterbus.co.uk)*.

Both Bus Éireann and Ulsterbus have a number of travel passes available including:

Emerald Card
Valid for combined bus and rail travel in the Republic of Ireland and Northern Ireland on the Bus Éireann, Ulsterbus, Iarnród Éireann and Northern Ireland Railways networks. This pass is also valid on Dublin's DART and suburban rail services and local bus services in Cork, Limerick, Galway and Waterford.

	Price
8 travel days in 15 days	€218
15 travel days in 30 days	€375

Irish Explorer
Valid for combined bus and rail travel in the Republic of Ireland on the Bus Éireann and Iarnród Éireann bus and rail networks. This pass is also valid on Dublin's DART and suburban rail services and local bus networks in Cork, Limerick, Galway and Waterford. The pass (costing €194) is good for 8 days travel in a 15 day period.

Irish Rambler
The Irish Rambler is valid for travel on Bus Éireann services in the Republic of Ireland as well as local bus services in Cork, Limerick, Galway and Waterford.

	Price
3 travel days in 8 days	€53
8 travel days in 15 days	€116
15 travel days in 30 days	€168

Irish Rover
The Irish Rover pass is valid for travel on Bus Éireann services in the Republic of Ireland and Ulsterbus services in Northern Ireland. The Irish Rover pass is also valid on local bus services in Belfast, Cork, Limerick, Galway and Waterford.

	Price
3 travel days in 8 days	€68
8 travel days in 15 days	€152
15 travel days in 30 days	€226

Open Road Pass
The Open Road Pass is a flexi pass that gives you unlimited travel on all scheduled Bus Éireann services including express, local, city and town buses. If you decide that you want extra travel days you can extend your pass by buying additional days once you have started travelling.

	Price
3 travel days in 6 days	€42
4 travel days in 8 days	€54
5 travel days in 10 days	€66
6 travel days in 12 days	€78
7 travel days in 14 days	€90
8 travel days in 16 days	€102

Alternative/Backpacker Transport
There are several companies in Ireland that offer an alternative to the scheduled bus operators. A lot of these companies seem to specialise in tours, which runs against the independent spirit of backpacking, however Paddywagon also offer more spontaneous hop-on hop-off

services. These allow you to follow a set route around Ireland, hopping on and off the bus at your leisure.

Paddywagon
Although Paddywagon is primarily a tour company, they do offer a hop on hop off service that gives you a little bit of flexibility although the buses only run four days a week. Overnight stops include Dublin, Galway, Doolin, Lahinch, Tralee, Killarney, Cork and Kilkenny.
☎ *(01) 672 6007*
Website *www.paddywagontours.com*
Fare *€89*
Valid *6 months*

Train Travel

Train travel is the most comfortable way to travel overland but it can be expensive if you don't have a rail pass.

Great Britain

The Brits complain about their rail network even more than the weather, which leaves visitors to the UK pleasantly surprised when they find such an extensive and well-developed train system. Britain's train network criss-crosses the land with services to even small towns and villages and there are almost 20,000 train services on a typical weekday. There are even trains running every 15 minutes on some intercity train routes.

Train Companies
The train system is comprised of over 25 different train operators that are collectively known as National Rail *(website www.nationalrail.co.uk)*. The train companies are:

Arriva Trains Northern
Arriva Trains Northern *(website www.arrivatrainsnorthern.co.uk)* run around 1200 daily train services with around half of them passing through Leeds. The company's routes include the scenic Settle-Carlisle line, the Carlisle-Newcastle line (which follows the course of Hadrian's Wall), as well as busy intercity routes connecting the big cities of Yorkshire and northern England including Bradford, Doncaster, Hull, Leeds, Manchester, Sheffield and York.

Arriva Trains Wales
Arriva Trains Wales *(**website** www.arrivatrainswales.co.uk)* operate an extensive train network in Wales with connecting services to Birmingham, Bristol, Manchester and a line running to Penzance in Cornwall.

c2c
c2c *(website www.c2c-online.co.uk)* run trains from London's Fenchurch Street and Liverpool Street stations to Southend and Shoeburyness.

Central Trains
Central Trains *(website www.centraltrains.co.uk)* operate an extensive network of routes in Midlands. Birmingham is the hub of the system but trains run as far as Norwich and Stansted Airport and also include the busy Liverpool-Manchester-Sheffield route.

Chiltern Railways
Chiltern Railways *(website www.chilternrailways.co.uk)* run trains between Birmingham and London's Marylebone Station.

Eurostar
Eurostar *(**website** www.eurostar.com)* has international services from London Waterlook to Brussels, Lille and Paris via the Channel Tunnel.

First Great Western
First Great Western *(website www.firstgreatwestern.co.uk)* runs trains from London's Paddington Station to Cornwall, South Wales and Hereford.

First Great Western Link
First Great Western Link *(website www.firstgreatwestern.co.uk/link)* trains go from London Paddington to Hereford, Oxford and Stratford-upon-Avon. They also run trains between Reading and Gatwick Airport.

First North Western
First North Western *(**website** www.firstnorthwestern.co.uk)* run train services

in northwest England. This includes extensive train services around Blackpool, Cumbria (the Lake District), Liverpool, Manchester and North Wales plus services connecting Birmingham and Manchester.

First ScotRail
First ScotRail (*website www.scotrail.co.uk*) is Scotland's main railway company with trains to most parts of the country.

Gatwick Express
Gatwick Express (*website www.gatwickexpress.com*) runs express trains between London Victoria and Gatwick Airport.

Great North Eastern Railway (GNER)
GNER (*website www.gner.co.uk*) have trains from London's King's Cross station to Leeds, York, Newcastle, Edinburgh, Glasgow, Aberdeen and Inverness.

Heathrow Express
Heathrow Express (*website www.heathrowexpress.co.uk*) run trains between London Paddington and Heathrow Airport.

Hull Trains
Hull Trains (*website www.hulltrains.co.uk*) run trains between Hull and London King's Cross.

Island Line
Island Line (*website www.island-line.co.uk*) run trains on the Isle of Wight.

Merseyrail
Merseyrail (*website www.merseyrail.org*) runs suburban trains in the Liverpool area.

Midland Mainline
Midland Mainline (*website www.midlandmainline.com*) run trains from London St Pancras to Leicester, Derby, Nottingham, Sheffield, Leeds and York.

One
One (*website www.onerailway.co.uk*) operates train services from London's Liverpool Street station to East Anglia. Their services include the Stansted Express plus trains to Cambridge, Norwich and Peterborough.

Silverlink
Silverlink (*website www.silverlink-trains.com*) run some London suburban trains plus trains from London Euston to Milton Keynes, Rugby, Coventry and Birmingham.

Southern
Southern (*website www.southernrailway.com*) run suburban trains in South London plus trains from London's Charing Cross, London Bridge and Victoria Stations to Gatwick Airport and Brighton. Southern also run trains on the coastal line linking Southampton and Portsmouth with Chichester, Brighton, Eastbourne and Hastings.

South Eastern Trains
South Eastern Trains (*website www.setrains.co.uk*) run train services in southeastern England.

South West Trains
South West Trains (*website www.southwesttrains.co.uk*) run trains from London Waterloo to southwest England including Portsmouth, Southampton, Reading, Salisbury, Exeter and Weymouth.

Thameslink
Thameslink (*website www.thameslink.co.uk*) run trains from London to Brighton, Bedford and Gatwick and Luton Airports stopping at the following London stations: Blackfriars, City Thameslink, King's Cross, London Bridge. There may be disruptions to the Thameslink service until May 2005 with Brighton and Gatwick Airport trains terminating at Blackfriars or King's Cross and Bedford and Luton trains terminating at St Pancras.

TransPennine Express
TransPennine Express (*website www.firstgroup.com/tpexpress*) operate train services in northern England with all their routes passing through Manchester Piccadilly. Their routes include Manchester to Barrow-in-Furness,

Durham, Huddersfield, Leeds, Liverpool, Manchester Airport, Middlesbrough, Newcastle, Scarborough, Windermere and York.

Virgin Trains
Virgin Trains *(website www.virgintrains.co.uk)* run trains to many of the bigger cities in Britain going as far north as Aberdeen in Scotland and as far south as Penzance in Cornwall.

WAGN
WAGN *(website www.wagn.co.uk)* run trains from London King's Cross to Cambridge, King's Lynn and Peterborough.

Wessex Trains
The Wessex Trains *(website www.wessextrains.co.uk)* network is centred on Bristol. There are trains to Brighton, Cardiff, Exeter, Penzance, Plymouth, Portsmouth, Southampton, Swindon and Worcester.

Tickets
Individual tickets are available at a confusing array of options and the more expensive tickets can sometimes cost the same as a multi-day rail pass.

Standard Single Ticket
A standard single ticket is valid for travel anytime on the date shown on the ticket.

Open Return
An open return is valid for travel anytime up to one calendar month from the ticket date.

Day Return
A day return is valid for one return journey with travel anytime on the date shown on the ticket.

Cheap Day Return
A cheap day return is similar to a day return, but with cheaper fares. On some journeys there are restrictions on times that you can travel (you usually have to travel outside peak hours).

Saver Retun
Similar to a cheap day return but you can usually make the return trip up to one month after your outward journey. On some journeys there are restrictions on times that you can travel (you usually have to travel outside peak hours).

SuperSaver Retun
This is a cheaper alternative to the Saver Return. These tickets are only available on some routes and can only be used to travel on off-peak days.

Network AwayBreak
This type of ticket is available on some routes in southeastern England. Network AwayBreak tickets are valid for outward travel on the date shown on the ticket with the return journey within five days. There are usually restrictions prohibiting travel at peak times on weekdays.

SuperAdvance
Limited numbers of SuperAdvance tickets are available on selected routes. These tickets must be booked by 6pm on the day before travel and are restricted to travel only on the date and train shown on the ticket. SuperAdvance tickets are available as both single and return tickets; the return voyage must be within one month of the outward journey. This type of ticket includes free compulsory seat reservations for both outbound and return journeys.

APEX
Limited numbers of APEX (Advance Purchase Excursion) tickets are available on selected routes. These tickets must be booked at least one week before travel (two days for travel on ScotRail trains) and are restricted to travel only on the date and train shown on the ticket. APEX tickets are available as both single and return tickets; the return voyage must be within one month of the outward journey. This type of ticket includes free compulsory seat reservations for both outbound and return journeys.

Travel Passes
The biggest drawbacks about British trains are the high prices and the fact that the Eurail pass isn't valid here.

However there is a large selection of other travel passes available that make train travel a much more affordable travel option than buying individual tickets. These include the BritRail passes and the more restricted Ranger and Rover tickets.

RANGER/ROVER TICKETS

There is a wide range of travel passes that are restricted to either a specific train company or a specified geographic area. These include:

Anglia Plus
Valid for one day travel in East Anglia after 8.45am weekdays and all day on weekends.
Train company One
Bus companies First buses in Norwich (zones 1-4), Anglia Coaches between Great Yarmouth station and the town centre or beach, First buses between Bury St Edmonds station and the town centre and First buses in Lowestoft
Adult fare £9
Valid 1 day

Cambrian Coaster Day Ranger
The Cambrian Coaster Day Ranger is valid for train travel in the area bordered by Aberystwyth, Machlynlleth and Pwllheli in Wales after 7.50am Mon-Fri and all day on weekends.
Train company Arriva Trains Wales
Adult fare £6.60
Valid 1 day

Central Scotland Rover (3 days in 7 days)
This is a flexi pass giving you unlimited three days travel on ScotRail trains in Central Scotland within a seven day period. It is useful for train travel in the region that includes Bathgate, Dunblane, Edinburgh, Falkirk, Glasgow, North Berwick and Markinch and all intermediate stations. It is also valid for travel on the Glasgow subway. However it is not valid for travel between Glasgow Central and Edinburgh Waverley.
Train companies ScotRail, SPT Glasgow Subway
Adult fare £29
Valid 3 travel days in a 7-day period

Coast and Peaks
The Coast and Peaks Rover is available in both a flexi pass offering three travel days in a seven day period and a rail pass offering seven consecutive travel days. It is good for train travel in North Wales and North West England in the area bounded by Liverpool, West Kirby, Wigan, Manchester, Glossop, Sheffield, Buxton, Stoke-on-Trent to Matlock via Derby, Tamworth, Shrewsbury, Telford Central, Blaenau Ffestiniog, Holyhead, and Llandudno. It is not valid for travel before 9am Mon-Fri.
Train companies Arriva Trains Northern, Arriva Trains Wales, Central Trains, First North Western, Merseyrail, Virgin Trains
Adult fare 3 in 7 day flexi pass £42.50; 7 day rover £52.50
Flexipass valid 3 travel days in a 7-day period; ***rover valid*** 7 consecutive days

Cornish Rover
This is a flexi pass that allows train travel in Cornwall including trains between Plymouth and Penzance and branch lines to Falmouth, Looe, Newquay and St Ives. It is not valid for travel before 9am Mon-Fri (8am Mon-Fri on trains from Falmouth and Looe).
Train companies Arriva Trains Wales, First Great Western, Virgin Trains, Wessex Trains
Adult fare 3 in 7 day flexi pass £18; 8 in 15 day flexi pass £33
Valid 3 travel days in a 7-day period, 8 travel days in a 15-day period

Devon Rover
This is a flexi pass that allows train travel in Devon between Plymouth and Weston-super-Mare including branch lines to Axminster, Barnstaple, Exmouth, Gunnislake and Paignton. It is not valid for travel before 9am Mon-Fri (8am on trains from Barnstaple, Dawlish, Dawlish Warren, Teignmouth and Weston-super-Mare).
Train companies Arriva Trains Wales, First Great Western, South West Trains, Virgin Trains, Wessex Trains
Adult fare 3 in 7 day flexi pass £24; 8 in 15 day flexi pass £39.50
Valid travel 3 days in a 7-day period, 8 travel days in a 15-day period

East Midlands Rover

This pass is available in both a flexi pass offering three travel days in a seven-day period and a rail pass offering seven consecutive travel days. It is good for train travel in the East Midlands in the area that is bordered to the south by Bedford, Bletchley, Milton Keynes and Peterborough; to the east by Skegness and Cleethorpes; to the north by Sheffield, Doncaster and Barton on Humber and to the west by New Mills, Chesterfield, Matlock, Stoke-on-Trent, Stafford, Lichfield Trent Valley, Tamworth and Coventry. It is not valid for travel before 9am Mon-Fri.
Train companies *Arriva Trains Northern, Central Trains, GNER, Midland Mainline, Silverlink, Virgin Trains*
Adult fare *3 in 7 day flexi pass £51.50; 7 day rover £67.30*
Valid *3 travel days in a 7-day period, 7 consecutive days*

East Midlands Day Ranger

This one-day travel pass is good for train travel in the East Midlands in the area that includes Crewe, Derby, Leicester, Lincoln, Loughborough, Matlock, Nottingham, Peterborough, Stamford, Stoke-on-Trent and Tamworth. It is not valid for travel before 9am Mon-Fri.
Train companies *Central Trains, First North Western*
Adult fare *£21*
Valid *1 day*

East Yorkshire Flexi Rover

This flexi pass is good for four travel days within an eight-day period in East Yorkshire. It is valid on the line linking Hull and Scarborough as well as on trains between Scarborough and York, York to Selby and Selby to Hull. It is not valid for travel before 9am Mon-Fri.
Train companies *Arriva Trains Northern, GNER, Midland Mainline, TransPennine Express*
Adult fare *£32.50*
Valid *4 travel days in an 8-day period*

Freedom of Scotland Travelpass

This flexipass is valid on all trains in Scotland including GNER and Virgin trains to and from Berwick-upon-Tweed and Carlisle. It is also good for bus travel on Bowmans Coaches services on the Isle of Mull, First buses between Edinburgh and the Scottish Borders; Highland Country Buses on the Isle of Skye as well as Thurso-Scrabster, Wick-John O'Groats, Thurso-John O'Groats; services on Scottish Citylink buses on the following routes Oban-Fort William-Inverness, Kyle of Lochalsh-Uig, Inverness-Ullapool, Oban-Cambeltown and Wick-Thurso and Stagecoach buses between Dundee and Leuchars/St Andrews. It is valid on all Caledonia MacBrayne ferries and it gives a 20% discount on the following Northlink Ferries routes Aberdeen-Kirkwall-Lerwick, Aberdeen-Lerwick and Scrabster-Stromness. It cannot be used before 9.15 Mon-Fri except between Glasgow and Oban/Fort William/Mallaig and Inverness and Kyle, Wick/Thurso.
Train companies *GNER, ScotRail, Virgin Trains*
Bus companies *some services operated by Bowmans Coaches, First, Highland Country Buses, Scottish Citylink, Stagecoach.*
Ferry companies *Caledonia MacBrayne, discount off Northlink Ferries*
Adult fare *4 in 8 day flexipass £89; 8 in 15 day flexipass £119*
Valid *4 travel days in an 8-day period, 8 travel days in a 15-day period*

Freedom of Settle-Carlisle Line

This flexi pass is good for train travel on the Leeds-Settle-Carlisle line. It is not valid for travel before 8.45am Mon-Fri.
Train companies *Arriva Trains Northern, First Great Western, GNER*
Adult fare *£35*
Valid *3 travel days in a 7-day period*

Freedom of South Wales Flexi Rover

The Freedom of South Wales is good for train travel in South Wales in the area bounded by Carmarthen, Fishguard, Hereford, Lydney, Newport and Swansea. It includes the Llanelli-Shrewsbury line. It is not valid for travel before 9am Mon-Fri.
Train companies *Arriva Trains Wales, Central Trains, First Great Western, First North Western, Virgin Trains,*

Wessex Trains
Adult fare *until £30-35*
Valid *3 travel days in a 7-day period*

Freedom of the North West

This flexi pass is good for train travel in northwest England covering Cheshire, Cumbria, Lancashire, Greater Manchester and West Yorkshire. The area this pass can be used is bounded by Chester, Manchester, Leeds, Hexham, Lockerbie and Dumfries. It is not valid for travel before 9am Mon-Fri.
Train companies *Arriva Trains Northern, First North Western, TransPennine Express, Virgin Trains*
Adult fare *3 in 7 day flexi pass £42.50; 7 day rover £52.50*
Valid *3 travel days in a 7-day period, 7 consecutive days*

Freedom of the South West

This flexi pass is good for travel in southwestern England. The area covered includes Cardiff, Bristol, Bath, Salisbury, Swindon and Romsey and all areas west to Cornwall. It is not valid for travel before 9am Mon-Fri (8am on trains from Barnstaple, Dawlish Warren Dawlish, Falmouth, Looe, Teignmouth and Weston-Super-Mare and 8.30am from Weymouth).
Train companies *Arriva Trains Wales, First Great Western, Virgin Trains, Wessex Trains*
Adult fare *£61*
Valid *8 travel days in a 15-day period*

Freedom of Wales

This flexi pass is good for travel on all mainline train services in Wales plus many bus services. It is not valid for travel before 9am Mon-Fri.
Train companies *Arriva Trains Wales, Central Trains, First Great Western, First North Western, Virgin Trains, Wessex Trains*
Bus companies *many bus services*
Adult fare *4 in 8 day flexi pass £45-55; 8 in 15 day flexi pass £75-92*
Valid *4 travel days in an 8-day period, 8 travel days in a 15-day period*

Greenways Day Ranger

This pass is good for one-day travel on the train line linking Pembroke Dock and Whitland in Pembrokeshire, Wales.
Train companies *Arriva Trains Wales, First Great Western*
Adult fare *£3.50*
Valid *1 day*

Hadrian's Wall Rover

This day rover ticket is good for travel on the Hadrian's Wall bus, travel on the Carlisle-Newcastle-Sunderland train line and travel on the Tyne & Wear metro. It is not valid for travel before 9am Mon-Fri.
Train companies *Arriva Trains Northern, Tyne & Wear Metro*
Bus companies *Hadrian's Wall Bus*
Adult fare *£12.50*
Valid *1 day*

Heart of England Flexi Rover

The Heart of England Flexi Rover is good for train travel in central England including travel to Birmingham, Cheltenham, Chester, Coventry, Derby, Gloucester, Hereford, Leicester, Ludlow, Matlock, Northampton, Nottingham, Oxford, Rugby, Shrewsbury, Stoke-on-Trent and Stratford-upon-Avon. It is not valid on direct Virgin Trains services between Birmingham and Cheltenham or on any train before 9am Mon-Fri.
Train companies *Arriva Trains Wales, Central Trains, First Great Western, First Great Western Link, First North Western, Midland Mainline, Silverlink, Virgin Trains and Wessex Trains.*
Adult fare *3 in 7 day flexipass £51.50; 7 day rover £67.30*
Valid *3 travel days in a 7 day period, 7 consecutive days*

Heart of Wales Circular Day Ranger

Heart of Wales Circular Day Ranger lets you make a circular journey in either direction along the following route: Cardiff Central–Craven Arms–Shrewsbury–Llandrindod Wells–Llanelli–Swansea–Cardiff Central. It is not valid before 9am Mon-Fri (except the 7.15am Cardiff Central–Manchester between Cardiff and Shrewsbury).
Train companies *Arriva Trains Wales*
Adult fare *£20-25*
Valid *1 day*

Highland Rover
This flexi pass lets you travel by train along the following routes: Glasgow-Oban-Mallaig, Fort William; Inverness-Aviemore-Kyle of Lochlash-Wick-Thurso-Aberdeen. It is also valid on Scottish Citylink buses between Fort William/Oban and Inverness and Caledonian MacBrayne ferries from Oban to the Isle of Mull and Mallaig to the Isle of Skye. It also includes some bus travel on the Isles of Mull and Skye. It is not valid for travel before 9.15am Mon-Fri.
Train companies *Glasgow Subway, GNER, Scotrail, Virgin Trains*
Bus companies *some services on Bowmans Coaches, Highland Country Buses and Scottish Citylink*
Ferry companies *Caledonian MacBrayne*
Adult fare *£59*
Valid *4 travel days in an 8-day period*

Lakes & Furness Day Ranger
This one-day pass is good for train travel from Lancaster and Heysham to Sellafield and Windermere in the Lake District. It is also good for travel on Stagecoach in Cumbria bus services and it includes a cruise from Ambleside, Bowness or Lakeside with Windermere Lake Cruises.
Train companies *First North Western*
Bus companies *Stagecoach*
Ferry companies *Windermere Lake Cruises*
Adult fare *£10.30*
Valid *1 day*

Lincolnshire Day Ranger
Lincolnshire Day Ranger is good for one-day travel in Lincolnshire with connections to some cities in neighbouring counties. It is not valid for travel before 9am Mon-Fri.
Train companies *Arriva Trains Northern, Central Trains*
Adult fare *£16*
Valid *1 day*

Mid Wales Day Rover
The Mid Wales Day Rover is good for train travel on the following routes: Aberystwyth-Machynlleth, Pwllheli-Shrewsbury and Chester-Wolverhampton. It is not valid on Saturdays in July and August or before 8.30am Mon-Fri.
Train companies *Arriva Trains Wales, Central Trains*
Adult fare *£18.50*
Valid *1 day*

Moorslink
This one day rover ticket lets you travel on the North York Moors using Moorsbus buses plus trains on the Esk Valley Railway and the North Yorkshire Moors Railway. It also includes transport to Bishop Auckland, Hull and York.
Train companies *Arriva Trains Northern, Esk Valley Railway (Middlesbrough-Whitby), North Yorkshire Moors Railway (Grosmont-Pickering).*
Bus companies *Moorsbus*
Adult fare *£12.50*
Valid *one day*

North Country Flexi Rover
The North Country Flexi Rover is good for travel in northern England in the area bounded by Carlisle and Newcastle to the north and Blackpool, Preston, Halifax, Bradford, Leeds and Hull to the south. It is not valid for travel before 9am Mon-Fri (except the 8.49 Leeds-Carlisle train).
Train companies *Arriva Trains Northern, First North Western, GNER, Virgin Trains*
Adult fare *£61.50*
Valid *4 travel days in an 8-day period*

North East Rover/Flexi Rover
This pass is valid for travel in northeastern England. It includes train travel in Yorkshire north to Northumbria as well as trains on the Leeds-Settle-Carlisle line and the Carlisle-Newcastle line. It is not valid for travel before 9am Mon-Fri (except the 8.49 Leeds-Carlisle train).
Train companies *Arriva Trains Northern, First North Western, GNER, Midland Mainline, TransPennine Express and Virgin Trains*
Adult fare *4 in 8 days flexipass £61.50, 7 day rover £73*
Valid *4 travel days in an 8-day period, 7 consecutive days*

North West Rover/Flexi Rover
The North West Rover/Flexi Rover is good for train travel in northwestern

England. It is not valid for travel before 9am Mon-Fri.
Train companies *Arriva Trains Northern, First North Western, ScotRail, TransPennine Express, Virgin Trains*
Adult fare *3 in 7 days flexi pass £42.50, 7 day rover £52.50*
Valid *3 travel days in a 7-day period, 7 consecutive days*

Settle & Carlisle Round Robin
The Settle & Carlisle Round Robin is good for one-day train travel in a circular route that includes the Leeds-Settle-Carlisle line and the Carlisle-Newcastle line, plus trains from Newcastle to York and York to Leeds. It is not valid for travel before 9am Mon-Fri (except the 8.49 Leeds-Carlisle train).
Train companies *Arriva Trains Northern, First North Western, GNER, Virgin Trains*
Adult fare *£32.50*
Valid *1 day*

Settle-Carlisle Rover
The Settle-Carlisle Rover gives you three days to travel along the Leeds-Settle-Carlisle train line. It is not good for travel before 8.45am Mon-Fri.
Train companies *Arriva Trains Northern, First North Western*
Adult fare *£20*
Valid *3 days*

Severn, Avon & Wessex Rover
This pass is good for train travel the area bounded by Cardiff, Cheltenham Spa, Swindon, Romsey, Weymouth and Weston-super-Mare. It is not valid for travel before 9am Mon-Fri (before 8am from Barnstaple, Dawlish, Dawlish Warren and Teignmouth, Falmouth, Looe and Weston-super-Mare, and before 8.30am from Weymouth).
Train companies *Arriva Trains Wales, First Great Western, Virgin Trains, Wessex Trains*
Adult fare *3 in 7 days flexi pass £24, 8 in 15 days flexi pass £39.50*
Valid *3 travel days in a 7-day period, 8 travel days in a 15-day period*

Shakespeare Country Explorer
The Shakespeare Country Explorer is good for travel from London to Leamington Spa, Warwick and Stratford-upon-Avon. It is not valid for travel from London Marylebone 5pm-6.30pm Mon-Fri or southbound before 8.30am Mon-Fri.
Train companies *Chiltern Railway, First Great Western Link*
Adult fare *1 day £25, 3 days £30*
Valid *1 day, 3 days*

Tees Dayrider
The Tees Dayrider is good for one-day train travel in the Tees Valley area bounded by Sunderland, Saltburn, Whitby, Darlington and Bishop Auckland. It is not valid for travel before 9am Mon-Fri.
Train companies *Arriva Trains Northern*
Adult fare *£11*
Valid *1 day*

Tees All Zone Dayrider Plus
The Tees All Zone Dayrider Plus is good for one day train travel in the Tees Valley area bounded by Sunderland, Saltburn, Whitby and the North York Moors plus Moorsbus feeder routes to Bishop Auckland, Hull and York. It is not valid for travel before 9am Mon-Fri.
Train companies *Arriva Trains Northern*
Bus companies *Moorsbus, Stagecoach Transit, Stagecoach Hartlepool*
Adult fare *£5.80*
Valid *1 day*

The Sunday Rover
The Sunday Rover gives you unlimited travel on Sundays on Chiltern Railways and London Underground trains in Buckinghamshire, plus most local buses in Buckinghamshire and Hertfordshire.
Train companies *Chiltern Railways, London Underground (stations in Buckinghamshire only)*
Bus companies *most local buses*
Adult fare *£6*
Valid *1 day (Sundays only)*

Tyne Valley Day Ranger
The Tyne Valley Day Ranger is good for one day train travel in the Tyne Valley area bounded by Morpeth, Sunderland and Durham plus trains on the Newcastle-Carlisle-Workington line. It is not valid for travel before 9am Mon-Fri.

Train companies Arriva Trains Northern, GNER, Virgin
Adult fare £11
Valid 1 day

Valley Lines Day Explorer

The Valley Lines Explorer is good for travel in the Cardiff area and out to Barry Island, Treherbert, Aberdare, Merthyr Tydfil, Coryton and Rhymney.
Train companies Arriva Trains Wales
Bus companies Rhondda Bus, Stagecoach Red, White Bus
Adult fare £6.50
Valid 1 day

West Midlands Day Ranger

The West Midlands Day Ranger pass is good for train travel in West Midlands and also includes trains to Shrewsbury, Crewe, Stoke-on-Trent, Lichfield, Tamworth, Nuneaton, Rugby, Northampton, Leamington Spa, Stratford-upon-Avon, Worcester, Great Malvern and Hereford. It is not valid for travel before 9am Mon-Fri.
Train companies Arriva Trains Wales, Central Trains, Chiltern Railways, First Great Western Link, First North Western, Silverlink
Adult fare £13.20
Valid 1 day

BRITRAIL PASSES

If you want to travel extensively by train throughout Great Britain, then the BritRail pass can be a good deal. You cannot buy the BritRail pass in the UK so it is best to organise this before leaving home. You can buy them online at the BUG Europe website *(www.bugeurope.com)*.

BritRail passes (including the Britrail Classic) can be used during consecutive travel days, but BritRail Flexipasses are restricted to a set number of travel days within a longer period.

BritRail Classic

The original BritRail pass is valid on most train services in England, Scotland and Wales offering unlimited travel on participating services within the validity of the pass.

Youth fares are applicable to people aged 16-25.

	Adult 1st class	Adult 2nd class	Youth 2nd class
4 days	US$315	US$209	US$157
8 days	US$455	US$299	US$299
15 days	US$679	US$449	US$337
22 days	US$859	US$575	US$432
30 days	US$1019	US$679	US$510

BritRail Flexipass

This pass is similar to the BritRail pass, except it restricts your travel to a specified number of travel days within a two-month period.

	Adult 1st class	Adult 2nd class	Youth 2nd class
4 days/ 2 mths	US$395	US$265	US$199
8 days/ 2 mths	US$579	US$385	US$289
15 days 2 mths	US$869	US$585	US$439

BritRail England Pass

The BritRail England Pass is a new rail pass similar to the BritRail Classic, except it doesn't include travel in Scotland or Wales. It is a more affordable option if you're only planning on travelling within England.

	Adult 1st class	Adult 2nd class	Youth 2nd class
4 days	US$249	US$169	US$127
8 days	US$365	US$239	US$180
15 days	US$545	US$365	US$274
22 days	US$689	US$459	US$345
30 days	US$815	US$539	US$405

BritRail England Flexipass

The BritRail England Flexipass is similar to the BritRail England Pass, except it restricts your travel to a specified number of travel days within a two-month period.

	Adult 1st class	Adult 2nd class	Youth 2nd class
4 days/ 2 mths	US$315	US$209	US$157
8 days/ 2 mths	US$465	US$309	US$232
15 days 2 mths	US$699	US$469	US$352

BritRail Days Out from London

This pass is similar to the BritRail Flexipass, except it is limited to southeast

England including London, Cambridge and Oxford.

	Adult 1st class	Adult 2nd class	Youth 2nd class
2 days/ 8 days	US$99	US$69	US$52
4 days/ 8 days	US$169	US$129	US$97
7 days 15 days	US$225	US$169	US$127

BritRail Pass + Ireland

The BritRail Pass + Ireland is similar to the BritRail Flexipass allowing the holder a set number of travel days within a longer period, however this pass is valid in England, Wales, Scotland and also Northern Ireland and the Republic of Ireland.

The BritRail Pass + Ireland includes return ferry service between Great Britain and Ireland.

	1st class	2nd class
5 days in 1 month	US$579	US$419
10 days in 1 month	US$959	US$669

Ireland

Train travel is a good way to get around Ireland with an efficient network operated by Iarnród Éireann *(website www.irishrail.ie)*, which connects most major towns and cities.

The train is an effective way of travelling between Dublin and other major cities, but the bus may be a more efficient option if you don't want to make a detour to Dublin when travelling between regional cities.

One-way tickets are the most expensive travel option, costing more than day and weekend return tickets. A regular return ticket allows you to return within one month.

Both Eurail and InterRail passes are valid in Ireland although there are a number of other passes and discount deals available.

BritRail Pass + Ireland

The BritRail Pass + Ireland is similar to the BritRail Flexipass allowing the holder a set number of travel days within a longer period. However not only is this pass is valid in England, Wales, Scotland but it also lets you travel in Northern Ireland and the Republic of Ireland.

The BritRail Pass + Ireland includes return ferry service between Great Britain and Ireland.

	1st class	2nd class
5 days in 1 month	US$579	US$419
10 days in 1 month	US$959	US$669

Emerald Card

The Emerald Card is a good deal if you want to explore all of Ireland. This pass is good for unlimited travel on bus and train services operated by Iarnród Éireann, Northern Ireland Railways, Bus Éireann and Ulsterbus. This pass costs €218 for eight travel days in a 15 day period and €375 for 15 travel days in a 30 day period.

Irish Explorer (Rail only)

The Irish Explorer pass is good for unlimited travel on Iarnród Éireann trains (including DART and Dublin suburban services) within the Republic of Ireland. It is not valid for cross border services or for travel in Northern Ireland. This pass costs €115.50 and is valid for five days of travel within a 15 day period.

Irish Explorer (Rail & Bus)

There is also a version of the Irish Explorer pass that includes both bus and train travel within the Republic of Ireland. It is good for unlimited bus travel on Bus Éireann and train travel on Iarnród Éireann trains (including DART and Dublin suburban services). This pass costs €194 and is valid for eight travel days within a 15 day period.

Irish Rover

The Irish Rover pass is good for unlimited train travel in both Northern Ireland and the Republic on Northern Ireland Railways and Iarnród Éireann trains (including DART and Dublin suburban services). The Irish Rover costs €143 and is valid for five days of unlimited train travel in a 15 day period.

Driving

Sometimes the best way to really discover a place is to buy or rent a car and get off the beaten track. Although a car can sometimes be an inconvenience, especially in cities where parking can be a problem, the independence to discover the countryside often outweighs any disadvantages.

Although the cost of buying or renting a car is often quite high, especially on shorter trips, this form of transport is much more affordable when split between a group of friends over a few months.

Motoring Organisations

There are two motoring organisations in the UK – the AA (☎ *0800 085 2721; website* www.theaa.co.uk) and RAC (☎ *0800 280 964; website* www.rac.co.uk). Both organisations offer roadside assistance.

If you've bought a car you may consider joining a motoring organisation to take advantage of their breakdown service. Membership in the AA costs between £42 and £155 depending on the level of service and the RAC costs from £34 to £149.

The RAC also offers coverage in the Republic of Ireland. If you're living in Ireland you can join the RAC for €90 to €145 depending on the level of cover. This gives you breakdown assistance throughout the Republic of Ireland, Northern Ireland and Great Britain.

If you're renting a car you should already be covered for some sort of roadside assistance.

Ireland

Driving is a great way to discover Ireland as most of the country's most scenic spots are in rural areas that are most easily accessed by car. This is particularly the case for the scenic Beara, Iveragh and Dingle Peninsulas.

Traffic in Ireland drives on the left. Fuel is expensive, but cheaper than in the UK.

In Ireland road distances are marked in kilometres but speed limits are still expressed in miles per hour.

The general speed limit is 60 mph (96 kph) on open roads, on motorways it is 70 mph (112 kph) and in built up areas it is 30 mph (48 kph). In some instances, such as an approach to a built up area, there may be speed limits of 40 or 50 mph (64 or 80 kph). The penalty for speeding offences is €80.

In Ireland the following roads have tolls: East Link Bridge (Dublin), West Link Bridge (Dublin), West Link Bridge 2 (Dublin) and the M1 Toll Drogheda By-Pass. Tolls on the East and West Link Bridges are €1.35 and the M1 Toll Drogheda By-Pass is €1.50.

Renting a Car in Ireland

For most travellers renting a car is the most practical option for driving around Ireland.

Car rental companies include:

Avis
1 Hanover Street, Dublin
☎ *(01) 605 7500*
Website *www.avis.ie*
Open *Mon-Fri 8.30am-5.45pm, Sat 8.30am-5pm, Sun 9am-2pm*

Budget
151 Lower Drumcondra Road, Dublin 9
☎ *(01) 837 9611*
Website *www.budget.ie*
Open *9am-5pm daily*

Europcar
Baggot Street Bridge, Dublin
☎ *(01) 614 2840*
Website *www.europcar.ie*
Open *Mon-Fri 8am-6.30pm, Sat 8am-4pm, Sun 9am-1pm*

Hertz
151 South Circular Road, Dublin
☎ *(01) 709 3060*
Website *www.hertz.ie*
Open *Jan-Mar Mon-Fri 9am-5.30pm, Sat 9am-4.30pm; Apr-Oct Mon-Fri 8.30am-5.30pm, Sat-Sun 9am-4pm; Nov-Dec Mon-Fri 9am-5.30pm, Sat 9am-4.30pm*

Irish Car Rentals
Harris Park, Old Airport Road, Cloughran, Co Dublin
☎ *(01) 862 2715*

Website *www.irishcarrentals.com*
Open *8.30am-5.30pm daily*

Thrifty
26 Lombard Street East, Dublin
☎ *(01) 874 5844*
Website *www.thrifty.ie*
Open *Mon-Fri 8.30am-5pm, Sat 8.30am-12.30pm*

Buying a Car in Ireland

If you are going to be spending a while in Ireland you may consider buying a car and selling it when you are ready to return home.

All drivers in Ireland have to have motor insurance and you cannot pay your motor tax without showing your motor insurance certificate. The minimum level of motor insurance covers you for third party damage that your car may cause. Motor insurance is available from most insurance companies.

Once you have your motor insurance you will need to pay motor tax.

When you buy a car in Ireland that was first registered in 1992 or earlier, you have to fill out part B of the RF 200 form and detach and retain part C, which is completed by the seller. The new details will be registered in the Log Book, which will then be returned to you.

If you are buying a car that was first registered in 1993 or later, the seller must fill in your details on part B of the Vehicle Licensing Certificate and return it to the Vehicle Registration Unit of the Department of Environment and Local Government. The new details will be registered and the amended certificate will be sent to you. The seller will give the Vehicle Registration Certificate to you when you buy the vehicle.

The rules for buying a brand new car are different but the paperwork for new cars is usually handled by the car dealer.

Selling your Car in Ireland

You will need to complete some paperwork when you sell your car at the end of your trip.

When you sell a car in Ireland you will need to register the change in ownership. If the car was first registered in 1992 or earlier you will need to complete a Change of Ownership for (RF200) from your local Motor Taxation Office. If the car was first registered in 1993 or later you will need to complete part B of the Vehicle Licensing Certificate, which you should have received when you bought the car, and send it to the Vehicle Registration Unit of the Department of Environment, Heritage and Local Government. You should also send the Vehicle Registration Certificate to the new owner.

The regulations are different if you are selling a car in Ireland that is registered in the United Kingdom or another country as the car will have to be first registered and given Irish number plates.

United Kingdom

Traffic congestion, parking hassles and expensive fuel mean that having a car can be a hassle if you're planning on spending a lot of time the in Britain's larger towns and cities. However having access to a car gives you a lot of freedom and it is still the best way to explore the countryside.

Driving in the countryside is characterised by picturesque country lanes that are very often harrowingly narrow, with stonewalls or high hedges defining either side. They are fun to drive; but when doing so you must be almost constantly prepared to bring your vehicle to a crawl and negotiate some sort of compromise with the oncoming traffic.

Britons drive on the left-hand side of the road. The driver and all passengers must wear seat belts. It is illegal for a driver to use a mobile phone while driving. Speed limits vary often; they are generally 30 mph (48 kph) where street lighting is in place in towns and cities, 40 mph (64 kph) in suburban areas, 60 mph (97 kph) on non-divided highways, and 70 mph (113 kph) on motorways and divided highways which provide multiple lanes in your direction.

It appears that no one pays much attention to the speed limit on motorways, however it is much more strictly enforced when you're driving on ordinary roads. Speed cameras are everywhere including the most out-of-the-way country lanes. You will also find red light cameras and bus lane cameras in the bigger cities and you may receive a fine in the mail if you're caught driving in a bus lane.

Free parking is difficult even in the smallest villages where pay-and-display machines are common and it is usually best to avoid driving into the centre of larger towns and cities and instead follow signs to a park and ride car park and catch a bus or train into the city centre. A £5 congestion charge has recently been introduced for any car driving into central London; see the London chapter for more details. If you have to take a car into London your best bet is to park at North Greenwich tube station (£5 per day) and take the tube into town.

Renting a Car in the UK

For most travellers renting a car is the most practical option for driving around Great Britain.

All the big international rental car chains are represented in the UK, most with offices at all the main airports. EasyCar is generally the cheapest rental car company for short rentals however the excess mileage charges can make them very expensive if you're planning on doing a lot of driving. Most of the larger rental car companies offer rental packages with unlimited mileage.

Rental car companies often try to upgrade your insurance cover, charging around £9 a day to reduce the excess that you would otherwise have to pay if you have an accident. This is really overpriced and it can substantially increase the cost of your car rental. It is a much better idea to take out travel insurance that covers this excess.

Car rental companies include:

Avis
181-183 Warwick Road, Kensington, London W14
☉ Earls Court, Kensington Olympia, West Kensington ☉ Kensington Olympia
☎ 0870 010 7968
Website www.avis.co.uk
Open Mon-Thu 8am-6pm, Fri 8am-7pm, Sat 8am-1pm

Budget
Park Road, Bracknell, Berkshire
☎ 0870 1539170
Website www.budget.co.uk

easyCar
245 Warwick Road, London W14
☎ 0906 333 3333
☉ Earls Court, Kensington Olympia, West Kensington ☉ Kensington Olympia
Website www.easycar.com
Open Mon 7am-noon & 1pm-6pm, Tue-Thu 8am-1pm & 2pm-7pm, Fri 9am-2pm & 3pm-8pm, Sat 8am-2pm, Sun 2pm-8pm

Europcar
245 Warwick Road, London W14
☎ (020) 7610 4347
☉ Earls Court, Kensington Olympia, West Kensington ☉ Kensington Olympia
Website www.europcar.co.uk
Open Mon 7am-noon & 1pm-6pm, Tue-Thu 8am-1pm & 2pm-7pm, Fri 9am-2pm & 3pm-8pm, Sat 8am-2pm, Sun 2pm-8pm

Hertz
201-203 Fulham Palace Road, London W6
☎ (020) 7381 8200
Website www.hertz.co.uk
Open Mon-Fri 8am-6pm, Sat 9am-1pm

Thrifty
Chelsea Cloisters Garage, Sloane Avenue, London SW3
☉ South Kensington
☎ (020) 7262 2223
Website www.thrifty.co.uk
Open Mon-Fri 8.30am-6pm, Sat 9am-1pm, Sun 9am-noon

Buying a Car in the UK

Many travellers base themselves in London for at least a few months before travelling around the UK and Europe, and often buy a car there. In London it is easy to buy, register and insure a car, mainly because of less bureaucracy and the ease of getting all the paperwork sorted out in a place where everyone speaks English. Because of the number of travellers looking to buy a car, London and other big cities in the

UK are the easiest places to sell your car when you have finished with it. There are a number of publications such as Auto Trader (*website www.autotrader.co.uk*), Exchange and Mart (*website www.exchangeandmart.co.uk*) and Loot (*website www.loot.co.uk*) that advertise second hand vehicles.

The UK is the most popular place in Europe for travellers to buy a second hand car, but vehicles made for British conditions are not always the most convenient for exploring the continent. Because England, Scotland, Wales, Ireland, the Channel Islands, the Isle of Man, Cyprus and Malta are the only European countries where people drive on the left, you will be stuck with a right-hand-drive vehicle which is less than ideal once you cross the Channel and have to drive on the right side of the road. If you plan on spending more than 70% of your time in continental Europe, you might find find it easier to buy your car in Europe. If you have friends on the continent, things will be much easier (and cheaper to insure) if you get the car in registered in their name.

All cars in the United Kingdom have a registration document that shows the car's registered keeper (but not necessarily the legal owner).

When you buy a used car you should fill in part of the registration document and send it to the Driver and Vehicle Licensing Agency (*DVLA; website www.dvla.gov.uk*).

If the car you are buying has a two part registration document you will be given the top half of the document when you buy the car, which should be completed and send to the DVLA.

If your car comes with a three-part registration document you will have to complete the blue section marked 'Your Details' and both you and the person selling the car will have to sign the declaration on the form. It is the person selling the car's responsibility to send this form into the DVLA.

If you don't have a registration document you will need to apply for one using form V62, which is available from any post office.

The person selling the car has to complete section six of the V5C registration certificate and you both need to sign the declaration in section eight of this form. It is the responsibility of the person selling the car to send this form into the DVLA.

After buying the car and transferring the registration documents you will need a vehicle licence (also known as a tax disc). The vehicle licence is affixed to the left-hand side of the car windscreen and it shows the car's registration number and the date until which you have paid the car's vehicle excise duty (VED). The rate of vehicle excise duty varies according to the type of car and you can buy a vehicle licence for either six or 12 months. A 12-month vehicle excise duty generally ranges from £65-160.

When you apply for your vehicle licence (tax disc) you will need to produce a valid MOT certificate. An MOT certificate shows that your car complies with roadworthiness and environmental requirements. All cars over three years old need to be tested for a MOT certificate once a year. The MOT test fee is £42.10, however you may need to pay for expensive repairs before your car can be retested if it fails the MOT.

Hitchhiking

Hitchhiking is a great way to travel that allows you to really get to know the locals. Many people prefer hitching to other forms of transport because it you can get dropped off anywhere, allowing you to discover places you may never have dreamed of visiting.

Both Ireland and the UK are countries to hitch in and it is a popular way of getting around. Most hitchers say that you don't have to wait much longer than 15 to 20 minutes for a lift although it may take longer on deserted country roads due to the lack of traffic.

Unfortunately hitchhiking gets a lot of bad press. It seems that everyone thinks that you'll get murdered if you hitch. This attitude has two negative effects – people are too frightened to pick you up and a lot of other travellers are scared to hitch-hike meaning less hitchers on the road which ultimately leads to hitch-hiking becoming a dying art.

Where to hitch

It is important to choose a good spot to hitchhike.

If you are leaving a big city it is a good idea to take a bus or train to the outskirts of town to get to a road leading to a motorway (expressway).

Choose a spot with plenty of room for the driver to safely stop. If possible try and stand in a spot where the traffic isn't too fast. It is much safer and also most drivers want to size you up before deciding whether to pick you up.

If you've got a lift on a motorway, try and get dropped off at a rest area rather than in town. If you're dropped off in town you may have to wait hours in local traffic before getting a lift back on to the motorway. If you hitch at a service area you have facilities like a restaurant, shop and toilets; you can chat to truck drivers and ask about getting a lift and you can get a good safe spot to stand where all the traffic is long distance.

Don't hitchhike on motorways, stick to the entrance ramps and service areas. Not only is hitching on motorways dangerous, it is difficult for cars to safely stop and in most places it is illegal.

Signs

A lot of hitchers debate whether to use signs or not. Some argue that drivers won't stop if they don't know where you want to go, while other hitchers say that it is safer to avoid using a sign. If you don't use a sign you can ask the driver where they are going before accepting a lift – the driver won't be able to lie about his destination to get you into the car.

A good compromise is to use a sign indicating the name of the road you want to travel on. This is especially useful if you are on a busy road before a major intersection, without a sign you may get a lift going in the wrong direction.

Tips for getting a ride

You'll find a lot of rides come from regular stoppers – people who've hitch-hiked themselves and are repaying the favour and frequent solo travellers like couriers and truck drivers who want some company. Although you'll find that different people have different reasons for picking you up, there are a number of things you can do to improve your chances of getting a lift.

- Look neat and respectable. Not only should you look non-threatening to any passing driver, but you also help to improve other people's impression of hitchhiking.
- Face the oncoming traffic and smile. It is important that people can see you, so avoid wearing sunglasses.
- Try and look smart and clean, but don't overdo it. If you dress up in a business suit, people will think you're a bit strange (or they might think that your car has broken down and give you a lift).
- When a car stops ask the driver where he is going to. At this point it is easy to decline the lift, if you don't like the look of the driver or if he/she isn't going your way.
- Never smoke in someone else's car.
- Travel light. The lighter your load, the quicker you travel.
- Take your drivers licence. Many people stop because they want someone to share the driving with.

Safety

Although hitchhiking is more hazardous than bus or train travel, it is still safer than many other forms of transport such as cycling.

The most dangerous thing about hitchhiking is the possibility of being involved in a car accident or being hit by a car if you stand too close to the side of the road.

There is also a very small danger posed by accepting a lift with a driver that you do not know. The driver could either be a dangerous character or simply a bad driver.

Despite the perceived danger, there are plenty of ways to minimise your risk.

If you're a single female you'll travel quickly, however you'll also attract your fair share of obnoxious drivers. It is a good idea to travel with someone else, preferably a guy. This way you will be perceived as a couple which means that you shouldn't have any sleazy old men trying to come on to you, and if they do at least there is someone to help you out.

Many hitchhikers travel with a mobile phone and only hitch where there is coverage. Being able to call for help makes hitching a safer transport option. For this to work you need to keep your phone charged and in your pocket and you need to know the emergency number (112 is the international emergency number from GSM mobile phones, although the British and Irish emergency number 999 should also work).

Don't let the driver put your backpack in the car boot. Try and keep all your stuff with you, even when you stop for food and fuel.

Don't feel compelled to accept a lift just because someone has stopped for you. If it doesn't feel right, don't get in. Another ride will come along.

Ride sharing

Ride sharing agencies are a good alternative to hitchhiking. These agencies act as a matchmaker between drivers and riders and cost around half what the bus fare would be.

BUG Ride *(website http://europe.bugride.com)* is BUG's own Internet-based ride sharing agency where you can offer lifts to other travellers or search for a lift. The lift is often free although it's also common to split fuel expenses with the driver.

England

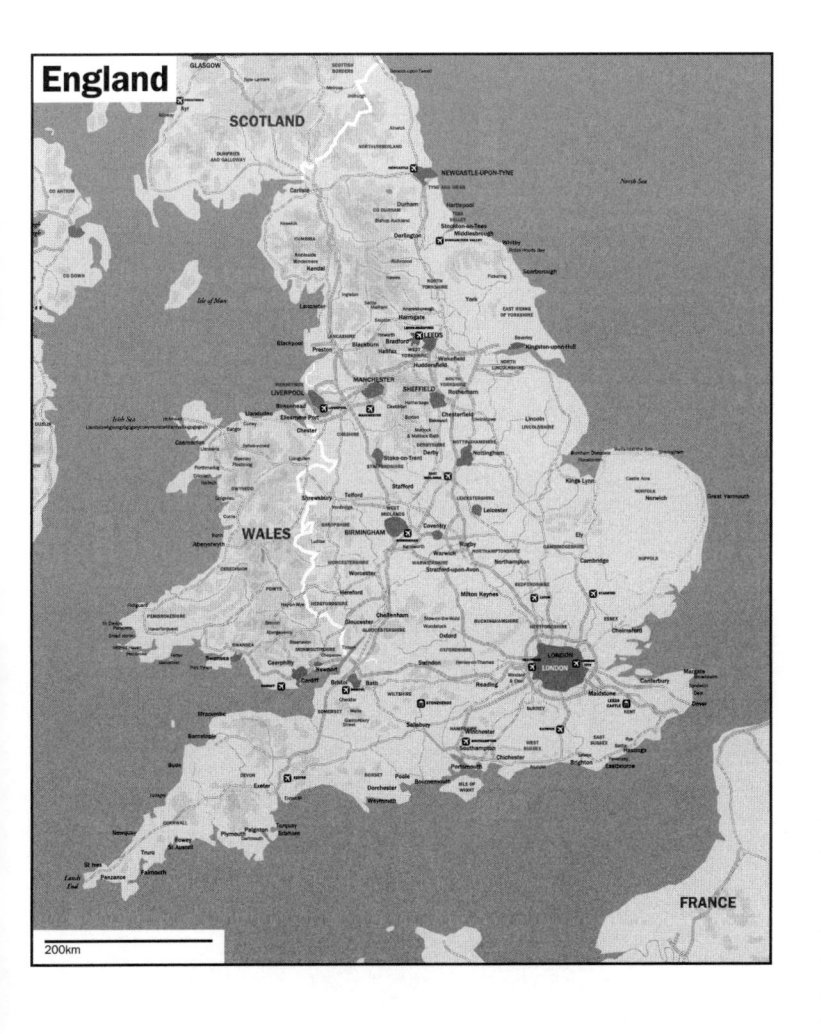

London

London is one of Europe's biggest cities and for many years was the centre of the English-speaking world. London today has a rich history with many remnants of its imperial past, yet it is a city facing the future with a diverse population and loads of attractions.

London is also most backpackers' gateway to Europe and is an enormously popular city to find work and it makes a great base with its cheap and frequent transport connections to the rest of the UK and Europe.

It is a very expensive city, particularly for accommodation, but there are many cheap places to eat and a lot of the major attractions (including many world-famous museums) are free.

Practical Information

For an up-to-date look at what's happening around London, including information on gigs and theatre plus finding work and accommodation, pick up a copy of one of the free weekly magazines such as *LAM* and *TNT* from your hostel or from boxes outside tube stations and pubs around town. For more in depth entertainment listings *Time Out* is available from newsagents for £2.35.

INFORMATION CENTRES
Britain & London Visitor Centre
1 Regent Street, Piccadilly Circus, London SW1
🚇 *Piccadilly Circus* 🚌 *3, 6, 9, 12, 13, 14, 15, 19, 22, 23, 38, 88, 94, 139, 159, 453*
Website *www.visitbritain.com*
Open *Jan-May Mon 9.30am-6.30pm, Tue-Fri 9am-6.30pm, Sat-Sun 10am-4pm; Jun-Oct Mon 9.30am-6.30pm, Tue-Fri 9am-6.30pm, Sat 9am-5pm, Sun 10am-4pm; Nov-Dec Mon 9.30am-6.30pm, Tue-Fri 9am-6.30pm, Sat-Sun 10am-4pm*

City of London Information Centre
St Paul's Churchyard, London
🚇 *Blackfriars, St Pauls* 🚆 *Blackfriars, City Thameslink* 🚌 *4, 8, 11, 15, 17, 23, 25, 26, 56, 76, 100, 172, 242, 521*
Open *Jan-Mar Mon-Fri 9.30am-5pm, Sat 9.30am-12.30pm; Apr-Sep 9.30am-5pm daily; Oct-Dec Mon-Fri 9.30am-5pm, Sat 9.30am-12.30pm*

Greenwich Tourist Information Centre
Pepys House, 2 Cutty Sark Gardens, Greenwich, London SE10
🚇 *Cutty Sark* 🚆 *Greenwich* 🚌 *177, 180, 188, 199, 286, 386* ⛴ *Greenwich Pier*
☎ *0870 608 2000*
Website *http://greenwich2000.com/*
Open *10am-5pm daily*

London Visitor Centre
Arrivals Hall, Waterloo International Terminal, London SE1
🚇🚆 *Waterloo* 🚌 *1, 4, 26, 59, 68, 76, 77, 139, 168, 171, 172, 176, 188, 211, 243, 341, 381, 507, 521, 705, RV1, X68*
Website *www.visitlondon.com*
Open *8.30am-10.30pm daily*

London Visitor Information Centre
Leicester Square, London
🚇 *Leicester Square* 🚌 *24, 29, 176*
☎ *(020) 7292 2333*
Website *www.londontown.com*
Open *Mon-Fri 8am-11pm, Sat-Sun 10am-6pm*

Southwark Tourist Information Centre
Vinopolis, 1 Bank End, London SE1
🚇🚆 *Cannon Street, London Bridge* 🚌 *381, RV1*
☎ *(020) 7357 9168*
Website *www.visitlondon.com*

Visit Scotland Centre
19 Cockspur Street, London SW1
🚇 *Charing Cross, Piccadilly Circus* 🚆 *Charing Cross* 🚌 *3, 6, 9, 12, 13, 15, 23, 88, 139, 159, 453*
Open *Jan-Apr Mon-Fri 10am-6pm, Sat noon-4pm; May-Sep Mon-Fri 9.30am-6.30pm, Sat 10am-5pm; Oct-Dec Mon-Fri 10am-6pm, Sat noon-4pm*

CREDIT CARDS
American Express
6 Haymarket, London SW1
🚇 *Piccadilly Circus* 🚌 *3, 6, 9, 12, 13, 14, 15, 19, 22, 23, 38, 88, 94, 139, 159, 453*
☎ *(020) 7930 4411*
Website *www.americanexpress.com*

Mastercard/Eurocard
Lost card hotline ☎ *0800 96 47 67*
Website *www.mastercard.com*

Diners Club
Lost card hotline ☎ *0800 460 800*
Website *www.dinersclub.com*

Visa International
Lost card hotline ☎ *0800 89 17 25*
Website *www.visa.com*

EMBASSIES & CONSULATES
Australian High Commission
Australia House, Strand, London WC2
🚇 *Charing Cross, Temple* 🚆 *Charing Cross* 🚌 *4, 11, 15, 23, 26, 76, 172*
☎ *(020) 7379 4334*
Website *www.australia.org.uk*
Open *Mon-Fri 9am-11am*

Canadian High Commission
38 Grosvenor Street, London W1
🚇 *Bond Street* 🚌 *6, 7, 8, 10, 12, 13, 23, 7388, 94, 98, 113, 139, 159, 189, 390*
☎ *(020) 7258 6600*
Website *www.canada.org.uk*
Open *Mon-Fri 8am-11am*

New Zealand High Commission
80 Haymarket, London SW1
🚇 *Piccadilly Circus* 🚌 *3, 6, 9, 12, 13, 14, 15, 19, 22, 23, 38, 88, 94, 139, 159, 453*
☎ *(020) 7930 8422*
Website *www.nzembassy.com*
Open *Mon-Fri 2pm-4pm*

South African Embassy
Trafalgar Square, London WC2
🚇🚆 *Charing Cross* 🚌 *3, 4, 9, 11, 12, 13, 15, 23, 24, 29, 53, 77A, 88, 91, 139, 159, 176, 453*
☎ *(020) 7451 7299*
Website *www.southafricahouse.com*
Open *Mon-Fri 9am-5pm*

United States Embassy
24 Grosvenor Street, London W1
🚇 *Bond Street* 🚌 *6, 7, 8, 10, 12, 13, 23, 7388, 94, 98, 113, 139, 159, 189, 390*
☎ *(020) 7499 9000*
Website *www.usembassy.org.uk*
Open *Mon-Fri 8.30am-5.30pm*

Home Office
(for visa extensions)
Lunar House, 40 Wellesley Road, Croydon, Surrey
🚆 *East Croydon* 🚌 *64, 119, 194, 197, 198, 312, 367, 409, 410, 466, 726, T33* 🚌 *1, 2, 3*
☎ *0870 606 7766*
Website *www.ind.homeoffice.gov.uk*
Open *Mon-Thu 9am-4.45pm, Fri 9am-4.30pm*

INTERNET ACCESS
Easy Internetcafé
160-166 Kensington High Street, London W8
🚇 *High Street Kensington* 🚌 *9, 10, 27, 28, 49*
Website *www.easyinternetcafe.com*
Open *7am-11pm daily*

Unit G1, Kings Walk, 120 Kings Road, London SW3
🚇 *Sloane Square* 🚌 *11, 19, 22, 137, 211*
Website *www.easyinternetcafe.com*
Open *Mon-Thu 9.30am-7pm, Fri-Sat 9.30am-10.30pm, Sun noon-6pm*

358 Oxford Street, London W1
🚇 *Bond Street* 🚌 *6, 7, 8, 10, 12, 13, 15, 23, 73, 94, 98, 113, 137, 139, 159, 189, 390*
Website *www.easyinternetcafe.com*
Open *Mon-Wed 8am-10pm, Thu-Sat 8am-midnight, Sun 8am-10pm*

Inside Burger King, 46 Regent Street, London W1
🚇 *Piccadilly Circus* 🚌 *3, 6, 9, 12, 13, 14, 15, 19, 22, 23, 38, 88, 94, 139, 159, 453*
Website *www.easyinternetcafe.com*
Open *Mon-Sat 8am-midnight, Sun 9am-midnight*

9-16 Tottenham Court Road, London W1
🚇 *Tottenham Court Road* 🚌 *10, 24,*

29, 73, 134, 390
Website www.easyinternetcafe.com
Open Mon-Wed 8am-midnight, Thu-Sat 8am-2am, Sun 8am-midnight

456/459 Strand, London WC2
🚇🚆 *Charing Cross* 🚌 *6, 9, 11, 13, 15, 23, 29, 77A, 91, 139*
Website www.easyinternetcafe.com
Open 8am-11pm daily

9-13 Wilton Road, London SW1
🚇🚆 *Victoria* 🚌 *C1, C10, 7, 8, 11, 16, 24, 36, 38, 52, 73, 82, 148, 185, 211, 239, 436, 507, 705*
Website www.easyinternetcafe.com
Open Mon 8am-11pm, Tue-Sat 8am-midnight, Sun 8am-11pm

Internet Café
19 Leinster Terrace, London W2
🚇 *Lancaster Gate* 🚌 *12, 94, 148*
Open 24 hours

Reload
197 Praed Street, Paddington, London W2
🚇🚆 *Paddington* 🚌 *7, 15, 23, 27, 36, 205, 436, 705*
☎ *(020) 7262 4113*
Open 9am-11pm daily

Coming & Going
AIR
London is served by five airports: Gatwick, Heathrow, London City, Luton and Stansted.

Gatwick
Gatwick Airport (☎ *0870 000 2468; website www.baa.com/main/airports/gatwick/*) is London's second busiest airport. It is located in Crawley, Sussex, about midway between London and Brighton. Gatwick Airport has two terminals that are connected by a transit system. When you arrive at the airport, signs will tell you which terminal to go to. Generally most flights, including charters, depart from the South Terminal, and the North Terminal handles Britain, Delta and British Airways.

There are over 900 train services each day from Gatwick Airport to London and other destinations in England. The following train companies serve Gatwick: First Great Western Link (*website www.firstgreatwestern.co.uk/link*), Gatwick Express (*website www.gatwickexpress.co.uk*), Southern Railway (*website www.southernrailway.com*), Thameslink (*website www.thameslink.co.uk*) and Virgin Trains (*website www.virgintrains.co.uk*).

Gatwick Express, Southern and Thameslink run the most frequent train services between Gatwick and London with each of these operators running trains every 15 minutes during the day, and hourly at night.

Both Gatwick Express and Southern have departures from Victoria station to Gatwick Airport, which is a 30-minute journey with Gatwick Express and 35 minutes with Southern Railway. Gatwick Express costs £12 one-way and £23.50 return. Southern Railway is cheaper at £8 one-way and £16 return. Southern Railway also operate a service between Gatwick and Kensington Olympia that stops at West Brompton (near Earls Court).

It is also possible to get to Gatwick from either London Bridge or Kings Cross train stations with Thameslink. Thameslink trains from London Bridge cost £10 one-way and £20 return; Thameslink trains from Kings Cross to Gatwick are £10 one-way and £20 for a one-month return. Keep in mind that Thameslink trains leave from Kings Cross Thameslink Station, which is on Pentonville Road, a two-minute walk from the main Kings Cross station. Thameslink trains also go between Gatwick and Luton Airports (£18 one-way, £36 return) and between Gatwick and Brighton.

Both Southern and Thameslink train services from Gatwick can be booked online at www.flybytrain.co.uk.

First Great Western Link trains go from Gatwick to Reading and Oxford. A one-way ticket between Gatwick and Oxford costs from £22.30 to £31.

If you have an early morning flight call 0845 7484950 for up-to-date information on train services to the airport.

Heathrow
Heathrow Airport (☎ *(020) 8759 4321; website www.baa.com/main/airports/*

heathrow/) is the world's busiest international airport and is located west of London.

Heathrow has four terminals. Terminals one, two and three are conveniently clustered together, but terminal four is at the other end of the airport.

You will need to use terminal four if you are flying on British Airways to Amsterdam, Basle, Brussels, Copenhagen, Geneva, Lyon, Oslo, Paris, Vienna or Zurich or longhaul British Airways flights (except flights to Hong Kong, Johannesburg, Los Angeles, Miami, San Francisco, Tokyo or Tripoli). Other airlines using terminal four include Air Malta, Asiana Airlines, SN Brussels, Emirates (to Abu Dhabi and flight EK6156 to Dubai), Iberia (to Bangkok only), Kenya Airways, KLM, Qantas, SriLankan Airlines and Swiss (flights LX3501-LX3541 only). All other flights depart from terminals one, two and three.

Heathrow is easily accessible from central London by tube, train and bus.

The most popular way to get to and from Heathrow is via the Piccadilly tube line that runs from central London to terminals one, two and three. Take the tube to Hatton Cross and hop on the terminal four shuttle bus if you need to get to terminal four. The tube takes approximately 45 minutes from central London and costs £3.80 one-way.

Alternatively you could take the Heathrow Express (*website* www.heathrowexpress.com) train, which is a more expensive option connecting Heathrow to Paddington Station in 15 minutes, with trains running every 15 minutes. Tickets are £13.

London City Airport

London City Airport (*website* www.londoncityairport.com) is the most centrally located airport but is almost exclusively used for business flights to northern Europe. City Airport's big advantage is that it only has a 10-minute check-in compared to two hours for most other airports.

The blue shuttle bus makes the 30-minute journey from Liverpool Street Station (£6 one-way) and a 10 minutes journey from Canary Wharf (£3.50 one-way) and the green bus from Canning Town station takes five minutes and costs £3.

Cheaper options include London transport's bus route 69 to Canning Town station, route 473 operates from the airport to Stratford, Silvertown, North Woolwich, and Prince Regent Station and bus 474, which goes to Canning Town, North Woolwich and East Beckton.

Luton Airport

London Luton Airport (☎ (01582) 405 100; *website* www.london-luton.co.uk) is in Luton, about 45 minutes north of central London. Luton is a smaller airport that mainly handles charter flights and budget airlines including easyJet.

Thameslink operate trains to Luton Airport Parkway station from Kings Cross, Blackfriars, London Bridge and Gatwick Airport train stations. Thameslink services from London cost £10.40 one-way or £20.80 return. If you are taking the Thameslink train from Kings Cross you will need to go to the Kings Cross Thameslink station on Pentonville Road rather than the main Kings Cross station (about a four minute walk away).

Greenline 757 is a bus service which operates from Buckingham Palace Road near Victoria Station, stopping at Brent Cross, Finchley Road station, Baker Street and Marble Arch. If you're flying with easyJet the Greenline bus costs £7.50 one-way or £8.50 return.

National Express operate direct coach connections from Luton Airport to Birmingham, Cambridge and Leicester.

Stansted Airport

Stansted Airport (☎ 0870 0000 303; *website* www.baa.com/main/airports/stansted) is London's third busiest airport. It is about halfway between London and Cambridge and handles many budget airlines including Ryanair.

Take the Stansted Express (☎ 0845 7484 950; *website* www.stanstedexpress.com) train from Liverpool Street station to get to the airport from London. Trains run every 15 to 30 minutes and the 45-minute journey costs £13.80 one-way or £24 return.

Central Trains *(website www.centraltrains.co.uk)* run trains from Stansted to Birmingham, Cambridge, Leicester and Liverpool. Central Trains' one-way fare to Cambridge is £6.80.

National Express (☎ *0870 5747 777; website www.nationalexpress.com)* run bus services linking Stansted with London, Cambridge, Colchester and Norwich. Its London services include the A6 bus, which runs every 20 minutes to Victoria Coach Station and the A7 bus, which also goes to Victoria but stops at Liverpool Street Station en route; both these services cost £10 one-way or £15 return. A cheaper alternative is the A9 service, which runs every half hour to Stratford in East London, costing £6 one-way. From Stratford you can hop onto the tube to virtually anywhere in London.

BUS

Victoria Coach Station on Buckingham Palace Road has National Express buses to destinations in the UK, Bus Eireann buses to Ireland and Eurolines to destinations in Europe. The cheap Megabus bus services and Green Line buses to Luton Airport and Windsor depart from the Green Line Coach Station, at the corner of Elizabeth Bridge and Bulleid Way just off Buckingham Palace Road.

TRAIN

London has lots of train stations, the main ones are: Charing Cross (trains to the south-east); Euston (trains to the Midlands, north-west England, and the west coast to Scotland); Kings Cross (trains to northern England, Yorkshire and Gatwick and Luton airports); Liverpool Street (trains to Essex, East Anglia and Stansted Airport); London Bridge (trains to Kent and Gatwick and Luton airports); Marylebone (trains to Birmingham and Oxfordshire); Paddington (trains to west England, the West Midlands, south Wales and Ireland (via Fishguard)); St Pancras (trains to the Midlands); Victoria (trains to Kent, Gatwick Airport and the south coast) and Waterloo Station (trains to southern England and Eurostar trains to Paris and Brussels).

For information on train departures in the UK call 0845 7484950.

HITCHHIKING

London is a reasonably easy city to hitch from. Because London has a number of motorways (expressways) that terminate in the suburbs, rather than run right through the centre you are able to get a good hitchhiking spot right near a motorway entrance.

If you're heading north, take the tube to Brent Cross (on the Northern line), then walk or take a bus to Brent Cross Shopping Centre and walk to Staples Corner. Staples Corner is a busy intersection with a number of big stores like PC World and Staples where Edgware Road, the M1 and the North Circular Road connect. When you get here, look for the entrance to the M1 Motorway.

If you're heading to the West of England or South Wales, you'll need to get to the entrance of the M4. Take the tube to Chiswick Park (on the District line) and walk to the A4 (which is also called Great West Road or Cedars Road). Because you need to hitch from the southern side of the road to catch traffic bound for the M4 Motorway, you'll need to walk down Sutton Court Road and cross at the lights. Check the area map at the tube station to get your bearings.

The M11 takes you to Cambridge and East Anglia. This motorway connects with the North Circular Road in the northeastern suburbs. Take the tube to Redbridge (on the Central line) and walk under the A406 overpass and stand near the on-ramp to both the M11 and the A406 (North Circular Road). You'll probably need a sign saying "M11 Please"; otherwise cars going to the North Circular Road might offer lifts.

If you want to go to the Southampton or Winchester, you'll need to get on the M3. You can either take a train from Waterloo to Sunbury and hitch from there or hitch from the A316 which carries a lot of traffic bound for the M3 Motorway. You'll need to get a train from Waterloo, Clapham Junction or Richmond to Whitton, walk to the A316 (Chertsey Road) and cross the footbridge to the southbound lane. Use a sign marked "M3 Please" to avoid getting picked up by suburban traffic.

If you're heading to the southeast to catch a ferry from one of the Channel ports of Folkstone or Dover, you'll want to get to the M20. Since the M20 doesn't start until you're well out of London, it's best to get on the A20 before it becomes a motorway. Catch a train from London Bridge Station to Mottingham in the southeastern suburbs. At Mottingham, walk to the A20 (Sidcup Road); at this point the A20 is still a suburban road so there is no problem finding a place to stand although you'll need a sign saying "M20 Please" otherwise you'll just get suburban traffic. A good ride on the M20 can get you all the way to France since the ferry ticket to Boulogne or Calais covers up to five passengers.

BUG Ride *(website http://europe.bugride.com)* is BUG's own free web-based ride sharing service, it allows travellers to both offer lifts and search for rides throughout Europe. This is a free service which links travellers to drivers – you contact the driver by email when you have found the ride you want.

Local Transport
Despite constant grumbling from Londoners, London has a brilliant public transport system that is comprised of buses, trains, trams and the underground.

BUS
London's double-decker buses are a tourist attraction in their own right and riding on the top deck is a must for every traveller. Although slower than the tube, buses are an excellent way to get around London since they give you a totally different perspective of the city.

The destination, along with major stops, is indicated on the panel on the front and sometimes the back of each bus. Although you can pay for each ride on board the bus, most people just flash their Travelcard which allows free transport on bus services provided by London Transport and a number of private bus operators.

Bus fares on London buses are £1.20 or £1 per journey if you buy a Bus Saver (a book of six single tickets that costs £6) in advance. It is also possible to buy a one-day bus pass for £3.

Although train and tube services stop shortly after midnight, there are a number of bus route that operate throughout the night. These night buses have route numbers prefixed with the letter "N" and run from around 11pm to 6am. Most night buses stop in Trafalgar Square, which makes this the place to head for, if you don't know which bus to get. Night buses cost more than regular buses and they don't accept one-day Travelcards although weekly and monthly passes are accepted.

There are also a number of touristy bus services that operate a circuit of the major tourist attractions. They give a running commentary, which some people may find entertaining and the open-top doubledeckers provide excellent photo opportunities. Although these tourist buses may seem like a good idea at first, they are a bit tacky, they don't give you the opportunity to mingle with the locals, and most importantly they are expensive. It's a much better idea to grab a travel card and take a regular bus and spend the money you've saved down at the pub!

TRAM
The Tramlink tram service operates around Croydon in the southern suburbs and it is unlikely that you will use this service. Fares are the same as the bus.

THE UNDERGROUND
The London Underground or the tube *(website http://tube.tfl.gov.uk/)* is the world's largest public transport network. Commonly referred to simply as 'the tube', the Underground network is made up of 12 lines plus Docklands Light Railway that provides an elevated network in the East End. Each line in the London Underground is named and indicated by a different colour on tube maps that appear at stations and on each train carriage. Because each line generally runs on its own tracks, you will have to follow the signs to transfer to a different line.

Following the fire at Kings Cross station in 1987, it is now illegal to smoke anywhere on the London Underground, even on stations above ground.

Some stations on the Underground network have curved platforms. This means that trains don't always stop flush to the edge to the platform creating a gap between the train and the platform. It is a good idea to pay attention to avoid falling in the gap when getting on and off your train. This has led to the Underground's most popular public safety announcement "mind the gap".

SUBURBAN TRAINS

London's suburban trains are run by around ten different companies and carry more commuters than the London Underground. Suburban train services fill in areas that aren't covered by the underground and generally run every 20 minutes or so, with more frequent trains operating the closer you get into central London. Trains on some routes (such as Waterloo to Clapham Junction) run almost as frequently as the tube. You probably won't be using these services unless you want to go to places in south London, if you want to get to the good hitchhiking spots or if you are travelling beyond or out of London. The Travelcard is accepted by virtually all suburban train services, the few exceptions include airport services such as the Heathrow Express and Gatwick Express.

FERRIES

There are ferry services that link piers along the River Thames. The three main commuter services run between Chelsea Harbour and Blackfriars Millennium Pier, between Savoy Pier and Greenwich (via Canary Wharf) and between Hilton Docklands and Canary Wharf.

FARES

Fares are based on a zone system with six zones in the London area. Everything you are likely to want to travel to is located in zones one and two.

A single ticket valid for zone one on the tube costs £2. Ticket prices for other zones are as follows:

Zones	Adult one-way fare
1	£2
1-2	£2.30
1-3	£2.80
1-4	£2.80
1-5	£3.80
1-6	£3.80

As you can tell from the above prices, the tube can be a very expensive way of getting around town. However, there are a number of ways of reducing the cost of getting around London.

It is possible to buy a carnet of ten tickets that discounts the fare to around 30% of the cost of buying individual tickets. Carnet tickets are only valid for journeys on the underground that start and finish in zone one. A carnet costs £17, which works out at £1.70 per trip.

Remember to validate your ticket or you could be up for a £10 fine.

Travelcards are a much better deal. These tickets allow unlimited travel during a set period.

Most visitors to London buy a travel card each day, although you may find a weekly ticket a better option if you're staying a five days or more. One-day Travelcards are good for unlimited travel on buses, the underground and suburban trains after 9.30am Monday to Friday and all day on Saturdays, Sundays and public holidays. Three-day Travelcards can be a good deal if you're visiting London for a few days, although they're not much cheaper than a weekly ticket.

One-day Travelcards are not valid on night buses, although travel on night buses is included in weekly and monthly Travelcards.

Zones	1 day off peak	1 day peak
1-2	£4.70	£6
1-4	£5.20	£8
1-6	£6	£12
2-6	£4	£7

Zones	3 day	weekly
1		£18.50
1-2	£15	£21.50
1-4	-	£30.40
1-6	£36 peak £18 off peak	£39.50
2-6	-	£25.30

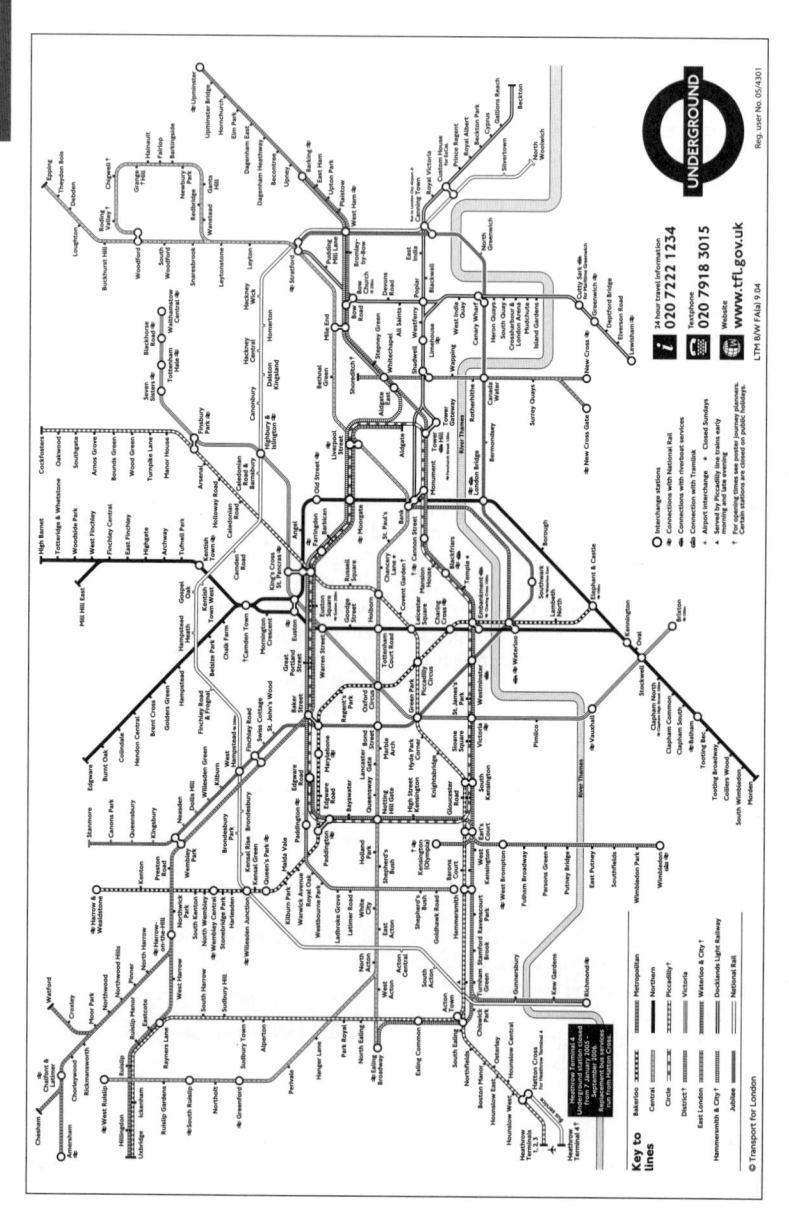

London

You will need a Photocard if you are buying a monthly Travelcard or a seven-day rail-only season ticket. Photocards are available from tube stations, Oyster ticket shops and London Travel Information Centres.

The pre-paid Oyster Card *(website www.oystercard.com)* is a smart card that can be used to buy tickets cheaper than the regular cash price. It isn't really worth the effort if you're in London for a short time, but it can be a good deal if you're planning on working in London. Monthly passes are only issued on Oyster Cards.

TAXIS

London's black cabs are as famous as its red double-decker buses, and many visitors consider a ride in a black cab all part of the London experience. Unlike taxi drivers elsewhere, London cabbies can't get their licence until they've passed a rigorous test called 'the knowledge'. Getting the knowledge involves two to three years of studying a map for three hours a day followed by another three hours whizzing around London on a moped. By the time taxi drivers have graduated they know the shortest distance between any two places in London. Tipping isn't really expected although many people add an extra 10%.

Minicabs are a cheaper alternative. Because they are unlicensed they are not allowed to pick up passengers off the street (although many minicabs hang around pubs at closing time) and you generally have to call them or wait for them at the office of a minicab company. Minicabs don't have meters so you'll have to negotiate a rate beforehand. Don't expect the professionalism of a black cab.

DRIVING

Although driving is one of the best ways to explore Great Britain, most travellers sensibly choose to avoid driving in central London. Although there is a fairly comprehensive network of motorways radiating from the outer suburbs, which are joined by the M21 Orbital Motorway (ring road), there are no motorways that run through the centre of town and this results in bottlenecks and traffic jams.

In an effort to reduce congestion, a daily congestion charge of £5 is levied on every car driven into a designated area in central London. You are required to pay the £5 congestion charge if you drive or park in the congestion-charging zone between 7am and 6.30pm Monday to Friday. Motorbikes and scooters are exempt from this levy.

The zone is bordered by Marylebone Road, Euston Road, Pentonville Road and City Road to the north, Commercial Street and Tower Bridge Road to the east, Vauxhall Bridge Road, Kennington Lane and New Kent Road to the south and Park Lane to the west. There are 174 entry and exit points on the congestion charging zone boundary and 230 automatic number plate recognition cameras placed throughout central London.

Victoria and Paddington Stations and the tourist areas of Bayswater, Earls Court and South Kensington are located outside the congestion charging zone.

Payment may be made by sending a text (SMS) message from your mobile phone; however you first have to register your name, address, credit card and vehicle details either by phone or online (☎ *0845 900 1234; website www.cclondon.com).* Alternatively you apply for a Fast Track card that can be swiped at participating retail outlets, although this card is designed more for residents and other frequent users and is not a popular option for visitors to London.

If you're planning on renting a car in London to explore Great Britain, it is a good idea to make sure that the rental car office you're picking the car up from is located outside the zone to avoid having to pay the charge.

Accommodation
BAYSWATER & PADDINGTON

The northern end of Hyde Park has a number of hostels and budget hotels, particularly in the Bayswater area and around Paddington Station. This area is close to Notting Hill, which is famous for its annual carnival.

Atlantic Paddington

The Atlantic Paddington is a large hostel with fairly standard facilities

that include a bar with pool table plus a TV lounge and Internet access. Most rooms have new bunk beds with real mattresses and all rooms have TVs.
1 Queens Gardens, Bayswater, London W2
🚇 *Bayswater, Lancaster Gate, Paddington, Queensway* 🚌 *12, 94, 148*
☎ *(020) 7262 4471*
Website *www.newatlantic.co.uk*
Dorm bed £21; **single room** £43-55; **double room** £60-73; **twin room** £55-73; *prices include breakfast*
Credit cards *JCB, MC, Visa*
📺 🅺 🅣

Maintenance & cleanliness	★★★
Facilities	★✩
Atmosphere & character	✩
Security	★★★
Overall rating	★★

Bayswater Hotel

This hostel offers good value accommodation. The rooms are quite nice with real mattresses and en suite showers but the common areas are rather limited, which detracts from the atmosphere.
60 Princes Square, Bayswater, London W2
🚇 *Bayswater, Royal Oak, Queensway*
🚌 *7, 23, 27, 70*
☎ *(020) 7229 6436*
Dorm bed £10; **single room** £25; **double room** £30; *prices include breakfast*
Reception open *24 hours*
🅺

Maintenance & cleanliness	★★✩
Facilities	★
Atmosphere & character	★✩
Security	★★
Overall rating	★★

Hyde Park Hostel

This large hostel is a comfortable place to stay that has the usual amenities such as a kitchen, TV lounge, laundry, Internet access plus a good bar; however it could be better maintained.
2-6 Inverness Terrace, Bayswater, London W2
🚇 *Bayswater, Queensway* 🚌 *12, 94, 148*
☎ *(020) 7229 5101*
Website *www.astorhostels.com*
Dorm bed £12.50-18; **twin room** £50; *prices include breakfast*

Credit cards *Amex, Diners, JCB, MC, Visa*
Reception open *24 hours*
📺 🅺 🅛 🅣

Maintenance & cleanliness	★★
Facilities	★★
Atmosphere & character	★★
Security	★★★★
Overall rating	★★✩

Hyde Park Inn

The Hyde Park Inn is a clean and well-maintained hostel with excellent security. Facilities include the usual kitchen, TV lounge and Internet access.
48-50 Inverness Terrace, Bayswater, London W2
🚇 *Bayswater, Queensway* 🚌 *12, 94, 148*
☎ *(020) 7229 0000*
Website *www.hydeparkinn.com*
Dorm bed £9-25; **double/twin** £48-50
Credit cards *Amex, JCB, MC, Visa*
Reception open *24 hours*
📺 🅺 🅛

Maintenance & cleanliness	★★★★✩
Facilities	★
Atmosphere & character	★★★
Security	★★★★★
Overall rating	★★★

Leinster Hostel

This hostel caters mostly to long-term guests on a working holiday in London. Accommodation consists of mostly small rooms with self-contained facilities. Although cheap, it's not such a good choice for travellers looking for somewhere to spend a few nights.
18 Leinster Gardens, London W2
🚇 *Bayswater, Queensway* 🚌 *12, 94, 148*
☎ *(020) 7262 3507*
Dorm bed £8.50 per night, £60-75 per week
Credit cards *Diners, JCB, MC, Visa*
Reception open *24 hours*
📺 🅺

Maintenance & cleanliness	★★★★✩
Facilities	★★✩
Atmosphere & character	-
Security	★★★✩
Overall rating	★★

Leinster Inn

The Leinster Inn is a miserable place that is in need of a thorough renova-

tion, although it has a good location and basic facilities that include a TV lounge, kitchen, and bar. The kitchen facilities are limited and you need to pay a deposit for pots and pans if you want to cook anything. The standard of accommodation varies from dingy and rundown to passable depending on what room you're staying in.
7-12 Leinster Square, Bayswater, London W2
🚇 *Bayswater, Royal Oak, Queensway*
🚌 *7, 23, 27, 70*
☎ *(020) 7229 9641*
Website *www.astorhostels.com*
Dorm bed *£15-18.50;* **single room** *£35-40;* **double/twin room** *£50-58*
Reception open *24 hours*
📺 🍳 🔒 🛏

Maintenance & cleanliness	★☆
Facilities	★★
Atmosphere & character	★
Security	★★★
Overall rating	★★

Millennium Lodge Central

This hostel is much nicer that the other Millennium Lodge (in Kensal Green) but it is also more expensive. It has a TV lounge at the reception and the kitchen is small, although it has new appliances.
26 Princes Square, Bayswater, London W2
🚇 *Bayswater, Royal Oak, Queensway*
🚌 *7, 23, 27, 70*
☎ *(020) 7727 5807*
Dorm bed *£10-16;* **single room** *£30;* **twin room** *£40; prices include breakfast*
Reception open *24 hours*
📺 🍳

Maintenance & cleanliness	★★★☆
Facilities	★☆
Atmosphere & character	★★★
Security	★★
Overall rating	★★★☆

Palace Hotel

The Palace Hotel is a good value hostel with a fully equipped kitchen and a small TV lounge with a wide screen telly.
48-49 Princes Square, Bayswater, London W2
🚇 *Bayswater, Royal Oak, Queensway*
🚌 *7, 23, 27, 70*
☎ *(020) 7229 1729*
Dorm bed *£9-10;* **single room** *£15;* **double room** *£25*
Reception open *24 hours*
📺 🍳 🔒

Maintenance & cleanliness	★★★
Facilities	★
Atmosphere & character	★★☆
Security	★★☆
Overall rating	★★☆

Princes Hotel

Princes Hotel is a good value hostel with TVs, fridges and en suite showers in the rooms. However minimal common areas and TVs in the rooms detract from the atmosphere.
63 Princes Square, Bayswater, London W2
🚇 *Bayswater, Royal Oak, Queensway*
🚌 *7, 23, 27, 70*
☎ *(020) 7229 4944*
Dorm bed *£8-11;* **double room** *£30*
Credit cards *MC, Visa*
Reception open *24 hours*
📺 🍳

Maintenance & cleanliness	★★★
Facilities	☆
Atmosphere & character	-
Security	★★☆
Overall rating	★☆

Quest Hostel

The Astor Quest Hostel has accommodation in small dorms with new bunk beds and en suite bathrooms in many rooms. The common room, with TV and Internet access, has a good atmosphere but the kitchen was dirty and poorly equipped.
45 Queensborough Terrace, London W2
🚇 *Bayswater, Queensway* 🚌 *12, 94, 148*
☎ *(020) 7229 7782*
Dorm bed *£12-17;* **twin room** *£46*
Credit cards *MC, Visa*
Reception open *24 hours*
📺 🍳

Maintenance & cleanliness	★★☆
Facilities	★☆
Atmosphere & character	★★★☆
Security	★★★
Overall rating	★★☆

West Two Hotel

The West Two offers basic accommodation and the furnishings are old and

tired, however it is great value considering the location.
22-23 Kensington Gardens Square, Bayswater, London W2
🚇 *Bayswater, Royal Oak, Queensway*
🚌 *7, 23, 27, 70*
☎ *(020) 7221 9171*
Dorm bed *£9-11;* **single bed** *£20;* **double room** *£35; prices include breakfast*
Reception open *24 hours*
📺🅺

Maintenance & cleanliness	★★☆
Facilities	★
Atmosphere & character	★
Security	★★★☆
Overall rating	★★☆

BLOOMSBURY & KINGS CROSS

Although a bit grotty, Kings Cross has excellent transport connections. Bloombury is a much nicer area than Kings Cross, is more central and is home to the British Museum.

Ashlee House

Ashlee House is a great hostel with a stylish décor and a hip atmosphere. Some dorms are large (the biggest has 16 beds) but the whole place is brightly painted, well maintained and has nice lounge areas.
261-265 Grays Inn Road, London WC1
🚇🚆 *Kings Cross St Pancras* 🚌 *17, 45, 46*
☎ *(020) 7833 9400*
Website *www.ashleehouse.co.uk*
Dorm bed *£13-19;* **single room** *£34-36;* **twin room** *£44-48; prices include breakfast*
Credit cards *MC, Visa*
Reception open *24 hours*
📺🅺🅻

Maintenance & cleanliness	★★★★
Facilities	★
Atmosphere & character	★★★★
Security	★★★
Overall rating	★★★

Astor Museum Inn

The Astor Museum Inn has a great location near the British Museum. It has a good atmosphere in the common rooms but the kitchen facilities are limited and the dorms look a little drab.
27 Montague Street, London WC1
🚇 *Russell Square, Holborn, Tottenham Court Road* 🚌 *7*
☎ *(020) 7580 5360*
Website *www.astorhostels.com*
Dorm bed *£15-19;* **twin room** *£48; prices include breakfast*
Credit cards *MC, Visa*
Reception open *24 hours*
📺🅺

Maintenance & cleanliness	★★★☆
Facilities	★
Atmosphere & character	★★★
Security	★★★★
Overall rating	★★★☆

Caledonia Hostel

Caledonia Hostel is a dreadful place offering very basic accommodation. The hostel is poorly maintained and furnishings are old and ratty. Facilities include a couple of lounges, one with a TV, and an old run down kitchen.
54-58 Caledonian Road, King's Cross, London N1
🚇🚆 *Kings Cross St Pancras* 🚌 *17, 91, 259*
☎ *(020) 7837 4602*
Website *http://indigo.ie/~breweryh/london/caledonia.htm*
Dorm bed *£11;* **double/twin room** *£30*
Reception open *24 hours*
📺🅺

Maintenance & cleanliness	★
Facilities	☆
Atmosphere & character	★★
Security	★★
Overall rating	★

The Generator

The Generator is a huge hostel with over 800 beds. It has a modern industrial décor and very extensive common areas with lots of TVs. There's also Internet access, a restaurant and a bar with activities like drinking games, karaoke, quiz nights and pool competitions. However there are no kitchen facilities other than a microwave and toaster in the corner of one of the common rooms and some parts of the hostel, including many of the dorm rooms, are a bit run down.
Compton Place, off 37 Tavistock Place, London WC1
🚇 *Russell Square, Kings Cross St Pancras* 🚆 *Kings Cross, St Pancras, Euston*

☎ (020) 7388 7666
Website www.generatorhostels.com
Dorm bed £10-17; ***single room*** £40;
twin room £47; *prices include breakfast*
Credit cards *MC, Visa*
Reception open *24 hours*

Maintenance & cleanliness	★★★
Facilities	★★☆
Atmosphere & character	★★★★
Security	★★★☆
Overall rating	★★★

St Pancras YHA

This is a very clean hostel with a high standard of accommodation. The rooms have good quality bunk beds and facilities include a common area on the ground floor with a TV, plus a kitchen and restaurant.
79-81 Euston Road, London NW1
🚇 *Kings Cross St Pancras* 🚌 *10, 30, 73, 91, 205, 390*
☎ *(020) 7388 9998*
Dorm bed £26.60 (£24.60 HI/YHA); ***double room*** £65.50 (£61.50 HI/YHA); ***twin room*** £60 (£56 HI/YHA); *prices include breakfast*
Credit cards *MC, Visa*
Reception open *7am-11pm daily*

Maintenance & cleanliness	★★★★★
Facilities	★★☆
Atmosphere & character	★★☆
Security	★★★★☆
Overall rating	★★★

THE CITY

London's financial district is the oldest part of the city and home to many major attractions such as St Paul's Cathedral, however it can feel a bit deserted during weekends.

City of London YHA

This centrally located hostel offers a good standard of accommodation but shared facilities are rather limited. Although it is an older building the hostel is clean and well maintained.
36 Carter Lane, London EC4
🚇 *Blackfriars, Mansion House, St Pauls* 🚆 *Blackfriars, City Thameslink, Cannon Street* 🚌 *4, 11, 15, 17, 23, 26, 76, 100, 172*
☎ *(020) 7236 4965*

Dorm bed £26.60 (£24.60 HI/YHA); *price includes breakfast*
Credit cards *Amex, MC, Visa*
Reception open *7am-10.30pm daily*

Maintenance & cleanliness	★★★★
Facilities	★
Atmosphere & character	★★
Security	★★★★☆
Overall rating	★★☆

EARLS COURT

Earls Court is close to the ritzy neighbourhoods of Kensington, South Kensington and Chelsea so it is surprising that it is also home to many of London's hostels and budget hotels. Many backpackers living in London rent flats and houses in Earls Court and the area has a bit of a reputation as an Australian ghetto.

Barmy Badger

Although nothing special the Barmy Badger is a good value hostel with decent facilities and a good atmosphere. It has a small TV lounge and a good kitchen plus a back garden with a barbecue.
17 Longridge Road, Earls Court, London SW5
🚇 *Earls Court* 🚌 *C1, C3, 74, 328*
☎ *(020) 7370 5213*
Website www.barmybadger.com
Dorm bed £15-16; ***double/twin room*** £34
Credit cards *MC, Visa*

Maintenance & cleanliness	★★☆
Facilities	★★
Atmosphere & character	★★★★☆
Security	★★☆
Overall rating	★★☆

Boka Hotel

The Boka offers basic accommodation in small rooms and has a big common area downstairs with a TV and small kitchen.
33 Eardley Crescent, Earls Court, London SW5
🚇 *Earls Court, West Brompton* 🚆 *West Brompton* 🚌 *74, 190, 430*
☎ *(020) 7370 1388*
Dorm bed £15; *price includes breakfast*
Credit cards *Amex, MC, Visa*

Maintenance & cleanliness	★★☆
Facilities	★
Atmosphere & character	★★
Security	★★★
Overall rating	★★

Earls Court Youth Hostel

This large well-appointed hostel features a small garden plus the usual kitchen and a couple of TV lounges.
38 Bolton Gardens, Earls Court, London SW5
🚇 *Earls Court* 🚌 *C1, C3, 74, 328*
☎ *(020) 7373 7083*
Website www.yha.org.uk
Dorm bed £21.50 (£19.50 HI/YHA); twin room £56 (£52 HI/YHA); prices include breakfast
Credit cards Amex, Diners, JCB, MC, Visa
Reception open 24 hours

Maintenance & cleanliness	★★★★★
Facilities	★★
Atmosphere & character	★★☆
Security	★★★★☆
Overall rating	★★★☆

Nevern Hotel

This friendly hostel has all the usual facilities including a TV lounge, a narrow kitchen and small dining room and a small backyard with a barbecue. Although relatively clean the décor feels dated. It sleeps around 100, mostly in three to four-bed dorms.
29-31 Nevern Place, Earls Court, London SW5
🚇 *Earls Court* 🚌 *C1, C3, 74, 328*
☎ *(020) 7244 8366*
Dorm bed £15; twin room £32-34; price includes breakfast
Reception open 24 hours

Maintenance & cleanliness	★★★
Facilities	★★
Atmosphere & character	★★★☆
Security	★★☆
Overall rating	★★★

O'Callaghan's

O'Callaghan's is a very friendly hostel with a good location on Earls Court Road right across from the tube station. Accommodation is in messy rooms and most guests are staying long term so everyone knows each other.
205 Earls Court Road, Earls Court, London SW5
🚇 *Earls Court* 🚌 *C1, C3, 74, 328*
☎ *(020) 7370 3000*
Website www.ocallaghans.co.uk
Dorm bed £15; double room £35; triple room £50; prices include breakfast
Credit cards MC, Visa
Reception open 8am-11pm daily

Maintenance & cleanliness	★★★☆
Facilities	★★☆
Atmosphere & character	★★★
Security	★★★☆
Overall rating	★★★☆

Silver Fern

This small hostel has accommodation in messy rooms and caters mostly to long-term guests on a working holiday. Facilities include a good TV lounge and kitchen.
29 Collingham Place, Earls Court, London SW5
🚇 *Earls Court, Gloucester Road* 🚌 *74*
☎ *(020) 7370 0943*
Website www.ocallaghans.co.uk
Dorm bed £15-16; double room £35; triple room £50; prices include breakfast
Credit cards JCB, MC, Visa
Reception open 24 hours

Maintenance & cleanliness	★★★★☆
Facilities	★
Atmosphere & character	★★☆
Security	★★
Overall rating	★★★☆

KENSINGTON

Kensington is one of London's most exclusive areas and it is home to many of its top museums. There is also a good selection of pubs.

Baden Powell House (South Kensington YHA)

This large hostel is operated by the Scout Association and offers accommodation in nine to 19-bed dormitories. It is very clean and well maintained but there is no atmosphere and no common areas other than the coffee shop on the

ground floor. It is also the UK's most expensive hostel.
65-67 Queens Gate Road, London SW7
🚇 *Gloucester Road, South Kensington* 🚌 *70, 74*
☎ *(020) 7584 7031*
Website *www.scoutbase.org.uk*
**Dorm bed £30.50; single room £72.50 (£58 HI/YHA); twin room £99 (£82 HI/YHA); prices include breakfast*
Credit cards *Amex, MC, Visa*

Maintenance & cleanliness	★★★★★
Facilities	★★
Atmosphere & character	-
Security	★★★★
Overall rating	★★★

Holland House YHA

Holland House YHA consists of three buildings, including the original Holland House, with a great location in a big park off High Street Kensington. Although the hostel incorporates the façade of the magnificent building, inside it is dull and lacking in character. Accommodation is mostly in 12 and 20-bed dormitories and common areas include a TV lounge, a quiet lounge, dining room and a kitchen.
Holland Walk, Kensington, London W8
🚇 *Holland Park, High Street Kensington, Kensington Olympia* 🚆 *Kensington Olympia* 🚌 *9, 10, 27, 28, 49*
☎ *(020) 7937 0748*
Website *www.hollhse.btinternet.co.uk*
**Dorm bed £23.60 (£21.60 HI/YHA); price includes breakfast*
Credit cards *MC, Visa*
Reception open *7am-11.30pm daily*
📺🇰🇱

Maintenance & cleanliness	★★★★
Facilities	★★
Atmosphere & character	★★
Security	★★★
Overall rating	★★★

MARYLEBONE & REGENTS PARK

This area, just north of the West End, is handy to Regents Park and London Zoo as well as Euston and Marylebone train stations.

International Student House

The ISH is a well-appointed hostel that is set up more like a posh hotel and as such it doesn't offer the social atmosphere that you would normally find in a hostel. It has very good facilities that include the usual kitchen, TV lounge and laundry plus a games room, a gym and a bar. It caters mostly to foreign students who are studying in London and you need to be a student to stay here. It is a very nice place but not really for backpackers.
229 Great Portland Street, London W1
🚇 *Great Portland Street* 🚌 *C2, 88, 453*
☎ *(020) 7631 8300*
Website *www.ish.org.uk*
**Dorm bed £12-18; single room £33; twin room £50; prices include breakfast*
Credit cards *Diners, JCB, MC, Visa*
Reception open *24 hours*
🏠♿📺🇰🇱🛗

Maintenance & cleanliness	★★★★
Facilities	★★★
Atmosphere & character	-
Security	★★★★★
Overall rating	★★★★

NORTH LONDON

Most people visit North London to hang out at Camden Town market. North London also includes many great live music venues and some great pubs although much of this part of London is bland suburbia.

Hampsted Heath YHA

This established hostel in the north London suburb of Golders Green is a good option for travellers with a car (even though the parking at this hostel is rather limited). The hostel has a nice garden area but much of the hostel's interior feels tired and drab. Facilities include the usual kitchen, TV lounge and games room and there's a big cooked breakfast included in the price.
4 Wellgarth Road, Golders Green, London NW11
🚇 *Golders Green* 🚌 *210, 268*
☎ *(020) 8458 9054*
Website *www.yha.org.uk*
**Dorm bed £22 (£20 HI/YHA); twin room £51 (£47 HI/YHA); prices include breakfast*
Credit cards *MC, Visa*
Reception open *7am-11pm daily*
🏠📺🇰🇱

Maintenance & cleanliness	★★★☆
Facilities	★★☆
Atmosphere & character	★★
Security	★★★★☆
Overall rating	★★★☆

Millennium Lodge

This large hostel opposite Kensal Green tube station has nice common areas, which include a bar/restaurant, TV lounge, Internet access and a small gym, but the kitchen is tiny and poorly equipped. The dorms are barren and run down with flimsy metal bunk beds and old worn-out mattresses.

639 Harrow Road, Kensal Green, London NW10
🚇🚆 *Kensal Green* 🚌 *18, 52*
☎ *(020) 8964 4411*
Website *www.millenniumlodge.com*
Dorm bed £10-12; **single room** £30; **twin room** £35
Reception open 24 hours
📺🍳🛏

Maintenance & cleanliness	★★☆
Facilities	★★
Atmosphere & character	★★☆
Security	★★☆
Overall rating	★★☆

North London Backpackers

North London Backpackers is near a busy intersection in Hendon in London's northern suburbs. It is in an old building that is a bit rough around the edges but it is good value for London and popular with travellers on a working holiday.

12 Queens Parade, Queens Road, Hendon, London NW4
🚇 *Hendon Central* 🚌 *83*
☎ *(020) 8203 1319*
Dorm bed £11; **single room** £23
Credit cards MC, Visa
Reception open 9am-10pm daily
📺🍳🛏

Maintenance & cleanliness	★★☆
Facilities	★★☆
Atmosphere & character	★★★
Security	★★
Overall rating	★★

Smart Camden Hostel

The Smart Camden Hostel is a good option for travellers visiting Camden Town markets. It is a clean hostel but facilities are limited to the usual kitchen and TV lounge.

55-57 Bayham Street, London NW1
🚇 *Camden Town, Mornington Crescent*
🚆 *Camden Road;* 🚌 *D 24, 27, 29, 88, 134, 168, 214, 253*
☎ *(020) 7229 0000*
Website *www.camdenhostel.com*
Dorm bed £9.99-23; *price includes breakfast*
Credit cards MC, Visa
Reception open 24 hours
📺🍳🛏

Maintenance & cleanliness	★★★
Facilities	★
Atmosphere & character	★★★
Security	★★★
Overall rating	★★★☆

St Christopher's (Camden)

St Christopher's Camden hostel is not quite as clean as the other St Christopher's hostels, but it is still a good option if you want to stay close to the Camden markets. It is located above a pub (you check in at the bar) and guests get discounted food and drinks. There is not kitchen but there's a laundry and a small TV lounge in the basement.

48-50 Camden High Street, Camden Town, London NW1
🚇 *Camden Town, Mornington Crescent*
🚆 *Camden Road* 🚌 *24, 27, 29, 88, 134, 168, 214, 253*
☎ *(020) 7407 1856*
Website *www.st-christophers.co.uk*
Dorm bed £15-17
Credit cards MC, Visa
📺🛏

Maintenance & cleanliness	★★★☆
Facilities	★
Atmosphere & character	★★★☆
Security	★★★★☆
Overall rating	★★

SOUTH LONDON

South London covers a vast area but most of the hostels here aren't too far south of the river. The three St Christopher's hostels and the Dover Castle are all within a five-minute walk to the City.

Dover Castle

This small hostel has accommodation above a pub near Borough tube station

in Southwark. It has a small kitchen with new appliances but the common area is cluttered and smoky. Guests get cheap drinks at the bar.
6A Great Dover Street, London SE1
🚇 *Borough* 🚌 *21, 35, 40, 133, 343*
☎ *(020) 7403 7773*
Website *www.dovercastlehostel.co.uk*
Dorm bed *£12-16*
Credit cards *MC, Visa*
Reception open *24 hours*

Maintenance & cleanliness	★★★☆
Facilities	★★
Atmosphere & character	★★★
Security	★★★
Overall rating	★★★☆

Journey's London Hostel
This hostel is a well-maintained place that has a large common area with a bar, Internet access and TVs. It is in a quiet part of South London close to the Imperial War Museum.
73 Lambeth Walk, Lambeth, London SE1
🚇 *Lambeth North* 🚌 *360*
☎ *(020) 7582 3088*
Website *www.london-hostel.co.uk*
Dorm bed *£13.50-14.50;* **double room** *£44*
Credit cards *MC, Visa*
Reception open *8am-midnight; 24 hour check in*

Maintenance & cleanliness	★★★★☆
Facilities	★★☆
Atmosphere & character	★★★
Security	★★★☆
Overall rating	★★★

Orient Espresso
The Orient Espresso consists of rooms above a café and it is the quietest of the three Southwark St Christopher's hostels. There are no shared facilities other than the café but guests have access to the facilities at the larger St Christopher's Village just a couple of minutes walk up the road.
59 Borough High Street, London SE1
🚇 *Borough, London Bridge* 🚆 *London Bridge* 🚌 *21, 35, 40, 133, 343*
☎ *(020) 7407 1856*
Website *www.st-christophers.co.uk*
Dorm bed *£15-18.50;* **twin room** *£46; prices include breakfast*
Credit cards *MC, Visa*
Reception open *24 hours*

Maintenance & cleanliness	★★★★
Facilities	★
Atmosphere & character	★
Security	★★★☆
Overall rating	★★★☆

Rotherhithe YHA
England's largest YHA hostel is a family-oriented place with lots of facilities for kids. Other amenities include a bar, TV lounge, Internet access and a games room. The largest dorm has 10 beds but most have six beds and there are TVs in the double and twin rooms. It's in a nice quiet neighbourhood with modern low-rise apartments and canals. There is a big shopping centre near Canada Water tube station and it is about a 30-minute walk into the City. It is one of the few areas in London where finding a parking spot on the street is no problem.
20 Salter Road, Rotherhithe, London SE16
🚇 *Canada Water, Rotherhithe* 🚌 *381*
☎ *(020) 7232 2114*
Website *www.yhalondon.org.uk*
Dorm bed *£17-26.60 (£15-24.60 HI/YHA);* **double/twin room** *£55.50 (£53.50 HI/YHA);* **family room** *£46 (£44 HI/YHA); prices include breakfast*
Credit cards *MC, Visa*
Reception open *24 hours*

Maintenance & cleanliness	★★★★★
Facilities	★★
Atmosphere & character	★
Security	★★★★
Overall rating	★★★★☆

St Christopher's (Greenwich)
This hostel, right next to Greenwich train station, is above a pub and has friendly staff and a good atmosphere. Facilities include a "chill out room" in the basement with a TV and Internet access but there is no kitchen.
189 Greenwich High Road, Greenwich, London SW10
🚇 *Greenwich DLR* 🚆 *Greenwich*
🚌 *177, 180, 199*
☎ *(020) 8858 3591*
Website *www.st-christophers.co.uk*
Dorm bed *£10-13;* **single room** *£42.50*

Credit cards MC, Visa
Reception open 7.30am-midnight

📺 🅛 🚻

Maintenance & cleanliness	★★★★½
Facilities	★★½
Atmosphere & character	★★★★★½
Security	★★★★½
Overall rating	★★★

St Christopher's Inn

This hostel is above between the two other St Christopher's hostels on Borough High Street. It is an old building with quite a bit of character and it features a small common room and a balcony area with a barbecue, but there is no kitchen.
121 Borough High Street, London SE1
🚇 *Borough, London Bridge* 🚆 *London Bridge* 🚌 *21, 35, 40, 133, 343*
☎ *(020) 7407 1856*
Website www.st-christophers.co.uk
Dorm bed £13-18.50; *twin room* £42.50-48
Credit cards MC, Visa

🚻

Maintenance & cleanliness	★★★
Facilities	★★½
Atmosphere & character	★★★½
Security	★★★★½
Overall rating	★★★½

St Christopher's Village

This is St Christopher's main London hostel. It is located above Belushi's Bar and has better facilities than the average London hostel. Facilities include a TV lounge with a big projection screen TV plus a deck with a spa pool and sauna, but there is no kitchen.
161-165 Borough High Street, London SE1
🚇 *Borough, London Bridge* 🚆 *London Bridge* 🚌 *21, 35, 40, 133, 343*
☎ *(020) 7407 1856*
Website www.st-christophers.co.uk
Dorm bed £13-18.50; *twin room* £42.50-48; *prices include breakfast*
Credit cards MC, Visa
Reception open 24 hours

📺 🅛 🚻

Maintenance & cleanliness	★★★★
Facilities	★★★
Atmosphere & character	★★★★½
Security	★★★★½
Overall rating	★★★★½

VICTORIA

As well as being the Queen's home turf – Buckingham Palace is just up the road – the Victoria area is a convenient spot for travellers as Victoria Coach Station and Victoria train station are both located here.

Astor Victoria

This is the nicest of the Astor hostels. It is well maintained and facilities include the usual TV lounge and Internet access but it has limited kitchen facilities.
71 Belgrave Road, London SW1
🚇🚆 *Victoria* 🚌 *24, N24*
☎ *(020) 7834 3077*
Website www.astorvictoria.com
Dorm bed £16-19 (£14.40-17.10 ISIC/VIP); *single room* £35 (£31.50 ISIC/VIP); *twin room* £40 (£36 ISIC/VIP); price includes breakfast
Credit cards MC, Visa
Reception open 24 hours

📺 🅛

Maintenance & cleanliness	★★★★½
Facilities	★
Atmosphere & character	★★★
Security	★★★
Overall rating	★★★½

WEST END
Oxford Street Youth Hostel

London's most centrally located YHA is not as nice as most other YHA hostels. It offers clean and simple accommodation with the standard TV lounge and kitchen facilities.
14 Noel Street, London W1
🚇 *Oxford Circus, Tottenham Court Road*
🚌 *7, 8, 10, 25, 55, 73, 98, 176, 390*
☎ *(020) 7734 1657*
Website www.yhalondon.org.uk
Dorm bed £24.60 (£22.60 HI/YHA)
Credit cards Amex, Diners, JCB, MC, Visa
Reception open 7am-11pm daily

📺 🅚 🅛

Maintenance & cleanliness	★★★★½
Facilities	★★
Atmosphere & character	★★
Security	★★★★★
Overall rating	★★★★½

Piccadilly Hotel

This hostel is a bit worn around the edges but the rooms are clean and the location

is unbeatable. The building is not well set up for a hostel but the staff tries hard to create an atmosphere with organised pub crawls and other activities.
12 Sherwood Street, London W1
🚇 *Piccadilly Circus* 🚌 *3, 6, 9, 12, 13, 14, 15, 19, 22, 23, 38, 88, 94, 139, 159, 453*
☎ *(020) 7942 0555*
Website *www.piccadillyhotel.net*
Dorm bed *£12-19;* **single room** *£35-36;* **double/twin room** *£50-52*
Reception open *24 hours*

Maintenance & cleanliness	★★★☆
Facilities	★★☆
Atmosphere & character	★★★☆
Security	★★★★
Overall rating	★★★

OTHER AREAS
Abercorn House
Abercorn House is a relatively clean and well-maintained hostel that caters for travellers working in London (the minimum stay is one week). It has the usual TV lounge plus a laundry and several small kitchens but there is not much atmosphere. It's on a quiet residential street in Hammersmith, west of central London.
28-30 Bute Gardens, Hammersmith, London W6
🚇 *Hammersmith* 🚌 *9, 10, 27, 72, 220, 283, 295, 391*
☎ *(020) 8563 8692*
Dorm bed *£55-60 per week;* **single room** *£110 per week;* **double/twin room** *£140 per week*
Reception open *24 hours*

Maintenance & cleanliness	★★★★
Facilities	★
Atmosphere & character	★★
Security	★★
Overall rating	★★☆

St Christopher's (Shepherd's Bush)
This hostel is above a pub next to a shopping centre surrounding the Shepherd's Bush tube station. It features a big common room, but there is no kitchen. Although there aren't a lot of facilities, it is a pretty good place to stay with clean rooms and good quality mattresses.
13-15 Shepherds Bush Green, Shepherds Bush, London W12
🚇 *Shepherd's Bush* 🚌 *49, 94, 148, 295*
☎ *(020) 7407 1856*
Website *www.st-christophers.co.uk*
Dorm bed *£15-19;* **double room** *£44; prices include breakfast*
Credit cards *MC, Visa*
Reception open *7.30am-11pm daily*

Maintenance & cleanliness	★★★☆
Facilities	★
Atmosphere & character	★★★☆
Security	★★★
Overall rating	★★☆

Eating & Drinking
EATING
London has never really been considered a culinary destination with most people's idea of British food consisting of overcooked veggies, corned beef, jellied eels, pork pies and fish & chips. Fortunately many Londoners have begun to appreciate their city's ethnic diversity and the wealth and variety of various national cuisines that have transplanted themselves here, which has led to a big improvement in the city's selection of restaurants.

If you're looking for something traditional, many of London's pubs serve inexpensive hearty meals; but for a uniquely London meal you may want to head to the East End and try some jellied eels (but watch out for the bones).

London's parks, gardens, squares and open spaces (there's 1,800 of them) provide a lovely setting for a picnic and Marks & Spencer's is the best spot to stock up on picnic food. There are branches in the Whitley's shopping centre in Bayswater, on Oxford Street near Oxford Circus or near Marble Arch (handy for a picnic in Hyde Park).

Cheaper options include the bigger supermarket s such as the Sainsbury on Cromwell Road and the Tesco on the corner of Cromwell and Earls Court Roads, both in Earls Court as well as the smaller Sainsbury Local and Tesco Metro supermarkets that are more plentiful in central London.

Notting Hill, Bayswater & Paddington

London **73**

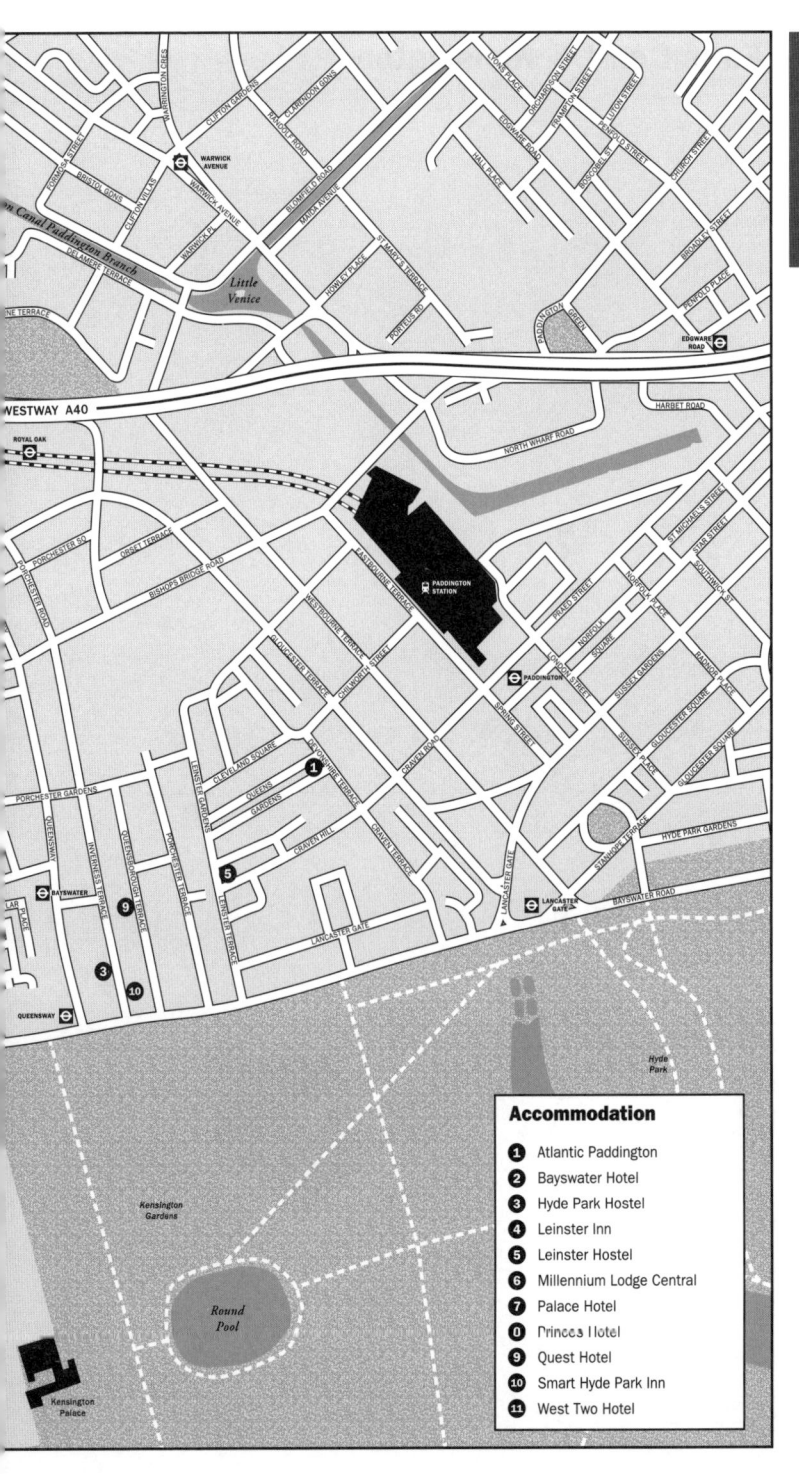

Accommodation

1. Atlantic Paddington
2. Bayswater Hotel
3. Hyde Park Hostel
4. Leinster Inn
5. Leinster Hostel
6. Millennium Lodge Central
7. Palace Hotel
8. Princess Hotel
9. Quest Hotel
10. Smart Hyde Park Inn
11. West Two Hotel

Earls Court & Kensington

Accommodation

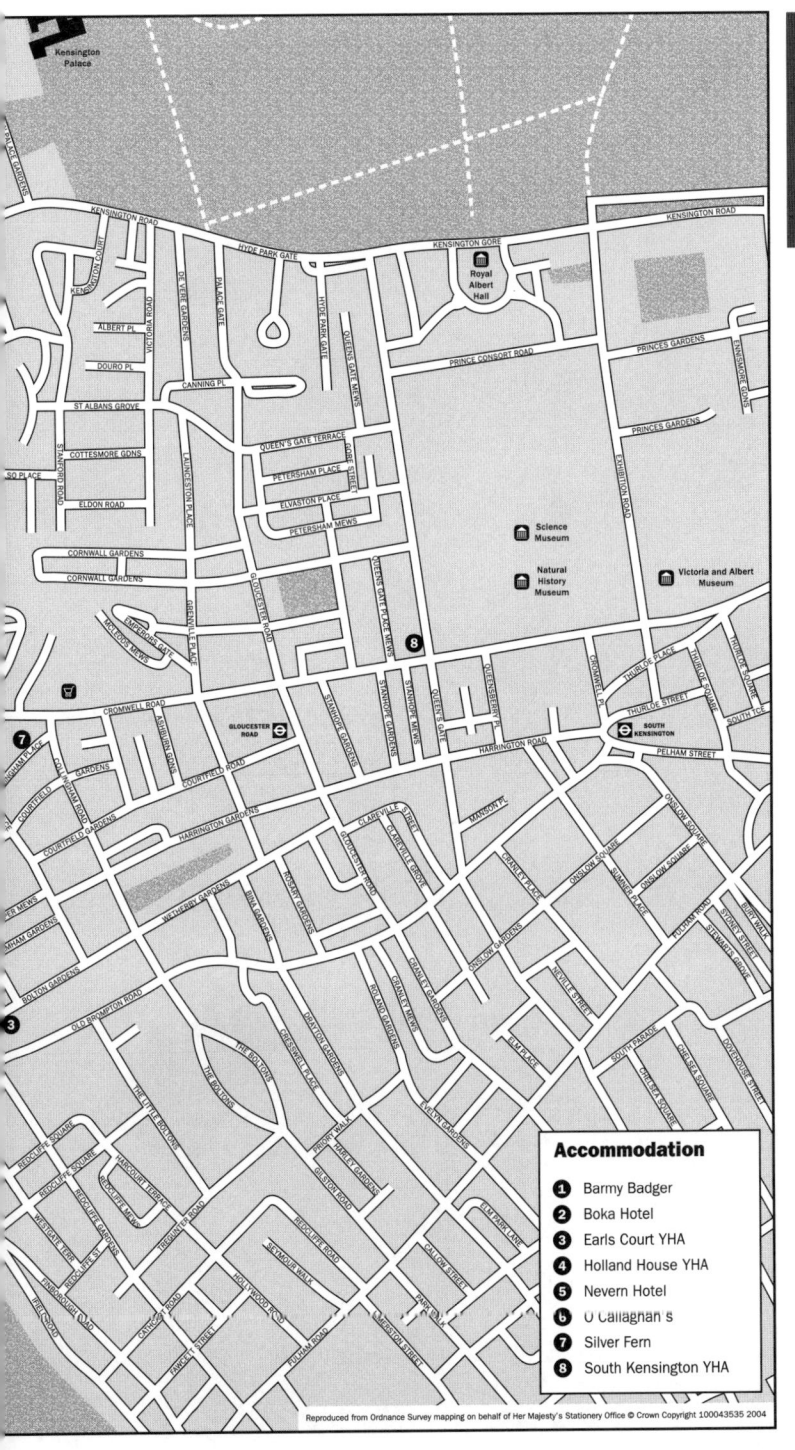

1. Barmy Badger
2. Boka Hotel
3. Earls Court YHA
4. Holland House YHA
5. Nevern Hotel
6. O'Callaghan's
7. Silver Fern
8. South Kensington YHA

Camden Town & Kings Cross

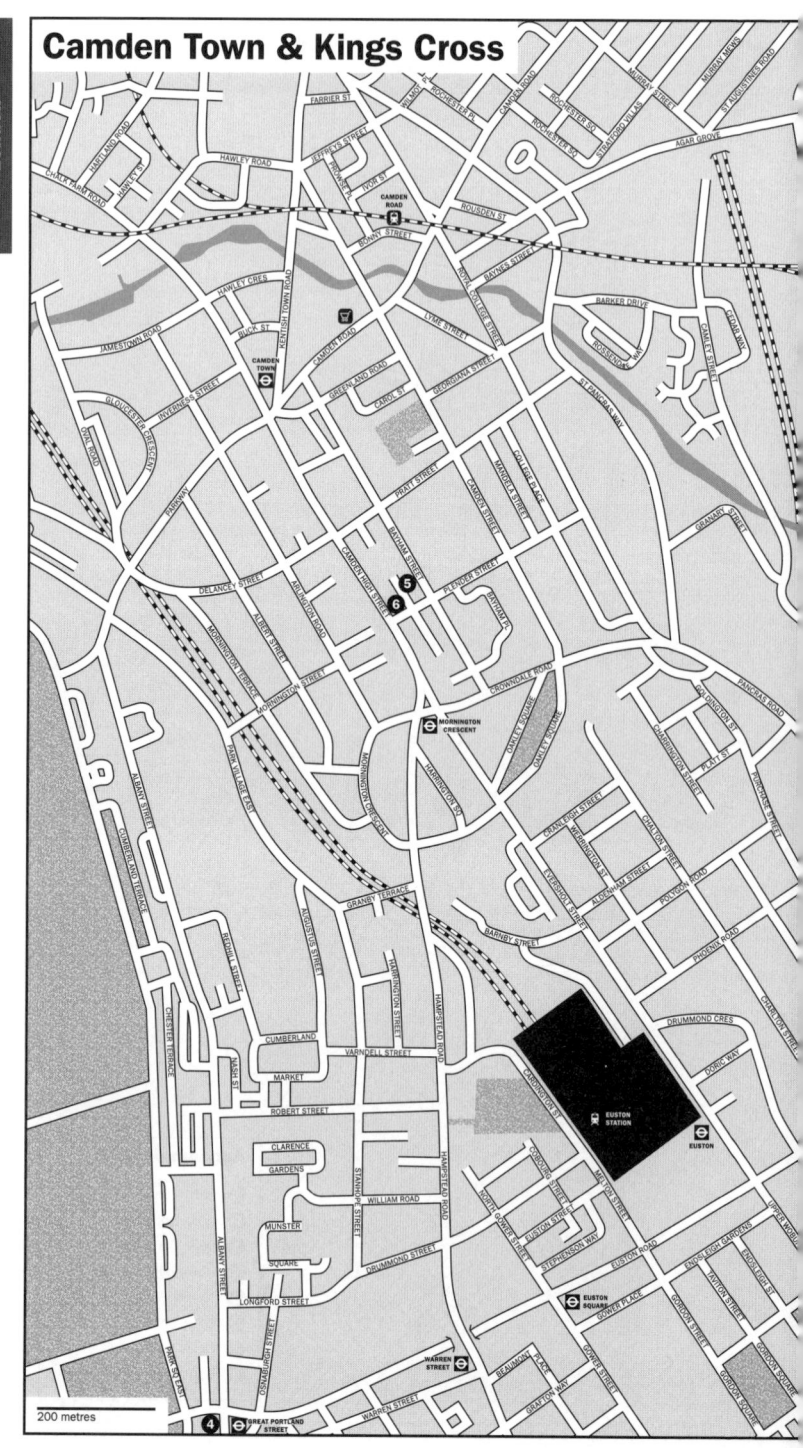

200 metres

London **77**

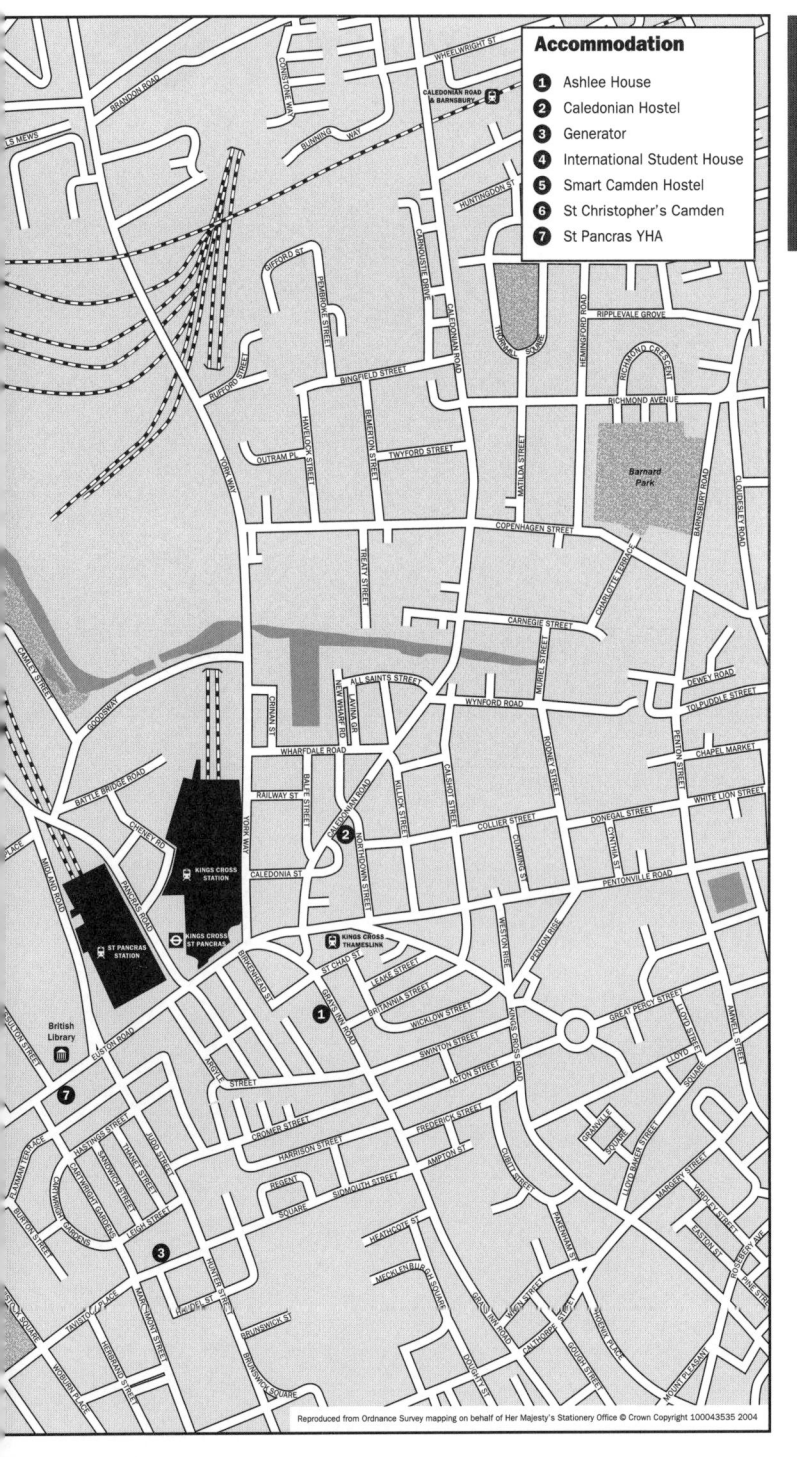

Accommodation
1. Ashlee House
2. Caledonian Hostel
3. Generator
4. International Student House
5. Smart Camden Hostel
6. St Christopher's Camden
7. St Pancras YHA

Bloomsbury & the West End

Accommodation

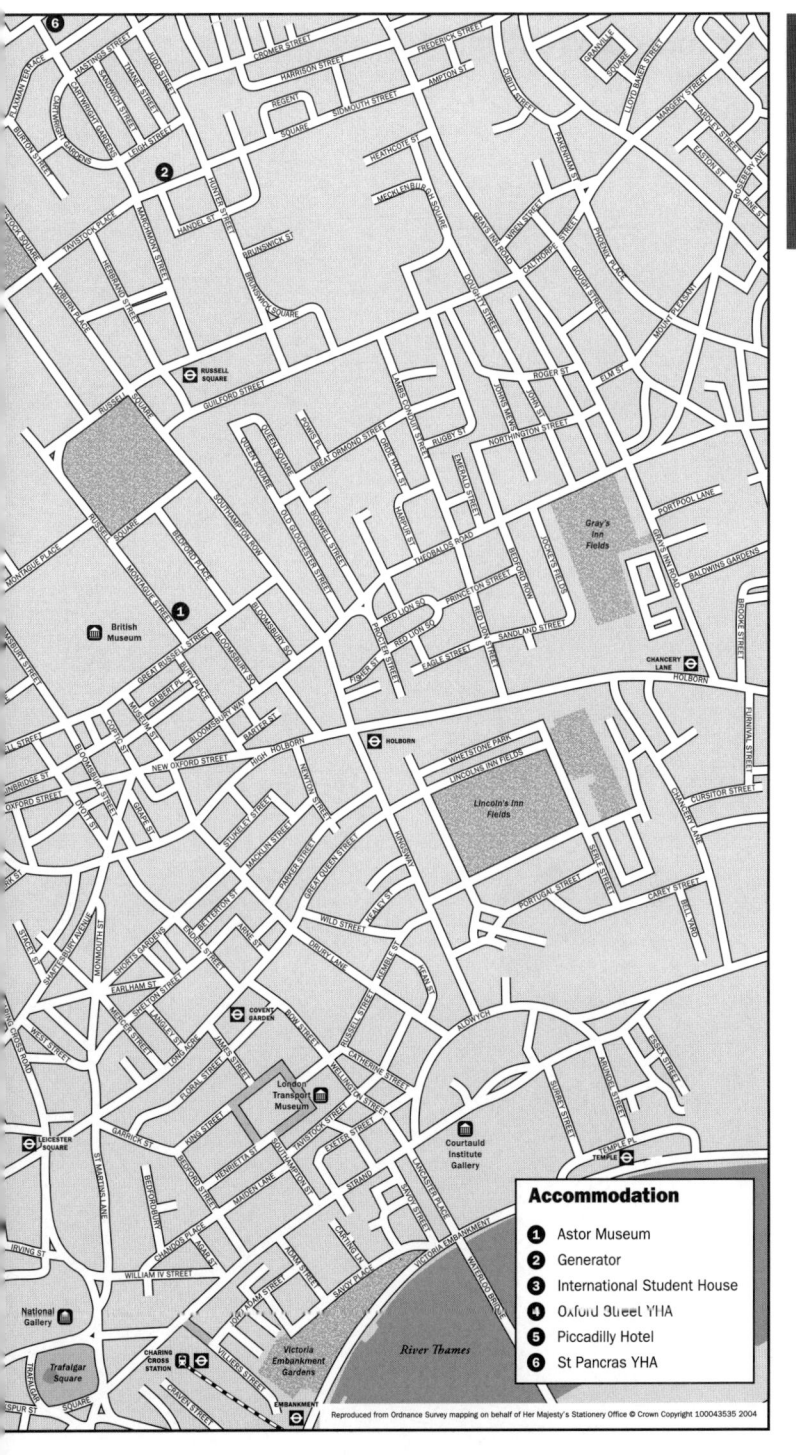

1. Astor Museum
2. Generator
3. International Student House
4. Oxford Street YHA
5. Piccadilly Hotel
6. St Pancras YHA

Victoria & Westminster

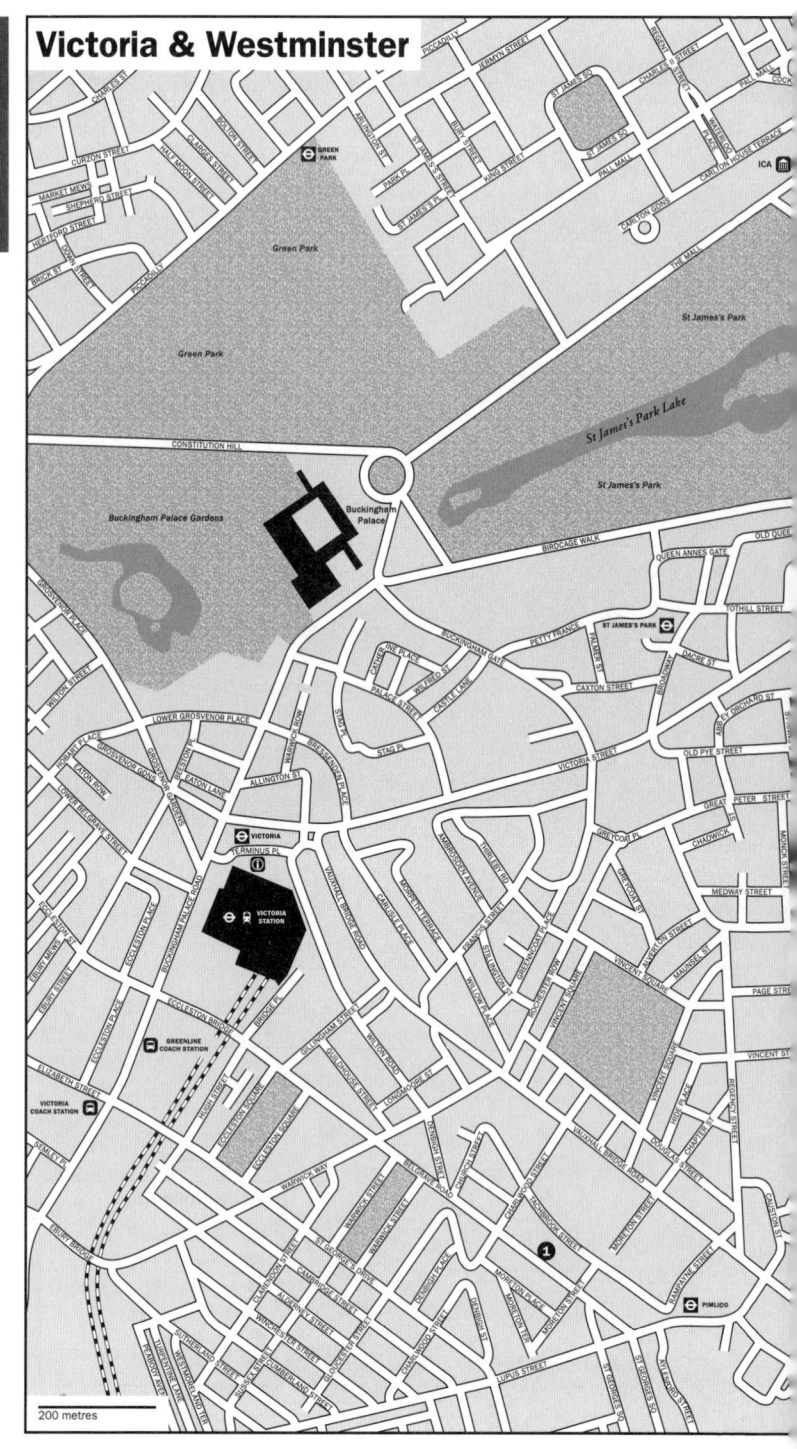

London

Accommodation

1. Astor Victoria
2. Journey's London Hostel

The City & Southwark

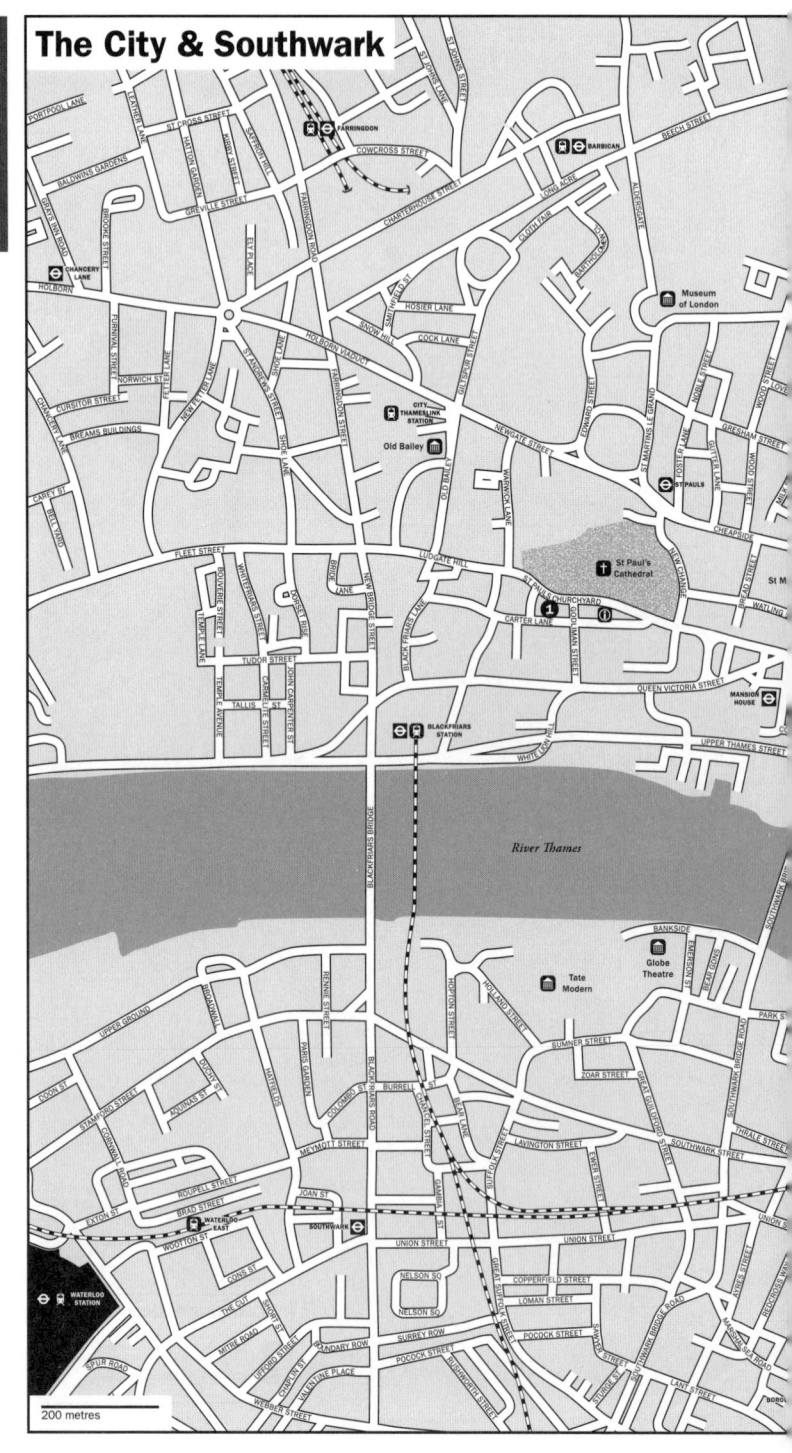

Accommodation

1. City of London YHA
2. Dover Castle
3. Orient Espresso
4. St Christopher's Inn
5. St Christopher's Village

DRINKING

London's pubs are among the city's main attractions and are some of the best places to immerse yourself in the local culture. Traditional British pubs offer an authentic ambience where you're almost guaranteed a good time and it is well worth the effort to sample as many pubs as you can afford. Some real gems include places like the Builder's Arms (*1 Kensington Court Place, Kensington, London W8;* ⊖ *High Street Kensington*) or Captain Kidd (*108 Wapping High Street, London E1;* ⊖ *Wapping*), although virtually every neighbourhood has a cosy pub with an unbeatable atmosphere.

With so many backpackers living and working in London it has a vibrant travellers' scene with lots of bars catering to the backpacking market, which means you can have a great time out on the town with other travellers although it can sometimes be too easy to miss out on meeting up with the locals. These pubs include the Redback Tavern in Acton Town (best known for its live music) and the popular Walkabout pub (with branches in Covent Garden, Islington and Shepherds Bush).

However the granddaddy of all the backpacker bars is undoubtedly the Church (*The Forum, 9-17 Highgate Road, Kentish Town;* ⊖ ⊖ *Kentish Town;* ☎ *(020) 7284 1001; website www.thechurch.co.uk*). This is like no other place you've ever seen. If you've come to London to party hard this is a place to get going on a Sunday afternoon but if you've come to London to get some culture and meet the locals over a quiet beer in a traditional pub, then you'll hate this place. The Church started back in 1979 when a group of Aussies living in London got together at a local pub every Sunday to get smashed. Over time this tradition gained a huge following and has moved location a number of times before settling at its most recent home at the Forum in Kentish Town. Every Sunday afternoon, the Church is packed with sweaty bodies trying to dance, get laid and sing along with Khe Sahn. Don't expect traditional pub decor, the management of The Church believe in interior decoration with alcohol – that is the more you drink the better it looks. Typical church decor consists of knee-deep beer cans complemented by pallets of beer next to the bar. Nothing will prepare you for the Church experience. Expect to be waiting in line at 11am on a Sunday morning for around an hour. When you get in the door you will be greeted by one of the Church Wardens who will take your £5 entry fee and point you in the direction of the bar. You will then head to the bar to get a six-pack and watch several thousand people fill the place. If it was cold outside, it will be hot and sweaty inside the Church. Entertainment consists of strippers and bad comedians although occasionally you get a good band.

Sights

London has over 300 museums, galleries and collections, including some of the greatest in the world as well as some of the most unusual and interesting. What's more, many of these superb cultural attractions are free (except for certain special exhibitions and events).

Like many other big cities, it is a good idea to allocate a day to each of London's various neighbourhoods. Each area has its own attractions, accommodation and work opportunities, as well as it's own unique ambience. This is why London has such a great cultural life such as the style of restaurants, pubs and bars, shopping and markets and live music venues.

THE CITY OF LONDON

Commonly referred to as The City, London's financial district contains one of the world's largest concentrations of banks and insurance companies and is a hive of activity during business hours and deserted on weekends. Although mainly a business district, The City has several major attractions including St Paul's Cathedral, the Tower of London and Tower Bridge.

Bank of England Museum

The Bank of England Museum presents a history of banking and money from 1694 to the present day.
Threadneedle Street, London EC2
⊖ *Bank, Cannon Street, Mansion*

House, Monument 🚇 *Cannon Street*
🚌 *8, 11, 23, 25, 26, 47, 48, 133, 141, 149, 242*
☎ *(020) 7601 5491*
Website *www.bankofengland.co.uk/museum/*
Admission *free*
Open *Mon-Fri 10am-5pm*

Barbican Centre
Conference and arts centre featuring theatre, cinema, music, restaurants, exhibitions and the Barbican Art Gallery.
Silk Street, London EC2
🚇🚌 *Barbican, Moorgate*
☎ *(020) 7638 4141*
Admission *£5*
Centre open *Mon-Sat 9am-11pm, Sun noon-11pm;* **gallery open** *Mon 10am-6.45pm, Tues 10am-5.45pm, Wed-Sat 10am-6.45pm, Sun noon-6.45pm*

Dr Johnson's House
This house just north of Fleet Street is one of the oldest surviving residential houses in the City of London. Built in 1700, Samuel Johnson lived here between 1748 and 1759 and compiled the first comprehensive English Dictionary here. The house contains a museum dedicated to Samuel Johnson's life and the English language.
17 Gough Square, London
🚇 *Blackfriars, Chancery Lane*
🚌 *Blackfriars* 🚌 *4, 11, 15, 17, 23, 26, 76, 172*
☎ *(020) 7353 3745*
Website *www.drjh.dircon.co.uk*
Admission *£4*
Open *Jan-Apr Mon-Sat 11am-5pm; May-Sep Mon-Sat 11am-5.30pm daily; Oct-Dec Mon-Sat 11am-5pm*

Museum of London
The Museum of London features 2,000 years of history from Roman times to the present day.
150 London Wall, London EC2
🚇 *Bank, Barbican, Moorgate, St Pauls*
🚌 *City Thameslink, Liverpool Street, Moorgate* 🚌 *4, 8, 25, 56, 100, 172, 242, 501, 521*
☎ *(020) 7600 3699*
Website *www.museumoflondon.org.uk*
Admission *free (charge for some temporary exhibitions)*
Open *Mon-Sat 10am-5pm, Sun noon-5.50pm*

Guildhall
This gothic building, dating from 1411, has historically been London's city hall and is now the home of the Corporation of London. Some of the more impressive parts of the building include the medieval Great Hall, which is the third largest civic hall in England and has entertained royalty and state visitors for hundreds of years, and the Old Library, which is now used as reception rooms.
Gresham Street, London EC2
🚇 *Bank, Moorgate, St Pauls*
☎ *(020) 7606 3030*
Admission *free*
Open *Jan-Apr Mon-Sat 10am-5pm; May-Sep 10am-5pm daily; Oct-Dec Mon-Sat 10am-5pm*

Monument
Designed by Christopher Wren and built to commemorate the Great Fire of 1666, this 61.5m-high tower is the tallest isolated stone column in the world. Breathtaking views of the city reward those who climb the 311 steps to the top.
🚇 *Bank, Monument* 🚌 *15, 17, 21, 25, 35, 40, 43, 47, 48, 133, 141, 149, 344, 521*
☎ *(020) 7626 2717*
Admission *£2; joint ticket with Tower Bridge £5.50*

Old Bailey
Dating from 1539, the Central Criminal Court (commonly known as Old Bailey) is one of the world's most famous criminal courts. Famous trials at Old Bailey include that of William Penn (founder of Pennsylvania), Oscar Wilde, Dr Crippen, the Krays and the Yorkshire Ripper.

It is still a functioning court and visitors are welcome to the public galleries. Daily case listings can be found at www.courtservice.gov.uk. Bags, cameras and mobile phones are not permitted in the courtroom and lockers are not available.
Old Bailey, London
🚇 *Blackfriars, St Pauls* 🚌 *Blackfriars,*

City Thameslink 🚇 *4, 11, 15, 23, 26, 76, 100, 172*
☎ *(020) 7248 3277*
Admission free
Open Mon-Fri 10am-1pm & 2pm-5pm

Prince Henry's Room

This is one of the few surviving houses predating the Great Fire of London in 1666. The building features a half-timbered front dating from the 17th century but its main feature is the large room with an ornate plaster ceiling and two stained glass windows. The room also houses the Samuel Pepys exhibition.
17 Fleet Street, London EC4
🚇 *Blackfriars*
Admission free
Open Mon-Fri 11am-2pm

St Mary-le-Bow

This Wren-designed church features a Norman crypt and chapel, but is best known as the home of the Bow Bells.
Cheapside, London EC2
🚇 *Mansion House, St Pauls* 🚌 *Cannon Street* 🚌 *11, 15, 23, 26, 76*
☎ *(020) 7248 5139*
Admission free
Open Mon-Wed 7.30am-6pm, Thu 7.30am-6.30pm, Fri 7.30am-3.30pm

St Paul's Cathedral

One of the City's most famous landmarks is the 108m-high St Paul's Cathedral, which was designed by Sir Christopher Wren after the Great Fire of London destroyed the original. Although the cathedral boasts an impressive interior, the attraction for many visitors is the enormous dome and the crypt, which holds the tombs of many famous Britons including TE Lawrence, Admiral Nelson, Florence Nightingale, the Duke of Wellington and St Paul's architect, Christopher Wren. Visitors can climb the 530 steps to the Golden Gallery above the famous dome. The climb will take you past the Whispering Gallery (30.2m) and the Stone Gallery (53.4m) to the Golden Gallery (85.4m) in the bell tower above the dome.
St Paul's Churchyard, London
🚇 *Blackfriars, Cannon Street, Mansion House, St Pauls* 🚌 *Blackfriars, Cannon Street* 🚌 *4, 11, 15, 23, 25, 26, 100, 242*
☎ *(020) 7248 2705*
Website www.stpauls.co.uk
Admission £7
Open Mon-Sat 8.30am-4pm

Tower Bridge

Built in 1894, it is one of London's top tourist attractions and perhaps the world's most well known bridge. Although you can drive to take a bus across it, walking across and visiting the Tower Bridge Exhibition gets you onto the high level walkways where you can take in breathtaking views and see exhibits on the history and construction of the bridge. Entry to the exhibition also lets you see the Victorian Engine Rooms, which house the original steam engines that once powered the bridge.
Tower Bridge, London SE1
🚇 *London Bridge, Tower Gateway, Tower Hill* 🚌 *Fenchurch Street, London Bridge* 🚌 *15, 25, 40, 42, 47, 78, 100, D1, P11, RV1*
☎ *(020) 7403 3761*
Website www.towerbridge.org.uk
Admission £5.50 exhibition and walkways; £4 walkways only; £6.50 combined entry with the Monument
Open Jan-Mar 9.30am-5pm daily; Apr-Sep 10am-5.30pm daily; Oct-Dec 9.30am-5pm daily

Tower of London

Since its foundation by William the Conqueror in 1066, the Tower of London has had many roles including palace, fortress, prison, mint, arsenal and jewel house, although it is best known as the place where Henry VIII sent his wife Anne Boleyn to be beheaded. The Tower features displays depicting its 900-year history, which include various torture tools, the medieval palace decked out to depict royal life during the reign of Edward I (1272-1397), a display of over 12,000 diamonds and the dazzling Crown Jewels. The Tower of London is well known for the famous Yeoman Warders (or Beefeaters) who guard the tower.
Tower Hill, London EC3
🚇 *Tower Hill, Tower Gateway*

🚉 Fenchurch Street, London Bridge
🚌 15, 25, 42, 78, 100, D1 ⛴ Tower Pier
☎ 0870 756 6060
Website www.hrp.org.uk
Admission £13.50 (£12.50 if booked by telephone or online); £10.50 students (£9.50 if booked by telephone or online); joint ticket with Kensington Palace £16.70 (£13.20 students); joint ticket with Hampton Court £17.50 (£14.20 students)
Open Jan-Feb Mon 10am-5pm, Tue-Sat 9am-5pm, Sun 10am-5pm (last admission 4pm); Mar-Oct Mon 10am-6pm, Tue-Sat 9am-6pm, Sun 10am-6pm (last admission 5pm)

THE WEST END

This is the area that most people talk about when they mean Central London. The area includes neighbourhoods such as Soho, Covent Garden and Bloomsbury. The main shopping streets are located here including Oxford and Regent Streets along with the major theatres and the bookshops of Charing Cross Road. Covent Garden is perhaps the most hip area of London with its market and loads of cool eateries and cafés and bars, pubs and live music venues. Landmarks in the West End include Piccadilly and Oxford Circuses, Leicester and Trafalgar Squares, along with the British Museum.

British Library

With over 150 million items on 625km of shelves on 14 floors, the British Library is one of the worlds great libraries. It contains a copy of every book published in Britain and Ireland plus a large range of exhibits that include a 2nd century Bible, Leonardo da Vinci's notebook, a copy of the *Magna Carta*, William Caxton's editions of Chaucer's *Canterbury Tales*, the Gutenburg Bible, hand written Beatles manuscripts and the *Diamond Sutra*, the world's earliest dated printed book (AD 868).
96 Euston Road, London NW1
🚇 *Kings Cross St Pancras* 🚉 *Euston, Kings Cross, St Pancras* 🚌 *10, 30, 73, 91*
☎ *0870 444 1500*
Website *www.bl.uk*
Admission free
Open Mon 9.30am-6pm, Tue 9.30am-8pm, Wed-Fri 9.30am-6pm, Sat 9.30am-5pm, Sun 11am-5pm

British Museum

The British Museum chronicles the story of the western world through an unmatched collection of antiques and exhibits than include the Elgin Marbles, the Rosetta Stone, the Iron Age Lindow Man and numerous Egyptian mummies and sarcophagi.
Great Russell Street, London WC1
🚇 *Tottenham Court Road*
☎ *(020) 7323 8299*
Website *www.thebritishmuseum.ac.uk*
Admission free
Open Mon-Wed 10am-5.30pm, Thu-Fri 10am-8.30pm, Sat-Sun 10am-5.30pm

Covent Garden

This neighbourhood in the heart of the West End evolved into London's principal produce market in the 18th century and the area was immortalised by George Bernard Shaw's play *Pygmalion*, and in screen versions of *My Fair Lady*, with Eliza Doolittle being discovered in the marketplace by Professor Henry Higgins.

Traffic congestion forced the relocation of the market south of the Thames more than 20 years ago. The original Central Market Building has been completely renovated and is now filled with boutiques, health food shops and trendy restaurants.

Covent Garden is now the undisputed heart of London's Theatreland. Some of the country's oldest theatres like the Theatre Royal Drury Lane and the Royal Opera House are found here and the surrounding area around Covent Garden is home to attractions that include the London Transport Museum.

However, it is out on the cobbled paving where the market life of old has been recaptured and where street performers make their livelihood through the passing tourists. The unique atmosphere of Covent Garden puts it alongside Camden Town as one of London's great areas for just hanging out.
🚇 *Covent Garden*

Courtauld Institute Gallery
The Courtauld Institute Gallery features paintings that range from the Old Masters to post-impressionism with works by Cézanne, Michelangelo, Rembrandt and Turner.
Somerset House, The Strand, London WC2
🚇 *Holborn*
☎ *(020) 7848 2526*
Website *www.courtauld.ac.uk*
Admission *£5; Mon 10am-2pm free*
Open *10am-6pm daily (last entry 5.15pm)*

Institute of Contemporary Art (ICA)
The ICA hosts an ever-changing programme of contemporary art exhibitions in addition to cinema, theatre and dance.
The Mall, London SW1
🚇 *Charing Cross, Piccadilly* 🚆 *Charing Cross* 🚌 *3, 6, 9, 11, 12, 13, 14, 15, 19, 22, 23, 24, 29, 38, 77a, 88, 91, 139, 176*
☎ *(020) 7930 3647*
Website *www.ica.org.uk*
Admission *prices vary*
Gallery open *noon-7.30pm daily*

London Transport Museum
The London Transport Museum features displays of the days when Londoners were transported by horse-drawn cab, to the introduction of the first underground railway, electrified trams and the arrival of motorised transport.

The story of the underground forms a large part of the museum's permanent exhibits. On show is the Metropolitan Railway locomotive number 23, built in 1866, which provided power for trains on the Metropolitan and Circle lines for 40 years. Another underground exhibit is the 'padded cell', an 1890 carriage that operated on the City and South London Railway. Displaying maps and archive material, the Beck Gallery tells the story of the world-famous London Underground map, designed in 1931 by draughtsman Harry Beck and now recognised as an icon of London itself.
The Piazza, Covent Garden
🚆 *Charing Cross* 🚇 *Charing Cross, Covent Garden*
☎ *(020) 7379 6344*
Website *www.ltmuseum.co.uk*
Admission *£5.95 (£4.50 students)*
Open *Mon-Thu 10am-6pm, Fri 11am-6pm, Sat-Sun 10am-6pm (last admission 5.15pm)*

Madame Tussaud's
Madame Tussaud's famous wax-works feature startlingly lifelike replicas of personalities from Nelson Mandela to Kylie Minogue. It also features the adjoining planetarium.
Marylebone Street, London NW1
🚇 *Baker Street* 🚆 *Marylebone* 🚌 *13, 18, 27, 30, 74, 82, 113, 139, 159, 274*
☎ *(020) 7486 1121*
Website *www.madame-tussauds.co.uk*
Admission *9am-3pm £19.99-21.99, 3pm-5pm £15.99-17.99, 5pm-6pm £11-13*
Open *Mon-Fri 9.30am-5.30pm, Sat-Sun 9am-6pm*

National Gallery
From Canaletto to Constable, the National Gallery holds more than 2,000 works of art including some of the great masterpieces of European art such as Botticelli's *Venus and Mars*, Monet's *Waterlilies*, Renoir's *Boating on the Seine* and Van Gogh's *Sunflowers*.
Trafalgar Square, London WC2
🚇🚆 *Charing Cross* 🚌 *3, 6, 9, 11, 12, 13, 15, 23, 24, 29, 33, 77A, 88, 91, 139, 159, 176, 453*
☎ *(020) 7747 2885*
Website *www.nationalgallery.org.uk*
Admission *free*
Open *Mon-Tue 10am-6pm, Wed 10am-9pm, Thu-Sun 10am-6pm*

National Portrait Gallery
The National Portrait Gallery features a large collection of portraits depicting prominent figures from British history.
St Martins Place, London WC2
🚇 *Charing Cross, Leicester Square*
🚆 *Charing Cross* 🚌 *24, 29, 176*
☎ *(020) 7306 0055*
Website *www.npg.org.uk*
Admission *free*
Open *Mon-Wed 10am-6pm, Thu-Fri 10am-9pm, Sat-Sun 10am-6pm*

Royal Academy of Arts
This art museum is housed in the magnificent Burlington House and features

a programme of art exhibitions that range from obscure to famous French impressionists.
Burlington House, Piccadilly, London W1
🚇 *Green Park, Piccadilly* 🚌 *9, 14, 19, 22, 38*
☎ *(020) 7300 8000*
Website *www.royalacademy.org.uk*
Admission *£7*
Open *Mon-Thu 10am-6pm, Fri 10am-10pm, Sat-Sun 10am-6pm*

WESTMINSTER AND VICTORIA

Within walking distance of Trafalgar Square, this is the administrative heart of the UK. It holds the Houses of Parliament, the Prime Ministers' residence on Downing Street, and New Scotland Yard along with Big Ben and Westminster Abbey. Further to the west, you'll find Buckingham Palace and a small cluster of budget hotels around Victoria Station.

Banqueting House

The Banqueting House is the only surviving building of the vast Whitehall Palace, destroyed by fire nearly 300 years ago. The Banqueting House is a welcome retreat from the bustle of the city and a hidden treasure for anyone interested in art and architecture – its Rubens ceiling painting is just one of the artworks on display.
Whitehall, London SW1
🚇 *Westminster*
☎ *0870 751 5178*
Website *www.hrp.org.uk*
Admission *£4 (students £3)*
Open *Mon-Sat 10am-5pm*

Buckingham Palace

Visitors are confined to only a small section of Buckingham Palace so it is unlikely that you'll catch the Queen on the Throne, however you will get to see a really spiffy staircase, the Guard's Room, the Green Drawing Room and the Picture Gallery.
Buckingham Palace Road, London SW1
🚇 *Victoria, Green Park, Hyde Park Corner* 🚌 *Victoria* 🚌 *11, 211, 239, C1, C10*
☎ *(020) 7766 7300*
Website *www.royal.gov.uk*
Admission *£12.95 (students £11)*
Open *31 Jul-26 Sep 9.30am-4.30pm daily*

Cabinet War Rooms

This fortified basement in Whitehall is where Winston Churchill, the Cabinet, and senior military figures coordinated Britain's war effort. During the war it was one of London's most secret installations, and very few people were allowed entry, today however, the site is open to the public with many fascinating exhibits.
Clive Steps, 1 King Charles Street, London SW1
🚇 *Westminster*
☎ *(020) 7930 6961*
Website *http://cwr.iwm.org.uk*
Admission *£7.50*
Open *Jan-Mar 10am-6pm daily; Apr-Sep 9.30am-6pm daily; Oct-Dec 10am-6pm daily*

Changing the Guard

You can watch the changing of the guard at Buckingham Palace *(Apr-Jul 11.30am daily; Aug 11.30am odd numbered dates; Sep-Oct 11.30am even numbered dates; Nov 11.30am odd numbered dates).*

There is also a changing of the Mounted Guard ceremony in Whitehall *(Horse Guards Parade, Whitehall, London SW1;* 🚇 *Green Park, St James; Mon-Sat 11am; Sun 10am).*

Houses of Parliament

The Palace of Westminster with its distinctive clock tower is one of London's most recognised attractions. It is an impressive building that has been at the centre of English politics since the 11th century. Parliament consists of several halls that include Westminster Hall, with a remarkably well-preserved wooden ceiling, and St Stephen's Hall, which you pass through en route to the two debating chambers – the House of Lords and the House of Commons. The clock tower is widely known as Big Ben, although this term technically refers only to the bell that famously tolls every hour.

Tours of parliament (officially known as the Line of Route tour) are conducted year round for UK residents and during the summer opening of parliament for foreign visitors. UK residents need to book a tour through their local Member of Parliament, but foreign visitors can book through the Keith Prowse ticket office on Abingdon Green (☎ 0870 906 3773; *website www.firstcalltickets.com*) opposite Parliament.

When Parliament is in session you may visit the Strangers Gallery of either the House of Commons or the House of Lords to witness parliamentary debate. You are able to sit in on a session of Parliament even when the summer tours aren't running. To obtain entry you need to join the queue at the St Stephen's entrance. There are two queues – one of the House of Commons and another for the House of Lords. The Lord's queue is usually shorter, although the wait may take around two hours during the afternoon and it is not always possible to secure a place for Question Time. Visitors who arrive around 1pm usually have the shortest wait. It is easy to get into the House of Commons on Fridays – often there isn't even a queue – although Parliament doesn't sit every Friday and you will need to check with the Commons Information Office (☎ *(020) 7219 4272; website www.parliament.uk)*. If you wish to avoid the queue you can get a card of introduction from your embassy or high commission, however cards are limited to no more than four per day per embassy and some nationalities may have to book several weeks in advance. Australian and Canadian citizens may apply for a card of introduction through the London office of their state or province. Question Time in the House of Commons takes place during the first hour of proceedings Mon-Thu (the Prime Minister's Question Time takes place on Wednesday) and Question Time at the House of Lords lasts for 40 minutes from 2.30pm Mon-Wed and 11am Thu.

St Stephen's Entrance, St Margaret Street, London SW1
☻ *Westminster* ☎ *3, 11, 12, 24, 53, 77A, 88, 148, 159, 211, 453*
☎ *(020) 7219 4272 (House of Commons), (020) 7219 3107 (House of Lords) for sitting times*
Website *www.parliament.uk*
Tours of parliament cost *£7 (English), £9 (French, Italian, German & Spanish)*
Tours of parliament depart *Jul-Sep, call 0870 906 3773 for exact dates and time*
Admission to Stranger's Galleries *free*
House of Commons open *Mon 2.30pm-10.30pm, Tue-Wed 11.30am-7.30pm, Thu 11.30am-6.30pm, Fri (occasionally) 9.30am-3pm; the Stranger's Gallery at the House of Commons is closed when Parliament is in recess. Recess dates vary but there are usually around six two to three-week recess periods per year, often around Easter, mid-summer and Christmas.*
House of Lords open *Mon-Wed from 2.30pm, Thu from 11am, Fri (occasionally) from 11am; the House of Lords doesn't sit Easter, Aug to early Oct and the week before and after Christmas.*

Parliament Clock Tower (Big Ben)

Tours of the clock tower feature a climb up 334 spiral steps to the famous bell known as Big Ben. Capacity on these tours is very limited and the tours must be booked at least three months in advance. UK residents can book tours through their local Member of Parliament and foreign visitors have to apply in writing to Amanda Leck, Clock Tower Tours, Parliamentary Works Services Directorate, 1 Canon Row, London SW1A 2JN. Where demand is high, preference is given to those who can prove an interest in clocks or bells.

St Stephen's Entrance, St Margaret Street, London SW1
☻ *Westminster* ☎ *3, 11, 12, 24, 53, 77A, 88, 148, 159, 211, 453*
Tour cost *free*
Tours depart *Mon-Fri 10.30am, 11.30am & 2.30pm*

Tate Britain

The original Tate Gallery features an extensive art collection spanning from 1500 to the present day and it is considered by many to be the foremost collection of British art. The gallery also hosts a programme of temporary exhibits.

Millbank, London SW1
🚇 *Pimlico* 🚇 *Vauxhall, Victoria* 🚌 *2, 3, 36, 77A, 88, 159, 185, 507, C10*
☎ *(020) 7887 8000*
Website *www.tate.org.uk*
Admission *free (permanent collection); charge for some special exhibitions*
Open *10am-5.50pm daily (last admission 5pm)*

Westminster Abbey

This fine Gothic cathedral has been the setting for the coronations, marriages and burials of Britain's royal family. It has been the scene for every British royal coronation since William the Conqueror in 1066 (except Edwards V and VIII) and most British kings and queens are buried here, a tradition started by Edward the Confessor who was buried here a few days after the church was consecrated in December 1065. Although Westminster Abbey has stood on this site for almost a thousand years, much of the present building dates from the 13th to 16th centuries.

Broad Sanctuary, London SW1
🚇 *St James's Park, Westminster* 🚌 *3, 11, 12, 24, 53, 77A, 88, 148, 159, 211, 453*
☎ *(020) 7654 4900*
Website *www.westminster-abbey.org*
Admission *£7.50; (students £5)*
Tours cost *£4*
Tours depart *Jan-Mar Mon-Fri 10am, 11am, 2pm, 3pm, Sat 10am, 10.30am, 11am; Apr-Oct Mon-Fri 10am, 10.30am, 11am, 2pm, 2.30pm, 3pm, Sat 10am, 10.30am, 11am; Nov-Dec Mon-Fri 10am, 11am, 2pm, 3pm, Sat 10am, 10.30am, 11am*
Open *Mon-Tue 9.30am-3.45pm, Wed 9.30am-7pm, Thu-Fri 9.30am-3.45pm, Sat 9.30am-1.45pm*

KENSINGTON, CHELSEA & WEST LONDON

Kensington, Chelsea and neighbouring Knightsbridge are traditionally known as London's most expensive addresses with loads of ritzy shops including the famous Harrods department store. Surprisingly this area is also home to most of London's hostels and budget hotels which are situated in Earls Court and neighbouring South Kensington. Many backpackers living in London rent flats and houses in Earls Court and the nearby western suburbs of Hammersmith and Acton. This area has a good selection of pubs with many of London's top museums situated in South Kensington. Other landmarks include Hyde Park and Kensington Palace (Princess Diana's former residence).

Natural History Museum

This fine Gothic revival building features a rich collection of exhibits from the animal and plant kingdoms, which include the huge dinosaurs that dominate the main exhibition halls, the impressive mammal balcony and the ecology gallery with its moonlit, replica rainforest.

Cromwell Road, South Kensington, London SW7
🚇 *South Kensington* 🚌 *14, 49, 70, 74, 345, C1*
☎ *(020) 7938 9123*
Website *www.nhm.ac.uk*
Admission *free*
Open *Mon-Sat 10am-5.50pm, Sun 11am-5.50pm (last admission 5.30pm)*

Royal Albert Hall

This famous concert venue has seen everyone from Eric Clapton to Nigel Kennedy and annually hosts the proms. Tours of the Royal Albert Hall take you inside the auditorium, the Royal Retiring Room and the Queen's Box.

Kensington Gore, London SW7
🚇 *High Street Kensington, South Kensington* 🚌 *9, 10, 52, 360*
☎ *(020) 7538 3105*
Website *www.royalalberthall.com*
Tours cost *£6*
Tours depart *from 10am to 3.30pm daily*

Science Museum

The Science Museum presents the world of science with interactive exhibits and important artefacts dating from around 1700 to the present day. The collection includes exhibits that relate to the fields of medicine, technology and the Industrial Revolution.

Exhibition Road, South Kensington, London SW7

🚇 *South Kensington* 🚌 *14, 49, 70, 74, 345, C1*
☎ *0870 870 4868*
Website *www.sciencemuseum.org.uk*
Admission *free*
Open *10am-6pm daily*

Victoria & Albert Museum

Many people regard the V&A as the world's greatest museum of the decorative arts; its permanent collections include fashion, sculpture, textiles, furniture, metalwork, ceramics, glass, jewellery, paintings, prints and photographs, reflecting centuries of achievement from Europe, the Far East, South East Asia and the Islamic World.
Cromwell Road, South Kensington, London SW7
🚇 *South Kensington* 🚌 *14, 49, 70, 74, 345, C1*
☎ *(020) 7938 8349*
Website *www.vam.ac.uk*
Admission *free*
Open *Mon-Tue 10am-5.45pm, Wed 10am-10pm, Thu-Sun 10am-5.45pm*

PADDINGTON, BAYSWATER & NOTTING HILL

The northern end of Hyde Park also has a number of hostels and budget hotels, particularly in the Bayswater area and around Paddington Station. Further to the west, you'll find Notting Hill with its famous annual street party and Portobello Road Market.

Hyde Park & Kensington Gardens

For an entertaining though not necessarily accurate view of the world, make a visit to Speakers' Corner on the northeast edge of Hyde Park (🚇 *Marble Arch*). For street theatre on a weekend mid-afternoon it is unrivalled entertainment, as there can be as many as a dozen speakers, pushing their own particular barrow in different languages to crowds of more than one hundred people at any one time. If you feel like speaking your own mind then heckling is an integral part of the Speakers' Corner tradition.

When you've had enough of hearing what other people think there is plenty of opportunity to just relax in Hyde Park and the adjoining Kensington Gardens. Rent a rowboat on the Serpentine, which is the long thin lake that arcs through the two parks, or rollerblade among the walking paths, or join the multitude lazing under a shady tree as they enjoy the springtime sunshine.

Further west, the park is known as Kensington Gardens, which are dominated by the Round Pond and Kensington Palace – Princess Diana's former home.

Kensington Palace

Princess Diana's former home has been a royal residence since 1689 and former residents have included King William III and Queen Victoria. Visitors to the palace can see the Kings and Queens Apartments as well as the Royal Ceremonial Dress Collection.
Kensington Gardens, London W8
🚇 *Bayswater, High Street Kensington, Queensway* 🚌 *9, 10, 12, 27, 28, 49, 52, 52A, 70, 94, 328, C1*
☎ *0870 751 5170*
Website *www.hrp.org.uk/webcode/kensington_home.asp*
Admission *£10.80, £9.80 if booked by telephone or online; students £8.20, £7.20 if booked by telephone or online; joint ticket with Hampton Court £15.70, students £12.20; joint ticket with Tower of London £16.70, students £13.20*
Open *Jan-Feb 10am-5pm daily (last admission 4pm); Mar-Oct 10am-6pm daily (last admission 5pm); Nov-Dec 10am-5pm daily (last admission 4pm)*

CAMDEN & NORTH LONDON

Most people visit North London to hang out at Camden Town market, however North London also includes many great live music venues and some great pubs, both in Camden Town and Upper Street Islington.

London's Canals

An often-overlooked part of London is its canal network that mostly comprises the Grand Union Canal and Regent's Canal. This canal system runs through Hackney and Islington, past Camden Town, Regent's Park, Paddington and Little Venice before heading out into the suburbs.

It is possible to cycle, walk and even travel by canal boat along the most attractive stretches of the canals. Three of the most attractive areas of Regent's Canal include Little Venice, west of Paddington; Regent's Park, which includes London Zoo; and Camden Town with its vibrant markets. You can walk the stretch from Camden Lock to Little Venice in around two and a half hours.

London Zoo
One of the oldest zoos in the world, the London Zoo is home to more than 12,000 animals and is a major centre for animal research. Free events are held daily in the Amphitheatre and around the grounds.
Outer Circle, Regents Park, London NW1
🚇 *Camden Town* 🚌 *274, C2*
☎ *(020) 7722 3333*
Website *www.londonzoo.co.uk*
Admission *£13 (£11 students)*
Open *8 Mar-24 Oct 10am-5.30pm daily; 25-31 Oct 10am-4.30pm daily; 1 Nov-26 Dec 10am-4pm daily*

Lord's Cricket Ground
Tread in the footsteps of cricketing giants at the legendary Lord's Cricket Ground. Visitors to Lord's take a guided tour that includes the cricketing art gallery, the Long Room, which includes portraits of Thomas Lord himself, Sir Donald Bradman and Sir Leonard Hutton. Cricket bats and balls used by some of the game's greats are on display and it may also be possible to view other parts of the Pavilion including the Committee Room and the Dressing Rooms. The story of cricket unfolds via changing displays, models and audiovisual commentary and in the Museum the Ashes are on view in their terracotta urn. The tour continues to the Mound Stand, with its fine view of the ground and of the Lord's weather vane "Father Time", then on to the Indoor School, described as one of the best in the world and used by many clubs and players. Visitors will also be able to see the Real Tennis Court.
Lord's Cricket Ground, London, NW8
🚇 *St Johns Wood* 🚌 *13, 82, 113, 139, 187, 189, 274*
☎ *(020) 7432 1033*
Website *www.lords.org*
Admission *£7*
Tours *Jan-Mar noon, 2pm daily; Apr-Sep 10am, noon, 2pm daily; Oct-Dec noon, 2pm daily; no tours during major matches*

Royal Air Force Museum
The Royal Air Force Museum chronicles over 100 years of aviation history and features 60 aircraft on display. The Royal Air Force Museum's exhibits include the Bomber Command and the Battle of Britain halls and a fighter simulator.
Graham Park Way, Hendon, London NW9
🚇 *Colindale* 🚉 *Mill Hill Broadway;*
🚌 *303*
☎ *(020) 8205 2266*
Website *www.rafmuseum.com*
Admission *free*
Open *10am-6pm daily (last admission 5.30pm)*

THE DOCKLANDS, GREENWICH & THE EAST END
The working class neighbourhoods to the east of The City have some fascinating sights, including the popular Jack the Ripper Walking Tour offering a different perspective of London. Further east, you'll find new developments at the Docklands, especially the area around Canary Wharf, which is fast becoming a new centre for the financial and media industries. To the south of the Docklands, walk through the foot-tunnel under the Thames to suburban Greenwich which is famous for its history of time keeping and navigation.

Cutty Sark
Launched in 1869, the *Cutty Sark* was one of the fastest tea clippers of her day and is still regarded as one of Britain's most famous sailing ships.
King William Walk, Greenwich, London SE10
🚇 *Cutty Sark* 🚌 *177, 180, 188, 199*
☎ *(020) 8858 3445*
Website *www.cuttysark.org.uk*
Admission *£4.25*
Open *10am-5pm daily (last admission 4.30pm)*

National Maritime Museum

The National Maritime Museum is home to the Royal Greenwich Observatory and is on the prime meridian where Greenwich Mean Time (GMT) is set. This museum of astronomy and time is where you can see the time-ball and working telescopes and visit the planetarium.
Greenwich Park, SE10
🚇 *Cutty Sark* 🚉 *Greenwich* 🚌 *53, 54, 188, 202, 380*
☎ *(020) 8858 4422*
Website *www.nmm.ac.uk*
Admission *free*
Open *10am-5pm daily*

SOUTH LONDON

The majority of South London's sights are clustered along the Thames, usually within walking distance of the busier areas to the north of the river.

Design Museum

This inspiring museum by the riverfront near Tower Bridge features displays of everyday items that feature outstanding design. Sure you could see the same thing for free in a department store, but the Design Museum has carefully amassed a collection that includes everything from furniture to can openers and vacuum cleaners. There is also a programme of exhibits featuring the work of leading designers.
28 Shad Thames, London SE1
🚇 *London Bridge, Tower Gateway, Tower Hill* 🚉 *London Bridge* 🚌 *15, 42, 47, 78, 100, 188, P11*
☎ *0870 833 9955*
Website *www.designmuseum.org*
Admission *£6*
Open *Mon-Thu 10am-5.45pm (last admission 5.15pm), Fri 10am-9pm (last admission 8.30pm), Sat-Sun 10am-5.45pm (last admission 5.15pm)*

Globe Theatre

William Shakespeare's Globe Theatre has been rebuilt on the banks of the Thames and it hosts performances of the Bard's work and is also home to an exhibition recounting the history of the famous theatre.
21 New Globe Walk, London SE1
🚇 *Blackfriars, Mansion House, St Pauls, Southwark* 🚉 *Blackfriars, Cannon Street, London Bridge* 🚌 *11, 15, 17, 23, 26, 45, 63, 76, 100, 344, 381, RV1* 🚉 *Bankside*
☎ *(020) 7902 1500*
Website *www.shakespeares-globe.org*
Admission *Jan-Apr £8 (£6.50 students); May-Sep £8.50 (£7 students); Oct-Dec £8 (£6.50 students)*
Open *daily 1 Jan-4 Apr 10am-5pm daily; 4 Apr-30 Sep 9am-noon daily (theatre tour & exhibition), 12.30pm-5pm daily (exhibition & visit to Rose Theatre site); 1 Oct-31 Dec 10am-5pm daily*

HMS Belfast

This impressive 11,000 tonne World War cruiser is now a floating museum with seven decks to explore. Many high quality naval exhibits are on board.
River Thames, off Morgans Lane, Tooley Street, London SW1
🚇 *London Bridge* 🚌 *21, 35, 40, 133, 343*
☎ *(020) 7940 6300*
Website *http://hmsbelfast.iwm.org.uk/*
Admission *£7 (£5 students)*
Open *Jan-Feb 10am-5pm (last admission 4.15pm) daily; Mar-Oct 10am-6pm (last admission 5.15pm) daily; Nov-Dec 10am-5pm (last admission 4.15pm) daily*

Imperial War Museum

This excellent museum features exhibits on Britain's military involvement from World War I to the present day.
Lambeth Road, London SE1
🚇 *Lambeth North* 🚌 *1, 3, 12, 45, 53, 59, 63, 68, 100, 159, 168, 171, 172, 176, 188, 344, C10*
☎ *(020) 7416 5000*
Website *www.iwm.org.uk*
Admission *£3*
Open *10am-6pm daily*

London Eye

The 135m-high London Eye is a huge Ferris wheel that rotates every thirty minutes offering brilliant views over London from the distinctive ellipsoid capsules.
🚇🚉 *Waterloo* 🚌 *11, 24, 211, RV1*
☎ *0870 500 0600*
Website *www.ba-londoneye.com*

Admission £11.50 (£9 ISIC)
Open May Mon-Thu 9.30am-8pm,
Fri-Sun 9.30am-9pm; Jun Mon-Thu
9.30am-9pm, Fri-Sun 9.30am-10pm,
Jul-Aug 9.30am-10pm daily; Oct-Dec
9.30am-8pm daily

London Dungeon
This tourist trap behind London Bridge station features displays about the gorier aspects of Britain's history with exhibits on Jack the Ripper, the Great Fire, the plague and royalty. It's cheesy but popular with kids.
28-34 Tooley Street, London SE1
🚇 *London Bridge* 🚌 *21, 35, 40, 133, 343*
☎ *(020) 7403 0606*
Website *www.london-dungeon.co.uk*
Admission £11 (£9.50 students)
Open daily Jan-Jul 10.30am-5.30pm daily; Aug-Sep 10.30am-8pm daily; Oct-Dec 10.30am-5.30pm daily

Old Operating Theatre
This museum in the attic of an old Baroque church shows the conditions in which surgeons operated in the early 1800s (without anaesthetic). This was originally an operating theatre where medical students would watch operations take place.
9A St Thomas Street, London SE1
🚇 *London Bridge* 🚌 *21, 35, 40, 133, 343*
☎ *(020) 7955 4791*
Website *www.thegarret.org.uk*
Admission £4.25
Open 10.30am-5pm daily

Southwark Cathedral
London's oldest Gothic church was established around 1220 and was attended by William Shakespeare (his brother Edmond is buried here). There is an exhibition of the history of Southwark in the cathedral's former chapter house building.
London Bridge, London SE1
🚇 *Bank, London Bridge, Monument*
🚌 *London Bridge* 🚌 *17, 21, 35, 40, 43, 47, 48, 133, 149, 501, 521, D1*
⛴ *Bankside*
☎ *(020) 7367 6722*
Website *www.dswark.org/cathedral/*
Admission free
Open Mon-Sat 10am-6pm (last admission 5.30pm), Sun 11am-5pm (last admission 4.30pm)

Tate Modern
This large modern art museum is housed in a former power station with seven floors of galleries including the huge Turbine Hall. Exhibits are organised by theme, which sees works by famous artists such as Picasso go up alongside relatively unknown artists.
Bankside, London SE1
🚇 *Blackfriars, Southwark* 🚇 *Blackfriars, London Bridge* 🚌 *45, 63, 100, 381, 344, RV1* ⛴ *Bankside*
☎ *(020) 7887 8000*
Website *www.tate.org.uk*
Admission free
Open Mon-Thu 10am-6pm (last admission 5.15pm), Fri-Sat 10am-10pm (last admission 9.15pm), Sun 10am-6pm (last admission 5.15pm)

WESTERN SUBURBS
London's affluent western suburbs extend far from the West End but include several important sights including Kew Gardens, Hampton Court Palace and Wimbledon.

Hampton Court Palace
It has been over 250 years since the Hampton Court Palace was home to Britain's royalty, but this opulent palace has been restored to show how monarchs including Kings Henry VIII and William III once lived. It features some of the world's finest Baroque style royal apartments and expansive gardens that include the popular maze, which was planted in 1702. Hampton Court is half an hour by train from Waterloo station.
A308, East Molesey, Surrey
🚇 *Hampton Court* 🚌 *111, 216, 411, 416, 451, 513, 726, R68*
☎ *0870 752 7777*
Website *www.hrp.org.uk*
Admission £11.80 (£10.80 if booked by telephone or online), student £8.70 (£7.70 if booked by telephone or online); joint ticket with Tower of London £17.50, student £14.20; joint ticket with Kensington Palace £15.70, student £12.20

Open *1 Jan-26 Mar Mon 10.15am-4.30pm, Tue-Sun 9.30am-4.30pm (last admission 3.30pm); 27 Mar-30 Oct Mon 10.15am-6pm, Tue-Sun 9.30am-6pm (last admission 5pm)*

Kew Gardens

Recognised by UNESCO as a World Heritage Site, the Royal Botanic Gardens at Kew are home to an outstanding collection of plantlife from around the world. The gardens were originally the grounds of Kew Palace but in 1752 Princess Augusta set about developing it into a serious botanic gardens and in 1793 Sir Joseph Banks expanded the gardens' role from a showpiece of exotic flora into a serious scientific and research role. The gardens now consist of several large temperature-controlled conservatories, each representing different climate zones.

Kew Gardens, Kew
🚇🚆 *Kew Gardens* 🚌 *65, 237, 267, 391*
Website www.rbgkew.org.uk
Admission £8.50
Open 1 Jan-6 Feb 9.30am-3.45pm daily; 7 Feb-5 Sep Mon-Fri 9.30am-6pm, Sat-Sun 9.30am-7pm; 6 Sep-30 Oct 9.30am-5.30pm daily; 1 Nov-31 Dec 9.30am-3.45pm daily

Walking Tours

A walking tour can be a good way to gain a unique perspective and a deeper appreciation of London. There are several walking tours to choose from including ones that specialise in ghosts, Jack the Ripper, music and literature.

The Blood and Tears Walk

Declan McHugh, a former actor, runs this entertaining walk that focuses on the dark side on London's history. This highly recommended walk covers the history of serial killers including Jack the Ripper and also conspiracy theories, execution, grave robbers and witchcraft.

Meet outside Barbican tube station
🚇 *Barbican*
☎ *(020) 8348 9022*
Website www.shockinglondon.co.uk
Tours cost £6
Tours depart Mon 2pm, Wed 7pm, Thu 2pm & 7pm, Fri 2pm & 7pm, Sat 11.30am & 2.30pm; phone to confirm times.

London Walks

London Walks has been guiding tours of the capital for more than 35 years, and in that time has devised routes and subject matter to attract anyone with the remotest interest in London's past. Themed walks include Darkest Victorian London, Ghosts of the West End, Hidden Pubs of Old London, Old Mayfair, Sir Christopher Wren's London, Shakespeare's London and of course the popular Jack the Ripper Haunts walking tour.

☎ *(020) 7624 9255*
Website www.walks.com
Tours cost £4.50

East Anglia

This region of eastern England stretches from London's outer northeastern suburbs to the North Sea. The main attractions in this mostly flat region include the cathedral cities of Ely and Norwich, the university city of Cambridge and Norfolk Broads National Park.

Cambridgeshire

Cambridge

This historic city shares many similarities with Oxford but it enjoys a much less hurried pace and attracts fewer tourists than its larger rival. Cambridge is also a thriving base for an increasing number of high-tech businesses although its famous university still dominates the city. The 31 colleges of Cambridge University – England's second-oldest – have educated many notable figures including Charles Darwin, Sir Isaac Newton and Stephen Hawking, not to mention John Cleese and Eric Idle.

Practical Information
Tourist Information Centre
Wheeler Street, Cambridge
☎ *0906 586 2526 (20p per minute)*
Website *www.visitcambridge.org*
Open *Mon-Fri 10am-5.30pm, Sat 10am-5pm, Sun 11am-4pm*

Coming & Going
AIR
Cambridge is close to Stansted Airport, which has flights to most European destinations including a large choice of destinations served by budget airline, Ryanair *(website www.ryanair.com)*.

Central Trains *(website www.centraltrains.co.uk)* operate a direct rail link between Cambridge and Stansted Airport. The airport is also served by frequent National Express bus services.

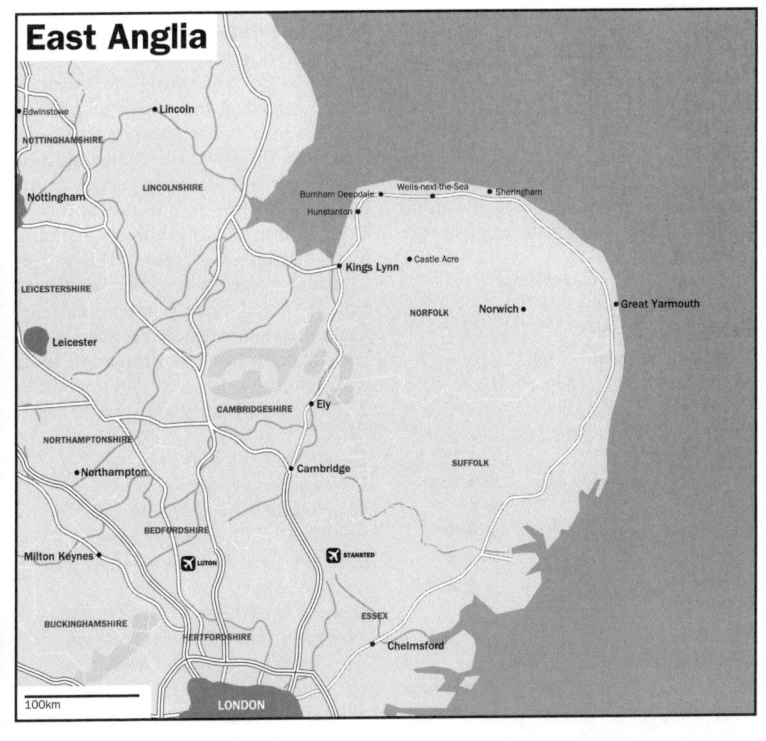

BUS
National Express *(website www.nationalexpress.co.uk)* has buses to Cambridge from Birmingham, London, Milton Keynes, Oxford and Stansted Airport. Buses arrive and depart at the coach stop on Drummer Street.

TRAIN
Central Trains *(website www.centraltrains.co.uk)* run trains to Birmingham, Ely, Norwich and Stansted Airport; One *(website www.onerailway.co.uk)* run trains to London (Liverpool Street) plus local trains in East Anglia with services to Ely, Ipswich and Norwich and WAGN *(website www.wagn.co.uk)* has trains to Ely, Kings Lynn and London (Kings Cross).

The train station is south of the city centre, accessible by buses 1, 3 and 7.

Local Transport
Stagecoach Citi *(website www.stagecoachbus.co.uk)* operate a comprehensive network of seven bus routes in the Cambridge area with buses running every 10 to 20 minutes.

Accommodation
Cambridge YHA
This is a large and very clean hostel that is close to the city centre and next to the train station. It has friendly and helpful staff and is popular with the younger age group. Facilities include the usual kitchen and TV lounge. It is a great base to explore the city.
97 Tension Road, Cambridge
🚌 *1, 3, 7*
☎ *(01223) 354 601*
Website *www.yha.org.uk*
Dorm bed *£18.50 (£16.50 HI/YHA)*
Credit cards *MC, Visa*
Reception open *7am-11pm daily*

Maintenance & cleanliness		★★★★½
Facilities		★★½
Atmosphere & character		★★★
Security		★★★
Overall rating		★★★

Sights
CAMBRIDGE UNIVERSITY
More than 60 Nobel Prize winners have graduated from Cambridge University, which is England's second oldest. The university is divided into 31 colleges, the most prestigious being King's and Trinity Colleges.

King's College
Henry VI founded King's College in 1441 to provide higher education to Eton students. Although it was restricted to former Eton students until 1861, King's College is now Cambridge's most liberal college, however its outward appearance is one of the most traditional. Its highlight is the impressive King's College Chapel, a Gothic masterpiece that is Cambridge's largest college chapel.
King's Parade, Cambridge
🚌 *1, 2, 5, 6*
☎ *(01223) 331 100*
Website *www.kings.cam.ac.uk*
Admission *£4*
Open *during term time Mon-Fri 9.30am-3.30pm, Sat 9.30am-3.15pm, Sun 1.15pm-2.15pm & 5pm-5.30pm; out of term Mon-Sat 9.30am-4.30pm, Sun 10am-5pm*

Trinity College
Henry VIII founded Trinity College in 1546 by combining two earlier buildings dating from 1317 and 1324, however most of the college's buildings date from the 16th and 17th centuries. Trinity College is the largest of Cambridge's colleges and is noted for its large courts and the library designed by Christopher Wren. Trinity has educated six British prime ministers and 31 Nobel Prize winners. Famous former students include Francis Bacon, Earl Grey, Sir Isaac Newton and Ernest Rutherford.
Trinity Street, Cambridge
🚌 *1, 2, 5, 6*
☎ *(01223) 338 400*
Website *www.trin.cam.ac.uk*
Admission *1 Jan-6 Mar free; 7 Mar-10 Jun £2; 19-23 Jun £2; 25 Jun-30 Sep £2; 6-24 Oct £2; 25 Oct-24 Dec free; 26-31 Dec free*
Open *1 Jan-10 Jun 10am-5pm daily; 19-23 Jun 10am-5pm daily; 25 Jun-30 Sep 10am-5pm daily; 6 Oct-24 Dec 10am-5pm daily; 26-31 Dec 10am-5pm daily*

OTHER ATTRACTIONS
Imperial War Museum at Duxford
The Duxford branch of the Imperial War Museum houses a huge collection of 180 aircraft ranging from World War I biplanes to the Concord. It is in Duxford, 15km south of Cambridge.
A505, Duxford
🚌 *7*
☎ *(01223) 835 000*
Website *http://duxford.iwm.org.uk*
Admission *£10 (£5 students)*
Open *1 Jan-12 Mar 10am-3.15pm daily; 13 Mar-30 Oct 10am-5.15pm daily; 31 Oct-31 Dec 10am-3.15pm daily*

Fitzwilliam Museum
Cambridge University's art museum has been described as Europe's finest small museum. The neoclassical building houses a collection that encompasses Egyptian, Greek and east Asian antiquities as well an art collection that includes works by the French Impressionists.
Trumpington Street, Cambridge
🚌 *4*
☎ *(01223) 322 900*
Website *www.fitzmuseum.cam.ac.uk*
Admission *free*
Open *Tue-Sat 10am-5pm, Sun noon-5pm*

Kettle's Yard
This small museum displays contemporary art through a programme of temporary exhibits.
Castle Street, Cambridge
🚌 *1, 2, 5, 6*
☎ *(01223) 352 124*
Website *www.kettlesyard.co.uk*
Admission *free*
Open *Jan-mid Apr Tue-Sun 2pm-4pm; mid Apr-mid Sep Tue-Sun 1.30pm-4.30pm; mid Sep-Dec Tue-Sun 2pm-4pm*

Museum of Classical Archaeology
This museum is home to the world's finest collection of plaster casts of ancient Greek and Roman sculpture.
Sidgwick Avenue, Cambridge
🚌 *1, 2, 3, 5, 6, 7*
☎ *(01223) 335 153*
Website *www.classics.cam.ac.uk/ark.html*
Admission *free*
Open *outside university term Mon-Fri 10am-5pm; during university term Mon-Fri 10am-5pm, Sat 10am-1pm*

Scott Polar Research Institute
The museum run by the Scott Polar Research Institute displays artefacts relating to polar exploration.
Lensfield Road, Cambridge
🚌 *1, 4, 7*
☎ *(01223) 336 540*
Website *www.spri.cam.ac.uk*
Admission *free*
Open *Tue-Sat 2.30pm-4pm*

Sedgwick Museum of Earth Sciences
This museum has a large collection of rocks and fossils from around the world. Exhibits include dinosaurs and other prehistoric wildlife plus specimens collected by Charles Darwin's 1831 voyage on the *Beagle*.
Downing Street, Cambridge
🚌 *1, 2, 3, 5, 6, 7*
☎ *(01223) 333 456*
Website *www.sedgwickmuseum.org*
Admission *free*
Open *Mon-Fri 9am-1pm & 2pm-5pm, Sat 10am-1pm*

Ely

This small city would just be another charming market town if it weren't for its majestic cathedral.

Practical Information
Ely Tourist Information Centre
Oliver Cromwell's House, 29 St Mary's Street, Ely
☎ *(01353) 662 062*
Open *Jan-Mar Mon-Fri 11am-4pm, Sat 10am-5pm, Sun 11am-4pm; Apr-Oct 10am-5.30pm daily; Nov-Dec Mon-Fri 11am-4pm, Sat 10am-5pm, Sun 11am-4pm*

Coming & Going
Central Trains *(website www.centraltrains.co.uk)* runs trains to Birmingham, Cambridge, Norwich and Stansted Airport; One *(website www.*

onerailway.co.uk) runs trains to Cambridge and London (Liverpool Street) plus local trains in East Anglia with services to Ipswich and Norwich and WAGN *(website www.wagn.co.uk)* operates trains to Cambridge, Kings Lynn and London (Kings Cross).

Sights
Ely Cathedral
Ely's eye-catching cathedral was founded in 1081 but its stained glass windows and elaborate ceiling date from the 19th century.
The College, Ely
☎ *(01353) 667 735*
Website *www.elycathedral.co.uk*
Admission *£4.80*
Open *summer 7am-7pm daily; winter Mon-Sat 7.30am-6pm, Sun 7.30am-5pm*

Ely Museum
This museum has exhibits about local history.
The Old Gaol, Market Street, Ely
☎ *(01353) 666 655*
Admission *£2*
Open *summer 10.30am-5.30pm daily; winter 10.30am-4.30pm daily*

Stained Glass Museum
Located inside Ely Cathedral, the Stained Glass Museum has displays about the history of stained glass.
The South Triforium, Ely Cathedral, Ely
☎ *(01353) 660 347*
Website *www.stainedglassmuseum.com*
Admission *£3.50*
Open *Jan-Easter Mon-Fri 10.30am-4.30pm, Sat 10.30am-5pm, Sun noon-4.30pm; Easter-Oct Mon-Fri 10.30am-5pm, Sat 10.30am-5.30pm, Sun noon-6pm; Nov-Dec Mon-Fri 10.30am-4.30pm, Sat 10.30am-5pm, Sun noon-4.30pm*

Norfolk
This largely flat county takes up most of the East Anglia region and it is renowned for its continental-style windmills. Its main attractions include the coastal towns, the Norfolk Broads National Park and the city of Norwich.

Kings Lynn
Lynn is a lovely town on the River Great Ouse that was a prosperous port in the 16th century when it controlled much of the trade between England and northern Germany.

Practical Information
Tourist Information Centre
Custom House, Corner King Street & Purfleet, Kings Lynn
☎ *(01553) 763 044*
Open *Mon-Sat 9.15am-5pm; Sun 10.15am-5pm*

Coming & Going
BUS
National Express *(website www.nationalexpress.co.uk)* have buses to Birmingham, Cambridge, London, Norwich and Peterborough.

First *(website www.firstgroup.com)* operate buses in Norfolk and neighbouring counties. The FirstTourist ticket costs £6 and gives you one day unlimited travel on First buses in East Anglia.

Buses stop at the Vancouver Centre.

TRAIN
WAGN *(website www.wagn.co.uk)* operates train services to Cambridge and London (Kings Cross).

Accommodation
Kings Lynn YHA
Kings Lynn YHA is in a college building in the historic part of Kings Lynn, close to a host of attractions from museums to Norman ruins. It has friendly and helpful staff and accommodation in basic dorms. A fantastic cooked breakfast is served every morning.
College Lane, Kings Lynn
☎ *(01553) 772 461*
Website *www.yha.org.uk*
Dorm bed *£13 (£11 HI/YHA);* ***double/twin room*** *£30 (£26 HI/YHA);* ***breakfast*** *£3.60*
Credit cards *MC, Visa*
Open *Easter-Sep;* ***reception open*** *7.30am-10am & 5pm-10.30pm daily;* ***lockout*** *10am-5pm daily;* ***curfew*** *11.30pm*

Maintenance & cleanliness		★★★½
Facilities		★

Atmosphere & character	★★★★
Security	★★
Overall rating	★★½

Sights
The Lynn Museum
This museum in a Victorian chapel houses a collection of exhibits on local history.
Market Street, Kings Lynn
☎ *(01553) 775 001*
Website www.museums.norfolk.gov.uk
Admission £1
Open Tue-Sat 10am-5pm

Sandringham Estate
The Queen's country retreat has been described as "the most comfortable house in England". The royal family regularly uses the house and the main ground floor rooms are open to the public. There is also a museum on the site that displays many items relating to the royal family including a collection of vintage cars.
Sandringham, near Kings Lynn
🚌 *411, coastliner*
☎ *(01553) 772 675*
Website www.sandringhamestate.co.uk
Admission £6.50
Open 10 Apr-23 Jul & 1 Aug-30 Sep 11am-4.45pm daily; Oct 11am-3pm daily

Town House Museum
This museum chronicles domestic life in Lynn from medieval times to the 1950s featuring reconstructed rooms from various periods in the town's history.
46 Queen Street, Kings Lynn
☎ *(01553) 773 450*
Website www.museums.norfolk.gov.uk
Admission £1.80
Open Jan-Apr Mon-Sat 10am-4pm; May-Sep Mon-Sat 10am-5pm, Sun 2pm-5pm; Oct-Dec Mon-Sat 10am-4pm

Castle Acre
This lovely village dates from the 10th century and boasts ruins of a Norman castle and a well maintained priory. Castle Acre is 30km east of Kings Lynn.

Accommodation
The Old Red Lion
The Old Red Lion is not a public house as the name might suggest, but lovely traditional accommodation set in a quiet and quaint medieval village just a stone's throw from the castle remains. The hostel offers homely dorms and cosy common areas, a peaceful garden and home cooked vegetarian whole food making it perfect for a relaxing retreat.
Bailey Street, Castle Acre
☎ *(01760) 755 557*
Website ww.oldredlion.here2stay.org.uk
Dorm bed £15; double/twin room £40-50; prices include breakfast

🚌 🅿 ♿ 📺 🅺

Maintenance & cleanliness	★★★★
Facilities	★★★½
Atmosphere & character	★★★★
Security	★★½
Overall rating	★★★★½

Sights
Castle Acre Castle
Castle Acre Castle was built in the 12th century as a Norman manor house, but was later fortified to become a castle.
Castle Acre
Website www.english-heritage.org.uk
Admission free
Always open

Castle Acre Priory
Castle Acre's well-preserved priory was built over a period of seven hundred years and it includes a 12th-century church and 15th-century gatehouse.
Castle Acre
☎ *(01760) 755 394*
Website www.english-heritage.org.uk
Admission £4.20 (£3.20 students)
Open Jan-Mar Wed-Sun 10am-4pm; Apr-Sep 10am-6pm daily; Oct-Dec Wed-Sun 10am-4pm

North Norfolk Coast
Norfolk's northern coast is one of Britain's more relaxed coastal regions. The main towns in this region stretch from Hunstanton, north of Kings Lynn, to Cromer, north of Norwich.

This part of Norfolk has a good selection of hostel accommodation.

Practical Information

Hunstanton Tourist Information Centre
Town Hall, The Green, Hunstanton
☎ *(01485) 532 610*
Open *Apr-Sep 10am-5pm daily*

Sheringham Tourist Information Centre
Station Approach, Sherringham
☎ *(01263) 824 329*

Wells-next-the-Sea Tourist Information Centre
Staithe Street, Wells-next-the-Sea
☎ *(01328) 710 885*

Coming & Going & Local Transport

First (*website www.firstgroup.com*) and Norfolk Green (*website www.norfolkgreen.co.uk*) operate local bus services in northern Norfolk. One of the more useful bus routes is Norfolk Greens bus 36, which runs along the coast from Cromer to King's Lynn.

One (*website www.onerailway.co.uk*) runs local train services from Cromer to Sheringham and Norwich.

Accommodation

HUNSTANTON
Courtyard Farm Bunkhouse Barn
Set amongst traditional farm buildings, this is a small hostel that provides a cosy, relaxed stay. It is popular with horse riders and is surrounded by beautiful countryside with plenty of nature walks. The dorm is a converted 17th century barn offering basic, but comfortable, accommodation.
Courtyard Farm, Ringstead, Hunstanton
☎ *(01485) 525 369*
Website *www.deepdalegranary.co.uk*
Dorm bed *£6*
Credit cards *MC, Visa*

Maintenance & cleanliness	★★★
Facilities	★★☆
Atmosphere & character	★★★★☆
Security	-
Overall rating	★★★☆

Hunstanton YHA
The hostel building is a converted Victorian house close to the picturesque seaside. It is popular with hikers of the Norfolk Coastal Path and offers a warm and sociable atmosphere with plenty of activities nearby.
15 Avenue Road, Hunstanton
🚌 *410, 411, 412, 413*
☎ *(01485) 532 061*
Website *www.yha.org.uk*
Dorm bed *£14.50 (£12.50 HI/YHA);*
twin room *£31.60 (£27.60 HI/YHA)*
Credit cards *MC, Visa*
Open *Easter-Oct; reception open 7.30am-10am & 5pm-10pm daily; lockout 10am-5pm daily*

Maintenance & cleanliness	★★★★☆
Facilities	★★
Atmosphere & character	★★★
Security	★★☆
Overall rating	★★★

BURNHAM DEEPDALE
Deepdale Backpackers
Located close to the sea in beautiful country surroundings, Deepdale Backpackers offers great facilities including an organic café, modern kitchen, spacious common room and a large reception area with very helpful staff and good local information. The dorms are housed in converted 17th-century farm buildings.
Deepdale Farm, Burnham Deepdale
☎ *(01485) 210 256*
Website *www.deepdalefarm.co.uk*
Dorm bed *£10-50-12.50*
Credit cards *JCB, MC, Visa*
Reception open *peak season 8am-8pm daily; off peak 10am-4pm daily; 24 hour check in available*

Maintenance & cleanliness	★★★★
Facilities	★★★☆
Atmosphere & character	★★★★★
Security	★★★
Overall rating	★★★★

WELLS-NEXT-THE-SEA
Wells-next-the-Sea YHA
This 1914 church hall was converted in 2002 and has become the YHA's most successful venture. What it lacks in atmosphere and charm is made up for in the maintenance of its facilities. There are pubs, restaurants and cafés nearby if you fancy a break from

cooking, though the kitchen is very well equipped. Pretty villages and nature reserves surround the hostel and it is just 10 minutes from the bustling harbour.
Church Plain, Wells-next-the-Sea
☏ *36 (Coast Hopper)*
☎ *0870 770 6084*
Website *www.yha.org.uk*
Dorm bed *£14.50 (£12.50 HI/YHA)*
Credit cards *JCB, MC, Visa*
Open *Easter-Oct; reception open 8am-10am & 5pm-9pm daily; curfew 11pm*

🚗♿📺Ⓚ🅻

Maintenance & cleanliness	★★★★
Facilities	★★
Atmosphere & character	-
Security	★★
Overall rating	★★★☆

SHERINGHAM
Sheringham YHA
This youth hostel has friendly staff and offers accommodation in clean and comfortable dorms. It has the usual hostel facilities including a TV lounge, Internet access, laundry and a kitchen. Sheringham is a traditional fishing village known for great pubs and several small beaches.
1 Cremers Drift, Sheringham
☎ *(01263) 823 215*
Website *www.yha.org.uk*
Dorm bed *£18 (£16 HI/YHA)*
Credit cards *MC, Visa*
Reception open *8am-10am & 1pm-10pm daily; lockout 10am-1pm daily; curfew 11.30pm*

🚗♿📺Ⓚ🅻🅹

Maintenance & cleanliness	★★★★
Facilities	★★★
Atmosphere & character	★★★☆
Security	★★
Overall rating	★★★☆

Norwich
Norwich is the UK's most complete medieval city and it is dominated by a 900-year-old Norman castle and cathedral.

During medieval times the city prospered from the wool trade, which resulted in 33 fine medieval churches including the stunning cathedral.

Practical Information
Norwich Tourist Information Centre
The Forum, Millennium Plain, Bethel Street, Norwich
☎ *(01603) 666 071*
Website *www.visitnorwich.co.uk*
Open *Jan-May Mon-Fri 9.30am-4.30pm, Sat 9.30am-1pm & 1.30pm-4.30pm; Jun-Sep Mon-Sat 9.30am-5pm; Oct-Dec Mon-Fri 9.30am-4.30pm, Sat 9.30am-1pm & 1.30pm-4.30pm*

Coming & Going
AIR
Norwich International Airport (☎ *(01603) 411923; website www.norwichinternational.com*) has flights to over 400 destinations; however it is hardly a busy hub for backpackers.

BUS
National Express (**website** *www.nationalexpress.co.uk*) runs buses from Norwich to Birmingham, London and Stansted Airport.

First (**website** *www.firstgroup.com*) operate buses in Norfolk and neighbouring counties. The FirstTourist ticket costs £6 and gives you one day unlimited travel on First buses in East Anglia.

Buses stop at the coach station on Drummer Street.

TRAIN
Norwich is about a 1½-hour train journey from London (Liverpool Street) with trains running every half hour. One (**website** *www.onerailway.co.uk*) operates most trains to and from London and Central Trains (**website** *www.centraltrains.co.uk*) runs trains to Birmingham, Cambridge, Ely, Leicester, Liverpool, Nottingham and Peterborough.

Local Transport
First (**website** *www.firstgroup.com*) operate local bus services in Cambridge. The most useful route is bus 25, which runs between the train station and the city centre.

The FirstDay Norwich ticket gives you one day unlimited bus travel on

First buses in Norwich (zones 1 to 4) for £2.80.

Accommodation

There are no hostels in Norwich. The closest hostels are in Great Yarmouth and Sheringham.

Sights
The Bridewell
This medieval building was once a prison for women and beggars and now operates as a museum with exhibits detailing Norwich's industrial heritage.
Bridewell Alley, Norwich
☎ *(01603) 493 636*
Website *www.museums.norfolk.gov.uk*
Admission *£2.20*
Open *Tue-Fri 10am-4.30pm, Sat 10am-5pm*

Dragon Hall
This historic house was built around 1430 and represents a superb example of medieval craftsmanship.
115-123 King Street, Norwich
☎ *(01603) 663 922*
Website *www.dragonhall.org*
Admission *£2.50*
Open *Jan-Mar Mon-Fri 10am-4pm; Apr-Oct Mon-Sat 10am-4pm; Nov-Dec Mon-Fri 10am-4pm*

Norwich Castle
Built by the Normans in 1067 as a royal palace, Norwich Castle is considered one of Europe's finest Norman buildings. The castle houses a museum and art gallery that feature exhibitions on loan from the Tate and a gallery dedicated to Queen Boudicca.
Castle Meadow, Norwich
☎ *(01603) 493 636*
Website *www.museums.norfolk.gov.uk*
Admission *£3.50-5.25*
Open *Mon-Fri 10am-4pm, Sat 10am-5pm, Sun 1pm-5pm*

Norwich Cathedral
This magnificent cathedral boasts England's second tallest spire and over 1000 medieval roof bosses.
The Close, Norwich
☎ *(01603) 218 321*
Website *www.cathedral.org.uk*
Admission *free*
Open *7.30am-6pm daily*

Origins
This excellent museum uses interactive exhibits to portray 2000 years of Norfolk's history.
The Forum, Millennium Plain, Norwich
🚌 *19, 20, 21, 22, 26, 27*
☎ *(01603) 727 920*
Website *www.originsnorwich.com*
Admission *£4.95*
Open *Jan-Mar Mon-Sat 10am-5.30pm, Sun 10.30am-4.30pm; Apr-Oct Mon-Sat 10am-6pm, Sun 10.30am-4.30pm; Nov-Dec Mon-Sat 10am-5.30pm, Sun 10.30am-4.30pm*

Strangers' Hall
This wealthy merchant's house dates from 1320 and features a Tudor Great Hall, a Georgian dining room and a splendid stone-vaulted undercroft.
Charing Cross, Norwich
☎ *(01603) 667 363*
Website *www.museums.norfolk.gov.uk*
Admission *£2.50*
Open *Wed & Sat 10.30am-4.30pm*

Great Yarmouth

Great Yarmouth is a seaside resort with the usual assortment of tacky amusement arcades. It is easily accessible from Norwich.

Practical Information
Great Yarmouth Tourist Information Centre
Marine Parade, Great Yarmouth
☎ *(01493) 842 195*
Open *Mon-Sat 9.30am-4pm, Sun 10am-4pm*

Coming & Going
BUS
First (**website** *www.firstgroup.com*) runs buses in and around Great Yarmouth including buses to Norwich. An all day bus pass for travel in the Great Yarmouth area costs £2.60.

TRAIN
One (**website** *www.onerailway.co.uk*) trains run between Norwich and Great Yarmouth.

Accommodation
Great Yarmouth YHA
Great Yarmouth's YHA was once an Edwardian family-run hotel. The hostel has the normal youth hostel facilities such as a TV lounge and kitchen and it is within walking distance of the traditional seaside attractions.
2 Sandown Road, Great Yarmouth
☎ *(01493) 843 991*
Website *www.yha.org.uk*
Dorm bed *£13 (£11 HI/YHA)*
Credit cards *MC, Visa*
Open *Easter-Sep; reception open 8am-10am & 5pm-10pm daily; lockout 10am-5pm daily*

Maintenance & cleanliness	★★★½
Facilities	★★½
Atmosphere & character	★★★½
Security	★★½
Overall rating	★★★

Sights
Elizabethan House Museum
This Elizabethan Quayside house depicts family life from Tudor to Victorian times.
Tolhouse Street, Great Yarmouth
☎ *(01493) 745 526*
Website *www.museums.norfolk.gov.uk*
Admission *£2.70*
Open *5 Apr-31 Oct Mon-Fri 10am-5pm, Sat-Sun 1.15pm-5pm*

Time & Tide – Museum of Great Yarmouth Life
This new museum has displays on local history including exhibits on Great Yarmouth's maritime and fishing heritage.
Blackfriars Road, Great Yarmouth
☎ *(01493) 743 930*
Website *www.museums.norfolk.gov.uk*
Admission *£5.45*
Open *14 Jul-31 Oct 10am-5pm daily*

Tolhouse Museum
This museum, housed in one of England's oldest prisons, has displays on the history of crime and punishment.
Tolhouse Street, Great Yarmouth
☎ *(01493) 745 526*
Website *www.museums.norfolk.gov.uk*
Admission *£2.70*
Open *5 Apr-31 Oct Mon-Fri 10am-5pm, Sat-Sun 1.15pm-5pm*

Southeast England

South and southeast England is easily accessible from London either as a daytrip, a weekend away for travellers working in the capital or a stopover on a longer trip. This region's attractions are varied and include beach resorts, castles and historic cities.

Kent

The Garden of England consists partly of London's southern suburbs but also includes historic cities like Canterbury, the channel ports of Dover and Folkstone as well as the decaying beach 'resorts' of Broadstairs and Margate. Most travellers just glimpse Kent from the window of a speeding Eurostar train or a bus en route between London and the south coast, however it is well worth visiting Kent's historic attractions such as Canterbury or Leeds Castle at Maidstone.

Maidstone

Although many people think of Maidstone as no more than an outer suburb of London, it has a pleasant historic centre with some lovely 14th century-buildings. Maidstone's main attraction is nearby Leeds Castle.

Practical Information
Maidstone Town Hall
Visitor Information Centre
Town Hall, High Street, Maidstone
☎ *(01622) 602169*
Website *www.tour-maidstone.com*
Open *Mon-Sat 9am-5pm, Sun 10am-4pm*

Coming & Going
Maidstone has two train stations. Maidstone East station has trains to London and Canterbury and Maidstone West has trains to Gatwick Airport.

Buses stop at the Chequers Centre Bus Station in the town centre. This includes National Express (☎ *0870 580 8080; website* www.nationalexpress.co.uk) services to London, Canterbury and Dover and local Stagecoach buses (*website www.stagecoachbus.co.uk*) to destinations within Kent.

Sights
Leeds Castle
Lord Conway called Leeds Castle "the loveliest castle in the world" and the castle's marketing people won't let you forget it. It certainly is a spectacular castle with a lovely setting encircled by a moat on 500 acres of lush parkland. Six queens have called the 1000-year-old castle home and it was one of Henry VIII's favourite places. Visitors to the castle can explore the castle's restored rooms, which include a Dog Collar Museum with a collection of collars dating back 400 years.
Leeds Castle, Maidstone
☎ *Bearsted*
☎ *0870 600 8880*
Website *www.leeds-castle.com*
Admission *£10.50-12.50 (£9-11*

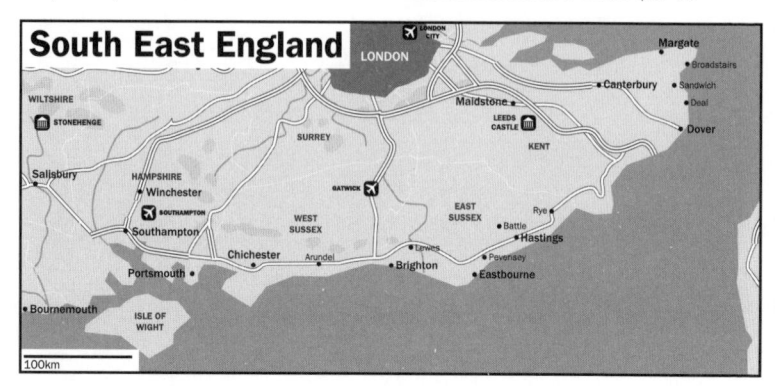

students)
Open *Jan-Mar 10am-3pm daily; Apr-Oct 10am-5pm daily; Nov-Dec 10am-3pm daily*

Museum of Kent Life
This open-air museum consists of restored historic buildings that depict rural life in Kent 100 years ago.
Cobtree, Lock Lane, Sandling
☎ *155*
☎ *(01622) 763936*
Website *www.museum-kentlife.co.uk*
Admission *£6*
Open *late Feb-early Nov 10am-5.30pm daily (last admission 4pm)*

Canterbury

This medieval town with its Tudor architecture and Roman city walls is a popular day trip from London. It is particularly famous for its cathedral, which was made famous in Chaucer's *Canterbury Tales* and T.S. Eliot's *Murder in the Cathedral*.

Practical Information
Canterbury Tourist Information Centre
The Buttermarket, 12-13 Sun Street, Canterbury
☎ *(01227) 378 100*
Website *www.canterbury.gov.uk*
Open *Mon-Sat 9.30am-5.30pm, Sun 10am-4pm*

Coming & Going
Canterbury has two train stations. East station is located south of the town centre and has trains to London Victoria and West station, northwest of the town centre, has trains to London Charing Cross and Waterloo.

National Express and Stagecoach buses stop at Canterbury bus station on St Georges Lane. National Express (☎ *0870 580 8080; **website** www.nationalexpress.co.uk*) has buses to London and Stagecoach *(**website** www.stagecoachbus.co.uk)* run local buses to destinations in Kent. Useful Stagecoach bus routes include bus 112 to Dover via Sandwich and Deal and route X82 to Ramsgate, Broadstairs and Margate.

Accommodation
Canterbury YHA
Canterbury's YHA is a clean place with a small kitchen plus a TV lounge, Internet access and a pool table. There's also a backyard with a barbecue and basketball hoop.
Ellerslie, 54 New Dover Road, Canterbury
☎ *(01227) 462911*
Dorm bed *£18 (£16 HI/YHA); price includes breakfast*
Credit cards *MC, Visa*
Open *1 Feb-20 Dec; reception open 7.30am-10am & 3pm-11pm daily; curfew 11pm daily*

🅿 🚗 📺 🅚 🅛

Maintenance & cleanliness	★★★★☆
Facilities	★★
Atmosphere & character	★★☆
Security	★★
Overall rating	★★★☆

KiPPs
KiPPs is a great little hostel with a cosy TV lounge and a fully equipped kitchen. This hostel has a friendly atmosphere and it is a five to 10-minute walk to the city walls.
40 Nunnery Fields, Canterbury
☎ *(01227) 786 121*
Website *www.kipps-hostel.com*
Dorm bed *£13; **single room** £18.50; **double/twin room** £32*
Credit cards *JCB, MC, Visa*
Reception open *Mon-Fri 7.30am-11am & 4pm-11pm, Sat-Sun 8am-11am & 4pm-11pm*

📺 🅚

Maintenance & cleanliness	★★★★☆
Facilities	★
Atmosphere & character	★★★★★
Security	★★☆
Overall rating	★★★

Sights
Canterbury Cathedral
Canterbury's major attraction is this cathedral that was founded in 597. It contains the tomb of the Black Prince and was the site of Thomas Becket's martyrdom. The cathedral was the subject of TS Eliot's *Murder in the Cathedral* and played a central role in Chaucer's *Canterbury Tales*.
The Precincts, Canterbury

☎ (01227) 762 862
Website *www.canterbury-cathedral.org*
Admission *£4*
Open *summer Mon-Fri 9am-6pm, Sun 9am-4pm; winter Mon-Fri 9am-4.30pm, Sun 9am-4pm*

Canterbury Roman Museum

Canterbury's Roman Museum shows what life was like in Canterbury during Roman times. The museum displays the remains of a Roman house featuring mosaics.

Longmarket, Butchery Lane, Canterbury
☎ *(01227) 785 575*
Website *www.canterbury-museums.co.uk*
Admission *£2.80*
Open *Jan-May Mon-Sat 10am-4pm; Jun-Oct Mon-Sat 10am-4pm, Sun 1.30pm-4pm; Nov-Dec Mon-Sat 10am-4pm*

The Canterbury Tales

This tourist attraction, inside St Margaret's Church, has displays depicting the

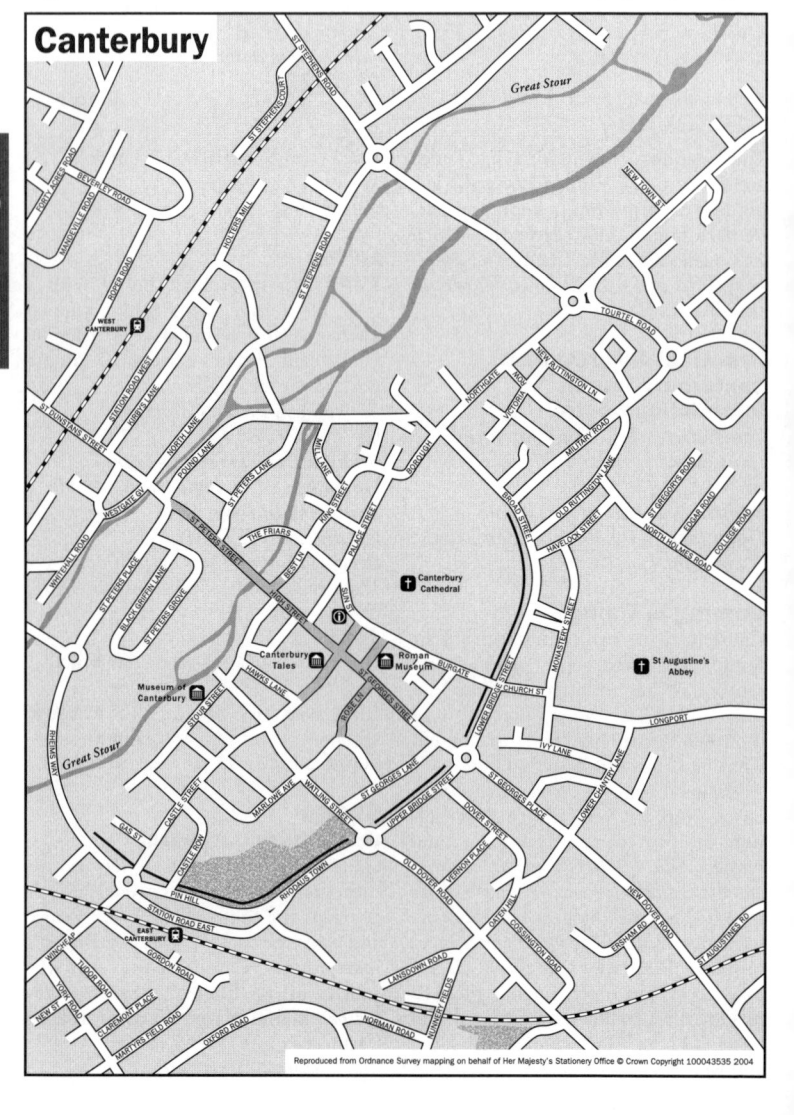

characters and storyline of Chaucer's *Canterbury Tales*.
St Margaret's Street, Canterbury
☎ *(01227) 479 227*
Website www.canterburytales.org.uk
***Admission** £6.95 (ISIC £5.95)*
***Open** Jan-Feb 10am-4.30pm daily; Mar-Jun 10am-5pm daily; Jul-Aug 9.30am-5pm daily; Sep-Oct 10am-5pm daily; Nov-Dec 10am-4.30pm daily*

Museum of Canterbury & Rupert Bear Museum

This museum tells the story of Canterbury from its medieval origins up to the present day and it incorporates a museum dedicated to one of Canterbury's most popular characters, Rupert Bear.
Stour Street, Canterbury
☎ *(01227) 452 747*
Website www.canterbury-museums.co.uk
***Admission** £3.10*
***Open** Jan-May Mon-Sat 10.30am-4pm; Jun-Oct Mon-Sat 10.30am-4pm, Sun 1.30pm-4pm; Nov-Dec Mon-Sat 10.30am-4pm*

St Augustine's Abbey

This World Heritage site marks the birthplace of English Christianity and it is where St Augustine first established a monastery in 598. In addition to the ruins of the monastery, there is a museum on site.
Longport, Canterbury
☎ *(01227) 767 345*
Website www.english-heritage.org.uk
***Admission** £3.50*
***Open** Jan-Mar Wed-Sun 10am-4pm; Apr-Sep 10am-6pm daily; Oct-Dec Wed-Sun 10am-4pm*

St Martin's Church

Before establishing his own monastery, St Augustine worshipped at St Martin's Church, which is the oldest parish church still in constant use.
North Holmes Road, Canterbury
☎ *(01227) 786 072*
***Admission** free*
***Open** Tue & Thu 10am-3pm, Sat 10am-1pm*

West Gate Towers

The West Gate Towers of Canterbury's city walls are considered to be among England's finest fortified gatehouses. The museum features armour exhibits plus scenic views from the battlements.
St Peter's Street, Canterbury
☎ *(01227) 452 747*
Website www.canterbury-museums.co.uk
***Admission** £1.10*
***Open** Mon-Sat 11am-12.30pm & 1.30pm-3.30pm*

Margate

This decaying seaside resort doesn't have much to offer the traveller, but it has a couple of hostels and you may pass through here if you're travelling along the Kent coast.

Practical Information
Tourist Information Centre

12-13 The Parade, Margate
☎ *(01843) 583334*
***Open** Jan-Mar Mon-Sat 9am-5pm; Apr-Sep Mon-Sat 9am-5pm, Sun 10am-4pm; Oct-Dec Mon-Sat 9am-5pm*

Coming & Going

National Express buses depart from the clock tower on Marine Parade.

Accommodation
Margate YHA

Margate's YHA is in an old building overlooking a sandy beach. It is an old fashioned but clean hostel with a TV lounge and a fully equipped kitchen.
3-4 Royal Esplanade, Westbrook Bay, Margate
☎ *(01843) 221616*
***Dorm bed** £14.50 (£12.50 HI/YHA)*
***Credit cards** MC, Visa*
***Open** daily 2-25 Apr; Fri-Sun 26 Apr-30 Jun; daily Jul-Aug; **reception open** 8am-10am & 5pm-10pm daily; **curfew** 11pm*

📺 🄺 🄻

Maintenance & cleanliness	★★
Facilities	★
Atmosphere & character	★★
Security	★★︎
Overall rating	★★︎

Old School House

This small independent hostel features a bar with an adjoining games room with pool table and table tennis plus a dining

room and balcony with sea views. The bunk beds are new but most other furnishings are old.
6 First Avenue, Cliftonville, Margate
☎ *(01843) 223905*
Website *www.oldschoolhouse-margate.co.uk*
Dorm bed *£14.50; price includes breakfast*
Credit cards *MC, Visa*
Reception open *8am-11pm daily*

Maintenance & cleanliness	★★★↲
Facilities	★★
Atmosphere & character	★★★
Security	★↲
Overall rating	★★★

Sights
Margate Old Town Hall Local History Museum
This small museum in the old town hall has exhibits on local history including the rise of Margate as a seaside resort and the town's maritime history.
Market Place, Margate
☎ *(01843) 231213*
Admission *£1*
Open *Jan-Mar Mon-Fri 11am-4pm; Apr-Sep Tue-Sun 10am-5pm; Oct-Dec Mon-Fri 11am-4pm*

Broadstairs

This bustling small town is one of England's oldest seaside resorts and it has much more charm than neighbouring Margate and Ramsgate. Broadstairs' most famous resident was Charles Dickens, who spent his summers here at Bleak House (now a museum) and the town has several Dickens-related attractions and it hosts an annual Dickens festival each June.

Practical Information
Tourist Information Centre
6B High Street, Broadstairs
☎ *(01843) 865650*
Open *Jan-Mar Mon-Sat 9am-5pm; Apr-Sep Mon-Sat 9am-5pm, Sun 10am-4pm; Oct-Dec Mon-Sat 9am-5pm*

Coming & Going
Broadstairs is accessible by bus and train. The train station is in the town centre . National Express coaches stop on High Street in the town centre.

Accommodation
Broadstairs YHA
This small youth hostel is a welcoming place with a small common rooms/TV lounge and a small, but fully equipped kitchen. The enthusiastic manager is very helpful and has a wealth of knowledge about things to see around town.
3 Osborne Road, Broadstairs
☎ *(01843) 604121*
Dorm bed *£13 (£11 HI/YHA)*
Credit cards *MC, Visa*
Open *Mar-Sep (flexible opening other times);* **reception open** *7.30am-10am & 5pm-11pm daily*

Maintenance & cleanliness	★★↲
Facilities	★
Atmosphere & character	★★★★
Security	★↲
Overall rating	★★↲

Sights
Bleak House
Charles Dickens former summer home has been turned into a museum showcasing the writer's life in Broadstairs. The museum also features exhibits on smuggling, which played an important role in the town's history.
Fort Road, Broadstairs
☎ *(01843) 862224*
Admission *£3*
Open *mid Mar-Nov 10am-6pm daily*

Dover

Thousands of travellers pass through this busy ferry port en route between London and France, seeing little more than the ferry terminal and a glimpse of the 12th century castle from a bus window. With the exception of the imposing castle, Dover isn't a particularly attractive town although it does offer quite a bit to see and it is a good base for exploring the surrounding region.

Practical Information
Dover Tourist Information Centre
The Old Town Gaol, Biggin, Dover
☎ *(01304) 205108*
Website *www.doveruk.com*
Open *Jun-Aug 9am-5.30pm daily*

Coming & Going

Most people come to Dover to make transport connections and the city is so well established as a transport hub that most travellers don't even see the town centre.

There are two train stations in Dover: Dover Priory is the closest station to the town centre and Dover Western Docks connects with some ferries. Both stations have frequent trains to Canterbury and London.

National Express and Stagecoach buses stop at Pencester Road between Maison Dieu Road and York Street in the town centre and National Express buses also continue right up to the Eastern Docks to meet ferries to France. The most useful of the Stagecoach bus routes is number 113, which goes to Canterbury via Sandwich and Deal.

There are two main ferry docks in Dover: Eastern and Western Docks. Although the Western Docks have a train station with good transport connections, most ferries depart from the Eastern Docks, which has frequent ferry departures to Calais, France and Oostend, Belgium.

Accommodation
Dover YHA

Dover's youth hostel is a neat and tidy hostel with a nice TV lounge, a common room with a pool table and a small kitchen. There's also a big backyard with a barbecue.

306 London Road, Dover
☎ *(01304) 201 314*
Website *www.yha.org.uk*
Dorm bed £18 (£16 HI/YHA); **twin room** £37.80 (£33.80 HI/YHA); prices include breakfast
Credit cards Diners, JCB, MC, Visa
Reception open 7am-11pm daily

Maintenance & cleanliness	★★★☆
Facilities	★☆
Atmosphere & character	★★★
Security	★★★☆
Overall rating	★★★☆

Sights
Dover Castle

This imposing castle is easily Dover's star attraction. The castle has played an important role in England's defence from its construction in 1066 right up to the Second World War when the Norman tunnels beneath the castle was the nerve centre for the evacuation of British and French troops from Dunkirk.

🚌 *90, 91, 111*
☎ *(01304) 211067*
Website *www.english-heritage.org.uk*
Admission £8.50
Open *Jan Mon & Thu-Sun 10am-4pm; Feb-Mar 10am-4pm daily; Apr-Jun 10am-6pm daily; Jul-Aug 9.30am-6.30pm daily; Sep 10am-6pm daily; Oct 10am-5pm daily; Nov-Dec Mon & Thu-Sun 10am-4pm*

Dover Museum

Dover Museum has exhibits covering the prehistory and history of Dover and the surrounding area including displays on the Bronze Age, artefacts from Dover's Roman sites, the Norman Conquest and Dover's role in World War II.

Market Square, Dover
☎ *(01304) 201066*
Website *www.dovermuseum.co.uk*
Admission £2
Open *Mon-Sat 10am-5.30pm*

Deal

This small town between Dover and Sandwich is famed for its castles, which were built by Henry VIII as part of southern England's defences.

Practical Information
Deal Tourist Information Centre

Deal Library, Broad Street, Deal
☎ *(01304) 369 576*
Open *Jan-May Mon-Fri 9am-12.30pm & 1.30pm-5pm; Jun-Sep Mon-Fri 9am-12.30pm & 1.30pm-5pm, Sat 10am-3pm; Oct-Dec Mon-Fri 9am-12.30pm & 1.30pm-5pm*

Sights
Deal Castle

This distinctive castle made up of rounded turrets was built between 1539 and 1540 by Henry VIII to defend England from European Catholics. Visitors are free to explore the castle including

the captain's residence and storerooms.
Deal Castle Road, Deal
🚉 *Deal* 🚌 *14, 14, 33, 112, 113, 114*
☎ *(01304) 372762*
Website *www.english-heritage.org.uk*
Admission *£3.50*
Open *Apr-Sep 10am-6pm daily*

Walmer Castle
Along with Deal Castle, Walmer Castle was built by Henry VIII to defend England against a feared attack by the Catholic powers in Europe. Walmer Castle is better preserved than Deal Castle and it was a favourite spot for the Duke of Wellington. Other former residents here include Winston Churchill, the Queen, the Queen Mother and WH Smith (who founded the newsagent chain).
A258, Walmer
🚉 *Walmer;* 🚌 *D 113*
☎ *(01304) 364288*
Admission *£5.80*
Open *Mar 10am-4pm daily; Apr-Sep 10am-6pm daily; Oct Wed-Sun 10am-4pm*

Sandwich
This well-preserved medieval town between Deal and Ramsgate has a lovely town centre with a couple of historic attractions. It is known as the home of the sandwich, however the food was named after the 4th Earl of Sandwich who had no connection with the town.

Practical Information
Sandwich Tourist Information Centre
The Guildhall, Sandwich
☎ *(01304) 613565*
Open *Apr-Oct Mon-Sat 9am-5pm*

Sights
Guildhall Museum
This small museum has exhibits on local history from Roman times to the present day.
The Guildhall, Sandwich
Open *Tue-Wed 10.30am-12.30pm & 2pm-4pm, Thu 10.30am-4pm, Fri 10.30am-12.30pm & 2pm-4pm, Sat 10.30am-4pm, Sun 2pm-4pm*

White Mill Rural Heritage Centre
This small museum is centred on a windmill dating from 1760 and also incorporates a miller's cottage and a wheelwright's workshop.
The Causeway, Ash Road, Sandwich
☎ *(01304) 612076*
Website *www.open-sandwich.co.uk/whitemill/*
Admission *£2*
Open *Jan-Easter Tue, Fri, Sun 10am-noon; Easter-mid Sep Tue & Fri 10am-noon, Sun 10am-noon & 2.30pm-5.30pm; mid Sep-Dec Tue, Fri, Sun 10am-noon*

East Sussex

Rye
This quaint small town is a popular spot for many travellers to pass through, although there isn't much to keep you busy for any longer than a day. It has a rich history dating prior to Roman times and several historic buildings that are worth a quick look.

Practical Information
Rye Tourist Information Centre
The Heritage Centre, Strand Quay, Rye
☎ *(01797) 226696*
Website *www.visitrye.co.uk*
Open *Mon-Sat 9.30am-5pm, Sun 10am-5pm*

Coming & Going
Rye is accessible by Stagecoach bus 71, which runs along the coast between Dover and Hastings. This bus runs hourly Mon-Sat and every two hours Sun.

Accommodation
The closest hostel is the Hastings YHA in the countryside at Guestling, 13km from Rye.

Sights
Camber Castle
This 16th century castle was part of Henry VIII's coastal defence, however it was used as a garrison for only a short period as the Camber harbour began to

silt up not too long after the castle was completed.
Open *Jul-Sep Sat-Sun 2pm-5pm*

Lamb House
The author Henry James lived in this 18th century house between 1898 and 1926. The house has a lovely garden and some of the writer's possessions are on display here.
West Street, Rye
🚉 *Rye*
Admission *£2.75*
Open *27 Mar-30 Oct Wed & Sat 2pm-5pm*

Rye Castle Museum
The Rye Castle Museum on East Street features an 18th century fire engine plus pottery and historic photos. The museum also maintains exhibits in the nearby Ypres Tower.
3 East Street, Rye
☎ *(01797) 226728*
Admission *£1.90; £2.90 joint admission with Ypres Tower*
Open *Apr-Oct Mon & Thu-Fri 2pm-5pm, Sat-Sun 10.30am-1pm & 2pm-5pm*

St Mary's Church
This 12th century church in the town centre is best known as home to England's oldest functioning church turret clock (dating from 1561). You can climb the tower for sweeping views of the surrounding countryside.
Lion Street, Rye
Admission *free*
Open *summer 9am-6pm daily; winter 9am-4pm daily*

Ypres Tower
Dating from the 14th century, the Ypres Tower is one of Rye's oldest structures, which was built as part of the town's defences and has been used as a prison and a private home before housing part of the museum's exhibits. Displays at the tower include iron and pottery as well as artefacts relating to the town's smuggling and law enforcement history.
☎ *(01797) 226728*
Admission *£1.90; £2.90 joint admission with Rye Castle Museum on East Street*

Open *Jan-Mar Sat-Sun 10.30am-3pm; Apr-Oct Mon & Thu-Sun 10.30am-1pm & 2pm-5pm; Nov-Dec Sat-Sun 10.30am-3pm*

Hastings
For almost a thousand years this town's name has been associated with the Battle of Hastings, which took place in 1066 at nearby Battle. Hastings' attractions include the ruins of Hastings Castle plus other attractions that relate to the Hastings' seafaring past.

Practical Information
Old Town Tourist Information Centre
The Stade, Old Town, Hastings
☎ *(01424) 781111*
Website *www.visithastings.com*
Open *Jan-Apr Sat-Sun 10am-4.30pm; May-Oct 10-4.30pm daily; Nov-Dec Sat-Sun 10am-4.30pm*

Queens Square Tourist Information Centre
Queens Square, Priory Meadow, Hastings
☎ *(01424) 781111*
Website *www.visithastings.com*
Open *Mon-Fri 8.30am-6.15pm, Sat 9am-5pm, Sun 10.30am-4.30pm*

Coming & Going
Hastings' local bus service is run mostly by Stagecoach (***website*** *www.stagecoachbuses.co.uk*).

Explorer tickets allow one day unlimited travel in the southeast for £6. These passes are good value for sightseeing around town and making day trips to places like Pevensey and Rye.

Accommodation
Hastings YHA
This hostel is a big old house in the countryside 6.5km from Hastings and 13km from Rye. It is clean with a reading room and a games room with a pool table and TV.
A259, Guestling, Hastings
🚌 *346, 711*
☎ *(01424) 812 373*
Website *www.yha.org.uk*
Dorm bed *£18 (£16 HI/YHA)*

Credit cards MC, Visa
Open 13 Feb-28 Jun Tue-Sat; 29 Jun-31 Aug Mon-Sun; 1 Sep-1 Nov Tue-Sat

Maintenance & cleanliness	★★★★☆
Facilities	★★
Atmosphere & character	★★☆
Security	★★☆
Overall rating	★★★☆

Sights
East Hill Lift
The 102-year-old East Hill Life is the United Kingdom's steepest funicular railway.
Fare 90p
Open summer 10am-5.30pm daily; winter 11am-4pm daily

Fisherman's Museum
This museum is housed in a former church by the waterfront in the Old Town. It has displays that include fishing tackle, model ships and historic photographs.
Rock-a-Nore Road, Hastings
☎ *(01424) 461446*
Admission free
Open Jan-Mar 11am-4pm daily; Apr-Oct 10am-5pm daily; Nov-Dec 11am-4pm daily

Hastings Castle & the 1066 Story
Hastings Castle dates from William of Normandy's coronation but less than half the original structure remains. It has a rich history that is closely linked with the Battle of Hastings. The 1066 Story is a 20-minute audio-visual presentation that covers much of the castle's history.
Castle Hill Road, West Hill, Hastings
☎ *(01424) 444412*
Website www.discoverhastings.co.uk/castle/
Admission £3.20
Open Jan-Mar 10am-3.30pm daily; Apr-Sep 11am-4pm daily; Oct-Dec 10am-3.30pm daily

Hastings Museum & Art Gallery
This museum has a range of exhibits that include a natural history section with fossils of dinosaurs and prehistoric crocodiles, Native American galleries and exhibits on local personalities John Logie Baird and Robert Tressell. The museum is noted for its excellent collection of exhibits relating to the Indian subcontinent, which consists of artefacts collected in the 19th century by the Brassey family.
Johns Place, Bohemia Road, Hastings
☎ *(01424) 781155*
Website www.hmag.org.uk
Admission free
Open Mon-Sat 10am-5pm, Sun 2pm-5pm

Old Town Hall Museum
This museum in Hastings' old town hall has exhibits on local history with an emphasis on the Old Town. It has exhibits depicting history from the middle ages to the 1930s and includes displays describing the town's role as a Napoleonic garrison and its rise as a Victorian resort.
High Street, Old Town, Hastings
☎ *(01424) 781166*
Website www.hmag.org.uk/oldTownHall/
Admission free
Open Jan-Mar 11am-4pm daily; Apr-Sep 10am-5pm daily; Oct-Dec 11am-4pm daily

The Stade and the Net Huts
The Stade is the beachside neighbourhood in the Old Town that is home to England's largest beach-launched fishing fleet, which has been in operation for around a thousand years. This area is home to many unique maritime buildings including the net huts. These weatherboard and tar buildings were built in the 17th century and were designed so fishermen could dry their nets.

Battle
Just a short distance north of Hastings is Battle, which was the site of the famous Battle of Hastings that took place here in 1066 between King Harold and William the Conqueror.

Practical Information
Battle Tourist Information Centre
Battle Abbey Gatehouse, High Street, Battle
☎ *5*

☎ *(01424) 773721*
Website *www.1066country.com*
Open *Jan-Mar 10am-4pm daily; Apr-Sep 9.30am-5.30pm daily; Oct 10am-5pm daily; Nov-Dec 10am-4pm daily*

Coming & Going
Battle is accessible from Hastings by train and bus 5.

Sights
Battle Abbey & Battlefield
Battle Abbey stands on the battlefield where the Battle of Hastings was fought in 1066, when invading Normans defeated the Anglo-Saxons. The abbey was founded in 1070, but little of the original Norman building remains and most of what you see today dates from the 14th century.
High Street, Battle
🚉 *Battle*
☎ *(01424) 773792*
Website *www.english-heritage.org.uk*
Admission £5
Open *Jan-Mar 10am-4pm daily; Apr-Sep 10am-6pm daily; Oct-Dec 10am-4pm daily*

Battle Museum
This small museum has exhibits relating to local history from the days of the dinosaurs to the present day.
The Almonry, High Street, Battle
☎ *(01424) 775955*
Website *www.battlemuseum.co.uk*
Admission £1
Open *Apr-Oct Mon-Sat 10.30am-4.30pm, Sun 2pm-5pm*

Pevensey

Pevensey's history dates to the 4th century when a Roman fort was built here, and on 28 September 1066 William the Conquerer landed here before marching to take part in the Battle of Hastings. Shortly afterwards, Robert de Mortain (William's half brother) built Pevensey Castle on the grounds of the original Roman fort.

Coming & Going
Pevensey lies on the train line between Rye and Hastings and is also served by buses 19, 710 and 711 from Hastings.

Sights
Pevensey Castle
This ancient castle incorporates fortifications from Roman and medieval periods.
A259, Pevensey
🚉 *Pevensey Bay, Pevensey & Westham*
🚌 *19, 710, 711*
☎ *(01323) 762604*
Website *www.english-heritage.org.uk*
Admission £3.50
Open *Jan-Mar Sat-Sun 10am-4pm; Apr-Sep 10am-6pm daily; Oct-Dec Sat-Sun 10am-4pm*

Herstmonceux

North of Pevensey is Herstmonceux, which is home to the magnificent 15th century Herstmonceux Castle.

Coming & Going
Herstmonceux lies on the A271 north of Pevensey and it is difficult to get to by public transport. Eastbourne Buses *(website www.eastbournebuses.co.uk)* route 22 stops nearby en route between Hailsham and Battle.

Sights
Herstmonceux Castle
This 15th century moated castle is considered England's oldest, notable, brick building. It is set among 550 acres of gardens and is a splendid spot for a picnic. Although you can visit the gardens, the castle is only accessible by guided tour.
Herstmonceux, Hailsham
☎ *(01323) 833816*
Website *www.herstmonceux-castle.com*
Admission grounds £4.50; castle tour £2.50
Gardens open *Apr-Sep 10am-5pm daily; Oct 10am-4pm daily;* ***tours*** *Mon-Fri & Sun (☎ (01323) 833816 for tour times)*

Brighton

Less than an hour from London, Brighton bucks the trend set by most other English beach resorts and is a surprisingly lively and cosmopolitan city. It is also a popular destination with European backpackers who come here to study English.

Practical Information
Brighton Tourist Information Centre
Bartholomew Square, Brighton
☎ *0906 711 2255*
Website *www.visitbrighton.com*
Open *Mon-Fri 9am-5pm, Sat-Sun 10am-5pm*

easyInternetcafé
McDonalds, 140 London Road, Brighton
Website *www.easyinternetcafe.com*

Coming & Going
AIR
Brighton is only half an hour from London Gatwick Airport (☎ *0870 000 2468; website www.baa.com/main/airports/gatwick/*). There are frequent transport connections between Brighton and Gatwick including trains operated by Southern and Thameslink and National Express buses. Buses to Gatwick take 45 minutes and cost £6.

National Express also run buses connecting Brighton with London

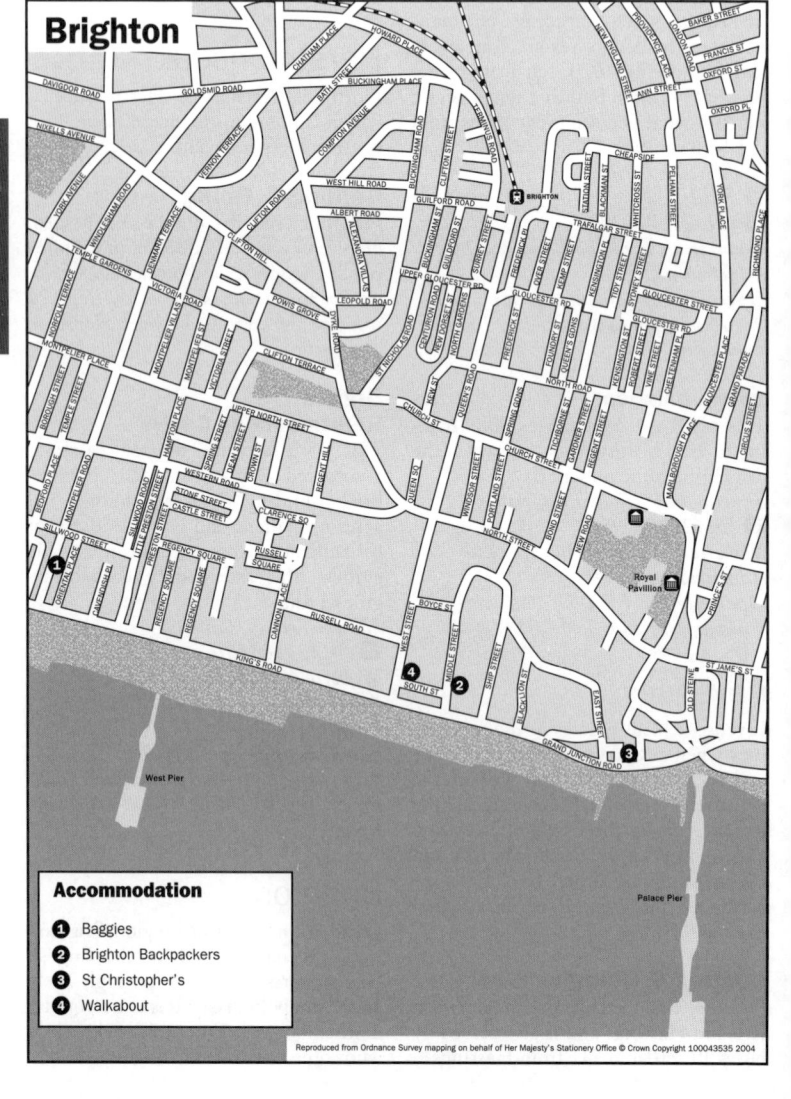

Brighton

Accommodation
1. Baggies
2. Brighton Backpackers
3. St Christopher's
4. Walkabout

Reproduced from Ordnance Survey mapping on behalf of Her Majesty's Stationery Office © Crown Copyright 100043535 2004

Heathrow Airport (☎ *(020) 8759 4321; website www.baa.com/main/airports/heathrow/)*, which is 1½ hour away. This bus costs £19.50.

BUS
Brighton has good bus connections with London and destinations in southern England with buses departing from the Pool Valley Coach Station near Grand Junction Road and the Palace Pier.

Megabus *(website www.megabus.com)* has several express buses a day to London with prices between £1 and £3 (plus 50p booking fee).

National Express (☎ *0870 580 8080; website www.nationalexpress.com)* has frequent buses to London and destinations in southern England including Portsmouth (£3.20 one-way).

Buses operated by Arriva and Stagecoach connect Brighton with other destinations throughout south and southeast England. The Explorer travel pass gives you one day unlimited travel in Kent and East Sussex for £6

TRAIN
Frequent train services connect Brighton and London in a little under an hour. They depart from London Victoria, Kings Cross and London Bridge, although the most frequent services depart from Victoria.

There is also a good coastal train route and services to the Midlands, South Wales and the West Country.

Brighton's train station is at the top of Queens Road in the city centre.

Local Transport
Brighton & Hove buses *(website www.buses.co.uk)* provide a comprehensive transport network linking most parts of the city. One-way fares are £1.30, but Saver tickets are better value if you're planning on making two or more trips in one day. A Saver ticket costs £2.50 for one day or £13 for one week and gives you unlimited travel on daytime bus routes

If you're making a day trip out of town or travelling on to other destinations on the south coast, the Explorer ticket is the best deal. This ticket gives you one day unlimited travel on most buses on the south coast including Brighton & Hove buses, Eastbourne Buses, Metrobus, Arriva and Stagecoach.

Accommodation
Baggies Backpackers
Baggies has a great atmosphere with cosy common areas and lots of knickknacks and interesting things on the walls. It has a TV lounge next to the reception on the ground floor, and a kitchen and another common room downstairs. Although the bunk beds are excellent many of the furnishings are eclectic, but the hostel is generally kept clean. Some travellers may not feel comfortable with the mixed showers.

33 Oriental Place, Brighton
☎ *(01273) 733 740*
Dorm bed *£12*
Credit cards *MC, Visa*
Reception open *9am-9pm daily*
📺 🅚

Maintenance & cleanliness	★★★
Facilities	★★
Atmosphere & character	★★★★★
Security	★★½
Overall rating	★★★

Brighton Backpackers
The bright yellow building is decorated with murals and it has a great atmosphere. There is a TV lounge near the reception and another downstairs with a pool table. However the carpet is filthy and the place could be kept much cleaner.

75-76 Middle Street, Brighton
☎ *(01273) 777 717*
Website *www.brightonbackpackers.com*
Dorm bed *£10-15*
Double/twin room *£24-30*
Reception open *9am-10pm daily*
📺 🅚 🅛

Maintenance & cleanliness	★★½
Facilities	★★½
Atmosphere & character	★★★★½
Security	★
Overall rating	★★

Brighton YHA
Brighton's YHA is housed in a 16th century Georgian Manor on the outskirts of town. It features the usual YHA facilities such as a TV lounge, games room and kitchen.

Patcham Place, London Road, Brighton
🚌 *5, 5A*
☎ *(01273) 556 196*
Website *www.yha.org.uk*
Dorm bed *£18 (£16 HI/YHA)*
Credit cards *MC, Visa*
Open *Jan-Feb Thu-Sat; Mar-Oct Mon-Sun; Nov-Dec Thu-Sat;* ***reception open*** *8am-10am & 4pm-11pm daily;* ***curfew*** *11pm*

📺 🅚 🅛

Maintenance & cleanliness	★★★½
Facilities	★★½
Atmosphere & character	★★
Security	★★
Overall rating	★★

St Christopher's Hostel

This hostel, located above Charlie's Bar, has accommodation in comfortable rooms with en suite bathrooms but shared facilities are limited to a TV and Internet access in the bar. However extensive renovations are planned, which will see an improvement in standards plus the addition of a real common area.
Palace Hotel, 10-12 Grand Junction Road, Brighton
☎ *(020) 7407 1856*
Website *www.st-christophers.co.uk*
Dorm bed *£13-22.25;* ***twin room*** *£40.50-44.50; prices include breakfast*
Credit cards *MC, Visa*
Reception open *24 hours*

📺 🆃

Maintenance & cleanliness	★★★
Facilities	★★½
Atmosphere & character	★★½
Security	★★★½
Overall rating	★★★½

Walkabout Backpackers

Walkabout has basic accommodation above an Australian pub in the city centre. The rooms aren't too bad but bathrooms could be better maintained and the hostel's facilities are limited to a small TV lounge.
78-81 West Street, Brighton
☎ *(01273) 719 364*
Website *www.walkabout.eu.com*
Dorm bed *£12;* ***double/twin room*** *£30*
Reception open *Mon-Thu 8.30am-8.30pm, Fri-Sat 8.30am-9.30pm, Sun 9.30am-3.30pm & 4.30pm-8.30pm*

📺 🅚 🅛 🆃

Maintenance & cleanliness	★★
Facilities	★
Atmosphere & character	★★½
Security	★★
Overall rating	★★

Sights

Booth Museum of Natural History

This museum houses a collection of over 500,000 specimens collected over three centuries. Exhibits include hundreds of butterflies and birds, a whale and dinosaur bones.
194 Dyke Street, Brighton
🚌 *27, 27A*
☎ *(01273) 292777*
Admission *free*
Open *Mon-Wed & Fri-Sat 10am-5pm, Sun 2pm-5pm*

Brighton Museum & Art Gallery

Brighton's Museum and Art Gallery adjoins the famous Royal Pavilion and features displays of art, fashion and contemporary design.
Church Street, Brighton
☎ *(01273) 290900*
Admission *free*
Open *Tue 10am-7pm, Wed-Sat 10am-5pm, Sun 2pm-5pm*

Brighton Toy & Model Museum

This large collection of toys and models features over 10,000 exhibits including impressive working model trains, model cars, ships and planes as well as dolls, dolls houses and toy soldiers.
52-55 Trafalgar Street, Brighton
🚆 *Brighton*
☎ *(01273) 749494*
Website *www.brightontoymuseum.co.uk*
Admission *£3.50*
Open *Tue-Fri 10am-4pm, Sat 11am-5pm*

Royal Pavilion

This extravagant building was built in 1787 for King George IV, but it was John Nash who transformed the building into an Indian style palace between 1815 and 1823. This exotic building is Brighton's major landmark and it features lavish Chinese inspired interiors and an opulent Banqueting Room.

Corner North Street & Old Steine, Brighton
☎ *(01273) 290900*
Website *www.royalpavilion.org.uk*
Admission £5.95
Open *Jan-Mar 10am-4.30pm daily; Apr-Sep 9.30am-5pm daily; Oct-Dec 10am-4.30pm daily*

West Sussex

West Sussex is the coastal region between Brighton and Portsmouth. Its main attractions include the historic city of Chichester and the small town of Arundel, with its large castle.

Arundel

This small town on the A27 between Brighton and Chichester is noted for its large castle, which dominates the town.

Practical Information
Arundel Tourist Information Centre
61 High Street, Arundel
☎ *(01903) 882268*
Website *www.arundel.org.uk*
Open *Jan-Easter 10am-3pm daily; Easter-Oct Mon 9.30am-5pm, Tue-Sun 9am-5pm; Oct-Dec 10am-3pm daily*

Coming & Going
Southern (**website** *www.southernrailway.com*) operate direct trains between Arundel and London Victoria (via Gatwick Airport) and there are also trains from Arundel to Brighton, Chichester and Portsmouth.

Stagecoach (**website** *www.stagecoachbuses.co.uk*) bus routes 315 stops in Arundel on the Coastliner route linking Eastbourne and Falmouth and route 702 also stops here en route between Brighton and Chichester.

Accommodation
Arundel YHA
Located 3.25km from Arundel, this neat and tidy youth hostel is in a lovely Georgian mansion. It has common areas that include a games room, TV lounge and several kitchens. This hostel is geared towards families and groups so independent travellers may sometimes feel out of place.
Warningcamp, Arundel
☎ *(01903) 882 204*
Dorm bed £20 (£18 HI/YHA); **camping** £7.75 (£5.75 HI/YHA)
Credit cards MC, Visa
Open *Apr-May;* **reception open** *7.30am-10am & 5pm-11pm*

📺 🅺 🅻

Maintenance & cleanliness	★★★★
Facilities	★★☆
Atmosphere & character	★★
Security	★★☆
Overall rating	★★★☆

Sights
Amberley Working Museum
This museum is comprised of reconstructed period buildings that include bus and train stations and a printing works. The museum features a wide range exhibits that range from old TVs and radios to vintage cars and locomotives.
B2139, Amberley,
🚉 *Amberley*
☎ *(01798) 831370*
Website *www.amberleymuseum.co.uk*
Admission £7.50
Open *17 Mar-4 Apr Wed-Sun 10am-4.30pm; 5-18 Apr 10am-4.30pm daily; 21 Apr-18 Jul Wed-Sun 10am-4.30pm daily; 19 Jul-5 Sep 10am-4.30pm daily; 8 Sep-24 Oct Wed-Sun 10am-4.30pm daily; 25-31 Oct 10am-4.30pm daily*

Arundel Castle
This impressive 11th century castle is home to the Dukes of Norfolk and has been open to visitors for nearly 200 years.
Arundel
☎ *(01903) 882173*
Website *www.arundelcastle.org*
Admission £9.50 (ISIC £7.50)
Open *Apr-Oct Mon-Fri & Sun noon-4pm*

Chichester

This historic cathedral city traces its history back to Roman times and its attractions include the 900-year-old Chichester cathedral and the brilliant Fishbourne Roman Palace.

Practical Information
Chichester Tourist Information Centre
29a South Street, Chichester
☎ *(01243) 539 449*
Website *www.chichester.gov.uk*
Open *Jan-Mar Mon-Sat 9.15am-5.15pm; Apr-Sep Mon-Sat 9.15am-5.15pm, Sun 11am-3.30pm; Oct-Dec Mon-Sat 9.15am-5.15pm*

Coming & Going
Chichester lies on the coastal train line linking Brighton with Portsmouth and Southampton and there are also regular trains to London (Victoria station). There are also good bus connections with National Express (☎ *0870 580 8080; website www.nationalexpress.co.uk*) buses to London and Stagecoach (*website www.stagecoachbuses.co.uk*) buses go to Brighton (route 702) and Portsmouth (routes 700 & 701).

Accommodation
There are no hostels in Chichester, however it can be visited as a daytrip from either Portsmouth or Arundel, which both have hostel accommodation.

Sights
Chichester Cathedral
Chichester's cathedral dates from 1091 but incorporates an eclectic range of architectural styles owing to additions to the cathedral that have been made over the past 900 years.
☎ *(01243) 782595*
Website *www.chichester-cathedral.org.uk*
Admission *£2 donation*
Open *summer 7.30am-7pm daily; winter 7.30am-5pm daily*

Chichester District Museum
This small museum has exhibits on local history.
26 Little London, Chichester
☎ *(01243) 784683*
Website *www.chichester.gov.uk/museum*
Admission *free*
Open *Jun-mid Sep Sat noon-4pm*

Fishbourne Roman Palace
Discovered by accident in 1960 while digging a water trench, the fascinating Fishbourne Roman Palace is Britain's largest Roman building dating from the 1st century. The site features Britain's largest collection of in-situ mosaics, which include the famous Cupid on a Dolphin. There are also formal gardens that have been replanted according to the original Roman plan and an adjoining museum with exhibits relating to the site.
Salthill Road, Fishbourne, Chichester
🚌 *11, 56, 700* 🚆 *Fishbourne*
☎ *(01243) 785859*
Website *www.sussexpast.co.uk*
Admission *£5.20 (student £4.50)*
Open *Jan-Feb 10am-4pm daily; Mar-Jul 10am-5pm daily; Aug 10am-6pm daily; Sep-Oct 10am-5pm daily; Nov-Dec 10am-4pm daily*

Pallant House Gallery
This elegant building is noted for its collection modern art, which is complemented by a programme of temporary exhibits.
9 North Pallant, Chichester
☎ *(01243) 77455*
Website *www.pallanthousegallery.com*
Admission *£4*
Open *Tue-Sat 10am-4pm*

Weald & Downland Open Air Museum
This open-air museum 11km north of Chichester has over 40 historic buildings that date from medieval to Victorian times. Highlights of the museum includes a Tudor farmhouse and a working 17th century waterwheel.
A286, Singleton, Chichester
🚌 *60*
☎ *(01243) 811348*
Website *www.wealddown.co.uk*
Admission *£7.50*
Open *Jan-Feb Sat-Sun 10.30am-4pm; Mar-Oct 10.30am-6pm daily; Nov-Dec Sat-Sun 10.30am-4pm*

Hampshire

Portsmouth & Southsea
Portsmouth is best known for its naval history and its historic seafront is home to several of the Royal Navy's grand old

ships including Henry VIII's *Mary Rose*, Admiral Nelson's *HMS Victory* and *HMS Warrior*.

Today it is a sprawling city that encompasses suburban Southsea with its own string of attractions along the Clarence Esplanade.

Practical Information
Tourist Information Centre (Clarence Esplanade)
Clarence Esplanade, Southsea
☎ *(023) 9282 6722*
Website *www.portsmouthand.co.uk*
Open *Jan-Jun 9.30am-5.15pm daily; Jul-Aug 9.30am-5.45pm daily; Sep-Dec 9.30am-5.15pm daily*

Tourist Information Centre (The Hard)
The Hard, Portsmouth
☎ *(023) 9282 6722*
Website *www.portsmouthand.co.uk*
Open *Jan-Mar 9.30am-5.15pm daily; Apr-Sep 9.30am-5.45pm daily; Oct-Dec 9.30am-5.15pm daily*

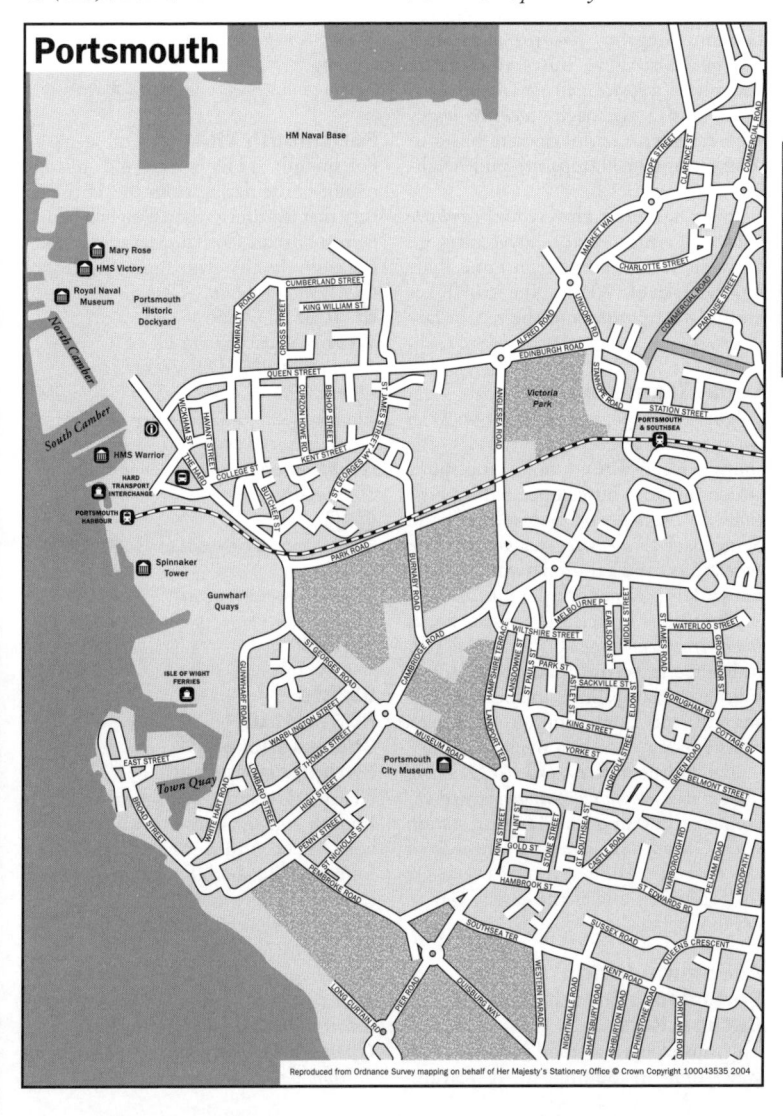

Coming & Going

Portsmouth has two train stations, Portsmouth and Southsea station on Commercial Road in Portsmouth city centre and Portsmouth Harbour station near the historic waterfront. There are frequent train services to London and also along the coast to Brighton and Southampton.

Buses terminate at the Hard Interchange, which is located adjacent Portsmouth Harbour train station. National Express (☎ *0870 580 8080; website www.nationalexpress.co.uk*) run buses to London; Megabus (*website www.megabus.com*) also have buses to London and First (*website www.firsthampshire.co.uk*) and Stagecoach (*website www.stagecoachbuses.co.uk*) operate buses to destinations in Hampshire and neighbouring counties.

Every half hour Hovertravel (*website www.hovertravel.co.uk*) hovercrafts go between Southsea Hoverport and Ryde on the Isle of Wight. The trip takes around 10 minutes and the return fare is £9.70.

Local Transport

Solent Transport (*website www.solent-transport.org.uk*) co-ordinates the south Hampshire's public transport, which includes buses operated by First (*website www.firsthampshire.co.uk*) and Stagecoach (*website www.stagecoachbuses.co.uk*) and a train network. A tram network is planned for the future.

The Solent Travelcard (*website www.solent-travelcard.org.uk*) is good for unlimited travel on all bus routes across southern Hampshire, including Portsmouth and Southampton. This pass costs £5 a day or £20 a week.

The Gosport ferry (☎ *(023) 9252 4551; website www.gosportferry.co.uk*) connects Portsmouth Harbour station with Gosport on the opposite side of the harbour. The ferry runs every 7½ to 15 minutes and is the easiest way to get to Gosport.

Accommodation
Portsmouth & Southsea Backpackers

This hostel is in a small lane near the waterfront in Southport. It features a big common area downstairs with a pool table, Internet access and TV plus a big commercial kitchen and a small backyard with a barbecue.
4 Florence Road, Southsea
☎ *(023) 9283 2495*
Website *www.portsmouthbackpackers.co.uk*
Dorm bed £12; **double room** £26-29; **twin room** £26
Reception open *8am-11.30pm daily*
📺 🅚 🅛

Maintenance & cleanliness	★★★★☆
Facilities	★★★☆
Atmosphere & character	★★★
Security	★★
Overall rating	★★★

Portsmouth YHA

Portsmouth YHA is an old historic manor house dating from the 11th century that features a wood panelled hall. It is in suburban Cosham, several kilometres from the city centre and waterfront.
Old Wymering Lane, Cosham
☎ *(023) 9237 5661*
Website *www.yha.org.uk*
Dorm bed £13 (£11 HI/YHA)
Open *3 Feb-6 Apr Tue-Sat; 7 Apr-30 Jun Mon-Sat; Jul-Aug every day; Sep-Oct Tue-Sat; 1 Nov-11 Dec Fri-Sat;* **reception open** *8am-10am & 5pm-10pm daily*
📺 🅚

Maintenance & cleanliness	★★★★☆
Facilities	☆
Atmosphere & character	★★☆
Security	★★☆
Overall rating	★★

Sights
PORTSMOUTH
Charles Dickens' Birthplace Museum

Charles Dickens was born in Portsmouth and the house in which he was born has been furnished as it was when John and Elizabeth Dickens first set up their home here in 1809.
393 Old Commercial Road, Portsmouth
☎ *(023) 9282 7261*
Website *www.charlesdickensbirthplace.co.uk*
Admission £2.50 (£1.50 students)
Open *7 Feb 10am-5pm; Apr-Sep 10am-5.30pm daily*

Natural History Museum

Portsmouth's Natural History Museum has exhibits on the wildlife that once lived in the Portsmouth area. The museum also features an aquarium and a butterfly house.
Cumberland House, Eastern Parade, Southsea
☎ *(023) 9282 7261*
Website www.portsmouthnaturalhistory.co.uk
Admission £
Open Jan-Mar 10am-4pm daily; Apr-Oct 10am-5.30pm daily, Nov-Dec 10am-4pm daily

Portsmouth City Museum

This museum has displays on the history and development of Portsmouth.
Museum Road, Portsmouth
☎ *(023) 9282 7261*
Website www.portsmouthcitymuseums.co.uk
Admission free
Open Jan-Mar 10am-5pm daily; Apr-Sep 10am-5.30pm daily; Oct-Dec 10am-5pm daily

Spinnaker Tower

Opened in late summer 2004, the massive 165m Spinnaker Tower is Portsmouth's newest and biggest landmark. The observation deck at the top of the tower offers breathtaking views of the harbour.
Website www.portsmouthand.co.uk/tower

PORTSMOUTH HISTORIC DOCKYARD

Portsmouth's main attraction is the historic dockyard that is home to many of Britain's most historic sailing ships. The Dockyard's outstanding attractions include:

Action Stations

This attraction provides an insight into today's Royal Navy. It features hands-on exhibits and a large format film that shows you what life is like aboard a Type 23 frigate.
Portsmouth Historic Dockyard, Portsmouth
🚌 *Hard Interchange* 🚆 *Portsmouth Harbour*
☎ *(023) 9286 1512*
Website www.historicdockyard.co.uk
Admission £9.70 (£8 ISIC); inclusive ticket to all Portsmouth Historic Dockyard attractions £15.50 (£12.50 ISIC)
Open Jan-Mar 10am-5pm daily; Apr-Oct 10am-5.30pm daily; Nov-Dec 10am-5pm daily

HMS Victory

The Royal Navy's best known warship was under the command of Vice Admiral Lord Horatio Nelson off Cape Trafalgar in 1805 and it has been restored to its original splendour to commemorate the 2005 bicentenary of the Battle of Trafalgar.
Portsmouth Historic Dockyard, Portsmouth
🚌 *Hard Interchange* 🚆 *Portsmouth Harbour*
☎ *(023) 9286 1512*
Website www.historicdockyard.co.uk
Admission £9.70 (£8 ISIC) includes entry to Royal Naval Museum; inclusive ticket to all Portsmouth Historic Dockyard attractions £15.50 (£12.50 ISIC)
Open Jan-Mar 10am-5pm daily; Apr-Oct 10am-5.30pm daily; Nov-Dec 10am-5pm daily

HMS Warrior 1860

When it was launched in 1861, *HMS Warrior* was the most advanced warship ever built. It has now been restore to its original glory.
Portsmouth Historic Dockyard, Portsmouth
🚌 *Hard Interchange* 🚆 *Portsmouth Harbour*
☎ *(023) 9286 1512*
Website www.historicdockyard.co.uk
Admission £9.70 (£8 ISIC); inclusive ticket to all Portsmouth Historic Dockyard attractions £15.50 (£12.50 ISIC)
Open Jan-Mar 10am-5pm daily; Apr-Oct 10am-5.30pm daily; Nov-Dec 10am-5pm daily

Mary Rose

Henry VIII's favourite warship was built between 1510 and 1511 and was sunk in battle against a French fleet in 1545. The *Mary Rose* lay in its watery grave for hundreds of years before being found by divers and raised in front of

a TV audience in 1982. There is an adjoining museum that features over 1200 items taken from the wreck and the museum's Bonaventure Gallery has hands-on exhibits that give you an idea of life aboard the *Mary Rose* in Tudor England.
Portsmouth Historic Dockyard, Portsmouth
☐ *Hard Interchange* ☐ *Portsmouth Harbour*
☎ *(023) 9286 1512*
Website *www.historicdockyard.co.uk*
Admission *£9.70 (£8 ISIC); inclusive ticket to all Portsmouth Historic Dockyard attractions £15.50 (£12.50 ISIC)*
Open *Jan-Mar 10am-5pm daily; Apr-Oct 10am-5.30pm daily; Nov-Dec 10am-5pm daily*

Royal Naval Museum

This excellent museum recounts 800 years of naval history with much of the museum focusing on Horatio Nelson, *HMS Victory* and the Battle of Trafalgar.
Portsmouth Historic Dockyard, Portsmouth
☐ *Hard Interchange* ☐ *Portsmouth Harbour*
☎ *(023) 9286 1512*
Website *www.historicdockyard.co.uk*
Admission *£9.70 (£8 ISIC) includes entry to HMS Victory; inclusive ticket to all Portsmouth Historic Dockyard attractions £15.50 (£12.50 ISIC)*
Open *Jan-Mar 10am-5pm daily; Apr-Oct 10am-5.30pm daily; Nov-Dec 10am-5pm daily*

SOUTHSEA
Blue Reef Aquarium

This aquarium on the sea front in Southsea features a walk-through aquarium with tropical marine life. There are open-top tanks where you can get close to rays and sharks and a freshwater area that features three Asian short claw otters.
Clarence Esplanade, Southsea
☎ *(023) 9287 5222*
Website *www.bluereefaquarium.co.uk*
Admission *£5.95 (£4.95 students)*
Open *Jan-Feb 10am-4pm daily; Mar-Oct 10am-5pm daily; Nov-Dec 10am-4pm daily*

D Day Museum

This excellent museum has displays depicting the events of 6 June 1944, which changed the course of World War II. The museum is also home to the *Overlord Embroidery*, an 83m-long embroidery that is intended to be a modern counterpart to the *Bayeux Tapestry*.
Clarence Esplanade, Southsea
☎ *(023)*
Website *www.ddaymuseum.co.uk*
Admission *£5 (£3 students)*
Open *Jan-Mar 10am-5pm daily; Apr-Oct 10am-5.30pm daily; Nov-Dec 10am-5pm daily*

Royal Marines Museum

This museum shows the history of the Royal Marines from their formation in 1664 to the present day.
Southsea Esplanade, Southsea
☎ *(023) 9281 9385*
Website *www.royalmarinesmuseum.co.uk*
Admission *£4.75*
Open *Jan-May 10am-4.30pm daily; Jun-Aug 10am-5pm daily; Sep-Dec 10am-4.30pm daily*

Southsea Castle

Southsea Castle was built in 1544 as part of Henry VIII's coastal fortifications. Throughout the centuries it was strengthened and used as a military base right up to 1960, when Portsmouth City Council restored the castle to how it looked in the 19th century.
Clarence Esplanade, Southsea
☎ *(023) 9287 7261*
Website *www.southseacastle.co.uk*
Admission *£2.50 (£1.50 students)*
Open *Apr-Oct 10am-5pm daily*

GOSPORT

Gosport lies across the harbour from Portsmouth and is easily reached by the Gosport ferry (☎ *(023) 9252 4551; website www.gosportferry.co.uk*), which departs from the dock behind Portsmouth Harbour station.

Explosion

This small museum focuses on the history of naval warfare and includes displays of gunpowder, explosives, mines,

guns, torpedos and missiles.
Priddy's Hard, Gosport
🚇 *Gosport*
☎ *(023) 9250 5600*
Website *www.explosion.org.uk*
Admission £5.50
Open *Jan-Mar 10am-4.30pm daily; Apr-Oct 10am-5.30pm daily; Nov-Dec 10am-4.30pm daily*

Royal Navy Submarine Museum
A visit to this museum gives you the opportunity to go inside a Royal Navy submarine, the *HMS Alliance*. The museum's collection features four submarines and one submersible survey vessel as well as over 4000 artefacts.
Royal Navy Submarine Museum, Haslar Jetty Road, Gosport
☎ *(023) 9252 9217*
🚇 *Gosport, then* 🚌 *9*
Website *www.rnsubmus.co.uk*
Admission £4.50
Open *Jan-Mar 10am-4.30pm daily; Apr-Oct 10am-5.30pm daily; Nov-Dec 10am-4.30pm daily*

Southampton

Southampton is a modern city that few tourists make the effort to visit. It was bombed heavily during World War II destroying many of the older buildings however remnants of the medieval city remain.

Practical Information
Southampton Tourist Information Centre
9 Civic Centre Road, Southampton
☎ *(023) 8083 3333*
Website *www.visit-southampton.co.uk*
Open *Mon-Sat 9.30am-5pm*

Coming & Going
AIR
Southampton Airport (**website** *www.baa.com/main/airports/southampton/*) is located just north of the city and has charter flights to many of the more popular European holiday destinations. The airport is easily accessible with direct train connections from London and Southampton and bus 101 runs between the airport and the city centre.

BUS
National Express (☎ *0870 580 8080*; **website** *www.nationalexpress.co.uk*) runs buses to Birmingham, Bournemouth and London; Megabus (**website** *www.megabus.com*) also have buses to London and First (**website** *www.firsthampshire.co.uk*), Stagecoach (**website** *www.stagecoachbuses.co.uk*) and Wilts & Dorset (**website** *www.wdbus.co.uk*) run buses to destinations in Hampshire and neighbouring counties.

The Explorer ticket is a great value pass that gives you one day unlimited bus travel in Wiltshire and parts of Dorset and Hampshire for just £6. This pass will take you as far as Bristol, Bath, Bournemouth and Winchester and is ideal if you're making a day trip into the countryside or if you want to go to Bath or Bristol with a stop en route.

FERRY
Red Funnel (**website** *www.redfunnel.co.uk*) ferries sail between Southampton and Cowes on the Isle of Wight. There are two ferry services: the fast ferry to West Cowes and the slower car ferry to East Cowes. A day return on either ferry costs £11 or £14 including a Rover bus ticket on the island.

TRAIN
South West Trains (**website** *www.swtrains.co.uk*) has trains from Southampton to Brighton, Bristol, London (Waterloo station) and Weymouth. The station is on Blechynden Terrace west of the centre.

Local Transport
Solent Transport (**website** *www.solent-transport.org.uk*) co-ordinates southern Hampshire's public transport, which includes a bus and train network. A tram network is planned for the future.

The Solent Travelcard (**website** *www.solent-travelcard.org.uk*) is good for unlimited travel on all bus routes across southern Hampshire, including Portsmouth and Southampton. This pass costs £5 a day or £20 a week.

Accommodation
There are no hostels in Southampton; the closest hostels are in Portsmouth and Winchester.

Sights
God's House Tower
Museum of Archaeology
This 13th century gatehouse originally stood at the southeast corner of the medieval city walls and now houses the city's museum of archaeology. The museum's displays depict Southampton's history with galleries dedicated to the Roman, Saxon and Medieval periods.
Town Quay, Southampton
☎ *(023) 8033 9601*
Admission *free*
Open *Jan-Mar Tue-Fri 10am-4pm, Sat 10am-noon & 1pm-4pm, Sun 1pm-4pm; Apr-Oct Tue-Fri 10am-noon & 1pm-5pm, Sat 10am-noon & 1pm-4pm, Sun 2pm-5pm; Nov-Dec Tue-Fri 10am-4pm, Sat 10am-noon & 1pm-4pm, Sun 1pm-4pm*

Medieval Merchant's House
The Medieval Merchant's House is one of the oldest buildings of its kind in England.
58 French Street, Southampton
☎ *(023) 8022 1503*
Admission *£3*
Open *Apr-Sep 10am-5pm daily*

Southampton Maritime Museum
Southampton was *Titanic's* home port and most of the ship's crew came from here. One of the museum's highlights is its *Titanic* gallery, which portrays this famous ship with artefacts and stories from local people who were affected by the tragedy. There are also exhibits about many of the other ocean liners that sailed from Southampton.
Bugle Street, Town Quay, Southampton
☎ *(023) 8063 5904*
Admission *free*
Open *Jan-Mar Tue-Fri 10am-4pm, Sat 10am-1pm & 2pm-4pm, Sun 1pm-4pm; Apr-Oct Tue-Fri 10am-1pm & 2pm-5pm, Sat 10am-1pm & 2pm-4pm, Sun 2pm-5pm; Nov Tue-Fri 10am-4pm, Sat 10am-1pm & 2pm-4pm, Sun 1pm-4pm*

Winchester
This small cathedral city north of Southampton has a rich history and Alfred the Great, William the Conqueror and Charles II have called it home.

Practical Information
Tourist Information Centre
Guildhall, Broadway, Winchester
☎ *(01962) 840500*
Website *www.visitwinchester.co.uk*
Open *Mon-Sat 9.30am-5.30pm, Sun 11am-4pm*

Coming & Going
Winchester has good bus and train connections throughout the south.

The train station is a 10-minute walk northwest of the city centre and there are trains to Brighton, Bournmouth, London (Waterloo station), Portsmouth and Southampton.

National Express (☎ *0870 580 8080; website www.nationalexpress.co.uk*) buses go to London and Southampton and buses operated by Stagecoach *(website www.stagecoachbus.com)* and Wilts & Dorset *(website www.wdbus.co.uk)* serve Hampshire and neighbouring counties.

The Explorer ticket is a great value pass that gives you one day unlimited travel on Stagecoach and Wilts & Dorset buses in Wiltshire and parts of Dorset and Hampshire for just £6. This pass will take you as far as Bristol, Bath, Bournemouth and Southampton and is ideal if you're making a day trip into the countryside or if you want to go to Bath or Bristol making a stop en route.

Accommodation
Winchester YHA
This youth hostel in a charming old 18th century watermill offers basic accommodation. It is conveniently located in the city centre near the bus station and the cathedral.
1 Water Lane, Winchester
☎ *(01962) 853723*
Website *www.yha.org.uk*
Dorm bed *£13 (£11 HI/YHA)*
Open *1 Mar-5 Apr Tue-Sat; 6 Apr-30 Jun Mon-Sat; Jul-Sep every day; 1-31 Oct Mon-Sat; reception open 8am-10am & 5pm-10pm; curfew 11pm*

Sights
City Museum
This museum has chronicles the history of Winchester from Roman times to the present day with exhibits that include the Middle Ages and the Saxon invasion.

☎ *(01962) 848 269*
Admission *free*
Open *Jan-Mar Tue-Sat 10am-4pm, Sun noon-4pm; Apr-Oct Mon-Sat 10am-5pm, Sun noon-5pm; Nov-Dec Tue-Sat 10am-4pm, Sun noon-4pm*

The Great Hall & Round Table

The 13th century Great Hall is all that remains of Winchester Castle (where Henry III was born). For years it was famous as the home of King Arthur's Round Table, however the Round Table is now known to date from the 14th century – too recent to be King Arthur's since the earliest written account of the King Arthur story dates from 1130.

The Great Hall, The Castle, Winchester
☎ *(01962) 846476*
Admission *free*
Open *10am-5pm daily*

Winchester Cathedral

The 900-year-old Winchester Cathedral has played a pivotal role in English history. It is the longest medieval building in Europe with a length of 170m and it also features a fine Norman crypt.
1 The Close, Winchester
☎ *(01962) 857200*
Website *www.winchester-cathedral.org.uk*
Open *Mon-Sat 8.30am-6pm, Sun 8.30am-5.30pm*

South West England

Wiltshire

Salisbury

This historic city in south Wiltshire is best known for it's cathedral, which boasts Britain's tallest spire.

Salisbury is also a popular base for travellers visiting the nearby Stonehenge stone circle.

Practical Information
Salisbury Tourist Information Centre
Fish Row, Salisbury
☎ *(01722) 334956*
Website *www.visitsalisbury.com*
Open *Jan-Apr Mon-Sat 9.30am-5pm; May Mon-Sat 9.30am-5pm, Sun 10.30am-4.30pm; Jun-Sep Mon-Sat 9.30am-6pm, Sun 10.30am-4.30pm; Oct-Dec Mon-Sat 9.30am-5pm*

Coming & Going
Although the centre of Salisbury is small enough to walk around, buses are essential for getting to outlying attractions such as Old Sarum and Stonehenge. Wilts & Dorset buses *(website www.wdbus.co.uk)* operate most bus services in the Salisbury area with services to towns and attractions such as Avebury, Old Sarum and Stonehenge.

The Explorer ticket is a great value pass that gives you one day unlimited bus travel in Wiltshire and parts of Dorset and Hampshire for just £6. This pass will take you as far as Bristol, Bath, Bournemouth, Southampton and Winchester and is ideal for a day trip encompassing Stonehenge and Avebury.

You can also buy a DayRider ticket, which gives you one day of unlimited bus travel within the Salisbury area for £3.

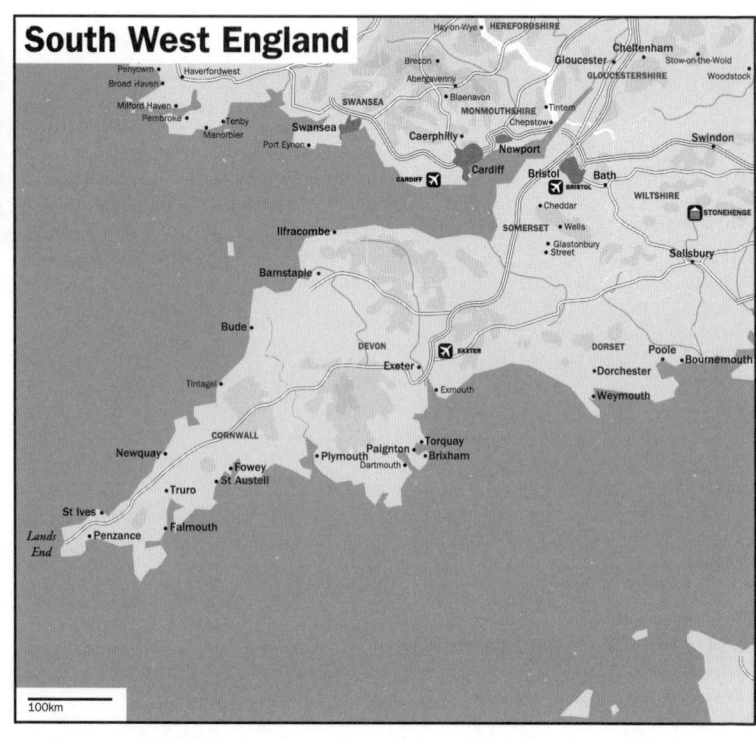

Accommodation
Matt & Tiggy's

Matt & Tiggy's is a small family-run hostel with a cosy atmosphere. It has a small kitchen and TV lounge and the dorms have single beds (not bunks).

51 Salt Lane, Salisbury
☎ *(01722) 327 443*
Dorm bed £11-13

📺🅚🅛

Maintenance & cleanliness	★★★★½
Facilities	★
Atmosphere & character	★★★★★
Security	★
Overall rating	★★★

Salisbury YHA

Salisbury's YHA hostel is in a 200-year-old building with a modern annex. It is newly renovated and very clean. Facilities include a good kitchen, a small TV lounge and a quiet common room on the ground floor.

Milford Hill, Salisbury
🚌 *63, 64, 66*
☎ *(01722) 327 572*

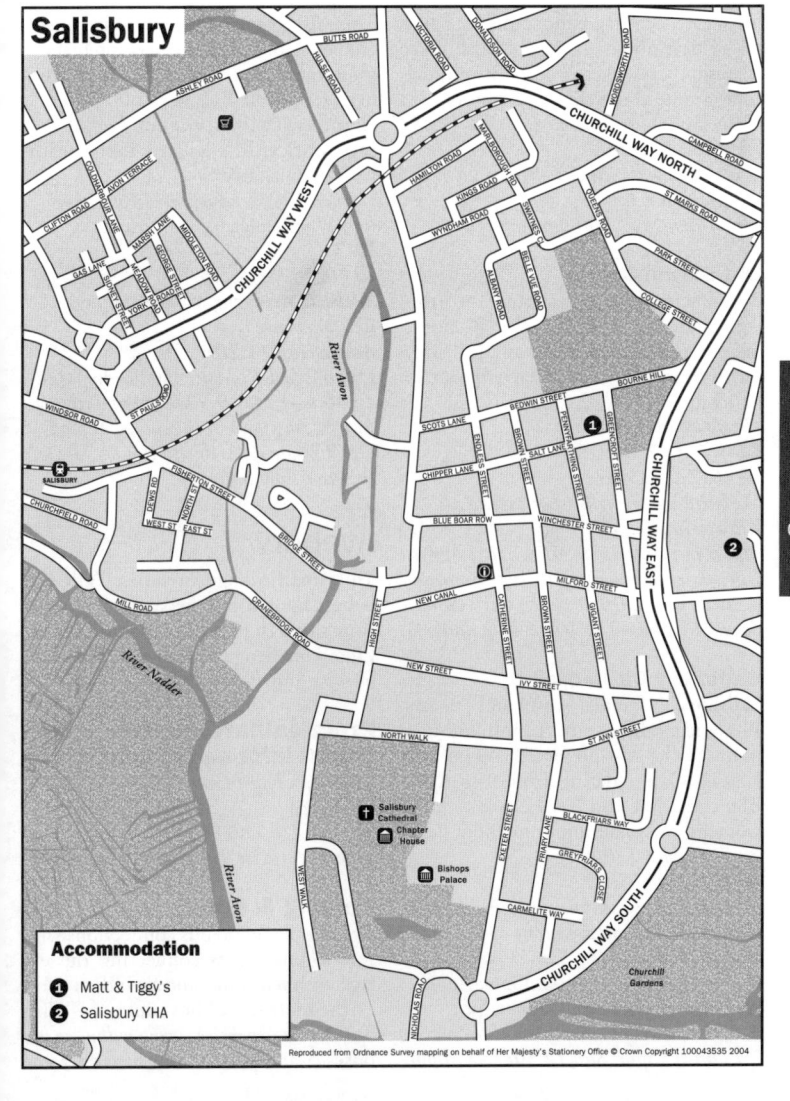

Salisbury

Accommodation
1. Matt & Tiggy's
2. Salisbury YHA

Dorm bed £18 (£16 HI/YHA); double room £37.80 (£33.80 HI/YHA); prices include breakfast
Credit cards MC, Visa
Reception open 7.30am-10.30pm daily
🚌 📺 🅺 🅻

Maintenance & cleanliness	★★★★★
Facilities	★★
Atmosphere & character	★★★
Security	★★
Overall rating	★★★½

Sights
The Medieval Hall
This 13th century banqueting hall has an exhibit about its history and construction and there's also 30-minute programme about the city's history.
Cathedral Close, Salisbury
☎ *(01722) 412472*
Website www.medieval-hall.co.uk
Admission £2.25
Open Apr-Sep 11am-5pm daily

Old Sarum Castle
This ancient site dates from the Iron Age and was used by the Romans, Saxons and Nomans. It is an ideal add-on to Stonehenge for a day trip out of Salisbury.
Castle Road, Salisbury
🚌 *3, 5, 6, 7, 8, 9*
☎ *(01722) 335398*
Website www.english-heritage.co.uk
Admission £2.50
Open Jan-Mar 10am-4pm daily; Apr-Jun 10am-6pm daily; Jul-Aug 9am-6pm daily; Sep 10am-6pm daily; Oct 10am-5pm daily; Nov-Dec 10am-4pm daily

Salisbury Cathedral
Salisbury's famous cathedral boasts England's tallest spire (123m) and it is home to the best-preserved copy of the Magna Carta (dating from 1215AD). The cathedral also has Europe's oldest working clock, dating from 1386.
33 The Close, Salisbury
☎ *(01722) 555120*
Website www.salisburycathedral.org.uk
Admission £3.80 donation
Open Jan-Mar Mon-Sat 7.15am-6.15pm, Sun 12.30pm-2.30pm; Apr-Aug Mon-Sat 7.15am-7.15pm, Sun 12.30pm-2.30pm; Sep-Dec Mon-Sat 7.15am-6.15pm, Sun 12.30pm-2.30pm

Salisbury & South Wiltshire Museum
This museum features exhibits on local history and archaeology including an exhibit about Stonehenge.
The King's House, 65 The Close, Salisbury
☎ *(01722) 332151*
Website www.salisburymuseum.org.uk
Admission £3.50
Open Jan-Jun Mon-Sat 10am-5pm; Jul-Aug Mon-Sat 10am-5pm, Sun 2pm-5pm; Sep-Dec Mon-Sat 10am-5pm

Stonehenge
This mysterious stone circle is considered to be one of the greatest prehistoric monuments on Earth. It dates from between 3000 BC and 1600 BC is is aligned with the rising sun at midsummer solstice. It is located 15km northwest of Salisbury
Corner A303 and A344/A360, 3km west of Amesbury
🚌 *3*
☎ *(01980) 624715*
Website www.english-heritage.org.uk/stonehenge
Admission £5.20
Open 2 Jan-15 Mar 9.30am-4pm daily; 16 Mar-31 May 9.30am-6pm daily; 1 Jun-31 Aug 9am-7pm daily; 1 Sep-15 Oct 9.30am-6pm daily; 16 Oct-31 Dec 9.30am-4pm daily

Avebury
This small village in north Wiltshire is best known for the stone circle that runs through part of the village centre. Like Stonehenge, Avebury can get very busy at Summer Solstice.

Practical Information
Tourist Information Centre
Avebury Chapel Centre, Green Street, Avebury
☎ *(01672) 539296*
Open Mar-Oct Tue-Sun 9.30am-5pm

Coming & Going
Avebury has good bus connections with several bus routes connecting the village with Salisbury and Swindon.

The most useful bus routes are Wilts & Dorset (*website www.wdbus.co.uk*) buses 5 and 6 that stop here en route between Salisbury and Swindon. Other buses include Stagecoach (*website www.stagecoachbus.co.uk*) bus 49 that stops here en route between Swindon and Trowbridge and Thamesdown (*website www.thamesdown-transport.co.uk*) buses 48A and 49A that come here from Marlborough.

Sights
Alexander Keiller Museum
This museum has two galleries with exhibits relating the Avebury's stone circle. This includes an audio-visual display in the Barn Gallery.
☎ (01672) 539250
Admission £4.20
Open Jan-Mar 11am-4pm daily; Apr-Oct 10am-6pm daily; Nov-Dec 10am-4pm daily

Stone Circle
This important megalithic monument consists of a stone circle enclosed by a ditch and an avenue of stones. Although the stones are smaller than Stonehenge, the monument is older and covers a larger area encompassing part of the village.
Website www.nationaltrust.org.uk
Admission free

Dorset

Bournemouth & Poole
The twin seaside cities of Bournemouth and Poole have grown into each other creating a relatively large seaside resort. Bournemouth is the larger and more modern of the two although Poole is a more interesting spot to wander around.

Practical Information
Bournemouth Tourist Information Centre
Westover Road, Bournemouth
☎ (01202) 451700
Website www.bournemouth.co.uk

Poole Tourist Information Centre
Enefco House, Poole Quay, Poole
☎ (01202) 253253
Website www.pooletourism.com
Open Jan-Apr Mon-Fri 10am-5pm, Sat 10am-4pm; May-Jun 10am-5pm daily; Jul-Aug 9.15am-6pm daily; Sep-Oct 10am-5pm daily; Nov-Dec Mon-Fri 10am-5pm, Sat 10am-4pm

Coming & Going
AIR
Bournemouth International Airport (*website www.flybournemouth.com*) has flights to destinations in Europe and the UK. Buses run between the airport and Bournemouth train station, the one-way bus fare to the airport is £4.

FERRY
Poole is a busy ferry port with departures by Brittany Ferries (*website www.brittany-ferries.co.uk*) sail to Cherbourg in France and Condor Ferries (*website www.condorferries.com*) to Guernsey and Jersey on the Channel Islands and St Malo and Cherbourg in France.

BUS
National Express (☎ *0870 580 8080; website www.nationalexpress.co.uk*) has buses from Bournemouth to Birmingham, Bristol and London. National Express buses depart from The Square in Bournemouth.

Megabus (*website www.megabus.com*) has several express buses a day to London with prices between £1 and £7 (plus 50p booking fee). Megabus departs from the Talbot Campus at Bournemouth University.

TRAIN
South West Trains (*website www.swtrains.co.uk*) have trains to London (Waterloo) as well as Dorchester, Southampton and Winchester and Virgin Trains (*website www.virgintrains.co.uk*) have trains to Birmingham, Manchester, Yorkshire and Scotland.

Local Transport
Bournemouth and Poole's local buses are run by Wilts & Dorset (*website www.wdbus.co.uk*).

The DayRider ticket is a good value pass that gives you one day unlimited bus travel in the Bournemouth, Poole and Christchurch area for £3.

Accommodation
Bournemouth Backpackers
Bournemouth Backpackers is a small homely hostel in an old house near the train station and just a short walk from a big Asda supermarket. It is a friendly place with the usual kitchen and TV lounge.
3 Frances Road, Bournemouth
☏ *17, 18, 33, 34, 41, 68*
☎ *(01202) 299 491*
Website *www.bournemouthbackpackers. co.uk*
Dorm bed £13-17; **double/twin room** £30-40
Reception open *1 Jan-17 May 5pm-6pm daily; 18 May-18 Sep 8.30am-10.30am & 4pm-7pm daily; 19 Sep-31 Dec 5pm-6pm daily*

[TV] [K]

Maintenance & cleanliness	★★★☆
Facilities	★
Atmosphere & character	★★★★☆
Security	★★☆
Overall rating	★★★☆

Sights
Oceanarium
Bournemouth's Oceanarium features a walk-through aquarium with marine life from the Mediterranean, the Great Barrier Reef, Hawaii and the Caribbean as well as river fish from the Amazon, the Ganges and the Nile.
West Undercliff Promenade, Bournemouth
☏ *3, 4, 5, 6, 9, 9A, 12, 20, 21, 22, 23, 32, 35, 89, 90, X94*
☎ *(01202) 311993*
Website *www.oceanarium.co.uk*
Admission £6.50 (£4.95 ISIC)
Open *10am-6pm daily*

Waterfront Museum
The Waterfront Museum has displays relating to Poole's local history.
4 High Street, Poole
☏ *152, 154*
☎ *(01202) 262600*
Website *www.poole.gov.uk*
Admission *free*
Open *Jan-Mar Mon-Sat 10am-3pm, Sun noon-3pm; Apr-Oct Mon-Sat 10am-5pm, Sun noon-5pm; Nov-Mar Mon-Sat 10am-3pm, Sun noon-3pm*

Devon

Exeter
Exeter is surrounded on three sides by Roman city walls, although it is mostly a Saxon/Norman and late medieval city. It also features an historic quayside and unique medieval underground passages.

Practical Information
Exeter Tourist Information Centre
Civic Centre, Paris Street, Exeter
☎ *(01392) 265700*
Open *Mon-Fri 9am-5pm, Sat 9am-1pm & 2pm-5pm*

Coming & Going
AIR
Exeter Airport (**website** *www.exeter-airport.co.uk*) has excellent connections throughout Britain and Europe with budget airline, Flybe (**website** *www.flybe.com*). Bus 56 runs between the airport and the city centre.

BUS
National Express (☎ *0870 580 8080;* **website** *www.nationalexpress.co.uk*) buses go to Bristol and London and Megabus (**website** *www.megabus.com*) has daily buses to London with prices between £1 and £9 (plus 50p booking fee). All buses depart from the Exeter Bus Station, which is near the corner of Paris and Cheeke Streets.

The First Bus and Rail Card costs £10 and allows one day travel on First Great Western Trains between Totnes and Penzance and all First buses in Devon.

TRAIN
Exeter has several train stations. Central Station in the city centre is the most convenient but more trains stop at Exeter St David's Station, which is about a 20-minute walk from the centre. Central Station has trains to London (Waterloo Station) and St David's has trains to Bristol and London (Paddington Station).

South West Trains (**website** *www.swtrains.co.uk*) stop at Central and St

David's Stations en route from London (Waterloo Station) to Torquay and Paignton and Wessex Trains *(website www.wessextrains.co.uk)* run trains from St David's Station to Penzance and Bristol with connecting services to London (Paddington and Waterloo).

Local Transport
Stagecoach *(website www.stagecoachbus.co.uk)* operates Exeter's local buses, which is handy if you're staying at the YHA or if you want to get to some of the bigger supermarkets in the suburbs. All buses (except some Park & Ride services) stop on High Street in the city centre.

Accommodation
Exeter YHA
Exeter's YHA is in a big 17th century building about a 10-minute bus ride from the city centre. It is a clean hostel with a big dining room, two lounges (one with a TV) and two kitchens (one normally used for groups).
Mount Wear House, 47 Countess Wear Road, Exeter

🚌 *57, 85, K, T*
☎ *(01392) 873 329*
Dorm bed £16 (£14 HI//YHA); **double room** £34.80 (£30.80 HI/YHA)
Credit cards MC, Visa
Reception open 8am-10am & 5pm-10pm daily

Maintenance & cleanliness	★★★½
Facilities	★★
Atmosphere & character	★★½
Security	★★½
Overall rating	★★★

Globe Backpackers
Globe Backpackers is a nice hostel with a friendly atmosphere, bright airy rooms and good solid bunk beds. There's a small TV lounge and a fully equipped kitchen. It is the closest hostel to the city centre, which makes it a good choice if you're travelling by public transport.
71 Holloway Road, Exeter
☎ *(01392) 215 521*
Website *www.exeterbackpackers.co.uk*

Dorm bed £12; *double/twin room* £32
Credit cards Amex, Diners, MC, Visa
Reception open 8am-11pm daily

Maintenance & cleanliness	★★★
Facilities	★½
Atmosphere & character	★★★★½
Security	★★½
Overall rating	★★★

Sights
Cathedral Church of St Peter
Exeter's 800-year-old Gothic cathedral is noted mainly for the Cathedral Library, whose collection includes the medieval *Exeter Book of Anglo-Saxon Poetry*, and its 15th century astronomical clock, which is believed to have been the inspiration for the nursery rhyme, *Hickory Dickory Dock*.
The Close, Exeter
☎ *(01392) 255 573*
Admission £3.50 donation
Open Mon-Fri 6.30am-6.30pm, Sat 7.30am-5pm, Sun 8am-7.30pm

Quay House Visitor Centre
This exhibition shows the development of the Quayside area with displays and an audio-visual presentation.
46 The Quay, Exeter
☎ *(01392) 265213*
Admission free
Open Jan-Mar Sat-Sun 11am-4pm; Apr-Oct 10am-5pm daily; Nov-Dec Sat-Sun 11am-4pm

Royal Albert Memorial Museum & Art Gallery
This museum has a large range of displays in 16 galleries. It covers everything from local history to exotic cultures and exhibits include Egyptian tombs and a stuffed elephant.
Queen Street, Exeter
☎ *(01392) 665 858*
Admission free
Open Mon-Sat 10am-5pm

Underground Passages
Britain's only medieval vaulted passages that are open to the public were constructed during the 14th century to bring water into the city.
Romangate Passage, off High Street, Exeter (next to Boots)
☎ *(01392) 665 887*
Admission £3.75
Open Feb-May Tue-Fri noon-5pm, Sat 10am-5pm; Jun-Sep Mon-Sat 10am-5pm; Oct-Dec Tue-Fri noon-5pm, Sat 10am-5pm

Torbay (Torquay/Paignton/Brixham)

Although it has an air of elegance there is certainly no comparison between the Torbay region and the French Riviera, which it likes to compare itself with. The region is comprised of several towns that sprawl from Torquay (the region's main city) south to Paignton and Brixham.

Practical Information
Brixham Tourist Information Centre
The Old Market House, The Quay, Brixham
☎ *0906 680 1268*
Website www.theenglishriviera.co.uk
Open summer Mon-Sat 9.30am-6pm, Sun 10am-6pm; winter Mon-Fri 9.30am-1pm & 2pm-5pm

Paignton Tourist Information Centre
The Esplanade, Paignton
☎ *0906 680 1268*
Website www.theenglishriviera.co.uk
Open summer Mon-Sat 9.30am-6pm, Sun 10am-6pm; winter Mon-Sat 9.30am-1pm & 2pm-5pm

Torquay Tourist Information Centre
Vaughan Parade, Torquay
☎ *0906 680 1268*
Website www.theenglishriviera.co.uk
Open Jan-Apr Mon-Sat 9.30am-5pm; May-Aug Mon-Sat 9.30am-6pm, Sun 10am-6pm; Sep-Dec Mon-Sat 9.30am-5pm

Coming & Going
BUS
National Express (☎ *0870 580 8080; website* www.nationalexpress.co.uk) has express services to Exeter and London that leave from the coach station on

Lymington Road in Torquay.

First *(website www.firstgroup.com)* and Stagecoach *(website www.stagecoachbus.co.uk)* operate local buses to destinations throughout Devon. Local buses depart from the Pavilion at the corner of the Stand and Torbay Road.

The First Bus and Rail Card costs £10 and allows one day travel on First Great Western Trains between Totnes and Penzance and all First buses in Devon.

TRAIN
Train stations in the Torbay region are located in Torquay and Paignton.

South West Trains *(website www.swtrains.co.uk)* run trains between Torbay and London (Waterloo) stopping en route at Exeter and Salisbury. Virgin Trains *(website www.virgintrains.co.uk)* have trains north to Birmingham and Bristol and west to Plymouth and Penzance. Wessex Trains *(website www.wessextrains.co.uk)* operate trains to Bristol, Cardiff and Exeter with connecting services to Plymouth and Penzance.

Local Transport
Stagecoach *(website www.stagecoachbus.com)* buses provide frequent services in the Torbay area.

You can buy a Dayrider ticket for £3.50 that gives you unlimited bus travel in the Torquay, Paignton and Brixham area and there is also a Dayrider ticket that includes ferry travel on the Kingswear and Dartmouth ferry (£5).

If you want to travel a little farther a field, the Dart Explorer ticket offers unlimited Stagecoach bus travel, a river cruise between Totnes and Dartmouth and a ferry connection between Dartmouth and Kingswear. The Dart Explorer costs £11.

Accommodation
Maypool YHA
This lovely youth hostel sits on a hill with spectacular views of Dartmouth and Kingswear. It is a big old house with lots of character and it features a kitchen, a big dining room, a TV lounge with pool table plus a quiet common room. It is a quiet retreat about 2km from Halpton village about midway between Brixham and Paignton, however the rural location makes it only convenient if you're driving.

Galmpton, Brixham
🚌 *12 to Churston Potter, then 3.25km walk*
☎ *(01808) 842 444*
***Dorm bed** £14.50 (£12.50 HI/YHA)*
***Credit cards** MC, Visa*

Maintenance & cleanliness				★★★½
Facilities				★★½
Atmosphere & character				★★★★
Security				★
Overall rating				★★★

Torquay Backpackers
Torquay Backpackers is a small friendly hostel that is a good base for exploring the English Riviera. It is a cluttered house with a homely atmosphere. The kitchen and TV lounge facilities are limited but it does have a sauna.

119 Abbey Road, Torquay
🚌 *32, 32H, 33*
☎ *(01803) 299 924*
***Website** www.torquaybackpackers.co.uk*
***Dorm bed** £10-12 (£9.50-11.40 VIP)*
***Credit card** MC, Visa*

Maintenance & cleanliness	★★
Facilities	★★½
Atmosphere & character	★★★★½
Security	★
Overall rating	★★★½

Sights
Living Coasts
Operated in conjunction with Paignton Zoo, Living Coasts is an excellent wildlife park focusing on coastal wildlife featuring reconstructed beaches and cliff-faces with penguins, puffins, sea ducks and fur seals.

Beacon Quay, Torquay
🚌 *63*
☎ *(01803) 202 470*
***Website** www.livingcoasts.org.uk*
***Admission** £5.70 (£4.40 students); joint ticket with Paignton Zoo £12.95 (£10.40 students)*
***Open** Jan-Feb 10am-3.30pm daily; Apr-Sep 10am-5pm daily; Oct 10am-4.30pm daily; Nov-Dec 10am-3.30pm daily*

Paignton Zoo
Paignton Zoo has the usual collection of African wildlife including giraffes, gorillas, rhinos and zebras.
Totnes Road, Paignton
🚌 *82, 100, 172, 179, X80, TC*
☎ *(01803) 697 500*
Website *www.paigntonzoo.org.uk*
Admission £8.50 (£7 students); joint ticket with Living Coasts £12.95 (£10.40 students)
Open *summer 10am-5pm daily; winter 10am-3pm daily*

Torquay Museum
Devon's oldest museum has been home to the Torquay Natural History Society since 1876. Its collection covers archaeology, ethnography and local history.
529 Babbacombe Road, Torquay
☎ *(01803) 293 975*
Website *www.torquaymuseum.org*
Admission £3 (£1.50 students)
Open *summer Mon-Sat 10am-5pm, Sun 1.30pm-5pm; winter Mon-Fri 10am-5pm, Sat 1.30pm-4pm*

Plymouth

There's a good chance that your ancestors passed through Plymouth on the way to the New World. Not only is this where Captain Cook set sail from before heading to Australia, New Zealand and Hawaii, but this historic port in Devon was also the departure point for the *Mayflower*.

Practical Information
Discovery Centre Tourist Information Centre
Plymouth Discovery Centre, Crabtree, Plymouth
☎ *(01752) 266030*
Website *www.visitplymouth.co.uk*
Open *Jul-Sep Mon-Sat 9am-5pm, Sun 10am-4pm*

Plymouth Mayflower Tourist Information Centre
Plymouth Mayflower Centre, 3-5 The Barbican, Plymouth
☎ *(01752) 304849*
Website *www.visitplymouth.co.uk*
Open *Jan-Easter Mon-Fri 9am-5pm, Sat 10am-4pm; Easter-Oct Mon-Sat 9am-5pm, Sun 10am-4pm; Nov-Dec Mon-Fri 9am-5pm, Sat 10am-4pm*

Coming & Going
BUS
National Express (☎ *0870 580 8080; website www.nationalexpress.co.uk*) buses go to Bristol, Exeter, London and Truro.

Stagecoach (*website www.stagecoachbus.com*) buses go to nearby towns in Devon and Cornwall and include buses X38 and X39, which run between Exeter and Plymouth.

National Express and Stagecoach buses depart from Bretonside coach station north of the Barbican.

Megabus (*website www.megabus.com*) has daily buses to London with prices between £1 and £9 (plus 50p booking fee). Megabus departs from outside Theatre Royal on Royal Parade in the city centre and in North Hill outside the main entrance to Plymouth University.

FERRY
Brittany Ferries (*website www.brittany-ferries.co.uk*) sail from Millbay Docks to Roscoff, France and Santander, Spain.

TRAIN
South West Trains (*website www.swtrains.co.uk*) run trains between Plymouth and London (Waterloo) stopping en route at Exeter and Salisbury. Virgin Trains (*website www.virgintrains.co.uk*) have trains north to Birmingham and Bristol and west to Penzance. Wessex Trains (*website www.wessextrains.co.uk*) operate trains to Bristol, Cardiff, Exeter and Penzance.

The train station is north of the city centre on North Road, accessible by buses 5 and 6.

TRAVEL PASSES
The First Bus and Rail Card costs £10 and allows one day travel on First Great Western Trains between Totnes and Penzance and all First buses in Devon.

Local Transport
Plymouth's local buses are run by Citibus (☎ *(01752) 222 221*), First (☎ *(01752) 402060; website www.firstgroup.com*) and Stagecoach (*website*

www.stagecoachbus.co.uk). Bus fares range from 50p to £1.80.

Accommodation
Globe Backpackers

Globe Backpackers is a good hostel near the Citadel. It has a fresh coat of paint and new carpets and facilities include a big common room, a TV lounge with Nintendo, plus a kitchen and a backyard with a barbecue.

172 Citadel Road, Plymouth
☎ *(01752) 225 158*

***Dorm bed** £12;* ***double room** £30*
Reception open *8am-11pm daily*

📺 🇰 🇱

Maintenance & cleanliness	★★★★½
Facilities	★★
Atmosphere & character	★★★★½
Security	★★½
Overall rating	★★★

Sights
Crownhill Fort

This fortified hill 6.5km north of Plymouth was built in the 1860s to defend

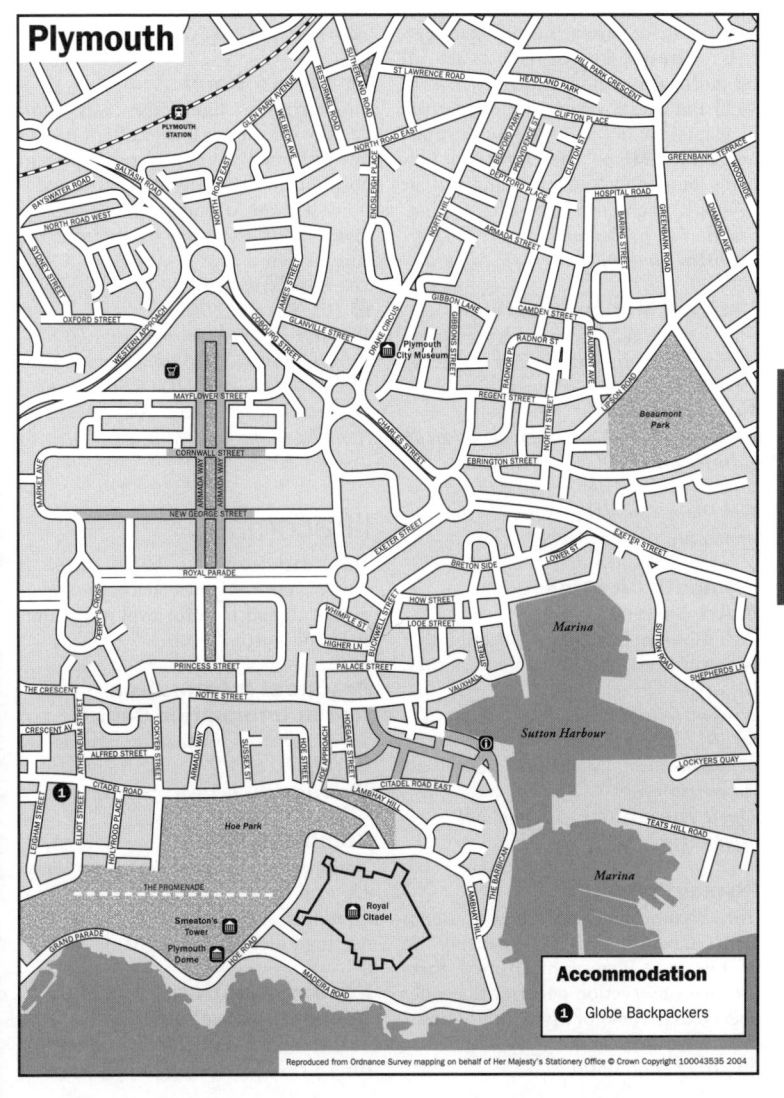

the city from attack by both land and sea. Crownhill has an impressive collection of artillery that includes the Moncrieff Counterweight Disappearing Gun.
Crownhill Road, Plymouth
☎ *(01752) 793 754*
Website *www.crownhillfort.co.uk*
Admission *£5*
Open *Apr-Oct Mon-Fri & Sun 10am-5pm*

Mayflower Steps
The Mayflower Steps marks the departure point for several historic journeys. It is where the Pilgrim Fathers set sail for North America in the *Mayflower* in 1620 and it also witnessed the departure of Captain Cook's voyage to Australia and New Zealand, Sir Humphrey Gilbert's journey to Newfoundland and Sir Walter Raleigh's trip to North Carolina.
The Barbican, Plymouth
Website *www.mayflowersteps.co.uk*

National Marine Aquarium
This aquarium is home to a large variety of marine life including several sharks.
Rope Walk, Coxside, Plymouth
☎ *(01752) 600 301*
Website *www.national-aquarium.co.uk*
Admission *£8.75 (£7.25 students)*
Open *Jan-Mar 10am-4pm daily; Apr-Oct 10am-5pm daily; Nov-Dec 10am-4pm daily*

Plymouth City Museum & Art Gallery
This museum has a large collection that covers fine art plus human and natural history.
Drake Circus, Plymouth
☎ *(01752) 304 774*
Website *www.plymouthmuseum.gov.uk*
Admission *free*
Open *Tue-Fri 10am-5.30pm, Sat 10am-5pm*

Plymouth Dome
The Plymouth Dome is a museum with hands-on exhibits focusing on 400 years of Plymouth's history. There are two observation galleries that offer spectacular views of Plymouth Sound.
Hoe Road, Plymouth
☎ *(01752) 603 300*
Website *www.plymouthdome.info*
Admission *£4.75; combined ticket with Smeaton's Tower £6.50 (£5.50 students)*
Open *Jan-Mar Tue-Sat 10am-4pm; Apr-Oct 10am-5pm daily; Nov-Dec Tue-Sat 10am-4pm*

Royal Citadel
This large fortress was built in the 17th century as a defence against the Dutch and is still in use today.
Plymouth Hoe, Plymouth
Website *www.english-heritage.org.uk*
Tours cost *£3*
Tours depart *May-Sep Tue 2.30pm*

Smeaton's Tower
This striking lighthouse was built 22.5km off the coast on Eddystone reef in 1759 but later moved to its present position on the Hoe after its foundations became unstable. The 22-metre tower offers stunning views from the lantern room.
The Hoe, Plymouth
☎ *(01752) 603 300*
Website *www.plymouthdome.info*
Admission *£2.25; combined ticket with Plymouth Dome £6.50 (£5.50 students)*
Open *Jan-Mar Tue-Sat 10am-3pm; Apr-Oct 10am-4pm daily; Nov-Dec Tue-Sat 10am-3pm*

Ilfracombe

This coastal town in north Devon is centred on a historic harbour and it makes a good base for exploring Somerset and north Devon.

Practical Information
Tourist Information Centre
The Landmark, The Seafront, Ilfracombe
☎ *(01271) 86301*
Website *www.northdevon.co.uk*

Coming & Going
National Express *(website www.nationalexpress.co.uk)* has daily buses to London. Change at Barnstaple for connecting buses to Birmingham.

Accommodation
Ocean Backpackers
This small centrally located hostel features a cosy bar/restaurant, plus a small

TV lounge and a kitchen with a mosaic floor. All rooms have en suite bathrooms and the hostel is undergoing constant renovation. It is a friendly place to stay with a warm atmosphere.
29 St James Place, Ilfracombe
☎ *(01271) 867 835*
Website *www.oceanbackpackers.co.uk*
***Dorm bed** £10;* ***double room** £30; linen £1 extra*
Credit cards *MC, Visa*

Maintenance & cleanliness	★★★
Facilities	★★☆
Atmosphere & character	★★★★
Security	★★☆
Overall rating	★★★☆

Sights
Ilfracombe Aquarium
Ilfracombe's aquarium focuses on the region's river and marine life with creatures from the Exmoor River, the Taw Estuary and Ilfracombe Harbour.
The Old Lifeboat House, The Pier, Ilfracombe
☎ *(01271) 864 533*
Website *www.ilfracombeaquarium.co.uk*
Admission *£2.75*
Open *Mar-Jun 10am-4.30pm daily; Jul-Aug 10am-6pm daily; Sep-Oct 10am-4.30pm daily;*

Ilfracombe Museum
This museum has an eclectic collection of artefacts that cover local and natural history.
Runnymede Gardens, Wilder Road, Sea Front, Ilfracombe
☎ *(01271) 863541*
Website *www.devonmuseums.net*
Admission *£1.50*
Open *Jan-Mar 10am-1pm daily; Apr-Oct 10am-5pm daily; Nov-Dec 10am-1pm daily*

Bath, Bristol & Somerset

Bath
Bath is one of Britain's most visited small cities, and with good reason as it is a charming place with a history dating back two thousand years when it was a Roman settlement. Although the city's two main landmarks are the Roman Baths and the 15th-century Bath Abbey, it was the Georgian period that saw Bath grow from a small town to the fashionable city that it is today.

Practical Information
Bath Tourist Information Centre
Abbey Chambers, Abbey Church Yard, Bath
☎ *0906 711 2000*
Website *www.visitbath.co.uk*
Open *Mon-Sat 9.30am-5pm, Sun 10am-4pm*

Coming & Going
BUS
National Express (☎ *0870 580 8080;* **website** *www.nationalexpress.co.uk*) has frequent buses to Bristol and London. First (**website** *www.firstgroup.com*) and Stagecoach (**website** *www.stagecoachbus.co.uk*) have buses to towns in Somerset and neighbouring counties.

Buses depart from the bus station near the train station on Manvers Street.

TRAIN
Bath Spa station at the southern end of the city centre has excellent train connections.

Train companies that serve Bath include First Great Western (**website** *www.firstgreatwestern.co.uk*) with trains to Bristol and London (Paddington); South West Trains (**website** *www.swtrains.co.uk*) with trains to Bristol, Salibury, London (Waterloo) and Southampton; and Wessex Trains (**website** *www.wessextrains.co.uk*), which goes to Brighton, Bristol, Cardiff, Exeter, Penzance, Plymouth, Portsmouth and Southampton.

Local Transport
First (**website** *www.firstgroup.com*) run local buses around Bath. All day passes cost £3 if purchased before 8.30am on weekdays or £2.50 if purchased after 8.30am on weekdays or all day on weekends.

The First Bus & Rail Card costs £7 and gives you one day unlimited travel on buses in Bath and Bristol plus travel on First Great Western trains between Bath, Bristol and Weston-super-Mare.

Accommodation
Bath Backpackers

Bath Backpackers is in a historic building in the city centre and it has been painted up with lots of murals, which give it a funky atmosphere. It is a bit grungy and has a smoky basement dungeon plus the usual kitchen and TV lounge but the brilliant location and atmosphere outweigh the negative aspects of this hostel.

13 Pierrepont Street, Bath
☎ *(01225) 446 787*
Website *www.hostels.co.uk*
Dorm bed *£12-13;* ***twin room*** *£34*
Credit cards *MC, Visa*
Reception open *8am-midnight daily*

TV K L

Maintenance & cleanliness ★★
Facilities ★★½

Accommodation
1. Bath Backpackers
2. Bath YMCA
3. St Christopher's Inn
4. The White Hart Inn

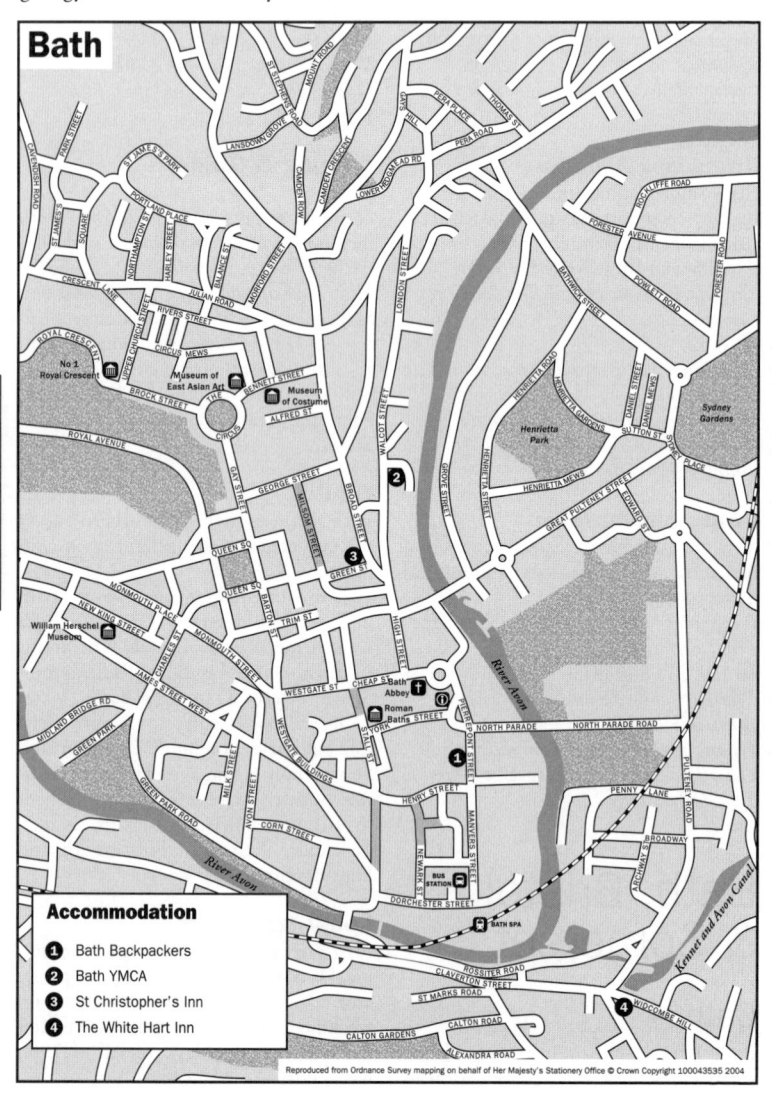

Atmosphere & character	★★★★★
Security	★★☆
Overall rating	★★★☆

Bath YMCA
Bath YMCA is in a modern building tucked in a quiet street behind Broad Street. It has a very clean well-maintained restaurant with TVs and good value meals and an excellent gym. The rooms have older furnishings but it is kept clean. There's no kitchen but there's a microwave that you can use when the restaurant is closed.
International House, Broad Street Place, Bath
☎ *(01225) 325 900*
Website *www.bathymca.co.uk*
Dorm bed £10-16; **single room** £22-26; **twin room** £34-40
Credit cards *JCB, MC, Visa*
Reception open *24 hours*
📺 L

Maintenance & cleanliness	★★★★
Facilities	★★
Atmosphere & character	★
Security	★★★
Overall rating	★★★

Bath YHA
Bath's YHA hostel is in a big mansion in expansive grounds overlooking the city. It features a quiet lounge plus a TV lounge with Internet access and a small kitchen with a big dining area. It is about a 25-minute walk uphill from the city centre but buses run every 15 minutes.
Bathwick Hill, Bath
🚌 *18*
☎ *(01225) 465 674*
Website *www.yha.org.uk*
Dorm bed £14.50 (£12.50 HI/YHA); **twin room** £36 (£32 HI/YHA)
Credit cards *JCB, MC, Visa*
Reception open *7am-11pm*
📺 K L

Maintenance & cleanliness	★★★★★
Facilities	★★
Atmosphere & character	★★★★☆
Security	★★☆
Overall rating	★★★★☆

St Christopher's Inn
St Christopher's Inn has hostel accommodation above a bar in the city centre. There is no kitchen, but the hostel has a TV lounge with Internet access on the top floor. The hostel's bar is bright and lacking in character but you can always just pop across the road to the Saracen's Head for a more authentic English pub. The dorms and bathrooms are clean and well maintained.
9 Green Street, Bath
🚌 *2, 6, 7, 20A, X71, X72, 700, 702, 706, 707, 716*
☎ *(020) 7407 1856*
Website *www.st-christophers.co.uk*
Dorm bed £13-19.50; **double/twin room** £42.50
Credit cards *MC, Visa*
Reception open *7am-11pm/midnight*
📺

Maintenance & cleanliness	★★★★
Facilities	★
Atmosphere & character	★★★☆
Security	★★★☆
Overall rating	★★★☆

The White Hart Inn
The White Hart Inn offers budget accommodation above a small pub just across the Avon River south of the train station. It's a neat and tidy place with basic facilities that include a kitchen and a lounge area in the bar.
Widcombe Hill, Bath
☎ *(01225) 313 985*
Website *www.whitehartbath.co.uk*
Dorm bed £13.50; **single room** £20; **double room** £40-50; **twin room** £35
Credit cards *MC, Visa*
Reception open *9am-11pm daily*
K

Maintenance & cleanliness	★★★
Facilities	★
Atmosphere & character	★★★☆
Security	★★★☆
Overall rating	★★★☆

Sights
The American Museum
This museum focuses on American decorative arts such as patchwork quilts and Shaker furniture.
Claverton Manor, Bath
🚌 *18*
☎ *(01225) 460503*
Website *www.americanmuseum.org*
Admission £6.50

Open 20 Mar-31 Oct Tue-Sun 2pm-5.30pm

Bath Abbey
Dominating the city centre, the 15th-century Bath Abbey is known for its 56 stained glass windows. A much larger cathedral that is believed to have been the site of King Edgars' (England's first king) coronation once stood on the site of Bath Abbey.
Cheap Street, Bath
☎ *(01225) 422 462*
Admission *£2 donation*
Open *Jan-Mar Mon-Sat 10am-4pm, Sun 8am-8pm; Apr-Oct Mon-Sat 10am-6pm, Sun 8am-8pm; Nov-Dec Mon-Sat 10am-4pm, Sun 8am-8pm*

Beckford's Tower & Museum
This lavishly restored building north of the city centre offers panoramic views from its tower.
Lansdown Road, Bath
🚌 *2, 702*
☎ *(01225) 460705*
Admission *£2.50*
Open *Easter-Oct Sat-Sun 10.30am-5pm*

Building of Bath Museum
This museum shows how – in a period of only 70 years – Bath developed into one of the most fashionable places in Georgian England.
The Countess of Huntingdon's Chapel, The Vineyards, The Paragon, Bath
☎ *(01225) 333 895*
Website *www.bath-preservation-trust.org.uk*
Admission *£4 (£3 students)*
Open *Tue-Sun 10.30am-4.15pm*

Jane Austen Centre
Bath's most famous resident is celebrated in this museum that has exhibits relating to her life and work.
40 Gay Street, Bath
☎ *(01225) 443000*
Website *www.janeausten.co.uk*
Admission *£4.45 (£3.65 students)*
Open *Mon-Sat 10am-5.30pm, Sun 10.30am-5.30pm*

Museum of Bath at Work
This museum details Bath's industrial heritage with a collection that includes manufacturing machinery and artefacts that illustrate the various industries that once thrived in Bath.
Julian Road, Bath
☎ *(01225) 318348*
Website *www.bath-at-work.org.uk*
Admission *£3.50*
Open *Jan-Mar Sat-Sun 10am-5pm; Apr-Oct 10am-5pm daily; Nov-Dec Sat-Sun 10am-5pm*

Museum of Costume
This museum exhibits fashion dating from 1600 to the present day.
Assembly Rooms, Bennett Street, Bath
☎ *(01225) 477785*
Website *www.museumofcostume.co.uk*
Admission *£6 (£5 students); joint ticket with Roman Baths £12 (£10.50 students)*
Open *Jan-Feb 11am-4pm daily; Mar-Oct 11am-5pm daily; Nov-Dec 11am-4pm daily*

Museum of East Asian Art
This museum features exhibits from throughout East Asia including bamboo carvings and one of Britain's largest collections of Chinese jade.
12 Bennett Street, Bath
☎ *(01225) 464640*
Website *www.meaa.org.uk*
Admission *£3.50 (£2.50 students)*
Open *Tue-Sat 10am-5pm, Sun noon-5pm*

No 1 Royal Crescent
The first house to be built on Bath's most prestigious street has been restored to show how it would have appeared in the 18th century.
1 Royal Crescent, Bath
☎ *(01225) 338727*
Website *www.bath-preservation-trust.org.uk*
Admission *£4 (£3.50 students)*
Open *10 Feb-30 Oct Tue-Sun 10.30am-5pm; 31 Oct-28 Nov Tue-Sun 10.30am-4pm; 4-5 & 11-12 Dec 10.30am-4pm*

Roman Baths
Bath's raison d'etre is the spa that was built by the Romans 2000 years ago. Considering its age, the Baths are very well preserved and the complex includes

several baths, the Sacred Spring, the Roman Temple and displays of objects found in the Sacred Spring.
Pump Room, Abbey Church Yard, Bath
☎ *(01225) 477785*
Website *www.romanbaths.co.uk*
Admission £9 (£8 students)
Open *Jan-Feb 9.30am-4.30pm daily; Mar-Jun 9am-5pm daily; Jul-Aug 9am-9pm daily; Sep-Oct 9am-5pm daily; Nov-Dec 9.30am-4.30pm daily*

William Herschel Museum
In 1781 William Herschel discovered Uranus using a home made telescope in the garden of his home, which is now a museum dedicated to the accomplishments of this distinguished astronomer.
19 New King Street, Bath
☎ *(01225) 311342*
Website *www.bath-preservation-trust.org.uk*
Admission £3.50
Open *10 Feb-30 Nov Mon-Tue & Th-Fri 2pm-5pm, Sat-Sun 11am-3pm*

Bristol
Bath's industrial neighbour is an increasingly popular travel destination with a couple of excellent hostels, some good museums and a vibrant nightlife. Its good transport connections to Bath, Cardiff and Glastonbury make it an excellent base for exploring the West Country.

Practical Information
Tourist Information Centre
The Annexe, Wildscreen Walk, Harbourside, Bristol
☎ *0906 711 2191 (50p per minute)*
Website www.visitbristol.co.uk
Open Jan-Feb Mon-Sat 10am-5pm, Sun 11am-4pm; Mar-Oct 10am-6pm daily; Nov-Dec Mon-Sat 10am-5pm, Sun 11am-4pm

Coming & Going
AIR
Bristol Airport (☎ *0870 1212747; website www.bristolairport.com*) has daily flights to many major European destinations. The Bristol International Flyer is an express bus that runs between Bristol city centre (with stops at the bus station and Temple Meads train station) and the airport. The bus costs £4 one-way or £6 return.

BUS
Bristol's Bus & Coach Station is located north of the old city between Marlborough Street and St James Park. National Express (☎ *0870 580 8080; website www.nationalexpress.co.uk*) and local First (*website www.firstgroup.com*) and Stagecoach buses (*website www.stagecoachbuses.co.uk*) depart from here.

Megabus (*website www.megabus.com*) has several buses a day to London with prices between £1 and £9 (plus 50p booking fee). Megabus departs from Colston Hall on Colston Street in the city centre.

TRAIN
Bristol has two main train stations, Temple Meads and Bristol Parkway, although Bristol Temple Meads is the more centrally located of the two stations. It is about a 15-minute walk from the city centre or you can take buses 8, 9 or 500.

Local Transport
First (*website www.firstgroup.com*) run local buses in Bristol. The most useful buses are routes 8, 9 and 500, which connect Temple Meads station with the city centre. Bus 8 also goes to Bristol Zoo Gardens and bus 500 connects both the city centre and the train station with Spike Island and *SS Great Britain*.

All day passes cost £3.20 if purchased before 9am, £2.60 if purchased after 9am or £1.70 if purchased after 7pm.

The First Bus & Rail Card costs £7 and gives you one day unlimited travel on buses in Bath and Bristol plus travel on First Great Western trains between Bath, Bristol and Weston-super-Mare.

There is also a ferry service (*website www.bristolferryboat.co.uk*) that connects Temple Meads station, the city centre and the harbour. Ferry fares range from 50p to £1.20.

Accommodation
Bristol Backpackers
This brilliant hostel has excellent common areas that include vault-style

Internet and TV rooms, a brand new kitchen and a great basement bar with a piano and drinks at off-licence prices. Although the carpets are a bit grotty, most of the hostel has been recently renovated and the dorms are nice with good sturdy bunk beds. It is a friendly hostel with a great social atmosphere.
17 Saint Stephen's Street, Bristol
☎ *(0117) 925 7900*
Website *www.bristolbackpackers.co.uk*
Dorm bed *£14*
Credit cards *Amex, Diners, MC, Visa*
Reception open *9am-11.30pm daily*

Maintenance & cleanliness	★★★★☆
Facilities	★★★
Atmosphere & character	★★★★★
Security	★★☆
Overall rating	★★★★☆

Bristol YHA
Bristol's YHA is a modern hostel with mostly en suite rooms. It features a TV lounge with lots of board games, a games room with a pool table and table football, a small kitchen and a big dining room. Its location by the waterfront is handy to several of Bristol's main attractions.
14 Narrow Quay, Bristol
☎ *(0117) 922 1659*
Website *www.yha.org.uk*
Dorm bed *£20 (£18 HI/YHA);*
twin room *£36.80-38.80 (£32.80-34.80 HI/YHA); prices include breakfast*
Credit cards *MC, Visa*
Reception open *24 hours*

Maintenance & cleanliness	★★★★☆
Facilities	★★★☆
Atmosphere & character	★★☆
Security	★★★☆
Overall rating	★★★

Sights
At Bristol
One of Bristol's best new attractions is the excellent At Bristol science and nature museum. At Bristol is split between several distinct galleries that include Explore, a science museum with plenty of interactive exhibits; an IMAX

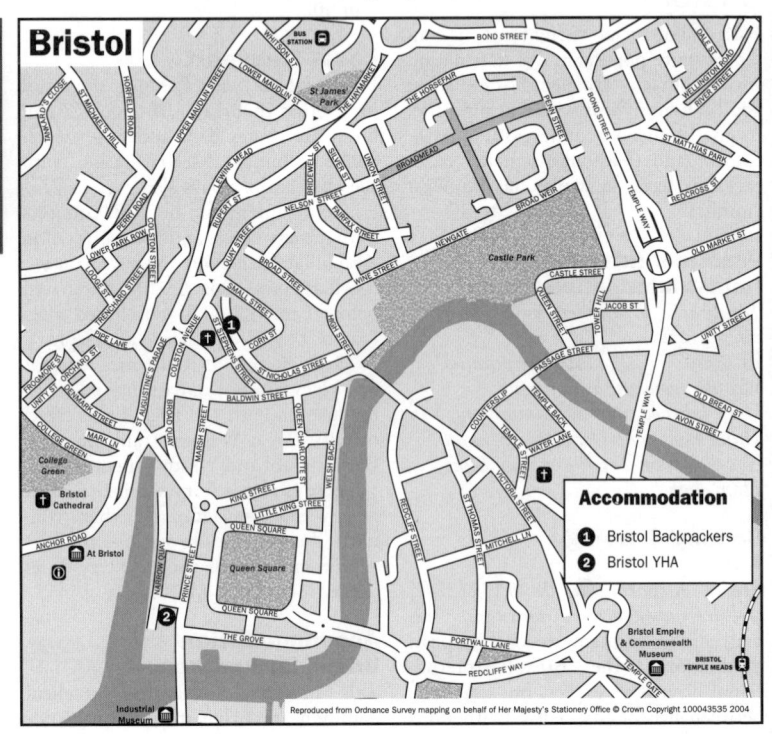

theatre and Wildwalk, which features a tropical forest complete with birds and butterflies. At Bristol also hosts a programme of temporary exhibits.
Anchor Road, Harbourside, Bristol
☎ *0845 345 1235*
Website *www.at-bristol.org.uk*
Admission *Explore £7.50; IMAX £6.50-8.50; Wildwalk £6.50; Explore & Wildwalk £12; Explore & IMAX £12; Wildwalk & IMAX £11; all three attractions £16.50*
Open *10am-6pm daily*

Blaise Castle House Museum
This 18th century house has displays relating to everyday life in Bristol.
Henbury Road, Henbury, Bristol
☎ *(0117) 903 9818*
Admission *free*
Open *Mon-Wed & Sat-Sun 10am-5pm*

Bristol Cathedral
Bristol Cathedral was built in 1140 as an Augustine monastery and has been a cathedral since 1542. The highlights include the English Lady Chapel and the Norman Chapter House.
College Green, Bristol
☎ *(0117) 926 4879*
Website *www.bristol-cathedral.co.uk*
Admission *free*
Open *Mon-Fri 8am-6pm, Sat 8am-5.0pm, Sun 7.30am-5pm*

Bristol Industrial Museum
This museum recounts Bristol's rich industrial heritage with exhibits that include the aircraft and automotive industries, printing and packaging, Bristol's involvement in the transatlantic slave trade and development of the Port of Bristol.
Princes Wharf, Wapping Road, Bristol
☎ *(0117) 925 1470*
Website *www.bristol-city.gov.uk/museums*
Admission *free*
Open *Mon-Wed & Sat-Sun 10am-5pm*

British Empire & Commonwealth Museum
This brilliant museum near Temple Meads station portrays the 500-year history of the rise and fall of the British Empire. The museum's galleries hold a huge collection of exotic artefacts from around the globe that are complemented by interactive exhibits.
Station Approach, Temple Meads, Bristol
🚌 *8, 9, 500* 🚆 *Bristol Temple Meads*
☎ *(0117) 925 4980*
Website *www.empiremuseum.co.uk*
Admission *£6.50 (£5.50 students)*
Open *10am-5pm daily*

Bristol Zoo
Bristol's award winning zoo has a large range of animals that range from the world's smallest and rarest tortoise to the largest ape.
Clifton Down, Clilfton, Bristol
🚌 *8, 9* 🚆 *Clifton Down*
☎ *(0117) 973 8951*
Website *www.bristolzoo.org.uk*
Admission *£9.50*
Open *summer 9am-5.30pm daily; winter 9am-4.30pm daily*

City Museum & Art Gallery
The City Museum & Art Gallery has a diverse range of exhibits that cover everything from natural history to fine art.
Queen's Road, Bristol
🚌 *1, 8, 9, 41, 42, 43, 54, 55, 99*
☎ *(0117) 925 1470*
Admission *free*
Open *10am-5pm daily*

Clifton Suspension Bridge
Bristol's iconic suspension bridge, designed by Isambard Kingdom Brunel, spans the breathtaking Avon Gorge. The bridge offers views of the gorge and a new visitor centre adjacent to the bridge will open in the summer of 2005.
Suspension Bridge Road, Clifton, Bristol
☎ *(0117) 974 4664*
Website *www.clifton-suspension-bridge.org.uk*
Open *summer 10am-5pm daily; winter Mon-Fri 11am-4pm, Sat-Sun 11am-5pm*

Georgian House
This restored Georgian townhouse is presented the way it would have appeared in the 18th century.
7 Great George Street, Bristol
☎ *(0117) 921 1362*
Admission *free*

Open Mon-Wed & Sat-Sun 10am-5pm

Red Lodge
This 400-year-old Elizabethan house features a Tudor style knot garden.
Park Row, Bristol
☎ *(0117) 921 1360*
Admission *free*
Open *Mon-Wed & Sat-Sun 10am-5pm*

St Mary Redcliffe Church
St Mary Redcliffe is one of Britain's largest parish churches and is a fine example of medieval architecture. Queen Elizabeth I called it "the fairest, goodliest and most famous Parish Church in England".
Redcliffe Way, Bristol
☎ *(0117) 929 1487*
Website *www.stmaryredcliffe.co.uk*
Admission *free*
Open *Jan-Apr 9am-4pm daily, May-Oct 9am-5pm daily; Nov-Dec 9am-4pm daily*

Severn Bridges Visitor Centre
This visitor centre has displays relating to the bridges crossing the River Severn.
Shaft Road, off Green Lane, Severn Beach
☎ *(01454) 633 511*
Website *www.onbridges.com*
Open *Easter-Sep 11am-4pm daily*

SS Great Britain
The *SS Great Britain* was the world's first steam powered, iron hulled passenger liner and she was twice the weight of any other ship when launched in 1843.
☎ *(0117) 929 1843*
Website *www.ss-great-britain.com*
Admission *£6.25*
Open *Jan-Mar 10am-4.30pm daily; Apr-Oct 10am-5.30pm daily; Nov-Dec 10am-4.30pm daily*

Glastonbury

This small town in Somerset is home to many legends that have given rise to its popularity as a "new age" destination. Various myths include Glastonbury as the final resting place for King Arthur and the Holy Grail. There's a lot to see for such a small town including Glastonbury Abbey, which dates from the 7th century, Glastonbury Tor and the Chalice Well. As well as all these attractions, Glastonbury is best known for the legendary Glastonbury Festival, which can be best described as Britain's original rock festival.

Practical Information
Tourist Information Centre
The Tribunal, 9 High Street, Glastonbury
☎ *(01458) 832954*
Website *www.glastonburytic.co.uk*
Open *Jan-Mar Mon-Thu 10am-4pm, Fri-Sat 10am-4.30pm, Sun 10am-4pm; Apr-Sep Mon-Thu 10am-5pm, Fri-Sat 10am-5.30pm, Sun 10am-5pm; Oct-Dec Mon-Thu 10am-4pm, Fri-Sat 10am-4.30pm, Sun 10am-4pm*

Coming & Going
First (*website* *www.firstgroup.co.uk*) runs buses 29 and 929 from Taunton, bus 173 from Bath, 376, 377, 929, 976, 977 from Bristol Temple Meads Station and 377 and 977 from Yeovil.

Accommodation
Glastonbury Backpackers
This hostel boasts an excellent location in a 16th century inn on the Market Place in Glastonbury town centre. The hostel is a bit rough around the edges but it has the basic amenities such as a smoky TV lounge and a small kitchen. There is a café and bar downstairs.
4 Market Place, Glastonbury
☎ *(01458) 833 353*
Website *www.glastonburybackpackers.com*
Dorm bed *£12;* ***double/twin room*** *£30-35*
Credit cards *MC, Visa*
Reception open *9am-11pm daily*
📺 🍳

Maintenance & cleanliness	★★
Facilities	★★☆
Atmosphere & character	★★★
Security	★★☆
Overall rating	★★

Street YHA
Street's youth hostel is a cute little Swiss-style chalet with views of Street. It has a small, but well stocked kitchen and a

small common room with a log-burning stove. It is a quiet hostel with no TV. It's in a rural setting 3.25km from Street and 6.5km from Glastonbury.
The Chalet, Ivythorn Hill, Street
🚌 *376, 676, 976*
☎ *(01458) 442 961*
Website *www.yha.org.uk*
Dorm bed *£13 (£11 HI/YHA)*
Credit cards *MC, Visa*
Open *Apr-May Wed-Sun; Jun Tue-Sun;* **reception open** *8.30am-10am & 5pm-9pm;* **lockout** *10am-5pm;* **curfew** *11pm*

🚗 K

Maintenance & cleanliness	★★★★
Facilities	★
Atmosphere & character	★★★
Security	★
Overall rating	★★

Sights
Glastonbury Abbey
Glastonbury Abbey claims to be the oldest above ground Christian church in the world and although it is in ruin, regular services are still held here. There are many legends surrounding the abbey and King Arthur and Queen Guinevere are buried here.
Abbey Gatehouse, Magdalene Street, Glastonbury
☎ *(01458) 832267*
Website *www.glastonburyabbey.com*
Admission *£4*
Open *Jan 10am-4.30pm daily; Feb 10am-5pm daily; Mar 9.30am-5.30pm daily; Apr-May 9.30am-6pm daily; Jun-Aug 9am-6pm daily; Sep 9.30am-6pm daily; Oct 9.30am-5pm daily; Nov 9.30am-4.30pm daily; Dec 10am-4.30pm daily*

Glastonbury Tor
The remaining 15th-century tower of the church of St Michael dominates this 159m-high hill just outside town. Legend has it that Joseph of Arimathea came to Glastonbury with the Holy Grail, which he buried under the Chalice Well near the Tor.
Wellhouse Lane, Glastonbury
☎ *(01934) 844518*
Website *www.nationaltrust.org.uk & www.glastonburytor.org.uk*
Admission *free*

Glastonbury Tribunal
This 14th-century house has a stone facade dating from the 16th century. The building now houses the tourist information centre, but there is also an area with displays on its history.
9 High Street, Glastonbury
🚌 *376, 377, 976, 977*
☎ *(01458) 832 954*
Website *www.glastonburytic.co.uk*
Admission *£2*
Open *Jan-Mar Mon-Fri 10am-4pm, Sat-Sun 10am-4.30pm; Apr-Sep Mon-Fri 10am-5pm, Sat-Sun 10am-5.30pm; Oct-Dec Mon-Fri 10am-4pm, Sat-Sun 10am-4.30pm*

Somerset Rural Life Museum
This open-air museum tells the life story of a farm worker in Victorian Somerset. The museum's highlight is a 14th century abbey barn.
Chilkwell Street, Glastonbury
☎ *(01458) 831197*
Website *www.somerset.gov.uk/museums/*
Admission *free*
Open *Jan-Mar Tue-Sat 10am-5pm; Apr-Oct Tue-Fri 10am-5pm, Sat-Sun 2pm-6pm; Nov-Dec Tue-Sat 10am-5pm*

Wells
England's smallest city is a charming place with Tudor buildings and a splendid cathedral.

Practical Information
Tourist Information Centre
Town Hall, Market Place, Wells
☎ *(01749) 672552*

Coming & Going
Local buses connect Wells to towns in Somerset and neighbouring counties. Bus 173 goes to Bath and bus 376 goes to Bristol.

Accommodation
There are no hostels in Wells. The closest are in Cheddar, Glastonbury and Street.

Sights
Bishop's Palace & Gardens
The Bishop's Palace has been the home to the Bishops of Bath and Wells since 1206, after Bishop Jocelin Trotman

received the licence to build the palace south of the cathedral. The palace is well maintained and features a Jacobean staircase and Victorian Gothic rooms where you can see the Coronation Cape and the Glastonbury Chair.
The Bishop's Palace, Wells
☎ (01749) 678691
Website *www.bishopspalacewells.co.uk*
Admission £4 (£1.50 students)
Open Apr-Oct Mon-Fri 10.30am-5pm, Sun noon-5pm

St Cuthbert's Church
This impressive church dates from the 13th century and is one of the largest in Somerset.
St Cuthbert Street, Wells
☎ (01749) 673136
Website *www.stcuthbertswells.co.uk*

Wells Cathedral
Wells Cathedral dates from 1180, although a church as been on the site since 705. It is an impressive building, particularly for such a tiny city.
Cathedral Green, Wells
☎ (01749) 674 483
Website *www.wellscathedral.org.uk*
Admission £4.50 donation (£1.50 students)
Open Jan-Mar 7am-6pm daily; Apr-Sep 7am-7pm daily; Oct-Dec 7am-6pm daily

Cheddar

This small town in England's largest gorge is world famous for its cheese. However it is also a tourist trap that's probably best avoided unless you really want to see the caves or if you really love tacky cheese and cider shops.

Practical Information
Tourist Information Centre
The Gorge, Cheddar
☎ (01934) 744071

Coming & Going
Buses 126 and 826 go to Cheddar from Wells.

Accommodation
Cheddar YHA
This small hostel 1km from Cheddar Gorge has a kitchen, laundry, TV lounge and a conservatory.
Hillfield, Cheddar
🚌 126, 826
☎ (01934) 744 724
Website *www.yha.org.uk*
Dorm bed £14.50 (£12.50 HI/YHA)
Open May-Sep; **reception open** 8am-10am & 5pm-10pm daily; **curfew** 11pm daily

📺 🇰 🇱

Sights
Cheddar Caves & Gorge
Britain's biggest gorge is not really that spectacular but the caves aren't too bad, although the way the caves are presented is a tad tacky. People have lived in these caves for thousands of years and the world-famous Cheddar Man – Britain's oldest complete skeleton – was discovered here. The site features a museum with displays relating to the 9000-year-old skeleton.
☎ (01934) 742343
Website *www.cheddarcaves.co.uk*
Admission £9.50
Open 10am-5pm daily

Cornwall

The southwestern corner of England is popular with international visitors who are drawn by surf beaches, history and unique Celtic culture. Although the Cornish language has all but died out, this county is distinct from other parts of England.

Fowey

This historic town at the mouth of the River Fowey was Daphne du Maurier's hometown. The town attracts fans of du Maurier's novels and it also makes a good base for visiting nearby attractions like the Eden Project and Restormel Castle.

Practical Information
Tourist Information Centre
5 South Street, Fowey
☎ (01726) 833 616
Website *www.fowey.co.uk*
Open Apr-Sep Mon-Sat 9.30am-5pm, Sun 10am-5pm

Coming & Going
First *(website www.firstgroup.com)* runs buses 24, 24B and 27between Fowey and St Austell where you can make bus and train connections to Bristol, London, Plymouth and destinations throughout Cornwall.

Accommodation
Golant YHA
This YHA hostel is in a big house in the countryside that makes a good base for visiting Fowey. It has a good kitchen, a TV lounge, Internet access and a conservatory looking onto the back garden.
Penquite House, Golant, Fowey
🚌 *24*
☎ *(01726) 833 507*
Website www.yha.org.uk
Dorm bed £16 (£14 HI/YHA)
Credit cards MC, Visa
Open Feb-Nov; reception open 7.30am-10.30am & 5pm-11pm daily

Maintenance & cleanliness	★★★
Facilities	★★☆
Atmosphere & character	★★
Security	★
Overall rating	★★

Sights
Daphne du Maurier Literary Centre
The centre has displays about Fowey's literary heritage and also shows videos about Fowey and Daphne du Maurier's ties with Cornwall.
5 South Street, Fowey
☎ *(01726) 833 616*
Website www.dumaurier.org
Open Apr-Sep Mon-Sat 9.30am-5pm, Sun 10am-5pm

Eden Project
The Eden Project is one of Cornwall's biggest attractions. This series of biomes has recreated the natural environment of various climatic regions including biomes with flora from the humid tropics and warm temperate regions.
Bodelva, St Austell
🚌 *T9, T10*
Website www.edenproject.com
Admission £12 (£6 students)
Open Jan-Mar 10am-3pm daily; Apr-Oct 9.30am-4.30pm daily; Nov-Dec 10am-3pm daily

Restormel Castle
This 14th century castle is surrounded by a moat and features a large circular keep with lovely views of the countryside. Edward, the Black Prince, once called this castle home. It is near Lostwithiel, 13km north of Fowey.
A390, Lostwithiel
☎ *(01208) 872687*
Website www.english-heritage.org.uk
Admission £2.20
Open Apr-Jun 10am-5pm daily; Jul-Aug 10am-6pm daily; Sep 10am-5pm daily; Oct 10am-4pm daily

Falmouth
This historic maritime centre is one of Cornwall's nicest large towns. It is built around the world's third-deepest harbour, which is guarded by castles on both sides and it is also home to the National Maritime Museum.

Practical Information
Falmouth Tourist Information Centre
28 Killigrew Street, Falmouth
☎ *(01326) 312300*
Website www.falmouth-cornwall.org
Open Jan-Mar Mon-Fri 9.30am-5.15pm; Apr-Sep Mon-Sat 9.30am-5.15pm; Oct-Dec Mon-Fri 9.30am-5.15pm

Coming & Going
First *(website www.firstgroup.com)* and Truronian *(website www.truronian.co.uk)* operate buses to neighbouring towns. Bus T11 goes to the Eden Project making it an ideal daytrip from Falmouth.

Falmouth has several train stations. Dell-Falmouth Town is the most centrally located station for both the hostel and the town centre but Falmouth Docks station is closest to the harbour and Pendennis Castle. Falmouth lies on a branch line with Wessex Trains *(website www.wessextrains.co.uk)* running trains to Truro where you can change for trains to Bristol, Exeter and Penzance.

Accommodation
Falmouth Lodge
This small 18-bed hostel near Falmouth Town Station is like a home. It has a nice lounge area and a small kitchen with an Aga. Accommodation is in small rooms (the largest has four beds) and some rooms have sea views. The manager is very helpful and enthusiastic about Falmouth.
9 Gyllyngvase Terrace, Falmouth
☎ *(01326) 319 996*
Website *www.falmouthbackpackers.co.uk*
Dorm bed *£13-14;* **twin room** *£32*

Maintenance & cleanliness	★★★★½
Facilities	★★½
Atmosphere & character	★★★★
Security	★
Overall rating	★★★

Sights
Falmouth Art Gallery
The small Falmouth Art Gallery has works by local artists but is best known for John William Waterhouse's *The Lady of Shalott*.
Municipal Buildings, The Moor, Falmouth
☎ *(01326) 313 863*
Website *www.falmouthartgallery.com*
Admission *free*
Open *Mon-Sat 10am-5pm*

National Maritime Museum
The excellent National Maritime Museum has a range of nautical themed exhibits that covers boatbuilding, yacht racing, navigation and Cornwall's fascinating maritime heritage. Visitors to the museum can watch boat builders restore boats, sail a radio-controlled yacht and take in panoramic views from the tower.
Discovery Quay, Falmouth
🚉 *Falmouth Town*
☎ *(01326) 313388*
Website *www.nmmc.co.uk*
Admission *£5.90*
Open *10am-5pm daily*

St Mawes Castle (Castel Lanvawseth)
The 16th century St Mawes Castle is located across the bay from Falmouth, facing Pendennis Castle. It considered the loveliest of Henry VIII's coastal fortresses and it offers lovely views of Falmouth.
A3078 St Mawes
☎ *(01326) 270526*
Website *www.english-heritage.org.uk*
Admission *£3.20*
Open *Jan-Mar Mon & Fri-Sun 10am-4pm; Apr-Jun 10am-5pm daily; Jul-Aug 10am-6pm daily; Sep 10am-5pm daily; Oct 10am-4pm daily; Nov-Dec 10am-4pm daily*

Pendennis Castle
This impressive Tudor Pendennis Castle bills itself as Cornwall's greatest fortress. It has witnessed 450 years of history and features a labyrinth of secret wartime defences.
Pendennis Headland, Falmouth
🚉 *Falmouth Docks*
☎ *(01326) 316594*
Website *www.english-heritage.co.uk*
Admission *£4.50*
Open *Jan-Mar 10am-4pm daily; Apr-Jun 10am-5pm daily; Jul-Aug 10am-6pm daily; Sep 10am-5pm daily; Oct-Dec 10am-4pm daily*

Penzance
Famed for its history of swashbuckling pirates, Penzance makes an ideal base for exploring Lands End and the Penwith Peninsula. It is very popular with tourists although there isn't a great deal to do in the town centre.

Practical Information
Penzance Tourist Information Centre
Station Road, Penzance
☎ *(01736) 362 207*
Website *www.go-cornwall.com*
Open *Jan-Apr Mon-Fri 9am-5pm, Sat 10am-1pm; May-Sep Mon-Sat 9am-6pm, Sun 10am-1pm; Oct-Dec Mon-Fri 9am-5pm, Sat 10am-1pm*

Coming & Going
BUS
First *(website www.firstgroup.com)* have frequent buses to destinations throughout Cornwall. Useful routes include buses 1, 1A, 1B and 300 to Lands End,

buses 9 and 300 to St Just and bus 16 to St Ives.

National Express (☎ 0870 580 8080; *website* *www.nationalexpress.co.uk*) has buses to Birmingham, Exeter, London, Plymouth.

Buses terminate near the train station on Wharf Road.

TRAIN

Virgin *(website www.virgintrains.co.uk)* run trains to Bristol, Cardiff and Birmingham; Wessex Trains *(website www.wessextrains.co.uk)* run trains from Penzance to Bristol, Exeter, Plymouth and St Ives. And First Great Western *(website www.firstgreatwestern.co.uk)* trains go to Bristol and London (Paddington). The train station is on Wharf Road near Albert Pier.

TRAVEL PASSES

The First Bus and Rail Card costs £10 and allows one day travel on First Great Western Trains between Totnes and Penzance and all First buses in Devon.

Accommodation
Penzance Backpackers (the Blue Dolphin)

This well maintained hostel has a big TV lounge, Internet access and a good kitchen.

Alexandra Road, Penzance
☎ *(01736) 363836*
Website *www.pzbackpack.com*
Dorm bed *£13;* ***double room*** *£28*
Credit cards *MC, Visa*
Reception open *8am-11pm daily*

📺 K L

Maintenance & cleanliness	★★★★½
Facilities	★★½
Atmosphere & character	★★★★
Security	★
Overall rating	★★★

Penzance YHA

The Penzance YHA is in a lovely restored manor house that boasts a fine Georgian staircase and 1000-year-old basement floors (it was built on the site of a Norman keep). It is clean and well maintained and features a good kitchen, a TV lounge, Internet access and a games

Penzance

Accommodation
1. Penzance Backpackers (the Blue Dolphin)

room with a pool table and table tennis.
Castle Horneck, Alverton, Penzance
🚌 5, 6
☎ (01736) 362 666
Website www.yha.org.uk
Dorm bed £16 (£14 HI/YHA)
Credit cards MC, Visa
Reception open *summer 8am-10pm & 5pm-10.30pm daily; winter 8am-10pm & 3pm-10.30pm daily*

🚌 📺 🇰 🇱

Maintenance & cleanliness	★★★★⯨
Facilities	★★
Atmosphere & character	★★★★
Security	★★
Overall rating	★★★⯨

Sights
St Michael's Mount
With a striking appearance similar to Mont St Michel in France this island off the coast from Marazion, 5km from Penzance, is home to a Benedictine monastery that incorporates a church, a castle and a small village at its base. At low tide you can walk across a causeway to get to the Mount; a ferry (£1) runs at other times.
🚌 2, 2A, 17A, 32
☎ (01736) 710 507
Website ww.stmichaelsmount.co.uk
Admission £4.80
Open *Apr-Oct 10.30am-4.45pm daily*

Lands End & the Penwith Peninsula

The Penwith Peninsula and Lands End – England's western most point – is a popular destination with many backpackers who come here for its mix of ancient Celtic monuments, quaint villages and surf beaches.

Practical Information
St Just Information Centre
The Library, Market Street, St Just
☎ (01736) 788 669
Open *Jun-Aug Mon-Wed & Fri 10am-5pm, Sat 10am-1pm, Sun 10am-5pm*

Coming & Going
& Local Transport
First *(website www.firstgroup.com)* run buses on the Penwith Peninsula with most buses terminating at Penzance and St Ives. Useful bus routes include bus 300, which runs along the coast between Penzance and St Ives stopping at Lands End and St Just; buses 1, 1A and 1B from Penzance to Lands End and bus 9 from Penzance to St Just.

Accommodation
Lands End YHA
This quiet hostel is set on three acres of Cornish countryside near the small village of St Just near Lands End. It has lovely sea views and facilities that include a lounge with fireplace and a small, but fully equipped kitchen.
Letcha Vean, St Just-in-Penwith
☎ (01736) 788 437
Website www.yha.org.uk
Dorm bed £14.50 (£12.50 HI/YHA)
Credit cards Amex, JCB, MC, Visa
Open *17 Feb-30 Apr Tue-Sat; May-Sep every day; Oct Tue-Sat; reception open 8.30am-10am & 5pm-10pm daily*

🚌 📺 🇰

Maintenance & cleanliness	★★★★⯨
Facilities	★★⯨
Atmosphere & character	★★★★⯨
Security	★
Overall rating	★★★⯨

The Old Chapel
This is a very well kept hostel above a café in a tiny village between St Ives and Lands End. It has a nice TV lounge with lots of books and most rooms have sea views.
The Old Chapel, Zennor
☎ (01736) 798 307
Website www.backpackers.co.uk/zennor/index.html
Dorm bed £12

🚌 📺 🇰

Maintenance & cleanliness	★★★★★
Facilities	★★
Atmosphere & character	★★★
Security	★★⯨
Overall rating	★★★★⯨

Whitesands Lodge
This cute hostel is painted with brightly coloured Cornish murals. It is very well maintained and has a great social atmosphere. Facilities include a small kitchen, a bar/restaurant and three common rooms (one with a TV, one

with a pool table and a quiet reading room).
Sennen
☎ *(01736) 871 776*
Website *www.whitesandslodge.co.uk*
Dorm bed *£12.50;* ***single room*** *£22;*
double room *£44-50;* ***twin room*** *£44*
Credit cards *MC, Visa*
Reception open *summer 9am-6pm daily; winter 9am-9pm daily*

Maintenance & cleanliness	★★★★⯪
Facilities	★★
Atmosphere & character	★★★★★
Security	★⯪
Overall rating	★★★⯪

Surfing

The area around Lands End has good surfing and you can learn to surf at the Sennen Surfing Centre.

The Sennen Surfing Centre

Based out of Whitesands Lodge, the Sennen Surfing Centre teaches you to surf on the uncrowded surf breaks at Sennen Beach.
Whitesands Lodge, Sennen
☎ *(01736) 871 458*
Website *www.whitesandslodge.co.uk*

Sights
Ballowall Barrow

This Bronze Age tomb features a series of burial chambers.
Near Carn Gloose, 1.5km west of St Just
Website *www.english-heritage.org.uk*
Admission *free*

Carn Euny Ancient Village

All that remains from this Iron Age settlement are the foundations of stone huts and an underground passage.
A30, 2km southwest of Sancreed
🚌 *10A, 10B*
Website *www.english-heritage.org.uk*
Admission *free*

Chysauster Ancient Village

This 2000-year-old Celtic settlement is made up of eight stone courtyard houses unique to Lands End and the Isles of Scilly.
B3311, 4km northwest of Gulval
☎ *07831 757934*
Website *www.english-heritage.org.uk*
Admission *£2*
Open *Apr-Jun 10am-5pm daily; Jul-Aug 10am-6pm daily; Sep 10am-5pm daily; Oct 10am-4pm daily*

Geevor Tin Mine

Geevor was a working tin mine until as recently as 1990 and has now been recreated as a heritage site that has underground tours plus displays of mining equipement.
Pendeen
🚌 *17, 300*
☎ *(01736) 788662*
Website *www.geevor.com*
Admission *£6.50*
Open *Jan-Easter 9am-3pm daily; Easter-Oct 9am-4pm daily; Nov-Dec 9am-3pm daily; tours Jan-Easter 11am, 1pm, 3pm daily; Easter-Oct 10am, 11am, noon, 1pm, 2pm, 3pm, 4pm daily; Nov-Dec 11am, 1pm, 3pm daily*

Tregiffian Burial Chamber

This chambered tomb is believed to date from the Neolithic or Bronze Age periods.
B3315, 3km southeast of St Buryan
Website *www.english-heritage.org.uk*
Admission *free*

St Ives

This medieval fishing village has become somewhat of an artists' colony with many art galleries including a local branch of the Tate Gallery. It is a lovely town although it can get crowded in summer.

Practical Information
St Ives Tourist Information Centre

The Guildhall, Street an Pol, St Ives
☎ *(01736) 796 297*
Open *Jan-Easter Mon-Fri 9am-5pm; Easter-Sep Mon-Sat 9.30am-6pm, Sun 10am-1pm; Oct-Dec Mon-Fri 9am-5pm*

Coming & Going

First (***website*** *www.firstgroup.com*) bus 16 runs directly between St Ives and Penzance while bus 300 takes the much longer route running along the coast to Penzance stopping en route at St Just and Lands End.

Wessex Trains *(website www.wessex trains.co.uk)* runs trains on the branch line between St Erth and St Ives.

Accommodation
St Ives Backpackers
St Ives Backpackers is a centrally located hostel in an old stone building. It is freshly painted and features the usual kitchen, TV lounge and Internet access plus a bar and a courtyard with a barbecue.
The Stennock, St Ives
☎ *(01736) 799 444*
Website *www.backpackers.co.uk/st-ives/index.htm*
Dorm bed *£10.95-15.95*
Credit cards *MC, Visa*
Reception open *Jan-May 10am-1pm & 5pm-10pm daily; Jun-Aug 10am-10pm daily; Sep-Dec 10am-1pm & 5pm-10pm daily*

Maintenance & cleanliness	★★★☆
Facilities	★★
Atmosphere & character	★★★
Security	★★☆
Overall rating	★★★☆

Sights
Barbara Hepworth Museum
Run as an extension of Tate St Ives, the Barbara Hepworth Museum features the artist's house and sculpture garden with exhibits of her artwork.
Barnoon Hill, St Ives
☎ *(01736) 796226*
Website *www.tate.org.uk/stives/hepworth.htm*
Admission *£4.50; joint admission with Tate St Ives £8.50*
Open *Jan-Feb Tue-Sun 10am-4.30pm; Mar-Oct 10am-5.30pm daily; Nov-Dec Tue-Sun 10am-4.30pm*

Tate St Ives
The St Ives branch of the Tate Gallery has exhibits of modern and contemporary art from both local and international artists.
Porthmeor Beach, St Ives
☎ *(01736) 796226*
Website *www.tate.org.uk/stives/*
Admission *£5.50; joint admission with Barbara Hepworth Museum £8.50*
Open *Jan-Feb Tue-Sun 10am-4.30pm; Mar-Oct 10am-5.30pm daily; Nov-Dec Tue-Sun 10am-4.30pm*

Newquay
England's surfing Mecca is hugely popular with backpackers and surfers and it has developed a good infrastructure to cater to surfing backpackers with a large selection of hostels, backpacker pubs and surf schools. However Newquay is also a tacky ugly town that is very unlike the rest of Cornwall and it is best avoided if you're not a surfer.

Practical Information
Tourist Information Centre
Marcus Hill, Newquay
☎ *(01637) 854 020*
Website *www.newquay.co.uk*
Open *Mon-Fri 9.30am-4.30pm, Sat 9.30am-12.30pm*

Coming & Going
First *(website www.firstgroup.com)* runs buses to destinations in Cornwall and Devon with services that include 21 and 21B to St Austell, buses X89 and X90 to Falmouth and bus X10 to Exeter.

Wessex Trains *(website www.wessex trains.co.uk)* runs trains on the branch line between Par and Newquay with connections from Plymouth and Penzance.

Accommodation
Note that accommodation prices in Newquay are very seasonal. The cheapest period is between October and April (except the Christmas/New Year period) and July and August is the most expensive time to stay here.

The Escape
This big new hostel features a bar with a 6am licence and a TV lounge with a massive cinema screen. It has been recently renovated and has brand new showers.
1 Mount Wise, Newquay
☎ *(01637) 873 387*
Website *www.escape2newquay.co.uk*
Dorm bed *£18-25; price includes breakfast*
Credit cards *MC, Visa*
Open *Mar-Nov*

Maintenance & cleanliness	★★★★
Facilities	★★☆
Atmosphere & character	★★★
Security	★★☆
Overall rating	★★★

Fistral Backpackers

This popular surfers' hostel is wallpapered with pictures from surfing magazines and features two TV lounges (one with a pool table) and a library of around 100 surfing magazines.
18 Headland Road, Newquay
☎ *(01637) 873 146*
Website *www.fistralbackpackers.co.uk*
Dorm bed *£7-15; double/twin room £16-33*
Reception open *7am-midnight*
📺🍳

Maintenance & cleanliness	★★☆
Facilities	★
Atmosphere & character	★★★★
Security	★
Overall rating	★★

Home Surf Lodge

Home Surf Lodge is a clean and well-maintained hostel near Fistral Beach that features a fully equipped kitchen and bar with a big flat screen TV.
18 Tower Road, Newquay
☎ *(01637) 873 387*
Website *www.homesurflodge.co.uk*
Dorm bed *summer £17.50-22, winter £12-15; during summer price includes breakfast*
Credit cards *MC, Visa*
📺🍳🍺

Maintenance & cleanliness	★★★★
Facilities	★★☆
Atmosphere & character	★★★★
Security	★★☆
Overall rating	★★★

Matt's Surf Lodge

Matt's Surf Lodge is a friendly hostel with a laid back atmosphere. It has a good TV lounge and pool table plus a good kitchen.
110 Mount Wise, Newquay
☎ *(01637) 874 651*
Website *www.mattssurflodge.co.uk*
Dorm bed *£8-15; double room £25-40; prices include breakfast*
Reception open *8.30am-11pm daily*
🚗📺🍳

Maintenance & cleanliness	★★★
Facilities	★★
Atmosphere & character	★★★★
Security	★★☆
Overall rating	★★★

Newquay Backpackers International

This hostel features brightly painted dorms, a fully equipped kitchen with new appliances and a cosy lounge that's wallpapered with maps. It has a great social atmosphere and is a fun place to stay.
69-73 Tower Road, Newquay
☎ *(01637) 879 366*
Website *www.backpackers.co.uk/newquay/*
Dorm bed *£8.95-14.95 (£8.50-14.20 VIP);* **double room** *£25.90-37.90 (£24.60-36 VIP);* **twin room** *£19.90-31.90 (£18.90-30.30 VIP)*
Credit cards *MC, Visa*
Reception open *10am-1pm & 5pm-10pm daily*
📺🍳🍺

Maintenance & cleanliness	★★★
Facilities	★★
Atmosphere & character	★★★★★
Security	★
Overall rating	★★★

Original Backpackers

The Original Backpackers is a great little hostel with a good kitchen, TV lounge and another lounge with a big fireplace. It doesn't look like much from the street but it is much nicer inside and it has a good atmosphere.
16 Beachfield Avenue, Newquay
☎ *(01637) 874 668*
Website *www.originalbackpackers.co.uk*
Dorm bed *£8-17*
📺🍳🍺

Maintenance & cleanliness	★★★
Facilities	★★☆
Atmosphere & character	★★★★☆
Security	★
Overall rating	★★★☆

SAFI Bunkhouse

The SAFI Bunkhouse offers budget accommodation in double, twin and dormitory rooms above a bar and café. In most cases you aren't put in a room with people you don't know so it doesn't

really have that communal hostel-style atmosphere.
Narrowcliff Seafront, Newquay
☎ *(01637) 872 8000*
Website www.mysafi.com
Dorm bed £15-25; ***double room*** *£30-50; prices include breakfast*
Credit cards MC, Visa
Reception open summer 8am-6pm daily; winter 9am-6pm daily; check in at the bar when the reception is closed

Maintenance & cleanliness	★★★
Facilities	★
Atmosphere & character	★★☆
Security	★★★☆
Overall rating	★★

St Christopher's Inn
St Christopher's is located above Belushi's Bar near the town centre and many rooms have views of Towan Beach. It features a chill out room under the bar, which has a pool table and TVs and there is a hot tub out the back. Like other St Christopher's hostels, it doesn't have a kitchen.
35 Fore Street, Newquay
☎ *(020) 7407 1856*
Website www.st-christophers.co.uk
Dorm bed £13-22; ***twin room*** *£42.50-51; prices include breakfast*
Credit cards MC, Visa

Maintenance & cleanliness	★★★
Facilities	★★
Atmosphere & character	★★★★☆
Security	★★★
Overall rating	★★★

The Zone
This hostel is in an old building near Fistral Beach that boasts lovely views of the golf course and the Cornish Coast. It has a large proportion of double and twin rooms making it a good option for couples travelling together. However the hostel could be better maintained and the kitchen was filthy.
Headland Road, Newquay
☎ *(01637) 872 089*
Website www.backpackers.co.uk/zone
Dorm bed £9.95-13.95; ***single room*** *£15.95-24.95;* ***double room*** *£27.90-51.90;* ***twin room*** *£25.90-47.90; prices include breakfast*
Credit cards MC, Visa
Reception open 9.30am-1pm & 5pm-9.30pm daily

Maintenance & cleanliness	★★☆
Facilities	★☆
Atmosphere & character	★★★
Security	★★★☆
Overall rating	★★☆

Surfing
Newquay has some of Europe's best surf with a choice of beaches that includes the famous Fistral Beach.

There are several surf schools in Newquay that include:

ESF Surf School
The Esplanade, South Fistral, Newquay
☎ *(01637) 851 800*
Website www.englishsurfschool.com
Lessons cost £25

King Surf School
King, Surfside stores, Mawgan Porth, Newquay
☎ *(01637) 860 091*
Website www.kingsurf.co.uk
½ day lesson £20; ***full day lesson*** *£30*

Sights
Blue Reef Aquarium
This aquarium on Towan Beach features a walk-through aquarium with tropical and Cornish marine life.
Towan Promenade, Newquay
☎ *(01637) 878134*
Website www.bluereefaquarium.co.uk
Admission £5.95 (£4.95 students)
Open Jan-Feb 10am-4pm daily; Mar-Oct 10am-5pm daily; Nov-Dec 10am-4pm daily

Newquay Zoo
Newquay's zoo features a range of exotic animals including pigmy marmosets, macaques, meerkats, penguins and zebras.
Edgcumbe Avenue, Trenance Gardens, Newquay
☎ *(01637) 873342*
Website www.newquayzoo.co.uk
Admission £6.95 (£5.45 students)
Open Jan-Mar 10am-dusk daily; Apr-Oct 9.30am-6pm daily; Nov-Dec 10am-dusk daily

Tintagel

This small village is steeped in legend and it has many close links with the King Arthur stories.

Practical Information
Tintagel Tourist Information Centre
Bossiney Road, Tintagel
☎ *(01840) 779 084*
Open *Jan-Feb 10.30am-4pm daily; Mar-Oct 9am-5pm daily; Nov-Dec 10.30am-4pm daily*

Sights
Tintagel Castle
Overlooking a rugged and spectacular coastline, this 13th-century castle is linked with many legends and many people believe it to be the birthplace of King Arthur.
Tintagel Head, Tintagel
🚌 *X10*
☎ *(01840) 770 328*
Website *www.english-heritage.org.uk*
Admission *£3.70*
Open *Jan-Mar 10am-4pm daily; Apr-Sep 10am-6pm daily; Oct 10am-5pm daily; Nov-Dec 10am-4pm daily*

Bude

This town near the Devon border in northern Cornwall has lovely coastal scenery and good surfing. Because of its close proximity to both Cornwall and Devon, many backpackers travelling by car use it as a base for making daytrips into the neighbouring counties.

Practical Information
Tourist Information Centre
The Crescent, Bude
☎ *(01288) 354240*
Website *www.visitbude.info*
Open *May-Sep Mon-Sat 10am-5pm, Sun 10am-4pm*

Coming & Going
First ***(website*** *www.firstgroup.com)* buses 319 and 372 go to Barnstaple, X8 goes to Plymouth, X9 goes to Exeter, X11 runs between Bude and Camelford, where you can transfer to the X10 to Newquay.

Accommodation
Northshore Bude Backpackers
Northshore Bude Backpackers is a brilliant hostel in a big house on a residential street near the town centre. It has very good facilities that include a fully equipped kitchen; Internet access, a big dining room and a good TV lounge. Everything here is maintained to a high standard and it has a great friendly atmosphere.
57 Killerton Road, Bude
☎ *(01288) 354 256*
Website *www.northshorebude.com*
Dorm bed *£12-14;* ***single room*** *£20;* ***double room*** *£30*
Reception open *8am-10pm daily*

Maintenance & cleanliness	★★★★½
Facilities	★★★☆
Atmosphere & character	★★★★½
Security	★★☆
Overall rating	★★★★½

Heart of England

Berkshire

Easily accessible from London, Berkshire is home to several top attractions that make an ideal daytrip from the capital.

Windsor & Eton

Windsor and the neighbouring town of Eton are a popular day trip from London. The main attraction is Windsor Castle where the Queen lives for six weeks each year as well as the posh Eton College, founded by Henry VI, and widely regarded as the country's most prestigious school.

Practical Information
Windsor Tourist Information Centre
24 High Street, Windsor
☎ *(01753) 743 900*
Website www.windsor.gov.uk
Open Jan-Apr Mon-Fri 10am-4pm, Sat 10am-5pm, Sun 10am-4pm; May-Jun 10am-5pm daily; Jul-Aug Mon-Fri 9.30am-6pm, Sat 10am-5.30pm, Sun 10am-5pm; Sep Mon-Sat 10am-5pm, Sun 10am-4pm; Oct-Dec Mon-Fri 10am-4pm, Sat 10am-5pm, Sun 10am-4pm

Coming & Going
BUS
Green Line (*website www.greenline.co.uk*) bus routes 700, 701 and 702 run between London and Windsor.

TRAIN
Windsor has two train stations – Windsor and Eton Central station and Windsor Riverside – both stations are centrally located near Windsor Castle and the town centre. South West Trains (*website www.swtrains.co.uk*) run between London (Waterloo) and Riv-

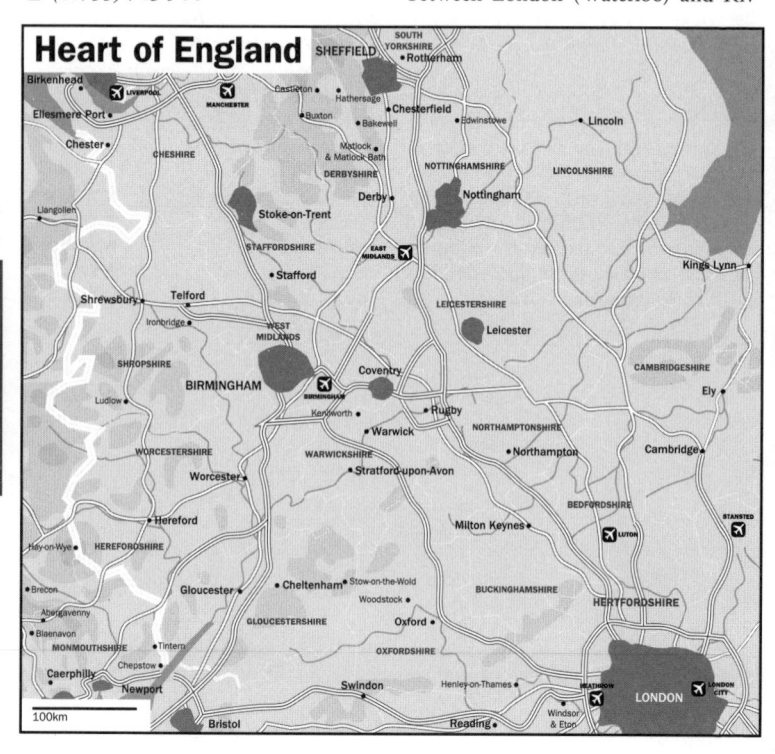

erside station and First Great Western Link *(website www.thamestrains.co.uk)* runs between London (Paddington) and Windsor and Eton Central station.

Sights
Eton College
In 1440 Henry VI founded Eton College and today it is widely regarded as the country's most prestigious school. Many famous people including much of the royal family have been educated here.
☎ *(01753) 671 177*
Website *www.etoncollege.com*
Admission *£3.80; tours £4.90*
Open *27 Mar-20 Apr 10.30am-4.30pm daily; 21 Apr-2 Jul 2pm-4.30pm daily; 3 Jul-7 Sep 10.30am-4.30pm daily; 8 Sep-3 Oct 2pm-4.30pm daily*

Legoland
The English branch of Denmark's Legoland theme park is one of the most popular new attractions, particularly for families with kids. It features over 50 rides but the main attractions are the Lego models that have been constructed from over 46.5 million Lego bricks. It has over 800 model buildings include many European landmarks.
Winkfield Road, Windsor
🚌 *Legoland shuttle bus from central Windsor*
☎ *0870 5040404*
Website *www.legoland.co.uk*
Admission *£21-23, £18.90-20.70 if booked in advance online*
Open *20 Mar-2 Apr 10am-5pm daily; 3-19 Apr 10am-5pm daily; 20 Apr-28 May 10am-5pm daily; 29 May-6 Jun 10am-6pm daily; 7 Jun-9 Jul 10am-5pm daily; 10 Jul-31 Aug 10am-7pm daily; 2 Sep-20 Oct Mon 10am-5pm, Thu-Fri 10am-5pm, Sat-Sun 10am-6pm; 21-31 Oct 10am-6pm daily*

Windsor Castle
The world's oldest and largest inhabited castle is easily Windsor's star attraction and one of the most popular day trips from London. The whole complex covers five hectares and includes the royal palace, which is used regularly by the royal family, and St George's Chapel, where Henry VIII is buried. Some of the castle's highlights include paintings by Canaletto, Rembrandt and Van Dyck; Henry VIII's armour; the bullet that killed Admiral Lord Nelson; and the amazing Queen Mary's Dolls' House, which took 1,550 craftspeople three years to build.
Thames Street, Windsor
🚉 *Windsor Royal*
☎ *(020) 7321 2233*
Website *www.royal.gov.uk*
Admission *£11.50 (£9.50 students)*
Open *Jan-Feb 9.45am-3pm daily; Mar-Oct 9.45am-4pm daily; Nov-Dec 9.45am-3pm daily*

Oxfordshire

Henley-on-Thames
Henley is home to the famous Henley Royal Regatta (29 Jun-3 Jul 2005). At other times of the year you can learn about the regatta's history at the River & Rowing Museum.

Practical Information
Henley-on-Thames Tourist Information Centre
King's Arms Barn
Kings Road, Henley-on-Thames
☎ *(01491) 578 034*
Open *Mon-Sat 10am-5pm*

Coming & Going
Henley on Thames is accessible by hourly train services from London (Paddington Station). Bus X39 runs hourly between Henley and Oxford.

Sights
River & Rowing Museum
This museum features exhibits about the history of rowing and the world famous Henley Regatta. There are also galleries devoted to Kenneth Grahame's *Wind in the Willows* that use models and audio-visual displays to bring alive the world of Badger, Mole, Toad and Ratty.
Mill Meadows, Henley on Thames
☎ *(01491) 415 600*
Website *www.rrm.co.uk*
Admission *£3 (£2.50 students);*

including entrance to the Wind & the Willows galleries £6 (£5 students)
Open *Jan-Apr 10am-5pm daily; May-Aug 10am-5.30pm daily; Sep-Dec 10am-5pm daily*

Oxford

Oxford is famous for its university, which is one of the world's oldest and most prestigious. The university is divided into 39 colleges and between them it has educated five kings, 25 British prime ministers, 40 Nobel Prize winners and many notable writers including CS Lewis, JRR Tolkien and Oscar Wilde. It is a bustling city with a youthful vibe that isn't dampened by the throngs of tourists that pass through town each day.

Practical Information
Oxford Tourist Information Centre
15-16 Broad Street, Oxford
☎ *(01865) 726 871*
Website *www.visitoxford.org*
Open *Mon-Sat 9.30am-5pm, Sun 10am-3.30pm*

Coming & Going
BUS
Several bus companies operate frequent services between London and Oxford. These include National Express, the Oxford Bus Company, the Oxford Tube and Megabus *(website www.megabus.co.uk)*. The competition between bus companies makes Oxford one of the cheapest excursions from London.

Megabus *(website www.megabus.com)* has several express buses a day to London with prices between £1 and £3 (plus 50p booking fee). Megabus departs from the Oxpens Coach Park on Oxpens Road next to the Ice Rink (which is accessible by walking up Queen Street from the city centre) and outside The Taylorian at St Giles, which is round the corner from the Ashmolean Museum and across the road from the Randolph Hotel. Their London terminus is outside the Allsop Arms near the corner of Gloucester Place and Marylebone Road *(🚇 Baker Street, Marylebone 🚆 Marylebone)*.

The Oxford Espress *(☎ (01865) 785 400; website www.oxfordbus.co.uk)* links London (Victoria Coach Station) with Oxford (Gloucester Green) daytime departures are every 20 minutes. This bus costs £9 one-way (£7 students); £11 day/next day return (£8 students); £13 three-month return (£10 students). A day/next day return costs £7 (£5 students) if you buy your ticket after 3pm. The Oxford Bus Company also runs the X70 bus between Oxford and Heathrow Airport and the X80 between Oxford and Gatwick Airport.

The Oxford Tube *(website www.stagecoach-oxford.co.uk/oxfordtube/)* has very frequent bus services linking Oxford with London. Oxford Tube fares are £9 one-way, £11 day return and £13 return. They stop at several locations in Oxford including High Street and St Clement's and their London terminus is on Buckingham Palace Road *(🚇🚆 Victoria)* with stops on Bayswater Road *(🚇 Notting Hill Gate)* and on Park Lane near Marble Arch *(🚇 Marble Arch)*.

TRAIN
First Great Western Link *(website www.firstgreatwestern.co.uk/link/home/index.php)* has frequent trains linking Oxford with London (Paddington) and Stratford-upon-Avon. Virgin Trains *(website www.virgintrains.co.uk)* connect Oxford with Birmingham, Brighton, Bournemouth, Northern England and Scotland.

The train station is conveniently located at the western edge of the city next the YHA hostel and just a short walk from the backpackers' hostel.

Local Transport
The Oxford Bus Company *(website www.oxfordbus.co.uk)* and Stagecoach *(website www.stagecoachbus.co.uk)* both operate local bus services in Oxford. Competition between the two bus operators keeps prices low and services competitive although you cannot use one company's pass on the other's buses.

Accommodation
Oxford Backpackers
This funky hostel has a small TV lounge and bar near the reception. It is

a bit worn around the edges but it has a good atmosphere. It's located midway between the train station and the city centre.
9a Hythe Bridge Street, Oxford
🚌 *Oxford Bus 2A, 2B, 4, 4A, 4B, 4C, 5, 10C, 10D, 400; Stagecoach 10, 10A, 11, 20, 44, 63, 66, X5, X31*
☎ *(01865) 721 761*
Website *www.hostels.co.uk*
Dorm bed *£13-14*
Credit cards *MC, Visa*
Reception open *8am-midnight*
📺 🇰 🇱 🛄

Maintenance & cleanliness	★★★½
Facilities	★★½
Atmosphere & character	★★★★★
Security	★★★½
Overall rating	★★★

Oxford YHA

This big new purpose-built hostel by the train station is a flash place with several lounges, a library, a small kitchen and a nice outdoor area. Accommodation is of a high standard and everything is clean and new.

2A Botley Road, Oxford
🚌 *Oxford Bus 2A, 2B, 4, 4A, 4B, 4C, 5, 10C, 10D, 400; Stagecoach 10, 10A, 11, 20, 44, 63, 66, X5, X31*
☎ *(01865) 727 182*
Website *www.yha.org.uk*
Dorm bed *£22.50 (£20.50 HI/YHA);*
twin room *£50 (£46 HI/YHA); prices include breakfast*
Credit cards *MC, Visa*
Reception open *7am-11pm daily*
🚌 📺 🇰 🇱

Maintenance & cleanliness	★★★★★
Facilities	★★
Atmosphere & character	★★★½
Security	★★★★
Overall rating	★★★★½

Sights
Ashmolean Museum

Open in 1683, the Ashmolean Museum is regarded as Britain's finest museum outside London. It's treasures include sketches by Michelangelo and paintings by Da Vinci, Manet, Monet, Matisse and Van Gogh.
Beaumont Street, Oxford

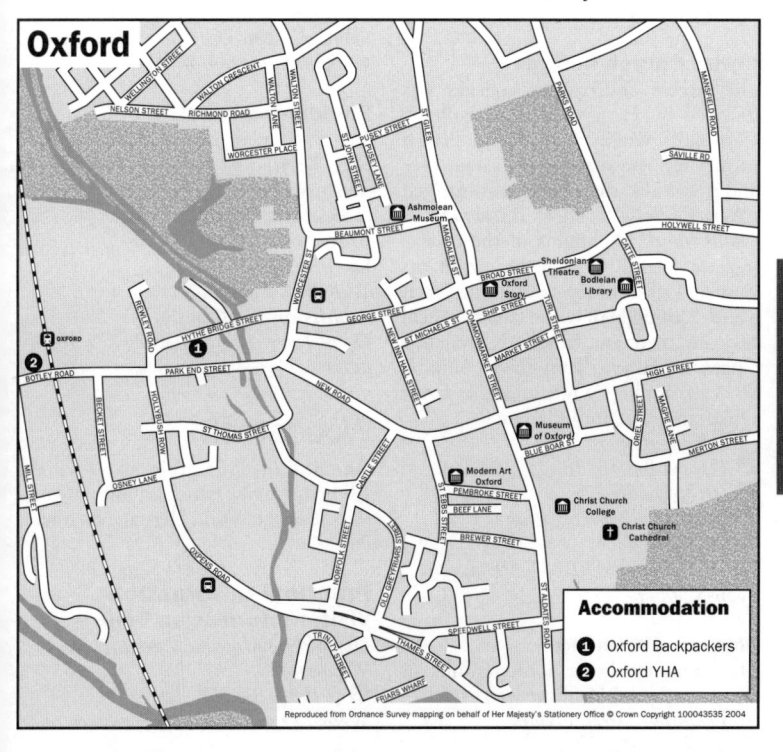

☎ (01865) 278 000
Admission free
Open Tue-Sat 10am-5pm, Sun 2pm-5pm

Bodleian Library
One of Europe's oldest libraries has been an important part of Oxford University since 1488. One-hour tours of the medieval library include a visit to the 17th century Convocation House and Court, which was the seat of parliament during the Civil War.
Catte Street, Oxford
☎ *(01865) 277 224*
Website www.bodley.ox.ac.uk
Tours cost £4
Open Mon-Fri 9am-4.45pm, Sat 9am-12.30pm

Carfax Tower
Great views over Oxford reward those who climb the 99 steps to the tower of the 14th-century Church of St Martin.
Carfax, Oxford
☎ *(01865) 792 653*
Admission £1.40
Open 10am-5pm daily

Christ Church College
The largest of Oxford's colleges was founded by Henry VIII and built by Cardinal Wolsey. Thirteen British prime ministers were educated here and it was also the college that inspired Lewis Carroll's *Alice's Adventures in Wonderland*. Highlights of the college include Oxford's cathedral with its vaulted 15th-century ceiling; the Great Tudor Dining Hall where Charles I held his parliament and Elizabeth I watched a play; the famous Tom Tower, built by Sir Christopher Wren and the Great Quadrangle, Oxford's largest.
St Aldgates, Oxford
🚌 Oxford Bus 16, 18, 35, 35A, X3
☎ *(01865) 286 573*
Website www.chch.ox.ac.uk
Admission £4
Open Mon-Sat 9.30am-5.30pm, Sun noon-5.30pm

Modern Art Oxford
This museum hosts a programme of temporary exhibits of modern art.
30 Pembroke Street, Oxford
☎ *(01865) 722 733*
Website www.modernartoxford.org.uk
Admission free
Open Tue-Sat 10am-5pm, Sun noon-5pm

Museum of Oxford
This museum recounts the history of the city and the university and it also hosts a programme of temporary exhibitions.
St Aldates, Oxford
☎ *(01865) 252761*
Website www.oxford.gov.uk/museum
Admission £2
Open Tue-Fri 10am-4pm, Sat 10am-5pm, Sun noon-4pm

The Oxford Story
This popular museum provides an insight into the city and its famous university.
Broad Street, Oxford
☎ *(01865) 728 822*
Website www.oxfordstory.co.uk
Admission £6.95
Open Jan-Jun Mon-Sat 10am-4.30pm, Sun 11am-4.30pm; Jul-Aug 9.30am-5pm daily; Sep-Dec Mon-Sat 10am-4.30pm, Sun 11am-4.30pm

Sheldonian Theatre
The Sheldonian is one of Sir Christopher Wren's first buildings, which was designed when he was an astronomy professor at Oxford.
Broad Street, Oxford
☎ *(01865) 277 299*
Website www.sheldon.ox.ac.uk
Admission £1.50
Open 10am-12.30pm & 2pm-4.30pm daily

Woodstock
Founded in 1163, this lovely village 13km north of Oxford is best known as the site of the World Heritage Blenheim Palace.

Practical Information
Visitor Information Centre
Oxfordshire Museum, Park Street, Woodstock
☎ *(01993) 813276*
Website www.wakeuptowoodstock.com

Coming & Going
Bus 20 (☎ *(01865) 772250*) runs between Oxford (Gloucester Green and the train station) and Woodstock. A day return costs £3.70.

Sights
Blenheim Palace
Sir John Vanbrugh designed the lavishly appointed Blenheim Palace in the baroque style and it is decked out with a collection of fine furniture, paintings, sculptures and tapestries. The palace was the birthplace of Sir Winston Churchill and there is an exhibition of his life and achievements.

This World Heritage Site also relates to the Battle of Blenheim in 1704 when John Churchill, Duke of Marlborough, saved Vienna and England from French rule.
A44 Evesham Road, Woodstock
☎ *20*
☎ *08700 602080*
Website *www.blenheimpalace.com*
Admission *£12.50 (£10 students); park & gardens £7.50 (£5.50 students)*
Open *9am-4.45pm daily*

Oxfordshire Museum
This museum has displays on Oxfordshire's history and culture and includes displays of Roman artefacts and the Stonesfield Carpet Textile Trail.
Park Street, Woodstock
☎ *(01993) 813276*
Open *Jan-Apr Tue-Fri 10am-4pm, Sat 10am-5pm, Sun 2pm-5pm; May-Sep Tue-Sat 10am-5pm, Sun 2pm-5pm; Oct-Dec Tue-Fri 10am-4pm, Sat 10am-5pm, Sun 2pm-5pm*

Gloucestershire

Stow-on-the-Wold
This "cute as a button" village in the heart of the Cotswolds boasts a lovely market square surrounded by old stone buildings.

It is home to one of the few hostels in Gloucestershire and it makes a good base for visiting Cheltenham and Gloucester.

Practical Information
Stow-on-the-Wold Tourist Information Centre
Hollis House, The Square, Stow-on-the-Wold
☎ *(01451) 831 082*
Open *Mon-Sat 9.30am-4.30pm*

Accommodation
Stow-on-the-Wold YHA
This small youth hostel is in an old stone building on the market square. It is a clean hostel with basic facilities that include the usual kitchen and TV lounge.
The Square, Stow-on-the-Wold
☎ *(01451) 830 497*
Website *www.yha.org.uk*
Dorm bed *£16 (£14 HI/YHA)*
Credit cards *MC, Visa*
Open *13 Feb-31 Oct every day; 1 Nov-18 Dec Fri-Sat; 27-31 Dec every day; reception open 7.30am-10am & 5pm-11pm daily*

Maintenance & cleanliness	★★★★½
Facilities	★★½
Atmosphere & character	★★★★½
Security	★★
Overall rating	★★★

Cheltenham
Cheltenham is an elegant spa town that makes a good base for visiting the Cotswold region.

Practical Information
Cheltenham Tourist Information Centre
77 Promenade, Cheltenham
☎ *(01242) 522 878*
Website *www.visitcheltenham.info*
Open *Mon-Tue 9.30am-5.15pm, Wed 10am-5.15pm, Thu-Sat 9.30am-5.15pm*

BUS
National Express (☎ *0870 580 8080; website www.nationalexpress.co.uk*) has buses to Birmingham, Bristol, Gloucester and London. The bus station is on Royal Wells Road in the town centre.

Stagecoach (***website*** *www.stagecoachbus.co.uk*) buses 10, 97, 98, N10 and X94 run between Cheltenham and Gloucester.

TRAIN
Cheltenham Spa station is at the corner of Gloucester and Queens Roads to the west of the city centre. There are frequent trains to Birmingham, Bristol, Gloucester, London (Paddington) and Penzance with services operated by First Great Western *(website www.firstgreatwestern.co.uk)*, Virgin Trains *(website www.virgintrains.co.uk)* and Wessex Trains *(website www.wessextrains.co.uk)*.

Local Transport
Cheltenham's local bus services are run by Stagecoach *(website www.stagecoachbus.co.uk)*. The most useful route is bus G, which runs between the train station and the town centre. This bus stops on High Street and St Georges Square in the town centre. Transfer tickets to any destination in Cheltenham cost £1.30 one way or £1.95 return.

Accommodation
Cheltenham YMCA
Cheltenham's YMCA offers basic accommodation in single rooms. Shared facilities include a TV lounge, table tennis table and a room with computers (but not Internet access). There's also a restaurant but there are no kitchen facilities other than a microwave in the TV lounge.
Vittoria Walk, Cheltenham
☎ *(01242) 524 024*
Single room *£19; price includes breakfast*
Credit cards *MC, Visa*
Reception open *Mon-Fri 7.30am-10pm, Sat-Sun 9am-10pm*

Maintenance & cleanliness	★★★★½
Facilities	★★
Atmosphere & character	★
Security	★★
Overall rating	★★★½

Sights
Cheltenham Art Gallery & Museum
Cheltenham's major museum features a variety of exhibits that cover local history, archaeology and art (including Dutch and Flemish paintings from the 17th and 19th-centuries).
Clarence Street, Cheltenham
🚌 *D, E*
☎ *(01242) 237 431*
Website *www.cheltenham.artgallery.museum*
Admission *free*
Open *Mon-Sat 10am-5.20pm, Sun 2pm-4.20pm*

Holst Birthplace Museum
Gustav Holst, who composed The Planets, was born here and his home has been made into a museum dedicated to his life and music.
4 Clarence Road, Cheltenham
☎ *(01242) 524 846*
Website *www.holstmuseum.org.uk*
Admission *£2.50*
Open *Tue-Sat 10am-4pm*

Gloucester
This city on the River Severn was once an important inland port. Its history goes back to Roman times when the city was a major provincial centre and its importance increased in the Norman period when William the Conqueror met here frequently; however in the Middle Ages the port began to decline as trade picked up in Bristol.

Nowadays Gloucester's waterways are popular with leisure craft travelling Britain's canal system and its historic docks have been revived with pubs, shops, cafés and the National Waterways Museum.

Practical Information
Gloucester Tourist Information Centre
28 Southgate Street, Gloucester
☎ *(01452) 396572*
Open *Jan-Jun Mon-Sat 10am-5pm; Jul-Aug Mon-Sat 10am-5pm, Sun 11am-3pm; Sep-Dec Mon-Sat 10am-5pm*

Coming & Going
BUS
National Express (☎ *0870 580 8080; website www.nationalexpress.co.uk*) buses go to Birmingham, Bristol and London. Stagecoach (*website www.stagecoachbus.co.uk*) buses 94 and X94 run between Cheltenham and Gloucester.

TRAIN

There are frequent trains to Birmingham, Bristol, Cheltenham, London (Paddington) and Penzance with services operated by First Great Western *(website www.firstgreatwestern.co.uk)*, Virgin Trains *(website www.virgintrains.co.uk)* and Wessex Trains *(website www.wessextrains.co.uk)*.

Accommodation

There are no hostels in Gloucester. The closest hostels are in Cheltenham and Stow-on-the-Wold.

Sights
Gloucester Cathedral

This beautiful cathedral features fan vaulted cloisters and the tomb of Edward II.
College Green, Gloucester
☎ *(01452) 528 095*
Website www.gloucestercathedral.uk.com
Admission £2.50 donation
Open summer 8am-6pm daily; winter 8am-5pm daily

Gloucester City Museum & Art Gallery

This museum has exhibits relating to Gloucestershire's history including dinosaur bones, Roman artefacts and the famous Birdlip mirror. The adjoining art gallery displays paintings by Gainsborough and Turner.
Brunswick Road, Gloucester
☎ *(01452) 396 131*
Website www.gloucester.gov.uk
Admission free
Open Tue-Sat 10am-5pm

Gloucester Folk Museum

Housed in a historic timber-framed Tudor building, this museum has displays on local history that include exhibits on the Port of Gloucester and the Civil War.
99-103 Westgate Street, Gloucester
☎ *(01452) 396 467*
Website www.gloucester.gov.uk
Admission free
Open Tue-Sat 10am-5pm

National Waterways Museum

Located on the historic Gloucester & Sharpness Canal, this museum recounts the 300-year history of Britain's canals and inland waterways. It features historic boats, hands-on exhibits and a floor dedicated to trade on the waterways.
Llanthony Warehouse, Gloucester Docks, Gloucester
☎ *(01452) 318054*
Website www.nwm.org.uk
Admission £5
Open 10am-5pm daily

Warwickshire

Shakespeare fans come to this county south of Birmingham to visit Stratford-upon-Avon but Warwickshire has several other attractions including Kenilworth and Warwick Castles.

Stratford-upon-Avon

In 1616 William Shakespeare was born in this lovely town of old Tudor-style buildings. The Shakespeare connection ensures that this is one of the most visited towns in the Midlands.

Practical Information
Stratford-upon-Avon Tourist Information Centre

Bridgefoot, Stratford-upon-Avon
☎ *0870 160 7930*
Website www.shakespeare-country.co.uk
Open Mon-Sat 9.30am-5pm

Coming & Going
BUS

Buses terminate at the Riverside Bus Station near Bridgeway Road.

National Express (☎ *0870 580 8080; website www.nationalexpress.co.uk)* buses connect Stratford with Birmingham, Cheltenham and London.

Stagecoach *(website www.stagecoachbus.co.uk)* buses go to destinations in Warwickshire and neighbouring counties. The most useful Stagecoach bus routes are X16 and X17, which go to Coventry, Kenilworth, Leamington Spa and Warwick.

TRAIN

Central Trains *(website www.centraltrains.co.uk)* run trains to Birmingham

(Moor Street and Snow Hill stations) and Warwick and First Great Western Link *(website www.firstgreatwestern. co.uk/link/home/index.php)* operates train services to Oxford and London (Paddington).

The Dayranger train pass is designed primarily for Birmingham and Coventry residents who want to make a day trip to nearby places like Stratford-upon-Avon but it can also be used to travel or make a daytrip north from Stratford. It costs £13.20 and gives you unlimited train travel after 9am on weekdays and all day on weekends in West Midlands county and parts of neighbouring counties. It lets you travel to Coventry, Crewe, Hereford, Leamington Spa, Northampton, Stafford, Stoke-on-Trent and Warwick.

Because of the lack of backpackers' accommodation in Birmingham, Coventry, Stoke and Warwick it can also be used to make a day trip into these cities from Stratford-upon-Avon.

Accommodation
Stratford-upon-Avon YHA
Stratford's youth hostel occupies a big white Georgian mansion on three acres of grounds about 3km outside Stratford-upon-Avon. It is popular with school groups and features the usual kitchen, TV lounge and Internet access.
Hemmingford House, Church Lane, Alveston, Stratford-upon-Avon
☎ *18, X18, 77*
☎ *(01789) 205 513*
Website *www.yha.org.uk*
Dorm bed *£20 (£19 HI/YHA);* ***double room*** *£50 (£46 HI/YHA);* ***twin room*** *£42 (£38 HI/YHA); prices include breakfast*
Credit cards *MC, Visa*
Reception open *7am-midnight*

Maintenance & cleanliness		★★★★½
Facilities		★★
Atmosphere & character		★★
Security		★★
Overall rating		★★★½

Sights
Most of Stratford's sights relate to William Shakespeare although the relationship can sometimes be rather distant. If you want to get the full Shakespeare experience then it is best to fork out the £13 for admission to all five Shakespeare properties or £10 (£8.70 HI/YHA) for the three properties in the town centre.

Anne Hathaway's Cottage
Shakespeare's wife, Anne Hathaway, lived in this thatched cottage 1.5km north of the town centre.
Shottery, Stratford-upon-Avon
☎ *(01789) 292100*
Website *www.shakespeare.org.uk*
Admission *£5.20; joint ticket to all five Shakespeare properties £13*
Open *Jan-Mar 10am-4pm daily; Apr-May Mon-Sat 9.30am-5pm, Sun 10am-5pm; Jun-Aug Mon-Sat 9am-5pm, Sun 9.30am-5pm; Sep-Oct Mon-Sat 9.30am-5pm, Sun 10am-5pm; Nov-Dec 10am-4pm daily*

Hall's Croft
This home of Shakespeare's daughter Susanna and her husband John Hall is a Tudor-style house in the old town that is furnished in the style of the early 17th-century.
Old Town, Stratford-upon-Avon
☎ *(01789) 292107*
Website *www.shakespeare.org.uk*
Admission *£3.50 (£3.50 HI/YHA); joint ticket to the three Shakespeare properties in town £10 (£8.70 HI/YHA); joint ticket to all five Shakespeare properties £13*
Open *Jan-Mar 11am-4pm daily; Apr-May 11am-5pm daily; Jun-Aug Mon-Sat 9.30am-5pm, Sun 10am-5pm; Sep-Oct 11am-5pm daily; Nov-Dec 11am-4pm daily*

Harvard House
The mother of the founder of Harvard University lived in this house, which is now a museum displaying 1500 years of British pewter history.
High Street, Stratford-upon-Avon
☎ *(01789) 204016*
Website *www.shakespeare.org.uk*
Admission *£2.50*
Open *29 May-4 Jul Wed & Sat-Sun noon-5pm; 7 Jul-5 Sep Wed-Sun noon-5pm; 8 Sep-31 Oct Wed & Sat-Sun noon-5pm*

Mary Arden's House & the Shakespeare Countryside Museum

Mary Arden, Shakespeare's mother, lived in this house 5km from the town centre. It now houses displays depicting country life in Shakespeare's time and it is also home to Rikki, the Snowy Owl that appeared in the Harry Potter films.

Wilmcote, 5km from Stratford-upon-Avon
☎ *(01789) 293 455*
Website *www.shakespeare.org.uk*
Admission *£5.70; joint ticket to all five Shakespeare properties £13*
Open *Jan-Mar Mon-Sat 10am-4pm, Sun 10.30am-4pm; Apr-May Mon-Sat 10am-5pm, Sun 10.30am-5pm; Jun-Aug Mon-Sat 9.30am-5pm, Sun 10am-5pm; Sep-Oct Mon-Sat 10am-5pm, Sun 10.30am-5pm; Nov-Dec Mon-Sat 10am-4pm, Sun 10.30am-4pm*

Nash's House & New Place

Shakespeare's granddaughter, Elizabeth Hall, and her husband, Thomas Nash, lived in this house in the town centre. The garden was the site of a house that William Shakespeare bought in 1597 and later retired and died in.

Henley Street, Stratford-upon-Avon
☎ *(01789) 292325*
Website *www.shakespeare.org.uk*
Admission *£3.50 (£3.40 HI/YHA); joint ticket to the three Shakespeare properties in town £10 (£8.70 HI/YHA); joint ticket to all five Shakespeare properties £13*
Open *Jan-Mar 11am-4pm daily; Apr-May 11am-5pm daily; Jun-Aug Mon-Sat 9.30am-5pm, Sun 10am-5pm; Sep-Oct 11am-5pm daily; Nov-Dec 11am-4pm daily*

Shakespeare's Birthplace

Shakespeare was born in this house right in the heart of the town centre, which has made this the most popular attraction in town.

Henley Street, Stratford-upon-Avon
☎ *(01789) 201823*
Website *www.shakespeare.org.uk*
Admission *£6.70 (£6 HI/YHA); joint ticket to the three Shakespeare properties in town £10 (£8.70 HI/YHA); joint ticket to all five Shakespeare properties £13*
Open *Jan-Mar Mon-Sat 10am-4pm, Sun 10.30am-4pm; Apr-May Mon-Sat 10am-5pm, Sun 10.30am-5pm; Jun-Aug Mon-Sat 9am-5pm, Sun 9.30am-5pm; Sep-Oct Mon-Sat 10am-5pm, Sun 10.30am-5pm; Nov-Dec Mon-Sat 10am-4pm, Sun 10.30am-4pm*

Teddy Bear Museum

Set in an Elizabethan house, Stratford's teddy bear museum has hundreds of teddy bears from around the world.

19 Greenhill Street, Stratford-upon-Avon
☎ *(01789) 293 160*
Website *www.theteddybearmuseum.com*
Admission *£2.50*
Open *9.30am-5.30pm daily*

Warwick

The small historic city of Warwick has an attractive town centre with Georgian and medieval architecture but it is best known for its castle.

Practical Information
Tourist Information Centre

The Court House, Jury Street, Warwick
☎ *(01926) 494837*
Open *9.30am-4.30pm daily*

Coming & Going
BUS

National Express (☎ *0870 580 8080; website www.nationalexpress.co.uk*) buses go to Birmingham, Coventry and Heathrow Airport.

Stagecoach (*website www.stagecoachbus.co.uk*) buses go to destinations in Warwickshire and neighbouring counties. Stagecoach buses X16 and X17 go to Stratford-upon-Avon, buses X16 and X18 go to Coventry and Kenilworth and buses 66, 75, 75a, 76, 76a, X16 and X18 go to Leamington Spa.

TRAIN

Warwick has two stations, Warwick station in the town centre and Warwick Parkway station near the M40 motorway, which is primarily used for park and ride services.

Central Trains *(website www.central-trains.co.uk)* runs trains from Warwick to Stratford-upon-Avon and Birmingham (Moor Street and Snow Hill stations), Chiltern Railways *(website www.chilternrailways.co.uk)* stop at Warwick Parkway on their route linking Birmingham (Moor Street and Snow Hill stations) and London (Marylebone station). First Great Western Link *(website www.firstgreatwestern.co.uk/link/home/index.php)* run trains from Warwick to Oxford and London (Paddington).

Accommodation
There is no hostel in Warwick. The closest hostel is the YHA in Stratford-upon-Avon, which is on the bus route into Warwick.

Sights
Doll Museum
Warwick's Doll Museum features a large collection of dolls, teddies and toys.
Oken's House, Castle Street, Warwick
☎ *(01926) 495546*
Admission £1
Open *Jan-Easter Sat 10am-dusk; Easter-Oct Mon-Sat 10am-5pm, Sun 11am-5pm; No-Dec Sat 10am-dusk*

St John's House
This old 17th-century house has been restored to show how people lived in Victorian times.
St John's, Warwick
☎ *(01926) 412021*
Admission *free*
Open *Jan-Apr Tue-Sat 10am-5.30pm; May-Sep Tue-Sat 10am-5.30pm, Sun 2.30pm-5pm; Oct-Dec Tue-Sat 10am-5.30pm*

Warwick Castle
This magnificent castle sits on over 60 acres of grounds and is a short distance to the town centre. Visitors to the castle can see the imposing Great Hall, lavishly appointed rooms; the dungeon and torture chamber and can take in sweeping views from the towers and ramparts.
☎ *0870 442 2000*
Website *www.warwick-castle.co.uk*
Admission £11.50-14.50 (£8.75-10.75 students)

Open *Jan-Mar 10am-5pm daily; Apr-Jul 10am-6pm daily; Aug Mon-Fri 10am-6pm, Sat-Sun 10am-7pm; Sep 10am-6pm daily; Oct-Dec 10am-5pm daily*

Warwickshire Museum
This museum has exhibits on the history of Warwickshire and its highlights include the Sheldon tapestry map. Other attractions include the usual assortment of fossils, bugs and ancient jewellery. The museum also hosts a programme of temporary exhibits.
Market Place, Warwick
☎ *(01926) 412 500*
Admission *free*
Open *Jan-Apr Mon-Sat 10am-5.30pm; May-Sep Mon-Sat 10am-5.30pm, Sun 11am-5pm; Oct-Dec Mon-Sat 10am-5.30pm*

Kenilworth
Located around midway between Warwick and Coventry, Kenilworth is best known for the impressive Kenilworth Castle.

Coming & Going
Stagecoach *(website www.stagecoachbuses.co.uk)* buses X12, X14, X16, X17 and X18 stop at Kenilworth on the Coventry to Stratford upon Avon and Travel West Midlands *(website www.travelwm.co.uk)* buses 12 and 112 stop here between Coventry and Leamington Spa.

Sights
Kenilworth Castle
Kenilworth Castle was built 50 years after the Norman Conquest and it has witnessed many important events in English history. It was home to much of England's royalty and at least four kings have called the castle home. The castle sits amid countryside between Warwick and Coventry.
Kenilworth (8km north of Warwick)
🚌 *12, 112, X12, X14, X16, X17, X18*
☎ *(01926) 852078*
Admission £4.80
Open *Jan-Feb 10am-4pm daily; Mar-May 10am-5pm daily; Jun-Aug 10am-6pm daily; Sep-Oct 10am-5pm daily; Nov-Dec 10am-4pm daily*

Rugby

This town near Coventry is home to the prestigious school where the game of rugby was first played. The town's market takes place each Monday, Friday and Saturday.

Practical Information
Tourist Information Centre
4 Lawrence Sheriff Street, Rugby
☎ *(01788) 534 979*
Open *Mon-Sat 9.30am-5pm, Sun 10am-3pm*

Coming & Going
BUS
National Express (☎ *0870 580 8080; website www.nationalexpress.co.uk*) buses go to Coventry and London.

Stagecoach (**website** *www.stagecoach bus.co.uk*) buses go to destinations in Warwickshire and neighbouring counties. Useful routes include buses 86 and 87 to Coventry and bus X40 to Leicester.

TRAIN
Central Trains (**website** *www.central trains.co.uk*) have frequent services into Birmingham (New Street) and Silverlink Trains (**website** *www.silverlink-trains.com*) go to Birmingham (New Street), Coventry, London (Euston) and Milton Keynes.

Sights
Rugby School Museum
This historic school educated several notable writers including Lewis Carroll and Salman Rushdie, although it is best known as the birthplace of rugby. The Rugby School Museum has exhibits about the Rugby and the game that originated here.
10 Little Church Street, Rugby
☎ *(01788) 556 109*

West Midlands

Birmingham

England's second-largest city is overlooked by most backpackers – partly because it has no hostels and also because of its reputation as a dull industrial centre. However the city is surprisingly vibrant with excellent shopping, great nightlife and some good attractions. Unfortunately a network of busy ring roads divides the city centre, which intimidates many first-time visitors.

Practical Information
ICC Tourism Centre
The Mall, The ICC, Broad Street, Birmingham
☎ *(0121) 616 1038*
Website *www.beinbirmingham.com*
Open *Mon-Sat 9.30am-5.30pm, Sun 10.30am-4.30pm*

The Tourism Centre
The Rotunda, 150 New Street, Birmingham
☎ *(0121) 202 5099*
Website *www.beinbirmingham.com*
Open *Mon-Sat 9.30am-5.30pm, Sun 10.30am-4.30pm*

The Welcome Centre
128 New Street, Birmingham
☎ *(0121) 202 5099*
Website *www.beinbirmingham.com*
Open *Mon-Sat 9am-6pm, Sun 10am-4pm*

Coming & Going
AIR
Birmingham International Airport (☎ *0870 733 511; website www.bhx.co.uk*) is a busy regional airport with around 50 airlines flying to over 100 destinations. It is a regional base for British Airways (**website** *www.britishairways.com*) and budget airline MyTravel Lite (**website** *www.mytravellite.com*) is based here. The airport is served by frequent train connections into Birmingham and Coventry. Trains between the airport and Birmingham New Street take 20 minutes and cost £3.10 although Centrocards and Daytripper travel passes are also valid.

BUS
Birmingham is enjoys excellent bus connections. National Express is headquartered here, Megabus run cheap buses to London and there are plenty of local bus services to neighbouring counties.

Megabus *(website www.megabus.com)* has several express buses a day to London with prices between £1 and £6 (plus 50p booking fee). Megabus departs from on Snow Hill, Queensway, near Colmore Circus and Snow Hill Station. Their London terminus is the Greenline Coach Station (*Victoria*).

National Express (☎ *0870 580 8080; website www.nationalexpress.co.uk*) has frequent bus services to most parts of the country including an hourly service to London. National Express coaches terminate at Digbeth Coach Station on Digbeth High Street about a 10-minute walk south of the city centre.

TRAIN

Birmingham has three main train stations with most mainline train services using the busy New Street station. New Street handles trains to Liverpool (Lime Street), London (Euston), Manchester (Piccadilly), Nottingham and Oxford while trains to Stratford-upon-Avon and Warwick and Chiltern Railways'

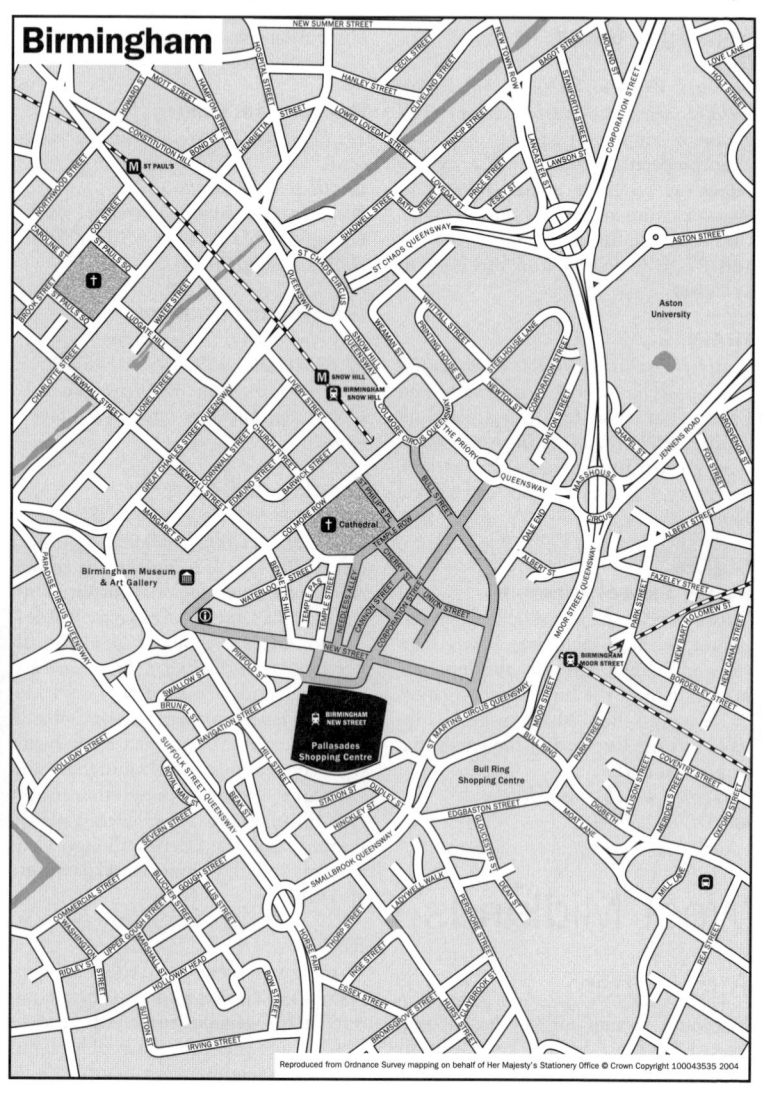

(website www.chilternrailways.co.uk) trains to London (Marylebone) use Snow Hill and Moor Street Stations.

The Dayranger train pass is a good deal if you want to make a daytrip out of Birmingham. It costs £13.20 and gives you unlimited train travel after 9am on weekdays and all day on weekends in West Midlands county and parts of neighbouring counties. It lets you travel as far as Coventry, Crewe, Hereford, Leamington Spa, Northampton, Stafford, Stoke-on-Trent, Stratford-upon-Avon and Warwick.

Because of the lack of backpackers' accommodation in Birmingham it can also be used to make a day trip into the city from Stratford-upon-Avon.

Local Transport

Centro (website www.centro.org.uk) organises Birmingham's public transport system, which is comprised of buses, a metro and suburban trains.

BUS

Buses are run by Travel West Midlands (website www.travelwm.co.uk) and several other companies that provide a good bus service in the Birmingham area and throughout West Midlands county.

One-way bus fares range from 70p to £1 and bus travel is included with several travel passes.

METRO

The one line metro (website www.midlandmetro.co.uk) runs between the city centre and Wolverhampton. In central Birmingham it stops at Snow Hill, St Pauls and Jewellery Quarter stations but once it leaves the city centre it runs along the street like a tram. One-way fares cost between 60p and £2.20. There are several travel passes (see below) that cover travel on the metro.

TRAIN

Birmingham has a good suburban rail network that is comprised of eight train lines. The train is a good way to get to places like the Formule 1 hotel at Bordesley, the Jewellery Quarter, Cadbury World in Bourneville and the Barber Institute at the University. The train is also the quickest way to Birmingham International Airport and Coventry.

TRAVEL PASSES

Birmingham's transport system is divided into five zones. Most places of interest are within zones one and two, but you'll need a ticket valid to zone five if you want to get to the airport, Coventry or Wolverhampton.

Centrocard   Ⓜ Ⓑ Ⓡ

The Centrocard covers unlimited travel on virtually all buses (except night buses) and suburban trains within the specified zones. Centrocards that cover travel outside zones one and two also allow unlimited travel on the metro. The most useful ticket for most travellers is the all-zone one-day Centrocard, which costs £5.20; however if you're planning on spending longer in Birmingham then the one week and four week cards are better value.

Prices for one-week Centrocards are as follows:

Zones	Fare
1	£14.50
1-2	£15.50
1-3	£16.70
1-4	£18.20
1-5	£19.70
2-5	£16.70

There is also an off-peak Centrocard that gives you two weeks unlimited travel Mon-Fri 9.30am-3.30pm and after 6pm and all day on weekends. It covers bus, metro and train travel within West Midlands country and costs £14.50.

Railmaster   Ⓡ

The Railmaster allows unlimited use of the suburban train network for periods of either one, four or 52 weeks. Prices for one-week Railmasters are as follows:

Zones	Fare
1	£6.30
1-2	£6.90
1-3	£11.70
1-4	£14.30
1-5	£15.80
2-5	£11.70

Birmingham Transport

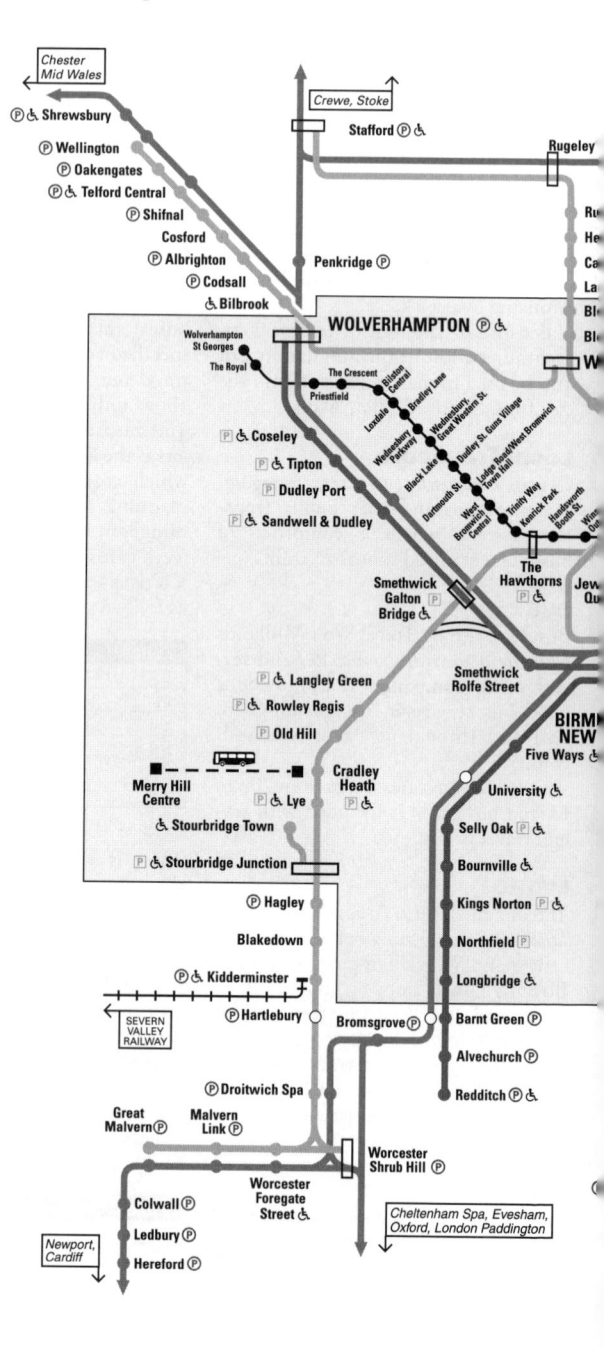

Chester / Mid Wales ←

- Ⓟ & Shrewsbury
- Ⓟ Wellington
- Ⓟ Oakengates
- Ⓟ & Telford Central
- Ⓟ Shifnal
- Cosford
- Ⓟ Albrighton
- Ⓟ Codsall
- & Bilbrook

Crewe, Stoke ↑

- Stafford Ⓟ &
- Penkridge Ⓟ
- Rugeley
- Ru...
- He...
- Ca...
- La...
- Bl...
- Bl...
- W...

WOLVERHAMPTON Ⓟ &

Wolverhampton St Georges — The Royal — Priestfield — Loxdale — Bilston Central — Dudley Lane — Wednesbury Parkway — Wednesbury Great Western St. — Black Lake — Dudley St. Guns Village — Dartmouth St. — Lodge Road/West Bromwich Town Hall — West Bromwich Central — Trinity Way — Kenrick Park — Handsworth Booth St. — Win... Oak...

- Ⓟ & Coseley
- Ⓟ & Tipton
- Ⓟ Dudley Port
- Ⓟ & Sandwell & Dudley
- Smethwick Galton Bridge Ⓟ &
- The Hawthorns Ⓟ &
- Jew... Qu...
- Ⓟ & Langley Green
- Ⓟ & Rowley Regis
- Ⓟ Old Hill
- Merry Hill Centre
- Cradley Heath
- Smethwick Rolfe Street
- Ⓟ & Lye
- & Stourbridge Town
- Ⓟ & Stourbridge Junction

BIRM... NEW...

- Five Ways &
- University &
- Selly Oak Ⓟ &
- Bournville &
- Kings Norton Ⓟ &
- Northfield Ⓟ
- Longbridge &
- Ⓟ Hagley
- Blakedown
- Ⓟ & Kidderminster
- Ⓟ Hartlebury
- ← SEVERN VALLEY RAILWAY
- Bromsgrove Ⓟ
- Barnt Green Ⓟ
- Alvechurch Ⓟ
- Redditch Ⓟ &
- Ⓟ Droitwich Spa
- Great Malvern Ⓟ
- Malvern Link Ⓟ
- Worcester Foregate Street &
- Worcester Shrub Hill Ⓟ
- Colwall Ⓟ
- Ledbury Ⓟ
- Hereford Ⓟ

Newport, Cardiff ↓

Cheltenham Spa, Evesham, Oxford, London Paddington ↓

Heart of England – Birmingham

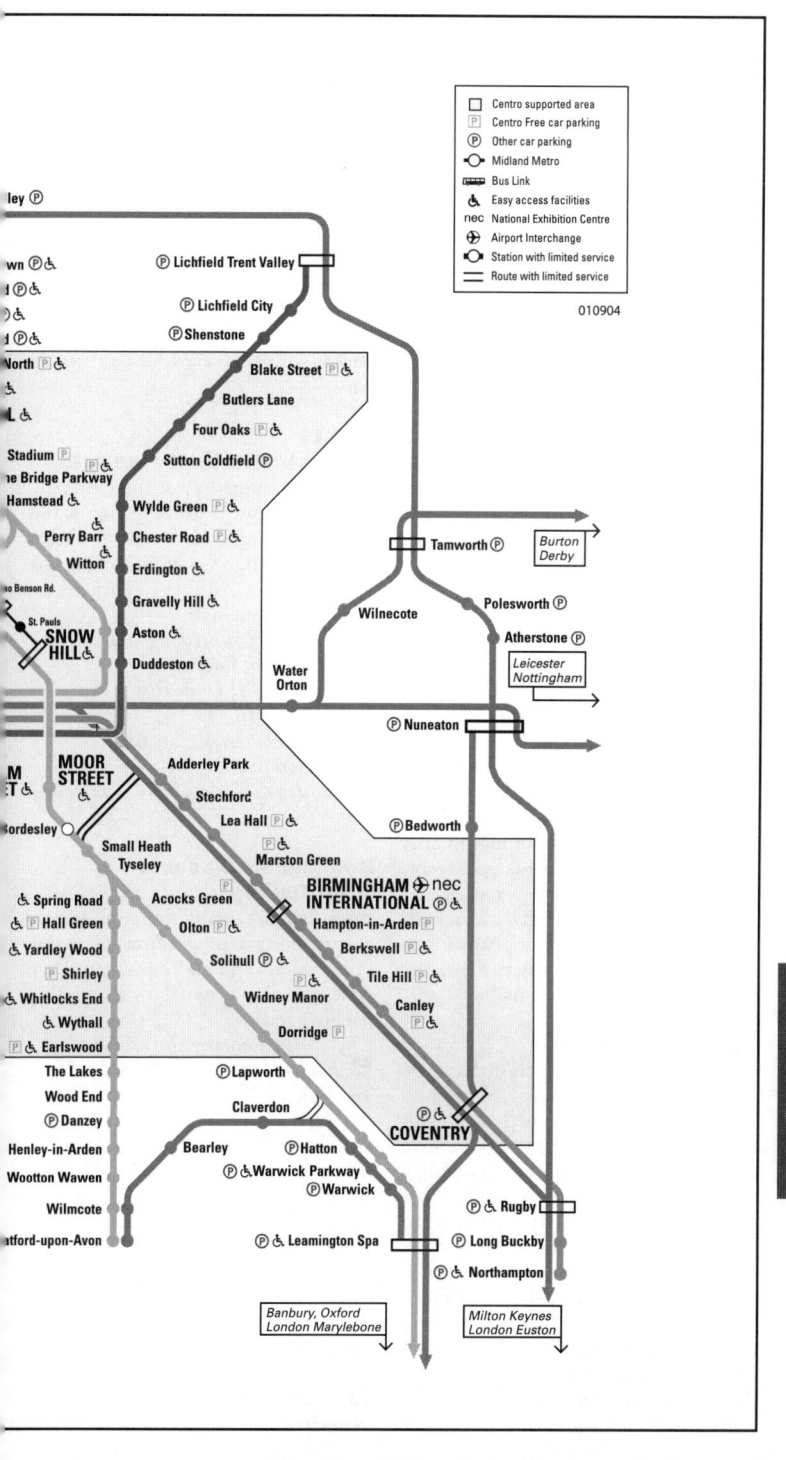

Legend:
- ☐ Centro supported area
- Ⓟ Centro Free car parking
- Ⓟ Other car parking
- ⊙ Midland Metro
- Bus Link
- ♿ Easy access facilities
- nec National Exhibition Centre
- ✈ Airport Interchange
- ⊙ Station with limited service
- ▬ Route with limited service

010904

Ⓟ Lichfield Trent Valley
Ⓟ Lichfield City
Ⓟ Shenstone
Blake Street Ⓟ ♿
Butlers Lane
Four Oaks Ⓟ ♿
Sutton Coldfield Ⓟ
Wylde Green Ⓟ ♿
Chester Road Ⓟ ♿
Erdington
Gravelly Hill ♿
Aston ♿
Duddeston ♿

...ley Ⓟ
...wn Ⓟ ♿
...Ⓟ ♿
...Ⓟ ♿
...North ♿
♿
...L ♿
Stadium Ⓟ
...e Bridge Parkway Ⓟ ♿
Hamstead ♿
Perry Barr
Witton
...o Benson Rd.
St. Pauls
SNOW HILL ♿

Tamworth Ⓟ → Burton / Derby
Wilnecote
Polesworth Ⓟ
Atherstone Ⓟ → Leicester / Nottingham
Water Orton
Ⓟ Nuneaton

MOOR STREET ♿
Adderley Park
Stechford
Lea Hall Ⓟ ♿
Small Heath
Tyseley
Marston Green Ⓟ ♿
Acocks Green Ⓟ
BIRMINGHAM ✈ nec
INTERNATIONAL Ⓟ ♿
Olton Ⓟ ♿
Hampton-in-Arden Ⓟ
Berkswell Ⓟ ♿
Solihull Ⓟ ♿
Tile Hill Ⓟ ♿
Widney Manor Ⓟ ♿
Canley Ⓟ ♿
Dorridge Ⓟ

...Bordesley
♿ Spring Road
♿ Ⓟ Hall Green
♿ Yardley Wood
Ⓟ Shirley
♿ Whitlocks End
♿ Wythall
Ⓟ ♿ Earlswood
The Lakes
Wood End
Ⓟ Danzey
Henley-in-Arden
Wootton Wawen
Wilmcote
...atford-upon-Avon

Ⓟ Lapworth
Claverdon
Bearley
Ⓟ Hatton
Ⓟ ♿ Warwick Parkway
Ⓟ Warwick
Ⓟ ♿ Leamington Spa

Ⓟ ♿ COVENTRY
Ⓟ Bedworth
Ⓟ ♿ Rugby
Ⓟ Long Buckby
Ⓟ ♿ Northampton

↓ Banbury, Oxford / London Marylebone
↓ Milton Keynes / London Euston

Heart of England

Busmaster 🚌 (Ⓜ)

The Busmaster gives you unlimited bus travel in West Midlands county for periods of one, four or 52 weeks. There is also a version of the pass that includes the metro. There is also a bus/metro day ticket that gives you one day unlimited bus and metro travel within West Midland county.

	1 day	1 week	4 weeks
bus only	-	£13.40	£45.65
bus & metro	£3.50	£15.40	£54.15

Daytripper Ⓜ🚇🚌

This pass is very similar to the one day Centrocard, but it cannot be used before 9.30am on weekdays. It costs £4.10 and lets you travel on the metro and all buses (except night buses) and suburban trains in West Midlands county.

Dayranger 🚇

The Dayranger is a good pass if you want to make a daytrip out of Birmingham. It costs £13.20 and gives you unlimited train travel after 9am on weekdays and all day on weekends in West Midlands county and parts of neighbouring counties. It lets you travel as far as Coventry, Crewe, Hereford, Leamington Spa, Northampton, Stafford, Stoke-on-Trent, Stratford-upon-Avon and Warwick.

Because of the lack of backpackers' accommodation in Birmingham it can also be used to make a day trip into the city from Stratford-upon-Avon.

Accommodation

The closest hostels to Birmingham are the YHAs in Ironbridge, Shropshire and Stratford-upon-Avon. It's difficult to get into Birmingham from both these hostels, however there are other budget accommodation options including a string of dodgy B&Bs on Hagley Road in the suburb of Edgbaston west of the city centre and the Formule 1 hotel in Bordesley, south east of the city centre.

Formule 1 Hotel

No atmosphere, but cheap clean rooms.
3 Bordesley Park Road, Small Heath Highway, Birmingham
🚇 *Bordesley*
☎ *(0121) 773 9583*
Website *www.hotelformule1.com*
Double/twin room £19.95-21.95
Credit cards *MC, Visa*

Eating & Drinking

Birmingham is the home of balti – a Kashmiri-Pakistani influenced cuisine that was invented here. There are a large number of balti restaurants in Birmingham with the highest concentration in the Balti Triangle south east of the city centre, which has over 50 balti restaurants.

Sights
Barber Institute of Fine Arts

This small art gallery at the University of Birmingham features a high standard of painting with works by Degas, Gainsborough, Gauguin, Magritte, Monet, Renoir, Rubens, Turner, Van Dyck and Van Gogh.
The University of Birmingham, Edgbaston Park Road, Edgbaston
🚌 *61, 62, 63 Q University*
☎ *(0121) 414 7333*
Website *www.barber.org.uk*
Admission *free*
Open *Mon-Sat 10am-5pm, Sun noon-5pm*

Birmingham Museum & Art Gallery

Birmingham's main museum and art gallery hosts a programme of temporary exhibits and also has a permanent collection that is noted for its pre-Raphaelite paintings.
Chamberlain Square, Birmingham
🚌 *1, 2, 4, 5, 6, 7, 9, 10, 12, 14, 15, 16, 16A, 17, 19, 21, 22, 23, 26, 29, 31, 33, 34, 34A, 35, 35S, 37, 41, 44, 44S, 44T, 45, 45A, 46, 46A, 47, 50, 50A, 51, 52, 52A, 55, 56, 57, 57A, 58, 58A, 60, 61, 62, 63, 63A, 65, 66, 66A, 67, 74, 78, 79, 80, 82, 84, 85A, 87, 88, 91, 92, 93, 94, 95, 96, 97, 99, 101, 103, 104, 104A, 105, 106, 107, 109, 113, 114, 120, 126, 128, 129, 140, 140A, 145, 158, 258, 626, 900, 902, 904, 905, 915, 921, 951, 951A, 952, 964, 994A, 995, 996, 997*
☎ *(0121) 303 2834*
Website *www.bmag.org.uk*

Admission free
Open Mon-Thu 10am-5pm, Fri 10.30am-5pm, Sat 10am-5pm, Sun 12.30pm-5pm

Cadbury World
Birmingham is the home of Cadbury chocolate and at Cadbury World in the southern suburb of Bourneville you can learn all about chocolate and take advantage of the free samples.
Linden Road, Bourneville
🚌 *11A, 11C, 35, 35S, 84* 🚆 *Bourneville*
☎ *(0121) 451 4180*
Website www.cadburyworld.co.uk
Admission £9 (£7.20 students)
Open call ☎ (0121) 451 4180 for current opening hours

Ikon Gallery
This art gallery in a neo-Gothic building on Oozells Square hosts a varied programme of temporary exhibits.
1 Oozells Square, Brindleyplace, Birmingham
🚌 *1, 9, 10, 19, 21, 22, 23, 29, 103, 109, 120, 126, 128, 129, 139, 140, 140A, 258*
☎ *(0121) 248 0708*
Website www.ikon-gallery.co.uk
Admission free
Open Tue-Sun 11am-6pm

Museum of the Jewellery Quarter
This museum has preserved jewellery workshops and features demonstrations by skilled jewellers.
75-79 Vyse Street, Hockley
🚌 *8A, 8C, 101* 🚆Ⓜ *Jewellery Quarter*
☎ *(0121) 554 3598*
Admission free
Open Easter-Oct Tue-Sun 11.30am-4pm

Sea Life Centre
Birmingham's Sea Life Centre features a walk-through aquarium plus sections dedicated to jellyfish, rays and seahorses. There is also an otter sanctuary.
The Waters Edge, Brindleyplace, Birmingham
🚌 *1, 9, 10, 19, 21, 22, 23, 29, 103, 109, 120, 126, 128, 129, 139, 140, 140A, 258*
☎ *(0121) 633 4700*
Website www.sealifeeurope.com
Admission £8 (£6 students)
Open 10am-5pm daily

Thinktank
Birmingham's science museum has 10 galleries of exhibits on four floors.
Millenium Point, Curzon Street, Digbeth, Birmingham
🚌 *55, 95*
☎ *(0121) 202 2222*
Website www.thinktank.ac
Admission £6.95
Open Mon-Thu & Sat-Sun 10am-4pm

Coventry
Coventry has a rich history dating from the late Saxon period but the city really started to boom during the Industrial Revolution when it became a major manufacturing centre, which in its heyday counted over 500 car, cycle and motorcycle manufacturers.

Practical Information
Tourist Information Centre
Bayley Lane, Coventry
☎ *(024) 7622 7264*
Website www.visitcoventry.co.uk
Open summer Mon-Fri 9.30am-5pm, Sat-Sun 10am-4.30pm; winter Mon-Fri 9.30am-4.30pm, Sat-Sun 10am-4.30pm

Coming & Going
AIR
Coventry has easy access to both Birmingham and Coventry Airports.

Birmingham International Airport *(☎ 0870 733 511; website www.bhx.co.uk)* is only 20 minutes by train from the centre of Coventry. It is a regional base for British Airways *(website www.britishairways.com)* and budget airline MyTravelLite *(website www.mytravellite.com)* is also based here.

Coventry Airport *(website www.coventryairport.co.uk)* is 5km south east of the city centre. It handles budget flights operated by Hapag Lloyd Express *(website www.hlx.com)*, Ryanair *(website www.ryanair.com)* and Thomsonfly *(website www.thomsonfly.com)*. Unfortunately there's no airport bus service so you'll have to catch a taxi from Coventry station.

BUS
National Express (☎ 0870 580 8080; *website* www.nationalexpress.co.uk) has buses from Coventry to Birmingham, Bristol, Leeds, Leicester, London and Manchester. Buses depart from Pool Meadow bus station.

TRAIN
There are frequent trains linking Coventry and Birmingham and there are also direct trains to Rugby, Milton Keynes and London (Euston).

Local Transport
Travel West Midlands *(website www.travelwm.co.uk)* run most buses in the Coventry area with one-way bus fares ranging from 70p to 90p.

Coventry is part of the Centro transport network that also covers Birmingham and Centro travel passes (see pages 171-174) can be used here.

Accommodation
Coventry doesn't have a hostel, although there is a cheap Formule 1 hotel.

Formule 1 Hotel
No atmosphere, but cheap clean rooms.
Mile Lane, Coventry
☎ *(024) 7623 4560*
Website *www.hotelformule1.com*
Double/twin room *£19.95-23.95*
Credit cards *MC, Visa*

Sights
Coventry Transport Museum
In its heyday Coventry hade over 500 car, cycle and motorcycle manufacturers so it stands to reason that Coventry's Transport Museum is among the world's best.
Hales Street, Coventry
🚌 *17, 27, 49* 🚉 *Coventry*
☎ *(024) 7683 2425*
Website *www.mbrt.co.uk*
Admission *free*
Open *10am-5pm daily*

Herbert Art Gallery & Museum
This museum has exhibits on Coventry's history with displays of archaeology, natural history and its industrial heritage.
Jordan Well, Coventry
☎ *(024) 7683 2381*

Admission *free*
Open *Mon-Sat 10am-5.30pm, Sun noon-5pm*

Lunt Roman Fort
This ancient Roman fort in Baginton, near Coventry, will reopen in April 2005 after a major refurbishment. The fort was established in 64 AD and was excavated between 1960 and 1973.
Coventry Road, Baginton
☎ *(024) 7683 2565*

St Mary's Guildhall
Built in the 1340s and altered in the 15th century, St Mary's Guildhall is one of England's best surviving medieval guildhalls. It was used as Coventry's city hall from 1421 until the 1860s.
Bayley Lane, Coventry
☎ *(024) 7683 2565*
Open *Easter-Sep Mon-Thu & Sun 10am-4pm*

Shropshire
Located between the West Midlands and Wales, Shropshire bills itself as the "nicest of England's quiet counties". Its main attractions include the quaint towns of Ludlow and Shrewsbury.

Ludlow
This 900-year-old Norman town boasts an 11th century castle and over 500 Georgian and half-timbered Tudor heritage buildings.

Practical Information
Ludlow Tourist Information Centre
Castle Street, Ludlow
☎ *(01584) 875053*
Website *www.ludlow.org.uk*
Open *Jan-Mar Mon-Sat 10am-5pm; Apr-Oct Mon-Sat 10am-5pm, Sun 10.30am-5pm; Nov-Dec Mon-Sat 10am-5pm*

Coming & Going
The train is the best way to get to Ludlow. Arriva Trains Wales *(website www.arrivatrainswales.co.uk)* stops in Ludlow en route between Cardiff and Crewe.

There are direct services to Shrewsbury, Hereford and Abergavenny. Change at Crewe for trains to Chester and Manchester and at Shrewsbury for trains to Aberystwyth and Birmingham (New Street).

Sights
Ludlow Castle
This 900-year-old castle has a long history that spans Norman, Medieval and Tudor periods. It was involved in the War of the Roses before becoming a royal palace and the seat of government for Wales and the Border Counties.
☎ (01584) 873355
Website www.ludlowcastle.com
Admission £3.50
Open Jan Sat-Sun 10am-4pm; Feb-Mar 10am-4pm daily; Apr-Jul 10am-5pm daily; Aug 10am-7pm daily; Sep 10am-5pm daily; Oct-Dec 10am-4pm daily

Shrewsbury
This lovely town boasts a Norman castle but is best known for its Jacobean and Tudor-style buildings that grace its streetscapes.

Practical Information
Shrewsbury Tourist Information Centre
The Music Hall, The Square, Shrewsbury
☎ (01743) 281200
Website www.visitshrewsbury.com
Open summer Mon-Sat 9.30am-5.30pm, Sun 10am-4pm; winter Mon-Sat 10am-5pm

Coming & Going
BUS
National Express (☎ 0870 580 8080; *website* www.nationalexpress.co.uk) buses go from Shrewsbury to Birmingham and London.

TRAIN
The train station on Castle Street has trains to Aberystwyth, Birmingham (New Street), Cardiff, Crewe, Hereford and Ludlow.

Local Transport
Arriva (*website* www.arriva.co.uk) runs Shrewsbury's local buses. A one-day ticket good for unlimited travel on Arriva buses costs £3. For £3.75 you can buy a day ticket valid on all Arriva buses in the Midlands allowing you to travel as far as Derby or Leicester.

Sights
Shrewsbury Castle & the Shropshire Regimental Museum
The castle was originally built in 1066 with many additions made during the following few hundred years. The castle is home to the Shropshire Regimental Museum, which has a collection of uniforms, medals and weapons from the 18th century to the present day.
☎ (01743) 358 516
Website www.shrewsburymuseums.com
Admission £2 (students free)
Open 18 Feb-31 Mar Wed-Sat 10am-4pm; Apr-May Tue-Sat 10am-5pm, Sun 10am-4pm; Jun-Sep Mon 10am-4pm, Tue-Sat 10am-5pm, Sun 10am-4pm

Shrewsbury Museum & Art Gallery
Shrewsbury Museum is housed in a 16th century timber-framed building and an adjoining 17th century stone and brick mansion. It features displays on archaeology, natural history, local history and fine art.
Barker Street, Shrewsbury
☎ (01743) 361 196
Website www.shrewsburymuseums.com
Admission free
Open Jan-Mar Tue-Sat 10am-4pm; Apr-May Tue-Sat 10am-5pm; May-Sep Mon-Sat 10am-5pm, Sun 10am-4pm

Ironbridge Gorge
This picturesque valley south of Telford is famed as the birthplace of the Industrial Revolution. Although originally a hive of activity with factories and belching smokestacks, it is now a quiet place with many interesting museums dedicated to the various items that were produced in the gorge.

There is no real town centre and Ironbridge Gorge is more a string of small villages clustered in the valley between Coalbrookdale and Coalport. These include Coalbrookdale where you'll find the Enginuity science museum, the

Museum of Iron and the Coalbrookdale YHA (groups only); Ironbridge with the Museum of the Gorge and the famous Iron Bridge; Jackfield and the Jackfield Tile Museum; Madeley and Blists Hill Victorian Village and Coalport, which is home to the China Museum, Tar Tunnel and the Coalport YHA.

Practical Information
Tourist Information Centre
The Wharfage, Ironbridge
☎ *(01952) 884391*
Website *www.ironbridge.org.uk*
Open *Mon-Fri 9am-5pm, Sat-Sun 10am-5pm*

Coming & Going
Ironbridge is 8km south of Telford and it is a relatively difficult place to get to without a car. The easiest way to get here is to take a train from Birmingham or Shrewsbury to Telford Central and then take a connecting bus to the gorge.

Telford Travelink (☎ *(01952) 200 005*) can give you up-to-date information about bus services between Telford and Ironbridge.

Local Transport
On weekends there is a shuttle bus (☎ *(01952) 200 005*) that runs between the Ironbridge museums.

Accommodation
Coalport YHA
Coalport YHA is housed in a former china factory (once the oldest china works in Europe) and is located next to the China Museum in the Ironbridge World Heritage site. It is a very well presented hostel, which is maintained to a high standard, however it does cater to a lot of school groups.
John Rose Building, High Street, Coalport, Ironbridge
☎ *895/9*
☎ *(01952) 588 755*
Website *www.yha.org.uk*
Dorm bed *£16 (£14 HI/YHA)*
Credit cards *MC, Visa*
Reception open *7.30am-11pm daily*

Maintenance & cleanliness ★★★★★
Facilities ★★☆
Atmosphere & character ★★★☆

Security ★★★☆
Overall rating ★★★★☆

Sights
If you plan on visiting several of the museums your best bet is the passport ticket, which costs £13.25 (£8.75 students) and allows admission to all the museums in Ironbridge Gorge.

Blists Hill Victorian Town
This open-air museum features restored cottages, factories and shops depicting life during Victorian times.
Madeley
☎ *(01952) 583 003*
Website *www.ironbridge.org.uk*
Admission *£8.50 (£5.30 students)*
Open *10am-5pm daily*

Clay Tobacco Pipe Museum
The Broseley Pipeworks closed its doors in 1957 and has now been reopened as museum showcasing 350 years of pipemaking.
Church Street, Broseley
Website *www.ironbridge.org.uk*
Admission *£3.10 (£1.70 students)*
Open *Apr-Oct 1pm-5pm daily*

Coalport China Museum
Located next to the Coalport YHA hostel, this former china factory shows how fine bone china was produced and features exhibitions about tableware and changes in dining etiquette.
High Street, Coalport
Website *www.ironbridge.org.uk*
Admission *£4.50 (£2.70 students)*
Open *10am-5pm daily*

Enginuity
This science museum has interactive exhibits that illustrate the engineering and technology behind the machines that powered the Industrial Revolution.
Coalbrookdale
Website *www.ironbridge.org.uk*
Admission *£5.30 (£3.70 students)*
Open *10am-5pm daily*

Iron Bridge & Tollhouse
Ironbridge's namesake is the world's first iron bridge that was cast in 1779 by Abraham Darby III and is still considered a great engineering feat.

Website *www.ironbridge.org.uk*
Open *10am-5pm daily*

Jackfield Tile Museum
This former tile factory shows how decorative tiles were produced in the 1870 and 1880s.
Jackfield
Website *www.ironbridge.org.uk*
Admission *£4.50 (£2.70 students)*
Open *10am-5pm daily*

Museum of the Gorge
This museum in a former warehouse houses a scale model of how the gorge appeared in 1796 and it is a good starting point for exploring Ironbridge Gorge.
Ironbridge
Website *www.ironbridge.org.uk*
Admission *£2.20 (£1.15 students)*
Open *10am-5pm daily*

Museum of Iron
The pioneering Darby family operated a furnace at Coalbrookdale that produced iron that was used by railways and the world's first iron bridge. The adjoining museum features exhibits on the history of iron with displays showing how iron was produced.
Coalbrookdale
Website *www.ironbridge.org.uk*
Admission *£4.50 (£2.70 students); including Darby Houses £5.30 (£3.40 students)*
Open *10am-5pm daily*

Staffordshire
Most travellers bypass this county between Birmingham and Manchester although some choose to stop for a break in Lichfield or Stoke-on-Trent.

Stoke-on-Trent
Made up of six separate towns – Burslem, Fenton, Hanley (the city centre), Longton, Stoke and Tunstall – Stoke-on-Trent is a unique city that is renowned as the world's leading centre for ceramics. Stoke-on-Trent is to crockery what Sheffield is to cutlery and Britain's leading potteries are all based here including Royal Doulton and Wedgewood. It is a popular spot with middle aged British tourists who come to tour the potteries and buy dinner settings from the factory outlets, however this isn't so practical for backpackers as that Wedgewood teapot you're thinking about buying for your mum will probably get smashed at the bottom of your backpack.

Practical Information
Stoke-on-Trent Tourist Information Centre
Quadrant Road, Hanley, Stoke-on-Trent
☎ *(01782) 236 000*
Website *www.visitstoke.co.uk*
Open *Mon-Sat 9.15am-5.15pm*

Coming & Going
Stoke-on-Trent lies about midway between Birmingham and Manchester, which are both around one hour away by train. The main train station is in the town of Stoke with local buses running between the train station and Hanley (the city centre).

National Express (☎ *0870 580 8080; website www.nationalexpress.com*) buses stop in Hanley (the city centre).

Local Transport
First *(website www.firstgroup.com)* operate Stoke-on-Trent's local bus service. Many travellers rely on the buses because Stoke is more spread-out than the average British city and very few attractions are within walking distance of each other. The Fareday ticket costs £3 and gives you unlimited travel on First buses in the Stoke-on-Trent area.

Sights
Ceramica
This new museum deals with all aspects of ceramics and it features hands-on exhibits and ancient artefacts.
Market Place, Burslem
☎ *(01782) 832 001*
Website *www.ceramicauk.com*
Admission *£3.75*
Open *Mon & Wed-Sat 9.30am-5pm, Sun 10.30am-4.30pm*

Etruria Industrial Museum
This museum houses Britain's only surviving steam-powered potter's mill and also has an interactive exhibition.

Lower Bedford Street, Etruria
☎ *(01782) 233 144*
Admission *£2*
Open *Mon-Wed & Sat-Sun noon-4.30pm*

Gladstone Pottery Museum
This museum is housed inside a Victorian pottery factory. Its displays include a new gallery that tells the story of the humble toilet.
Uttoxeter Road, Longton
☎ *(01782) 319 232*
Admission *£4.95*
Open *10am-5pm daily*

Potteries Museum & Art Gallery
The Potteries Museum hosts art exhibitions and also features the world's best collection of Staffordshire ceramics.
Bethesda Street, Hanley
☎ *(01782) 232 323*
Admission *free*
Open *Jan-Feb Mon-Sat 10am-4pm, Sun 1pm-4pm; Mar-Oct Mon-Sat 10am-5pm, Sun 2pm-5pm; Nov-Dec Mon-Sat 10am-4pm, Sun 1pm-4pm*

Royal Doulton Visitor Centre
Royal Doulton maintain a visitor centre with exhibits pertaining to its ceramics and they also run tours of their factory.
Nile Street, Burslem
☎ *(01782) 292 434*
Visitor centre admission *£3;* **tours cost** *£6.50*
Visitor centre open *Mon-Sat 9.30am-5pm, Sun 10.30am-4.30pm;* **tours depart** *Mon-Thu 10.30am, 2pm, Fri 10.30am, 1.30pm*

The Wedgewood Story
Visitors to the Wedgewood Story can see pottery being made on its factory floor, which features the latest robots, laser guided vehicles and 100 metre long kilns.
Barlaston
☎ *(01782) 204 218*
Admission *£7.25*
Open *Mon-Fri 9am-5pm, Sat-Sun 10am-5pm*

Lichfield

This small city boasts a beautiful triple-spire cathedral dating from the 11th century. Charles Darwin's grandfather, Erasmus, lived here and it was also the birthplace of Samuel Johnson, who wrote the first English dictionary.

Practical Information
Tourist Information Centre
Donegal House, Bore Street, Lichfield
☎ *(01543) 308209*
Website *www.visitlichfield.com*
Open *Apr-Sep Mon-Fri 9am-5pm, Sat 9am-4pm*

Coming & Going
BUS
Buses stop at Levetts Field Bus Station. National Express (☎ *0870 580 8080;* **website** *www.nationalexpress.co.uk*) has buses to Birmingham, Burton-upon-Trent, Derby, London and Sheffield.

TRAIN
Lichfield has two train stations. Lichfield City station is the most centrally located but many trains use Lichfield Trent Valley station north of the city centre. Both stations have trains from Birmingham, Burton-upon-Trent and Derby and Trent Valley station has trains to Tamworth, Stafford and Stoke-on-Trent.

Sights
Darwin House
This restored Georgian house was the home of Charles Darwin's grandfather, Erasmus. A leading doctor and scientist, Dr Erasmus Darwin was a major figure in the Lunar Society and he came up with the theory of evolution 70 years before his grandson refined it.
Beacon Street, Lichfield
☎ *(01543) 306 260*
Website *www.erasmusdarwin.org*
Admission *£2.50*
Open *Thu-Sat 10am-3.45pm, Sun noon-3.45pm*

Lichfield Cathedral
Lichfield's major attraction is its triple-spire cathedral that dates from the 11th century.
19A The Close, Lichfield
☎ *(01543) 306 100*
Website *www.lichfield-cathedral.org*
Admission *by donation*
Open *7.30am-6.15pm daily*

The Lichfield Story
This heritage centre on the Market Square has displays about Lichfield's history and it features audio-visual presentations and the Staffordshire Millennium Embroideries, which represents 1000 years of Staffordshire's history.
Market Square, Lichfield
☎ *(01543) 306 100*
Website *www.lichfieldheritage.org.uk*
Admission *£3.50*
Open *Mon-Sat 10am-5pm, Sun 10.30am-5pm*

Samuel Johnson Museum
Samuel Johnson, who wrote the first English dictionary, was born in this house that is now a museum focusing on Samuel Johnson's life and work.
Breadmarket Street, Lichfield
☎ *(01543) 264 972*
Website *www.lichfield.gov.uk/sjmuseum/*
Admission *£2.20*
Open *Jan-Mar noon-4pm daily; Apr-Sep 10.30am-4pm daily; Oct-Dec noon-4pm daily*

Leicestershire

The county in the East Midlands is a fairly anonymous place that most travellers pass through en route to somewhere more exciting, however its central location makes it an ideal base for exploring the Midlands.

Leicester

Although Leicester appears to be an uninteresting modern city, it actually has rich history dating back to Roman times when it was a major stop on the Fosse Way.

Practical Information
Tourist Information Centre
7/9 Every Street, Town Hall Square, Leicester
☎ *0906 294 1113*
Website *www.discoverleicester.co.uk*

Coming & Going
AIR
Leicester is 30 minutes from Nottingham East Midlands Airport (☎ *(01332) 852 852; website www.eastmidlandsairport.com*) and 45 minutes from Birmingham International Airport (☎ *(0121) 767 5511; website www.bhx.co.uk*).

BUS
National Express (☎ *0870 580 8080; website www.nationalexpress.co.uk*) and local buses terminate at St Margaret's Bus Station, near the corner of Gravel Street and New Road in the city centre.

Megabus (*website www.megabus.com*) has a daily express bus to London with prices between £1 and £3 (plus 50p booking fee). Megabus departs from Gravel Street outside St Margaret's Bus & Coach Station. Their London terminus is the Greenline Coach Station (🚇🚆 *Victoria*).

TRAIN
Midland Mainline trains (*website www.midlandmainline.com*) stop in Leicester en route from London to Manchester, Leeds and Sheffield and Central Trains (*website www.centraltrains.co.uk*) connect Leicester with Birmingham and other cities in the Midlands. The train station is a 10 to 15-minute walk from the city centre.

Local Transport
Leicester has a good city bus network with buses operated by Arriva (*website www.arriva.co.uk*), Centrebus and First (*website www.firstgroup.com*). Many buses use the Haymarket and St Margaret's Bus Stations as their central termini.

The FirstDay ticket costs £2 and allows one day unlimited travel on First buses.

Accommodation
Richard's Backpackers' Hostel
This tiny hostel offers basic accommodation in a suburban house 3km north of the city centre.
157 Wanlip Road, Birstall
🛏 *99*
☎ *(0116) 267 3107*
Dorm bed *£9*

Sights
Abbey Pumping Station
A 19th century sewage pumping station is the site of Leicester's science and technology museum. The museum fea-

tures England's largest working steam beam engines, which were originally used to pump almost one million litres of sewage every hour. Related exhibits can be found in the Flushed With Pride exhibition, which includes the country's only interactive toilet as well as a display of sewers, water pipes and a talking toilet! Other displays include an historic car collection and a display of old cinema equipment.
Corporation Road, Leicester
☎ (0116) 299 5111
Website *www.leicestermuseums.ac.uk*
Admission *free*
Open *Jan-Mar Mon-Sat 10am-4pm, Sun 1pm-4pm; Apr-Sep Mon-Sat 10am-5pm, Sun 1pm-5pm; Oct-Dec Mon-Sat 10am-4pm, Sun 1pm-4pm*

Guildhall
The Guildhall is one of Leicester's most notable buildings. It was built around 1390 for a guild of prominent businessmen and by the end of the 14th century it was used as Leicester's town hall. Today it is a venue of performing arts and it also houses a museum with exhibits on the city's history.
Guildhall Lane, Leicester
☎ (0116) 253 2569
Website *www.leicestermuseums.ac.uk*
Admission *free*
Open *Jan-Mar Mon-Sat 10am-4pm, Sun 1pm-4pm; Apr-Sep Mon-Sat 10am-5pm, Sun 1pm-5pm; Oct-Dec Mon-Sat 10am-4pm, Sun 1pm-4pm*

Jewry Wall
This 2000-year-old Roman wall was originally part of the city's Roman baths. There is an adjoining museum that chronicles the city's history from the Iron Age to the present day.
St Nicholas Circle, Leicester
☎ (0116) 225 4971
Website *www.leicestermuseums.ac.uk*
Admission *free*
Open *Jan-Mar Mon-Sat 10am-4pm, Sun 1pm-4pm; Apr-Sep Mon-Sat 10am-5pm, Sun 1pm-5pm; Oct-Dec Mon-Sat 10am-4pm, Sun 1pm-4pm*

National Space Centre
This attraction is dedicated to astronomy and space exploration and features five galleries of exhibits that include satellites and rockets as well as hands-on displays.
Exploration Drive, Leicester
🚌 54
☎ 0870 6077223
Website *www.spacecentre.co.uk*
Admission *£8.95*
Open *school term Tue-Fri 10am-5pm (last entry 3.30pm), Sat-Sun 10am-6pm (last entry 4.30pm); school holidays Mon noon-6pm (last entry 4.30pm), Tue-Sun 10am-6pm (last entry 4.30pm)*

New Walk Museum & Art Gallery
This museum is impressive for a small city. It features an excellent Ancient Egypt Gallery with mummies and a natural history section with dinosaur skeletons. Art exhibits include a notable collection of European art with an emphasis on German Expressionist art.
53 New Walk, Leicester
☎ (0116) 225 4900
Website *www.leicestermuseums.ac.uk*
Admission *free*
Open *Jan-Mar Mon-Sat 10am-4pm, Sun 1pm-4pm; Apr-Sep Mon-Sat 10am-5pm, Sun 1pm-5pm; Oct-Dec Mon-Sat 10am-4pm, Sun 1pm-4pm*

Lincolnshire
Lincolnshire bridges the divide between Cambridgeshire and Yorkshire. Its main attraction is the history city of Lincoln.

Lincoln
Lincoln has a lot going for it. Over 2000 years of history has left it endowed with a 3rd-century Roman town wall, several buildings dating from the medieval period and England's third-largest cathedral.

Practical Information
Castle Hill Tourist Information Centre
9 Castle Hill, Lincoln
☎ (01522) 873213
Website *www.lincoln-info.org.uk*
Open *Mon-Fri 9.30am-5.30pm, Sat-Sun 10am-5pm*

Cornhill Tourist Information Centre
21 Cornhill, Lincoln
☎ *(01522) 873256*
Website www.lincoln-info.org.uk
Open Mon-Fri 9.30am-5.30pm, Sat 10am-5pm

Coming & Going
BUS
National Express (☎ *0870 580 8080; website www.nationalexpress.co.uk*) have buses from Lincoln to Birmingham, Leeds, Leicester, London and Sheffield.

TRAIN
Central Trains (*website www.centraltrains.co.uk*) run trains from Lincoln to Cleethorpes, Doncaster, Nottingham and Peterborough.

Accommodation
Lincoln YHA
Lincoln's youth hostel is an elegant Victorian mansion with a conservatory that offers lovely views of the city centre.
77 South Park, Lincoln
☎ *(01522) 522076*
Website www.yha.org.uk
Dorm bed £13 (£11 HI/YHA)
Open Jul-Aug; reception open 8am-10am & 5pm-10pm daily; curfew 11pm

Sights
Bishop's Palace
Dating from the 12th century, this medieval bishop's palace was once the centre of England's largest diocese.
Minster Yard, Lincoln
☎ *(01522) 527 468*
Website www.english-heritage.org.uk
Admission £3.50
Open Jan-Mar Mon & Thu-Sun 10am-4pm; Apr-Jun 10am-5pm daily; Jul-Aug 10am-6pm daily; Sep-Oct 10am-5pm daily; Nov-Dec Mon & Thu-Fri 10am-4pm

Lincoln Castle
Dating from the 12th to 19th centuries, Lincoln Castle is a former prison that houses one of the four remaining copies of the *Magna Carta*.
Castle Hill, Lincoln
☎ *(01522) 511 068*
Admission £2.50
Open Jan-Mar Mon-Sat 9.30am-4pm, Sun 11am-4pm; Apr-Oct Mon-Sat 9.30am-5.30pm, Sun 11am-5.30pm; Nov-Dec Mon-Sat 9.30am-4pm, Sun 11am-4pm

Lincoln Cathedral
Lincoln Cathedral was built over a period of 300 years and when complete it was Europe's tallest building and it remains the country's third-largest church.
Minster Yard, Lincoln
☎ *(01522) 544 544*
Admission £3.50
Open Jan-May Mon-Sat 7.15am-6pm, Sun 7.15am-5pm; Jun-Aug Mon-Sat 7.15am-8pm, Sun 7.15am-6pm; Sep-Dec Mon-Sat 7.15am-6pm, Sun 7.15am-5pm

Nottinghamshire

This county in the East Midlands is most often associated with Robin Hood, a ruthless outlaw who terrorised the county in medieval times but who is now treated almost as a hero due to the Robin Hood legend that has spawned countless movies.

Nottingham

Nottingham is a vibrant city with loads of history and a thriving nightlife scene. Most of the city's main attractions revolve around glorifying a medieval criminal, Robin Hood.

Practical Information
Nottingham Tourist Information Centre
1-4 Smithy Row, Nottingham
☎ *(0115) 915 5330*
Website www.profilenottingham.com
Open Jan-Jul Mon-Fri 9am-5.30pm, Sat 9am-5pm; Aug-Sep Mon-Fri 9am-5.30pm, Sat 9am-5pm, Sun 10am-3pm; Oct-Dec Mon-Fri 9am-5.30pm, Sat 9am-5pm

Coming & Going
AIR
Nottingham East Midlands Airport (☎ *(01332) 852 852; website www.eastmidlandsairport.com*) is located near

Loughborough, south of the Nottingham. The Skylink bus *(website www.skylink.co.uk)* runs between the airport and Friar Lane, Market Square in Nottingham's city centre every half hour. The Skylink bus costs £3.50 but for £4.50 you can get a DayRider ticket that also allows you unlimited travel within Nottingham.

BUS
National Express (☎ *0870 580 8080; website www.nationalexpress.co.uk*) buses terminate at the Broad Marsh Bus Station, which is located at the southern edge of the city centre between the train station and Broad Marsh Shopping Centre.

TRAIN
Both Midland Mainline trains *(website www.midlandmainline.com)* and Central Trains *(website www.centraltrains.co.uk)* use Nottingham Midland Station, south of the city centre. Midland Mainline trains run north-south connecting Nottingham with London and Sheffield and Central Trains go to destinations throughout the Midlands including Birmingham and Lincoln.

Local Transport
Nottingham has a good public transport system that is comprised of tram and bus services.

BUS
Nottingham City Transport *(NCT;* ☎ *(0115) 950 6070; website www.nctx.co.uk)* operates over 300 bus lines in the Nottingham area. Single tickets range in price from 60p to £1.10 and several good value travel passes are available that include the Kangaroo pass (£2), which is good for one day unlimited bus travel within the city area.

Travel Centre
NCT's Travel Centre sells tickets and travel passes and can help with transport information.
5 South Parade, Nottingham
☎ *(0115) 950 6070*
Website *www.nctx.co.uk*
Open *Mon 9am-6pm, Tue-Fri 9am-5.30pm, Sat 9am-5pm*

TRAM
Nottingham Express Transit *(NET;* ☎ *(0115) 942 7777; website www.thetram.net)* runs Nottingham's trams. Trams depart from Station Street, near the train and bus stations, and stop at Lace Market, Old Market Square, Royal Centre and Nottingham Trent University in the city centre and run to park and ride car-parking areas in the suburbs.

One-way tram fares range from 80p to £1.20. Other options include an all-day TramRider ticket that costs £2.

FARES
In addition to the bus-only and tram-only travel passes outlined above there are several other travel passes available.

City Rider
The CityRider ticket that gives you one day unlimited travel on NET trams and NCT buses and costs £2.20.

Day Rider
The DayRider Plus travel card gives you one day unlimited travel on NCT buses, the Skylink airport bus and NET trams. These passes must be bought in advance and cost £4.50.

EasyRider
This pass is aimed mostly at residents but may be useful if you're planning on spending a while in Nottingham. The EasyRider is offers cheap travel for £10 for seven days or £33 for 28 days plus an initial fee of £3 for the card.

Kangaroo Pass
The Kangaroo Pass lets you hop on and off buses and trams and costs £3.20 for a one-day pass. A bus-only version of the pass is available for £2.

Accommodation
The Igloo
The Igloo is in a large Victorian house north of the city centre. It has a good TV lounge but the kitchen and dormitories are fairly basic.
110 Mansfield Road, Nottingham
🚌 *56, 57, 58, 59, 141, 200*
☎ *(0115) 947 5250*
Website *www.igloohostel.co.uk*

Dorm bed £13
Reception open 9am-midnight daily; check in 9am-6pm daily

📺 🇰 🇱

Maintenance & cleanliness	★★★
Facilities	★★
Atmosphere & character	★★★
Security	★★
Overall rating	★★★

Eating & Drinking
Nottingham has the usual array of restaurants, sandwich shops and fast food places, particularly around Goosgate, Mansfield Road and Milton Street. The city is home to England's oldest pub, Ye Olde Trip to Jerusalem Inn, which dates from 1189 and boasts rooms carved into the Castle Rock.

If you're preparing your own food, head to the Tesco supermarket in the Victoria Shopping Centre between the city centre and the Igloo hostel.

Sights
City of Caves
Nottingham was built upon a labyrinth of sandstone caves that people have lived in for over a thousand years. A section of the caves beneath the Broadmarsh Shopping Centre is open to visitors with exhibits depicting how people lived in the caves during medieval times and how the caves were used as an air raid shelter during World War II.
Broadmarsh Centre, Nottingham
☎ *(0115) 952 0555*
Website *www.cityofcaves.com*
Admission *£4*
Open *10.30am-4pm daily*

Galleries of Justice
This museum depicts 300 years of crime and punishment through interactive displays and activities.
High Pavement, The Lace Market, Nottingham
☎ *(0115) 952 0555*
Website *www.galleriesofjustice.org.uk*
Admission *£6.95*
Open *summer 10am-5pm daily; winter 10am-4pm daily*

Museum of Nottingham Lace
Nottingham has been a major lace producer for over 250 years. This museum details the history of Nottingham's lace industry and has displays showing how lace is made.
2-5 High Pavement, Nottingham
☎ *(0115) 989 7365*
Admission *£3*
Open *Jan-Mar Tue-Sun 10am-4pm; Apr-Oct Tue-Sun 10am-5pm; Nov-Dec Tue-Sun 10am-4pm*

Nottingham Castle
This 17th century mansion was built on the grounds of the original castle that features in the Robin Hood stories. It houses a museum and boasts a spectacular setting high on Castle Rock offering sweeping views of the surrounding countryside.
Castle Road, Nottingham
☎ *(0115) 915 3700*
Website *www.nottinghamcity.gov.uk/whatson/museums/castle.asp*
Admission *free Mon-Fri, £2 Sat-Sun*
Open *10am-5pm daily*

Tales of Robin Hood
This attraction takes you back 700 years to relive the stories of Robin Hood through a variety of interactive displays.
30-38 Maid Marian Way, Nottingham
☎ *(0115) 948 3284*
Website *www.robinhood.uk.com*
Admission *£6.95*
Open *10am-4.30pm daily*

Edwinstowe & Sherwood Forest

This town is believed to have been the home of Robin Hood and it is close to the last remaining patch of Sherwood Forest, which once covered a fifth of Nottinghamshire. According to legend, Maid Marian and Robin Hood were married here in the local parish church.

Practical Information
Sherwood Forest Tourist Information Centre
Forest Corner, Edwinstowe
☎ *(01623) 824 490*
Website *ww.nottinghamshiretourism.co.uk*

Coming & Going

Stagecoach (*website www.stagecoach-bus.co.uk*) bus Sherwood Arrow 33 runs between Nottingham and Edwinstowe and bus 10A runs between Edwinstowe and Mansfield, which has train connections to Nottingham.

The Sherwood Forester bus network runs additional services during summer with Day Ranger tickets that give you one day unlimited travel on the network for £5, allowing you to travel as far as Matlock or Nottingham.

The Day Rover ticket costs £4.75 and gives you one day unlimited travel on Stagecoach buses in the East Midlands. This travel pass will let you travel to Nottingham and Sheffield.

Accommodation
Sherwood Forest Youth Hostel

The Sherwood Forest Youth Hostel is a good purpose-built hostel with modern amenities and brand new furnishings. Accommodation is in small dorms, mostly with en suite facilities.
Forest Corner, Edwinstowe
☎ *13, 15, 33, 110, 113*
☎ *(01623) 825 794*
Website *www.yha.org.uk*
Dorm bed *£16 (£14 HI/YHA)*
Credit cards *MC, Visa*
Open *Feb-Mar Tue-Sat; Apr-Oct every day; Nov-Dec Tue-Sat; reception open 7.30am-10am & 1pm-11pm daily*

Maintenance & cleanliness	★★★★★
Facilities	★★☆
Atmosphere & character	★★
Security	★★☆
Overall rating	★★★

Sights
Major Oak

The Major Oak in Sherwood Forest, 20 minutes walk from the Sherwood Forest Visitor Centre, is reputed to have been Robin Hood's hideout. The tree is estimated to be 800 years old and has a girth of 10m.

Sherwood Forest Country Park & Visitor Centre

The Sherwood Forest Visitor Centre has exhibits about the forest and the Robin Hood story. A series of trails run from the centre into the forest, the most popular being the track to Major Oak.
Forest Corner, Edwinstowe
☎ *(01623) 823 202*
Admission *free*
Open *Jan-Mar 10.30am-4.30pm daily; Apr-Oct 10.30am-5pm daily; Nov-Dec 10.30am-4.30pm daily*

Derbyshire

Most of Derbyshire is taken up by the Peak District National Park, a region of pleasant rolling hills, stone fences and picturesque towns and villages.

Derby

Located west of Nottingham and south of the Peak District, Derby is a bustling city that is dominated by its cathedral tower.

Practical Information
Derby Tourist Information Centre

Assembly Rooms, Market Place, Derby
☎ *(01332) 255802*
Website *www.visitderby.co.uk*
Open *Mon-Fri 9.30am-5.30pm, Sat 9.30am-5pm, Sun 10.30am-2.30pm*

Coming & Going

National Express (☎ *0870 580 8080; website www.nationalexpress.co.uk*) has buses to Derby from Bakewell, Birmingham, Buxton, Leeds, Leicester, London and Nottingham. Buses stop at Morledge Bus Station. Trent Barton (*website www.trentbuses.co.uk*) operates buses from Derby to Burton-on-Trent, Buxton, Manchester and Nottingham.

Central Trains (***website*** *www.centraltrains.co.uk*) have trains from Derby to Birmingham, Liverpool, Matlock, Nottingham and Stoke-on-Trent.

The Derbyshire Wayfarer pass allows one day's virtually unlimited bus and train travel throughout Derbyshire and includes travel to the following cities in neighbouring counties: Burton-on-Trent, Leek, Macclesfield, Sheffield and Uttoxeter. The pass costs £7.50 and is available from bus and train stations and the tourist information centre.

Local Transport
Although the city centre is compact enough to walk around there is a good local bus network that is run by Arriva *(website www.arriva.co.uk)* and Trent Barton *(website www.trentbuses.co.uk)*.

Sights
Derby Cathedral
Derby Cathedral's medieval tower dominates the city centre.
18-19 Iron Gate, Derby
☎ *(01332) 341201*
Website *www.derbycathedral.org*
Admission *free*
Open *8.30am-6pm daily*

Derby City Museum & Art Gallery
This museum features displays relating to natural history and local history and its art exhibits include a collection of Joseph Wright oil paintings.
The Strand, Derby
☎ *(01332) 716659*
Website *www.derby.gov.uk/museums*
Admission *free*
Open *Mon 11am-5pm, Tue-Sat 10am-5pm, Sun 1pm-5pm*

Derby Industrial Museum
This excellent museum has exhibits about coal mining, the development of the railways and Rolls-Royce aero-engines.
Full Street, Derby
☎ *(01332) 255308*
Website *www.derby.gov.uk/museums*
Admission *free*
Open *Mon 11am-5pm, Tue-Sat 10am-5pm, Sun 2pm-5pm*

Peak District National Park

Britain's first and the world's second-most-visited national park lies within easy access of many of England's biggest cities and is popular on weekends and school holidays. It is an area of rolling countryside criss-crossed with hiking trails and ubiquitous stone fences. Although a pleasant area, there is nothing spectacular about the park and most travellers see it as simply a place to pass through.

Although most of the park is in Derbyshire, parts of it fall within Staffordshire and South Yorkshire. However we have included all information about the park within the Derbyshire section.

Coming & Going & Local Transport
For a largely rural county, Derbyshire and the Peak District have a good public transport system *(website www.derbysbus.net)* with regular bus and train services. There are several county-wide travel passes available that make it an affordable county to travel around.

Derbyshire Wayfarer
This travel pass allows one day's virtually unlimited bus and train travel throughout Derbyshire and includes travel to the following cities in neighbouring counties: Burton-on-Trent, Leek, Macclesfield, Sheffield and Uttoxeter. The pass costs £7.50 and is available from most major bus and train stations (including Burton-on-Trent, Buxton, Chesterfield, Derby and Sheffield) and at tourist information centres in Ashbourne, Bakewell, Burton-on-Trent, Buxton, Castleton, Chesterfield, Derby, Edale, Glossop, Hayfield, Leek, Matlock, Matlock Bath, New Mills and Uttoexeter.

East Midlands Day Rover
This pass costs £4.75 and is valid for one day's travel on Stagecoach East Midlands buses in Derbyshire, Nottinghamshire and South Yorkshire (except D 909).

South Yorkshire Peak Explorer
The South Yorkshire Peak Explorer costs £6.25 and gives you one day's bus travel in South Yorkshire and the northern part of the Peak District bounded by Bakewell, Baslow, Buxton, Holmfirth, Hayfield, Owler Bar and Sparrowpit. It also includes tram travel in Sheffield.

Bakewell
This pleasant town is famous for its Bakewell pudding and it is a good base for travellers who would rather not stay in the countryside.

Practical Information
Bakewell Tourist Information Centre
Old Market Hall, Bridge Street, Bakewell
☎ *(01629) 813227*
Website *www.visitpeakdistrict.com*
Open *Jan-Feb 10am-5pm daily; Mar-Oct 9.30am-5.30pm daily; Nov-Dec 10am-5pm daily*

Coming & Going
National Express (☎ *0870 580 8080; website www.nationalexpress.co.uk*) buses go to Derby, Leicester, London, Manchester and Matlock. Buses stop at the corner of Buxton Road and Matlock Street.

Accommodation
Bakewell YHA
This small hostel, in a quiet corner of the town on a hill with fine views, feels homely with its sociable common/dining room, good kitchen and friendly staff.
Fly Hill, Bakewell
☎ *0870 770 5682*
Website *www.yha.org.uk*
Dorm bed *£13 (£11 HI/YHA)*
Credit cards *MC, Visa*
Open *Jul-Aug; flexible opening at other times; reception open 10am-5pm daily; curfew 11pm*

Maintenance & cleanliness	★★★★½
Facilities	★★
Atmosphere & character	★★
Security	★★½
Overall rating	★★★

Sights
Haddon Hall
This stately home southeast of Bakewell was built 800 years ago and is one of the country's best-preserved historic houses.
A6, 3.25km southeast of Bakewell
☎ *(01629) 812855*
Website *www.haddonhall.co.uk*
Admission *£7.25*
Open *Apr-Sep 10.30am-5pm daily; Oct Thu-Sun 10.30am-4.30pm*

Old House Museum
This small museum has a variety of exhibits relating to local history.
Cunningham Place, North Church Street, Bakewell
☎ *(01629) 813 642*
Admission *£2.50*
Open *Apr-Jun 1.30pm-3.30pm daily; Jul-Sep 11am-3.30pm; Oct 1.30pm-3.30pm daily*

Buxton
Buxton is one of the biggest towns in the Peak District with all the trappings of a cultured destination including a grand opera house and museum.

Practical Information
Buxton Tourist Information Centre
The Crescent, Buxton
☎ *(01298) 25106*
Website *www.visitpeakdistrict.com*
Open *Jan-Feb noon-4pm daily; Mar-Aug 9.30am-5.30pm daily; Sep 9.30am-5pm daily; Oct-Dec noon-4pm daily*

Coming & Going
National Express (☎ *0870 580 8080; website www.nationalexpress.co.uk*) buses go to Derby, Leicester and Manchester. Trent Barton buses *(website www.trentbuses.co.uk)* stop at Buxton en route between Derby and Manchester.

There are frequent trains between Buxton and Manchester (Piccadilly) that you can travel on with a Wayfarer ticket, which allows unlimited travel on buses, trains and trams in the Greater Manchester area and to parts of Cheshire, Derbyshire, Lancashire and Staffordshire. The Wayfarer ticket costs £7.80 for one-day or £11 for a weekend pass.

Castleton
This tiny village is surprisingly busy and it is one of the main tourism centres of the Hope Valley in the northern Peak District. Castleton attractions include several caves plus the ruins of the 11th and 12th century Peveril Castle, which overlooks the village.

Practical Information
Tourist Information Centre
Buxton Road, Castleton
☎ *(01433) 620679*

Website *www.visitpeakdistrict.com*
Open *Jan-Mar Sat-Sun 10am-5pm; Apr-Oct 10am-1pm & 2pm-5.30pm daily; Nov-Dec Sat-Sun 10am-5pm*

Coming & Going
The closest train station to Castleton is 3.25km away in Hope, which is served by several bus routes. Bus routes 272, 273 and 274 connect Castleton and Sheffield.

Accommodation
Castleton YHA
Castleton YHA consists of several old stone buildings in Castleton village centre. There is a big dining room plus a games room and a small kitchen/TV lounge. Double and twin rooms are in an annex next door.
Castle Street, Castleton
☎ *A625, 272/4*
☎ *(01433) 620 235*
Website *www.yha.org.uk*
Dorm bed *£14.50 (£12.50 HI/YHA)*
Credit cards *MC, Visa*
Open *2 Feb-24 Dec;* ***reception open*** *7am-11pm daily*

Maintenance & cleanliness	★★☆
Facilities	★★
Atmosphere & character	★★☆
Security	★☆
Overall rating	★★☆

Sights
Peveril Castle
Founded by William Peveril shortly after the Norman Conquest, this castle sits on a hilltop overlooking Castleton and offering breathtaking views of the Peak District.
A6187, Castleton
☎ *(01433) 620 613*
Website *www.english-heritage.org.uk*
Admission *£2.70*
Open *Jan-Mar Mon & Thu-Sun 10am-4pm; Apr 10am-5pm daily; May-Jul 10am-6pm aily; Aug 10am-7pm daily; Sep-Oct 10am-5pm daily; Nov-Dec 10am-4pm daily*

Treak Cliff Cavern
This is the best of the caves around Castleton. It features the usual collection of stalactites and stalagmites plus the unique mineral known as Blue Johnstone.
Buxton Road, Castleton
☎ *(01433) 620 571*
Website *www.bluejohnstone.com*
Admission *£5.80*
Open *from 10am daily, closing time varies call* ☎ *(01433) 620 571 for up-to-date opening times*

Hathersage
This village at the northern part of the Peak District claims to be the home of Little John of Robin Hood fame. Its main advantage for many travellers is that it's the closest town with a hostel to Sheffield.

Coming & Going
Hathersage is on a major road with several buses stopping here en route between Sheffield and the Peak District. It also lies on the Manchester-Sheffield train line with frequent trains in both directions. It is only 25 minutes by train into the centre of Sheffield, making Hathersage a convenient base for visiting Sheffield.

Accommodation
Hathersage YHA
This is a cheerful-feeling hostel in a Victorian house in the centre of Hathersage close to shops and transport, with a bright dining room, a pleasant lounge with TV, and a well-equipped kitchen. The dorms are bright and spacious. If you arrive early there's a shelter area and a garden with picnic tables but you can't get into the main hostel till 5pm.
Castleton Road, Hathersage
☎ *0870 770 5852*
Website *www.yha.org.uk*
Dorm bed *£13 (£11 HI/YHA; £8 HI/YHA & student)*
Credit cards *MC, Visa*
Open *Apr-Aug Mon-Sat; Sep-Oct Tue-Sat;* ***reception open*** *7.30am-10am & 5pm-11pm daily;* ***lockout*** *10am-5pm;* ***curfew*** *11pm*

Maintenance & cleanliness	★★★★☆
Facilities	★★★
Atmosphere & character	★★☆
Security	★★☆
Overall rating	★★★

Thorpe Farm Bunkhouses

There are several bunkhouses on this working farm, which is a good half-hour walk from Hathersage, and you need to bring all your food and a sleeping bag (though they keep a few for loan). The cost is low and the bunkhouses are well but simply equipped with kitchens and bunkrooms and comfortable common rooms without TV. You won't be sharing a building with a large group, but you might be on your own. If there are several of you with a car you can have a great time here.
Thorpe Farm, Hathersage
☎ *(01433) 650 659*
Website *www.thorpe-bunk.co.uk*
Dorm bed *£8*

Maintenance & cleanliness	★★★½
Facilities	★
Atmosphere & character	★★½
Security	★
Overall rating	★★½

Matlock & Matlock Bath

Although these two towns lay only 3km apart they each have quite a different character. Matlock is a lovely little historic town but Matlock Bath is a tacky tourist town.

Practical Information
Matlock Tourist Information Centre
Crown Square, Matlock
☎ *(01629) 583388*
Website *www.visitpeakdistrict.com*
Open *Mar-Oct 9.30am-5pm daily*

Matlock Bath Tourist Information Centre
The Pavillion, Matlock Bath
☎ *(01629) 55082*
Website *www.visitpeakdistrict.com*
Open *Jan-Feb Sat-Sun 10am-4pm; Mar-Oct 9.30am-5pm daily; Nov-Dec Sat-Sun 10am-4pm*

Coming & Going
National Express (☎ *0870 580 8080; website www.nationalexpress.co.uk*) runs buses from Matlock to Derby, Leicester and Manchester. Trains operated by Central Trains (***website*** *www.centraltrains.co.uk*) run from Matlock to Birmingham via Derby.

Accommodation
Matlock YHA
This is a good-quality hostel. It's 300m from the centre of Matlock with good transport. It has several lounges, a large dining room with meals available, an equipped self-catering kitchen, Internet, drying room, and an evening bar. It's a very comfortable and super-clean hostel.
40 Bank Road, Matlock
☎ *0870 770 5960*
Website *www.yha.org.uk*
Dorm bed *£14.50 (£12.50 HI/YHA; £9.50 HI/YHA & student)*
Credit cards *MC, Visa*
Open *12 Feb-31 Oct every day; 1 Nov-31 Dec Fri-Sat;* ***lockout*** *10am-1pm;* ***curfew*** *11pm*

Maintenance & cleanliness	★★★★
Facilities	★★★½
Atmosphere & character	★★★½
Security	★★½
Overall rating	★★★

Elsewhere in the Peak District

The open countryside is one of the region's most popular attractions, which draws thousands of British walkers from neighbouring cities every weekend.

Accommodation
Many of the Peak District hostels are in the countryside away from the main towns, which makes them difficult to get to by public transport but idyllic if you are cycling, driving or walking.

Alstonefield YHA
This small hostel is in an old stone farmhouse. It is a very well presented hostel, which is kept immaculate inside.
Gypsy Lane, Alstonefield, near Ashbourne, Staffordshire
☎ *(01629) 592 708*
Website *www.yha.org.uk*
Dorm bed *£14.50 (£12.50 HI/YHA)*
Reception open *8am-10am & 5pm-10pm daily;* ***curfew*** *11pm*

Heart of England – Peak District National Park

Maintenance & cleanliness	★★★★★
Facilities	★★
Atmosphere & character	★★★
Security	★½
Overall rating	★★★

Bretton YHA

This is a small cosy hostel in a fabulous spot, off the road high on a windswept ridge with spacious views. Run by voluntary managers, it is very clean and has a superb kitchen and a sociable dining/common room with books, games and magnificent views. The dorms are cosy and comfortable, but the bathrooms are on a separate floor. There's a pub 100m away and buses come within 2km.
Near Eyam, Hope Valley
☎ *0870 770 5720*
Website *www.yha.org.uk*
Dorm bed *£12 (£10 HI/YHA; £7 HI/YHA & ISIC)*
Open *Jul-Aug;* **reception open** *7.30am-10am & 5pm-11pm daily;* **lockout** *10am-5pm daily;* **curfew** *11pm*

Maintenance & cleanliness	★★★★½
Facilities	★★½
Atmosphere & character	★★★½
Security	★★½
Overall rating	★★★

Dimmingsdale YHA

This small hostel is in a remote-feeling field location 3km from anywhere, with lots of pleasant walks around. Its opening dates are limited and a bit iffy; if a group is staying it may be closed to others. It has a pleasant common room with books and a small TV, and an equipped kitchen. It is just 4km from Alton Towers theme park but you really need your own transport to stay here.
Oakamoor, Staffordshire
☎ *(01538) 702 304*
Website *www.yha.org.uk*
Dorm bed *£13 (£11 HI/YHA)*
Open *8 Apr-20 Sep flexible opening, call first to make sure it isn't booked by a group*

Maintenance & cleanliness	★★★★½
Facilities	★★½
Atmosphere & character	★★★½
Security	★
Overall rating	★★★½

Edale YHA

Edale YHA operates primarily as an activity centre running accommodation/activity packages that include kayaking, rock climbing and caving. The hostel is set in three buildings and has several common rooms plus a kitchen and a number of activity-focussed facilities such as a climbing tower and high ropes course.
Edale
☎ *(01433) 670 302*
Website *www.yha.org.uk*
Dorm bed *£14.50 (£12.50 HI/YHA)*
Credit cards *MC, Visa*
Reception open *8.30am-10am & 10.30am-noon & 1pm-7.30pm & 8.30pm-10pm daily*

Maintenance & cleanliness	★★★
Facilities	★★★
Atmosphere & character	½
Security	★★
Overall rating	★★★½

Gradbach Mill YHA

This former mill is set in a peaceful valley with many scenic walks around, and there is a nearby grotto used as a secret church by the Luddites. It has everything you want in a country spot – a well laid-out kitchen/dining area, a lounge with large TV, bedside lights, picnic tables and a playing field. You can eat hostel meals in the large dining/common room, and buy organic beer and wine. School groups often stay there, but they sleep in a different building from individuals. It's spotlessly clean and the staff are friendly. There is even a stuffed wallaby that was caught locally!
Gradbach Mill, Gradbach, Quarnford
☎ *(01260) 227 625*
Website *www.yha.org.uk*
Open *Apr-Oct;* **reception open** *8am-10am & 1pm-10pm daily*
Dorm bed *£14.50 (£12.50 HI/YHA)*
Credit cards *Amex, MC, Visa*

Maintenance & cleanliness	★★★★★
Facilities	★★★½
Atmosphere & character	★★★★½
Security	★★★½
Overall rating	★★★★

Hartington Hall Youth Hostel

Hartington Hall YHA is a historic manor house with loads of character. It features dark wood panelling, stained glass windows and it is maintained to a very high standard. Facilities include several common rooms with fireplaces, a TV lounge, games room and a kitchen.
Hall Bank, Hartington, near Buxton, Derbyshire
☎ *(01298) 84223*
Website *www.yha.org.uk*
Dorm bed *£18 (£16 HI/YHA)*
Open *1-3 Jan & 16 Jan-31 Dec;* **reception open** *7am-10pm daily;* **curfew** *11.30pm*

Maintenance & cleanliness	★★★★★
Facilities	★★★
Atmosphere & character	★★★
Security	★★★
Overall rating	★★★★

Meerbrook YHA

This is one of YHA's delightful small hostels run by volunteers. It is a former village school and has one large room including a good kitchen, dining tables and easy chairs, books and games, so is very sociable. The garden has picnic tables, a barbecue and a wildlife pond. The only snag is that to get from dorm to bathrooms you have to walk down stairs and through the common room.
Old School, Meerbrook, Leek, Staffordshire
☎ *(01538) 300 244*
Website *www.yha.org.uk*
Dorm bed *£13 (£11 HI/YHA)*
Apr-May Fri-Sat; Jun-Aug every day; Sep-Oct Fri-Sat; **reception open** *7am-10am & 5pm-10pm daily;* **lockout** *10am-5pm daily; lockout 11pm*

Maintenance & cleanliness	★★★★★
Facilities	★
Atmosphere & character	★★
Security	★
Overall rating	★★★

Ravenstor YHA

This hostel is a beautiful building set in its own grounds near a river amid some of the best Peak District scenery, with fine walks all around. The hostel takes school groups but usually not on the same days as individuals. There is a TV lounge, a lounge with books, a games room, a large dining room with good hostel meals, and a small kitchen where you can self-cater. The staff are friendly. They sell beer, which you can drink on a terrace with a delightful restful view.
Millers Dale, near Buxton
☎ *(01298) 871 826*
Website *www.yha.org.uk*
Dorm bed *£14.50 (£12.50 HI/YHA)*
Credit cards *JCB, MC, Visa*
Open *Feb-Oct Sat-Sun & school holidays;* **reception open** *7am-10am & noon-10.30pm;* **curfew** *11pm*

Maintenance & cleanliness	★★★★★
Facilities	★★★
Atmosphere & character	★★★
Security	★★
Overall rating	★★★★

Youlgreave YHA

Youlgreave is a small town that is a bit out-of-the-way but it has hourly buses from Bakewell during daytime on weekdays. There are walking paths all around. The youth hostel is a character building that was once a co-op grocery store. It is in superb condition with a large bright dining/sitting room overlooking the town square, an excellent kitchen with eating area, and spacious dorms with washbasins. There's no TV.
Fountain Square, Youlgreave, near Bakewell
☎ *(01629) 636 518*
Website *www.yha.org.uk*
Dorm bed *£14.50 (£12.50 HI/YHA)*
Credit cards *MC, Visa*
Open *Apr-Oct Mon-Sat; Nov-Dec Fri-Sat;* **reception open** *8am-10am & 5pm-10pm daily;* **curfew** *11pm*

Maintenance & cleanliness	★★★★★
Facilities	★★
Atmosphere & character	★★
Security	★★
Overall rating	★★★

North West England

Manchester

England's third-largest city is experiencing somewhat of a revival and has become a hip destination known for its cutting edge nightlife.

Practical Information
Manchester Visitor Centre
Town Hall Extension, Lloyd Street, Manchester
☎ *(0161) 234 3157*
Website www.destinationmanchester.com
Open *Mon-Sat 10am-5.30pm, Sun 10.30am-4pm*

INTERNET ACCESS
easyInternetcafé
8 Exchange Street, Manchester
☎ *(0161) 832 9200*
Website www.easyinternetcafe.com
Open *Mon-Sat 8am-6pm, Sun 10am-6pm*

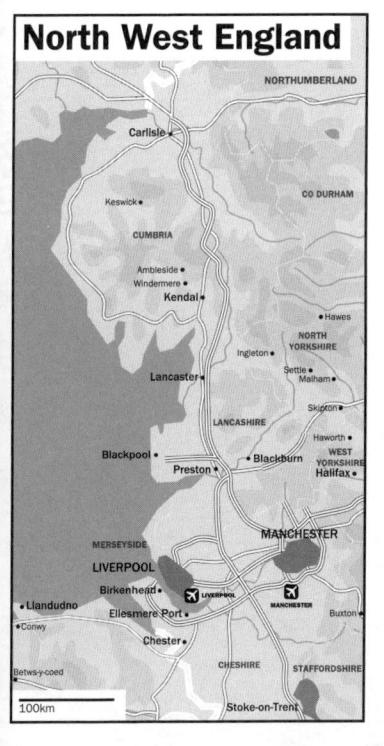

Coming & Going
AIR
Manchester Airport (☎ *(0161) 489 3000; website www.manchesterairport.co.uk*) is England's busiest airport outside London with flights to all corners of the globe. It is 16km south of the city centre. Trains run into the Manchester Piccadilly station every 15 minutes and cost £2.35 or £2.80 before 9.30am Mon-Fri.

BUS
National Express (☎ *0870 580 8080; website www.nationalexpress.co.uk*) has frequent bus services to most major destinations including Birmingham, Leeds, Liverpool, London and Sheffield. Buses depart from Chorlton Street Coach Station on Chorlton Street in the city centre.

Megabus (*website www.megabus.com*) is a cheap option if you want to travel to Leeds and London or to Dundee, Glasgow and Perth in Scotland. Megabus departs opposite the coach station on Chorlton Street. Fares start at £1 (plus 50p booking fee).

TRAIN
Manchester has several stations with most long distance trains stopping in either Piccadilly or Victoria stations. Piccadilly station, east of the city centre, has trains to Birmingham (New Street), Chester, Edinburgh, the Lake District, Leeds, London (Euston) and York. Victoria Station on Victoria Street north of the city centre has trains to Liverpool.

Local Transport
Manchester has a good public transport network (*website www.gmpte.com*) that is comprised of buses, trains and trams.

BUS
Manchester has an extensive bus network with many routes terminating at Piccadilly Gardens bus station. Bus only Day Saver tickets cost £3.30 for one day unlimited bus travel in Greater Manchester or £2.95 after 9.30am Mon-Fri or all day on weekends.

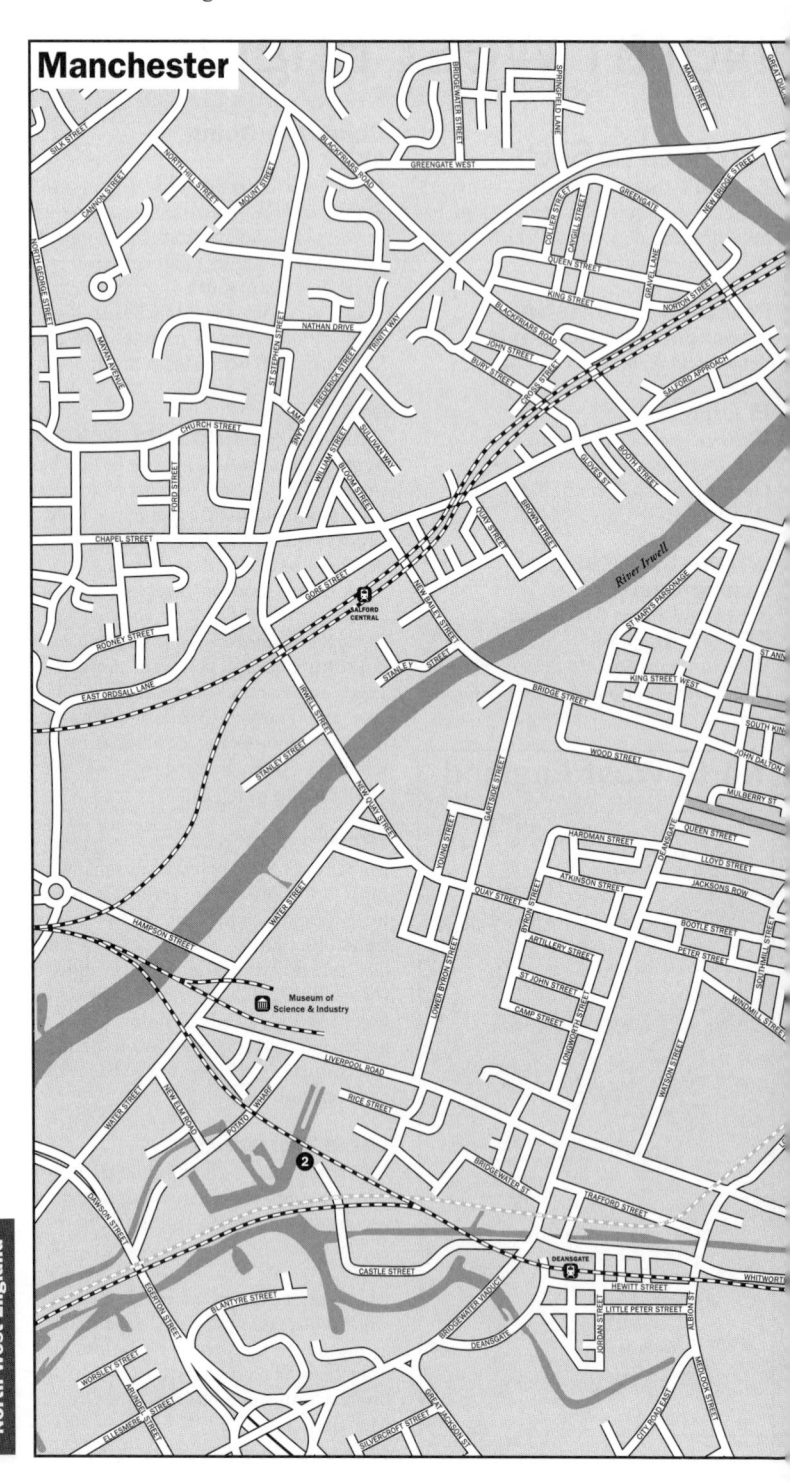

Manchester

Northwest England – Manchester

Accommodation
1. The Hatters
2. Manchester YHA

A free bus service runs between Piccadilly and Victoria Stations.

TRAIN
There are 98 stations on Manchester's suburban train system, which many people take to the airport or the Peak District.

TRAM
The Metrolink tram network *(website www.metrolink.co.uk)* provides good coverage in the city centre and extends out to some suburbs. It is a useful mode of transport for many travellers with eight stops in the city centre including the two main train stations. One-way fares range from 50p to £1.80.

FARES
There are several good value travel passes available that give you unlimited travel on buses, trains and trams.

Day Saver
The Day Saver is a flexible travel pass that gives you unlimited travel on a

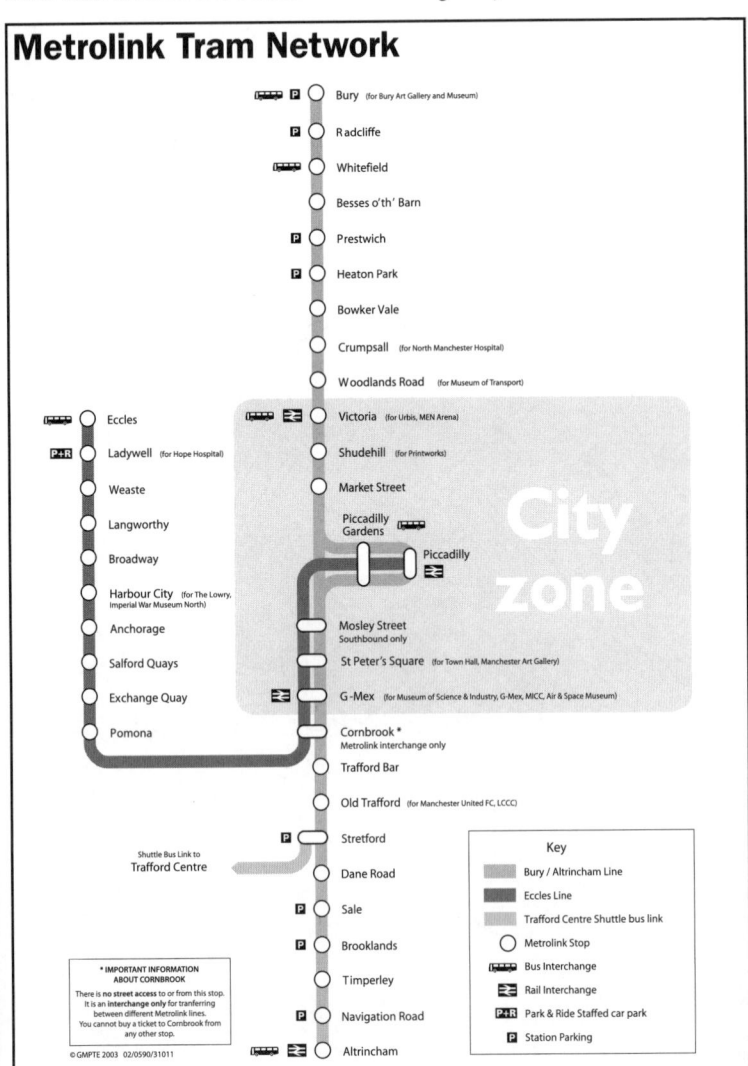

Metrolink Tram Network

Bury (for Bury Art Gallery and Museum)
Radcliffe
Whitefield
Besses o'th' Barn
Prestwich
Heaton Park
Bowker Vale
Crumpsall (for North Manchester Hospital)
Woodlands Road (for Museum of Transport)

Eccles
Ladywell (for Hope Hospital)
Weaste
Langworthy
Broadway
Harbour City (for The Lowry, Imperial War Museum North)
Anchorage
Salford Quays
Exchange Quay
Pomona

Victoria (for Urbis, MEN Arena)
Shudehill (for Printworks)
Market Street
Piccadilly Gardens
Piccadilly
Mosley Street (Southbound only)
St Peter's Square (for Town Hall, Manchester Art Gallery)
G-Mex (for Museum of Science and Industry, G-Mex, MICC, Air & Space Museum)

City zone

Cornbrook *
Metrolink interchange only
Trafford Bar
Old Trafford (for Manchester United FC, LCCC)
Stretford — Shuttle Bus Link to Trafford Centre
Dane Road
Sale
Brooklands
Timperley
Navigation Road
Altrincham

Key
- Bury / Altrincham Line
- Eccles Line
- Trafford Centre Shuttle bus link
- Metrolink Stop
- Bus Interchange
- Rail Interchange
- P+R Park & Ride Staffed car park
- P Station Parking

* IMPORTANT INFORMATION ABOUT CORNBROOK
There is **no street access** to or from this stop. It is an interchange only for transferring between different Metrolink lines. You cannot buy a ticket to Cornbrook from any other stop.

© GMPTE 2003 02/0590/31011

combination of buses, trains and trams in the Greater Manchester area. It is valid after 9.30am Mon-Fri and all day on weekends.

Fare	
Bus only	£2.95-3.30
Bus & train	£3.80
Bus & tram	£4.50
Train & tram	£5
Bus, train & tram	£6.50

Wayfarer
The Wayfarer ticket is similar to the Day Saver but it allows travel beyond the Greater Manchester area allowing you to travel to parts of Cheshire, Derbyshire, Lancashire and Staffordshire. Like the Day Saver, it gives you unlimited travel on buses, trains and trams. It is ideal if you want to make excursions to the Peak District.

The Wayfarer costs £7.80 for one-day unlimited travel or £11 for a weekend pass.

Accommodation
The Hatters
This new hostel is housed in a renovated building that was built as a hat factory in 1907. Facilities include a good kitchen and a lounge with a pool table and TV. It has very friendly staff and a good atmosphere. It was still undergoing development when we visited but it looks promising.
50 Newton Street, Manchester
◉ *Manchester Piccadilly*
☎ *(0161) 236 9500*
Website *www.hattersgroup.com*
Dorm bed *£14-17.50;* **double/twin room** *£45; prices include breakfast*
Credit cards *Amex, Diners, JCB, MC, Visa*
Reception open *24 hours*

Maintenance & cleanliness	★★★★
Facilities	★★☆
Atmosphere & character	★★★★
Security	★★★★
Overall rating	★★★★☆

Manchester YHA
Manchester's YHA offers good facilities for all ages but it is rather too spread out to have a great atmosphere. It has a good kitchen, although the lighting is poor, and the dining area has a nice view and is good for chatting with other travellers. There is also a patio with tables.
Potato Wharf, Castlefield, Manchester
◉ *G-Mex* ◉ *Deansgate*
☎ *(0161) 839 9960*
Website *www.yha.org.uk*
Dorm bed *£22.50 (£20.50 HI/YHA); price includes breakfast*
Credit cards *Amex, Diners, JCB, MC, Visa*
Reception open *7am-11pm daily*

Maintenance & cleanliness	★★★★
Facilities	★★
Atmosphere & character	★★★☆
Security	★★★★
Overall rating	★★★

Peppers Hostel
Peppers is a small hostel with friendly staff and a cosy feel although some travellers may find it a little cramped. It has a good kitchen, a small TV lounge and a smoker's lounge. There is a second building down the road that is used for long term guests.
17 Great Stone Road, Stretford, Manchester
◉ *Old Trafford*
☎ *(0161) 848 9770*
Dorm bed *£12;* **twin room** *£28; prices include breakfast*
Credit cards *Amex, Diners, MC, Visa*
Reception open *7am-midnight*

Maintenance & cleanliness	★★★
Facilities	★★
Atmosphere & character	★★★★
Security	★★★☆
Overall rating	★★★

Eating & Drinking
Manchester has a good choice of restaurants, pubs and bars including trendy canal-side bars and cafés as well as more traditional English pubs.

If you're preparing your own food, head to the Tesco at 58-66 Market Street or Sainsbury at Piccadilly Station.

Sights
Imperial War Museum North
Manchester's branch of the Imperial War Museum is housed in a striking

building at The Quays in Trafford Park. The museum's galleries feature exhibits focusing on how war changes people's lives and it includes a timeline of 20th and 21st century conflict.
The Quays, Trafford Wharf Road, Trafford Park, Manchester
☎ *(0161) 836 4000*
Website *www.iwm.org.uk/north/*
Admission *free*
Open *10am-6pm daily*

The Lowry

This new arts centre at Salford Quays features art exhibitions including works by LS Lowry.
Pier Eight, Salford Quays, Salford
🚇 *Harbour City* 🚌 *51, 52, 69, 91, 92, 250*
☎ *(0161) 876 2000*
Website *www.thelowry.com*
Admission *free*
Open *Mon-Fri 11am-5pm, Sat 10am-5pm, Sun 11am-5pm*

Manchester Art Gallery

This art museum displays a collection of Victorian art including works by the Pre-Raphaelites and it features an excellent decorative art collection.
Mosley Street, Manchester
🚇 *Mosley Street, St Peter's Square*
☎ *(0161) 235 8888*
Website *www.manchestergalleries.org*
Admission *free*
Open *Tue-Sun 10am-5pm*

Manchester Jewish Museum

This restored synagogue has displays about Manchester's Jewish history.
190 Cheetham Hill Road, Manchester
☎ *(0161) 832 9879*
Website *www.manchesterjewishmuseum.com*
Admission *£2.50*
Open *Mon-Thu 10.30am-4pm, Sun 10.30am-5pm*

Manchester Museum

This large museum has archaeology and natural history displays and is best known for its excellent Egyptology exhibits.
Oxford Road, Manchester
🚌 *11, 16, 41, 42, 47, 190, 191*
☎ *(0161) 275 2634*
Website *www.museum.man.ac.uk*
Admission *free*
Open *Mon-Sat 10am-5pm, Sun 11am-4pm*

Manchester United Museum & Tour

This museum is dedicated to Manchester United, the world's richest and most famous football team. It has displays depicting the club's history and the tour allows you to go behind the scenes at Old Trafford.
Sir Matt Busby Way, Old Trafford
🚇 *Old Trafford*
☎ *(0161) 442 1994*
Admission *£5.50, £8.50 including tour*
Open *9.30am-5pm daily*

Museum of Science & Industry

This museum focuses on the Industrial Revolution and the technological achievements that made it possible. The museum's highlights include the world's largest collection of working steam mill engines and the world's first computer, developed in Manchester in 1948.
Liverpool Road, Castlefield, Manchester
🚇 *Deansgate* 🚇 *G-Mex* 🚌 *33*
☎ *(0161) 832 244*
Website *www.msim.org.uk*
Admission *free*
Open *10am-5pm daily*

Museum of Transport

The Museum of Transport has exhibits about public transport in Greater Manchester including old horse-drawn buses and the Metrolink tram.
Boyle Street, Manchester
🚌 *135* 🚇 *Woodlands Road*
☎ *(0161) 205 2122*
Website *www.gmts.co.uk*
Admission *£3*
Open *Jan-Feb Wed, Sat-Sun 10am-4pm; Mar-Oct Wed, Sat-Sun 10am-5pm; Nov-Dec Wed, Sat-Sun 10am-4pm*

Urbis Museum of the Modern City

Urbis features four floors of exhibits about life in Manchester and other cities.
Cathedral Gardens, Manchester
🚇🚇 *Victoria*
☎ *(0161) 605 8200*

Website www.urbis.org.uk
Admission free
Open 10am-4.30pm daily

Merseyside

Liverpool

The home of the Beatles is one of the most popular northwestern cities with backpackers. It is a little run down with a lot of boarded up buildings but it is developing into a vibrant city with excellent – and affordable – nightlife, good shopping and popular attractions.

Liverpool makes a big deal of its musical heritage especially its connection with the Beatles, who originated in the city. There are plenty of Beatles related attractions such as the Beatles Story and walking tours around the band's old haunts.

Other attractions include Albert Dock, a redeveloped dockside area that is home to the Beatles Story, HM Customs & Excise Museum, Merseyside Maritime Museum, Museum of Liverpool Life and the Tate Liverpool.

Practical Information
Tourist Information Centres
Merseyside Maritime Museum
Albert Dock, Liverpool
Ⓜ *James Street*
☎ *(0151) 709 5111 or 0906 680 6886*
(25p per minute)
Website www.visitliverpool.com
Open 10am-5.30pm daily

Queen Square, Roe Street, Liverpool
Ⓡ Ⓜ *Lime Street*
☎ *(0151) 709 5111 or 0906 680 6886*
(25p per minute)
Website www.visitliverpool.com
Open Mon 9am-5.30pm, Tue 10am-5.30pm, Wed-Sat 9am-5.30pm, Sun 10.30am-4.30pm

INTERNET ACCESS
Caffè Latte.net
4 South Hunter Street, Liverpool
☎ *(0151) 708 9610*

Accommodation
❶ International Inn
❷ Liverpool YHA

Open Mon-Fri 8am-9pm, Sat-Sun 9am-5.30pm

Coming & Going
AIR
Liverpool John Lennon Airport *(website www.liverpooljohnlennonairport.com)* has flights to destinations in Britain, Ireland and Europe and is served by budget airlines including easyJet *(website www.easyjet.com)* and Ryanair *(website www.ryanair.com)*. The airport is 13km south east of the city centre and express bus 500 runs every 30 minutes between the airport and the city centre. Alternatively you can take the train to Hunts Cross and transfer to bus 81A to the airport.

Manchester Airport *(website www.manchesterairport.co.uk)* is also close with direct trains linking it to Liverpool Lime Street Station.

BUS
National Express *(☎ 0870 5808080; website www.nationalexpress.co.uk)* operate buses to Manchester every 30 minutes, Birmingham and London every two hours and York every hour. Buses depart from the coach station on Norton Street in the city centre.

FERRY
SeaCat *(☎ 0870 5523523; website www.seacat.co.uk)* ferries sail from Liverpool to Dublin and the Isle of Man Steam Packet Company *(☎ 0870 5523523; website www.steam-packet.com)* sails to Douglas on the Isle of Man. These ferries depart from Princes Landing Stage near the Pier Head, about 600 metres from James Street station.

NorseMerchant Ferries *(☎ 0870 6004321; website www.norsemerchant.com)* sail from Birkenhead (on the other side of the Mersey) to Belfast and Dublin. Take the train to Hamilton Square and walk down Canning Street to get to the Birkenhead ferry terminal.

TRAIN
Virgin Trains *(website www.virgin-trains.co.uk)* and Central Trains *(website www.centraltrains.co.uk)* run trains from Liverpool Lime Street station to Birmingham, London (Euston station), Manchester and Stoke-on-Trent.

Local Transport
Mersey Travel *(☎ 0870 608 2608; website www.merseytravel.org)* operates an extensive public transport service comprised of buses and trains and Mersey Ferries run ferries across the Mersey.

BUS
Liverpool has an extensive bus network, which is a handy way to get to the airport and destinations throughout the city. Apart from taking a tour, the bus is the best way to get to many of the Beatles' sites like Penny Lane and Strawberry Fields.

FERRY
Mersey Ferries *(☎ (0151) 330 1444; website www.merseyferries.co.uk)*, which sail between Liverpool and Birkenhead on the opposite side of the Mersey, have been famous ever since Gerry and the Pacemakers had their 1964 hit with Ferry Across the Mersey. The ferry costs £1.25 one-way or £2.05 return.

TRAIN
Merseytravel's train network runs as far as Chester and Ellesmere Port and has underground stops at Central, James Street, Lime Street and Moorfields in the city centre.

TRAVEL PASSES
Pre-paid Saveaway tickets are a good value way to get around. They offer unlimited bus and train travel in Liverpool for £2.10, Liverpool and Birkenhead for £3.20 or the entire Merseyside area for £3.70. The Saveaway ticket doesn't cover travel to Merseytravel stations outside Merseyside (such as Chester or Ellesmere Port).

Zone	Fare
Area A, B, C or D	£2.10
Cross River (Area B-Zone E)	£3.20
All areas (whole of Merseyside)	£3.70

Accommodation
Embassie Hostel
The Embassie is in a quiet location facing Falkner Square – a 15-minute walk to the city centre. It has a warm and cosy atmosphere with exposed brick walls

and it is a little bit cluttered but this just adds to the ambience. Facilities include a kitchen and two TV lounges including a basement lounge with a pool table. The biggest dorm has 20 beds.
1 Falkner Square, Liverpool
🚌 *80, 86, 88*
☎ *(0151) 707 1089*
Website *Dorm bed £13 (£11 HI/YHA; £8 HI/YHA & student)*
Dorm bed *£13.50 first night, £12.50 subsequent nights*
Reception open *24 hours*

Maintenance & cleanliness	★★★☆
Facilities	★★
Atmosphere & character	★★★★★
Security	★
Overall rating	★★★

International Inn

International Inn is an excellent hostel with good quality facilities that include a TV lounge with pool table and table football plus a kitchen and adjoining Internet café. However the en suite showers aren't very well ventilated and can get very stuffy.
4 South Hunter Street, Liverpool
☎ *(0151) 709 8135*
Website *www.internationalinn.co.uk*
Dorm bed *£16; twin room £36*
Credit cards *MC, Visa*
Reception open *24 hours*

Maintenance & cleanliness	★★★★☆
Facilities	★★
Atmosphere & character	★★★★
Security	★★★★
Overall rating	★★★★☆

YHA Liverpool

Liverpool's YHA is a modern hostel near the docks. Facilities include a kitchen (no oven), a big dining room, a TV area near the reception and a room with a pool table.
25 Tabley Street, Wapping, Liverpool
☎ *(0151) 709 8888*
Website *www.yha.org.uk*
Dorm bed *£22.50 (£20.50 HI/YHA; £17.50 HI/YHA & ISIC);* **double/twin room** *£46 (£42 YHA/HI; £36 HI/YHA & ISIC); prices include breakfast*
Credit cards *MC, Visa*
Reception open *7am-11pm daily*

Maintenance & cleanliness	★★★★☆
Facilities	★★
Atmosphere & character	★★☆
Security	★★★★☆
Overall rating	★★★

Sights
BEATLES SIGHTS

Many of Liverpool's attractions are based around the Beatles. These include Paul McCartney's house where John Lennon and Paul first met, the Cavern Club where the band played, and of course Penny Lane and Strawberry Fields.

20 Forthlin Road

Paul McCartney lived at this house on Forthlin Road and it is here that he first met John Lennon. Many early Beatles songs where written here.
20 Forthlin Road, Allerton; entry only by minibus from Albert Dock or Speke Hall (advance booking essential
☎ *(0151) 708 8574 morning tours or (0151) 427 7231 afternoon tours)*
☎ *0870 900 0256*
Website *www.nationaltrust.org.uk*
Admission *£12 including entry to Mendips*
Tours run *27 Mar-31 Oct*

Beatles Story

This popular attraction has displays on various aspects of the Beatles including Liverpool in the 60s, the Abbey Road studios and their Hamburg era. Some of the highlights include a replica of the Cavern Club, George Harrison's first guitar, John Lennon's original glasses and the Beatles' jackets.
Britannia Vaults, Albert Dock
☎ *(0151) 709 1963*
Website *www.beatlesstory.com*
Admission *£7.95*
Open *10am-5pm daily*

Cavern Club

The Beatles, and many other prominent Merseyside acts, played here. Matthew Street and the surrounding area have a lot of other Beatles sights including the Beatles Shop and the Matthew Street Gallery, which exhibits art by John Lennon.
Matthew Street, Liverpool

☎ 0871 222 1957
Website www.cavern-liverpool.co.uk
Open Mon-Wed noon-6pm, Thu-Sat noon-2am, Sun noon-12.30am

Magical Mystery Tour
Several companies operate tours to Liverpool's main Beatles sights but the main tour operator is Beatles Magical Mystery Tour, which runs two-hour tours to sites connected to the Beatles. Tours depart from the Beatles Story (Britannia Vaults, Albert Dock) and finish at the Cavern Club (Matthew Street, Liverpool)
☎ 0871 222 1963
Website www.cavern-liverpool.co.uk/mmt/
Tours cost £11.95

Mendips
John Lennon grew up in this house with his Aunt Mimi and Uncle George and some early Beatles songs were written here.
Entry is only by minibus from Albert Dock or Speke Hall (advance booking essential ☎ *(0151) 708 8574 morning tours or (0151) 427 7231 afternoon tours).*
☎ 0870 900 0256
Website www.nationaltrust.org.uk
Admission £12 including entry to 20 Forthlin Road
Tours run 27 Mar-31 Oct

Penny Lane & Strawberry Fields
Many travellers make the trip to Penny Lane (🚍 33, 35, 86A) and Strawberry Fields (🚍 176).

OTHER SIGHTS
Conservation Centre
The Conservation Centre is a museum about museums. More specifically it is about the work of museums' conservators with exhibits about how Merseyside's museum collections are cared for and presented.
Whitechapel, Liverpool
🚍Ⓜ *Lime Street*
☎ (0151) 478 4499
Website www.conservationcentre.org.uk
Admission free
Open Mon-Sat 10am-5pm, Sun noon-5pm

Historic Warships
The Historic Warships at Birkenhead features a museum and several historic warships that include *HMS Plymouth*, a Type 12 frigate; *HMS Onyx*, an 'O' class submarine and *U534*, a German World War II U-boat.
East Float, Dock Road, Birkenhead
🚢 *Seacombe, then* 🚍 *401*
☎ (0151) 650 1573
Website www.warships.freeserve.co.uk
Admission £6; ***U534 tour*** *£8.50;*
admission & U534 tour *£14.50*
Open Jan-Mar 10am-4pm daily; Apr-Aug 10am-5pm daily; Sep-Dec 10am-4pm daily

HM Customs & Excise Museum
This museum is dedicated to those friendly folk who guard Britain's borders and extort VAT and customs duties. It has displays about the customs officers' job and smugglers they catch.
Merseyside Maritime Museum, Albert Dock, Liverpool
Ⓜ *James Street*
☎ (0151) 478 4499
Website www.customsandexcisemuseum.org.uk
Admission free
Open 10am-5pm daily

Liverpool Cathedral
This massive Anglican Cathedral offers sweeping views from its 101-metre tower.
St James Mount, Liverpool
Ⓜ *Central*
Admission free; tower £2
Open 8am-6pm daily

Liverpool Football Club Museum
Fans of Liverpool FC will love this museum that includes a cinema showing highlights from the club's history. You can also take a tour of Anfield stadium that takes you behind the scenes giving you a chance to visit the dressing room and walk down the tunnel onto the pitch.
Anfield Road, Liverpool
☎ (0151) 260 6677
Website www.liverpoolfc.tv/club/tour.htm
Museum admission £4; **museum &**

tour £9
Open *10am-4pm daily; no stadium tours on match days*

Liverpool Museum
This major museum features exhibits from around that world that include artefacts from Egypt, Greece and Cyprus plus an award-winning Natural History Centre and Planetarium.
William Brown Street, Liverpool
🚆Ⓜ *Lime Street*
☎ *(0151) 478 4399*
Website *www.liverpoolmuseum.org.uk*
Admission *free*
Open *Mon-Sat 10am-5pm, Sun noon-5pm*

Merseyside Maritime Museum
This museum in a former warehouse at Albert Dock tells the story of Liverpool's status as one of the world's great ports. It includes displays about the nine million emigrants who sailed from Liverpool between 1830 and 1930, the slave trade and artefacts salvaged from the *Titanic*.
Albert Dock, Liverpool
Ⓜ *James Street*
☎ *(0151) 478 4499*
Website *www.merseysidemaritimemuseum.org.uk*
Admission *free*
Open *10am-5pm daily*

Museum of Liverpool Life
This museum celebrates the city's diversity and features exhibits on Liverpool's culture including football, music and television.
Pier Head, Liverpool
Ⓜ *James Street*
☎ *(0151) 478 4080*
Website *www.museumofliverpoollife.org.uk*
Admission *free*
Open *10am-5pm daily*

Speke Hall
This half-timbered Tudor house dates from 1530 and is surrounded by fine gardens. Minibuses to 20 Forthlin Road and Mendips depart from here.
The Walk
🚌 *80, 82, 180*
☎ *(0151) 427 7231*
Website *www.nationaltrust.org.uk*
Admission *£6; grounds only £3*
Open *20 Mar-31 Oct Wed-Sun 1pm-5.30pm; 6 Nov-5 Dec Sat-Sun 1pm-4.30pm*

Tate Liverpool
The Tate Liverpool is Britain's largest modern art gallery outside London. It has a collection of art by international and British artists and hosts a programme of rotating exhibits taken from the gallery's archives.
Albert Dock, Liverpool L3
Ⓜ *James Street;* 🚌 *1, 4, 222*
☎ *(0151) 702 7400*
Website *www.tate.org.uk/liverpool/*
Admission *free; special exhibitions £4*
Open *Tue-Sun 10am-5.50pm*

The Walker
This large art museum has an extensive collection that includes works from the 14th to 20th centuries. The gallery's highlights feature European art including works by Degas and Rembrandt; 18th and 19th century British art including works by the Pre-Raphaelites and 20th century art including work by David Hockney.
William Brown Street, Liverpool
🚆Ⓜ *Lime Street*
☎ *(0151) 478 4199*
Website *www.thewalker.org.uk*
Admission *free*
Open *Mon-Sat 10am-5pm, Sun noon-5pm*

Cheshire
The historic walled city of Chester is the main attraction in this county between Liverpool and Wales.

Chester
Chester boasts Britain's most complete city walls and is widely known for its wealth of Tudor-style architecture. It also home to the country's largest Roman amphitheatre.

Practical Information
Tourist Information Centre
Vicar's Lane, Chester

☎ (01244) 402 111
Website www.chestertourism.com
Open *Jan-Mar Mon-Sat 10am-5pm, Sun 10am-4pm; Apr-Sep Mon-Sat 9am-5.30pm, Sun 10am-4pm; Oct-Dec Mon-Sat 10am-5pm, Sun 10am-4pm*

Coming & Going
National Express (☎ *0870 580 8080; website www.nationalexpress.co.uk*) buses stop outside the tourist information centre on Vicar's Lane. Merseytravel (*website www.merseytravel.org*) trains connect Chester with Liverpool (James Street).

Accommodation
Chester Backpackers
Chester Backpackers is a small hostel with a good atmosphere. It has new carpets and solid metal bunk beds and facilities include a small TV lounge, Internet access, a tiny kitchen and dining room and a small rooftop terrace.
67 Boughton Street, Chester
☎ (01244) 400 185
Website www.chesterbackpackers.co.uk
Dorm bed *£13;* **single room** *£18.50;* **double/twin room** *£34*
Credit cards *Amex, JCB, MC, Visa*
Reception open *9am-late*
📺 Ⓚ

Maintenance & cleanliness	★★★★½
Facilities	★
Atmosphere & character	★★★★
Security	★★
Overall rating	★★★

YHA Chester
Chester's YHA hostel is in a grand old building with a large ornate staircase. Facilities include a cafeteria, a narrow kitchen, a big dining room, a TV lounge, a quiet reading room and a games room with a pool table and table football.
40 Hough Green, Chester
🚌 *4, 4A*
☎ (01244) 680056
Website www.yha.org.uk
Dorm bed *£18 (£16 HI/YHA; £13 HI/YHA & ISIC)*
Credit cards *MC, Visa*
Open *9 Jan-18 Dec;* **reception open** *7am-10.30pm;* **curfew** *11pm*
🍽️ 📺 Ⓚ Ⓛ

Maintenance & cleanliness	★★★★½
Facilities	★★★½
Atmosphere & character	★★★
Security	★★★
Overall rating	★★★

Sights
Chester Cathedral
Originally a Benedictine Abbey, the 1000-year-old Chester Cathedral is noted for its fine 800-year-old quire stalls and the 200-year-old cobweb picture.
☎ (01244) 324 756
Website www.chestercathedral.com
Admission *£4*
Open *Mon-Sat 9am-5pm, Sun 1pm-6pm*

Chester Zoo
This popular zoo features over 6000 animals including elephants, black rhinos, chimpanzees and jaguar.
Upton-by-Chester, Chester
🚌 *4, 8, 411, 412, X8*
☎ (01244) 380 280
Website www.chesterzoo.org
Admission *£12*
Open *1 Jan-13 Feb 10am-3.30pm daily; 14 Feb-28 Mar 10am-4pm daily; 29 Mar-2 Apr 10am-4.30pm daily; 2-18 Apr 10am-5pm daily; 19-30 Apr 10am-4.30pm daily; 1-3 May 10am-5.30pm daily; 4-28 May 10am-4.30pm daily; 29 May-6 Jun 10am-5.30pm daily; 7 Jun-16 Jul 10am-4.30pm daily; 17 Jul-5 Sep 10am-5.30pm daily; 6-26 Sep 10am-4.30pm daily; 27 Sep-31 Oct 10am-4pm daily; 1 Nov-23 Dec 10am-3.30pm daily*

Grosvenor Museum
This museum has exhibits on local history with a strong focus on Chester's Roman heritage.
Grosvenor Street, Chester
☎ (01244) 402 008
Admission *free*
Open *Mon-Sat 10.30am-5pm, Sun 1pm-4pm*

Roman Amphitheatre
Located just outside the city walls near the tourist information centre are the 2000-year-old ruins of the largest Roman amphitheatre in Britain.
Vicars Lane, Chester

Ellesmere Port

This city is considered by many as a southern suburb of Liverpool. The main attraction here is the excellent Boat Museum.

Practical Information
Ellesmere Port Tourist Information Centre
Unit 22b, McArthur Glen Outlet Village, Kinsey Road, Ellesmere Port
☎ *(0151) 356 7879*
Open *Mon-Fri 10am-8pm, Sat 10am-7pm, Sun 11am-5pm*

Coming & Going
Ellesmere Port is easily accessible from Chester and Liverpool. Merseytravel (*website www.merseytravel.org*) trains connect Chester with Liverpool (James Street).

Accommodation
There are no hostels in Ellesmere Port with the closest budget accommodation in Chester or Liverpool.

Sights
The Boat Museum
The Boat Museum has an extensive collection of boating related exhibits with an emphasis on canal boats and Britain's inland waterways. It includes the world's largest collection of traditional canal boats and you are able to step aboard most of the boats on display.
South Pier Road, Ellesmere Port
🚉 *Ellesmere Port*
☎ *(0151) 355 5017*
Website *www.boatmuseum.org.uk*
Admission *£5.50 (£4.30 students)*
Open *Jan-Mar Mon-Wed & Sat-Sun 11am-4pm; Apr-Oct 10am-5pm daily; Nov-Dec Mon-Wed & Sat-Sun 11am-4pm*

Lancashire

This county between Manchester and the Lake District is best known for the tacky beach resort of Blackpool. Another attraction is the historic city of Lancaster, which is bypassed by most travellers although it is well worth a visit.

Blackpool

More than any other seaside resort, Blackpool typifies the tacky English seaside resort. There is nothing tasteful about Blackpool, which is cluttered with souvenir shops, fast food restaurants, and amusement arcades and it is dominated by Blackpool Tower and the Blackpool Pleasure Beach amusement park with its roller coasters and sideshows. Although there is nothing quaint about this city, it can be a lot of fun and is worth visiting to see how cheerfully tacky it really is.

Blackpool is also famous for its illuminations, which take place each year between September and early November when the tower and 8km of the Promenade is lit with bright lights.

Practical Information
Blackpool Tourist Information Centre
1 Clifton Street, Blackpool
☎ *(01253) 478 222*
Website *www.visitblackpool.com*
Open *Jan-Apr Mon-Sat 8.45am-4.45pm; May-Oct Mon-Sat 9am-5pm, Sun 10am-4pm; Nov-Dec Mon-Sat 8.45am-4.45pm*

Coming & Going
AIR
Blackpool's small airport has Ryanair (*website www.ryanair.com*) flights from Dublin and London (Stansted). The airport is only 4km south of the town centre. Buses 7 and L1 stop outside the terminal building and the tram and Squires Gate train station are nearby.

BUS
Local buses go to destinations throughout Lancashire and neighbouring counties and include the X61 bus to Manchester and National Express (☎ *870 580 8080; website www.nationalexpress.co.uk*) buses go to Birmingham and London.

TRAIN
Blackpool has several train stations accessed by a branch line from Preston that splits in two running to Blackpool North and Blackpool South. Blackpool North is the best station for the city

centre but Pleasure Beach Station is on the Blackpool South line.

First North Western (*website www.firstnorthwestern.co.uk*) run most train services with trains to Liverpool and Manchester; change at Preston for trains north to Lancaster, the Lake District and Scotland.

Local Transport
Metro Coastlines (*website www.blackpooltransport.com*) run bus and tram services in the Blackpool area. The tram, which runs between the city centre and Pleasure Beach, is probably the easiest way to get around although bus L1 runs along a similar route. A Blackpool Transport Travelcard costs £5 for one day, £13 for three days, £17 for five days and £18 for seven days unlimited bus and tram travel in the Blackpool area.

Sights
Blackpool Tower
Looking like a low budget replica of the Eiffel Tower, the 171m-high Blackpool Tower was erected in 1894 by a London businessman impressed by the original, which he saw in Paris in 1880. At the base of the tower is an eclectic collection of garish attractions including amusement arcades, a casino, aquarium and a Victorian ballroom.
Promenade, Blackpool
🚇 *Blackpool North* 🚌 *5, 6, 7, 11, 14*
☎ *(01253) 292 029*
Website *www.theblackpooltower.co.uk*
Admission *£12*
Open *3 Jul-7 Nov 10am-11pm daily*

Pleasure Beach
This big amusement park boasts 13 roller coasters, which include historic wooden ones such as the Big Dipper and Grand National and the more modern Big One, Europe's tallest rollercoaster at 72m and its fastest, reaching speeds of 140km/h.
Ocean Boulevard, Blackpool
🚇 *Pleasure Beach* 🚌 *2, L1*
☎ *0870 444 5566*
Website *www.blackpoolpleasurebeach.com*
Admission *free, but charge for individual rides; all day unlimited ride pass £30; two-day unlimited ride pass £45; seven-day unlimited ride pass £90*
Open *Mar-Nov opening times vary, call* ☎ *0870 444 5566 for current opening times*

Lancaster
Although its history dates thousands of years, Lancaster's heyday was the Georgian era when it was an important port. The city's main draw is the castle and other attractions include the City and Maritime Museums.

Practical Information
Tourist Information Centre
29 Castle Hill, Lancaster
☎ *(01524) 32878*
Website *www.visitlancaster.co.uk*
Open *Apr-Sep Mon-Sat 10am-5pm*

Coming & Going
Lancaster is on the main west coast rail line and is served by several train companies including TransPennine Express (*website www.firstgroup.com/tpexpress/*) and Virgin Trains (*website www.virgintrains.co.uk*).

Stagecoach (*website www.stagecoachbus.co.uk*) operate buses in Lancashire and neighbouring counties and National Express have buses from Lancaster to Birmingham, Glasgow, London and Preston.

Local Transport
Stagecoach (*website www.stagecoachbus.co.uk*) also runs local buses in the Lancaster and Morecambe area. The Bay Dayrider ticket costs £3.50 and is good for unlimited travel on Stagecoach buses in the Lancaster and Morecambe area (Dayrider tickets cannot be used before 9am Mon-Fri).

Sights
Lancaster Castle
One of England's best-preserved castles is also one of Europe's longest running prisons. It houses an historic courthouse where the Lancashire Witches were tried in addition to many convicts that were subsequently transported to Australia.
Shire Hall, Castle Parade, Lancaster
☎ *(01524) 64998*

Website www.lancastercastle.com
Admission £4 (£2.50 students)
Open 10am-5pm daily

Lancaster City Museum
This museum in Lancaster's former town hall has exhibits detailing the city's history with artefacts from the Neolithic age to the present day.
Market Square, Lancaster
☎ *(01524) 64637*
Website www.lancsmuseums.gov.uk
Admission free
Open Mon-Sat 10am-5pm

Lancaster Maritime Museum
This museum has exhibits relating to Lancaster's maritime history including the history of the port and Lancaster Canal, the maritime trade and the fishing industry.
Customs House, St George's Quay, Lancaster
☎ *(01524) 64637*
Website www.lancsmuseums.gov.uk
Admission £2
Open Jan-Easter 12.30pm-4pm daily; Easter-Oct 11am-5pm daily; Nov-Dec 12.30pm-4pm daily

Cumbria

This largely rural county is one of England's most visited, with people coming for the fabulous Lake District National Park.

Kendal

This busy town is a popular gateway to the Lake District. It is a nice town with good transport connections but it can become crowded on weekends.

Practical Information
Kendal Tourist Information Centre
Corner Highgate & Lowther Street, Kendal
☎ *(01539) 725 758*
Website www.kendaltown.org.uk

Coming & Going
Both National Express (☎ *0870 580 8080; website www.nationalexpress.co.uk)* and Stagecoach *(website www.stagecoachbus.co.uk)* run buses linking Kendal with the Lake District and cities like Lancaster, Carlisle and Manchester. Stagecoaches routes include the useful bus 106 that goes to Penrith and the 555 to Lancaster and Keswick.

The Cumbria Goldrider is a good value pass that costs £20.50 and gives you seven days unlimited travel on Stagecoach buses throughout Cumbria.

Trans Pennine Express *(website www.firstgroup.com/tpexpress/)* run trains to Lancaster and Manchester (Piccadilly) every two hours. Change at Oxenholme for trains to Carlisle and Glasgow.

Local Transport
Stagecoach *(website www.stagecoachbus.co.uk)* run local bus services in Kendal. All buses run a circular route around the town centre and buses 42, 43 and 43A run between the town centre and the train station.

A seven-day Megarider ticket costs £7.80. This ticket gives you unlimited travel on Stagecoach buses in the Kendal area.

Accommodation
YHA Kendal
Kendal's YHA hostel is a Georgian town house in the town centre that has facilities that include the usual kitchen and TV lounge plus a games room with pool tables and table football.
118 Highgate, Kendal
☎ *(01539) 724 906*
Website www.yha.org.uk
Dorm bed £18 (£16 HI/YHA; £13 HI/YHA & ISIC); ***twin room*** £37.80 (£33.80 HI/YHA; £27.80 HI/YHA & ISIC); prices include breakfast
Credit cards MC, Visa
Open 2 Jan-20 Mar check with hostel; 21 Mar-28 Aug every day; 29 Aug-18 Dec Fri-Sat; reception open 7am-10am & 1pm-11.30pm daily; curfew 11.30pm

[TV] [K] [L]

Maintenance & cleanliness	★★★★☆
Facilities	★★
Atmosphere & character	★★
Security	★★★☆
Overall rating	★★★☆

Sights
Kendal Museum
This small museum depicts Kendal's history from prehistoric times to the present day.
Station Road, Kendal
☎ *(01539) 721 374*
Website *www.kendalmuseum.org.uk*
Admission *£2.50*
Open *12 Feb-31 Mar Mon-Sat 10.30am-4pm; 1 Apr-31 Oct Mon-Sat 10.30am-5pm; 1 Nov-23 Dec 10.30am-4pm*

Museum of Lakeland Life
This museum has displays about people's lives in Cumbria during the 19th and early 20th centuries.
Kirkland, Kendal
☎ *(01539) 722 464*
Website *www.lakelandmuseum.org.uk*
Admission *£3.50 (£2 students)*
Open *20 Jan-Mar Mon-Sat 10.30am-4pm; Apr-Oct Mon-Sat 10.30am-5pm; Nov-23 Dec Mon-Sat 10.30am-4pm*

Lake District National Park

The most scenic of England's national parks is popular with both locals and international visitors. It is famed for its lakes, which are visited by thousands of tourists, most of whom stay in the cluster of towns that include Ambleside, Coniston, Grasmere, Hawkshead and Windermere; however you can escape the crowds if you venture away from this area to lakes such as Buttermere, Crummock Water and Wastwater.

Ambleside
This small town north of Windermere is a well-located base for exploring the Lake District.

Practical Information
Ambleside Tourist Information Centre
Central Buildings, Market Cross
☎ *(015394) 32582*
Website *www.ambleside online.co.uk/adverts/tic/main.html*
Open *9am-5pm daily*

Accommodation
Ambleside Backpackers
This hostel is in a quiet lane and it has a big kitchen, dining room and a cosy common room with a TV and piano. It has new bunk beds. The biggest dorm has 16 beds but most dorms are smaller.
Old Lake Road, Ambleside
☎ *(015394) 32340*
Website *www.englishlakesbackpackers.co.uk*
Dorm bed *£13.75; price includes breakfast*
Credit cards *MC, Visa*
Reception open *8.30am-1pm & 4pm-8.30pm daily*

Maintenance & cleanliness	★★★★
Facilities	★★
Atmosphere & character	★★★★
Security	★★½
Overall rating	★★★

YHA Ambleside
Ambleside YHA is one of the Lake District's more popular hostels and it boasts a peaceful lakeside setting. It has the usual kitchen and dining room plus two cosy TV lounges and a games room with pool tables and table football.
A591, Waterhead, Ambleside
☎ *(015394) 32304*
Website *www.yha.org.uk*
Dorm bed *£20 (£18 HI/YHA; £15 HI/YHA & ISIC);* **twin room** *£36.80 (£32.80 HI/YHA; £26.80 HI/YHA & ISIC)*
Credit cards *MC, Visa*
Reception open *7.15am-11.30pm daily*

Maintenance & cleanliness	★★★½
Facilities	★★
Atmosphere & character	★★½
Security	★★★★½
Overall rating	★★★

Sights
Armitt Museum & Library
This museum presents 2000 years of Ambleside's history through the eyes of local people.
Rydal Road, Ambleside
☎ *(015394) 31212*
Website *www.armitt.com*
Admission *£2.50 (£1.80 students)*
Open *10am-4.30pm daily*

Borrowdale

This quiet locale in the countryside alongside the River Derwent between Buttermere and Derwent Water is a pleasant place with several good hiking trails.

Accommodation
YHA Borrowdale

Borrowdale Youth Hostel is a wooden building with a newer annex. It features a cosy lounge, a fully equipped kitchen, a big dining room and a TV lounge with table tennis.
Longthwaite, Borrowdale
☎ *(0870) 770 5706*
Dorm bed *£16 (£14 HI/YHA; £11 HI/YHA & ISIC)*
Credit cards *MC, Visa*
Reception open *7.30am-10am & 1pm-10.30pm daily*

Maintenance & cleanliness	★★★★
Facilities	★★
Atmosphere & character	★★
Security	★★★½
Overall rating	★★★

Sights
Honister Slate Mine

This Honister Slate Mine features underground mine tours.
B5289, Borrowdale
🚌 *77, 77A, 491*
☎ *(017687) 77230*
Website *www.honister-slate-mine.co.uk*
Tours cost *£7*
Tours depart *10.30am, 12.30pm, 3.30pm*

Buttermere

This quiet corner of the Lake District is wedged between two lakes – Buttermere and Crummock Water. There are several good hiking trails that depart from here.

Accommodation
YHA Buttermere

This hostel is a slate house in the countryside with facilities that include several lounges and a kitchen and dining room.
B5289, Buttermere
🚌 *77/A (May-Oct)*
☎ *(017687) 70245*
Website *www.yha.org.uk*
Dorm bed *£18 (£16 HI/YHA; £13 HI/YHA & ISIC); price includes breakfast*
Credit cards *MC, Visa*
Reception open *7am-10am & 5pm-10.30pm daily;* **curfew** *11pm*

Maintenance & cleanliness	★★★★½
Facilities	★★½
Atmosphere & character	★★½
Security	★★
Overall rating	★★★½

Coniston

Coniston, in the southern Lake District is easily accessible from Kendal, Hawkshead and Windermere.

Practical Information
Coniston Tourist Information Centre

Main Car Park, Coniston
☎ *(015394) 41533*
Website *www.coniston-net.com*
Open *Jan-Easter Sat-Sun 10am-3.30pm; Easter-Oct 9.30am-5.30pm daily; Nov-Dec Sat-Sun 10am-3.30pm*

Accommodation
YHA Coniston Holly How

This big stone house has mostly eight-bed dormitories and common areas that include a large, but basic, kitchen, a lounge with a fireplace and a room upstairs with a TV, table football and video games.
Far End, Coniston
☎ *(015394) 41323*
Website *www.yha.org.uk*
Dorm bed *£14.50 (£12.50 HI/YHA; £9.50 HI/YHA & ISIC)*
Credit cards *MC, Visa*
Open *23 Jan-30 Jun check with hostel; 1 Jul-31 Aug every day; 1 Sep-25 Nov check with hostel;* **reception open** *7.30am-10am & 5pm-10.30pm daily;* **curfew** *11pm*

Maintenance & cleanliness	★★★★½
Facilities	★★½
Atmosphere & character	★★½
Security	★★½
Overall rating	★★★½

Grasmere

Grasmere is a popular spot, just a short distance north of Ambleside and Windermere, with three good hostels in the countryside.

Practical Information
Grasmere Tourist Information Centre
Red Bank Road, Grasmere
☎ *(015394) 35245*
Open *Jan-Easter Sat-Sun 10am-3.30pm; Easter-Oct 9.30am-5.30pm daily; Nov-Dec Sat-Sun 10am-3.30pm*

Accommodation
Grasmere Independent Hostel
This outstanding hostel is in a stone building with lots of charm. Everything here is maintained to a very high standard and it features a fully equipped kitchen and a cosy TV/common room with lovely views from the big circular windows. All the dorms have en suite bathrooms, good solid bunk beds and a locker for each bed.
Broadrayne Farm, A 591 Keswick Road, Grasmere
☎ *(015394) 35055*
Dorm bed *£14.50*
Credit cards *MC, Visa*

Maintenance & cleanliness	★★★★★
Facilities	★★★
Atmosphere & character	★★★★★
Security	★★☆
Overall rating	★★★★

YHA Grasmere Butharlyp How
This hostel is comprised of a couple of stone buildings. The main building has most accommodation as well as the dining room, a games room with pool table and table football and a cosy lounge with an open fire and the smaller room has the kitchen.
Easedale Road, Grasmere
☎ *(015394) 35316*
Website *www.yha.org.uk*
Dorm bed *£16 (£14 HI/YHA; £11 HI/YHA & ISIC)*
Credit cards *MC, Visa*
Open *1-3 Jan every day; 4 Jan-28 Feb Fri-Sat; 1 Mar-31 Oct every day; 1 Nov-19 Dec Fri-Sat; 27-31 Dec every day;* ***reception open*** *8am-10.30pm daily;* ***curfew*** *11pm*

Maintenance & cleanliness	★★★☆
Facilities	★★
Atmosphere & character	★★
Security	★★★
Overall rating	★★★

YHA Grasmere Thorney How
This hostel is smaller than the other YHA in Grasmere. It features the standard kitchen and a cosy lounge with a fireplace.
Easedale Road, Grasmere
☎ *(0870) 770 5836*
Website *www.yha.org.uk*
Dorm bed *£13 (£11 HI/YHA; £8 HI/YHA & ISIC)*
Credit cards *MC, Visa*

Maintenance & cleanliness	★★★☆
Facilities	★
Atmosphere & character	★★★★
Security	★★
Overall rating	★★★

Keswick

This quaint market town is quieter than Kendal and its easy access to tranquil Derwent Water makes it a relaxing spot to stay while exploring the northern Lake District.

Practical Information
Keswick Tourist Information Centre
Moot Hall, Market Square, Keswick
☎ *(017687) 72645*
Website *www.keswick.org*
Open *9.30am-5.30pm daily*

Coming & Going
Although there is no train station, Keswick is a busy transport hub for the northern Lake District. Buses 36A, 491, X4 and X5 run between Keswick and Cockermouth; buses 77 and 77A run a circular route taking in Derwent Water, Borrowdale, Buttermere and Crummock Water; and buses 555, NE, X8 and X72 go to Ambleside and Windermere. The Cumbria Goldrider is a good value pass that costs £20.50 and gives you seven days unlimited travel on Stagecoach buses throughout Cumbria.

The closest train station is in Penrith, which is served by buses 87, X4, X5, X50.

Accommodation
Denton House
This independent hostel has accommodation in solid wooden bunks. Common areas include a small kitchen and a TV room with table football. The rooms are OK, but the furnishings in the common room are old and worn. It is about a 10-minute walk into the town centre.
Penrith Road, Keswick
☎ *(017687) 75351*
Website *www.vividevents.co.uk*
Dorm bed *£12*

Maintenance & cleanliness	★★★½
Facilities	★★½
Atmosphere & character	★★½
Security	★
Overall rating	★★

YHA Derwentwater
This 200-year-old mansion is in a lovely setting overlooking picturesque Derwentwater, 3.25km south of Keswick. It is on expansive grounds that include a waterfall and football pitch.
Barrow House, Borrowdale, Keswick
🚌 *79* ⛴ *Derwentwater*
☎ *(017687) 77246*
Website *www.yha.org.uk*
Dorm bed *£14.50 (£12.50 HI/YHA; £9.50 HI/YHA & ISIC)*
Credit cards *MC, Visa*
Open *1 Jan-4 Feb Fri-Sat; 5 Feb-8 Nov every day;* **reception open** *8am-10pm daily;* **curfew** *11pm*

YHA Keswick
This nice riverside hostel has the usual kitchen and dining room plus a big common room with a pool table and TV and a smaller quiet reading room. It is just a couple of minutes walk to the town centre.
Station Road, Keswick
🚌 *X4/5/5-, 555*
☎ *(017687) 72484*
Website *ww.yha.org.uk*
Dorm bed *£14.50 (£12.50 HI/YHA; £9.50 HI/YHA & ISIC)*
Credit cards *MC, Visa*
Reception open *7.30am-11pm daily;* **curfew** *11.30pm*

Maintenance & cleanliness	★★★★½
Facilities	★★
Atmosphere & character	★
Security	★★
Overall rating	★★★½

Sights
Keswick Museum & Art Gallery
This small museum features displays on local history and some of the town's famous residents.
Fitz Park, Station Road, Keswick
☎ *(017687) 73263*
Admission *free*
Open *Mar-Oct Tue-Sat 10am-4pm*

Pencil Museum
Aside from tourism, Keswick's main industry is the Cumberland Pencil Factory, which churns out the famous Derwent colouring pencils. Adjoining the factory is a museum dedicated to pencils that includes displays about how pencils are made as well as machinery, exhibits about artistic techniques and the world's largest coloured pencil.
Southey Works, Greta Bridge, Keswick
☎ *(017687) 73626*
Website *www.pencils.co.uk*
Admission *£2.50*
Open *9.30am-4pm daily*

Patterdale

This rural location south of Ullswater makes a good base for energetic travellers who come here to climb Helvellyn.

Accommodation
YHA Patterdale
This hostel has accommodation in mostly eight to ten-bed dormitories with solid bunk beds. There's also the usual kitchen and dining room and a big common room with a log fire, pool table and a TV.
A592, Patterdale.
☎ *(017684) 82394*
Website *www.yha.org.uk*
Dorm bed *£14.50 (£12.50 HI/YHA; £9.50 HI/YHA & ISIC)*
Credit cards *MC, Visa*

🚗📺🔑🛗

Maintenance & cleanliness	★★★⯪
Facilities	★★⯪
Atmosphere & character	★★★
Security	★⯪
Overall rating	★★★

Wastwater

England's deepest lake is in the lesser-visited western end of the national park. It is a lovely spot that's worth heading to if the eastern part of the Lake District is too crowded for you. The nearby village of Nether Wastwater has a couple of excellent pubs but the nearest shop is 8km away.

Accommodation
YHA Wastwater

This grand stone and half-timbered house stands on the shores of Wastwater, England's deepest lake. The charming lounge features an ornate carved fireplace and plenty of books and there is also a small kitchen and dining room.
Wasdale Hall, Wastwater
☎ *(019467) 26222*
Website *www.yha.org.uk*
Dorm bed *£13 (£11 HI/YHA; £8 HI/YHA & ISIC)*
Credit cards *MC, Visa*
Open *1 Jan-10 Feb Fri-Sat; 11 Feb-31 Mar Thu-Mon; Apr-Aug every day; Sep-Oct Thu-Mon; Nov-Dec Fri-Sat;* **reception open** *7.30am-10am & 5pm-10.30pm daily;* **curfew** *11pm*

🚗🔑

Maintenance & cleanliness	★★★
Facilities	★★⯪
Atmosphere & character	★★
Security	★★⯪
Overall rating	★★★⯪

Windermere

This busy town just north of Kendal is a popular base for exploring the Lake District, particularly for those without their own transport.

Practical Information
Windermere Tourist Information Centre
Victoria Street, Windermere
☎ *(015394) 46499*
Open *Jan-Easter 9am-5pm daily; Easter-Jun 9am-6pm daily; Jul-Aug 9am-7.30pm daily; Sep-Oct 9am-6pm daily; Nov-Dec 9am-5pm daily*

Coming & Going

Trains run from Windermere to Lancaster and Manchester every two hours and Windermere is also well served by buses to all parts of the Lake District including bus 555, which stops here en route between Lancaster and Keswick and bus 599 that runs between Windermere and Ambleside.

The Cumbria Goldrider is a good value pass that costs £20.50 and gives you seven days unlimited travel on Stagecoach buses throughout Cumbria.

Accommodation
Lake District Backpackers

This clean and centrally located hostel has facilities that include a small TV lounge with Internet access and a small kitchen.
High Street, Windermere
☎ *(015394) 46374*
Website *www.lakedistrictbackpackers.co.uk*
Dorm bed *£12.50;* **double/twin room** *£30; prices include breakfast*

📺🔑🛗

Maintenance & cleanliness	★★★★
Facilities	★★
Atmosphere & character	★★★
Security	★★⯪
Overall rating	★★★

YHA Windermere

This hostel is in a quiet setting 3.25km from Windermere and it boasts lovely views of Lake Windermere. It has a small kitchen, a lounge with a log fire, a small reading room and a dining room with a TV.
Bridge Lane, Troutbeck, Windermere
☎ *(015394) 43543*
Dorm bed *$14.50 (£12.50 HI/YHA; £9.50 HI/YHA & ISIC)*
Credit cards *MC, Visa*
Open *Feb-Nov every day; 1-13 Dec Fri-Sat; 23-27 Dec every day;* **reception open** *8.0am-10am & 1pm-10.30pm daily;* **curfew** *11pm*

🚗📺🔑

Maintenance & cleanliness	★★★★
Facilities	★★
Atmosphere & character	★★★★½
Security	★★
Overall rating	★★★

Carlisle

Cumbria's only major city is located just south of the Scottish border near the western end of Hadrian's Wall. It is a historic city dominated by a 900-year-old castle and cathedral.

Practical Information
Carlisle Visitor Centre
Old Town Hall, Carlisle
☎ *(01228) 625600*
Website *www.historic-carlisle.org.uk*
Open *Jan-Feb Mon-Sat 10am-4pm; Mar-Apr Mon-Sat 9.30am-5pm; May Mon-Sat 9.30am-5pm, Sun 10.30am-4pm; Jun-Aug Mon-Sat 9.30am-5.30pm, Sun 10.30am-4pm; Sep-Oct Mon-Sat 9.30am-5pm; Nov-Dec Mon-Sat 10am-4pm*

INTERNET ACCESS
Internet Café @ Almond's Bistro
16 Scotland Street, Stanwix, Carlisle
☎ *(01228) 523 546*
Open *Mon-Sat 9am-9pm*

Coming & Going

Carlisle has excellent train services including hourly trains to Edinburgh, Glasgow, London (Euston) and Newcastle. The train station is on Botchergate near the castle.

National Express (☎ *0870 580 8080;* **website** *www.nationalexpress.co.uk*) have a daily bus to London and Stagecoach (**website** *www.stagecoachbus.co.uk*) have frequent bus services to the Lake District including the useful bus 555, which goes to Keswick, Ambleside, Windermere, Kendal and Lancaster. The Cumbria Goldrider is a good value pass that costs £20.50 and gives you seven days unlimited travel on Stagecoach buses throughout Cumbria.

During summer the Hadrian's Wall Bus (route AD122) runs several times each day between Carlisle and Hexham following the course of the wall and stopping at visitor attractions en route. One bus each day goes all the way from Bowness on Solway to Newcastle-upon-Tyne and Wallsend. It connects with train and other bus services at Carlisle, Haltwhistle and Hexham. A one-day ticket on this bus costs £6 and a three-day pass costs £10.

Local Transport

Carlisle's local buses are run by Stagecoach (**website** *www.stagecoachbus.co.uk*) who have a Dayrider pass that costs £2.65 and gives you one day unlimited travel on Stagecoach buses within the Carlisle area. The Megarider, a seven-day version of this pass costs £7.

Accommodation
YHA Carlisle

Carlisle's youth hostel is situated in the university's halls of residence and occupies the building that was once used as the Theakston's Brewery. It has a good location near the city centre but is only open in summer.
Old Brewery Residences, Bridge Lane, Caldewgate, Carlisle
☎ *(01228) 597 352*
Website *www.yha.org.uk*
Dorm bed *£18 (£16 HI/YHA; £13 HI/YHA & ISIC)*
Credit cards *MC, Visa*
Open *3 Jul-4 Sep; reception open 8am-10am & 5pm-10pm daily*

Sights
Carlisle Castle

This 900-year-old fortress at the northern end of the city centre has witnessed a rich history of conflict between England and Scotland. It was here that Mary, Queen of Scots was imprisoned as were prisoners of the 1746 Jacobite uprising.
Castle Way, Carlisle
☎ *(01228) 591 922*
Website *www.english-heritage.org.uk*
Admission *£3.80*
Open *Jan-Mar 10am-4pm daily; Apr-Sep 9.30am-6pm daily; Oct-Dec 10am-4pm daily*

Carlisle Cathedral

Carlisle Cathedral was founded in 1122 and it features exquisite woodcarving

and stained glass windows from the 14th centuries.
Castle Street, Carlisle
☎ *(01228) 548 151*
Admission *free*
Open *Mon-Sat 7.30am-6.15pm, Sun 7.30am-5pm*

Tullie House Museum & Art Gallery
The Tullie House Museum has exhibits on local history including extensive displays about Hadrian's Wall as well as Cumbria in Roman times, the Dark Ages and the medieval period. There is also an art gallery with a large collection of decorative and fine arts.
Castle Street, Carlisle
☎ *(01228) 534 781*
Website *www.tulliehouse.co.uk*
Admission *£5.20*
Open *Jan-Mar Mon-Sat 10am-4pm, Sun noon-4pm; Apr-Jun Mon-Sat 10am-5pm, Sun noon-5pm; Jul-Aug Mon-Sat 10am-5pm, Sun 11am-5pm; Sep-Oct Mon-Sat 10am-5pm, Sun noon-5pm; Nov-Dec Mon-Sat 10am-4pm, Sun noon-4pm*

Dentdale

Part of the Yorkshire Dales National Park, this region of rolling countryside lies between the Lake District and the more visited parts of the Yorkshire Dales. You can often find accommodation here on busy weekends when the hostels in the Lake District are full.

Coming & Going
Dentdale is served by bus 564B, which runs occasionally through the dale but Dent station (about 3km north of the youth hostel) on the Carlisle-Settle railway is an easier option for travellers using public transport.

Accommodation
YHA Dent
This former shooting lodge offers comfortable accommodation in small dorms. Facilities include the usual kitchen, dining room, and TV lounge.
Cowgill, Dent
☎ *(015396) 25251*
Website *www.yha.org.uk*
Dorm bed *£14.50 (£12.50 HI/YHA; £9.50 HI/YHA & ISIC)*
Credit cards *MC, Visa*
Feb-Nov check with hostel; **reception open** *7.45am-10am & 5pm-10.30pm daily;* **lockout** *10am-noon;* **curfew** *11pm*

Maintenance & cleanliness	★★★
Facilities	★★½
Atmosphere & character	★★★½
Security	★★★½
Overall rating	★★★½

Yorkshire

This well-known region is comprised of the counties of East Riding of Yorkshire, North East Lincolnshire, North Lincolnshire, North Yorkshire, South Yorkshire, and West Yorkshire. Yorkshire's varied attractions include a rugged coastline, the rolling countryside of the Yorkshire Dales and North York Moors National Parks and the vibrant cities of Bradford, Leeds, Sheffield and York.

West Yorkshire

Much of West Yorkshire is made up of the Bradford-Leeds urban area although one of the county's main attractions is the small town of Haworth.

Leeds

England's fourth-largest city is a vibrant metropolis renowned for its shopping and nightlife.

Practical Information
Leeds Tourist Information Centre
Gateway Yorkshire, The Arcade, City Station, Leeds
☎ *(0113) 242 5242*
Open *Mon-Sat 9am-5.30pm, Sun 10am-4pm*

Coming & Going
BUS
National Express (☎ *0870 580 8080; website www.nationalexpress.co.uk)* runs buses from Leeds to most major British destinations including Birmingham, London, Manchester, Newcastle, Sheffield and York.

Megabus *(website www.megabus.com)* have cheap buses from Leeds to London and Manchester with fares starting at £1 (plus 50p booking fee). The Leeds Megabus stop is at bus stand S1 on Wellington Street near the Queens Hotel.

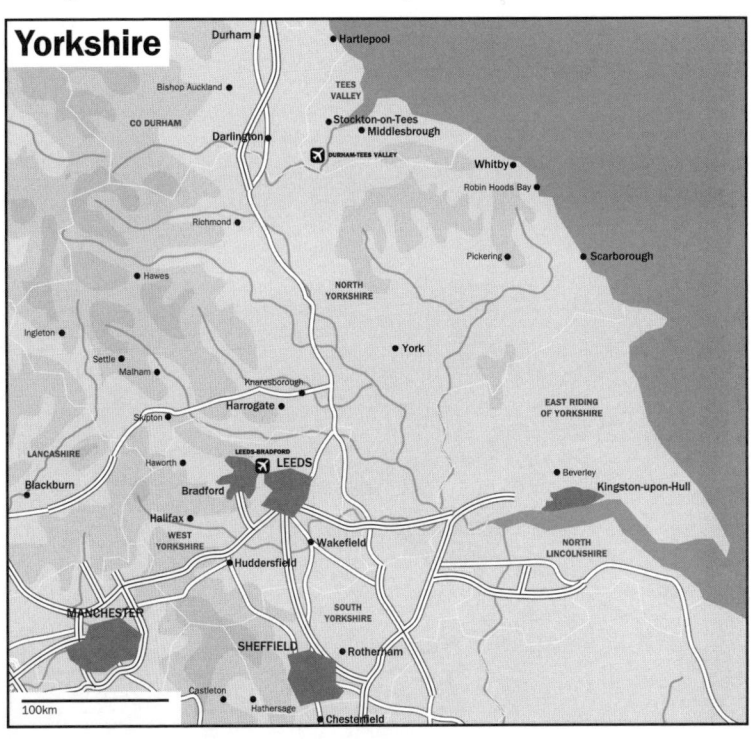

TRAIN

Leeds is well served by trains with services run by Arriva Trains Northern *(website www.arrivatrainsnorthern.co.uk)* going to Manchester (Victoria) and destinations throughout Yorkshire including Harrogate, Hull and York. Arriva Trains Northern also runs trains from Leeds on the scenic Settle-Carlisle Railway. GNER *(website www.gner.co.uk)* going to London (Kings Cross) and TransPennine Express *(website www.tpexpress.co.uk)* trains go to Hull, Manchester (Piccadilly), Newcastle and Scarborough. Local trains on the West Yorkshire Metro system have frequent services to nearby cities including Bradford.

Local Transport

West Yorkshire's Metro transport network (☎ *(0113) 245 7676; website www.wymetro.com)* is comprised of buses and trains and is an efficient way to get around Leeds and to other destinations in West Yorkshire such as Bradford and Haworth.

The excellent DayRover pass gives you unlimited bus travel in West Yorkshire for £3.80, unlimited train travel for £3.80 or unlimited bus and train travel for £4.50. It is only valid after 9.30am on weekdays or all day on weekends.

Accommodation

There are no hostels – not even cheap Formule 1-style hotels – in Leeds and the closest affordable accommodation is in Haworth or York. If you want to stay in Leeds, try the B&Bs on Cardigan Road in Headingly (a 20-minute bus ride into the suburbs).

Sights
Armley Mills – Leeds Industrial Museum

This industrial museum is housed inside what was once the world's largest woollen mill. The museum has exhibits on the city's industrial heritage with displays on engineering and the textile and clothing industries.
Canal Road, Leeds

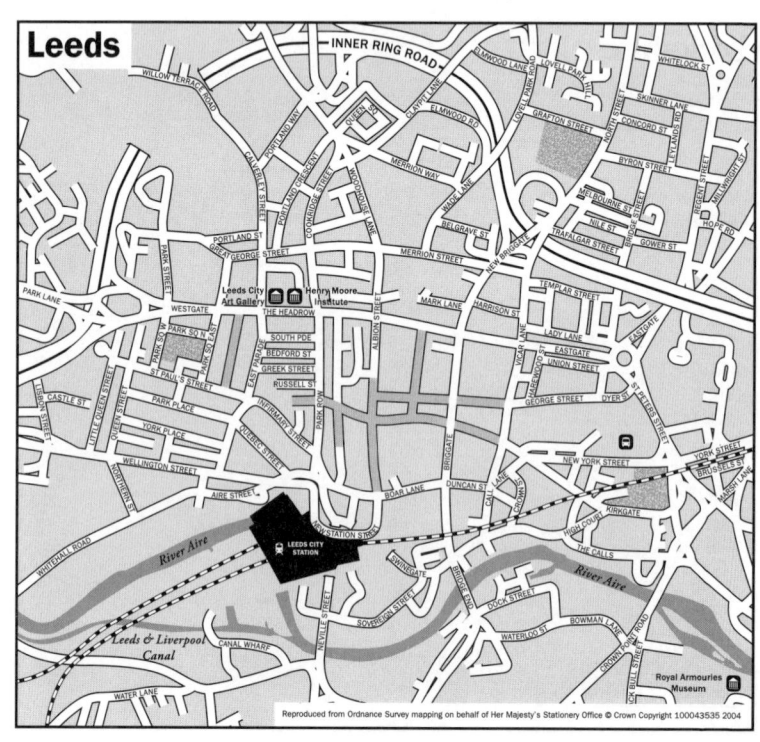

☎ *(0113) 263 7861*
Admission *£2*

Henry Moore Institute
The Henry Moore Institute is one of the country's leading art museums devoted to sculpture. It contains four galleries that host a programme of temporary exhibitions.
74 The Headrow, Leeds
☎ *(0113) 246 7467*
Website *www.henry-moore.ac.uk*
Admission *free*
Open *Mon-Tue 10am-5.30pm, Wed 10am-9pm, Thu-Sun 10am-5.30pm*

Leeds City Art Gallery
This art gallery displays a large collection of British artworks from the 19th and 20th centuries.
The Headrow, Leeds
☎ *(0113) 247 8248*
Admission *free*
Open *Mon-Tue 10am-5pm, Wed 10am-8pm, Thu-Sat 10am-5pm, Sun 1pm-5pm*

Royal Armouries Museum
Leeds' top attraction is this excellent museum that houses an unsurpassed collection of arms and armour and also features demonstrations that include jousting tournaments.
Armouries Drive, Leeds
☎ *(0113) 220 1999*
Website *www.armouries.org.uk*
Admission *free*
Open *10am-5pm daily*

Thackray Museum
This excellent museum has interesting displays focusing on the history of medicine.
Beckett Street, Leeds
🚌 *11, 41, 42, 50*
☎ *(0113) 244 4343*
Website *www.thackraymuseum.org*
Admission *£4.90*
Open *10am-3pm daily*

Bradford
Birthplace of the Brontë sisters and artist David Hockney, Bradford is part of the sprawling Bradford-Leeds metropolitan area. However it is a vibrant city in its own right and is home to several top attractions including National Museum of Photography, Film & Television and the Saltaire World Heritage Site is nearby.

Practical Information
Bradford Tourist Information Centre
City Hall, Bradford
☎ *(01274) 433678*
Website *www.visitbradford.com*
Open *Mon 10am-5pm, Tue-Wed 9.30am-5pm, Thu 8.30am-5pm, Fri-Sat 9.30am-5pm*

Coming & Going
TRAIN
Bradford has two main train stations, Forster Square and Interchange. Trains depart Forster Square for Carlisle, Settle and Keighley (where you can change for a bus to Haworth). The busier Interchange station has mainline and Metro services to Manchester, Leeds and York.

Local Transport
West Yorkshire's Metro transport network (☎ *(0113) 245 7676;* **website** *www.wymetro.com*) is comprised of buses and trains and is an efficient way to get around Bradford and to other destinations in West Yorkshire such as Haworth and Leeds.

The excellent DayRover pass gives you unlimited bus travel in West Yorkshire for £3.80, unlimited train travel for £3.80 or unlimited bus and train travel for £4.50. It is only valid after 9.30am on weekdays or all day on weekends.

Accommodation
There is no cheap accommodation in Bradford and the nearest hostel is in Haworth, which is a 20-minute train trip followed by a 15-minute bus ride away.

YHA Haworth
This relatively basic hostel is housed in an imposing Victorian mansion and has facilities that include a kitchen, games room and a nice garden area. To get here from Bradford Forster Square train

station, take the train to Keighley and then hop on bus 663, 664, 665 or 720.
Longlands Drive, Lees Lane, Haworth
☏ *Keighley, then* ☏ *500, 663, 664, 665, 698, 720, M1, M2, M3, M4*
☏ *(01535) 642234*
Website *www.yha.org.uk*
Dorm bed *£14.50 (£12.50 HI/YHA; £9.50 HI/YHA & ISIC)*
Open *13 Feb-31 Oct every day; 5 Nov-18 Dec Fri-Sat; 28 Dec-1 Jan every day; reception open 7.30am-10.30pm daily; curfew 11pm*

🚗 Ⓚ Ⓛ

Sights
Bradford Cathedral
Bradford's ancient cathedral is one of the city centre's main landmarks. Highlights include embroidery by Ernest Sichel and William Morris windows.
1 Stott Hill, Bradford
☏ *(01274) 777 720*
Admission *free*
Open *Mon-Fri 8.30am-4.30pm*

Bradford Industrial Museum
Housed in a 19th century spinning mill, the Bradford Industrial Museum has exhibits that include stables with working horses. Spinning and weaving demonstrations take place daily and steam engines run on Wednesdays.
Moorside Mills, Moorside Road, Bradford
☏ *(01274) 435 900*
Admission *free*
Open *Tue-Sat 10am-5pm, Sun noon-5pm*

Brontë Birthplace
Anne, Branwell, Charlotte and Emily Brontë were born in this house, which has been restored with furnishings from the period when the Brontë sisters grew up in the house.
72-74 Market Street, Thornton, Bradford
☏ *(01274) 830 849*
Website *www.brontebirthplace.org.uk*
Admission *£3*
Open *Apr-Sep Tue-Sun noon-4pm*

Cartwright Hall Art Gallery
This Baroque-style art gallery houses mostly 19th and 20th century British art, although it also has a notable South Asian collection.
Lister Park, Bradford
☏ *(01274) 431 212*
Admission *free*
Open *Tue-Sat 10am-5pm, Sun 1pm-5pm*

The Colour Museum
Run by the Society of Dyers and Colourists, this unique museum is dedicated to the history and technology of colour and it features a gallery with exhibits about Textiles and Colour.
Pekin House, Providence Street, Bradford
☏ *(01274) 390 955*
Website *www.sdc.org.uk*
Admission *£2*
Open *Tue-Sat 10am-4pm*

National Museum of Photography, Film & Television
This museum has 10 galleries depicting various aspects of the history, art and science of photography, film and television.
Bradford
☏ *0870 701 0200*
Website *www.nmpft.org.uk*
Admission *free*
Open *Tue-Sun 10am-6pm*

Saltaire
This World Heritage Site north of Bradford was an important site during the Industrial Revolution.

Practical Information
Saltaire Tourist Information Centre
2 Victoria Road, Saltaire
☏ *(01274) 774993*
Website *www.visitsaltaire.com*
Open *10am-5pm daily*

Coming & Going
Saltaire is served by West Yorkshire's Metro transport network (☏ *(0113) 245 7676; website www.wymetro.com*) with frequent trains from Bradford.

The excellent DayRover pass gives you unlimited bus travel in West Yorkshire for £3.80, unlimited train travel for £3.80 or unlimited bus and train travel for £4.50. It is only valid after 9.30am on weekdays or all day on weekends.

Sights
1853 Gallery & Salts Mill
This is a popular art museum that houses three galleries devoted to the work of Bradford-born artist, David Hockney.
Salts Mill, Victoria Road, Saltaire
☎ *(01274) 531 163*
Admission *free*
Open *Mon-Fri 10am-6pm*

Saltaire United Reformed Church
Open in 1859, this Classical-style church was the first public building in the village.
7 Highfield Mews, Saltaire
☎ *(01274) 597894*
Website *www.saltaireurc.info*
Admission *free*
Open *Jan-Mar Sun 2pm-4pm; Apr-Sep 2pm-4pm daily; Oct-Dec Sun 2pm-4pm*

Haworth

Haworth is best known for its literary connection with the works of the Brontë sisters. Although it can get touristy, it is a pleasant town and home to the closest youth hostel to Bradford and Leeds.

Practical Information
Haworth Tourist Information Centre
2/4 West Lane, Haworth
☎ *(01535) 642329*
Website *www.visitbrontecountry.com*
Open *May-Aug Mon-Tue 9.30am-5.30pm, Wed 10am-5.30pm, Thu-Sun 9.30am-5.30pm*

Coming & Going
Haworth's proximity to Bradford and Keighley means that it enjoys good public transport connections. There are frequent buses between Haworth and Keighley, where there is a train station with good connections to Bradford and Leeds.

The excellent DayRover pass gives you unlimited bus travel in West Yorkshire for £3.80, unlimited train travel for £3.80 or unlimited bus and train travel for £4.50. It is only valid after 9.30am on weekdays or all day on weekends. The DayRover is not valid on trains operated by Keighley and Worth Valley Railway.

Alternatively there is the pricy but popular Keighley and Worth Valley Railway *(website www.kwvr.co.uk)* that operates steam trains between Haworth and Keighley. A return ticket on this delightful railway costs £7 or £10 for a day rover pass, which also entitles you to entry to the Museum of Rail Travel at Ingrow West.

Accommodation
YHA Haworth
Haworth's YHA is a relatively basic hostel that is housed in an imposing Victorian mansion. It's facilities include a kitchen, games room and a nice garden area.
Longlands Drive, Lees Lane, Haworth
🚌 *500, 663, 664, 665, 698, 720, M1, M2, M3, M4*
☎ *(01535) 642234*
Website *www.yha.org.uk*
Dorm bed *£14.50 (£12.50 HI/YHA; £9.50 HI/YHA & ISIC)*
Open *13 Feb-31 Oct every day; 5 Nov-18 Dec Fri-Sat; 28 Dec-1 Jan every day;* **reception open** *7.30am-10.30pm daily;* **curfew** *11pm*

Sights
Brontë Parsonage Museum
The Brontë family lived in this Georgian Parsonage between 1820 and 1861 and both *Jane Eyre* and *Wuthering Heights* were written here.
Haworth
☎ *(01535) 642 323*
Admission *£4.80*
Open *Feb-Mar 11am-4.30pm daily; Apr-Sep 10am-5pm daily; Oct-Dec 11am-4.30pm daily*

Museum of Rail Travel
This museum at Ingrow train station – on the Keighley and Worth Valley Railway – has a collection of vintage train carriages from the 19th and 20th centuries.
Ingrow
🚂 *Ingrow* 🚌 *500, 502, 663, 664, 665, 696, 697*
☎ *(01535) 680 425*
Website *www.vintagecarriagestrust.org*
Admission *£1.50*
Open *11am-4.30pm daily*

South Yorkshire

South Yorkshire borders the Peak District although few travellers make it up this way.

Sheffield

Stainless steel was invented in Sheffield making it an industrial powerhouse that has produced much of the world's cutlery. The city went into a depression in the late 20th century although it is experiencing a renaissance and is now a lovely city with a vibrant centre and well worth a visit if you have the time.

Practical Information
Sheffield Tourist Information Centre
Winter Garden, Surrey Street, Sheffield
☏ *(0114) 221 1900*
Website *www.sheffieldcity.co.uk*
Open *Mon-Thu 9.30am-5.15pm, Fri 10.30am-5.15pm, Sat 9.30am-4.15pm*

Coming & Going
BUS
National Express (☏ *0870 580 8080; website www.nationalexpress.co.uk*) goes from Sheffield to Birmingham, Leeds, London, Manchester, Nottingham and York. National Express buses stop at the Interchange Bus Station between Pond and Sheaf Streets near the train station.

Megabus (*website www.megabus.com*) have cheap buses from Sheffield to London via Chesterfield. Fares start at £1 (plus 50p booking fee) but can increase to around £9. Megabus stops outside the Adsetts Centre building on Arundel Gate near Sheffield Hallam University.

Stagecoach (*website www.stagecoachbus.co.uk*) operates local buses in South Yorkshire and neighbouring counties including the Peak District. There are several travel passes available for travel on Stagecoach buses; these include:

East Midlands Day Rover
This pass costs £4.75 and is valid for one day's travel on Stagecoach buses in Derbyshire, Nottinghamshire and South Yorkshire (except D 909). This pass is a good option if you're planning on travelling between Sheffield and destinations in Derbyshire and Nottinghamshire.

South Yorkshire Peak Explorer
The South Yorkshire Peak Explorer costs £6.25 and gives you one day's bus travel in South Yorkshire and the northern part of the Peak District bounded by Bakewell, Baslow, Buxton, Holmfirth, Hayfield, Owler Bar and Sparrowpit. It also includes tram travel in Sheffield. This pass is a good option if you're planning on travelling between Sheffield and the northern Peak District.

TRAIN
Arriva Trains Northern (*website www.arrivatrainsnorthern.co.uk*) connects Sheffield to destinations in northern England; Central Trains (*website www.centraltrains.co.uk*) go to Manchester, Liverpool, Nottingham and Leicester; Midland Mainline (*website www.midlandmainline.com*) have trains to Derby, Leeds, Leicester, London (St Pancras), Nottingham and York and TransPennine Express has trains to Manchester (Piccadilly).

Trains leave from Midland Station on Sheaf Square east of the city centre.

Local Transport
Sheffield's public transport system is made up of bus, train and tram services.

Sheffield's Supertram (*website www.supertram.com*) has three tram routes covering the main transport corridors in the city. For many travellers trams are the easiest way to get around although the coverage isn't as extensive as the bus. One-way tram fares start at 70p in the city centre.

Buses operated by Arriva (*website www.arriva.co.uk*), First (*website www.firstgroup.com*) and Stagecoach (*website www.stagecoachbus.co.uk*) provide a good bus service in the Sheffield area.

The following travel passes are a good option if you're planning on doing a lot of sightseeing in Sheffield and South Yorkshire:

Dayrider
This pass costs £2.40 and is good for one day's unlimited tram travel. The weekly Megarider ticket costs £7.50.

TravelMaster

The TravelMaster pass is a one-day pass good for unlimited bus, train and tram travel.

TravelMaster passes are available for travel in either Sheffield or all of South Yorkshire.

Zone	1 day	5x1 day	week
Sheffield	-	-	£15
South Yorkshire	£4.95	£22.50	£16.50

FlexiMaster

This pass gives you three days bus and tram travel in South Yorkshire within a seven-day period. It costs £8.75

TRAVEL INFORMATION CENTRES

The following centres sell passes and help out with public transport information:

Cambridge Street, Sheffield
☎ *(01709) 515151*
Website *www.sypte.co.uk*
Open *Mon-Sat 9am-5pm*

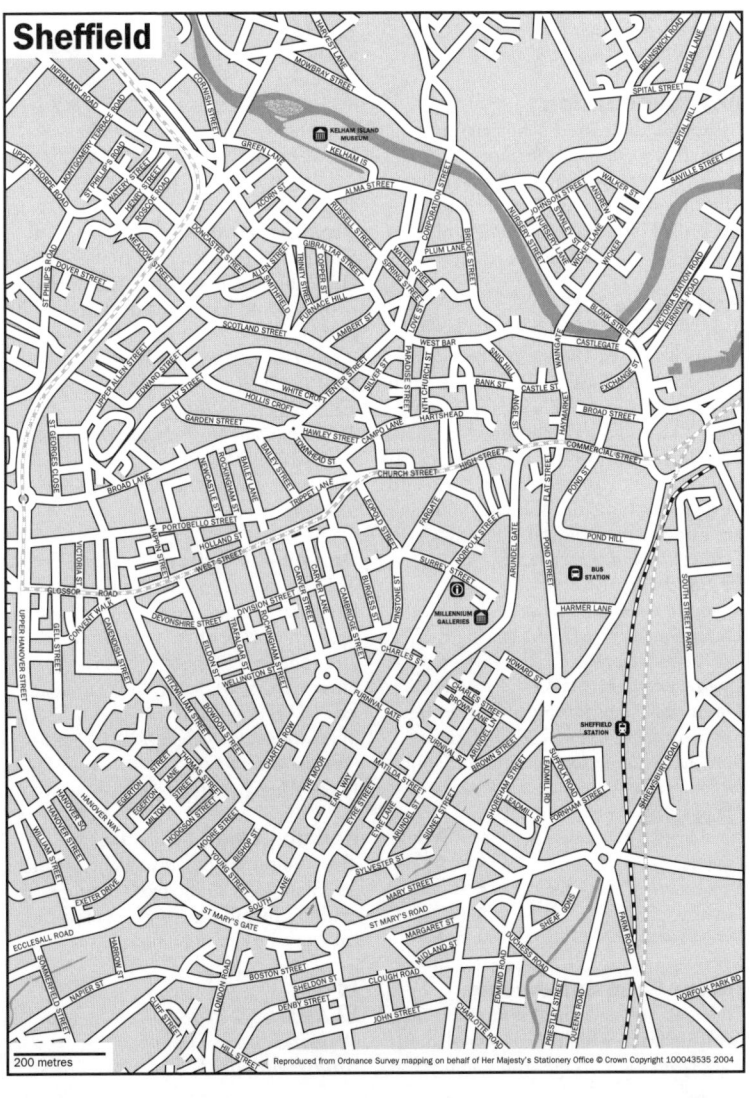

Sheffield

200 metres

Exchange Street, Sheffield
☎ *(01709) 515151*
Website *www.sypte.co.uk*
Open *Mon-Sat 9am-5pm*

Meadowhall Interchange, Meadowhall
☎ *(01709) 515151*
Website *www.sypte.co.uk*
Open *Mon-Fri 8am-8pm, Sat 9am-6pm, Sun 10.30am-6pm*

Sheffield Interchange, Sheffield
☎ *(01709) 515151*
Website *www.sypte.co.uk*
Open *Mon-Fri 8am-5.30pm, Sat 9.30am-5pm, Sun 9am-5pm*

Accommodation

Although there are no hostels in Sheffield, there are plenty of hostels in the Peak District, which isn't too far away. The closest town with hostel accommodation is Hathersage, about 25 minutes by train from Sheffield.

Hathersage YHA

This is a cheerful-feeling hostel in a Victorian house in the centre of Hathersage close to shops and transport, with a bright dining room, a pleasant lounge with TV, and a well-equipped kitchen. The dorms are bright and spacious. If you arrive early there's a shelter area and a garden with picnic tables but you can't get into the main hostel till 5pm.
Castleton Road, Hathersage
☎ *0870 770 5852*
Website *www.yha.org.uk*
Dorm bed *£13 (£11 HI/YHA; £8 HI/YHA & student)*
Credit cards *MC, Visa*
Open *Apr-Aug Mon-Sat; Sep-Oct Tue-Sat;* **reception open** *7.30am-10am & 5pm-11pm daily;* **lockout** *10am-5pm; lockout 11pm*

Maintenance & cleanliness	★★★★☆
Facilities	★★★
Atmosphere & character	★★☆
Security	★★☆
Overall rating	★★★

Thorpe Farm Bunkhouses

There are several bunkhouses on this working farm, which is a good half-hour walk from Hathersage, and you need to bring all your food and a sleeping bag (though they keep a few for loan). The cost is low and the bunkhouses are well but simply equipped with kitchens and bunkrooms and comfortable common rooms without TV. You won't be sharing a building with a large group, but you might be on your own. If there are several of you with a car you can have a great time here.
Thorpe Farm, Hathersage
☎ *(01433) 650 659*
Website *www.thorpe-bunk.co.uk*
Dorm bed *£8*

Maintenance & cleanliness	★★★★☆
Facilities	★
Atmosphere & character	★★☆
Security	★
Overall rating	★★☆

Sights

Bishops' House

Sheffield's best-preserved timber-framed house has been restored to show how people would have lived during the 17th century.
Norton Lees Lane, Sheffield
🚌 *13, 39*
☎ *(0114) 278 2600*
Website *www.sheffieldgalleries.org.uk*
Admission *free*
Open *Sat 10am-4.30pm, Sun 11am-4.30pm*

Graves Art Gallery

This art museum has a programme of temporary exhibitions plus a permanent collection that includes works by Cezanne and Picasso.
Surrey Street, Sheffield
☎ *(0114) 278 2600*
Website *www.sheffieldgalleries.org.uk*
Admission *free*
Open *Mon-Sat 10am-5pm*

Kelham Island Museum

This museum has excellent displays on Sheffield's industrial heritage. Its exhibits include Europe's most powerful working steam engine.
Alma Street, Sheffield
🚌 *53*
☎ *(0114) 272 2106*
Website *www.simt.co.uk*
Admission *£3.50*

Open Mon-Thu 10am-3pm, Sun 11am-3.45pm

Millennium Galleries
Sheffield's new Millennium Galleries features a programme of temporary exhibitions plus permanent galleries feature metalwork and the Ruskin Gallery with its collection of drawings, paintings and medieval manuscripts.
Arundel Gate, Sheffield
☎ *(0114) 278 2600*
Website www.sheffieldgalleries.org.uk
Admission permanent collection free; charge for temporary exhibitions
Open Mon-Sat 10am-5pm, Sun 11am-5pm

Hull & East Riding of Yorkshire

Many travellers pass through the least visited part of Yorkshire but few stop unless it is to catch the ferry from Hull. If you are passing through you should consider stopping in Beverley, just north of Hull.

Kingston-upon-Hull

Hull – locals never call it by its full name – has a reputation as a dull city and it attracts very few tourists. With low expectations most visitors to Hull are pleasantly surprised to find a vibrant riverside city with an old town and a rejuvenated dockside area. The city's major attraction is The Deep aquarium, but Hull's old town – home to several free museums – is also worth a look.

Practical Information
Hull Tourist Information Centre
1 Paragon Street, Hull
☎ *(01482) 223559*
Website www.hullcc.gov.uk/visithull
Open Mon-Sat 10am-5pm, Sun 11am-3pm

Coming & Going
AIR
Humberside International Airport *(website www.humberside-airport.co.uk)* is 30 minutes south of Hull and has flights to Amsterdam and Mediterranean holiday destinations.

BUS
National Express (☎ *0870 580 8080; website www.nationalexpress.co.uk*) buses go to Leeds, London, Manchester, Nottingham and York with the most frequent services to Leeds. Hull's bus station is on Paragon Street, which runs between the train station and Queen Victoria Square.

TRAIN
Arriva Trains Northern (*website www.arrivatrainsnorthern.co.uk*) run trains to Leeds, Scarborough, Sheffield and York; Hull Trains (*website www.hulltrains.co.uk*) have five daily trains between Hull and London (Kings Cross) and Trans Pennine Express (*website www.firstgroup.com/tpexpress/*) run hourly trains to Leeds and Manchester (Piccadilly).

FERRY
P & O Ferries (*website www.poferries.com*) sail from Hull to Rotterdam (Netherlands) and Zeebrugge (Belgium). Hull's port is about 10 minutes by bus from the city centre.

Local Transport
East Yorkshire Motor Services (*website www.eyms.co.uk*) run buses in Hull and East Riding of Yorkshire. A Day Rover ticket gives you one day unlimited bus travel within Hull for £2; a Weekly Saver ticket costs £6.

Accommodation
Although there is no hostel in Hull, the excellent Beverley Friary hostel is only a 20-minute train trip or 40-minute bus ride away.

YHA Beverley Friary
The Beverley Friary YHA is in a restored historic friary that dates from the 1330s. The building has lots of character and it features a history room with an exhibition on the building's history as well as the oldest wall paintings in Yorkshire (dating from the 1550s). Facilities include a good kitchen and a large lounge room.

Friars Lane, Beverley
🚆 *Beverley* 🚌 *6*
☎ *(01482) 881751*
Website www.yha.org.uk
Dorm bed £13 (£11 HI/YHA; £8 HI/YHA & ISIC)
Credit cards JCB, MC, Visa
Reception open 8am-10am & 5pm-11pm daily

🚗 Ⓚ Ⓛ

Maintenance & cleanliness	★★★★½
Facilities	★★½
Atmosphere & character	★★★★½
Security	★★½
Overall rating	★★★★½

Sights
The Deep
The Deep, which bills itself as "the world's only Submarium", is Hull's star attraction. It boasts the world's only underwater lift and Europe's deepest walk-through aquarium with an emphasis on marine life on the ocean floor.
The Deep, Hull
🚌 *90*
☎ *(01482) 381000*
Website www.thedeep.co.uk
Admission £6.75
Open 10am-5pm daily

Hull & East Riding Museum
Hull's museum houses artefacts from the Bronze Age, Iron Age and Roman periods and also has natural history exhibits that feature the only dinosaur bones to have been found in East Yorkshire.
36 High Street, Hull
☎ *(01482) 613902*
Website www.hullcc.gov.uk/museums/hulleast/
Admission free
Open Mon-Sat 10am-5pm, Sun 1.30pm-4.30pm

Maritime Museum
Hull's Maritime Museum features a collection of paintings, models and artefacts relating it the city's maritime history.
Queen Victoria Square, Hull
Website www.hullcc.gov.uk/museums/maritime/
Admission free
Open Mon-Sat 10am-5pm, Sun 1.30pm-4.30pm

Spurn Lightship
This floating lighthouse acted as a navigation aid at the mouth of the River Humber for 48 years and is now operated as a museum moored at Hull's marina.
Hull Marina, Hull
Website www.hullcc.gov.uk/museums/spurn/
Admission free
Open Mon-Sat 10am-5pm, Sun 1.30pm-4.30pm

Streetlife Museum of Transport
Hull's transport museum has displays of vintage cars and a hands-on interactive exhibition area.
High Street, Hull
Website www.hullcc.gov.uk/museums/streetlife/
Admission free
Open Mon-Sat 10am-5pm, Sun 1.30pm-4.30pm

Wilberforce House Museum
William Wilberforce, who campaigned to abolish slavery, was born in this 17th-century building that now houses a museum dedicated to his fight.
Open Mon-Sat 10am-5pm, Sun 1.30pm-4.30pm
Website www.hullcc.gov.uk/museums/wilberforce/
Admission free
Open Mon-Sat 10am-5pm, Sun 1.30pm-4.30pm

Beverley
This historic market town boasts the beautiful 13th-century Beverley Minster as well as several notable medieval buildings. Its charming youth hostel and convenient location makes it an ideal base for visiting Hull.

Practical Information
Beverley Tourist Information Centre
34 Butcher Row, Beverley
☎ *(01482) 867430*
Website www.inbeverley.co.uk
Open Jan-Jun Mon-Fri 9.30am-5.30pm, Sat 10am-5pm; Jul-Aug Mon-Fri 9.30am-5.30pm, Sat 10am-5pm, Sun 10am-2pm; Sep-Dec Mon-Fri 9.30am-5.30pm, Sat 10am-5pm

Coming & Going
Beverley lies just 15-minutes by train north of Hull although there are also frequent buses (route numbers 121, 122 and X46) between Beverley and Hull. From Hull there are mainline train services to most major cities in England. Call (01482) 22 22 22 for up-to-date transport information.

Accommodation
YHA Beverley Friary
The Beverley Friary YHA is in a restored historic friary that dates from the 1330s. The building has lots of character and it features a history room with an exhibition on the building's history as well as the oldest wall paintings in Yorkshire (dating from the 1550s). Facilities include a good kitchen and a large lounge room.
Friars Lane, Beverley
☎ 6
☎ *(01482) 881751*
Website *www.yha.org.uk*
Dorm bed *£13 (£11 HI/YHA; £8 HI/YHA & ISIC)*
Credit cards *JCB, MC, Visa*
Reception open *8am-10am & 5pm-11pm daily*

Maintenance & cleanliness	★★★★⯪
Facilities	★★⯪
Atmosphere & character	★★★★⯪
Security	★★⯪
Overall rating	★★★★⯪

Sights
Beverley Minster
This magnificent Gothic structure dates from 1220 when it was built to replace an earlier building that was destroyed by fire in 1188.
Minster Yard North, Beverley
☎ *(01482) 868 540*
Website *www.beverleyminster.co.uk*
Admission *£2 donation*
Open *winter Mon-Sat 9am-4pm, Sun noon-4pm; spring Mon-Sat 9am-5pm, Sun noon-4pm; summer Mon-Sat 9am-6pm, Sun noon-4pm; autumn Mon-Sat 9am-5pm, Sun noon-4pm*

St Mary's Church
This 12th-century church is regarded as one of England's greatest parish churches.
Hengate, Beverley
☎ *(01482) 865 709*
Website *www.stmarysbeverley.org.uk*

North Yorkshire
The largest and most visited county in Yorkshire has a diverse range of attractions that include the historic city of York, the seaside towns of Scarborough and Whitby and the rolling hills of the Yorkshire Dales and the North York Moors National Parks.

York
Originally a Viking settlement, York was also an important centre in the Anglo-Saxon and Roman eras and has several important sights that drawn on its rich heritage. Although one of the country's most visited historic cities, this medieval walled city hasn't lost its charm and it is still a great place to wander along cobblestone lanes in search of yet another pub.

Practical Information
INFORMATION CENTRES
York Tourist Information Centre
The De Grey Rooms
Exhibition Square, York
☎ *(01904) 621756*
Website *www.york-tourism.co.uk*
Open *summer Mon-Sat 9am-6pm, Sun 10am-5pm; winter Mon-Sat 9am-5pm, Sun 10am-4pm*

York Tourist Information Centre
Outer Concourse, York Train Station, Station Road, York
☎ *(01904) 621756*
Website *www.york-tourism.co.uk*
Open *summer Mon-Sat 9am-6pm, Sun 9.30am-4.30pm; winter Mon-Sat 9am-5pm, Sun 10am-4pm*

INTERNET ACCESS
Gateway Internet Cafe-Bar
26 Swinegate, York
☎ *(01904) 646446*
Website *www.ymn.net/gateway*
Open *Mon-Wed 10am-8pm, Thu-Sat 10am-11pm, Sun noon-4pm*

Coming & Going
BUS
National Express (☎ *0870 580 8080; website www.nationalexpress.co.uk*) runs buses from York to Edinburgh, Leeds, London and Newcastle.

TRAIN
Arriva Trains Northern (*website www.arrivatrainsnorthern.co.uk*) have trains to York from destinations in Yorkshire including Harrogate, Hull and Leeds; GNER (*website www.gner.co.uk*) operate trains to London (Kings Cross), Newcastle, Edinburgh and Glasgow; Midland Mainline (*website www.midlandmainline.com*) have trains to Sheffield, Derby, Leicester, London (St Pancras) and Nottingham and TransPennine Express trains go to Leeds, Manchester (Piccadilly), Newcastle and Scarborough.

Local Transport
First (*website www.firstgroup.com*) runs 22 local bus routes around York. One way tickets cost from 50p to £1.70 and the FirstDay ticket gives you one day unlimited travel on First buses for £2.20.

Accommodation
YHA York
York's YHA is a big hostel that features a large TV lounge with table football, a games room with a pool table, a large kitchen and a small bar with Internet access.

Water End, Clifton, York
🚌 *2, 17*
☎ *(01904) 653 147*
***Dorm bed** £20 (£18 HI/YHA; £15 HI/YHA & ISIC)*
***Credit cards** MC, Visa*
***Reception open** 7am-10.30pm daily*

Maintenance & cleanliness	★★★★☆
Facilities	★★
Atmosphere & character	★
Security	★★★
Overall rating	★★★☆

York Backpackers
York Backpackers is in an old building with lots of character. It features a bar in

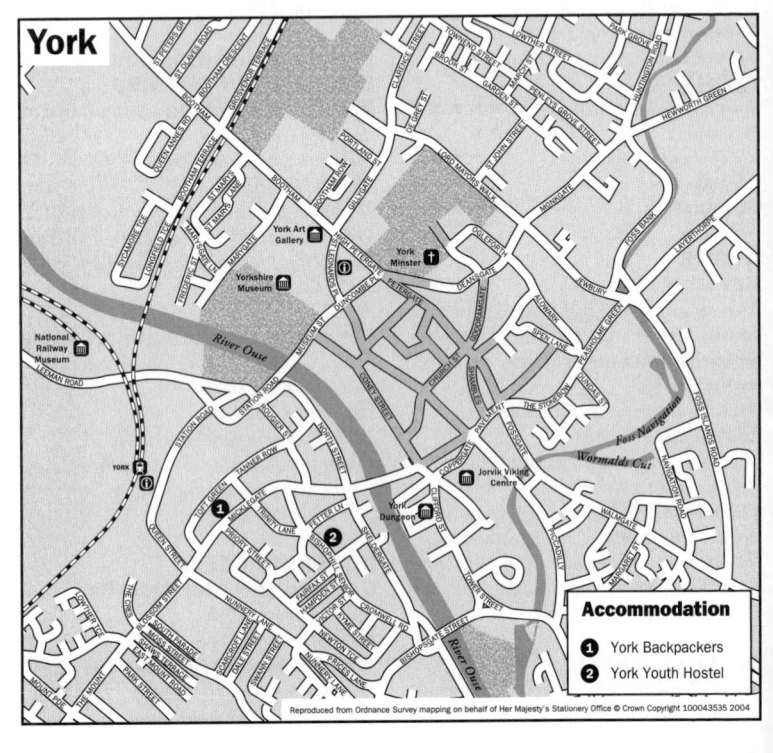

the basement with a brilliant atmosphere plus a cosy TV lounge. It is an excellent choice for backpackers visiting York.
88-90 Micklegate, York
☎ *(01904) 627 720*
Website *www.yorkbackpackers.mcmail.com*
Dorm bed £13-14; **double/twin room** £34; *prices include breakfast*
Credit cards *MC, Visa*
Reception open *8am-10pm daily; 24 hour check in available*

📺 🔑 L 🅿️

Maintenance & cleanliness	★★★
Facilities	★★☆
Atmosphere & character	★★★★★
Security	★★
Overall rating	★★★

York Youth Hotel

This hostel has good facilities that include a TV lounge with books and board games, a big games room with pool table, table tennis, table football and video games plus a kitchen and laundry. However the showers don't offer much privacy and the hostel lacks atmosphere.
Bishophill House, 11-13 Bishophill Senior, York
☎ *(01904) 625 904*
Website *www.yorkyouthhotel.com*
Dorm bed £12-18; **single room** £25
Credit cards *Amex, Diners, MC, Visa*
Reception open *24 hours*

📺 🔑 L

Maintenance & cleanliness	★★★
Facilities	★★☆
Atmosphere & character	★★☆
Security	★★★
Overall rating	★★★☆

Sights
Barley Hall

This unique medieval townhouse was only discovered in the 1980s. In the 15th century it was home to Alderman William Snawsell, a goldsmith who was also Mayor of York.
Coffee Yard, York
☎ *(01904) 610 275*
Website *www.barleyhall.org.uk*
Admission £3.50
Open *Tue-Sun 10am-4pm*

Clifford's Tower

Built by William the Conqueror as York Castle's central stronghold, Clifford's Tower has displays on the city's turbulent history.
Tower Street, York
☎ *(01904) 646 940*
Admission £2.50
Open *Jan-Mar 10am-4pm daily; Apr-Sep 10am-6pm daily; Oct-Dec 10am-4pm daily*

Jorvik Viking Centre

This popular attraction relives York's Viking past with reconstructed Viking streets and a large collection of 1000-year-old Viking artefacts.
Coppergate, York
☎ *(01904) 543 403*
Website *www.vikingjorvik.com*
Admission £7.20
Open *10am-5pm daily*

Micklegate Bar Museum

For over 800 years visiting royalty have passed through this gateway on the city's walls.
Bar Walls, York
☎ *(01904) 634 436*
Admission £2
Open *Jan 9am-dusk daily; Feb-Oct 9am-5pm daily; Nov-Dec 9am-dusk daily*

National Railway Museum

The world's largest railway museum features a replica of Stephenson's Rocket and a superb collection of royal trains.
Leeman Road, York
☎ *(01904) 621 261*
Website *www.nrm.org.uk*
Admission *free*
Open *10am-6pm daily*

Richard III Museum

This museum about Richard III, King of England from 1483 to 1485, focuses on the trial of the murders of the Princes in the Tower. The museum is located inside Monk Bar – the tallest of the medieval gatehouses on York's city walls.
Monkbar, York
☎ *(01904) 634 191*
Website *www.richardiiimuseum.co.uk*
Admission £2
Open *Jan-Feb 9.30am-4pm daily; Mar-Oct 9am-5pm daily; Nov-Dec 9.30am-4pm daily*

York Art Gallery
This art museum has paintings and ceramics dating from the War of the Roses, six hundred years ago, to the present day.
Exhibition Square, York
☎ *(01904) 687 687*
Website *www.yorkartgallery.org.uk*
Admission *free*
Open *10am-5pm daily*

York Castle Museum
This museum chronicles six hundred years of York's history with an emphasis on the lives of everyday people.
The Eye of York, York
☎ *(01904) 687 687*
Website *www.yorkcastlemuseum.org.uk*
Admission *£6*
Open *9.30am-5pm daily*

York Dungeon
York Dungeon uses wax models to illustrate the macabre side of England's history with exhibits on the Plague as well as criminals like Dick Turpin and Guy Fawkes.
12 Clifford Street, York
☎ *(01904) 632 599*
Website *www.thedungeons.com*
Admission *£8.50*
Open *10.30am-5pm daily*

York Minster
Northern Europe's largest medieval cathedral dominates the city centre. It features fine stained glass and a tower with views of the city centre.
St William's College, 5 College Street, York
☎ *(01904) 557 216*
Website *www.yorkminster.org*
Admission *£4.50*
Open *Mon-Sat 9am-6.30pm, Sun noon-6.30pm*

Yorkshire Air Museum
Aviation enthusiasts will love this museum, which features a restored World War II Halifax bomber and replicas of the *Cayley Glider* and the *Wright Flyer*.
Halifax Way, Elvington, York
☎ *(01904) 608 595*
Website *www.yorkshireairmuseum.co.uk*
Admission *£5*
Open *Jan-Mar 10am-3.30pm daily; Apr-Oct 10am-5pm daily; Nov-Dec 10am-3.30pm daily*

Yorkshire Museum & Gardens
This museum tells the history of Yorkshire from dinosaurs to the present day with displays of Viking and Roman artefacts.
Museum Gardens, York
☎ *(01904) 687 687*
Website *www.yorkshiremuseum.org.uk*
Admission *£4*
Open *10am-5pm daily*

Harrogate & Knareborough

Harrogate has long been the more upscale of Yorkshire's bigger towns and cities. The neighbouring town of Knaresborough is only 5km from the centre of Harrogate and is a quainter alternative with its own charm and unique attractions.

Practical Information
Harrogate Tourist Information Centre
Royal Baths Crescent Road, Harrogate
☎ *(01423) 537 300*
Website *www.harrogate.gov.uk/tourism/*
Open *Jan-Mar Mon-Fri 9am-5pm, Sat 9am-4pm; Apr-Sep Mon-Sat 9am-6pm, Sun 10am-1pm; Oct-Dec Mon-Fri 9am-5pm, Sat 9am-4pm*

Knaresborough Tourist Information Centre
9 Castle Courtyard, Knaresborough
☎ *(01423) 866 886*
Website *www.harrogate.gov.uk/tourism/*
Open *Apr-Jun Mon-Sat 10am-1pm & 1.30pm-5pm; Sun 1pm-4pm; Jul-Aug Mon-Sat 10am-1pm & 1.30pm-6pm, Sun 1pm-4pm; Sep Mon-Sat 10am-1pm & 1.30pm-5pm; Sun 1pm-4pm; Oct Mon-Sat 10am-1pm & 1.30pm-4pm*

Coming & Going
BUS
National Express (☎ *870 580 8080; website www.nationalexpress.co.uk*) run buses from Harrogate to Leeds

Harrogate & District (*website www.harrogateanddistrict.co.uk*) bus 36 runs frequent services connecting Harrogate with Ripon and Leeds with services at least once every 20 minutes on weekdays and every half hour on Sundays.

The good value Leeds Connection ticket is a day return between Harrogate or Knaresborough and Leeds that costs £4.20.

An Explorer ticket costs £6 and is valid for one day of unlimited travel on all Harrogate and District buses and on Arriva buses between Ripon and Darlington.

TRAIN

Arriva Trains Northern (*website www.arrivatrainsnorthern.co.uk*) run trains to Harrogate and Knaresborough from Leeds and York.

Local Transport

Local buses in the Harrogate and Knaresborough area are run by Harrogate & District (*website www.harrogateanddistrict.co.uk*). Buses 56, 57, 58, 101 and 102 run between Harrogate and Knaresborough. An all day ticket for travel in the central area of Harrogate and Knareborough costs £2.60 before 9am Mon-Fri or £2.10 after 9am Mon-Fri and all day on weekends.

Sights
Royal Pump Room Museum

The Royal Baths were built over a sulpher well and the museum depicts the history of the spa and also has a programme of changing exhibits.
Crown Place, Harrogate
☎ *(01423) 556 188*
Admission £2.50

St Robert's Cave

St Robert of Knaresborough is believed to have lived in this 12th century hermit's cave.
Abbey Road, Knaresborough
☎ *(01423) 556 188*
Admission free

Ripon

The spectacular Fountains Abbey is the main attraction in this market town.

Practical Information
Ripon Tourist Information Centre
Minster Road, Ripon
☎ *(01765) 604 625*
Website www.harrogate.gov.uk/tourism/
Open Apr-Jun Mon-Sat 10am-1pm & 1.30pm-5pm, Sun 10am-1pm; Jul-Aug Mon-Sat 10am-1pm & 1.30pm-6pm, Sun 10am-1pm; Sep Mon-Sat 10am-1pm & 1.30pm-5pm, Sun 10am-1pm; Oct Mon-Sat 10am-1pm & 1.30pm-4.30pm

Coming & Going

Harrogate & District (*website www.harrogateanddistrict.co.uk*) bus 36 runs frequent services to Harrogate and Leeds with services at least once every 20 minutes on weekdays and every half hour on Sundays.

Sights
Couthouse Museum

This museum is housed in the former courthouse where criminals were sentenced to transportation to Australia. The courtroom is presented as it was in the 1830s and there are audio visual presentations depicting actual cases.
Minster Road, Ripon
☎ *(01765) 690 799*
Website www.riponmuseums.co.uk
Admission £1; £5 including Prison & Police Museum & Workhouse Museum
Open Apr-Jun 1pm-4pm daily; Jul-Aug 11am-4pm daily; Sep-Oct 1pm-4pm daily

Fountains Abbey

This impressive World Heritage Site encompasses an Elizabethan mansion, St Mary's church and the remains of Britain's largest Cistercian abbey, which was founded by Cistercian monks in 1132. The grounds cover 800 acres and are home to 500 deer.
Fountains, Ripon
☎ *(01765) 608 888*
Website www.nationaltrust.org.uk
Admission £5.50
Open Jan-Mar 10am-4pm daily; Apr-Sep 10am-6pm daily; Oct-Dec 10am-4pm daily

Prison & Police Museum

This museum cronicles the history of the police force and prison service from the 17th century to the present day.

27 St Marygate, Ripon
☎ *(01765) 690 799*
Website *www.riponmuseums.co.uk*
Admission *£2.50; £5 including Courthouse Museum & Workhouse Museum*
Open *Apr-Jun 1pm-4pm daily; Jul-Aug 11am-4pm daily; Sep-Oct 1pm-4pm daily*

Workhouse Museum of Poor Law

This museum shows how vagrants were treated 100 years ago. It includes cells where they were locked up at night, the day room and the work yard.
Sharow View, Allhallowgate, Ripon
☎ *(01765) 690 799*
Website *www.riponmuseums.co.uk*
Admission *£2; £5 including Courthouse Museum & Prison & Police Museum*
Open *Apr-Jun 1pm-4pm daily; Jul-Aug 11am-4pm daily; Sep-Oct 1pm-4pm daily*

North York Moors National Park

The northern part of North Yorkshire doesn't have the spectacular landscape you find in Snowdonia or the Lake District, but the North York Moors is still a lovely area that is home to several charming small towns and a unique weather-beaten landscape that is covered in heather between early July and mid August.

Coming & Going & Local Transport

The North York Moors is most easily accessible from Helmsley, Middlesbrough, Pickering, Scarborough and Whitby and it has good public transport within the park including the historic North York Moors Railway.

Moorbus *(website www.moorsbus.net)* operates a good bus network connecting most towns in the park between April and October.

Arriva *(website www.arriva.co.uk)* supplements Moorsbus services in the northern area of the park and Yorkshire Coastliner *(website www.yorkshirecoastliner.co.uk)* connects the principal towns in the park with Leeds, Whitby and York.

Helmsley

Helmsley makes an ideal gateway to the North York Moors National Park. It is a picturesque market town that boasts some top class attractions including Helmsley Castle and – just 5.5km up the road – Rievaulx Abbey. Helmsley's market takes place each Friday.

Practical Information
Helmsley Tourist Information Centre
The Town Hall, Market Place, Helmsley
☎ *(01439) 770173*
Open *Jan-Feb Fri-Sun 10am-4pm; Mar-Oct 9.30am-5pm daily; Nov-Dec Fri-Sun 10am-4pm*

Accommodation
YHA Helmsley
This cosy stone hostel is close to the town centre and offers the usual hostel facilities such as a kitchen and TV lounge.
Carlton Lane, Helmsley
☎ *(01439) 770433*
Website *www.yha.org.uk*
Dorm bed *£14.50 (£12.50 HI/YHA; £9.50 HI/YHA & ISIC)*
Credit cards *MC, Visa*
Open *check with hostel;* ***reception open*** *8am-10am & 5pm-10pm daily;* ***curfew*** *11pm*

Sights
Helmsley Castle
This 900-year-old castle was built as a defence against the Scots but didn't see military action until the Civil War when it was blown in half.
Helmsley
☎ *(01439) 770 442*
Website *www.english-heritage.org.uk*
Admission *£4*
Open *Jan-Mar Mon & Thu-Sun 10am-4pm; Apr-Sep 10am-6pm daily; Oct-Dec Mon & Thu-Sun 10am-4pm*

Rievaulx Abbey
The magnificent Rievaulx Abbey is located 5.5km outside Helmley. It was founded around 1132 and became one of England's most powerful abbeys.
Rievaulx, Helmsley
☎ *(01439) 798 228*

Website www.english-heritage.org.uk
Admission £4
Open Jan-Mar Mon & Thu-Sun 10am-4pm; Apr-Sep 10am-6pm daily; Oct-Dec Mon & Thu-Sun 10am-4pm

Rievaulx Terrace & Temples
This 18th century terrace is home to two classical temples and it offers views of Rievaulx Abbey.
Rievaulx, Helmsley
☎ *(01423) 780 688*
Website www.nationaltrust.org.uk
Admission £3.80
Open 20 Mar-30 Sep 10.30am-6pm daily; 1-31 Oct 10.30am-5pm daily

Pickering
This nice market town is known as the starting point for the North Yorkshire Moors Railway. The town's other attraction is the Norman Pickering Castle. Monday is market day.

Practical Information
Pickering Tourist Information Centre
Ropery House, The Ropery, Pickering
☎ *(01751) 473791*
Open Jan-Feb Mon-Sat 9.30am-4pm; Mar-Oct Mon-Sat 9.30am-5pm, Sun 9.30am-4pm; Nov-Dec Mon-Sat 9.30am-4pm

Sights
North Yorkshire Moors Railway
England's most popular heritage railway runs through 29km of the North York Moors National Park between Pickering and Grosmont. Goathland station has featured in the TV show *Heartbeat* and also in the film *Harry Potter and the Philosopher's Stone*.
Pickering Station, Park Street, Pickering
☎ *(01751) 473 799*
Website www.northyorkshiremoorsrailway.com
Return fare £12.50

Parish Church of St Peter & St Paul
This Norman church is famed for having the country's most complete collections of medieval wall paintings.
Hallgarth, Pickering
☎ *(01751) 472 983*
Admission free

Pickering Castle
The original keep, towers and walls survive in this well-preserved 12th-century Norman castle.
Pickering
🚌 *128, 840, 842*
☎ *(01751) 474 989*
Website www.english-heritage.org.uk
Admission £3
Open Apr-Sep 10am-6pm daily; Oct Mon & Thu-Sun 10am-4pm

Whitby
This seaside town in the North York Moors has more to offer than the average English seaside resort. For a start it is home to the majestic Whitby Abbey, which overlooks the historic old town with its narrow cobblestone streets. Whitby has also been home to many famous people including Captain James Cook and writers Bram Stoker and Lewis Carroll.

Practical Information
Tourist Information Centre
Langborne Road, Whitby
☎ *(01723) 383637*
Open Jan-Apr 10am-12.30pm & 1pm-4.30pm daily; May-Sep 10.30am-5.30pm daily; Oct-Dec 10am-12.30pm & 1pm-4.30pm daily

Coming & Going
BUS
Arriva *(website www.arriva.co.uk)* buses connect Whitby with nearby towns. Buses 93, 93A and 93B go to Middlesbrough and Scarborough, bus X60 goes to Newcastle and bus X61 goes to Durham.

TRAIN
Arriva Trains Northern *(website www.arrivatrainsnorthern.co.uk)* run trains from Whitby to Middlesbrough and Newcastle.

Accommodation
Harbour Grange Backpackers
This small 24-bed hostel by the riverfront has a TV lounge and a small but

fully equipped kitchen and accommodation in mostly small dorms.
Spital Bridge, Whitby
☎ *(01947) 600817*
Website *www.harbourgrange.co.uk*
Dorm bed *£10-12*
Reception open *8am-10am & 5pm-9pm daily;* **curfew** *11.30pm*

Maintenance & cleanliness	★★★★
Facilities	★★½
Atmosphere & character	★
Security	★
Overall rating	★★★½

Whitby Backpackers
This small hostel has clean and comfortable accommodation with facilities that include a cosy front lounge with a TV and a small but fully equipped kitchen.
28 Hudson Street, Whitby
☎ *(01947) 601 794*
Website *www.thewhitbybackpackers.co.uk*
Dorm bed *£10-15; double/twin room £30*

Maintenance & cleanliness	★★★★½
Facilities	★★½
Atmosphere & character	★★★★½
Security	★
Overall rating	★★★½

YHA Whitby
This traditional youth hostel is in an old building next to Whitby Abbey. It has a basic but spacious kitchen and a big lounge with comfortable sofas. The biggest dorm has 18 beds but most are smaller.
East Cliff, Whitby
☎ *(01947) 602 878*
Website *www.yha.org.uk*
Dorm bed *£13 (£11 HI/YHA; £8 HI/YHA & ISIC)*
Credit cards *MC, Visa*
Open *1 Jan-27 Mar Fri-Sat; 28 Mar-4 Sep every day; 5 Sep-30 Oct Mon-Sat; 31 Oct-4 Dec Fri-Sat; reception open 7.15am-10am & 5pm-10.30pm daily*

Maintenance & cleanliness	★★★★
Facilities	★
Atmosphere & character	★★★½
Security	★★
Overall rating	★★★½

Sights
Captain Cook Memorial Museum
Captain Cook lived in this house while serving his seaman's apprenticeship. It is now a museum with exhibits relating to Cook's achievements and artefacts from his voyages.
Grape Lane, Whitby
☎ *(01947) 601 900*
Website *www.cookmuseumwhitby.co.uk*
Admission *£3*
Open *Mar Sat-Sun 11am-3pm; Apr-Oct 9.45am-5pm daily*

Whitby Abbey
The haunting ruins of Whitby Abbey is perched high on a hill overlooking Whitby and the abbey is accessible by climbing 199 steps from the old town. St Hilda founded Whitby Abbey in 657 and it is here in 664 that an agreement on the date of Easter was reached between the Synod of Celtic and Roman Christians, however Vikings destroyed it in 857 and the present structure was built in 1078. The Abbey's visitor centre houses a museum with artefacts tracing the site's history.
☎ *(01947) 603 568*
Admission *£4*
Open *Jan-Mar Mon & Thu-Sun 10am-4pm; Apr-Sep Mon & Thu-Sun 10am-4pm; Oct-Dec Mon & Thu-Sun 10am-4pm*

Whitby Museum
This museum has exhibits on local history including Jurassic fossils and displays about Captain Cook and whaling.
Pannett Park, St Hilda's Terrace, Whitby
☎ *(01947) 602 908*
Website *www.durain.demon.co.uk*
Admission *£3*
Open *Jan-Apr Tue 10am-1pm, Wed-Sat 10am-4pm, Sun 2pm-4pm; May-Sep Mon-Fri 9.30am-5.30pm, Sat-Sun 2pm-5pm; Oct-Dec Tue 10am-1pm, Wed-Sat 10am-4pm, Sun 2pm-4pm*

Robin Hoods Bay

This tiny village by the sea on the coastal road between Whitby and Scarborough doesn't offer many things to see or do but it is home to a secluded waterfront hostel, which is a lovely place to relax and unwind.

Coming & Going
Arriva bus 93A passes Robin Hoods Bay en route between Scarborough and Whitby.

Accommodation
YHA Boggle Hole
This youth hostel is in a quiet setting on a secluded bay a 20-minute walk along the beach from Robin Hoods Bay. It consists of two buildings and features a kitchen and a quiet lounge. Most dorms have four beds but there are a couple of larger rooms.
Mill Beck, Fylingthorpe, Robin Hoods Bay
☎ *(01947) 880 352*
Website www.yha.org.uk
Dorm bed *£14.50 (£12.50 HI/YHA; £9.50 HI/YHA & ISIC)*
Credit cards *MC, Visa*
Open *Jan-Jun contact hostel; Jul-Aug every day; Sep-Dec contact hostel;* **reception open** *8am-10am & 1pm-10.30pm daily*

Maintenance & cleanliness	★★★
Facilities	★★
Atmosphere & character	★★
Security	★★
Overall rating	★★½

Scarborough
Like many other English seaside resort, Scarborough has its share of tacky attractions. However it has a richer history than most other seaside towns and boasts a large 12th-century castle.

Practical Information
Scarborough Tourist Information Centre
Unit 3, Pavilion House, Valley Bridge Road, Scarborough
☎ *(01723) 383636*
Open *Jan-Apr Mon-Sat 10am-4.30pm; May-Sep 9.30am-6pm daily; Oct-Dec Mon-Sat 10am-4.30pm*

Harbourside Tourist Information Centre
Sandside, Scarborough
☎ *(01723) 383636*
Open *Jan-Apr Sun 10am-4.30pm; May-Oct 10am-5pm daily; Nov-Dec Sun 10am-4.30pm*

Coming & Going
BUS
National Express (☎ *0870 580 8080; website www.nationalexpress.co.uk*) run buses from the train station to Birmingham, Leeds, London and York.

TRAIN
Arriva Trains Northern (**website** *www.arrivatrainsnorthern.co.uk*) run trains to Hull and Trans Pennine Express (**website** *www.tpexpress.co.uk*) run hourly trains to Leeds and Manchester (Piccadilly).

Local Transport
Arriva (**website** *www.arriva.co.uk*) and Scarborough and District (**website** *www.eyms.co.uk/scarborough.htm*) run bus services around Scarborough.

Accommodation
YHA Scarborough
Scarborough's YHA is a basic hostel in a former water mill dating from around 1600. It is located in a riverside setting 3.25km from the town centre.
Burniston Road, Scarborough
☎ *(01723) 361176*
Website *www.yha.org.uk*
Dorm bed *£13 (£11 HI/YHA; £8 HI/YHA & ISIC)*
Credit cards *MC, Visa*
Open 20 Mar-31 Aug every day; 1 Sep-31 Oct Tue-Sat; **reception open** *8am-10am & 5pm-10pm daily;* **curfew** *11pm*

Sights
Rotunda Museum
The Rotunda Museum has exhibits on local history including artefacts from Roman times.
Vernon Road, Scarborough
☎ *(01723) 374 839*
Website *www.scarboroughmuseums.org.uk*
Admission *£2.50 includes entry to Scarborough Art Gallery & Wool End Museum*
Open *Jan-May Tue & Sat-Sun 11am-4pm; Jun-Sep Tue-Sun 10am-5pm; Oct-Dec Tue & Sat-Sun 11am-4pm*

Scarborough Castle
The 12th-century Scarborough Castle 1.5km east of the town centre was built by William Le Gros, Earl of Albemarle but was expanded in the 13th century by King John and Henry III as a defence.
Castle Road, Scarborough
☎ *(01723) 372 451*
Website www.english-heritage.org.uk
Admission £3.20
Open Jan-Mar Mon & Thu-Sun 10am-4pm; Apr-Sep 10am-6pm daily; Oct-Dec Mon & Thu-Sun 10am-4pm

Wood End Natural History Museum
This natural history museum has displays about the rocks, fossils and wildlife of the Yorkshire coast and the North York Moors National Park.
The Crescent, Scarborough
☎ *(01723) 367 326*
Website www.scarboroughmuseums.org.uk
Admission £2.50 includes entry to Rotunda Museum & Scarborough Art Gallery
Open Jan-May Wed & Sat-Sun 11am-4pm; Jun-Sep Tue-Sun 10am-5pm; Oct-Dec Jan-May Wed & Sat-Sun 11am-4pm

Yorkshire Dales National Park

This scenic region is characterised by stonewalls that mark ancient field boundaries. It represents a slice of English countryside that just begs to be explored, as it combines picturesque valleys and rolling hills with quaint villages.

Coming & Going & Local Transport
Considering that it is a largely rural area, the Yorkshire Dales has a good public transport infrastructure with the Settle-Carlisle Railway running from Leeds to Carlisle with a branch line to Lancaster as well as bus services into the park.

Travel Dales (*website* www.traveldales.org.uk) provides public transport information for the Yorkshire Dales.

There are several travel passes available that include:

Dales Rover
The Dales Rover ticket is good for on day travel on the Dales Connections bus network on weekends during summer. It is valid on the following bus services 24, 25, 67A, 159, 800, 802, 803, 804, 804T, 805, 807, 812, 830 and 843 and also on the following Saturday service 210, 804, 804T. The Dales Rover ticket is divided into four zones with tickets costing between £3.50 for one zone to £8 for all zones.

Settle-Carlisle Country Freedom of the Line Rover Ticket
This ticket gives you three consecutive days travel on the entire Settle-Carlise train line between Leeds and Carlisle. This pass costs £30 but needs to be booked one week in advance.

Skipton
Located at the southern edge of the national park, Skipton is a handy transport hub that makes a good base for exploring the Dales. Skipton Castle is the town's main attraction.

Practical Information
Skipton Tourist Information Centre
35 Coach Street, Skipton
☎ *(01756) 792809*
Open Mon-Sat 10am-5pm, Sun 11am-3pm

Sights
Skipton Castle
This fully roofed castle is one of England's best-preserved medieval castles, despite having withstood a three-year siege during the Civil War.
High Street, Skipton
☎ *(01756) 792 442*
Website www.skiptoncastle.co.uk
Admission £5
Open Jan-Feb Mon-Sat 10am-4pm, Sun noon-4pm; Mar-Sep Mon-Sat 10am-6pm; Sun noon-6pm; Oct-Dec Mon-Sat 10am-4pm, Sun noon-4pm

Settle

This small town in Ribblesdale has a couple of hostels and is a good base for visiting Malham Tarn. Settle's market day is Tuesday.

Practical Information
Settle Tourist Information Centre
Town Hall, Cheapside, Settle
☎ *(01729) 825192*
Open *9.30am-4.30pm daily*

Accommodation
Dalesbridge
This bunkhouse has accommodation in self-contained units, each with en suite bathroom and kitchenette (usually just a microwave, toaster and kettle). There is a bar, but not much else in the way of common areas. Bring your own sleeping bag and pillow. It is 8km from Settle near the Shell service station on the A65.
A65, Austwick, Settle
☎ *(015242) 51021*
Website *www.dalesbridge.co.uk*
Dorm bed *£11*
Credit cards *Amex, JCB, MC, Visa*
Reception open *Mon-Thu 9am-6pm, Fri 9am-9pm, Sat 8am-9pm, Sun 8am-noon*

Maintenance & cleanliness	★★½
Facilities	★
Atmosphere & character	½
Security	★
Overall rating	★★½

YHA Stainforth
YHA Stainforth is a youth hostel in a Georgian country house 3.25km north of Settle. The house has been recently refurbished and its facilities include the usual lounge, dining room and kitchen.
Stainforth, Settle
☎ *(01729) 823 577*
Website *www.yha.org.uk*
Dorm bed *£14.50 (£12.50 HI/YHA; £9.50 HI/YHA & ISIC)*
Credit cards *MC, Visa*
Open *Fri-Sat & school holidays only;* **reception open** *8am-10am & 1pm-10pm daily;* **curfew** *11pm*

Maintenance & cleanliness	★★★½
Facilities	★★½
Atmosphere & character	★★★
Security	★★½
Overall rating	★★★

Malham

This small village has a couple of hostels and is also home to the national park centre and makes a good base for visiting Malham Tarn.

Practical Information
National Park Centre
Malham
☎ *(01729) 830363*
Website *www.yorkshiredales.org*
Open *Jan-Mar Fri-Sun 10am-4pm; Apr-Oct 10am-5pm daily; Nov-Dec Fri-Sun 10am-4pm*

Accommodation
Hill Top Farm Bunk Barns
This bunk barn offers basic accommodation in large dorms in a stone barn with old metal bunk beds with plastic-coated mattresses. Facilities are limited to a kitchen and a large common room.
Malham
☎ *(01729) 830 320*
Dorm bed *£9*

Maintenance & cleanliness	★★★
Facilities	½
Atmosphere & character	★★★★½
Security	½
Overall rating	★★

YHA Malham
Malham's YHA consists of a couple of buildings and it provides clean accommodation. Facilities include a good kitchen, a dining room and a cosy lounge.
Malham
☎ *(01729) 830 321*
Website *www.yha.org.uk*
Dorm bed *£14.50 (£12.50 HI/YHA; £9.50 HI/YHA & ISIC)*
Credit cards *MC, Visa*
Open *1-4 Jan every day; 23 Jan-14 Feb Fri-Sat; 15 Feb-9 Nov every day; 10 Nov-18 Dec Fri-Sat;* **reception open** *9am-10am & 5pm-10pm daily;* **curfew** *11pm*

🚗 🆒 🅛

Maintenance & cleanliness	★★★★
Facilities	★
Atmosphere & character	★★★
Security	★★½
Overall rating	★★★½

Sights
Malham Tarn
This estate consists of six farms with striking limestone features and a large lake. It is located north of Malham village and can be visited from either Malham or Settle.
🚌 *Pennine 210, Arriva 804*
☎ *(01729) 830 416*
Website *www.nationaltrust.org.uk*
Admission *free*

Ingleton
This small market town at the southwest corner of the park is home to Britain's longest show cave. Ingleton's market takes place on Fridays.

Accommodation
YHA Ingleton
This big Victorian house in the village centre has good quality accommodation but shared facilities are limited to a lounge and a fully equipped kitchen.
Sammy Lane, Ingleton
☎ *(015242) 41444*
Website *www.yha.org.uk*
Dorm bed *£14.50 (£12.50 HI/YHA; £9.50 HI/YHA & ISIC)*
Credit cards *MC, Visa*
Open *13-29 Feb Tue-Sat; 2 Mar-1 Sep every day; 2 Sep-30 Oct Mon-Sat; 1 Nov-17 Dec Fri-Sun;* **reception open** *8am-11am & 5pm-10.30pm daily;* **curfew** *11pm*

🚗 🆒 🅛

Maintenance & cleanliness	★★★★
Facilities	★★★½
Atmosphere & character	★
Security	★★
Overall rating	★★★

Sights
White Scar Cave
Britain's longest show cave features a 1.6km-long tour that takes you past stalactites and underground waterfalls.
Admission *£6.50*

Richmond
Richmond is an historic market town in Swaledale that has an expansive cobbled market square plus the ruins of Richmond Castle.

Practical Information
Richmond Tourist Information Centre
Friary Gardens, Victoria Road, Richmond
☎ *(01748) 850252*
Open *Apr-Oct 9.30am-5.30pm daily*

Sights
Richmond Castle
The ruins of the impressive Richmond Castle loom over Richmond's market square. William the Conqueror built the castle, which features 11th century walls and a 30m-high 12th century keep.
Castle Wynd, Richmond
☎ *(01748) 822 493*
Website *www.english-heritage.org.uk*
Admission *£3.50*
Open *Jan-Mar Mon & Thu-Sun 10am-4pm; Apr-Sep 10am-6pm daily; Oct-Dec Mon & Wed-Sun 10am-4pm*

Richmondshire Museum
This museum has exhibits on local history from the Stone Age to the 1950s. Displays include the surgery set from the Herriot film, *All Creatures Great and Small*.
Ryders Wynd, Richmond
☎ *(01748) 822 271*
Admission *£1.50*
Open *Easter-October 11am-5pm daily*

Wensleydale & Hawes
Wallace and Grommit's love of Wensleydale cheese has made Wensleydale the most well known of the Yorkshire Dales. The main town in the dale is Hawes, which is England's highest market town.

Practical Information
Hawes Tourist Information Centre
Dales Countryside Museum, Station Yard, Hawes
☎ *(01969) 667450*
Open *10am-5pm daily*

Accommodation
YHA Hawes
This purpose-built youth hostel features open plan living areas with a dining area and small lounge plus a kitchen and a separate room with a TV and pool table.
Lancaster Terrace, Hawes
☎ *(01969) 667 368*
Website *www.yha.org.uk*
Dorm bed *£13 (£11 HI/YHA; £8 HI/YHA & ISIC)*
Credit cards *MC, Visa*
Open *13 Feb-30 Mar Tue-Sat; 31 Mar-31 Oct every day; 1 Nov-19 Dec Fri-Sat;* **reception open** *8am-10am & 5pm-10pm daily;* **curfew** *11pm*

🚗 📺 🅚 🅛

Maintenance & cleanliness	★★★★☆
Facilities	★★
Atmosphere & character	★★★☆
Security	★
Overall rating	★★★☆

Sights
Dales Countryside Museum
This small museum has excellent exhibits on life in the Yorkshire Dales. It features a Time Tunnel depicting 10,000 years of history, an old steam train, a recreation of an old kitchen and doctor's surgery and a programme of changing exhibitions.
Station Yard, Hawes
☎ *(01969) 667450*
Website *www.yorkshiredales.org.uk*
Admission *£3*
Open *10am-5pm daily (last entry 4pm)*

Wensleydale Creameries
Cistercian monks first settled in Wensleydale in 1150, bringing their unique cheese recipe with them. Except for a brief period in 1992, the cheese has been produced in Wensleydale ever since. Wensleydale Creameries have a museum with displays about the history of the cheese and a viewing gallery where you can see the cheese being made.
Gayle Lane, Hawes
☎ *(01969) 667 664*
Website *www.wensleydale.co.uk*
Admission *£2*
Open *Mon-Sat 9am-5pm, Sun 10am-4.30pm*

Northumbria

England's northeastern corner is one of the country's least visited regions. The main attractions here are the historic city of Durham, vibrant Newcastle-upon-Tyne and the countryside alongside Hadrian's Wall.

Tees Valley

Most travellers pass straight through this largely industrial county between Newcastle and Yorkshire.

Middlesbrough & Stockton-on-Tees

These twin cities on the Tees River hold little interest to most travellers, however Captain James Cook was born in the Middlesbrough suburb of Marton where there is now a museum dedicated to the famous explorer.

Practical Information
Tourist Information Centre
The Old Town Hall Box Office, Albert Road, Middlesbrough
☎ *(01642) 729 700*
Open *Mon-Thu 9am-5pm, Fri 9am-4.30pm, Sat 9am-1.30pm*

Coming & Going
AIR
Durham Tees Valley Airport *(website www.teessideairport.com)* handles scheduled flights to Aberdeen, Amsterdam, Belfast, Dublin, Jersey, London, Nice and Prague and charter flights to Greece, Spain and Florida. Budget airlines that use this airport include bmibaby *(website www.bmibaby.com)* and Ryanair *(website www.ryanair.com)*. Arriva Trains Northern *(website www.arrivatrainsnorthern.co.uk)* operate trains to Durham Tees Valley Airport from Middlesbrough and Stockton and Arriva bus 76 runs between the airport and Darlington train station.

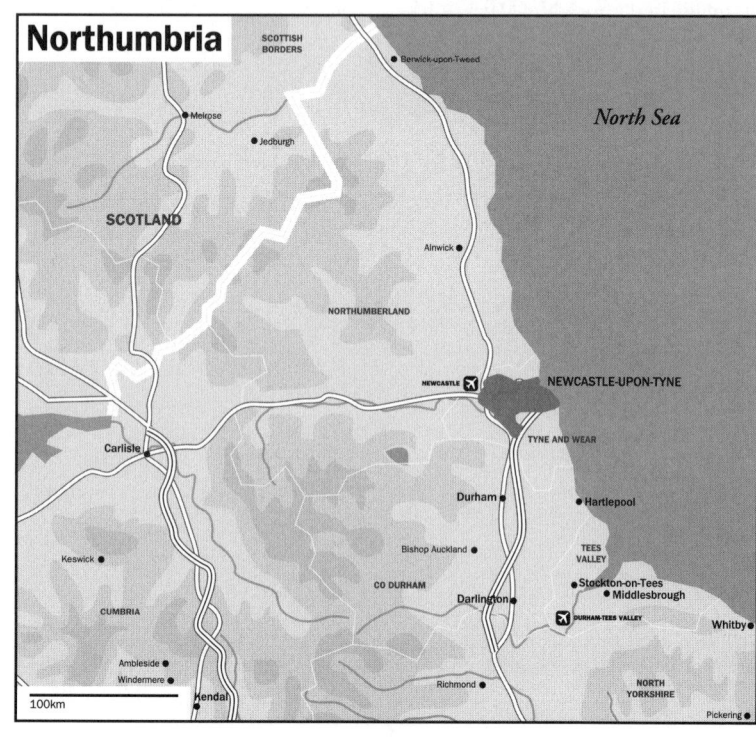

BUS

National Express (☎ 0870 580 8080; *website www.nationalexpress.co.uk*) has bus services from Middlesborough to Birmingham, Glasgow, Leeds, Liverpool, London, Manchester and York. Arriva *(website www.arriva.co.uk)* and Stagecoach *(website www.stagecoachbus. co.uk)* run buses to nearby towns and cities including Durham, Hartlepool, Newcastle, Scarborough and Whitby. Buses depart from Middlesbrough Bus Station, which is next to the Captain Cook Square Shopping Centre.

TRAIN

Arriva Trains Northern *(website www. arrivatrainsnorthern.co.uk)* run trains to Darlington, Durham, Hartlepool, Newcastle, Sunderland and Whitby and Trans Pennine Express *(website www. firstgroup.com/tpexpress/)* run trains to York, Leeds and Manchester.

Local Transport

Local buses and train services in Middlesbrough and Stockton on Tees are operated by Arriva *(website www.arriva. co.uk)*. Arriva One Day tickets cost £4.50 and give you one day's unlimited travel on Arriva buses in the northeast.

Accommodation

There aren't any hostels here, but there is a cheap Formule 1 hotel in Stockton-on-Tees.

Formule 1 Hotel

No atmosphere, but cheap clean rooms.
Teesway, North Tees Industrial Estate, Stockton on Tees
☎ *(01642) 606 560*
Double/twin room *£19.95-21.95*
Website *www.hotelformule1.com*
Credit cards *MC, Visa*

Sights
Captain Cook Birthplace Museum

Captain Cook's birthplace on the grounds of Stewart Park, 6km from Middlesbrough city centre, features displays and audio-visual presentations on the life of Captain James Cook, who is credited with discovering Australia, Hawaii and New Zealand.

Stewart Park, Marton, Middlesbrough
🚌 *27, 27A, 29, 66, 67*
☎ *(01642) 311 211*
Admission *£2.40*
Open *Jan-Feb Tue-Sun 9am-3.30pm; Mar-Oct Tue-Sun 10am-5.30pm; Nov-Dec Tue-Sun 9am-3.30pm*

Dorman Museum

This museum has displays that include natural history and Victorian art and craft.

Linthorpe Road, Middlesbrough
☎ *(01642) 813 781*
Website *www.dormanmuseum.co.uk*
Admission *free*
Open *Tue-Wed 10am-5.30pm, Thu 11am-6.30pm, Fri-Sun 10am-5.30pm*

Transporter Bridge Visitor Centre

Located just south of Middlesbrough's famous Transporter Bridge, this museum has interactive displays about Middlesbrough's industrial heritage.

Ferry Road, Middlesbrough
☎ *(01642) 248 566*
Admission *50p (students 30p)*

Hartlepool

This maritime town boasts a brilliant historic quayside that features Britain's oldest floating warship.

Practical Information
Tourist Information Centre

Hartlepool Art Gallery, Church Square, Hartlepool
☎ *(01429) 869 706*
Website *www.destinationhartlepool.com*
Open *Tue-Sat 10am-5.30pm, Sun 2pm-5pm*

Sights
Hartlepool Historic Quay & Museum

Hartlepool's historic quayside has been restored to recreate the 18th century seaport. It features Britain's oldest floating warship, *HMS Trincomalee* as well as the restored paddle steamer, *PSS Wingfield Castle*. The Museum of Hartlepool is also on the site and it has displays on local history from prehistoric times to the present day.

Jackson Dock, Maritime Avenue, Hartlepool
☎ *(01429) 860 006*
Admission *£5.50*
Open *10am-5pm daily*

Newgate, Barnard Castle
🚌 *8, 75*
☎ *(01833) 690 606*
Website *www.bowesmuseum.org.uk*
Admission *£6*
Open *11am-5pm daily*

County Durham

County Durham has a fascinating history and during medieval times it was an autonomous region, with its own army, courts and currency that was ruled by the Prince Bishops for almost 800 years.

Barnard Castle

This market town 32km south of Durham is home to the ruins of the large Barnard Castle and it also makes a good base for exploring other castles in Teesdale.

Practical Information
Barnard Castle Tourist Information Centre
Woodleigh, Flatts Road, Barnard Castle
☎ *(01833) 690 909*
Website *www.teesdalediscovery.com*
Open *Mon-Sat 9.30am-5pm, Sun 11am-5pm*

Coming & Going
Arriva (**website** *www.arriva.co.uk*) run buses to other destinations in north east England. Useful routes include bus 76 to Darlington and Durham Tees Valley Airport.

Sights
Barnard Castle
The town's namesake consists of the rambling ruins of this Norman castle. It features a three-storey keep, a round tower and the 14th century great hall.
Barnard Castle
☎ *(01833) 638 212*
Admission *£2.50*
Open *Jan-Mar Wed-Sun 10am-4pm; Apr-Sep 10am-6pm daily; Oct 10am-4pm daily; Nov-Dec Wed-Sun 10am-4pm*

Bowes Museum
This large museum features an extensive art collection with a particularly impressive collection of Spanish paintings.

Durham

Durham is the gem of the north. Durham's Prince Bishops once ruled County Durham for almost 800 years. This city is home to England's third oldest university (only Cambridge and Oxford are older) and its castle and cathedral have been recognised by UNESCO as a World Heritage Site.

Practical Information
Durham Tourist Information Centre
2 Millennium Place, Durham City
☎ *(0191) 384 3720*
Open *Mon-Sat 9.30am-5.30pm, Sun 11am-4pm*

Coming & Going
BUS
National Express (☎ *0870 580 8080; website www.nationalexpress.co.uk*) buses go to Leeds, London and Newcastle.

Arriva (**website** *www.arriva.co.uk*) operates buses to most destinations in northeastern England. Some of the more useful Arriva bus routes include buses 1X, 123, 223, 723, X1, X2 and X41 to Newcastle and bus X61 to Scarborough.

The bus station is on North Road east of the city centre across Framwellgate Bridge.

TRAIN
Arriva Trains Northern (**website** *www.arrivatrainsnorthern.co.uk*) run trains to Durham from other destinations in the north of England including Carlisle, Newcastle and Whitby. GNER (**website** *www.gner.co.uk*) stops in Durham en route from London (Kings Cross) to Edinburgh and Glasgow. The train station is north west of the city centre.

Accommodation
YHA Durham City
Durham's YHA provides accommodation in historic surroundings at St Chad's

College in the University of Durham. All the rooms have either one or two beds and there is also a bar on site.
St Chad's College, University of Durham, 18 North Bailey, Durham
☎ *(0191) 334 3358*
Dorm bed *£24 (£22 HI/YHA; £19 HI/YHA & ISIC)*
Open *Jul-Sep & 27 Dec-16 Jan*

Sights
Durham Castle
Dating from 1072, Durham's Prince Bishops used Durham Castle as a fortress and the castle is home to University College, the first college of the University of Durham.
University of Durham, Palace Green, Durham
☎ *(0191) 334 4106*
Website *www.durhamcastle.com*
Admission *£5*
Open *20 Jan-29 Mar Mon, Wed, Sat 2pm-4.30pm; 22 Mar-23 Apr 10am-noon & 2pm-4.30pm daily; 26 Apr-23 Jun Mon, Wed, Sat 2pm-4.30pm; 5 Jul-15 Oct 10am-noon & 2pm-4.30pm daily; 11 Oct-15 Dec Mon, Wed, Sat 2pm-4.30pm*

Durham Cathedral
Durham's exquisite 12th-century cathedral has been compared with cathedrals in Chartres, Cologne and Salzburg making it one of Europe's great religious buildings. The cathedral houses the 7th century tomb of St Cuthbert as well as a display of the Treasures of St Cuthbert and an exhibition about the construction of the cathedral. You can also climb the 325 steps to the top of the tower.
The College, Durham
☎ *(0191) 386 4266*
Website *www.durhamcathedral.co.uk*
Admission *free; Treasures of St Cuthbert £2; exhibition on the building of the church 80p; tower £2*
Cathedral open *Mon-Sat 9.30am-6.15pm, Sun 12.30pm-5pm; Treasures of St Cuthbert open Mon-Sat 10am-4.30pm, Sun 2pm-4.30pm;* **exhibition on the building of the church open** *Mon-Sat 10am-4pm;* **tower open** *Jan-Mar Mon-Sat 10am-3pm; Apr-Sep Mon-Sat 9.30am-4pm; Oct-Dec Mon-Sat 10am-3pm*

Durham Heritage Centre
This museum has displays on local history from the 10th century.
Saint Mary-le-Bow, North Bailey, Durham
☎ *(0191) 384 5589*
Open *Apr-May Sat-Sun 2pm-4.30pm; Jun 2pm-4.30pm daily; Jul-Sep 11am-4.30pm daily; Oct Sat-Sun 2pm-4.30pm*

Finchale Priory
Located 5km north east of Durham, this 13th-century Benedictine priory was built around the tomb of St Godric who lived here until he was 105.
Brasside, Durham
🚌 *737*
☎ *(0191) 386 3828*
Website *www.english-heritage.org.uk*
Open *Apr-Sep 10am-6pm daily*

The Old Fulling Mill Museum of Archaeology
This museum has archaeological exhibits from northeast England as well as from ancient Greece and Rome.
The Old Fulling Mill, The Banks, Durham
☎ *(0191) 334 1823*
Website *www.dur.ac.uk/fulling.mill*
Admission *£1*
Open *Jan-Mar Mon & Fri-Sun 11.30am-3.30pm; Apr-Oct 11am-4pm daily; Nov Mon & Fri-Sun 11.30am-3.30pm*

Oriental Museum
This museum has exhibits on ancient Egypt and eastern Asia.
University of Durham, Elvet Hill, Durham
🚌 *5, 6, 41, 722*
☎ *(0191) 334 5694*
Website *www.dur.ac.uk/oriental.museum*
Admission *£1.50*
Open *Mon-Fri 10am-5pm, Sat-Sun noon-5pm*

Beamish
This small town, 13km south of Newcastle and 21km north of Durham is

home to the excellent Beamish open-air museum, which makes a worthwhile daytrip.

Coming & Going
Beamish is about halfway between Durham and Newcastle. To get here take bus 709 from Newcastle, bus 775 or 778 from Sunderland or bus 720 from Durham.

Sights
Beamish Museum
This excellent open-air museum depicts life in northeast England in the 19th and early 20th centuries. The museum is set on 300 acres and features a re-created town and mining village and a working steam railway.

☎ *(0191) 370 4000*
Website *www.beamish.org.uk*
Admission *Jan-Mar £5; Apr-Oct £14; Nov-Dec £5*
Open *Jan-Mar Tue-Thu & Sat-Sun 10am-4pm; Apr-Oct 10am-5pm daily; Nov-Dec Tue-Thu & Sat-Sun 10am-4pm*

Newcastle-upon-Tyne

The northeast's largest city is becoming a popular destination with many travellers searching for the genuine England away from the tourist hoards down south. Its metropolitan area, which includes the suburbs of Gateshead, Sunderland, South Shields, North Shields and Tynemouth, offers an impressive array of attractions with many of Newcastle's top sights relating to its Roman heritage at the eastern end of Hadrian's Wall.

Practical Information
Gateshead Quays Visitor Centre
St Mary's Church, Gateshead
☎ *(0191) 478 4222*
Open *Mon-Fri 9am-5pm, Sat 10am-5pm, Sun 11am-5pm*

Newcastle Tourist Information Centre
Main Concourse, Central Station, Newcastle-upon-Tyne
🚆 Ⓜ *Central Station*
☎ *(0191) 277 8000*
Open *Jan-May Mon-Fri 10am-5pm, Sat 9am-5pm; Jun-Sep Mon-Fri 10am-8pm, Sat 9am-5pm; Oct-Dec Mon-Fri 10am-5pm, Sat 9am-5pm*

Newcastle Tourist Information Centre
132 Grainger Street, Newcastle-upon-Tyne
Ⓜ *Monument*
☎ *(0191) 277 8000*
Open *Jan-May Mon-Wed 9.30am-5.30pm, Thu 9.30am-7.30pm, Fri-Sat 9.30am-5.30pm; Jun-Sep Mon-Wed 9.30am-5.30pm, Thu 9.30am-7.30pm, Fri-Sat 9.30am-5.30pm, Sun 10am-4pm; Oct-Dec Mon-Wed 9.30am-5.30pm, Thu 9.30am-7.30pm, Fri-Sat 9.30am-5.30pm*

Coming & Going
AIR
Newcastle International Airport *(website www.newcastleairport.com)* handles flights to most major European destinations including flights on many budget airlines including easyJet *(website www.easyjet.com)*, Flybe *(website flybe.com)* and Hapag Lloyd Express *(website www.hlx.com)*. The metro runs between the airport and the city centre

FERRY
Ferries operated by DFDS Seaways *(☎ 0900 333 000; website www.dfdsseaways.co.uk)* go to Ijmuiden (the Netherlands) and Kristiansand (Norway) and Fjord Line *(☎ (0191) 296 1313; website www.fjordline.co.uk)* has ferries to Bergen and Stavanger in Norway. Ferries depart from the ferry terminal at Royal Quays in North Shields, 11.25km east of the city centre.

BUS
National Express *(☎ 0870 580 8080; website www.nationalexpress.co.uk)* has buses from Newcastle to Edinburgh, Glasgow, Leeds, Leicester, Liverpool, London, Manchester and York.

Buses depart from the coach station on St James Boulevard *(Ⓜ St James)*.

During summer the Hadrian's Wall Bus (route AD122) runs several times each day between Carlisle and Hexham following the course of the wall and stopping at visitor attractions en route. One bus each day goes all the way from Bowness on Solway to Newcastle-upon-Tyne and Wallsend. It connects with train and other bus services at Carlisle, Haltwhistle and Hexham. A one-day ticket on this bus costs £6 and a three-day pass costs £10.

TRAIN

Newcastle's train station is on Neville Street in the city centre. Arriva Trains Northern *(website www.arrivatrain-snorthern.co.uk)* goes to destinations in northern England including Carlisle, Durham, Middlesbrough and Whitby and GNER *(website www.gner.co.uk)* has trains to Edinburgh, Glasgow, London (Kings Cross) and York.

Local Transport

The Newcastle area has an excellent public transport system that is comprised of buses and a metro *(website www.tyneandwearmetro.co.uk)*.

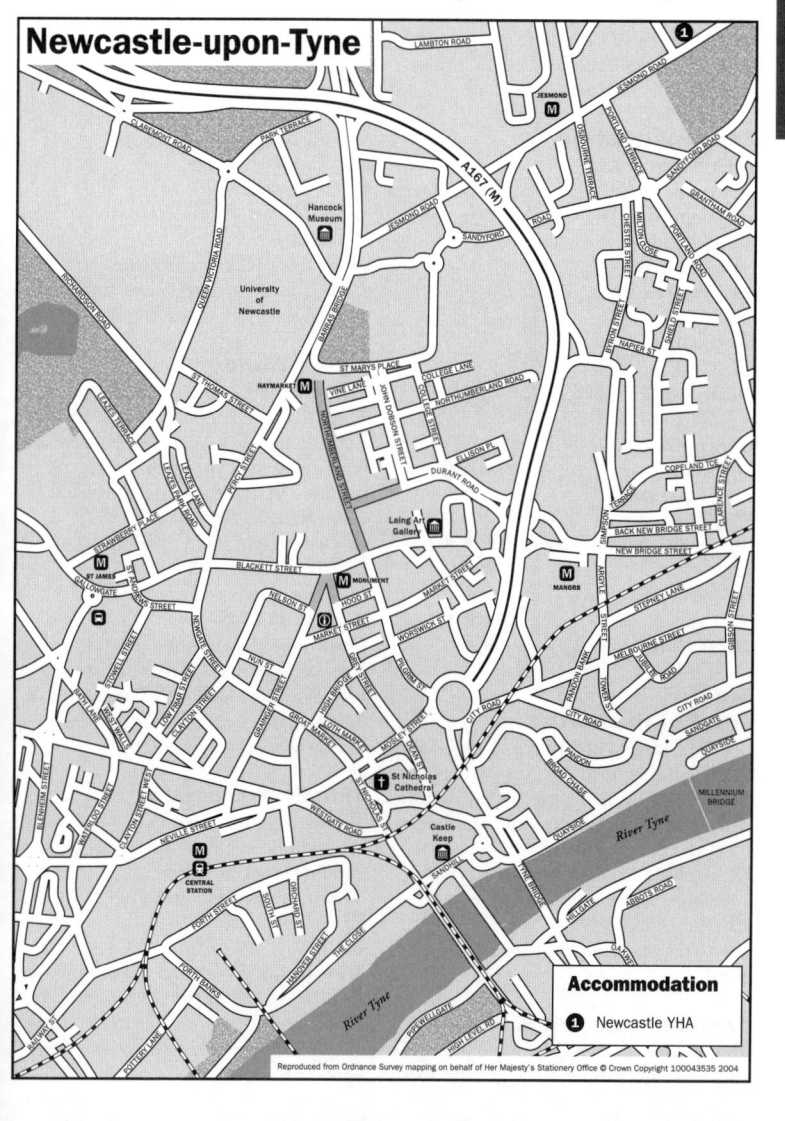

Newcastle-upon-Tyne

Accommodation

1 Newcastle YHA

There are several travel passes available that include:

DaySaver Ⓜ
This pass gives you unlimited metro travel after 9am on weekdays and all day on weekends. The DaySaver costs £3.20, £2 after 6pm in the evening or after 9am Wednesdays or £4 if you buy it before 9am on weekdays.

Day Rover 🚂Ⓜ🚌⛴
The Day Rover gives you one day's unlimited travel in Tyne and Wear on the metro, buses, the Shields ferry and trains between Sunderland and Blaydon. £4.20.

Accommodation
YHA Newcastle
Newcastle's YHA is a basic but clean and comfortable hostel with facilities that include a cosy lounge, a dining room and kitchen.
107 Jesmond Road, Newcastle-upon-Tyne
Ⓜ *Jesmond*
☎ *(0191) 281 2570*
Dorm bed £18 (£16 HI/YHA; £13 HI/YHA & ISIC)
Credit cards MC, Visa
Open 22 Jan-23 Dec; **reception open** 7am-11pm daily

🚗 Ⓚ

Maintenance & cleanliness	★★★
Facilities	★
Atmosphere & character	★★
Security	★★½
Overall rating	★★

Sights
Angel of the North
Britain's largest sculpture is in Gateshead, 8km south of Newcastle. The steel sculpture is 20 metres tall with a wingspan of 54 metres and can be seen from the A1 motorway.
🚌 *any bus (except express buses) from Gateshead Interchange stand J*
☎ *(0191) 433 8400*
Website *www.gateshead.gov.uk/angel/*

Arbeia Roman Fort & Museum
This Roman fort was built in 160 AD and was the supply base for the forts along Hadrian's Wall. The museum features artefacts depicting life in Roman times.
Baring Street, South Sheilds
Ⓜ *South Sheilds*
☎ *(0191) 456 1369*
Website *www.twmuseums.org.uk/arbeia/*
Admission *free*
Open *Mon-Sat 10am-5.30pm, Sun 1pm-5pm*

Baltic Centre for Contemporary Art
This former warehouse on the south bank of the Tyne hosts a programme of temporary exhibits in its five exhibition galleries.
South Stone Road, Gateshead
Ⓜ *Manors*
☎ *(0191) 478 1810*
Website *www.balticmill.com*
Admission *free*
Open *Mon-Wed 10am-7pm, Thu 10am-10pm, Fri-Sat 10am-7pm, Sun 10am-5pm*

Bede's World
This open-air museum depicts life in Anglo-Saxon Northumbria. It includes a recreated 7th-century village and farm and a museum with artefacts from the late 7th and early 8th centuries.
Church Bank, Jarrow
Ⓜ *Bede, then D 526, 527*
☎ *(0191) 489 2106*
Website *www.bedesworld.co.uk*
Admission £4.50
Open *Jan-Mar Mon-Sat 10am-4.30pm, Sun noon-4.30pm; Apr-Oct Mon-Sat 10am-5.30pm, Sun noon-5.30pm; Nov-Dec Mon-Sat 10am-4.30pm, Sun noon-4.30pm*

Blue Reef Aquarium
This aquarium overlooking the North Sea is home to a wide variety of tropical and local marine life.
Grand Parade, Tynemouth
Ⓜ *Cullercoates*
☎ *(0191) 258 1031*
Website *www.bluereefaquarium.co.uk*
Admission £4.95 (£4.25 students)
Open *Jan-Feb 10am-4pm daily; Mar-Oct 10am-5pm daily; Nov-Dec 10am-4pm daily*

Castle Keep
Built by Henry II in the 12th century, Newcastle's Castle Keep is one of the country's finest remaining examples of Norman keep.
Castle Garth, St Nicholas Street, Newcastle-upon-Tyne
🚇Ⓜ *Central Station*
☎ *(0191) 232 7938*
Website *www.castlekeep-newcastle.org.uk*
Admission *£1.50 (50p students)*
Open *9.30am-4.30pm daily*

Discovery Museum
This museum has lots of interactive science exhibits aimed at kids, but there are other displays including Turbinia, the first ship to be powered by steam turbines, and exhibits on Newcastle that include artefacts from Roman times and reconstructed city scenes.
Blandford Square, Newcastle-upon-Tyne
🚇Ⓜ *Central Station*
☎ *(0191) 232 6789*
Website *www.twmuseums.org.uk/discovery*
Admission *free*
Open *Mon-Sat 10am-5pm, Sun 2pm-5pm*

Gateshead Millennium Bridge
This pedestrian and cycle bridge links Baltic Square, Gateshead with Newcastle Quayside. It is unique in that it can tilt to form an archway allowing ships to sail underneath.
Ⓜ *Manors*
Website *www.gateshead.gov.uk*

Hancock Museum
This museum of natural history has a collection that includes a couple of Egyptian mummies, dinosaurs and live animals.
Barras Bridge, Newcastle-upon-Tyne
Ⓜ *Haymarket*
☎ *(0191) 222 6765*
Website *www.twmuseums.org.uk/hancock/*
Admission *£2.50*
Open *Mon-Sat 10am-5pm, Sun 2pm-5pm*

Laing Art Gallery
The recently refurbished Laing Art Gallery is noted for its watercolour collection.
New Bridge Street, Newcastle-upon-Tyne
Ⓜ *Monument*
☎ *(0191) 232 7734*
Website *www.twmuseums.org.uk/laing/*
Admission *free*
Open *Mon-Sat 10am-5pm, Sun 2pm-5pm*

Life Science Centre
This science museum has interactive exhibits that try to explain the wonders of life.
Times Square, Newcastle-upon-Tyne
🚇Ⓜ *Central Station*
☎ *(0191) 243 8210*
Website *www.lifesciencecentre.co.uk*
Admission *£6.95*
Open *Mon-Sat 10am-6pm, Sun 11am-6pm*

Monkwearmouth Station Museum
This former train station depicts rail travel in Victorian England.
North Bridge Road, Sunderland
Ⓜ *St Peter's*
☎ *(0191) 567 7075*
Website *www.twmuseums.org.uk/monkwearmouth/*
Admission *free*
Open *Mon-Sat 10am-5pm, Sun 2pm-5pm*

Museum of Antiquities
This museum focuses on the archaeology of Northern England with prehistoric, Bronze Age and Anglo-Saxon artefacts, a reconstructed 3rd century temple to Mithras and exhibits relating to Hadrian's Wall.
University of Newcastle-upon-Tyne, Newcastle-upon-Tyne
Ⓜ *Haymarket*
☎ *(0191) 222 7846*
Website *www.ncl.ac.uk/antiquities*
Admission *free*
Open *Mon-Sat 10am-5pm*

St Nicholas' Cathedral
Although dating from the 13th century, St Nicholas' Cathedral also has additions from the 18th and 20th century. Its highlights include 15th century lantern tower.
Mosley Street, Newcastle-upon-Tyne
🚇Ⓜ *Central Station*

☎ *(0191) 232 1939*
Website *www.newcastle-ang-cathedral-stnicholas.org.uk*
Admission *free*
Open *Mon-Fri 7am-6pm, Sat 8am-4pm, Sun 7am-noon & 4pm-7pm*

Segedunum Roman Fort, Baths & Museum

Built in 122 AD as the eastern-most outpost on Hadrian's Wall, Segedunum Roman Fort was home to 600 soldiers during 300 years of Roman rule.
Buddle Street, Wallsend
Ⓜ *Wallsend*
☎ *(0191) 295 5757*
Website *www.twmuseums.org.uk/segedunum/*
Admission *£3.50*
Open *Apr-Oct 9.30am-5.30pm daily*

Shipley Art Gallery

The Shipley Art Gallery has displays of ceramics, glass, jewellery and metalwork as well as a collection of paintings from the Dutch and Flemmish masters.
Prince Consort Road, Gateshead
Ⓜ *Gateshead, then* 🚌 *27*
☎ *(0191) 477 1495*
Website *www.twmuseums.org.uk/shipley/*
Admission *free*
Open *Mon-Sat 10am-5pm, Sun 2pm-5pm*

South Shields Museum & Art Gallery

The South Shields Museum feature exhibits on local history and include the Tales of South Tyneside gallery and the adjoining art gallery has interactive exhibits that allow you to learn more about the paintings and their artisits.
Ocean Road, South Shields
Ⓜ *South Shields*
☎ *(0191) 456 8740*
Website *www.twmuseums.org.uk/southshields/*
Admission *free*
Open *Mon-Sat 10am-5.30pm, Sun 1pm-5pm*

Stephenson Railway Museum

A must of railway enthusiasts, the Stephenson Railway Museum is home to many notable steam engines including George Stephenson's "Billy". Steam train rides are available.
Middle Engine Lane, North Shields
Ⓜ *Wallsend, then* 🚌 *337*
☎ *(0191) 200 7146*
Website *www.twmuseums.org.uk/stephenson/*
Admission *free;* **steam train rides** *£2*
Open *Tue-Thu 11am-3pm, Sat-Sun 11am-4pm*

Sunderland Museum & Winter Gardens

This museum has an eclectic collection of exhibits depicting the history of Sunderland from its prehistoric past to the present day. There is also an art gallery with a focus on Victorian paintings and the works of LS Lowry and an impressive Winter Garden that is home to over 1500 plants.
Burdon Road, Sunderland
Ⓜ *Park Lane*
☎ *(0191) 553 2323*
Website *www.twmuseums.org.uk/sunderland/*
Admission *free*
Open *Mon-Sat 10am-5pm, Sun 2pm-5pm*

Tynemouth Priory & Castle

This medieval castle and fort offers lovely coastal views.
Front Street, North Shields
Ⓜ *Tynemouth*
☎ *(0191) 257 1090*
Website *www.english-heritage.org.uk*
Admission *£3*
Open *Jan-Mar Mon & Thu-Sun 10am-4pm; Apr-Sep 10am-6pm daily; Oct 10am-4pm daily; Nov-Dec Mon & Thu-Sun 10am-4pm*

Northumberland

The history of England's most north-eastern county has born witness to a long and bitter struggle between the English and Scots. This has resulted in a large number of castles, historic battlefields and other fortifications including Hadrian's Wall. Despite all this, it remains one of England's least visited regions.

Alnwick

This small town north of Newcastle is best known for its castle, which featured in the Harry Potter films.

Practical Information
Alnwick Tourist Information Centre
2 The Shambles, Alnwick
☎ *(01665) 510 665*
Website www.alnwick.gov.uk
Open Mon-Sat 9am-5pm, Sun 10am-4pm

Coming & Going
The closest train station is 8km away at Alnmouth with buses 518 and 519 running between Alnwick and Alnmouth. Alternatively bus 505 runs directly from Newcastle to Alnwick.

Sights
Alnwick Castle
Alnwick is England's second largest inhabited castle – only Windsor Castle is larger. This well-preserved castle has been home to the Dukes of Northumberland for almost 700 years and was used as a location for several films including *Elizabeth* and the *Harry Potter* movies. The castle features paintings by Canaletto, Titian and Van Dyck and there is a Regimental Museum in the Abbot's Tower.
Alnwick Castle, Alnwick
☎ *(01665) 511 100*
Website www.alnwickcastle.com
Admission £7.50 house, £4 gardens, £10 house and gardens
Open Apr-Oct 11am-5pm daily

Bailiffgate Museum
This museum has displays relating to local history of Alnwick and the surrounding district.
14 Bailiffgate, Alnwick
☎ *(01665) 605 847*
Website www.bailiffgatemuseum.co.uk
Admission £2.20
Open Jan-Easter Tue-Sun 10am-4pm; Easter-Oct 10am-5pm daily; Nov-Dec Tue-Sun 10am-4pm

Berwick-upon-Tweed

Located about midway between Newcastle and Edinburgh, Berwick-upon-Tweed has been at the front line of conflict between England and Scotland and has changed rulership several times during its turbulent history. It is a quaint place with an old town surrounded by 16th century walls but very few travellers make the effort to visit.

Practical Information
Berwick-upon-Tweed Tourist Information Centre
106 Marygate, Berwick-upon-Tweed
☎ *(01289) 330 733*
Website www.berwickonline.org.uk
Open Mon-Sat 10am-6pm, Sun 11am-4pm

Coming & Going
BUS
National Express (☎ *0870 580 8080; website www.nationalexpress.co.uk*) has buses from Berwick to Edinburgh, London and Newcastle.

Buses stop in Golden Square.

TRAIN
GNER *(website www.gner.co.uk)* trains stop at Berwick en route from Edinburgh to Newcastle, York and London (Kings Cross). Virgin Trains *(website www.virgintrains.co.uk)* run along the same route but their London terminus is Euston station instead of Kings Cross.

Accommodation
Berwick Backpackers
This very small hostel has a small kitchen and a sociable TV lounge with plenty of books. It has low ceilings that give it a cosy atmosphere.
56 Bridge Street, Berwick-upon-Tweed
☎ *(01289) 331 481*
***Dorm bed** £10*
***Reception open** Mon-Wed 4pm-7pm, Thu-Sat 10am-5pm*
📺 🇰

Sights
Berwick Castle
The 12th-century Berwick Castle features a 16th-century gun tower.
Website www.english-heritage.org.uk
***Admission** free*
***Open** Mon-Sat 6.30am-7.50pm, Sun 10.15am-7.30pm*

Berwick-upon-Tweed Main Guard
This Georgian Guard House features an exhibition about the Berwick-upon-Tweed's history as a border garrison town.
Website www.english-heritage.org.uk
Admission free
Open Jun-Sep Mon-Tue & Thu-Sun 1pm-5pm

Berwick-upon-Tweed Museum & Art Gallery
Housed in Berwick's historic barracks, this museum has exhibits on local history as well as contemporary and decorative art.
Ravensdowne Barracks, off Church Street, Berwick-upon-Tweed
☎ *(01289) 301 869*
Admission £3
Open Jan-Mar Wed-Sun 10am-1pm & 2pm-4pm; Apr-Sep 10am-6pm daily; Oct 10am-5pm daily; Nov-Dec Wed-Sun 10am-1pm & 2pm-4pm

Berwick Ramparts
Berwick's extensive fortifications surrounding the old town were built between 1558 and 1570 to replace earlier medieval defences.
Website www.english-heritage.org.uk

Hadrian's Wall

In 122 AD, Roman emperor Hadrian ordered an 117km-long wall to be built between Bowness on Solway (near Carlisle) and Wallsend (near Newcastle-upon-Tyne) to define the Roman Empire's boundaries. Don't expect anything as impressive as the Great Wall of China though, as large portions of the wall have been dismantled and even the best-preserved parts of the wall are only half their original height.

Practical Information
Hexham Tourist Information Centre
Wentworth Car Park, Hexham
☎ *(01434) 652 220*
Website www.hadrianswallcountry.org
Open Jan-Mar Mon-Sat 9am-5pm; Apr-mid May Mon-Sat 9am-5pm, Sun 10am-5pm; mid May-Sep Mon-Sat 9am-6pm, Sun 10am-5pm; Oct Mon-Sat 9am-5pm, Sun 10am-5pm; Nov-Dec Mon-Sat 9am-5pm

Once Brewed National Park & Tourist Information Centre
Military Road, Bardon Mill
☎ *(01434) 344 396*
Website www.northumberland-national-park.org.uk
Open Jan-Mar Sat-Sun 9.30am-5pm; Apr-May 9.30am-5pm daily; Jun-Aug 9.30-am-5.30pm daily; Sep-Oct 9.30am-5pm daily; Nov-Dec Sat-Sun 9.30am-5pm

Local Transport
During summer the Hadrian's Wall Bus (route AD122) runs several times each day between Carlisle and Hexham following the course of the wall and stopping at visitor attractions en route. One bus each day goes all the way from Bowness on Solway to Newcastle-upon-Tyne and Wallsend. It connects with train and other bus services at Carlisle, Haltwhistle and Hexham. A one-day ticket on this bus costs £6 and a three-day pass costs £10.

Accommodation
YHA Acomb
This small hostel in the countryside near Hexham is a converted stable with very basic facilities that include a small kitchen and common area. The toilets and showers are outside.
Main Street, Acomb
☎ *(01434) 602864*
Website www.yha.org.uk
Dorm bed £10.50 (£8.50 HI/YHA; £5.50 HI/YHA & ISIC)
Open Apr-Nov; **reception open** 8am-10am & 5pm-10pm daily; **curfew** 11pm

YHA Greenhead
This former Methodist Chapel offers the usual hostel facilities such as a kitchen and common room. The building has a lot of character and a convenient location in the small village of Greenhead about 2km south of Hadrian's Wall.
Greenhead, Brampton
☎ *(016977) 47401*
Website www.yha.org.uk
Dorm bed £13 (£11 HI/YHA; £8 HI/YHA & ISIC)

Open *Apr-Jun contact hostel; Jul-Aug every day; Sep-Oct contact hostel;* ***reception open*** *8am-10am & 5pm-10pm;* ***curfew*** *11pm*

🅚 🅛

YHA Once Brewed
This purpose-built hostel is well situated for exploring the best-preserved sections of Hadrian's Wall. Accommodation consists mostly of four-bed rooms and facilities include a kitchen, games room and a TV lounge.
Military Road, Bardon Mill
☎ *(01434) 344360*
Website *www.yha.org.uk*
Dorm bed *£14.50 (£12.50 HI/YHA; £9.50 HI/YHA & ISIC)*
Credit cards *MC, Visa*
Open *6 Feb-31 Mar Tue-Sat; 1 Apr-30 Oct every day; 31 Oct-22 Nov Tue-Sat;* ***reception open*** *8am-10am & 1pm-10.30pm;* ***curfew*** *11pm*

🅟 🅣🅥 🅚 🅛

Sights
Chesters Roman Fort
This Roman cavalry fort includes barracks and a Roman bathhouse plus a museum with Roman artefacts.
B6318, 1.5km west of Chollerford
☎ *(01434) 681 379*
Website *www.english-heritage.org.uk*
Admission *£3.50*
Open *Jan-Mar 10am-4pm daily; Apr-Sep 9.30am-6pm daily; Oct-Dec 10am-4pm daily*

Corbridge Roman Site
Predating Hadrian's Wall, Corbridge Roman Site was an important supply base for the garrisons on the central section of Hadrian's Wall.
1km west of Corbridge
☎ *(01434) 632 349*
Website *www.english-heritage.org.uk*
Admission *£3.50*
Open *Jan-Mar Sat-Sun 10am-4pm; Apr-Sep 10am-6pm daily; Oct 10am-4pm daily; Nov-Dec Sat-Sun 10am-4pm*

Housesteads
Britain's best-preserved Roman fort is the best of the historic sites alongside Hadrian's Wall. It was built to house 800 soldiers and sits on a ridge offering sweeping views and it adjoins one of the best-preserved stretches of the wall.
B6318, northeast of Bardon Mill
☎ *(01434) 344 363*
Website *www.english-heritage.org.uk*
Admission *£3.50*
Open *Jan-Mar 10am-4pm daily; Apr-Sep 10am-6pm daily; Oct-Dec 10am-4pm daily*

Roman Army Museum
This museum features exhibits about Hadrian's Wall including many artefacts found here.
Walltown, 1.5km northeast of Greenhead
☎ *(016977) 47485*
Website *www.vindolanda.com*
Admission *£3.50; joint admission to Vindolanda £6.50*
Open *15 Feb-30 Mar 10am-5pm daily; Apr-Sep 10am-6pm daily; 1 Oct-8 Nov 10am-5pm daily*

Vindolanda
Excavations at this Roman fort, predating Hadrian's Wall, have unearthed an impressive collection of artefacts and rare documents that provide an insight into life in the Roman army. Visitors can visit a reconstructed temple, a section of the wall that has been rebuilt to its original size and a museum that displays many artefacts found here.
2.5km north of Bardon Mill
☎ *(01434) 344 277*
Website *www.vindolanda.com*
Admission *£4.50; joint admission to Roman Army Museum £6.50*
Open *Feb-Mar 10am-5pm daily; Apr-Sep 10am-6pm daily; Oct-Nov 10am-5pm daily*

Northumberland National Park

Adjoining the Scottish border, the national park is England's least visited. It features parts of Hadrian's Wall, several castles and the Cheviot Hills.

Practical Information
Bellingham Tourist Information Centre
Main Street, Bellingham
☎ *(01434) 220 616*

Website www.hadrianswallcountry.org
Open 17 May-30 Sep Mon-Sat
9.30am-5.30pm, Sun 1pm-5pm; Oct
Mon-Sat 9.30am-1pm & 2pm-5.30pm,
Sun 1pm-5pm

Ingram National Park Information Centre
☎ (01669) 578 248
Website www.northumberland-national-park.org.uk
Open Apr-May 10am-5pm daily; Jun-Aug 10am-6pm daily; Sep 10am-5pm daily; Oct Sat-Sun 10am-3pm

Once Brewed National Park & Tourist Information Centre
Military Road, Bardon Mill
☎ (01434) 344 396
Website www.northumberland-national-park.org.uk
Open Jan-Mar Sat-Sun 9.30am-5pm; Apr-May 9.30am-5pm daily; Jun-Aug 9.30-am-5.30pm daily; Sep-Oct 9.30am-5pm daily; Nov-Dec Sat-Sun 9.30am-5pm

Rothbury National Park Information Centre
Church Street, Rothbury
☎ (01669) 620 887
Website www.northumberland-national-park.org.uk
Open Jan-Mar Sat-Sun 10am-3pm; Apr-May 10am-5pm daily; Jun-Aug 10am-6pm daily; Sep-Oct 10am-5pm daily; Nov-Dec Sat-Sun 10am-3pm

Wooler Tourist Information Centre
The Cheviot Centre, 12 Padgepool Place, Wooler
☎ (01668) 282 123
Website www.berwickonline.org.uk
Open 4 May-16 Jul 10am-1.30pm & 2pm-5pm daily; 17 Jul-31 Aug Mon-Sat 10am-5pm, Sun 10am-4pm; Sep-Oct 10am-4pm daily

Accommodation
There are several youth hostels in and around the Northumberland National Park. These include:

Bellingham Youth Hostel
This cedar cabin on the Pennine Way has a small kitchen and common room.
Woodburn Road, Bellingham
☎ (01434) 220 313
Website www.yha.org.uk
Dorm bed £12 (£10 HI/YHA)
Credit cards MC, Visa
Open 6 Feb-30 Jun Tue-Sat; 1 Jul-31 Aug every day; 1-31 Sep Tue-Sat; *reception open* 8am-10am & 5pm-10pm daily; *curfew* 11pm

Byrness Youth Hostel
This basic youth hostel is comprised of two adjoining houses just 8km from the Scottish border.
7 Otterburn Green, Byrness
☎ (01830) 520 425
Website www.yha.org.uk
Dorm bed £12 (£10 HI/YHA)
Credit cards MC, Visa
Open Mar-Sep; *reception open* 8am-10am & 5pm-10pm daily; *curfew* 11pm

Kielder Youth Hostel
This relatively new hostel offers a high standard of accommodation but facilities are limited to a kitchen and lounge.
Butteryhaugh, Kielder
☎ (01434) 250 195
Website www.yha.org.uk
Dorm bed £14.50 (£12.50 HI/YHA)
Credit cards MC, Visa
Open Jul-Aug; *reception open* 8am-10am & 5pm-10pm; *curfew* 11pm

Wooler Youth Hostel
This comfortable hostel has the usual common room and kitchen.
30 Cheviot Street, Wooler
☎ (01668) 281 365
Website www.yha.org.uk
Dorm bed £13 (£11 HI/YHA)
Credit cards MC, Visa
Open Mar-May Tue-Sat; Jun-Aug every day; Sep-Oct Tue-Sat; *reception open* 8am-10am & 5pm-10pm daily; *curfew* 11pm

Wales

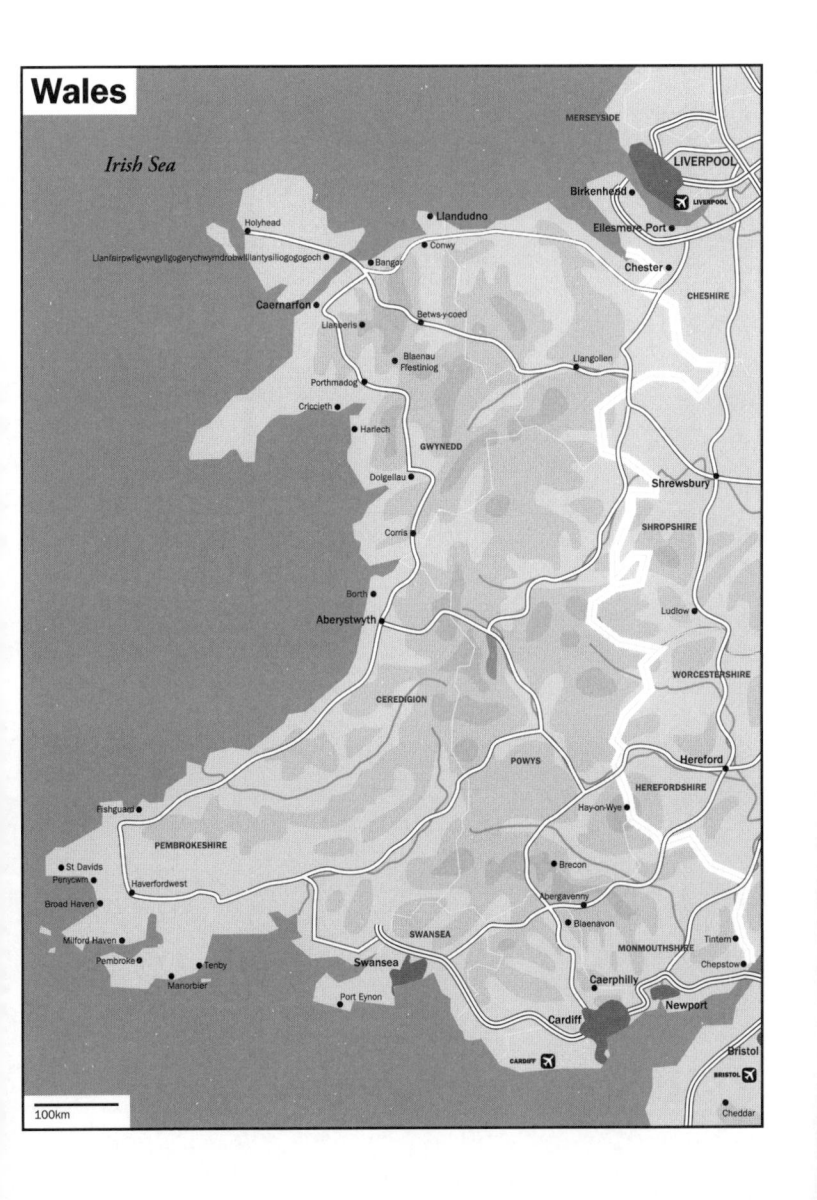

Wales (Cymru)

Not a lot of backpackers make it to Wales, which is a small country with a beautiful countryside and quaint little towns. The country boasts its own strong culture and a unique language that has survived after years of influence from its powerful neighbour. The Welsh language, which is related to Breton and Cornish, is spoken by around half a million people or around 17% of the population.

Wales' attractions include a large number of preserved steam railways and impressive castles. A lot of people visit Wales for the outdoors, particularly to walk in the Brecon Beacons, Pembrokeshire Coast and Snowdonia National Parks.

Cardiff (Caerdydd)

The Welsh capital isn't typical of the rest of Wales, but many travellers find themselves passing through to make transport connections and inevitably end up spending some time exploring the city.

Cardiff's main attraction is the castle, which dominates the city centre and there are also some good museums. The Millennium Waterfront at Cardiff Bay is a new development that is home to the Welsh National Assembly as well as several other attractions.

Practical Information
Cardiff Tourist Information Centre
16 Wood Street, Cardiff
🚌 *8, 9, 9A, 12, 12A, 13, 17, 18, 21, 23, 24, 25, 27, 28, 29, 29B, 30, 30D, 44, 45, 49, 50, 57, 58, 60, 61, 62, 92, 93, 94* 🚉 *Cardiff Central*
☎ *(029) 2022 7281*
Website *www.visitcardiff.info*
Open *10am-5pm daily*

Cardiff Bay Tourist Information Centre
The Tube, Harbour Drive, Cardiff
🚌 *7, 8, 35, 89, Bay Express.*
☎ *(029) 2046 3833*
Open *Jan-Feb Mon-Fri 9.30am-5pm, Sat-Sun 10.30am-5pm; Mar-Oct Mon-Fri 9.30am-5pm, Sat-Sun 10.30am-6pm; Nov-Dec Mon-Fri 9.30am-5pm, Sat-Sun 10.30am-5pm.*

American Express
3 Queen Street, Cardiff CF10 2AE
🚉 *Cardiff Queen Street*
☎ *(029) 2064 9301*
Open *Mon-Fri 9am-5.30pm, Sat 9am-5pm*

Coming & Going
AIR
Cardiff Airport (☎ *(01446) 711 111; website www.cardiffairportonline.com*), 20km southwest of the city centre has flights to destinations throughout the UK and Europe. Budget airlines that use this airport include bmibaby (☎ *(0870) 264 2229; website www.bmibaby.com*), which flies to Alicante, Belfast, Edinburgh, Glasgow, Jersey, Malaga, Milan (Bergamo), Munich, Palma, Paris and Toulouse and Ryanair (*website www.ryanair.com*), which flies between Cardiff and Dublin.

Bus routes 95, X91 run between the airport and the city centre every 30 minutes during peak periods and hourly in the evenings and on weekends. The 40-minute journey costs £2.70.

BUS
Cardiff Central Bus Station near Central Station on Wood Street handles local buses and also National Express services to Birmingham, Manchester and London. There are also a number of regional bus companies that operate bus and coach services throughout Wales.

HITCHHIKING
The M4 is the motorway that runs east west through Cardiff. This is the route that you'll take if you're headed to east to England or west to Swansea and Pembrokeshire. The easiest way to get to the M4 is to first hitch a ride on the A48, which is the most direct route from the centre of Cardiff to the M4.

The A470 is the most direct route going north to the Brecon Beacons

National Park, but some travellers find it best to take a train to Merthyr Tydfil to bypass most local traffic and hitch from there.

No matter which direction you're going, the Gabalfa interchange where the A470 and the A48 meet is a good hitching spot; but this spot does have a problem with a lot of suburban traffic. Take bus 8, 21, 23, 24, 35, 37, 53 or 53A to get to the interchange.

TRAIN
Cardiff has good rail connections to destinations in England and south Wales.

London (Paddington and Waterloo) is less than two hours away and trains run every half hour. Trains to England are run by Central Trains (*☎ (0121) 654 1200; website www.centraltrains.co.uk*), Virgin Trains (*website www.virgintrains.co.uk*) and Wessex Trains (*website www.wessextrains.co.uk*). Most of the services within Wales are run by Arriva Trains Wales (*website www.arrivatrainswales.co.uk*).

Local Transport
Cardiff's public transport system is comprised of buses and a suburban train network.

Cardiff Bus (*☎ (029) 2066 6444; website www.cardiffbus.com*) runs most bus services although other companies operate some services.

The Bay Express bus is a handy route that runs between Cardiff bay and the city centre. This bus runs every 10 minutes and fares are 60p one-way or £1.10 return.

Arriva Trains Wales (*website www.arrivatrainswales.co.uk*) runs Cardiff's suburban train network, which extends as far as Merthyr Tydfil and Rhymney.

There are a number of travel passes that allow unlimited travel around Cardiff.

Rider Tickets
These tickets allow one day's unlimited bus travel in the Cardiff area.

The City Rider costs £3.30 and allows travel on Cardiff Bus services in Cardiff.

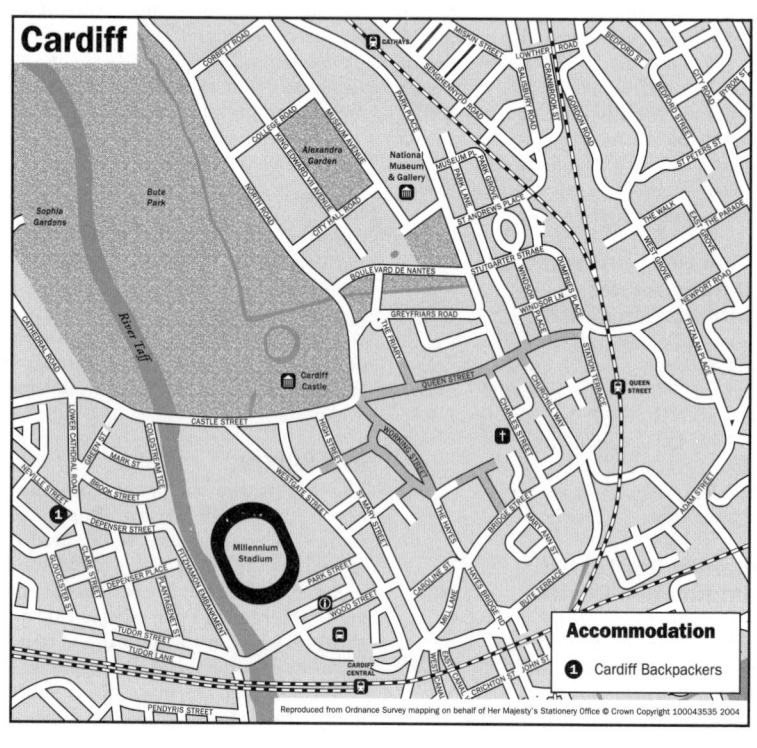

Accommodation
1. Cardiff Backpackers

The Network Rider pass allows you to travel further afield on services operated by Cardiff Bus and other bus companies that include Newport Transport and Stagecoach South Wales. The Network Rider costs £5.

Multiride Tickets
Multiride tickets are similar to the Rider tickets but they offer bus travel for weekly, monthly, quarterly and annual periods. They are geared to commuters but are a handy option if you're planning on spending a while in the Cardiff area. A one-week pass for bus travel in the Cardiff and Penarth areas costs £11.20.

Capital Card
The Capital Card is the best deal since it combines both bus and train travel. It is available in daily, weekly, monthly and annual passes to a range of destinations that extend into the surrounding countryside. Most visitors to Cardiff will find the £4.30-4.80 one day off peak passes the best value.

Cardiff Welcome Card
The Cardiff Welcome Card gives you unlimited bus travel in Cardiff and Penarth for one, two or three days. This pass also comes with a book of discount coupons that give you discounts off various attractions around Cardiff. The Welcome Card costs £7 for one day, £11 for two days and £15 for three days.

Accommodation
Cardiff Backpackers
Cardiff Backpackers is a fantastic hostel, a 10-minute walk from the city centre. It has brilliant common areas that include a bar with a big cinema screen, a kitchen and a TV lounge with Internet access and a pool table. There's also a rooftop deck with a barbecue and hammocks. The whole place is clean and well maintained.
98 Neville Street, Riverside, Cardiff
☎ *(029) 2034 5577*
Website www.cardiffbackpackers.co.uk
***Dorm bed** £16; **single room** £24;*
***double/twin room** £38; prices include breakfast*
Credit cards *MC, Visa*
Reception open *7.30am-2.30am daily;*
curfew *Mon-Fri 2.30am*

Maintenance & cleanliness	★★★★★
Facilities	★★★
Atmosphere & character	★★★★
Security	★★★
Overall rating	★★★★

Cardiff YHA
Cardiff's YHA has the usual facilities such as a TV lounge, Internet access and kitchen. However it has an institutional feel and is outside the city centre.
2 Wedal Road, Roath Park, Cardiff
🚌 *28, 29, 29B*
☎ *(029) 2046 2303*
Website www.yha.org.uk
***Dorm bed** £18 (£16 HI/YHA); price includes breakfast*
Credit cards *MC, Visa*
Reception open *7am-11pm daily*

Maintenance & cleanliness	★★★
Facilities	★★½
Atmosphere & character	★★½
Security	★★
Overall rating	★★

Sights
CITY CENTRE
Cardiff Castle
Cardiff Castle claims 2000 years of history and it features medieval fortification dating from soon after the Norman Conquest. Despite the castle's impressive history, most of what you see was built in the 19th century under the direction of John Patrick Crichton-Stuart, the third Marquess of Bute, and his architect William Burges. The modifications created an awe-inspiring structure that has dominated the city ever since. The castle's grounds are home to ducks, geese and peacocks and the interiors are lavishly opulent.
Castle Street, Cardiff
☎ *(029) 2087 8100*
Website www.cardiffcastle.com
Admission to castle and grounds *£6 (£4.85 students); **admission to grounds only** £3, (£2.45 students)*
Open *Jan-Feb 9.30am-5pm daily (last admission 4pm); Mar-Oct 9.30am-6pm daily (last admission 5pm); Nov-Dec 9.30am-5pm daily (last admission 4pm)*

National Assembly
The National Assembly features a visitors' centre with interactive displays that explain the Welsh political process. It is possible to observe the National Assembly when it is in session (usually Tue-Wed).
Pierhead Building, Cardiff Bay
🚌 *7, 8, 35, Bay Express* 🚉 *Cardiff Bay*
☎ *(029) 2089 8200*
Website www.wales.gov.uk/assembly-building/
Admission free

National Museum & Gallery
This excellent National Museum features natural history and science exhibits and the gallery has the largest Impressionist art collection outside France.
Museum Avenue, Cathays Park, Cardiff
☎ *(029) 2039 7951*
Website www.nmgw.ac.uk/nmgc/
Admission free
Open Tue-Sun 10am-5pm.

OUTSIDE THE CITY CENTRE
Caerphilly Castle
The largest castle in Wales is located in Caerphilly, about 10km north of the city centre.
Castle Street, Caerphilly
☎ *(029) 2088 3143*
Website www.caerphillycastle.org
Admission £3
Open Jan-Mar Mon-Sat 9.30am-4.30pm, Sun 11am-4pm; Apr-May 9.30am-5pm daily; Jun-Sep 9.30am-6pm daily; Oct-Dec Mon-Sat 9.30am-4.30pm, Sun 11am-4pm.

Castell Coch
The fairy tale style Castell Coch dates from the 13th century but was embellished by the third marquess of Bute and William Burges in the 19th century. It boasts a serene setting in the Taff Valley 8km north of the city centre.
Tongwynlais, Cardiff
🚉 *Taff Wells*
☎ *(029) 2081 0101*
Admission £3 (£2.50 students)
Open 1 Jan-31 Mar Mon-Sat 9.30am-4pm, Sun 11am-4pm; 1 Apr-1 Jun 9.30am-5pm daily; 2 Jun-28 Sep 9.30am-6pm daily; 29 Sep-26 Oct 9.30am-5pm daily; 27 Oct-31 Dec Mon-Sat 9.30am-4pm, Sun 11am-4pm

Museum of Welsh Life
This big open-air museum features over 30 buildings complete with staff in traditional costume. The museum provides a good introduction to traditional Welsh culture. It is located 6.5km west of the city centre.
St Fagans, Cardiff
🚌 *32, 320*
☎ *(029) 2057 3500*
Website www.nmgw.ac.uk/mwl/
Admission free
Open 10am-5pm daily

Llandaff Cathedral
Llandaff Cathedral was bombed in World War II and is comprised of a number of architectural styles but has a tranquil setting by the River Taff, 3km north of the city centre. It was founded in 560, and its history stretches back further than most other cathedrals in Britain.
Cathedral Green, Llandaff, Cardiff
🚌 *25, 33, 33A, 62*
☎ *(029) 2022 5877*
Website www.llandaffcathedral.org.uk
Admission free.

Swansea (Abertawe)
Wales' second largest city isn't a very popular place with tourists and most travellers bypass it in favour for the Pembrokeshire coast.

Birthplace of Dylan Thomas, the second most quoted writer after Shakespeare, this maritime city boasts a lovely seaside promenade and a couple of museums that focus on its industrial and maritime past.

Practical Information
Swansea Tourist Information Centre
Plymouth Street, Swansea SA1 3QG
☎ *(01792) 468321*
Website www.swansea.gov.uk
Open Mon-Sat 9.30am-5.30pm

American Express
28 The Kingsway, Swansea SA1 5JY
☎ *(01792) 455006*

Open *Mon-Fri 9am-5pm, Sat 9am-4pm*

Coming & Going
Buses and coaches leave from the Quadrant Bus Station near the Quadrant Shopping Centre. Trains stop at High Street Station.

Accommodation
There aren't any backpackers' hostels in the city although there is a youth hostel and an independent backpackers hostel in Swansea County, both a little under an hour by bus from the city centre.

Merlin's Backpackers
Merlin's offers accommodation in clean rooms with good quality fittings. Shared facilities include a bar with a TV and comfy leather sofas.
44/46 Commercial Street, Ystradgynlais
X20, 24, 25, 63, 68, 122, 146
(01639) 845 676
Dorm bed *£11;* ***twin room*** *£22*

Maintenance & cleanliness	★★★★
Facilities	★★
Atmosphere & character	★★★
Security	★★
Overall rating	★★★

Port Eynon YHA
This former lifeboat station enjoys an absolute beachfront setting. Facilities include the usual common room and kitchen.
Old Lifeboat House, Port Eynon
18/A, 49
(01792) 391 794
Website *www.yha.org.uk*
Dorm bed *£13.80 (£11.80 HI/YHA)*
Credit cards *MC, Visa*
Open *5 Apr-6 Nov; reception open 8am-10am & 5pm-10pm daily; curfew 11pm*

Sights
Dylan Thomas Centre
The Dylan Thomas Centre features an exhibition about the life and work of Swansea's most famous son.
Somerset Place, Swansea
(01792) 463980
Website *www.swansea.gov.uk/dylanthomas/*
Admission *free*
Open *Tue-Sun 10.30am-4.30pm.*

Swansea Museum
The oldest museum in Wales features a large and eclectic collection that includes an Egyptian mummy and an Ichthyosaur skeleton as well as exhibits on local history.
Victoria Road, Swansea
(01792) 653 763
Admission *free*
Open *Tue-Sun 10am-5pm.*

Pembrokeshire Coast National Park

The 583 sq km Pembrokeshire Coast National Park is the smallest of Wales' three national parks. It consists of a breathtaking rugged coastline with superb sandy beaches.

Many people come here to walk the Pembrokeshire Coast Path, which hugs the coast for over 300km between Poppit Sands and Amroth. It can take up to 15 days to walk the complete path, but many people split it into more manageable sections and hike each part separately.

There are several towns around the park that are worth visiting. These include Fishguard, Haverfordwest, Pembroke and St Davids.

Practical Information
Pembrokeshire Coast National Park Authority
Winch Lane, Haverfordwest
(01437) 764636
Website *www.pembrokeshirecoast.org.uk*

Accommodation
There are quite a number of youth hostels scattered around the park, which are popular places for people walking the Pembrokeshire Coast Path to stay.

Broad Haven YHA
Broad Haven is a popular destination for a host of water sports with a beautiful sandy beach nearby. The hostel has good all round facilities and

bubbly staff and there's a good social atmosphere with a pool table and large common area.
Broad Haven, 11km from Haverfordwest
☎ *(01437) 781 688*
Website *www.yha.org.uk*
Dorm bed *£13.80 (£11.80 HI/YHA)*
Credit cards *MC, Visa*
Open *Mar-Oct; reception open 8am-noon & 3pm-10pm daily*

Maintenance & cleanliness	★★★★☆
Facilities	★★
Atmosphere & character	★★★
Security	★★☆
Overall rating	★★★

Caerhafod Lodge

Caerhafod Lodge has outstanding, modern, comfortable and well-furnished dorms and common areas making it possibly the best accommodation you can find for the money anywhere. It has a very friendly and helpful owner and is in a lovely small rural village about 12km from St Davids.
Llanrhiah, near St Davids
411
☎ *(01348) 837 859*
Website *www.caerhafod.co.uk*
Dorm bed *£12*

Maintenance & cleanliness	★★★★☆
Facilities	★★★★☆
Atmosphere & character	★★★★★
Security	★★☆
Overall rating	★★★★

Lawrenny YHA

Lawrenny YHA is a former village school overlooking Milford Haven in the Pembrokeshire Coast National Park. It has basic facilities but good clean dorms and peaceful surroundings.
☎ *(01646) 651 270*
Website *www.yha.org.uk*
Dorm bed *£11.30 (£9.30 HI/YHA)*
Open *Apr-Oct; reception open 8am-10am & 5pm-10pm daily; lockout 10am-5pm daily*

Maintenance & cleanliness	★★★★☆
Facilities	★
Atmosphere & character	★★★
Security	★★☆
Overall rating	★★★☆

Marloes Sands YHA

This hostel is comprised of converted farm buildings and an old cottage in a National Trust reserve with a friendly welcome and accommodation is in small but comfortable dorms. It is close to a famous bird sanctuary and a marine reserve and there are good walking trails in the surrounding area.
Runwayskiln, Marloes
☎ *(01646) 636 667*
Website *www.yha.org.uk*
Dorm bed *£10.50 (£8.50 HI/YHA)*
Credit cards *MC, Visa*
Open *Easter-Sep; reception open 8am-10am & 5pm-10.30pm daily; lockout 10am-5pm daily; curfew 11.30pm*

Maintenance & cleanliness	★★★
Facilities	★
Atmosphere & character	★★★☆
Security	★
Overall rating	★★

Manorbier YHA

Manorbier YHA is on the cliffs of the Pembrokeshire Coast National Park in a converted, futuristic looking, Ministry of Defence building. It has good facilities and helpful staff and boasts great views out to sea.
Manorbier, about halfway between Manorbier and Tenby
First 349 to Skrinkle Manorbier
☎ *(01834) 871 803*
Website *www.yha.org.uk*
Dorm bed *£14.50 (£12.50 HI/YHA)*
Credit cards *MC, Visa*
Open *Mar-Oct flexible opening; reception open 7.30am-10am & 5pm-10.30pm daily*

Maintenance & cleanliness	★★★
Facilities	★★
Atmosphere & character	★★☆
Security	★★
Overall rating	★★★☆

Penycwm YHA

Penycwm YHA is a great hostel with superb facilities, good food and comfortable dorms. The staff are very helpful and friendly and the common room and kitchen areas are spacious and well kept. It is close to several beaches with coastal walks and various water sport activities.

Whitehouse, Penycwm
☎ *(01437) 721 940*
Website *www.yha.org.uk*
Dorm bed *£16 (£14 HI/YHA)*
Credit cards *MC, Visa*
Open *Easter-Sep;* **reception open**
8am-10am & 5pm-10pm daily; **lockout**
10am-5pm daily

🚗 📺 Ⓚ Ⓛ

Maintenance & cleanliness	★★★★
Facilities	★★
Atmosphere & character	★★★
Security	★★
Overall rating	★★★

Pwyll Deri YHA

This hostel is located on a cliff and there are spectacular views from the common room with its windows facing out to sea. It is a very small hostel in a desolate area but it has a nice atmosphere, friendly staff and cosy dormitories.
Castell Mawr, Trefasser, near Goodwick
☎ *(01348) 891 385*
Website *www.yha.org.uk*
Dorm bed *£12 (£10 HI/YHA)*
Credit cards *MC, Visa*
Open *Apr-Jun Mon-Tue & Thu-Sun; Jul-Aug every day; Sep-Oct Mon & Thu-Sun;* **reception open** *8.30am-10am & 5pm-11pm daily;* **lockout** *10am-5pm daily;* **curfew** *11pm*

🚗 ♿ 📺 Ⓚ Ⓛ

Maintenance & cleanliness	★★★
Facilities	★★
Atmosphere & character	★★★
Security	★★
Overall rating	★★★

Trefdraeth YHA

Trefdraeth YHA is an old village schoolhouse converted into a comfortable, traditional youth hostel. It has a good, well-equipped kitchen, a modern furnished common room and clean, comfortable dorms. Newport (Trefdraeth) is a small pleasant town with the beach, shops and pubs close by.
Lower St Mary Street, Newport (Trefdraeth)
🚌 *412*
☎ *(01239) 820 080*
Website *www.yha.org.uk*
Dorm bed *£14.50 (£12.50 HI/YHA)*
Credit cards *MC, Visa*
Open *Easter-Sep;* **reception open**
8am-10am & 5pm-10pm daily; **lockout**
10am-5pm daily

🚗 📺 Ⓚ

Maintenance & cleanliness	★★★
Facilities	★
Atmosphere & character	★★★
Security	★★
Overall rating	★★

Trefin YHA

This hostel is in a converted farmhouse in a tiny village 17km from St Davids. The hostel has a good social atmosphere and the dormitories and common rooms are small but well looked after.
Ffordd-yr-Afon, Trefin (17km from St Davids)
☎ *(01348) 831 414*
Website *www.yha.org.uk*
Dorm bed *£12 (£10 HI/YHA)*
Open *Easter-Sep;* **reception open**
8am-10am & 5pm-10pm daily; **lockout**
10am-5pm daily

🚗 📺 Ⓚ

Maintenance & cleanliness	★★★
Facilities	★
Atmosphere & character	★★★
Security	★★
Overall rating	★★

Pembroke (Penfro)

This walled town is a pleasant spot with quaint medieval streets and a 14th century castle. Ferries to Rosslare, Ireland departs from the port 2½km from here.

Practical Information
Pembroke Tourist Information Centre
Commons Road, Pembroke
☎ *(01646) 622388*
Website *www.visitwales.com*
Open *summer 10am-5.30pm daily*

Pembroke Dock Tourist Information Centre
Ferry Terminal, Pembroke Dock
☎ *(01646) 622753*
Website *www.visitwales.com*
Open *summer 11am-3pm daily*

Coming & Going

Pembroke's train station is located on Lower Lamphey Road and has several trains a day to Swansea and Cardiff.

Eastbound buses stop outside the Somerfield supermarket and westbound buses stop at the castle.

Irish Ferries (☎ *(08705) 329543; web-site www.irishferries.com*) sail between Pembroke Dock and Rosslare, Ireland.

Accommodation

The closest hostel to Pembroke is the YHA hostel 11km away in Manorbier.

Manorbier YHA

Manorbier YHA is on the cliffs of the national park in a converted, futuristic looking, Ministry of Defence building. It has good facilities and helpful staff and boasts great views out to sea.
Manorbier, about halfway between Manorbier and Tenby
🚌 *First 349 to Skrinkle* 🚉 *Manorbier*
☎ *(01834) 871 803*
Website www.yha.org.uk
Dorm bed £14.50 (£12.50 HI/YHA)
Credit cards MC, Visa
Open Mar-Oct flexible opening; reception open 7.30am-10am & 5pm-10.30pm daily

Maintenance & cleanliness	★★★
Facilities	★★
Atmosphere & character	★★☆
Security	★★
Overall rating	★★★☆

Sights
Pembroke Castle

This massive fortress was the birthplace of Henry VII and its Norman keep offers lovely views of the surrounding countryside.

St Davids (Tyddewi)

With a population of 1700, St Davids is Britain's smallest city. It was the home of Wales' patron saint and it is here that St David established a church in the sixth century. This tiny city has great historical significance among the Welsh and its cathedral is considered by many to be the country's finest.

Practical Information
National Park Visitor Centre

The Grove, St Davids
☎ *(01437) 720392*
Open winter Mon-Sat 10am-4pm; summer 9.30am-5.30pm daily

Accommodation
St Davids YHA

St Davids YHA offers homely accommodation in old farm buildings 3.25km from St Davids. It is a well-maintained and very relaxed hostel that is popular with hikers and nature enthusiasts.
Llaethdy, Whitesands, St Davids
☎ *(01437) 720 345*
Website www.yha.org.uk
Dorm bed £12 (£10 HI/YHA)
Credit cards MC, Visa
Open Mar-Nov; reception open 8am-10am & 5pm-11pm daily; lockout 10am-5pm daily; curfew 11.30pm

Maintenance & cleanliness	★★★
Facilities	★★☆
Atmosphere & character	★★★
Security	★
Overall rating	★★★☆

Sights
Bishop's Palace

Bishop Thomas Bek and Bishop Henry Gower built this palace in the 13th and 14th centuries. It is located near the cathedral and there is an exhibition centre on the site.
☎ *(01437) 720517*
Admission £2.50 (£2 students)
Open Jan-Mar Mon-Sat 9.30am-4pm, Sun 11am-4pm; 1 Apr-1 Jun 9.30am-5pm daily; 2 Jun-28 Sep 9.30am-6pm daily; 29 Sep-26 Oct 9.30am-5pm daily; 27 Oct-31 Dec Mon-Sat 9.30am-4pm, Sun 11am-4pm

St Non's Chapel

The ruins of this small chapel are located just under a kilometre south of St Davids. It was built on the site of the birthplace of St David to commemorate St Non, the traditional mother of St David.
Admission free
Always open.

St Davids Cathedral

Many people consider this to be Wales' finest cathedral. The 12th century cathedral contains the bones of St David and St Justinian.
Website www.stdavidscathedral.org.uk

Admission free; tours £3
Tours Jul-Aug Mon, Tue, Thu, Fri, Sun 2.30pm

Fishguard (Abergwaun)

Most travellers visit this seaside town to catch the ferry across the Irish Sea to Rosslare, Ireland. Fishguard also makes a good base for exploring the Pembrokeshire Coast National Park.

Practical Information
Fishguard Harbour Tourist Information Centre
Ocean Lab, The Parrog, Goodwick, Fishguard
☎ *(01348) 872037*
Website www.visitwales.com
Open winter 10am-4pm daily; summer 10am-5pm daily

Fishguard Town Tourist Information Centre
Town Hall, The Square, Fishguard
☎ *(01348) 873484*
Website www.visitwales.com
Open winter Mon-Sat 10am-4pm; summer 10am-5.30pm daily

Coming and Going
Stena Line ferries (☎ *(08705) 707 070; website www.stenaline.com*) between Fishguard and Rosslare, Ireland.

Local Transport
Fishguard is a small place and the only bus you're likely to need is bus 410, which operates a shuttle service between the harbour and the town centre.

Accommodation
Hamilton Backpackers Lodge
Hamilton Backpackers Lodge has extremely knowledgeable staff with lots of local knowledge. The building's character and comfortable accommodation with a quiet garden area and good, homely facilities make this hostel a superb place to stay. It is in the centre of Fishguard close to good local pubs and shops.
21-23 Hamilton Street, Fishguard
☎ *(01348) 874 797*
Website www.fishguard-backpackers.com
Dorm bed £12; double room £30

Maintenance & cleanliness	★★★★
Facilities	★★★
Atmosphere & character	★★★★★
Security	★★★
Overall rating	★★★★

Wye Valley

The Wye River marks the England/Wales border between Hay-on-Wye and the Severn Estuary. The Wye Valley is often your first stop in Wales if you are travelling by car.

The main attractions are Chepstow Castle and Tintern Abbey at the south of the valley and the book lovers' town of Hay-on-Wye at the valley's north.

Chepstow (Cas-gwent) & Tintern

Chepstow is the first town in Wales after crossing the Severn Bridge. It is a nice place that is dominated by the ruins of one of Britain's oldest stone castles.

Tintern and the impressive Tintern Abbey are located 8km north of Chepstow. Tintern is a much smaller town without the choice of shops and pubs that you can find in Chepstow, but there are some lovely walking trails around town.

Practical Information
Tourist Information Centre
Castle Car Park, Bridge Street, Chepstow
☎ *(01291) 623772*
Website www.visitwales.com
Open winter 10am-4pm daily; summer 10am-5.30pm daily

Coming & Going & Local Transport
The main train line linking Cardiff with Birmingham runs through Chepstow and National Express coaches stop here on their Cardiff to London route. Stagecoach bus routes 65 and 69 run between Chepstow and Monmouth, stopping en route at Tintern.

Accommodation
Although there is no backpackers accommodation in Chepstow or Tintern,

the excellent St Briavel's Castle youth hostel in England is just 6.5km across the border from Tintern.

St Briavel's Castle YHA
St Brivel's Castle YHA is an amazing youth hostel that is housed inside a moated Norman castle dating from 1205 that was once King John's hunting lodge.
St Briavels, Lydney, Gloucestershire
🚌 *69*
☎ *(01594) 530 272*
Website www.yha.org.uk
Dorm bed £13.80 (£11.80 HI/YHA)
Credit cards MC, Visa
Open during school holidays only; reception open 8am-10am & 5pm-10pm daily; curfew 11pm

Sights
Chepstow Castle
Chepstow Castle is one of the oldest stone castles in Britain and went through extensive renovations during the Middle Ages and the mid-17th century. Although it is now in ruins, it is still an impressive site and worth a look if you're in the area.
Chepstow
☎ *(01291) 624 065*
Admission £3 (£2.50 students)
Open Jan-Mar Mon-Sat 9.30am-4pm, Sun 11am-4pm; 1 Apr-1 Jun 9.30am-5pm daily; 2 Jun-28 Sep 9.30am-6pm daily; 29 Sep-26 Oct 9.30am-5pm daily; 27 Oct-31 Dec Mon-Sat 9.30am-4pm, Sun 11am-4pm

Tintern Abbey
This Cistercian abbey was founded in 1131 and rebuilt in the 13th and 14th centuries but began to fall into ruin during Henry VIII's reign. There is an exhibition centre on site and audio tours are also available.
A466, Tintern
☎ *(01291) 689 251*
Admission £2.50 (£2 students)
Open Jan-Mar Mon-Sat 9.30am-4pm, Sun 11am-4pm; 1 Apr-1 Jun 9.30am-5pm daily; 2 Jun-28 Sep 9.30am-6pm daily; 29 Sep-26 Oct 9.30am-5pm daily; 27 Oct-31 Dec Mon-Sat 9.30am-4pm, Sun 11am-4pm

Hay-on-Wye (Y Gelli)
This tiny town has the surprisingly claim to the title of the book capital of Britain, or perhaps even the world. The town has over 40 bookshops, mostly specialising in second hand books. Most of the bookshops are small but there are a few biggies including the original Hay bookshop, Booth's Books, which has 400,000 titles making it the world's largest second hand bookshop.

Hay boasts an annual literary festival each June when thousands of visitors descend on the town to see famous authors read their work.

Practical Information
Tourist Information Centre
Oxford Road, Hay-on-Wye
☎ *(01497) 820144*
Open Easter-Oct 10am-5pm daily; Nov-Easter 11am-1pm & 2pm-4pm daily

Accommodation
Capel-y-Ffin Youth Hostel
Capel-y-Ffin YHA is a stone farmhouse with loads of character. It has fairly basic facilities that include a small kitchen and a cosy lounge with books, board games and a fireplace. It is the closest hostel to Hay-on-Wye – 13km away – but there is no access by public transport.
Capel-y-Ffin, Llanthony
☎ *(01873) 890 650*
Website www.yha.org.uk
Dorm bed £12 (£10 HI/YHA)
Credit cards MC, Visa
Open Apr-Aug; reception open 7.30am-10am & 5pm-9.30pm daily; curfew 11pm
🚗 🇰

Maintenance & cleanliness	★★★½
Facilities	★
Atmosphere & character	★★★★½
Security	½
Overall rating	★★½

Brecon Beacons National Park (Parc Cenedlarthol Bannau Brycheiniog)
The Brecon Beacons National Park is one of Wales' major visitor attractions. It is

a scenic area with lakes, mountains and rolling hills. There are some good hiking trails and several hostels in the park.

Brecon is the main town inside the park, but many travellers stay in Abergavenny and Llandovery, which are located on the edge of the park's boundary.

Practical Information
Brecon Tourist Information Centre
Cattle Market Car Park, Brecon
☎ *(01874) 622485*
Website *www.visitwales.com*
Open *winter Mon-Sat 9am-5pm; summer 10am-6pm daily*

Craig-y-nos Country Park Information Centre
Craig-y-nos, Brecon Road, Penycae
☎ *(01639) 730395*
Website *www.breconbeacons.org/english/visitor-cyn01.html*

Llandovery Tourist Information Centre
Heritage Centre, Kings Road, Llandovery
☎ *(01550) 720693*
Website *www.visitwales.com*
Open *winter 10am-4pm daily; summer 10am-5.30pm*

Libanus Mountain National Park Information Centre
A470, Libanus, Brecon Beacons National Park
☎ *(01874) 623366*
Website *www.breconbeacons.org/english/visitor-mc01.html*
Open *Jan-Feb 9.30am-4.30pm daily; Mar-Jun 9.30am-5pm daily; Jul-Aug 9.30am-6pm daily; Sep-Oct 9.30am-5pm daily; Nov-Dec 9.30am-4.30pm daily*

Brecon (Aberhonddu)
With around 8000 people, Brecon is the biggest town within the park and it makes an obvious base for people hiking in the Brecon Beacons.

Accommodation
Bikes & Hikes
Bikes & Hikes occupies a charming building in the centre of Brecon. It features a cosy common area with a TV and a small kitchen plus a front lounge with a pool table.
The Elms, 10 The Struet, Brecon
☎ *(01874) 610 071*
Website *www.bikesandhikes.co.uk*
Dorm bed *£12.50;* **twin room** *£25*

Maintenance & cleanliness	★★★½
Facilities	★★½
Atmosphere & character	★★★★½
Security	★★
Overall rating	★★★

Ty'n-y-Caeau YHA
This youth hostel is in a Victorian country house in the countryside 5km from Brecon. It features a TV room, a dining room and a cosy lounge with a fireplace and piano. Accommodation is mostly in four-bed dormitories but there are also some big 18-bed dorms.
Groesffordd, Brecon
☎ *(01874) 665 270*
Website *www.yha.org.uk*
Dorm bed *£14.50 (£12.50 HI/YHA)*
Credit cards *MC, Visa*
Open *Jan-Feb Fri-Sun; Mar Tue-Sun; Apr-Sep every day; Oct Tue-Sun; Nov-Dec Fri-Sun;* **reception open** *8am-10am & 5pm-10pm daily;* **curfew** *11pm*

Maintenance & cleanliness	★★★★
Facilities	★★
Atmosphere & character	★★★½
Security	★★½
Overall rating	★★★

Star Bunkhouse
The Star Bunkhouse is a 300-year-old former pub that has been thoroughly renovated to a high standard. Communal areas include a small kitchen, dining room and a lounge. Accommodation is in tidy rooms with solid bunk beds. This hostel is on the A40 about halfway between Brecon and Abergavenny.
Brecon Road (A40), Bwlch
☎ *(01874) 730080*
Website *www.starbunkhouse.com*
Dorm bed *£12-15*

Maintenance & cleanliness	★★★★★
Facilities	★★
Atmosphere & character	★★★★½
Security	★★
Overall rating	★★★★

Abergavenny (Y Fenni)

This town of 10,000 lies at the eastern edge of the Brecon Beacons and it is an accessible base for exploring the park and the nearby Blaenavon World Heritage site.

Practical Information
Abergavenny Tourist Information Centre
Swan Meadow, Monmouth Road, Abergavenny
☎ *(01873) 857588*
Website *www.abergavenny.co.uk*
Open *winter 10am-4pm daily; summer 10am-5.30pm daily*

Coming & Going
Abergavenny has a train station that lies on the main line that links Cardiff with Strewsbury and Liverpool. There are also frequent buses to Brecon, Cardiff and Hereford.

Accommodation
Black Sheep Backpackers
This hostel is above a pub near the train station. The pub has a pool table and common areas downstairs include a small kitchen and a dining area/TV lounge. Accommodation is in very nice clean rooms with comfortable beds.
The Great Western Hotel, 24 Station Road, Abergavenny
🚆 *Abergavenny*
☎ *(01873) 859 125*
Website *www.blacksheepbackpackers.com*
Dorm bed *£11-12;* **twin room** *£28*
Credit cards *MC, Visa*

📺 🅺 🛜

Maintenance & cleanliness	★★★★⯪
Facilities	★★⯪
Atmosphere & character	★★★
Security	★★⯪
Overall rating	★★★⯪

Smithy's Bunkhouse
Smithy's Bunkhouse is a small rural hostel on a farm 3km north of Abergavenny. It is comprised of a couple of stone buildings including a bunkhouse with two big 12-bed dormitories and a building with two common rooms, one with a log fire and another with a pool table.
Lower House Farm, Pantygelli, Abergavenny
☎ *(01873) 853 432*
Website *www.smithysbunkhouse.com*
Dorm bed *£9.50*

🚗 🅺

Maintenance & cleanliness	★★★★★
Facilities	★★⯪
Atmosphere & character	★★★
Security	⯪
Overall rating	★★★

Sights
Abergavenny Castle
The ruins of the Norman Abergavenny Castle offer scenic views of the adjacent countryside.

Abergavenny Museum
This museum has exhibits on local history the Brecon Beacons and the Abergavenny area.
☎ *(01873) 854 282*
Admission *£1*
Open *Jan-Feb Mon-Sat 11am-1pm & 2pm-4pm; Mar-Oct Mon-Sat 11am-1pm & 2pm-5pm, Sun 2pm-5pm; Nov-Dec Mon-Sat 11am-1pm & 2pm-4pm*

Blaenavon

Many people visit this World Heritage site as a day trip from Abergavenny, which is only 15km away.

Practical Information
Tourist Information Centre
Blaenavon Ironworks, Stack Square, Blaenavon
☎ *(01495) 792615*
Website *www.visitwales.com*
Open *summer 10am-4.30pm daily*

Coming & Going
It is easiest to reach Blaenavon with your own car but if you're relying on public transport take bus X4 from Abergavenny to Bryn Mawr and then transfer to bus 30 to Blaenavon.

Sights
Blaenavon Ironworks
This site includes the ruins of five blast furnaces dating from 1788. There is also an exhibit on site that explains its significance.

A4043, Blaenavon
☎ *(01495) 792615*
Admission *£2 (£1.50 students)*
Open *Apr-Oct 9.30am-4.30pm daily*

The Big Pit National Mining Museum
The Big Pit National Mining Museum is part of the Blaenavon Industrial Landscape UNESCO World Heritage Site, 15km south west of Abergavenny. It is set in a coal mine that was operational for over 200 years and which once employed 1300 miners. The highlight of a visit is the underground tour that takes you 90 metres below the ground to the heart of the mine.
Blaenarfon,
☎ *(01495) 790311*
Website *www.nmgw.ac.uk/bigpit/*
Admission *free*
Open *Mar-Nov 9.30am-5pm daily, underground tours run 10am-3.30pm*

Aberystwyth

This seaside resort and university town on the central coast has several attractions that include a castle, a cliff railway and the National Library of Wales. It is a halfway stop for many backpackers travelling between South and North Wales.

Practical Information
Aberystwyth Tourist Information Centre
Terrace Road, Aberystwyth
☎ *(01970) 612125*
Website *www.visitwales.com*
Open *winter Mon-Sat 10am-5pm; summer 10am-6pm daily*

Coming & Going
Aberystwyth is a busy transport hub, which lies on the rail line to goes to Strewsbury with onward connections to Birmingham, Liverpool and Manchester. It is also possible to take a train to the north coast, but this requires a change at Minffordd for the narrow gauge Festiniog tourist railway to Blaenau Festiniog where you can transfer to another train to Llandudno.

Buses run up and down the coast going to places where there are no train lines. Destinations include Cardigan and Fishguard. The bus is also the quickest way to reach destinations in north Wales including Holyhead and Llandudno.

Accommodation
Borth Youth Hostel
This hostel has the usual facilities that include a TV lounge, kitchen, dining room and a smoking room and it has an institutional feel to it. It is located directly across the road from the sea and it's 15km north of Aberystwyth.
B4353, Marlais, Borth
☎ *(01970) 871 498*
Website *www.yha.org.uk*
Dorm bed *£13 (£11 HI/YHA)*
Credit cards *MC, Visa*
Open *12 Mar-31 Oct; reception open 8am-10am & 5pm-10pm daily; lockout 10am-5pm; curfew 11pm*

🅿️🍴📺🅺🅻

Maintenance & cleanliness	★★★½
Facilities	★
Atmosphere & character	★
Security	★★★
Overall rating	★★

Plas Dolau
This lovely hostel is in a big house in the countryside 5km from Aberystwyth. It has a games room with table tennis and a pool table, a cosy TV lounge with a piano and a bigger lounge with a fireplace and a grand piano. It has a brilliant kitchen with an Aga and a dishwasher. It is a clean hostel that is maintained to a high standard.
Lovesgrove, Aberystwyth
🚌 *501, 531*
☎ *(01970) 617 834*
Website *www.dolau-holidays.co.uk*
Dorm bed *£13.50 with continental breakfast, £17.50 with cooked breakfast*

🅿️🍴📺🅺🅻

Maintenance & cleanliness	★★★★★
Facilities	★★★½
Atmosphere & character	★★★★
Security	★★½
Overall rating	★★★★

Sights
Aberystwyth Arts Centre
Wales's largest arts centre hosts a varied programme of exhibitions and performances.
University of Wales, Penglais Campus,

Aberystwyth
☎ *(01970) 622822*
Website *www.aber.ac.uk/artscentre/*

Aberystwyth Castle
Edward II built this castle by the waterfront in 1277, however the castle now lies in ruins.
Admission *free*

Ceredigion Museum
The Ceredigion County Museum features a varied programme of exhibitions that focus on art and local history and culture.
Coliseum, Terrace Road, Aberystwyth
☎ *(01970) 633 088*
Website *www.ceredigion.gov.uk*
Admission *free*
Open *Mon-Sat 10am-5pm*

Cliff Railway & Constitution Hill
A steep cliff railway climbs 130 metres to the top of Constitution Hill where there are breathtaking views of the town and coastline. The top of Constitution Hill also features the world's largest camera obscura, which portrays this view from a different perspective.
☎ *(01970) 617642*
Admission *free to all attractions at the top of Constitution Hill*
Open *10am-5pm daily*

National Library of Wales
It may seem strange for a small seaside town to be home to the country's National Library, which houses virtually every book every published in Welsh including some important historical documents. Exhibitions of Welsh art and photography are also held here.
☎ *(01970) 632 800*
Website *www.llgc.org.uk*
Admission *free*
Open *Mon-Fri 9.30am-6pm, Sat 9.30am-5pm*

Snowdonia National Park (Parc Cenedlaethol Eryri)

Mount Snowdon, Wales' tallest mountain, lies at the heart of Snowdonia National Park. This is the biggest and most visited national park in Wales and, after the Lake District, is the second largest national park in Britain. There are some excellent hiking trails in the park, but climbing Mount Snowdon is the main objective of most visitors.

Like much of Wales, the park is home to some brilliant little railways including the famous Ffestiniog Railway and also the Snowdon Mountain Railway, which runs from Llanberis to the summit of Mount Snowdon.

Practical Information
Betws-y-Coed Tourist Information Centre
Royal Oak Stables, Betws-y-Coed
☎ *(01690) 710426*
Website *www.visitwales.com*
Open *winter 9.30am-4.30pm daily; summer 10am-6pm daily*

Blaenau Ffestiniog Tourist Information Centre
Unit 3, High Street, Blaenau Ffestiniog
☎ *(01766) 830360*
Website *www.visitwales.com*
Open *summer 10am-6pm daily*

Llanberis Tourist Information Centre
41b High Street, Llanberis
☎ *(01286) 870765*
Website *www.visitwales.com*
Open *winter Wed, Fri, Sun 11am-4pm; summer 10am-6pm daily*

Local Transport
The Snowdonia area is well served by Snowdon Sherpa buses, which are a handy way to travel between towns in the park. The Red Rover travel pass allows you to travel all day on bus routes 1 to 99 including buses to and from Aberystwyth.

If you can't be fagged climbing Mount Snowdon, you may want to take the Snowdon Mountain Railway (☎ *0870 458 033; website www.snowdonrailway. co.uk*) to the summit. This train costs £18 for a return ticket or £13 one-way.

Accommodation
The area around Mount Snowdon is home to a bunch of great little hostels.

BETWS-Y-COED
Betws-y-Coed Youth Hostel
This hostel is part of a complex that also includes a hotel and pub. It is a spotless hostel that is maintained to a very high standard but there aren't a lot of common areas other than the pub and a small, but fully equipped, kitchen.
A5, Swallow Falls, Betws-y-Coed
☎ *(01690) 710 796*
Website www.yha.org.uk
Dorm bed £14.50 (£12.50 HI/YHA)
Credit cards MC, Visa
Reception open 8am-11pm daily

Maintenance & cleanliness	★★★★★
Facilities	★★
Atmosphere & character	★★★☆
Security	★★
Overall rating	★★★★☆

CAPEL CURIG
Capel Curig YHA
Capel Curig YHA is in a house on a hill overlooking Capel Curig village. It has two lounges, a big dining room and a good kitchen.
A5, Plas Curig, Capel Curig
☎ *(01690) 720 225*
Website www.yha.org.uk
Dorm bed £18 (£16 HI/YHA)
Credit cards MC, Visa
Open Jan-Feb Fri-Sat; Mar-Oct daily; Nov-Dec Fri-Sat; **reception open** 8am-10am & 5pm-10pm daily; **curfew** 11pm

Maintenance & cleanliness	★★★
Facilities	★★☆
Atmosphere & character	★★☆
Security	★★☆
Overall rating	★★

CORRIS
Braich Goch Bunkhouse
Braich Goch is a tidy bunkhouse catering to outdoorsy types. It features a fully equipped kitchen; a dining room with a fireplace and a cosy bar/lounge with pool table, table football and a climbing wall.
A487, Corris
☎ *(01654) 761 229*
Website www.braichgoch.co.uk
Dorm bed £12.50

Maintenance & cleanliness	★★★★☆
Facilities	★★★
Atmosphere & character	★★★★★☆
Security	★
Overall rating	★★★★☆

Canolfan Corris
This hostel is an old stone schoolhouse on a hill overlooking Corris village. It has a lot of character and a laid back atmosphere. Accommodation is in big dorms with old metal bunk beds and facilities include a small kitchen and a cosy lounge with a log fire.
Old School, Corris
☎ *0870 770 5778*
Website www.canolfancorris.com
Dorm bed £10.60

Maintenance & cleanliness	★★★★☆
Facilities	★★☆
Atmosphere & character	★★★
Security	★
Overall rating	★★★☆

DOLGELLAU
Kings (Dolgellau) Youth Hostel
Kings YHA is made up of several stone and concrete buildings in a natural setting by a stream. Facilities are basic and limited to the usual kitchen and lounge.
Kings, Penmaenpool
☎ *(01341) 422 392*
Website www.yha.org.uk
Dorm bed £13 (£11 HI/YHA)
Credit cards MC, Visa
Open 5 Mar-1 Apr Fri-Sat; 2 Apr-27 Sep daily; 28 Sep-31 Oct Fri-Sat; **reception open** 8am-10am & 5pm-10pm daily; **curfew** 11pm

Maintenance & cleanliness	★★★☆
Facilities	★
Atmosphere & character	★★
Security	★
Overall rating	★★

LLANBERIS
Heights Hotel
The Heights Hotel has backpacker accommodation above a pub. The accommodation is clean but basic and there aren't any common areas apart from the bar. It is the most centrally located of the Llanberis hostels.
74 High Street, Llanberis

☎ (01286) 871 179
Website www.heightshotel.co.uk
Dorm bed £14
Credit cards MC, Visa
Reception open 8am-11pm daily
🚗📱

Maintenance & cleanliness	★★★★½
Facilities	★
Atmosphere & character	★★
Security	★★
Overall rating	★★★½

Jesse James' Bunkhouse
This small hostel is a bit rough around the edges and has basic facilities including a cluttered kitchen and lounge and a Spartan dining area.
A4244, Penisarwaen Nr Llanberis
🚌 76, 77
☎ (01286) 870521
Dorm bed £8
🚗 K L

Maintenance & cleanliness	★★½
Facilities	★
Atmosphere & character	★★★
Security	½
Overall rating	★★½

Llanberis YHA
This neat and tidy hostel just outside Llanberis has nice views and facilities that include a big dining room, a kitchen and a common room with TV, pool table and table football. To get here follow the signs from the Spar supermarket on High Street in the village centre.
Llwyn Celyn, Llanberis
☎ (01286) 870 280
Website www.yha.org.uk
Dorm bed £14.50 (£12.50 HI/YHA)
Credit cards MC, Visa
Reception open 7am-10pm & 5pm-10.30pm daily
🚗 TV K

Maintenance & cleanliness	★★★★
Facilities	★★
Atmosphere & character	★★★
Security	★★
Overall rating	★★★

Snowdon House
This small bunkhouse has been going since 1958. It is a stone building that sleeps 18 in three-tier bunk beds and there is a basic kitchen. Toilets and showers are in an outhouse.

A4086, Nant Peris
☎ (01286) 870 284
Website www.snowdonhouse.co.uk
Dorm bed £7.50
🚗 K

Maintenance & cleanliness	★★
Facilities	★½
Atmosphere & character	★★
Security	★
Overall rating	★★½

NANT GWYNANT
Bryn Dinas Bunkhouse
Bryn Dinas Bunkhouse is comprised of a large bunkhouse (that is used for groups) and several small tidy cabins. The main building features spotless bathrooms, a kitchen and a spartan lounge and there's also another kitchen that people staying in the cabins can use.
A496, Bryn Dinas, Nant Gwynant
🚌 97A
☎ (01766) 890 234
Website www.bryndinasbunkhouse.co.uk
Dorm bed £12.50
Credit cards MC, Visa
🚗 K

Maintenance & cleanliness	★★★★½
Facilities	★
Atmosphere & character	★★★
Security	★
Overall rating	★★★½

Bryn Gwynant Youth Hostel
This youth hostel is in a big mansion overlooking Llyn Gwynant. It consists of two buildings on 40 acres of woodland. Shared facilities include a lounge with comfy sofas, open fireplace and views of the lake; two dining rooms and a small kitchen.
A496, Bryn Dinas, Nant Gwynant
🚌 97A
☎ (01766) 890 251
Website www.yha.org.uk
Dorm bed £13 (£11 HI/YHA)
Credit cards MC, Visa
Open *1 Jan-15 Feb Fri-Sat; 16 Feb-31 Oct every day;* **reception open** *8am-10am & 5pm-10pm daily;* **curfew** *11pm*
🚗 K

Maintenance & cleanliness	★★★★
Facilities	★
Atmosphere & character	★★★½
Security	★
Overall rating	★★★½

Pen-y-Pass YHA

This well located hostel sits in a spectacular setting at Pen-y-Pass, which makes it a good base for climbing Mount Snowdon. It is a relatively large hostel with several lounges, a games room with pool table and table football and a bar.
A4086, Pen-y-Pass, Nant Gwynant
Sherpa
☎ *(01286) 870 428*
Website *www.yha.org.uk*
Dorm bed *£14.50 (£12.50 HI/YHA)*
Reception open *8am-10am & 5pm-10pm daily;* **curfew** *11pm*

Maintenance & cleanliness	★★★★
Facilities	★★☆
Atmosphere & character	★★★★☆
Security	★
Overall rating	★★★

Sights
Welsh Slate Museum

Slate has been described as 'the most Welsh of Welsh industries' and slate quarries were common throughout the country in the 19th century. Remnants of the industry can be found today, particularly in the Snowdonia region in places like Blaenau Ffestiniog and Llanberis. The Welsh Slate Museum is set in the Dinorwig slate quarry and it features Britain's largest working waterwheel, restored workshops and slate-splitting demonstrations. There is also a 3D multimedia presentation about the lives of the quarry workers.
Padarn Country Park, Llanberis
☎ *(01286) 870630*
Website *www.nmgw.ac.uk/wsm/*
Admission *free*
Open *Jan-Easter Sun-Fri 10am-4pm; Easter-Oct 10am-5pm daily; Nov-Dec Sun-Fri 10am-4pm*

Porthmadog

Porthmadog, and neighbouring Tremadog, is a good base for exploring the southern part of Snowdonia National Park, but most visitors come here to travel on the Ffestiniog Railway.

The World Heritage Harlech Castle is located a half hour drive south of here.

Practical Information
Porthmadog Tourist Information Centre

High Street, Porthmadog
☎ *(01766) 512981*
Website *www.visitwales.com*
Open *winter Thu-Tue 10am-5pm; summer 10am-6pm daily*

Accommodation
Snowdon Lodge

This excellent hostel is in an old stone house that was the birthplace of Lawrence of Arabia. Accommodation is in good quality sturdy bunk beds with real mattresses and the extensive common areas feature a cosy bar, a café/dining room, a small but fully-equipped kitchen and a TV lounge with a log fire.
Lawrence House, Church Street, Tremadog
☎ *(01766) 515 354*
Website *www.snowdonlodge.co.uk*
Dorm bed *£13.50;* **double room** *£35;* **twin room** *£30; prices include breakfast*
Credit cards *MC, Visa*

Maintenance & cleanliness	★★★★
Facilities	★★★☆
Atmosphere & character	★★★★★
Security	★★
Overall rating	★★★★☆

Stone Barn

This small hostel has an open-plan design inside a stone barn with exposed wooden beams. Accommodation is in alpine-style sleeping platforms and showers are in a separate building that is shared with the adjoining caravan park. The barn has a small TV, a wood burning stove and basic kitchen facilities but furnishings are old and worn. It is 2.5km from Criccieth and 8km from Porthmadog.
Tyddyn Morthwyl, Criccieth
☎ *(01766) 522 115*
Dorm bed *£5*

Maintenance & cleanliness	★★☆
Facilities	★
Atmosphere & character	★★★★
Security	☆
Overall rating	★★

Sights
Ffestiniog Railway
This narrow gauge steam railway chugs its way through the Vale of Ffestiniog, terminating at the slate mining town of Blaenau Ffestiniog where you can transfer to a regular train to Wales' northern coast.
Harbour Station, Porthmadog
☎ *(01766) 516024*
Website www.festrail.co.uk
Fare £14 all day rover ticket.

Harlech
This small town, about a half hour drive south of Porthmadog, is known for the World Heritage Harlech Castle.

Practical Information
Harlech Tourist Information Centre
Llys y Graig, Harlech
☎ *(01766) 780658*
Website www.visitwales.com
Open summer 10am-6pm daily

Sights
Harlech Castle
This spectacular castle was built between 1283 and 1289 for Edward I. It features four massive round towers at each corner and UNESCO has classified it as a World Heritage site.
Harlech
☎ *(01766) 780552*
Admission £3 (£2 students)
Open Jan-Mar Mon-Sat 9.30am-4pm, Sun 11am-4pm; 1 Apr-1 Jun 9.30am-5pm daily; 2 Jun-28 Sep 9.30am-6pm daily; 29 Sep-26 Oct 9.30am-5pm daily; 27 Oct-31 Dec Mon-Sat 9.30am-4pm, Sun 11am-4pm

Caernarfon
This major centre in north Wales has an old centre surrounded by medieval city walls and an outstanding castle that dates from 1283.

Practical Information
Tourist Information Centre
Oriel Pendeitsh, Castle Street, Caernarfon
☎ *(01286) 672232*
Website www.visitwales.com
Open winter Thu-Tue 9.30am-4.30pm; summer 10am-6pm daily

Accommodation
Totters
This classy hostel has an excellent location inside the medieval town walls. There's a cosy lounge with a small TV and lots of books and downstairs there's a fully equipped kitchen with a dishwasher and a lovely dining area with games and music. The rooms are spacious and tastefully decorated.
Plas Proth Yr Aur, 2 High Street, Caernarfon
☎ *(01286) 672 963*
Website www.totters.co.uk
Dorm bed £12; price includes breakfast
Credit cards MC, Visa

Maintenance & cleanliness	★★★★
Facilities	★★½
Atmosphere & character	★★★★★
Security	★★★½
Overall rating	★★★★½

Sights
Caernarfon Castle
Breathtaking Caernarfon Castle dominates the old town with its massive fortifications and polygonal towers. It was originally constructed in 1283 as a royal residence for Edward I and it has been the site of much royal pageantry. The castle is home to the Royal Welch Fusiliers Museum, a regimental museum and the Eagle and the Dragon audiovisual display. It is a World Heritage Site along with another three of Edward I's castles.
☎ *(01286) 677 617*
Admission £4.50 (£3.50 students)
Open Jan-Mar Mon-Sat 9.30am-4pm, Sun 11am-4pm; 1 Apr-1 Jun 9.30am-5pm daily; 2 Jun-28 Sep 9.30am-6pm daily; 29 Sep-26 Oct 9.30am-5pm daily; 27 Oct-31 Dec Mon-Sat 9.30am-4pm, Sun 11am-4pm

Segontium Roman Museum
This museum portrays the Roman conquest and occupation of Wales. Exhibits include artefacts unearthed at the Segontium fort.
Beddgelert Road, Caernarfon
☎ *(01286) 675 625*

Admission *free*
Open *Jan-Easter Mon-Sat 10am-4pm, Sun 2pm-4pm; Easter-Sep Mon-Sat 10am-5pm, Sun 2pm-5pm; Nov-Dec Mon-Sat 10am-4pm, Sun 2pm-4pm*

Conwy & Llandudno

These two towns on Wales' north coast are only a short distance apart and are both very popular with tourists, but for entirely different reasons.

Conwy is a historic town that is dominated by a 13th century castle, but it also boasts an eclectic variety of other sights. On the other hand, Llandudno, which is only 6.5km away, is a Victorian seaside resort with an assortment of tacky attractions but it also features a pleasant beachfront promenade.

Practical Information
Conwy Tourist Information Centre
Conwy Castle Visitor Centre, Conwy
☎ *(01492) 592248*
Website *www.visitwales.com*
Open *winter Thu-Sat 9.30am-4pm; summer 9.30am-5pm daily*

Llandudno Tourist Information Centre
1-2 Chapel Street, Llandudno
☎ *(01492) 876413*
Website *www.visitwales.com*
Open *winter Mon-Fri 9.30am-4.30pm; summer 9.30am-5.30pm daily*

Coming & Going
Conwy and Llandudno have good train connections to Chester, Liverpool and Manchester. There are stations at Conwy and Llandudno but most trains stop at Llandudno Junction station, which is the area's transport hub.

National Express coaches go to Holyhead, Chester, Manchester and London.

Local Transport
Arriva buses *(website www.arriva.co.uk)* run throughout North Wales and they're the best option for getting around Conwy and Llandudno. Buses 5, 5X, 14, 15, 19, 19A and 25 run between Conwy and Llandudno. An Arriva Day Pass costs £5 and lets you travel on most Arriva buses, but not long distance coach services.

Accommodation
Conwy YHA
This modern hostel is perched upon a hill with views of Conwy Castle. It is maintained to a high standard and has a games room with Internet access, pool table and table football and several lounge areas including a rooftop terrace. The beds have new mattresses and there are showers in all rooms.
Larkhill, Sychnant Pass Road, Conwy
☎ *(01492) 593 571*
Website *www.yha.org.uk*
Dorm bed *£16 (£14 HI/YHA)*
Credit cards *JCB, MC, Visa*
Open *16 Feb-31 Oct daily; 1 Nov-20 Dec Fri-Sun;* **reception open** *8am-noon & 2pm-11pm daily*

Maintenance & cleanliness		★★★★½
Facilities		★★★
Atmosphere & character		★★½
Security		★★★★½
Overall rating		★★★★½

Sights
Aberconwy House
This medieval merchant's house has endured six centuries of turbulent history. The house has been restored to represent life here in different historical periods. There is also an audiovisual presentation.
Castle Street, Conwy
☎ *(01492) 592 246*
Admission *£2.20*
Open *29 Mar-2 Nov Wed-Mon 11am-5pm*

Conwy Castle
The World Heritage listed Conwy Castle was built between 1283 and 1287 for Edward I. It stands on a rocky outcrop overlooking Conwy and Llandudno and it features eight immense towers and a bow-shaped hall.
☎ *(01492) 592358*
Admission *£3.50 (£3 students); joint ticket for Conwy Castle & Plas Mawr £6.50 (£5.50 students)*
Open *Jan-Mar Mon-Sat 9.30am-4pm, Sun 11am-4pm; 1 Apr-1 Jun 9.30am-*

5pm daily; 2 Jun-28 Sep 9.30am-6pm daily; 29 Sep-26 Oct 9.30am-5pm daily; 27 Oct-31 Dec Mon-Sat 9.30am-4pm, Sun 11am-4pm

Conwy Suspension Bridge
This tasteful suspension bridge, near Conwy Castle spans the River Conwy. It designed by Thomas Telford and built in 1826. The toll-keeper's house has been restored and furnished, as it would have looked 100 years ago.
☎ *(01492) 573 282*
Website *www.nationaltrust.org.uk*
Admission *£1.20*
Open *27 Mar-31 Oct 10am-5pm daily*

Plas Mawr
Plas Mawr claims to be Great Britain's best-preserved Elizabethan townhouse. It features a gatehouse and tower and the interior reflects the style of the late 16th century.
☎ *(01492) 580 167*
Admission *£4.50 (£3.50 students); joint ticket for Conwy Castle & Plas Mawr £6.50 (£5.50 students)*
Open *1 Apr-1 Jun Tue-Sun 9.30am-5pm; 2 Jun-31 Aug Tue-Sun 9.30am-6pm; 1-28 Sep Tue-Sun 9.30am-5pm; 29 Sep-26 Oct Tue-Sun 9.30am-4pm*

Llangollen
This pretty town by the River Dee is famous for the International Musical Eisteddfod *(**website** www.international-eisteddfod.co.uk)* that has been held here each July since 1947. The festival see the town's population explode from 3,000 to 80,000 people who come here for a hectic week of song and dance.

Practical Information
Tourist Information Centre
Town Hall, Castle Street, Llangollen
☎ *(01978) 860828*
Website *www.visitwales.com*
Open *winter Mon-Sat 9.30am-5pm; summer 10am-6pm daily*

Bangor
This university town makes a convenient base for exploring Anglesey and north Wales.

Practical Information
Tourist Information Centre
Town Hall, Deniol Road, Bangor
☎ *(01248) 352 786*
Website *www.visitwales.com*
Open *10am-6pm daily*

Accommodation
Bangor Youth Hostel
Bangor's YHA is a clean and functional hostel with a cosy TV lounge, a games room with a pool table and table football plus a kitchen and a big dining room.
Tan-y-Bryn, Bangor
☎ *(01248) 353 516*
Website *www.yha.org.uk*
Dorm bed *£14.50 (£12.50 HI/YHA)*
Credit cards *MC, Visa*
Open *Jan-Mar Tue-Sat; Apr-Oct every day; Nov Tue-Sat; **reception open** 7.30am-10.30pm daily*

Maintenance & cleanliness	★★★★⯪
Facilities	★★
Atmosphere & character	★★⯪
Security	★★
Overall rating	★★⯪

Isle of Anglesey (Ynys Môn)
Many travellers visit Anglesey to catch the ferry to Ireland from Holyhead; but many others come here for the wealth of prehistoric sites that are located here.

Another attraction is the small town of Llanfairpwllgwyngyllgogerychwyrndrobwllllantysiliogogogoch, which claims Britain's longest place name. The town is often abbreviated to Llanfairpwll or Llanfair P G.

Practical Information
Holyhead Tourist Information Centre
Stena Line Terminal 1, Holyhead
☎ *(01407) 762622*
Open *winter Mon-Sat 10am-4.30pm; summer Mon-Sat 8.30am-6pm*

Llanfairpwllgwyngyllgogerych- wyrndrobwllllantysiliogogogoch Tourist Information Centre
Station Road, Llanfairpwllgwyngyllgo- gerychwyrndrobwllllantysiliogogogoch

station, Llanfairpwllgwyngyllgogerychwyrndrobwllllantysiliogogogoch
☎ (01248) 713177
Website www.visitwales.com
Open 10am-5pm daily

Local Transport
Although there are local bus services in Anglesey, the island is best explored with a car and it can be difficult to appreciate it fully by public transport. Bangor on the mainland is the best spot to make transport connections to Anglesey.

Sights
Plas Newydd
This graceful 18th century mansion was built in classical and Gothic styles and it features paintings by Rex Whistler including his largest work. In addition to an exhibition on Whistler's works, there is a military museum with relics from the Battle of Waterloo.
3.25km south west of Llanfairpwllgwyngyllgogerychwyrndrobwllllantysiliogogogoch
☎ (01248) 715272
Admission £4.70; garden only £2.80
Open 29 Mar-2 Nov Sat-Wed noon-5pm

Scotland

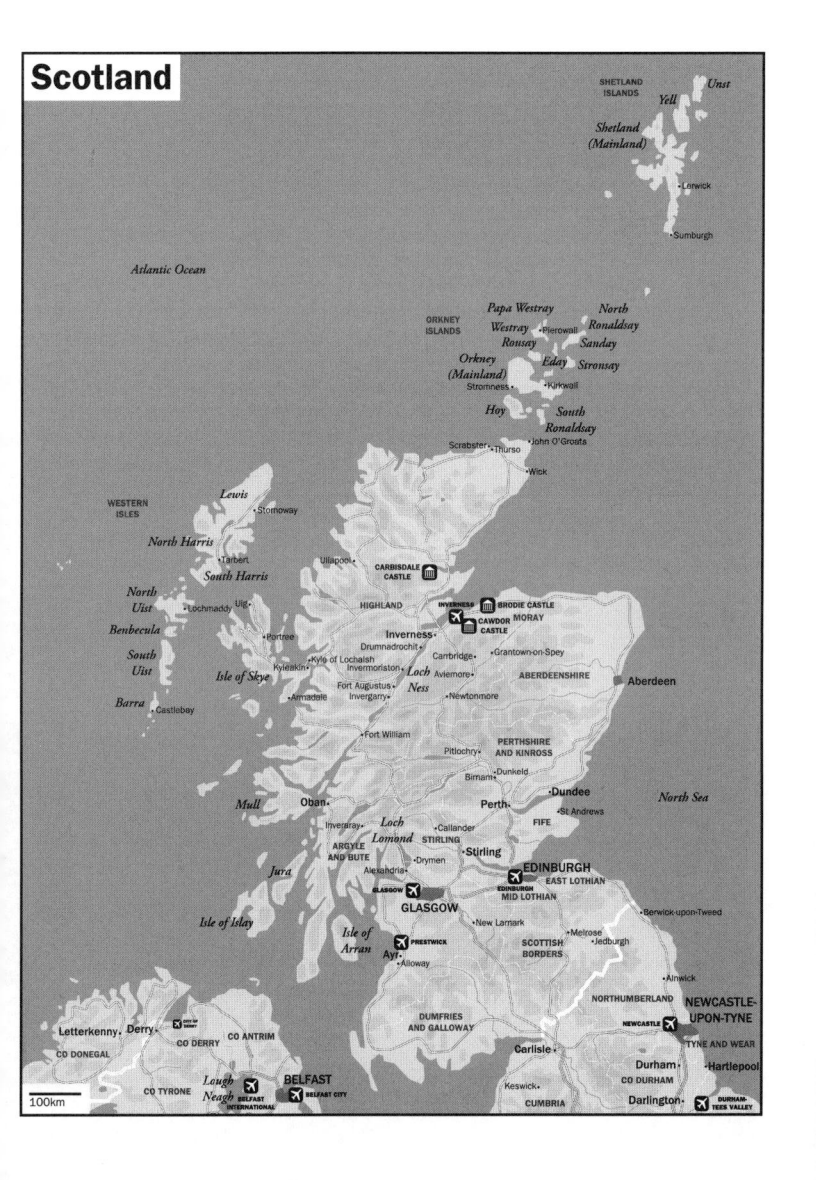

Scottish Borders

The area between Edinburgh and the border with England is one of Scotland's least visited regions. This is partly because of poor transport, but mostly because most travellers bypass the Borders in order to spend more time in the Highlands and cities.

Jedburgh

This agreeable town 21km south of Melrose is home to the splendid Jedburgh Abbey and several other attractions.

Practical Information
Tourist Information Centre
Murray's Green, Jedburgh TD8 6BE
☎ *(0870) 6080404*
Website www.discovertheborders.co.uk
Open Mon-Sat 9.30am-4.30pm

Coming & Going
Munro's of Jedburgh (☎ (01835) 862253; *website* www.munrosofjedburgh.sageweb.co.uk) bus 29 runs hourly between Jedburgh and Edinburgh.

Sights
Jedburgh Abbey
Founded by David I in 1138, the superb Jedburgh Abbey is built in the Romanesque and Gothic styles. Several important artefacts, including the ivory Jedburgh Comb, have been unearthed here.
Abbey Bridgend, Jedburgh
☎ *(01835) 863 925*
***Admission** £3.50 (£2.50 students)*
***Open** Apr-Sep 9.30am-6pm daily*

Jedburgh Castle Jail & Museum
This 19th century prison features displays of local history and prison life.
Castlegate, Jedburgh
☎ *(01450) 373457*
***Admission** £2*
***Open** Easter-Oct Mon-Sat 10am-4.45pm, Sun 1pm-4pm*

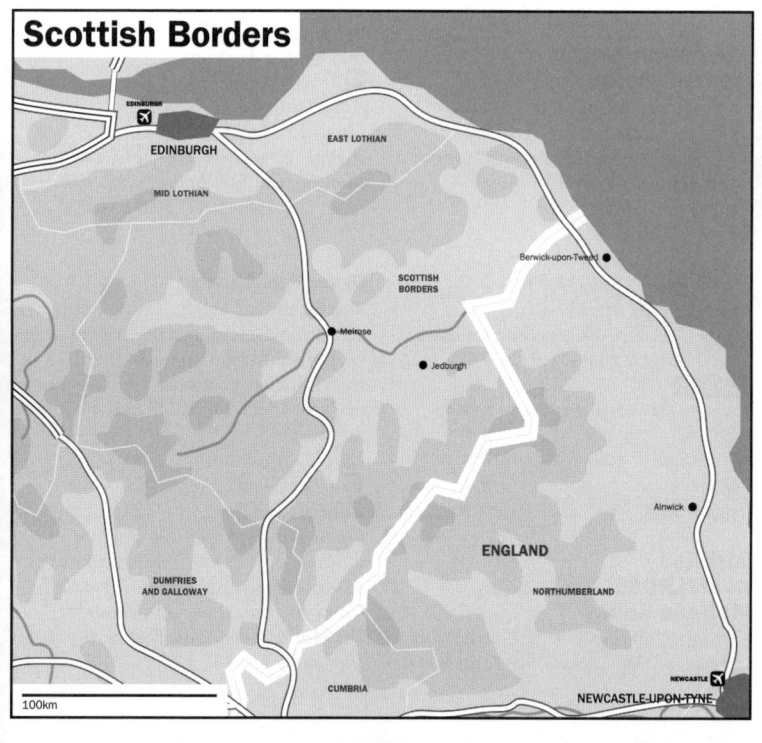

Mary, Queen of Scots Visitors' Centre
A 16th century bastel house is home to exhibits about Mary, Queen of Scots, who visited Jedburgh in 1566.
Queen Street, Jedburgh
☎ *(01835) 863331*
Admission *£3*
Open *Mar-Nov Mon-Sat 10am-4.30pm, Sun 11am-4.30pm*

Melrose

This enchanting town is one of the nicer places in the Scottish Borders. Melrose Abbey is the major attraction and Dryburgh Abbey and Thirlestane Castle are just a short distance away.

There is a SYHA hostel here, which makes it the only interesting town in the Borders with a hostel.

Practical Information
Tourist Information Centre
Abbey House, Abbey Street, Melrose
☎ *(0870) 6080404*
Website *www.discovertheborders.co.uk*
Open *Mon-Sat 9.30am-4.30pm*

Accommodation
Melrose SYHA
The Melrose Youth Hostel is a big mansion just outside town. It has a big kitchen and dining room, a spacious common room and a separate TV lounge.
Priorwood, Melrose
☎ *0870 004 1141*
Website *www.syha.org.uk*
Dorm bed *£11.50-12.75*
Credit cards *MC, Visa*
Open *5 Mar-31 Oct; reception open 7am-10am & 5pm-11pm daily*

Maintenance & cleanliness	★★★
Facilities	★★☆
Atmosphere & character	★★☆
Security	★★☆
Overall rating	★★

Sights
IN MELROSE
Melrose Abbey
Dating from 1136, this Gothic abbey is famous throughout Scotland for its elegance and also as the home of Robert the Bruce's embalmed heart.
Abbey Street, Melrose
☎ *(01896) 822562*
Admission *£3.50 (£2.50 students)*
Open *Jan-Mar Mon-Sat 9.30am-4.30pm (last entry 4pm); Apr-Sep 9.30am-6.30pm daily (last entry 6pm); Oct-Dec Mon-Sat 9.30am-4.30pm (last entry 4pm)*

Trimontium Exhibition
The Trimontium Exhibition is a small museum that explains the region's Roman history.
Market Square, Melrose
☎ *(01896) 822651*
Website *www.trimontium.freeserve.co.uk/exhibition.html*
Admission *£1.50*
Open *Apr-Oct 10.30am-4.30pm*

AROUND MELROSE
Abbotsford House
The former home of 19th century author Sir Walter Scott has a collection of Scott memorabilia and exhibits of other memorabilia that include Rob Roy's gun.
5km west of Melrose
☎ *(01896) 752043*
Admission *£4.50*
Open *15 Mar-31 May Mon-Sat 9.30am-5pm, Sun 2pm-5pm; Jun-Sep Mon-Sat 9.30am-5pm, Sun 9.30am-5pm; Oct Mon-Sat 9.30am-5pm, Sun 2pm-5pm*

Dryburgh Abbey
This beautiful abbey, 11km south east of Melrose, is a fascinating place to visit. In addition to substantial ruins, the Abbey's grounds are the burial place of Field Marshall Earl Haig and Sir Walter Scott.
B6356, St Boswells
☎ *(01835) 822381*
Admission *£3*
Open *Jan-Mar Mon-Sat 9.30am-4.30pm, Sun 2pm-4.30pm (last entry 4pm); Apr-Sep 9.30am-6.30pm daily (last entry 6pm); Oct-Dec Mon-Sat 9.30am-4.30pm, Sun 2pm-4.30pm (last entry 4pm)*

Edinburgh

After London, Edinburgh is Britain's most popular big city with backpackers. Although not everyone who visits London gets the chance to make it to Scotland, virtually everyone who visits Scotland will also visit Edinburgh.

The Scottish capital is a beautiful city with an imposing castle, Holyrood Palace and the majestic Royal Mile that connects the two. Apart from impressive old buildings and centuries of tradition, Edinburgh is a city that knows how to party. The city is home to an endless array of festivals including the Edinburgh Festival and the Festival Fringe, which has grown into the world's largest arts festival plus numerous other arts, entertainment and music festivals. Strong Scottish tradition has fused with Edinburgh's party culture to turn Edinburgh's Hogmanay from a traditional Scottish celebration to the world's largest New Year's Eve party.

The city has plenty of things to do, including great pubs and world-class attractions that make this an unbeatable destination.

Practical Information
Edinburgh Tourist Information Centre
3 Princes Street, Edinburgh
☎ *1, 3, 3A, 4, 5, 7, 8, 10, 11, 12, 14, 15, 15A, 16, 17, 19, 22, 24, 25, 26, 29, 30, 31, 33, 34, 37, 37A, 44, 44A, 49, Airlink100, X26, X31, X37, X47 & all Night Buses*
☎ *(0131) 473 3800*
Website www.edinburgh.org
Open *Jan-Apr Mon-Wed 9am-5pm, Thu-Sat 9am-6pm, Sun 10am-5pm; May-Jun Mon-Sat 9am-7pm, Sun 10am-7pm; Jul-Aug Mon-Sat 9am-8pm, Sun 10am-8pm; Sep Mon-Sat 9am-7pm, Sun 10am-7pm; Oct-Dec Mon-Wed 9am-5pm, Thu-Sat 9am-6pm, Sun 10am-5pm*

American Express
139 Princes Street, Edinburgh
☎ *1, 3, 3A, 4, 5, 7, 8, 10, 11, 12, 14, 15, 15A, 16, 17, 19, 22, 24, 25, 26, 29, 30, 31, 33, 34, 37, 37A, 44, 44A, 49, Airlink100, X26, X31, X37, X47 & all Night Buses*
☎ *(0131) 718 2503*
Website www.americanexpress.com
Open *Mon-Fri 9am-5.30pm, Sat 9am-4pm*

Showers
Public showers are available at the train station.
Shower *£2*
Open *4.15am-1am daily*

Coming & Going
Edinburgh has great transport connections with air, coach and train connections to destinations throughout the UK.

AIR
Edinburgh Airport (☎ *(0131) 333 1000; website www.baa.co.uk/main/airports/edinburgh/*) is a busy airport with flights to most major destinations in the UK and Ireland and major European cities. It is served by major airlines as well as cut prices carriers like easyJet and Ryanair.

The airport is located around 11km west of the city centre and Lothian Buses route 100 makes the 25-minute journey between the airport and Waverley Bridge in the city centre every 10-30 minutes. The one-way fare is £3.40.

Glasgow's two airports are also nearby and are an alternative gateway for people travelling to Edinburgh.

BUS
Express coaches arrive at the coach station on St Andrews Square. National Express (☎ *0870 580 8080; website www.nationalexpress.co.uk*) has coaches to London and other destinations in England and Scottish Citylink (☎ *08705 50 50 50; website www.citylink.co.uk*) have coaches to places in Scotland. The cheapest option is buses run by Megabus (*website www.megabus.com*), which go to Dundee, Glasgow, Perth and St Andrews. Megabus fares start at £1 (plus 50p booking fee).

HITCHHIKING

It's not too difficult to get a lift out of Edinburgh but you'll need to take a bus to the outer suburbs to get to the best hitching spots.

The A1 is the main road to Berwick-upon-Tweed, Durham, Leeds, Newcastle and York. Many hitchers take buses 15 26 40 44 44A X26 X44 N26 N44 to Musselburgh and try their luck there but there is still a lot of local traffic here and it may be better to take bus 15 26 X44 N44 a little farther to Tranent and try your luck on the A1 roundabout where there is more long distance traffic. Also the roundabout slows the traffic down making it safer for cars to stop for you.

If you're heading to most other destinations in England take bus 4 11 15 32 32A N27 to Fairmilehead and try your luck on the A702. The A702 passes Biggar and then joins the M74, which becomes the M6 after passing Carlisle. This is the best route if you're headed for Liverpool, Manchester, Stoke-on-Trent, Birmingham, Oxford or London.

Hitchers heading north to Perth, Aberdeen and the Highlands will want to take the A90/M90. Take bus 18 to the corner of Maybury and Queensferry Roads and stick your thumb out on Queensferry Road (the A90).

TRAIN

Edinburgh's main station is Waverley Station, which is right in the city centre near Waverley Bridge. From here trains go to England and most parts of Scotland. Haymarket Station is a couple of kilometres west of the centre and it has trains to Glasgow and southwest Scotland.

Local Transport

Edinburgh's transport network is made up of buses operated by First Edinburgh (☎ *(08708) 727 271; website www.firstgroup.com*) and Lothian Buses (☎ *(0131) 555 6363; website www.lothianbuses.co.uk*) although Lothian Buses offer the most extensive route network. Fares range from 80p to £1 per trip. A one-week RideCard costs £12 and gives you unlimited transport on Lothian Buses. Lothian Buses

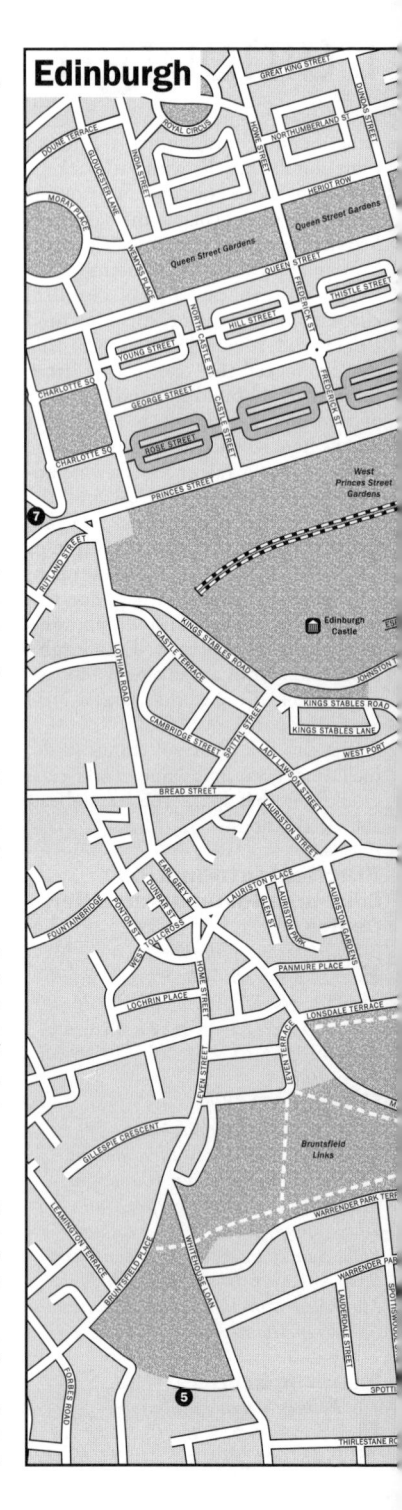

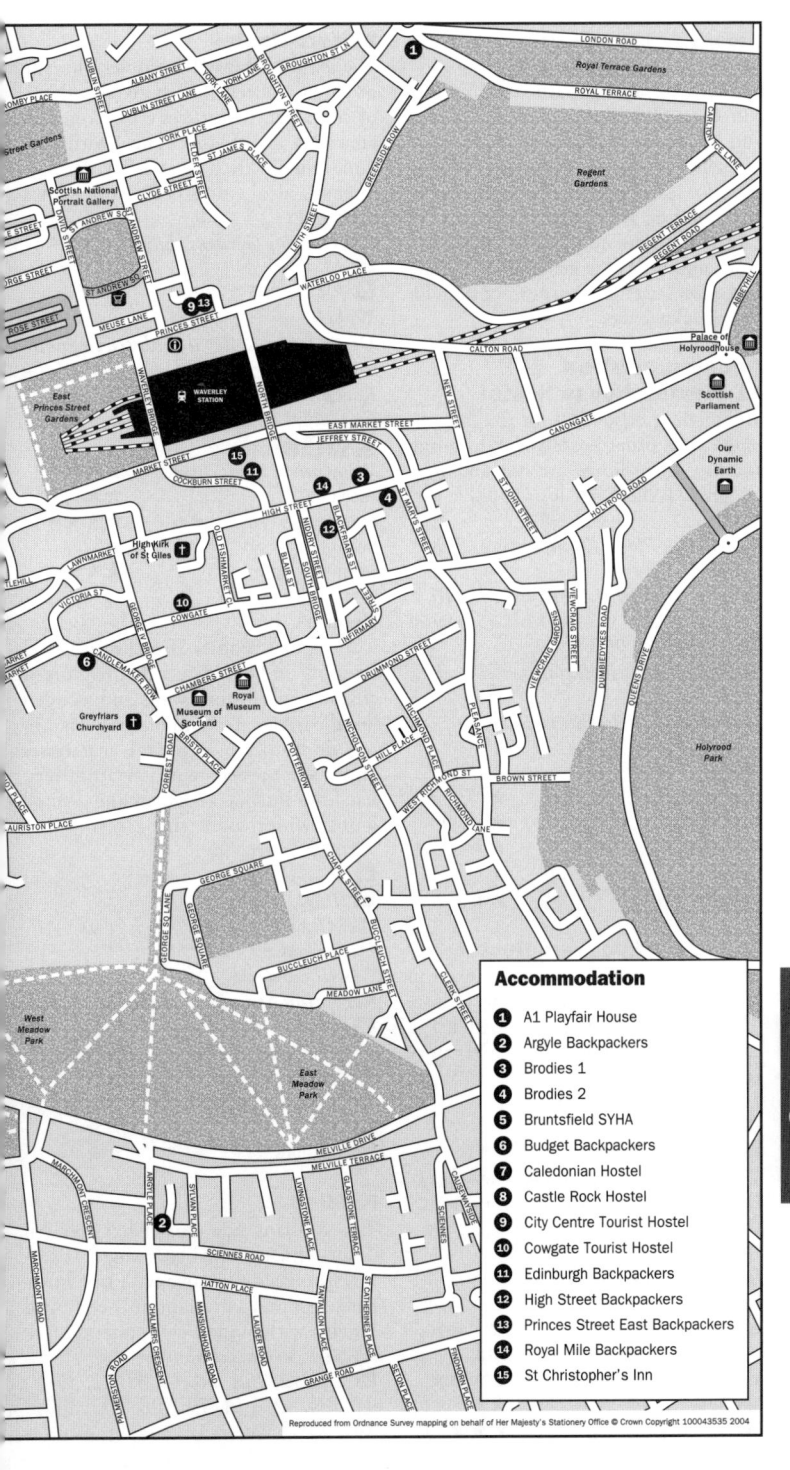

Accommodation

1. A1 Playfair House
2. Argyle Backpackers
3. Brodies 1
4. Brodies 2
5. Bruntsfield SYHA
6. Budget Backpackers
7. Caledonian Hostel
8. Castle Rock Hostel
9. City Centre Tourist Hostel
10. Cowgate Tourist Hostel
11. Edinburgh Backpackers
12. High Street Backpackers
13. Princes Street East Backpackers
14. Royal Mile Backpackers
15. St Christopher's Inn

also sell a CitySingle ticket, which is a carnet of 20 tickets for £18.

There are also suburban trains that run every 30 minutes during the day and hourly during the evening and on weekends. This is comprised of long distance trains passing through the city and stopping at local stations so it's not a real suburban rail system like Glasgow's and buses are generally a cheaper and more useful transport option for most backpackers.

Accommodation
A1 Playfair House Hostel
This mangy hostel is a bit rough compared with other hostels in Edinburgh and the furnishings are old and mismatched. It has a TV lounge and a tiny kitchen.
8 Blenheim Place, Royal Terrace, Edinburgh
🚌 *1, 4, 5, 7, 10, 12, 14, 15, 15A, 16, 19, 22, 25, 26, 34, 44, 44A, 45, 49, 64*
☎ *(0131) 478 0007*
Website *www.a1-playfairhousehostel.co.uk*
Dorm bed *£11-14.50;* **twin room** *£38*
TV K

Maintenance & cleanliness	★
Facilities	★
Atmosphere & character	★★
Security	★
Overall rating	★½

Argyle Backpackers Hostel
Arglye Backpackers is a nice hostel in Marchmont south of the city centre that has a big Internet room with a TV, plus two good kitchens, a conservatory and a small back yard.
14 Argyle Place, Edinburgh
🚌 *40, 41, 41A*
☎ *(0131) 667 9991*
Website *www.argyle-backpackers.co.uk*
Dorm bed *£15;* **double/twin room** *£40*
Credit cards *MC, Visa*
Reception open *9am-11pm daily*
TV K

Maintenance & cleanliness	★★★½
Facilities	★★
Atmosphere & character	★★★★
Security	★★½
Overall rating	★★★

Belford Hostel
The Belford Hostel occupies the site of an old church, which gives it plenty of character. It features a big common area with a bar (3am licence) with pool table plus a kitchen and TV lounge. There is also a nice courtyard with a barbecue.
6-8 Douglas Gardens, Edinburgh
🚌 *13*
☎ *(0131) 225 6209*
Website *www.hoppo.com*
Dorm bed *£10-17;* **double/twin room** *£30-52*
Reception open *Mon-Thu 8am-3am; Fri-Sat 24 hours; Sun 8am-3am*
TV K L B

Maintenance & cleanliness	★★★½
Facilities	★★
Atmosphere & character	★★★★½
Security	★
Overall rating	★★★

Brodies 1
The original Brodies Hostel is in an old building on High Street that has lots of character with stone walls and wooden floorboards. Accommodation is in big dormitories with real mattresses and made up beds with tartan duvets. Facilities include a kitchen and a small lounge with free Internet access.
12 High Street, Edinburgh
🚌 *35, 64*
☎ *(0131) 556 6770*
Website *www.brodieshostels.co.uk*
Dorm bed *£9.50-18.50*
Credit cards *MC, Visa*
Reception open *7am-midnight*
K

Maintenance & cleanliness	★★★
Facilities	★★½
Atmosphere & character	★★★★½
Security	★★
Overall rating	★★★

Brodies 2
This brilliant new hostel has modern décor with top quality fittings. It features a nice lounge area with free Internet access and a brilliant fully equipped kitchen with brand new appliances.
93 High Street, Edinburgh
🚌 *1, 3, 12, 15A, 26, 30, 31, 32, 35, 37, 37A, 42, 44A, 49, X26, X31, X37, X47, N26, N30, N37, N44*

☎ *(0131) 556 2223*
Website *www.brodieshostels.co.uk*
Dorm bed *£10.50-15;* ***double room***
£35-45
Credit cards *MC, Visa*
Reception open *7am-midnight*
🆂 🅺 🅻

Maintenance & cleanliness	★★★★★
Facilities	★★★☆
Atmosphere & character	★★★★
Security	★★☆
Overall rating	★★★★

Bruntsfield SYHA

The Bruntsfield SYHA is in a couple of terrace houses facing a park. It features a TV lounge with Internet access, a pool table, a big kitchen and dining room plus a nice backyard with a barbecue. Most dorms have six beds and the hostel also has wireless Internet access.
7 Bruntsfield Crescent, Edinburgh
🚌 *11, 15, 16, 17*
☎ *0870 004 1114*
Website *www.syha.org.uk*
Dorm bed *£14-17.50 (£13-16.50 HI/SYHA)*
Credit cards *MC, Visa*
Reception open *24 hours*
📺 🅺 🅻

Maintenance & cleanliness	★★★★☆
Facilities	★★
Atmosphere & character	★★★☆
Security	★★★★☆
Overall rating	★★★

Budget Backpackers

This hostel is a former block of flats and has a bathroom and small kitchen for each two rooms. It is a freshly painted place with a small TV lounge and new furnishings.
15 Cowgatehead, Edinburgh
🚌 *2*
☎ *(0131) 226 6351*
Website *www.budgetbackpackers.com*
Dorm bed *£10-20;* ***double/twin room***
£32-54
Credit cards *MC, Visa*
Reception open *8am-8pm daily*
🔒 📺 🅺 🅻

Maintenance & cleanliness	★★★
Facilities	★★☆
Atmosphere & character	★★★☆
Security	★★★
Overall rating	★★★☆

Caledonian Hostel

This big hostel features a brilliant bar with a pool table and cheap drinks, an Internet lounge and a kitchen with a big dining room. Accommodation is in big bright – but basic – dorms. It's a bit rough around the edges but improvements are being made to the place.
3 Queensferry Street, Edinburgh
🚌 *1, 4, 10, 11, 12, 13, 15A, 16, 17, 19, 22, 24, 25, 26, 28, 30, 31, 33, 34, 35, 36, 37, 37A, 41, 44, 44A, X26, X31, X37, X47, N16, N22, N25, N26, N30, N33, N37, N44*
☎ *(0131) 226 2939*
Dorm bed *£10-15;* ***double/twin room***
£32-34
Credit cards *MC, Visa*
Reception open *24 hours*
📺 🅺 🅻 ℹ

Maintenance & cleanliness	★★
Facilities	★★☆
Atmosphere & character	★★★★
Security	★★★☆
Overall rating	★★★☆

Castle Rock Hostel

Castle Rock is a great hostel near the castle. Facilities include a cinema-style TV lounge, a lounge with a pool table and a 'posh' lounge with a piano and fireplace. There's also a kitchen and a dining area with a big banquet table. It has big spacious dorms with high ceilings that range from four to 14 beds.
15 Johnstone Terrace, Edinburgh
🚌 *28*
☎ *(0131) 225 9666*
Website *www.scotlands-top-hostels.com*
Dorm bed *£12-15;* ***double room***
£40-45
Credit cards *Amex, Diners, MC, Visa*
Reception open *24 hours*
📺 🅺

Maintenance & cleanliness	★★★☆
Facilities	★★
Atmosphere & character	★★★★★☆
Security	★★
Overall rating	★★★

City Centre Tourist Hostel

This clean and well-maintained hostel is in the same building as Princes Street East Backpackers. It has a small kitchen with brand new appliances and the dorms have new beds. The largest dorm has 10 beds but most have four beds.

5 West Register Street, Edinburgh
🚌 *1, 3, 3A, 4, 5, 7, 8, 10, 11, 12, 14, 15, 15A, 16, 17, 19, 22, 24, 25, 26, 29, 30, 31, 33, 34, 37, 37A, 44, 44A, 49, Airlink100, X26, X31, X37, X47 & all Night Buses*
☎ *(0131) 556 8070*
Website *www.scotland-hostels.com*
Dorm bed *£12-18*
Reception open *24 hours*
📺 🔑

Maintenance & cleanliness	★★★★★
Facilities	★☆
Atmosphere & character	★★★★½
Security	★★☆
Overall rating	★★★★½

Cowgate Tourist Hostel

This hostel is made up of self-contained apartments, each with its own bathroom, kitchen and a small lounge. The outside and corridors look a little run down but inside the apartments are newly renovated and very well maintained.

96-112 Cowgate, Edinburgh
☎ *(0131) 226 2153*
Dorm bed *£12-17 (£11-16 VIP);* **twin room** *£30-42 (£28-40 VIP)*
Credit cards *MC, Visa*
Reception open *8am-11pm daily*
📺 🔑

Maintenance & cleanliness	★★★★
Facilities	★★☆
Atmosphere & character	★★☆
Security	★★☆
Overall rating	★★★☆

Edinburgh Backpackers

This good hostel features a games room with pool table, a TV lounge with Internet access and a small kitchen.

65 Cockburn Street, Edinburgh
🚌 *35, 64*
☎ *(0131) 220 1717*
Dorm bed *£13.40-19.50;* **double/twin room** *£40-50*
Credit cards *MC, Visa*
Reception open *24 hours*
📺 🔑

Maintenance & cleanliness	★★★★½
Facilities	★★
Atmosphere & character	★★★
Security	★★★½
Overall rating	★★★

Eglinton SYHA

This youth hostel is a lovely old building with lots of charm. It has several lounges including a TV lounge with a log fire and another with Internet access. There's also a nice big kitchen. The hostel also has WiFi Internet access.

8 Eglinton Crescent, Edinburgh
🚌 *13*
☎ *0870 004 1116*
Dorm bed *£14-17.50 (£13-16.50 HI/SYHA)*
Credit cards *JCB, MC, Visa*
Reception open *7am-midnight*
📺 🔑

Maintenance & cleanliness	★★★★
Facilities	★★
Atmosphere & character	★★★½
Security	★★
Overall rating	★★★

Globetrotters Inn

Globetrotters Inn is an unusual hostel that has its own bizarre way of doing things. It is a relatively clean place with very good facilities that include a bar, TV lounges, pool tables, Internet access, spa, sauna and a gym. The dormitories are very well laid out with well-designed bunks that feature individual lights and curtains. However the kitchen has no oven and only four hobs for around 400 people, although there is a huge bank of 16 microwaves. Also you have to pay for things inside the hostel using a smart card, which is bloody annoying when you have to run to the reception to top up your card just so you can buy another drink from the bar. It is miles from the centre of Edinburgh (a good 20 minute drive), but there's a free shuttle bus into town and the location ensures that there are plenty of parking spaces making it a good option for travellers with cars.

Marine Drive, Cramond Foreshore, Edinburgh
🚌 *42*
☎ *(0131) 336 4934*
Website *www.globetrotterinns.com*
Dorm bed *£15-17;* **double/twin room** *£42; prices include breakfast*
Credit cards *MC, Visa*
Reception open *24 hours*
🚌 ♿ 📺 🔑

Maintenance & cleanliness	★★★★
Facilities	★★★★

Atmosphere & character	★
Security	★★★★½
Overall rating	★★★½

High Street Backpackers

This cosy hostel off High Street has a snug lounge with Internet access near the reception, a bigger lounge downstairs with a pool table and also a large kitchen. Accommodation is in plain dormitories, but overall the hostel has a good atmosphere.

8 Blackfriars Street, Edinburgh
🚌 *3, 3A, 5, 7, 8, 14, 29, 30, 31, 33, 35, 37, 37A, 49, 64, X31, X37, X47, N30, N33, N37*
☎ *(0131) 557 3984*
Website *www.scotlands-top-hostels.com*
Dorm bed *£12-15*
Credit cards *Amex, Diners, MC, Visa*
Reception open *24 hours*

Maintenance & cleanliness	★★½
Facilities	★
Atmosphere & character	★★★★½
Security	★½
Overall rating	★★★½

Highlander Backpackers

This good value hostel caters mostly to long-term guests. It has a TV lounge and a small, but nice, kitchen.

22 Annandale Street, Edinburgh
🚌 *7, 10, 12, 13, 14, 16, 22, 25, 49*
☎ *0800 073 0558*
Website *www.highlanderbackpackers.com*
Dorm bed *£10-12*
Credit cards *MC, Visa*
Reception open *9am-11.30pm daily*

Maintenance & cleanliness	★★½
Facilities	★
Atmosphere & character	★★★★
Security	★½
Overall rating	★★★½

Princes Street East Backpackers

This grungy hostel has a funky party atmosphere and is painted with lots of murals. Common areas include the 'cave' lounge with table football, a TV room and a dining room with Internet access.

5 West Register Street, Edinburgh
🚌 *1, 3, 3A, 4, 5, 7, 8, 10, 11, 12, 14, 15, 15A, 16, 17, 19, 22, 24, 25, 26, 29, 30, 31, 33, 34, 37, 37A, 44, 44A, 49, Airlink100, X26, X31, X37, X47 & all Night Buses*
☎ *(0131) 556 6894*
Website *www.edinburghbackpackers.com*
Dorm bed *£11-14;* **double/twin room** *£30-40*
Credit cards *MC, Visa*
Reception open *24 hours*

Maintenance & cleanliness	★
Facilities	★★½
Atmosphere & character	★★★★★
Security	★★★★½
Overall rating	★★★½

Royal Mile Backpackers

This small 38-bed hostel has a brilliant location on the Royal Mile. It has neat and tidy dorms plus a small lounge at the reception with a fireplace. There is also a tiny kitchen (just a toaster, microwave and a fridge) and a little dining room.

105 High Street, Edinburgh
🚌 *3, 3A, 5, 7, 8, 14, 29, 30, 31, 33, 35, 37, 37A, 49, 64, X31, X37, X47, N30, N33, N37*
☎ *(0131) 557 6120*
Website *www.scotlands-top-hostels.com*
Dorm bed *£12-13.50*
Credit cards *Amex, Diners, MC, Visa*
Reception open *7am-3am daily*

Maintenance & cleanliness	★★★½
Facilities	★
Atmosphere & character	★★★★
Security	★★
Overall rating	★★★

St Christopher's Inn

St Christopher's is a good hostel in the old town close to Waverley Station. It is located above two bars and features a good chill out lounge with TV and Internet access, but there is no kitchen. The biggest dormitory has 10 beds but most have four beds.

9-13 Market Street, Edinburgh
🚌 *64* 🚇 *Waverley*
☎ *(020) 7407 1856*
Website *www.st-christophers.co.uk*
Dorm bed *£11-17.50 (£9.90-15.75 ISIC/VIP);* **double/twin room** *£42-46 (£37.80-41.40 ISIC/VIP); prices*

include breakfast
Credit cards *MC, Visa*
Reception open *24 hours*

Maintenance & cleanliness	★★★★☆
Facilities	★★☆
Atmosphere & character	★★★☆
Security	★★★★☆
Overall rating	★★★

West End Hostel

This is a clean hostel with limited, but well maintained, facilities that include a TV lounge with Internet access and a tiny, but fully equipped, kitchen. The dorms are cramped but they have new beds.
3 Clifton Terrace, Edinburgh
2, 3, 3A, 4, 12, 25, 26, 31, 33, 44, 44A Haymarket
(0131) 441 6628
Website *www.edinburghcitycentre hostels.co.uk*
Dorm bed *£12;* ***double/twin room*** *£30*
Credit cards *MC, Visa (10% charge)*
Reception open *24 hours*

Maintenance & cleanliness	★★★★☆
Facilities	★
Atmosphere & character	★★☆
Security	★★
Overall rating	★★☆

Eating & Drinking

Edinburgh boasts a good choice of restaurants and there is a good range of cheap dining options with some pubs running backpacker and student specials offering cheap food in the hope that it will draw in young people who will hang around to drink the place dry.

The Sainsbury's supermarket on St Andrew's Square is the best spot to stock up on groceries.

Festivals

Edinburgh is famous for its festivals (*website www.edinburghfestivals.com*), which range from the pomp and splendour of the Military Tattoo to the world's greatest arts festival. August is the main festival month and during this time it can be difficult and expensive to find a place to stay.

Edinburgh International Festival

Edinburgh's International Festival features world-class music, opera, theatre and dance performances. This is the original festival and the most sophisticated.
14 Aug-3 Sep 2005
The Hub, Castlehill, Edinburgh
(0131) 473 2001
Website *www.eif.co.uk*
There are some free events but most cost between £6 and £40

Edinburgh Festival Fringe

The Festival Fringe originally started as an offshoot of the International Festival is now the biggest and most popular festival and it features a programme to suit every conceivable taste and persuasion. This festival has a more youthful orientation that the international festival and many of the events are cheaper.
7-29 August 2005
Festival Office, 180 High Street, Edinburgh
(0131) 226 0026
Website *www.edfringe.com*

Edinburgh Military Tattoo

Set against the stunning backdrop of Edinburgh Castle, this unique Scottish event is one of the finest exhibitions of military pomp and splendour in the world. The event features military bands from around the world but the kilted Massed Military Bands from the Scottish Regiments with their blaring bagpipes always steal the show.
5-27 Aug 2005
The Tattoo Office, 32 Market Street, Edinburgh
(0131) 225 1188)
Website *www.edinburgh-tattoo.co.uk*
Tickets £9-28.50.

Hogmanay

New Year's Eve in Scotland is steeped in tradition and Edinburgh has the biggest New Year's Eve party you're likely to ever find. The main street party is only accessible by a free pass that is issued by a ballot system with 75% of tickets going to Edinburgh residents. If you have missed the deadline for the free pass, you will need to pay £15 to

join the First Foot Club, whose membership benefits include a pass.
31 Dec-1 Jan
☎ *(0131) 473 2056*
Website *www.edinburghshogmanay.org*

Sights
THE OLD TOWN & ROYAL MILE
The Old Town comprises the bulk of its tourist sights, most of which are located along the Royal Mile. The Royal Mile is the 1.7km long thoroughfare that connects Edinburgh Castle with the Palace of Holyroodhouse. It consists of five connected streets – Castlehill, Lawnmarket, High Street, Canongate and Abbey Street. These streets and the lanes that run off them have a rich history and there are many walking tours that explore the Royal Mile's history in depth.

Arthur's Seat
This rocky outcrop in Holyrood Park offers a spectacular vantage point with great views of Edinburgh and as far a field as Fife and the Trossachs. Arthur's Seat is around a 45-minute walk from the Palace of Holyroodhouse.
Queens Drive, Edinburgh

Edinburgh Castle
Edinburgh's big attraction is the castle that dominates the city. Like many castles, it was built over many centuries. St Margaret's Chapel, the oldest part of Edinburgh Castle, dates from the 12th century, and the Great Hall and the Half Moon Battery were built in the 16th century. The castle features Scotland's crown jewels, the Stone of Destiny (also known as the Stone of Scone) and it is also home to the National War Museum of Scotland.
Castle Hill, Edinburgh
🚌 *23, 27, 28, 35, 41, 42, 45*
☎ *(0131) 225 9846*
Website *www.historic-scotland.gov.uk*
Admission *£9.50 (£7 students)*
Open *Jan-Mar 9.30am-5pm daily (last entry 4.15pm); Apr-Oct 9.30am-6pm daily (last entry 5.15pm); Nov-Dec 9.30am-5pm daily (last entry 4.15pm)*

Edinburgh Dungeon
Edinburgh's version of London's Dungeon uses actors, rides and exhibits to portray Scotland's bloody past.
31 Market Street, Edinburgh
🚌 *64*
☎ *(0131) 240 1000*
Website *www.thedungeons.com*
Admission *£9.95*
Open *Jan-Mar Mon-Fri 11am-4pm, Sat-Sun 10.30am-4.30pm; Apr-Jun 10am-5pm daily; Jul-Aug 10am-7pm daily; Sep-Oct 10am-5pm daily; Nov-Dec Mon-Fri 11am-4pm, Sat-Sun 10.30am-4.30pm*

Gladstone's Land
The National Trust for Scotland has restored this 17th century merchant's house on the Royal Mile to show how Edinburgh's wealthy lived almost 400 years ago.
477B Lawnmarket, Edinburgh
🚌 *23, 27, 28, 35, 41, 42, 45*
☎ *(0131) 226 4851*
Website *www.nts.org.uk*
Admission *£5 (£3.75 HI/SYHA)*
Open *Apr-Oct Mon-Sat 10am-5pm, Sun 2pm-5pm*

Greyfriar's Churchyard
The 17th century Grey Friar's Kirk is famous for its cemetery, which is the final resting place for many notable Scots. Its claim to fame, however, is a loyal Skye terrier named Bobby whose life-size statue stands guard outside the churchyard.

This loyal dog belonged to a farmer named Jock Gray who is buried in the churchyard. For 14 years following his master's death in 1858 Bobby refused to leave his masters' grave except to be fed by locals at the Grassmarket Inn where Jock Gray regularly dined.

The story of Greyfriars' Bobby was immortalised by a children's book written by American author Eleanor Atkinson, which was later made into a 1961 Disney film.
Candlemakers' Row, Edinburgh
🚌 *2*

High Kirk of St Giles
This church was originally built in the 12th century but was burnt down by the English in 1385. It was subsequently rebuilt with the distinctive crowned steeple going up in 1495 and extensive

additions were built in the 19th century. In 1911 the Knights of the Thistle built the most recent addition, a chapel honouring their Order. John Knox was a minister here during the Reformation and the church has played a central role in Scottish history.
Lawnmarket, Edinburgh
🚌 *23, 27, 28, 35, 41, 42, 45*
☎ *(0131) 225 4363.*

Museum of Edinburgh

This museum, housed in a 16th century mansion, has exhibits on local history and industries that have played an important role in the city's development. The more important exhibits include the original National Covenant dating from 1638 and the Greyfriars' Bobby's collar and bowl.
142 Canongate, Edinburgh
🚌 *35*
☎ *(0131) 529 4143*
Admission *free*
Open *Mon-Sat 10am-5pm; during Edinburgh Festival Mon-Sat 10am-5pm, Sun 2pm-5pm.*

Museum of Scotland & the Royal Museum

This striking new museum chronicles Scottish history with a rich collection of over 10,000 artefacts. The adjoining Royal Museum features exhibits of a more international nature including natural history displays.
Chambers Street, Edinburgh
🚌 *3, 7, 8, 14, 21, 30, 31, 33, 36, 69, 87*
☎ *(0131) 220 4819*
Website *www.nms.ac.uk*
Admission *free*
Open *Mon 10am-5pm, Tue 10am-8pm, Wed-Sat 10am-5pm, Sun noon-5pm.*

National Gallery of Scotland

This gallery houses Scotland's best collection of European paintings with works that span from the Renaissance to Impressionism. It also boats the world's largest collection of Scottish paintings including the works of McTaggart, Raeburn, Ramsay and Wilkie.
The Mound, Edinburgh
🚌 *23, 27, 28, 42, 45*
☎ *(0131) 624 6200*
Website *www.nationalgalleries.org*
Admission *free*
Open *Mon 10am-5pm, Tue 10am-8pm, Wed-Sat 10am-5pm, Sun noon-5pm.*

National Library of Scotland

Scotland's largest library is home to rare documents that include the Gutenburg Bible and Blind Harry's the *Wallace*, both dating from the 15th century as well as Mary, Queen of Scots' last letter.
George IV Bridge, Edinburgh
🚌 *23, 27, 35, 41, 42, 45*
☎ *(0131) 226 4531*
Website *www.nls.uk*
Admission *free*
Exhibition hall open Jun-Oct Mon-Sat 10am-5pm, Sun 2pm-5pm; during Edinburgh Festival Mon-Fri 10am-8pm, Sat 10am-5pm, Sun 2pm-5pm.

Our Dynamic Earth

This new natural history museum features user-friendly exhibits that show the story of our planet focussing on how life, and the continents themselves, has evolved since the Big Bang. The museum also examines different environments such as the oceans, Polar Regions and the tropics.
Holyrood Road, Edinburgh
🚌 *35, Mac60*
☎ *(0131) 550 7800*
Website *www.dynamicearth.co.uk*
Admission *£8.95 (£6.50 students)*
Open *Jan-Mar Wed-Sun 10am-5pm (last entry 3.50pm); Apr-Oct 10am-5pm daily (last entry 3.50pm); Nov-Dec Wed-Sun 10am-5pm (last entry 3.50pm)*

Palace of Holyroodhouse

Queen Elizabeth II's official Scottish residence is located at the end of the Royal Mile under the shadow of Arthur's Seat. This baroque palace has a rich history and many British and Scottish monarchs have lived here including Mary, Queen of Scots, whose secretary David Rizzio was murdered here in the 16th century. The palace remains the hub of Royal events in Scotland and the Queen is normally in residence from late June to early July when she carries out a variety of official engagements. For visitors, the palace's main attrac-

tions include the State Apartments; Mary, Queen of Scots' Chambers; the Queen's Gallery and the palace's largest room, the Great Gallery.
Royal Mile, Edinburgh
🚌 35
☎ (0131) 557 5256
Website *www.royal.gov.uk*
Admission *Palace £8.80 (£6.50 students); Queen's Gallery £4 (£3 students); Palace & Queen's Gallery £11 (£9 students)*
Open *Jan-Mar 9.30am-4.30pm daily (last entry 3.45pm); Apr-Oct 9.30am-6pm daily (last entry 5.15pm); Nov-Dec 9.30am-4.30pm daily (last entry 3.45pm)*

The People's Story Museum
The 16th century Canongate Tolbooth houses a museum about the lives of ordinary people living in Edinburgh from the 18th to the 20th centuries.
163 Canongate, Canongate Tolbooth, Edinburgh
🚌 35
☎ (0131) 529 4057
Admission *free*
Open *Mon-Sat 10am-5pm; during Edinburgh Festival Mon-Sat 10am-5pm, Sun 2pm-5pm*

Scottish Parliament
The Scottish Parliament Visitors' Centre has displays on the history and current role of Scotland's parliament. You can also book tickets here to sit in on chamber sessions.
George IV Bridge, Edinburgh
🚌 35
☎ (0131) 348 5411
Website *www.scottish.parliament.uk*
Admission *free*
Open *during parliamentary session Mon 10am-5pm, Tue-Thu 9am-5pm, Fri 10am-5pm; during parliamentary recess Mon-Fri 10am-5pm*

The Writers' Museum
This museum focuses on the life and works of Scottish writers with an emphasis on the country's three leading literary figures: Robert Burns, Sir Walter Scott and Robert Louis Stephenson.
Lady Stairs Close, Lawnmarket, Edinburgh
🚌 23, 27, 28, 35, 41, 42, 45
☎ (0131) 529 7868
Admission *free*
Open *Mon-Sat 10am-5pm; during Edinburgh Festival Mon-Sat 10am-5pm, Sun 2pm-5pm*

THE NEW TOWN
In contrast to the narrow medieval streets of the Old Town, Edinburgh's New Town features wide, carefully planned streets, which were popular with the city's well-heeled residents in Georgian times. Edinburgh's main shopping street – Princes Street – runs along the southern edge of the New Town.

Georgian House
This restored home in Edinburgh's New Town features furnishings from the 18th century showing how the well off lived during the late 18th century.
7 Charlotte Square, Edinburgh
🚌 13, 19, 36, 37, 37A, 41
☎ (0131) 226 3318
Admission *£5*
Open *Mar 11am-3pm daily; Apr-Oct 10am-5pm daily; Nov 11am-3pm daily*

Scottish National Portrait Gallery
This art gallery features portraits of Scottish historical figures that range from criminals to royalty. Although many of the paintings are by Scots, there are also works by Dalí, Gainsborough, Matisse and Picasso.
1 Queen Street, Edinburgh
☎ (0131) 623 7126
Website *www.nationalgalleries.org*
Admission *free, charge for temporary exhibits*
Open *Mon-Wed 10am-5pm, Thu 10am-7pm, Fri-Sun 10am-5pm*

Walter Scott Monument
This ornate Gothic monument in Princes Street Gardens offers superb views of the city. The monument features a statue of Sir Walter Scott (1771-1832), a prominent author who, among many other novels, wrote *Rob Roy*. He took a great interest in promoting Scottish culture and is responsible for rediscovering the Scottish crown and sceptre in Edinburgh Castle, for retaining

Scotland's own banknotes and for promoting Highland clan tartans.
Princes Street, Edinburgh
🚍 *1, 3, 3A, 4, 8, 10, 11, 12, 15, 15A, 16, 17, 19, 22, 23, 24, 25, 26, 27, 28, 29, 30, 31, 33, 34, 37, 37A, 41 42 44, 44A, 45, X26, X31, X37, X47 and all Night Buses*
Admission *free*

OTHER AREAS
Dean Gallery
Adjoining the Scottish National Gallery of Modern Art, the Dean Gallery features exhibits of Dada and Surrealist art and a large collection of Sir Eduardo Paolozzi's sculptures.
73 Belford Road, Edinburgh
🚍 *3, 4, 13, 30, 31, 32, 33, 36, 40, 41, 43, 44, 52, 69, 82*
☎ *(0131) 624 6200*
Website *www.nationalgalleries.org*
Admission *free*
Open *Mon 10am-5pm, Tue 10am-8pm, Wed-Sat 10am-5pm, Sun noon-5pm*

Edinburgh Zoo
The zoo is home to over 1000 animals and it has the world's largest penguin pool.
Murrayfield Road, Edinburgh
🚍 *12, 26, 31*
☎ *(0131) 314 0320*
Website *www.edinburghzoo.org.uk*
Admission *£8.50 ($6.50 students)*
Open *Jan-Feb 9am-4.30pm daily; Mar 9am-5pm daily; Apr-Sep 9am-6pm daily; Oct 9am-5pm daily; Nov-Dec 9am-4.30pm daily*

Royal Botanic Gardens
Edinburgh's botanic gardens feature plants from around the world and Britain's largest palm house.
20a Inverleith Row, Edinburgh
🚍 *8, 17, 23, 27*
☎ *(0131) 248 2901*
Website *www.rbge.org.uk*
Admission *free*
Open *Jan-Feb 10am-4pm daily; Mar 10am-6pm daily; Apr-Sep 10am-7pm daily; Oct 10am-6pm daily; Nov-Dec 10am-4pm daily*

Royal Yacht Britannia
Located beside the Ocean Terminal shopping complex at Leith Docks, the *Royal Yacht Britannia* was used by the royal family between 1953 and 1997. During its service, the *Royal Yacht Britannia* travelled over 1½ million kilometres on official state visits and royal holidays before making itself home in Edinburgh.
Ocean Terminal, Leith, Edinburgh
🚍 *1, 11, 22, 34, 35, 36*
☎ *(0131) 555 5566*
Website *www.royalyachtbritannia.co.uk*
Admission *£8.50 (£4.50 students)*
Open *Jan-Mar 10am-3.30pm daily; Apr-Sep 9.30am-4.30pm daily; Oct-Dec 10am-3.30pm daily*

Scottish National Gallery of Modern Art
This gallery features an extensive collection of 20th century art including works by Bacon, Hockney, Lichtenstein, Matisse, Picasso and Warhol.
75 Belford Road, Edinburgh
🚍 *3, 4, 13, 30, 31, 32, 33, 36, 40, 41, 43, 44, 52, 69, 82*
☎ *(0131) 624 6200*
Website *www.nationalgalleries.org*
Admission *free*
Open *Mon 10am-5pm, Tue 10am-8pm, Wed-Sat 10am-5pm, Sun noon-5pm*

Glasgow & Strathclyde

The Strathclyde region includes Glasgow and the surrounding area. Although Glasgow dominates the region, there is a lot more to Clydesdale than Scotland's biggest city. Other attractions include Ayrshire and the New Lanark World Heritage Site.

Glasgow

Once known as the 'second city of the Empire', Glasgow is Scotland's largest (and Britain's second largest) city. It may not be quite as impressive or as popular with tourists as Edinburgh, less than an hour to the east; but there are plenty of top attractions. It is also home to Scotland's best nightlife and the best shopping in Britain outside of London.

Glasgow is a popular destination with architecture buffs that come here to see the uniquely Glaswegian art nouveau creations of Charles Rennie Mackintosh.

Practical Information
Glasgow Tourist Information Centre
11 George Square, Glasgow
☎ *(0141) 204 4400*
Website *www.glasgowguide.co.uk*
Open *Jan-Jun Mon-Sat 9am-7pm, Sun 10am-6pm; Jul-Aug Mon-Sat 9am-8pm, Sun 10am-6pm; Sep-Dec Mon-Sat 9am-7pm, Sun 10am-6pm*

American Express
115 Hope Street, Glasgow
☎ *(0141) 222 1401*
Open *Mon-Fri 8.30am-5.30pm, Sat 9am-noon*

INTERNET ACCESS
easyInternetcafé
57-61 St Vincent Street, Glasgow
Ⓢ *Buchanan Street* Ⓜ *Central, Queen Street*
☎ *(0141) 222 2365*
Website *www.easyinternetcafe.com*
Open *Mon-Fri 7am-10pm, Sat-Sun 8am-9pm*

Coming & Going
AIR
Two airports serve Glasgow: Glasgow Airport in Paisley 13km west of the city centre and Prestwick Airport in Ayrshire 48km south of Glasgow. Edinburgh airport is also less than an hour away.

Glasgow Airport
Most flights use the more conveniently located Glasgow airport (☎ *(0141) 887 1111;* ***website*** *www.baa.co.uk/main/airports/glasgow/*), which is by far the busier of the two airports. It handles trans-Atlantic flights to Chicago, New York and Toronto and more than 200 flights each week to London. All the big, established airlines use this airport.

Paisley Gilmour Street is the closest train station to the airport. At Gilmour Street station you can transfer to a connecting bus to the airport. You can buy a ticket to Glasgow Airport from any train station in Scotland; this ticket will include the connecting bus from Gilmour Street.

The SPT travel centre in the terminal building sells a ticket that combines both the bus to Gilmour Street station and train travel to Central Station. If you want to travel to a different station you will need to hand over your bus ticket at Gilmour Street station and the value of this ticket will be discounted off your train ticket.

Scottish Citylink (☎ *08705 505050;* ***website*** *www.citylink.co.uk*) operates a frequent shuttle bus between the airport and Buchanan Bus Station. Buses run every 10 minutes during peak periods and the 25-minute journey costs £3.30 one-way or £5 return.

Prestwick International Airport
Prestwick Airport (☎ *(01292) 511006;* ***website*** *www.gpia.co.uk*) is a popular airport with charter and budget airlines like Ryanair.

There are direct train connections from Central Station that bring the airport within 45 minutes of central Glasgow. A big advantage of flying into Prestwick is that you can get a 50%

discount off the train fare to anywhere in Scotland if you show your airline ticket when you buy your ticket for the train. This deal is only valid on the same day as your flight.

BUS

Buses depart from Buchanan Bus Station on the corner of North Hannover Street and Killermont Street. There is a frequent bus service that links Central and Queen Street train stations with Buchanan Bus Station.

FERRY

Ferries to Belfast in Northern Ireland depart from several ports close to Glasgow.

The most convenient is the Seacat ferry *(website www.seacat.co.uk)* from Troon, only 30 minutes from central Glasgow and easily accessible by train.

Stena Line ferries (☎ *(08705) 707070; website www.stenaline.com)* sail from Stranraer, which is around two hours south of Glasgow by train, but it is a shorter ferry trip.

P&O Irish Ferries *(website www.poirishsea.com)* is probably the least convenient as the ferries sail from Cairnryan, which is near Stranraer but not accessible by train, to Larne near Belfast.

HITCHHIKING

The M74 is the main road heading south to England. The M74 becomes the M6 after passing Carlisle and you'll want to hitch a ride on this motorway if you're going to Liverpool, Manchester, Stoke-on-Trent, Birmingham, Oxford or London. You can find a good hitching spot close to the city centre at the Carmyle Road entrance to the M74. Take a train to Carmyle and you'll find the motorway entrance just north of the station.

The Bothwell motorway service area is just south of Glasgow and is also a good place to wait for a southbound lift. To get to the services, take the train to Bellshill and walk 2km up Hamilton Road.

The A80/M80 is the main route north. Thumb a lift on this road if you want to go to Stirling, Aberdeen or anywhere in the Highlands. The M80 becomes the A80 at Stepps, north of the city and at this point most of the traffic will be long distance. Take the train to Stepps and then bus 36, X3, X37 or X39 to Crow Wood Golf Club.

If you want to go to Edinburgh, you may want to try hitching on the Glasgow and Edinburgh Road (A8), which later becomes the M8. Take a train to Bredisholm Road and walk south down Langmuir Road until you reach the A8. However Edinburgh and Glasgow are so close and there are frequent and cheap transport connections between the two so it hardly seems worth your while to hitch.

TRAIN

Glasgow has two train stations. Central Station has trains to England and southern Scotland. Queen Street Station has trains to northern Scotland. Trains to Edinburgh leave from both stations.

Local Transport

Glasgow has a good public transport system, operated by Strathclyde Passenger Transport *(SPT;* ☎ *(0141) 332 7133; website www.spt.co.uk)*, which is comprised of buses, ferries, suburban trains and the subway.

BUS

There are a large number of bus routes that are operated by SPT and several private companies. However most travellers find trains and the subway to be an easier way to get around.

FERRY

SPT also operate a couple of ferry services across the Clyde but these are of little use to most travellers. The Renfrew-Yoker ferry crosses the Clyde just west of the city centre and it has been running for over 500 years making it one of Scotland's longest running ferry services. The one-way fare is 90p.

TRAINS & SUBWAY

Glasgow's subway consists of a single circular line that is nicknamed the Clockwork Orange. After London and Budapest, the Glasgow subway is the world's third oldest metro system.

Trains run every five to eight minutes. Because it is a circular system, clockwise trains are referred to as running on the Outer Circle and anti-clockwise trains, the Inner Circle.

A single fare on the subway costs £1, you can also buy a 10-trip ticket for £8 or a 20-trip ticket for £13. A Discovery ticket allows one day unlimited travel for £1.70, but you cannot travel before 9.30am Mon-Sat. Weekly passes (£8) are also available.

A good suburban train network that also has underground stations in the city centre complements the subway. Transfer stations between the subway and suburban train networks are at Partick to the west of the city centre and Buchanan Street subway station, which connects with Queen Street train station at the eastern end of the city. Most travellers will only use the train between stations within the city centre, although there are some handy services such as to Balloch on Loch Lomond and also to Prestwick Airport.

Train fares vary depending on the length of the journey.

TRAVEL PASSES

In addition to individual tickets and passes restricted to a single mode of transport, there are some useful passes that make it easy and affordable to get around Glasgow.

Roundabout

The Roundabout ticket gives you unlimited travel for one day on trains and the subway after 9am Mon-Fri and all day on weekends. Travel is only valid within a limited area, but this covers most of suburban Glasgow including Glasgow Airport. The Roundabout ticket costs £4.50.

Daytripper

The Daytripper is useful if you want to make long daytrips to the surrounding countryside. It allows you to travel as much as you want on most buses, some ferries, on the subway and on trains in a large area that covers Glasgow and the surrounding countryside including Loch Lomond, Ayr and Lanark. It costs £8.50 or £15 for two people and is valid after 9am Mon-Fri and all day on weekends.

ZoneCard

If you're planning on working in Glasgow or staying at least a week, then a ZoneCard is a better idea. These allow unlimited travel on most buses and ferries plus trains and the subway within a specified area and are excellent value. A one-week ZoneCard ranges in price from £12.40 for travel in the two zones that comprise central Glasgow and £44.50 for travel in all zones.

Accommodation
Blue Sky Hostel

This small hostel has facilities that include the usual TV lounge and kitchen. It is a little rough around the edges but it has a good party atmosphere.

65 Berkeley Street, Glasgow
🚇 *Charing Cross*
☎ *(0141) 221 1710*
Website *www.blueskyhostel.com*
Dorm bed £8-12; **twin room** £25-30; *prices include breakfast*

📺 🇰

Maintenance & cleanliness	★★
Facilities	★
Atmosphere & character	★★★★
Security	★★½
Overall rating	★★

Bunkum Backpackers

Bunkum Backpackers is a good mix of comfort and atmosphere, making it a good spot to stay in Glasgow. It is in a lovely old building in a quiet street northwest of the city centre and it has a big TV lounge plus a fully equipped kitchen.

26 Hillhead Street, Glasgow
🚌 *41, 66* 🚇 *Hillhead*
☎ *(0141) 581 4481*
Website *www.bunkumglasgow.co.uk*
Dorm bed £12
Credit cards *MC, Visa*
Reception open *8.30am-10.30pm daily*

📺 🇰

Maintenance & cleanliness	★★★★½
Facilities	★★½
Atmosphere & character	★★★★
Security	★★
Overall rating	★★★

Glasgow

Strathclyde – Glasgow

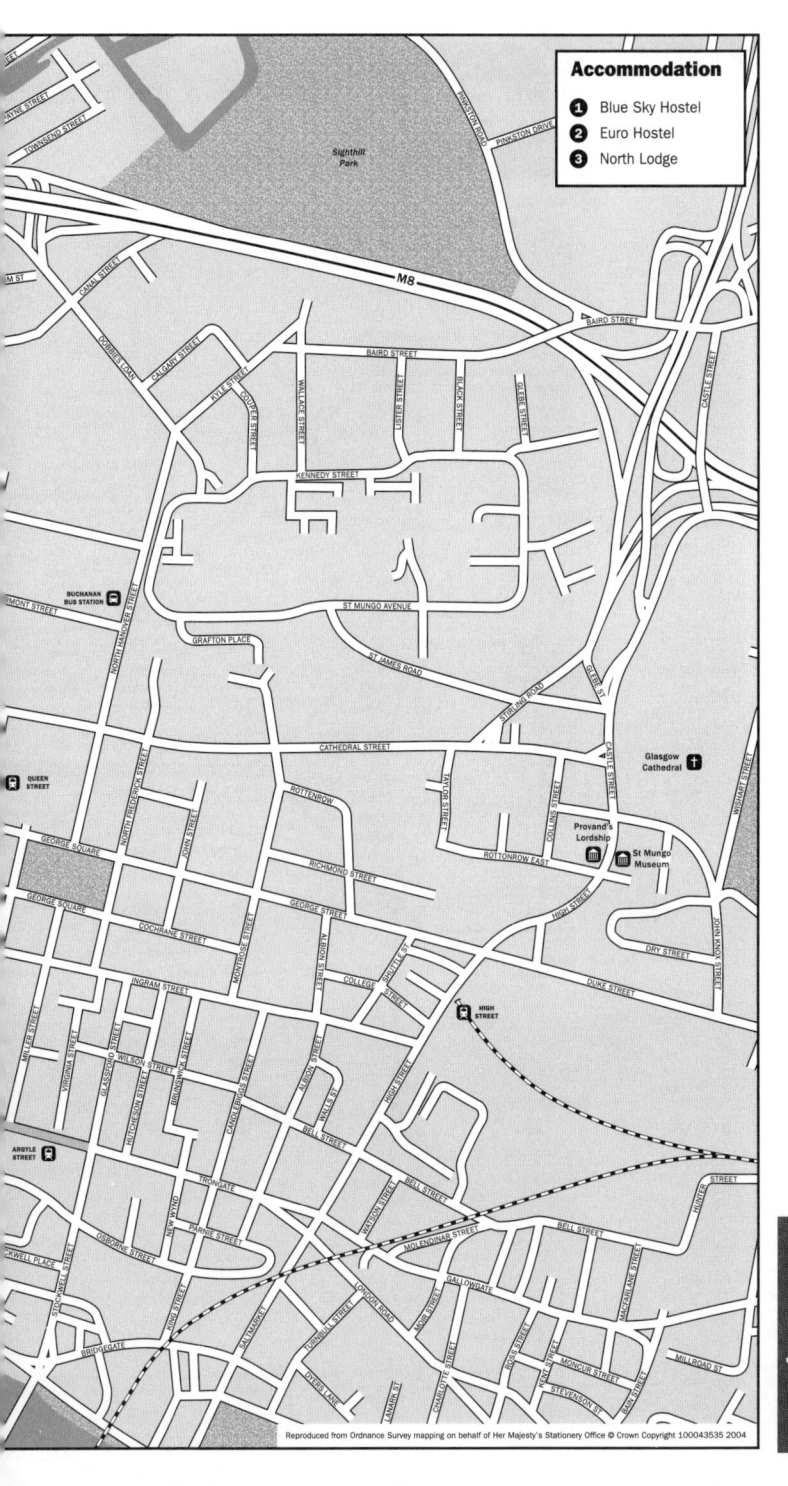

Accommodation
1. Blue Sky Hostel
2. Euro Hostel
3. North Lodge

296 Strathclyde – Glasgow

joining up journeys — SPT rail

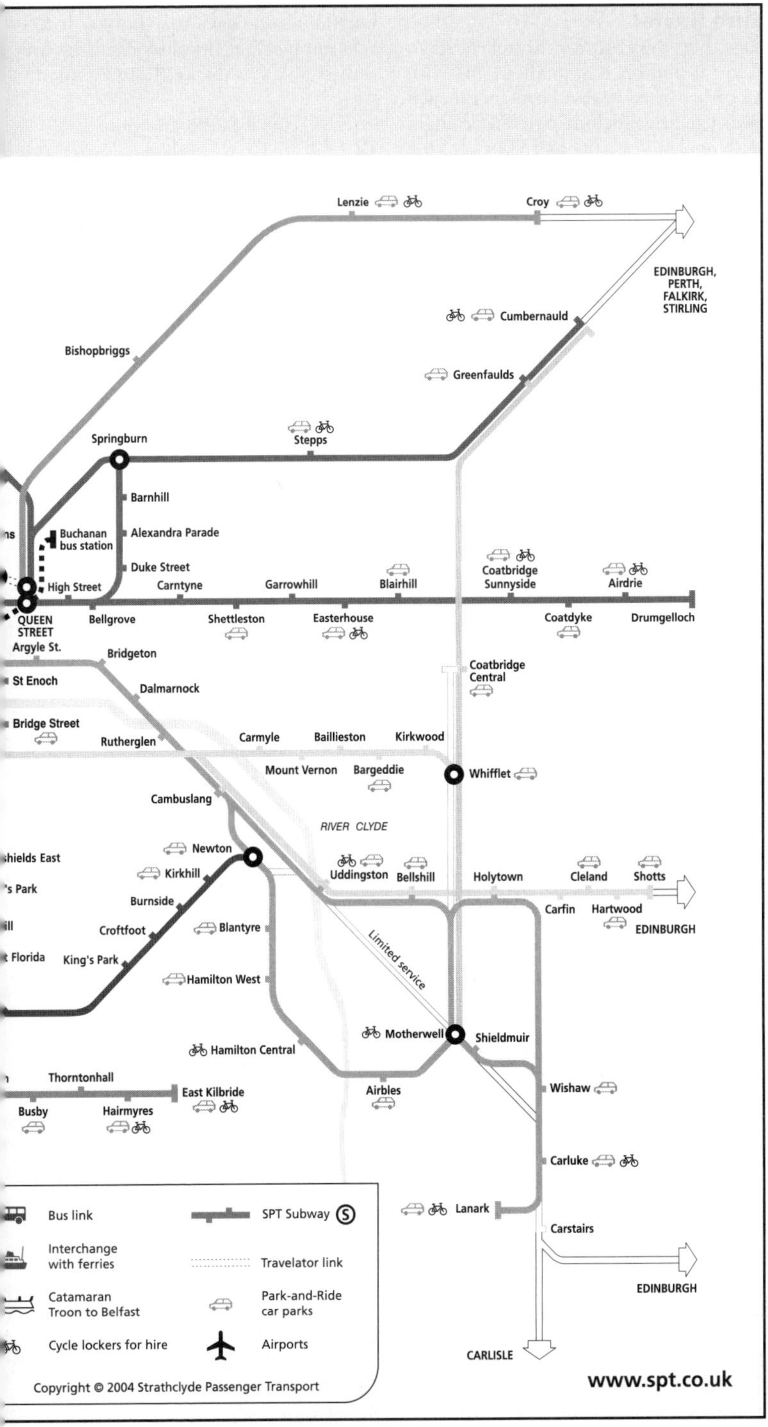

Strathclyde

Euro Hostel

This big multi-storey hostel next to Central Station has small dorms with en suite bathrooms and lockers for each bed. Facilities include two TV lounges with pool tables, a bar and a kitchen that is tiny considering the size of the hostel. Unfortunately the hostel's size and the design of the common areas ensure that it has very little social atmosphere.
318 Clyde Street, Glasgow
Ⓢ *St Enoch* 🚉 *Central*
☎ *(0141) 222 2828*
Website *www.euro-hostels.co.uk*
Dorm bed £13.75-16.75; **single room** £29-33; **double/twin room** £33-35; *prices include breakfast*
Credit cards *MC, Visa*
Reception open *25 hours*

Maintenance & cleanliness	★★★★
Facilities	★★★½
Atmosphere & character	★★½
Security	★★★★★
Overall rating	★★★

Glasgow Backpackers Hostel

This hostel near Kelvingrove Park is set in a Georgian terrace house and has the usual kitchen, common room and Internet access.
17 Park Terrace, Glasgow
🚌 *11, 44* Ⓢ *St George's Cross* 🚉 *Charing Cross*
☎ *(0141) 332 9099*
Website *www.scotlands-top-hostels.com*
Dorm bed £12; **twin room** £30
Open *early Jul-early Sep*

Glasgow SYHA

Glasgow's SYHA hostel has been recently renovated. Facilities include a kitchen, TV lounge and Internet access.
8 Park Terrace, Glasgow
🚌 *11, 44* Ⓢ *St George's Cross* 🚉 *Charing Cross*
☎ *0870 004 1119*
Website *www.syha.org.uk*
Dorm bed £14-15.75 *(£13-14.75 HI/ SYHA)*

North Lodge

This small 36-bed hostel feels a little grungy with old mismatched furniture but the rooms have new bunks. It has two lounges but 'kitchen' facilities are limited to a toaster, kettle and a microwave.
161-167 North Street, Glasgow
🚉 *Charing Cross*
☎ *(0141) 221 3852*
Dorm bed £9-12.50
Credit cards *MC, Visa*
Reception open *9am-10pm daily*

Maintenance & cleanliness	★★½
Facilities	★
Atmosphere & character	★★½
Security	★
Overall rating	★★½

Eating & Drinking

Glasgow is best known for its Indian food and there are plenty of cheap curry joints to choose from.

Head to the Willow Tea Rooms *(217 Sauchiehall Street;* ☎ *(0141) 332 0521; website www.willowtearooms.co.uk)* for a more British ambience, this Glasgow institution was designed by Charles Rennie Mackintosh and it offers the chance to relax over a pot of tea in regal surroundings.

Sights
Burrell Collection

In 1944 Sir William Burrell gave his extensive art collection to the city of Glasgow. The Burrell Collection is one of Britain's most impressive art museums and it features an eclectic, but high quality, collection that encompasses antiques, tapestries, ceramics, sculpture and paintings.
Pollock Country Park, Glasgow
🚌 *45, 56, 57* 🚉 *Pollokshaws West*
☎ *(0141) 287 2597*
Admission *free*
Open *Mon-Thu 10am-5pm, Fri 11am-5pm, Sat 10am-5pm, Sun 11am-5pm*

Gallery of Modern Art

This solid classical building houses the city's contemporary art collection and plays host to temporary art exhibits.
Queen Street, Glasgow
Ⓢ *Buchanan Street, St Enoch* 🚉 *Argyle Street, Queen Street*
☎ *(0141) 229 1996*
Admission *free*

Open Mon-Thu 10am-5pm, Fri 11am-5pm, Sat 10am-5pm, Sun 10am-5pm.

Glasgow Cathedral & Necropolis

This cathedral was built from the 13th to 15th centuries over what is believed to be the tomb of St Kentigern and it is the only medieval cathedral in mainland Scotland to have been spared during the Reformation. The necropolis behind the cathedral has an eerie atmosphere and is worth a look.
Cathedral Street, Glasgow
☎ *(0141) 552 6891*
Ⓢ *Buchanan Street* 🚆 *Queen Street*
Website *www.historic-scotland.gov.uk*
Admission *free*
Open *Jan-Mar Mon-Sat 9.30am-4pm, Sun 1pm-4pm; Apr-Sep Mon-Sat 9.30am-6pm, Sun 1pm-5pm; Oct-Dec Mon-Sat 9.30am-4pm, Sun 1pm-4pm*

Glasgow Science Centre

This impressive science museum complex is comprised of three distinct buildings: the Glasgow Tower, the Science Mall and an IMAX theatre.

The Glasgow Tower is Scotland's tallest structure and the only tower in the world that can completely rotate 360º. It is closed for maintenance but when open it offers brilliant views of the city and out to Ben Lomond and Lanarkshire.

Both the Science Mall and IMAX theatre are striking in their titanium construction. The Science Mall is the heart of the complex and it features hundreds of interactive exhibits making it one of the world's top science museums.
50 Pacific Quay, Glasgow
🚌 *Arriva 24, First Bus 89, 90*
Ⓢ *Cessnock* 🚆 *Exhibition Centre*
☎ *(0141) 420 5011*
Website *www.gsc.org.uk*
Admission *single attraction (either Glasgow Tower, Science Mall or IMAX) £6.95 (£4.95 students); two attractions (any two of Glasgow Tower, Science Mall or IMAX) £9.95 (£7.95 students)*
Glasgow Tower open *11am-6pm daily;* **Science Mall open** *10am-6pm daily*

Hunterian Museum

Scotland's first public museum was opened in 1807 to house a collection of books, coins and anatomical specimens bequeathed by Dr William Hunter. The museum, which is part of the University of Glasgow, now also houses Roman antiquities, natural history exhibits and an art collection, but its main attraction is a reproduction of the interior of Charles Rennie Mackintosh's house complete with original furniture.
University of Glasgow, Glasgow
🚌 *44, 59* Ⓢ *Hillhead*
☎ *(0141) 330 4221*
Website *www.hunterian.gla.ac.uk*
Admission *free*
Open *Mon-Sat 9.30am-5pm.*

Pollok House

This Victorian mansion houses paintings and furnishings from the Edwardian period. It is located in Pollok Country Park near the Burrell Collection
Pollok Country Park, 2060 Pollokshaws Road, Glasgow
🚌 *45, 47, 48, 57* 🚆 *Pollokshaws West*
☎ *(0141) 616 6410*
Website *www.nts.org.uk*
Admission *£6 (£4 HI/SYHA)*
Open *10am-5pm daily*

Provand's Lordship

In 1927 a museum opened in Glasgow's oldest house, which was built in 1471. The exhibits are mainly antique furniture donated by Sir William Burrell. There is also a medieval herb garden behind the building.
3 Castle Street, Glasgow
🚌 *11, 36, 37, 38, 42, 89, 138* 🚆 *High Street*
☎ *(0141) 552 8819*
Admission *free*
Open *Mon-Thu 10am-5pm, Fri 11am-5pm, Sat 10am-5pm, Sun 11am-5pm*

Scottish Football Museum

Sports fans will love this museum that explains the history and culture behind Scottish football (soccer). A visit is essential if you want to know more about the century-old rivalry between Glasgow Celtic and the Glasgow Rangers. Tours of the stadium run on non-event days.
Hampden Park Stadium, Aikenhead Road, Glasgow
🚌 *5, 12, 31, 37, 44, 66, 74, 75, 89, 90*

🚇 *Mount Florida*
☎ *(0141) 616 6139*
Website *www.scottishfootballmuseum.org.uk*
Admission *museum £5 (£2.50 students); museum & stadium tour £7.50 (£5 students); stadium tour only £5*
Open *Mon-Sat 10am-5pm, Sun 11am-5pm*

St Mungo Museum of Religious Life and Art

This museum, across the road from Glasgow Cathedral, has exhibits on a wide range of religious topics that encompass Buddhism, Christianity, Hinduism, Islam, Judaism and Sikhism. The museum features a Japanese Zen garden and a series of stained glass windows but its main attraction is the Salvador Dalí painting *Christ of St John on the Cross*, which was bought in 1952 using the city's entire budget.
2 Castle Street, Glasgow
🚌 *11, 36, 37, 38, 42, 89, 138* 🚇 *High Street*
☎ *(0141) 553 2557*
Admission *free*
Open *Mon-Sat 10am-5pm, Sun 11am-5pm*

South Lanarkshire

New Lanark

New Lanark was established in 1785 by industrialist Robert Owen as a company town to house workers for his cotton mill. It is similar to other Industrial Revolution-era World Heritage Sites such as Ironbridge (Shropshire) and Saltaire (West Yorkshire) and it is now run as a living community with the restored 18th century cotton mill plus a visitor centre with displays depicting life in New Lanark during the Industrial Revolution.

Coming & Going

Frequent trains make the 45-minute journey between Glasgow and Lanark. It's a 20-minute walk from the station to New Lanark or you can take a shuttle bus.

Accommodation
New Lanark SHYA
This excellent hostel is in a listed building dating from 1785, which is part of the New Lanark World Heritage Site. It is maintained to a very high standard and it has a good kitchen, a big dining area and a cosy TV lounge. All the rooms have en suite bathrooms and most dormitories have four beds. Dorms face the river and the soothing sound of the rapids ensures a quiet night sleep.
Wee Row, Rosedale Street, New Lanark
☎ *0870 004 1143*
Website *www.syha.org.uk*
Dorm bed *£12.75-14 (£11.75-13 HI/SYHA)*
Credit cards *MC, Visa*
Open *Mar-Oct*

Maintenance & cleanliness	★★★★★
Facilities	★★
Atmosphere & character	★★★★☆
Security	★★
Overall rating	★★★★☆

Ayrshire

This region south of Glasgow is comprised of three unitary authorities: East, North and South Ayrshire. Most attractions here can be visited as an easy daytrip from Glasgow, but a longer visit is best if you want to explore the Isle of Arran.

Ayr & Alloway

Located just south of Prestwick International Airport, this town of 50,000 boasts a sandy beach and it was a seaside resort in Victorian times. Robert Burns, who wrote *Auld Lang Syne*, was born 5km south of Ayr in the pretty village of Alloway and many people visit Ayr to tour the area's Burns related sights.

Practical Information
Ayr Tourist Information Centre
22 Sandgate, Ayr
☎ *(01292) 288 688*

Website www.ayrshire-arran.com
Open Jan-Jun Mon-Sat 9am-5pm;
Jul-Aug Mon-Sat 9am-6pm, Sun 10am-5pm;
Sep-Dec Mon-Sat 9am-5pm

Coming & Going
The train is the best way to get to Ayr. There are frequent trains to Glasgow as it is part of its suburban rail network. The train runs via Prestwick International Airport, which is just a short distance north of town.

Sights
Burns Cottage & Museum
Robert Burns was born in this cottage in 1759; two years after his father built it. Both the cottage and the adjoining museum are packed with Burns memorabilia.
Murdoch's Lone, Alloway
☎ *(01292) 441215*
Website www.burnsheritagepark.com
Admission £3
Open Jan-Mar 10am-5pm daily; Apr-Sep 9.30am-5.30pm daily; Oct-Dec 10am-5pm daily

Kirk Alloway
The ruins of this 16th century church are the setting for the Burns' tale *Tam O'Shanter*.
Murdoch's Lone, Alloway
Admission free
Always open

Tam O'Shanter Experience
This visitors' centre features exhibits and audio-visual displays about the life and works of Robert Burns.
Murdoch's Lone, Alloway
☎ *(01292) 443700*
Website www.burnsheritagepark.com
Admission £1.50
Open Jan-Mar 10am-5pm daily; Spr-Oct 9.30am-5.30pm daily; Nov-Dec 10am-5pm daily

Culzean Castle
Located around 20km south of Ayr, this majestic castle features an opulent interior and a dramatic cliff top setting.
Maybole, South Ayrshire
🚌 *60 from Ayr*
☎ *(01655) 884400*
Website www.nts.org.uk
Admission £10 (£7.50 HI/SYHA)
Open Apr-Oct 10.30am-5pm daily (last entry 4pm)

Isle of Arran
Easily accessible from Glasgow, this picturesque island is popular with many tourists who don't have the time to make it to the Highlands or the more northern islands. The compact island offers contrasting scenery that ranges from granite peaks to rolling hills and sandy beaches. Attractions include stone circles that date from the Bronze Age as well as a wide variety of wildlife that make it a popular destination for outdoors enthusiasts.

Brodick, Lamlash and Lochranza are the island's main villages. Most attractions are in Brodick, where the ferry from Ardrossan arrives, but most backpackers stay at the hostels in Lochranza and Lamlash.

Practical Information
Tourist Information Centre
Brodick, Isle of Arran
☎ *(01770) 302 140*
Website www.ayrshire-arran.com
Open Jan-May Mon-Fri 9am-5pm, Sat 10am-5pm; Jun-Sep Mon-Sat 9am-7.30pm, Sun 10am-5pm; Oct-Dec Mon-Fri 9am-5pm, Sat 10am-5pm

Coming & Going
Caledonian MacBrayne ferries (☎ *08457) 484950; website www.calmac.co.uk*) make the one-hour trip between Brodick and Ardrossan, which is easily accessible by train from Glasgow.

Local Transport
Stagecoach (☎ *(01770) 302000; website www.stagecoachbus.co.uk*) runs most bus services on the island.

Accommodation
Aldersyde Hostel
This quaint purpose-built bunkhouse has two dormitories and a small common room.
Lamlash, Isle of Arran
☎ *(01770) 600 959*
Dorm bed £10

Lochranza SYHA
This lovely waterfront hostel is well positioned for walking holidays on the Isle of Arran.
Lochranza, Isle of Arran
🚌 *324*
☎ *0870 004 1140*
Website *www.syha.org.uk*
Dorm bed *£12-12.50 (£11-11.50 HI/SYHA)*
Open *Mar-Oct*

Whiting Bay SYHA
This good hostel is in a big house south of Whiting Bay. The hostel's facilities include a kitchen, dining room and a couple of lounges. It is well located to many hiking trails but it's 13km from the ferry.
Shore Road, Whiting Bay, Isle of Arran
🚌 *323*
☎ *0870 004 1158*
Website *www.syha.org.uk*
Dorm bed *£12-12.50 (£11-11.50 HI/SYHA)*
Open *Apr-Oct*

Sights
Brodick Castle
Brodick Castle is a former Viking fortress that has had major additions made in the 13th, 16th and 17th centuries. The castle is the ancient seat of the Dukes of Hamilton and it boasts extensive grounds that feature walking trails, wildlife pools and waterfalls.
Brodick, Isle of Arran
☎ *(01770) 302 202*
Website *www.nts.org.uk*
Admission *£8 (£6 HI/SYHA), garden only £4 (£3 HI/SYHA)*
Open *Apr-Sep 11am-4.30pm daily; Oct 11am-3.30pm daily*

Isle of Arran Heritage Museum
The small Isle of Arran Heritage Museum features displays on local history that date back 5000 years.
A841, Rosaburn, Brodick, Isle of Arran
☎ *(01770) 302 636*
Website *www.arranmuseum.co.uk*
Admission *£2.50*
Open *Apr-Oct 10.30am-4.30pm daily*

Central Scotland

The area of central Scotland bordered by Edinburgh and Glasgow to the south and to the north by the Highlands is comprised of Aberdeenshire, Angus, Argyll and Bute, Fife, Perth and Kinross and Stirling.

Argyll & Bute

Argyll and Bute encompasses an area that includes the western Highlands and the Inner Hebrides including Colonsay, Islay, Jura and Mull. Although many travellers pass through here en route to the Highlands, not many people stop for longer than a day.

Loch Lomond

Scotland's largest loch is a popular weekend getaway for Glaswegians. It comprises part of Loch Lomond and the Trossachs National Park, which is Scotland's first national park even though it wasn't officially opened until July 2002. There are some good hiking trails around Loch Lomond and it makes a good excursion from Glasgow, which is only 30km away.

The Loch covers three unitary authorities, the Scottish equivalent of a county; these are Argyll and Bute, which includes the heavily visited western shore; Stirling to the east and Dumbarton and Clydebank, which includes Balloch and the easily accessible south shore. The main towns in the region are Balloch, Dryman, Luss and Tarbet.

Practical Information
Balloch Tourist Information Centre
Balloch Road, Balloch
☎ *(01389) 753 533*
Open *Apr-May 10am-5pm daily; Jun-Sep 9.30am-6pm daily; Oct 10am-5pm daily*

Loch Lomond & the Trossachs National Park Headquarters
The Old Station, Balloch G83 8SS
☎ *(01389) 722600*
Website *www.lochlomond-trossachs.org*
Open *Apr-May 10am-5pm daily; Jun-Sep 9.30am-6pm daily; Oct 10am-5pm daily*

Coming & Going
Loch Lomond's close proximity to Glasgow means that many people commute so there are frequent transport connections between Glasgow and the larger towns on the loch.

Balloch has the best transport connections with frequent Scottish Citylink buses and a half-hourly train service to Glasgow, which is 35-45 minutes away.

The train is the best option if you're headed for Balloch because buses don't stop near the centre. However the bus is a better option if you're headed farther north to Luss and Tarbet.

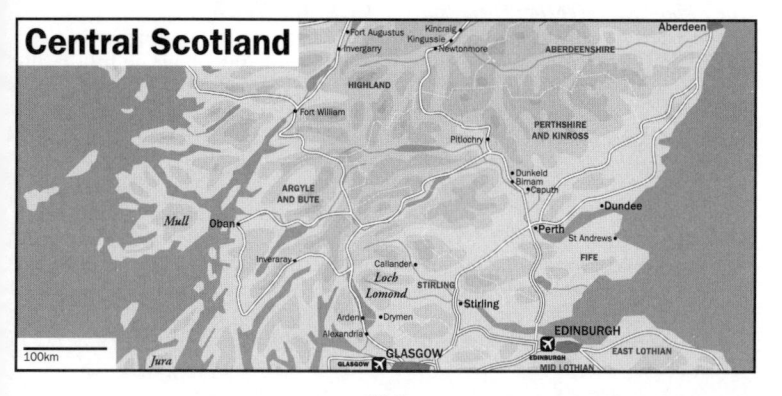

Accommodation
Loch Lomond SYHA
This impressive mansion dates from 1864 and is sumptuously appointed with exquisite detail that includes leather wallpaper and intricate woodwork. The hostel also boasts lovely views of Loch Lomond and features several lounges including a TV lounge, a big dining room, a games room with pool table and the awe inspiring 'Great Hall'. This opulent building is sometimes used as a film set and is a popular wedding venue.
Auchendennan, Arden, Alexandria
☎ *0870 004 1136*
Website *www.syha.org.uk*
Dorm bed *£114-15.50 (£13-14.50 HI/SYHA)*
Credit cards *JCB, MC, Visa*
Open *Mar-Oct;* **reception open** *24 hours*

Maintenance & cleanliness	★★★★★
Facilities	★★
Atmosphere & character	★★★★★
Security	★★★★☆
Overall rating	★★★★

Rowardennan SYHA
The small Rowardennan SYHA hostel is within the national park. The hostel has the usual youth hostel facilities including a small kitchen and a TV lounge and it boasts lovely views of Loch Lomond.
By Drymen
☎ *0870 004 1148*
Website *www.syha.org.uk*
Dorm bed *£12-13.50 (£11-12.50 HI/SYHA)*
Credit cards *MC, Visa*
Open *Mar-Oct;* **reception open** *7am-10.30am & 5pm-midnight*

Maintenance & cleanliness	★★★
Facilities	★★☆
Atmosphere & character	★★
Security	★★
Overall rating	★★★☆

Hiking
There are several good hiking trails in the Loch Lomond area including the West Highland Way as well as the popular hikes up Ben Lomond and Ben Vorlich.

Sights
Loch Lomond Shores Visitors' Centre
This striking building overlooking the Loch features audiovisual presentations about the wildlife and the legends that surround Loch Lomond.
Balloch
🚌 *204, 205* 🚂 *Balloch*
☎ *(01389) 721500*
Website *www.lochlomondshores.com*
Admission *£5.95*
Open *Jan-Mar 11am-5pm daily; Apr-Sep 9am-7pm daily; Oct-Dec 10am-5pm daily*

Inveraray
Noted for its Georgian architecture, this small town features several engaging attractions including a castle and the Inveraray Jail.

Practical Information
Tourist Information Centre
Front Street, Inveraray
☎ *(01499) 302063*
Open *Jan-Mar Mon-Fri 10am-4pm, Sat-Sun noon-4pm; Apr Mon-Sat 9am-5pm, Sun noon-5pm; May-Jun Mon-Sat 9am-5pm, Sun 11am-5pm; Jul-Aug 9am-6pm daily; Sep-Oct Mon-Sat 9am-5pm, Sun noon-5pm; Nov-Dec Mon-Fri 10am-4pm, Sat-Sun noon-4pm*

Coming & Going
Scottish Citylink (☎ *(08705) 505050; website www.citylink.co.uk*) run coaches from Glasgow and Oban.

Accommodation
Inverary SYHA
This alpine-style wooden hut is clean and tidy offering simple no frills facilities and dorm accommodation. It is located next door to the tennis courts bequeathed by the Duchess of Argyll and guests can enjoy a set or two before strolling down to the village to enjoy some freshly caught oysters and a wee nip. A wide range of travellers stay here so you're bound to meet someone interesting.
Dalmally Road, Inverary
☎ *(01499) 302 454 or 0870 004 1125*
Website *www.syha.org.uk*

Dorm bed *£11.50-12 (£10.50-11 HI/ SYHA)*
Credit cards *MC, Visa*
Open *Feb-Oct;* ***reception open*** *8am-10.30am & 5pm-11.30pm daily; lockout 10.30am-5pm daily;* ***curfew*** *11.30pm*

🏠 📺 🄺 🄻 ⚙ ✈

Maintenance & cleanliness	★★★
Facilities	★★★½
Atmosphere & character	★★
Security	★
Overall rating	★★★½

Sights
Inveraray Castle
The fairy-tale Inveraray Castle sits among immaculate gardens and is home to the Duke of Argyll.
☎ *(01499) 302203*
Website *www.inveraray-castle.com*
Admission *£5.90 (£4.90 students)*
Open *Apr-May Mon-Thu 10am-1pm (last entry 12.30pm) & 2pm-5.45pm (last entry 5pm), Sat 10am-1pm (last entry 12.30pm) & 2pm-5.45pm (last entry 5pm), Sun 1pm-5.45pm (last entry 5pm); Jun-Sep Mon-Sat 10am-5.45pm (last entry 5pm), Sun 1am-5.45pm (last entry 5pm); Oct Mon-Thu 10am-1pm (last entry 12.30pm) & 2pm-5.45pm (last entry 5pm), Sat 10am-1pm (last entry 12.30pm) & 2pm-5.45pm (last entry 5pm), Sun 1pm-5.45pm (last entry 5pm)*

Inveraray Jail
This impressive restored 19th century prison features several interactive displays and exhibits that include the popular Torture, Death and Damnation exhibition.
☎ *(01499) 302 381*
Website *www.inverarayjail.co.uk*
Admission *£5.75*
Open *Jan-Mar 10am-5pm daily (last entry 4pm); Apr-Oct 9.30am-6pm daily (last entry 5pm); Nov-Dec 10am-5pm daily (last entry 4pm)*

Inveraray Maritime Museum (the Arctic Pengiun)
Inveraray's maritime museum is housed inside the *Arctic Penguin*, a three-mast schooner, built in 1911, which is one of the last iron sailing ships.
☎ *(01499) 302 213*
Website *www.skwebpages.com/arctic/*
Admission *£3*
Open *Jan-Mar 10am-5pm daily; Apr-Sep 10am-6pm daily; Oct-Dec 10am-5pm daily*

Oban
This busy ferry port doesn't have a lot to see and do, but it is a pleasant enough place to spend a day or two.

Practical Information
Tourist Information Centre
Argyle Square, Oban
☎ *(01631) 563 122*
Website *www.oban.org.uk*
Open *Jan-Mar Mon-Fri 9.30am-5pm, Sat-Sun noon-4pm; Apr Mon-Fri 9am-5pm, Sat-Sun noon-5pm; May-Jun Mon-Sat 9am-6.30pm, Sun 10am-5pm; Jul-Aug Mon-Sat 9am-9pm, Sun 9am-7pm; Sep Mon-Sat 9am-6.30pm, Sun 10am-5pm; Oct Mon-Sat 9am-5.30pm, Sun 10am-4pm; Nov-Dec Mon-Fri 9.30am-5pm, Sat-Sun noon-4pm*

Coming & Going
Oban is well connected with trains to Fort William and Glasgow.

Scottish Citylink (☎ *(08705) 505 050;* ***website*** *www.citylink.co.uk*) has coach services from Oban to Fort William, Glasgow and Inverness.

Caledonian MacBrayne ferries (☎ *(01631) 566688;* ***website*** *www.calmac.co.uk*) depart from Railway Pier for the Western Isles and the southern Hebrides.

Accommodation
Corran House
If you're looking for somewhere quiet but don't want to be too far from the pubs, this is ideal as there is a nice bar downstairs. This unhurried hostel is targeted towards those who want a good nights sleep. Its rooms are bright and clean and some have en suite facilities. The kitchen is well equipped and the TV room is snug.
1 Victoria Crescent, Corran Esplanade, Oban
☎ *(01631) 566 040*
Website *www.corranhouse.co.uk*
Dorm bed *£12-14;* ***double/twin room***

£30-45
Credit cards *MC, Visa*

Maintenance & cleanliness		★★★★★
Facilities		★★★★☆
Atmosphere & character		★★★★★
Security		★
Overall rating		★★★★

Jeremy Inglis Hostel

This hostel isn't the easiest to find, but once there you'll always remember it. It's short on common areas (it doesn't have a lounge) but the artworks on the wall and the truly endearing homeliness of it all makes it work experiencing. If you're looking for sterile, gleaming kitchens and bathrooms forget it. If you're looking for the archetypical 60s independent hostel complete with an eccentric owner – Jeremy Inglis is your man.
21 Airds Crescent, Oban
☎ *(01631) 565 065*
Dorm bed *£6.50-7.50; price includes breakfast*

Maintenance & cleanliness	★★
Facilities	★★
Atmosphere & character	★★★★
Security	★
Overall rating	★★★☆

Oban Backpackers

Oban Backpackers is perhaps the liveliest hostel in town. Its layout lends itself to the social with the reception, kitchen, dining room and lounge all together. The dorms feel roomy and the bathrooms are fresh and bright. This place buzzes all day and at night the lounge is hopping, however upstairs you can sleep through it all.
Breadalbane Street, Oban
☎ *(01631) 562 107*
Website *www.scotlands-top-hostels.com*
Dorm bed *£11-12*
Credit cards *Amex, MC, Visa*
Open *Mar-Oct & Christmas/New Year;* ***reception open*** *7am-11.30pm daily;* ***curfew*** *2am*

Maintenance & cleanliness	★★★☆
Facilities	★★
Atmosphere & character	★★★★★☆
Security	★
Overall rating	★★★☆

Oban Youth Hostel

This big old mansion right on the most northerly part of the seafront has big windows that allow you to appreciate the amazing views towards the Western Isles. The rooms are bright and clean and the bathrooms fresh. The kitchen has every kind of pot, pan and utensil you could need.
Esplanade, Oban
☎ *(01631) 562 025 or 0870 004 1144*
Website *www.syha.org.uk*
Dorm bed *£11.50-14.50 (£10.50-13.50 HI/SYHA)*
Credit cards *MC, Visa*
Reception open *7.30am-11am & 4.30pm-11pm daily*

Maintenance & cleanliness	★★★★
Facilities	★★★☆
Atmosphere & character	★★★
Security	★
Overall rating	★★★

Sights
Dunollie Castle

Dating from 1150, Oban's oldest building lays in ruin a couple of kilometres north of the city centre. This castle is not officially open to the public, but it is a popular spot with visitors.

McCaig's Tower

The Colosseum-like McCaig's tower dominates Oban and also offers great views of the city.
Laurel Street, Oban
Admission *free*
Always *open*

Stirling

Stirling is the district north of the area between Edinburgh and Glasgow and it includes the Trossachs region as well as the city of Stirling with its famous castle.

Stirling

The capital of the Stirling district has played an important role in Scottish history. In 1297 it was here that William Wallace defeated the English at the Battle of Stirling Bridge and 17 years later Robert the Bruce regained Scotland's independence at Bannockburn, 3.25km southeast of the city centre.

The jewel in Stirling's crown is its castle, which many people regard as Scotland's best. Other attractions include the old town and the battlefield at Bannockburn.

Stirling is close enough to Edinburgh and Glasgow to visit as a daytrip, but many travellers choose to stay overnight.

Practical Information
Tourist Information Centre
41 Dunbarton Road, Stirling
☎ *(01786) 475019*
Website *www.visitscottishheartlands.com*
Open *Jan-May Mon-Sat 10am-5pm; Jun Mon-Sat 9am-6pm, Sun 10am-4pm; Jul-Aug Mon-Sat 9am-7.30pm, Sun 9.30am-6.30pm; Sep Mon-Sat 9am-6pm, Sun 10am-4pm; Oct-Dec Mon-Sat 10am-5pm*

Coming & Going
Stirling's close proximity to Edinburgh and Glasgow makes it an easy place to get to. There are several trains each hour to both Edinburgh and Glasgow as well as regular trains to Aberdeen, Inverness and London.

Scottish Citylink (☎ *(0870) 505 050; website www.citylink.co.uk*) run hourly coaches to Edinburgh and Inverness and several coaches each hour to Glasgow.

Both the train and coach stations are on Goosecroft Road.

Local Transport
Although the city centre is compact enough to walk around, buses are a handy way to get to the Wallace Monument and the Bannockburn Heritage Centre.

Accommodation
Stirling SYHA
Stirling's SYHA youth hostel is a modern hostel that incorporates the façade of an 18th century church. It has a good kitchen, a big dining room, a TV lounge and WiFi Internet access.
St John Street, Stirling
☎ *0870 004 1149*
Website *www.syha.org.uk*
Dorm bed *£13-15 (£12-14 HI/SYHA)*
Credit cards *MC, Visa*
Reception open *7am-11.30pm daily; 24 hour check in*

Maintenance & cleanliness	★★★★★
Facilities	★★☆
Atmosphere & character	★★★★☆
Security	★★★★
Overall rating	★★★★☆

Willy Wallace Backpackers
This small hostel is in a Victorian building in the city centre just a couple of minutes from the bus and train stations. It has a good social atmosphere with a good kitchen and a cosy lounge with books, games, Internet access and a tiny TV.
77 Murray Place, Stirling
☎ *(01786) 446 773*
Website *www.willywallacehostel.com*
Dorm bed *£12;* **double room** *$30*
Credit cards *MC, Visa*
Reception open *9am-1pm & 2pm-10pm*

Maintenance & cleanliness	★★★
Facilities	★★☆
Atmosphere & character	★★★★★☆
Security	★★
Overall rating	★★★

Sights
Bannockburn
In 1314 Robert the Bruce overpowered the English at Bannockburn, giving Scotland independent rule. The battlefield, which is around 2.5km south of the city centre, is the site of the Bannockburn Heritage Centre where an audiovisual display relives the historic battle.
Glasgow Road, Whins of Milton, Stirling
🚌 *51, 52*
☎ *(01259) 211701*
Website *www.nts.org.uk*
Admission *£3.50 (£2.60 HI/SYHA)*
Open *20 Jan-24 Mar 10.30am-4pm daily; 25 Mar-27 Oct 10am-6pm daily; 28 Oct-24 Dec 10.30am-4pm daily*

Church of the Holy Rude
In 1567 this old church was the site of the coronation of James VI (son of Mary Queen of Scots) and it has also held witness to John Knox during the

Reformation. The church features a medieval timber roof and it often hosts organ recitals.
Corner Castle Wynd & St John Street, Stirling
☎ *(01786) 475275*
Admission *free*
Open *May-Sep 10am-5pm daily*

Cowane's Hospital
John Cowane, a successful 17th century merchant, financed this almshouse that was built for members of a merchant guild. Nowadays it is used for concerts and ceilidhs.
49 St John Street, Stirling
☎ *(01786) 472247*
Admission *free*
Open *Jan-Mar 10am-4pm daily; Apr-Sep Mon-Sat 9am-5pm, Sun 10am-5pm; Sep-Dec 10am-4pm daily*

Old Town Jail
This prison has displays and re-enactments showing the life of a former inmate.
St John Street, Stirling
☎ *(01786) 471301*
Admission *£3.95*
Open *Feb 9.30am-3.30pm daily; Mar 9.30am-4.30pm daily; Apr-Sep 9.30am-5pm daily; Oct 9.30am-4.30pm daily; Nov 9.30am-3.30pm daily*

Stirling Castle
The castle dominates the city and offers spectacular views of Stirling and the Forth Valley. Many people regard it as the grandest of Scotland's castles and it is the highlight of a visit to Stirling. The castle dates from the 14th century and there are frequent guided tours (included in admission price) that give visitors an in depth history of the castle.
Castle Wynd, Stirling
☎ *(01786) 450 000*
Website *www.historic-scotland.gov.uk*
Admission *£8*
Open *Jan-Mar 9.30am-5pm daily (last entry 4.15pm); Apr-Oct 9.30am-6pm daily (last entry 5.15pm); Nov-Dec 9.30am-5pm daily (last entry 4.15pm)*

Stirling Visitors' Centre
The Visitors' Centre features an audio-visual presentation that provides a good introduction to the city.
Castle Esplanade, Stirling
☎ *(01786) 479901*
Admission *free*
Open *Jan-Mar 9.30am-5pm daily; Apr-Oct 9.30am-6pm daily; Nov-Dec 9.30am-5pm*

Wallace Monument
This monument, 3km north of the city centre, has exhibits about the Battle of Stirling Bridge and the life and achievements of William Wallace, the champion of Scottish freedom that was the inspiration for the film Braveheart. The monument also has a 67m tower that offers great views of the city.
Abbey Craig, Stirling
🚌 *62, 63*
☎ *(01786) 461322*
Admission *£3.95, students £3*
Open *Jan-Feb 10.30am-4pm daily; Mar-May 10am-5pm daily; Jun 9.30am-5pm daily; Jul-Aug 9.30am-6.30pm; Sep 9.30am-5pm; Oct 10am-5pm daily; Nov-Dec 10.30am-4pm daily*

The Trossachs
This region in western Stirling is part of Loch Lomond and Trossachs National Park *(website www.lochlomond-trossachs.org)*, which is Scotland's first national park. The region was the home of Rob Roy Macgregor and its popularity with tourists surged when the film *Rob Roy*, starring Liam Neeson, was released. The main towns in the region are Aberfoyle and Callander.

Practical Information
Tourist Information Centre
The tourist information centre in Callander also houses the Rob Roy & Trossachs Visitor Centre; see the listing under Sights for more information.
Ancaster Square, Callander
☎ *(01877) 330342*
Open *Jan-Feb Sat-Sun 11am-4.30pm; Mar-May 10am-5pm daily; Jun 9.30am-6pm daily; Jul-Aug 9.30am-8pm daily; Sep 10am-6pm daily; Oct-Dec 10am-5pm daily*

Coming & Going
First *(☎ (08708) 727 271; website www.firstgroup.com)* run regular buses

between Callander and Stirling, and less frequently, to Aberfoyle. Ask the bus driver for the Stirling and Trossachs Day Rover pass, which gives you unlimited transport on First bus services between Stirling and Callander.

The Trossachs Trundler (☎ *(01786) 442 707)* provides a convenient alternative by running a shuttle service between Stirling, Callander, Aberfoyle and Port of Menteith. The Trundler bus costs £8 from Stirling or £5.50 for transport within the Trossachs area.

The above transport services are supplemented by post bus (☎ *08457 740 740; website www.postbus.co.uk)* services.

Accommodation
Trossachs Backpackers
This alpine-style building is in the countryside 3.25km from Callander. The property is home to sheep, goats and geese and it features a fully equipped kitchen, a dining room with pianos, a small TV lounge and a big lounge with lots of comfortable chairs. Accommodation is in spacious rooms with en suite bathrooms.
Invertrossachs Road, Callander
☎ *(01877) 331 200*
Website *http://members.aol.com/trosstel/hostel.htm*
Dorm bed £13.50-16; **twin room** £37; prices include breakfast
Credit cards MC, Visa

Maintenance & cleanliness	★★★★★	
Facilities	★★	
Atmosphere & character	★★★★½	
Security	★	
Overall rating	★★★½	

Sights
Rob Roy & Trossachs Visitor Centre
This museum and visitors' centre features displays and an audiovisual presentation about Rob Roy.
Ancaster Square, Callander
☎ *(01877) 330 342*
Admission £2.90
Open *Jan-Feb Sat-Sun 11am-4.30pm; Mar-May 10am-5pm daily; Jun 9.30am-6pm daily; Jul-Aug 9am-10pm daily; Sep 10am-6pm daily; Oct-Dec 10am-5pm daily*

Fife
The Kingdom of Fife comprises most of the peninsula east of Stirling. The main draw card is the university town of St Andrews where golf was first played.

St Andrews
Visitors to St Andrews will find that there's no escaping the influence that golf has made to this historic university town. The game has been played here since at least as early as 1457 and the rules of the game were first written down at the Royal and Ancient Golf Club and that club's Old Course is regarded as the mecca of the golfing world.

It will cost you a bundle if you want to play a round on the Old Course, and you'll need an introduction from your club back home and a reservation made at least a year in advance.

Practical Information
Tourist Information Centre
70 Market Street, St Andrews
☎ *(01334) 472021*
Website *www.standrews.com*
Open *Jan-mid Mar Mon-Sat 9.30am-5pm; mid Mar-Jun Mon-Sat 9.30am-6pm, Sun 10am-5pm; Jul-Aug Mon-Sat 9.30am-7pm, Sun 10am-5pm; Sep-Oct Mon-Sat 9.30am-6pm, Sun 10am-5pm; Nov-Dec Mon-Sat 9.30am-5pm*

Coming & Going
The most extensive bus and coach services in Fife are operated by Stagecoach Buses (☎ *(01592) 642 394; website www.stagecoachbus.com/fife)*, which have buses from St Andrew to Dundee (routes 96, 96a, 99, 99a, 99b) and Glasgow (routes X24, X26). Buses and coaches terminate at St Andrews Bus Station (☎ *(01334) 474 238)* on City Road.

The closest train station, on the Edinburgh-Aberdeen line, is 8km away at Leuchars. Buses 96, 96a, 99, 99a, 99b run between St Andrew and Leuchars train station.

Accommodation
St Andrews Tourist Hostel
This small hostel in the town centre offers a high standard of accommodation

in freshly painted rooms. Facilities include a fully equipped kitchen and a TV lounge with comfy sofas.
Inchape House, St Marys Place, St Andrews
☎ *(01334) 479 911*
Website *www.hostelsaccommodation.com*
Dorm bed *£12-16*
Credit cards *JCB, MC, Visa*
Reception open *summer 8am-11pm daily; winter 8am-3pm & 6pm-10pm daily*

📺 🅚 🅛

Maintenance & cleanliness	★★★★½
Facilities	★★½
Atmosphere & character	★★★★
Security	★★½
Overall rating	★★★★½

Sights
British Golf Museum
Chronicling the history of golf, the British Golf Museum's exhibits cover all aspects of the game from its origins to the present day. A new gallery entitled 'The 18th Hole' offers a more hands-on approach with a putting green and replicas of some of the clubs and balls in the museum's collection.
Bruce Embankment, St Andrews
☎ *(01334) 460 046*
Website *www.britishgolfmuseum.co.uk*
Admission *£4 (£3 students)*
Open *Jan-Easter Thu-Mon 11am-3pm; Easter to mid-Oct 9.30am-5.30pm daily; mid-Oct to Dec Thur-Mon 11am-3pm*

St Andrews Castle
This 13th century castle is the former home of the archbishops of St Andrews and it features a unique bottle dungeon and siege tunnels. The adjoining visitors' centre has displays about both the castle and cathedral.
The Scores, St Andrews
☎ *(01334) 477 196*
Website *www.historic-scotland.gov.uk*
Admission *£4 (£3 students), ticket also allows entry to St Andrews Cathedral*
Open *Jan-Mar 9.30am-4.30 daily (last entry 4pm); Apr-Sep 9.30am-6.30pm (last entry 6pm); Oct-Dec 9.30am-4.30pm (last entry 4pm)*

St Andrews Cathedral
Once Scotland's largest cathedral, the ruins of St Andrews Cathedral features St Rules Tower, which offers superb views over the town. There is also a museum on the site and an adjoining visitors' centre that has displays about both the castle and cathedral.
The Pends, St Andrews
☎ *(01334) 472563*
Website *www.britishgolfmuseum.co.uk*
Admission *£4 (£3 students)*
Open *Jan-Mar 9.30am-4.30pm daily (last entry 4pm); Apr-Sep 9.30am-6.30pm daily (last entry 6pm); Oct-Dec 9.30am-4.30pm daily (last entry 4pm)*

St Andrews Museum
This museum has exhibits on local history with displays on medieval times and the town's growth in the 20th century.
Kinburn Park, Doubledyke Road, St Andrews
☎ *(01334) 412 820*
Website *www.visit-standrews.co.uk/pages/kinburn.htm*
Admission *free*
Open *Jan-Mar Mon-Fri 10.30am-5pm, Sat-Sun 12.30pm-5pm; Apr-Sep 10am-5pm daily; Oct-Dec Mon-Fri 10.30am-5pm, Sat-Sun 12.30pm-5pm*

Perthshire & Kinross
Perthshire and Kinross is bordered by Stirling and Fife to the south, Highland and Aberdeenshire to the north and Angus to the east. It encompasses the Tayside region and the Grampians are in the north. It isn't a big destination with budget travellers but many backpackers pass through here on the M90 motorway and A9 highway en route to the Highlands.

Perth
Although it's a pleasant place, Scotland's former capital doesn't offer much for the average backpacker and most travellers stop here to take a look at Scone Palace and then move on.

Practical Information
Tourist Information Centre
Lower City Mills, Perth
☎ *(01738) 450600*

Open *Jan-Mar Mon-Sat 10am-4pm; 1 Apr-7 Jul Mon-Sat 9.30am-5.30pm, Sun 11am-4pm; 8 Jul-1 Sep Mon-Sat 9.30am-6.30pm, Sun 11am-5pm; 2 Sep-27 Oct Mon-Sat 9.30am-5.30pm, Sun 11am-4pm; 28 Oct-31 Dec Mon-Sat 10am-4pm*

Coming & Going

There are frequent trains and coaches from Perth to the Scottish major towns and cities with several trains and coaches every hour to Aberdeen, Edinburgh and Glasgow. Because Perth is on the main route to the Highlands there are also frequent coaches and trains to Inverness via Pitlochry.

Sights
Black Watch Museum

This museum is dedicated to the Black Watch regiment of the British Army. Exhibits include uniforms, weapons and a number of interesting artefacts.
Dalhousie Castle, Hay Street, Perth
☎ *(0131) 310 8530*
Website *www.theblackwatch.co.uk/museum/*
Admission *free*
Open *Jan-Apr Mon-Fri 10am-3.30pm; May-Sep Mon-Sat 10am-4.30pm; Oct-Dec Mon-Fri 10am-3.30pm*

Perth Museum & Art Gallery

Perth Museum is one of the world's oldest and it features exhibits that include local history, silver, glass making and a 29kg salmon that was caught in 1922 from the River Tay. The adjoining art galleries boast over 4000 works of art.
78 George Street, Perth
☎ *(01738) 632 488*
Website *www.pkc.gov.uk/ah/perth_museum.htm*
Admission *free*
Open *Mon-Sat 10am-5pm*

St John's Kirk

Dating from 1127, St John's Kirk played an important role during the Reformation and even today it remains the focus of the town.
St John's Place, Perth
☎ *(01738) 638482*
Website *www.st-johns-kirk.co.uk*
Admission *free*
Open *May-Sep Mon-Fri 10am-4pm*

Scone Palace

Perth's most important attraction is Scone Palace, 4½km north of the city centre. This was the site of the coronation ceremonies of Scotland's kings and nowadays is the home of the Lord and Lady of Mansfield. The interior and grounds of the palace are open to visitors and the palace features an impressive collection of lace, fine china and antiques. The Palace's most famous artefact was the 'Stone of Destiny', which is now housed in Edinburgh Castle, after being kept in Westminster Abbey for many centuries. The Palace's extensive grounds feature formal and wild gardens and an excellent maze.
A93, Perth
☎ *(01738) 552300*
Website *www.scone-palace.net*
Admission *£6.75 ($5.70 students); grounds only £3.40 (£2.80 students); joint ticket with entry to Blair Castle, Glamis Castle and Dewars World of Whisky £12*
Open *Apr-Oct 9.30am-5.30pm daily (last entry 5pm)*

Dunkeld & Birnam

These two villages, located only a short walk apart, are rich in history and also make a good base for walking in the surrounding countryside. The main attraction is Dunkeld Cathedral while Birnam has influenced Beatrix Potter's the *Tale of Peter Rabbit* and has also featured in Shakespeare's *Macbeth*.

Practical Information
Tourist Information Centre

The Cross, Dunkeld PH8 0AN
☎ *(01350) 727 688*
Open *25 Mar-7 Jul Mon-Sat 9.30am-5.30pm, Sun 11am-4pm; 8 Jul-1 Sep Mon-Sat 9.30am-6.30pm, Sun 11am-5pm; 2 Sep-27 Oct Mon-Sat 9.30am-5.30pm, Sun 11am-4pm.*

Coming & Going

Of the two villages, Birnam is the main transport hub and the majority of coaches and all trains stop here.

Scottish Citylink coaches on the Edinburgh and Glasgow to Inverness route stop outside the train station in Birnam. The local Stagecoach buses are a handy way of getting to either Perth or Pitlochry and they have the benefit of also stopping in Dunkeld.

Birnam's small train station is on the Edinburgh-Inverness line.

Accommodation
Wester Caputh Independent Hostel
This wee hostel has a huge list of things going for it. The local area offers excellent fishing, walking and canoeing while the hostel itself is packed with things to do, from books to card games, to musical instruments, so you can settle down in front of the fire and create your own ceilidh band. Your fellow guests will love you for it! It's an environmentally friendly hostel too.
Maise Road, Caputh, near Dunkeld
☎ *(01738) 710 449*
Website *www.westercaputh.co.uk*
Dorm bed *£12-15*

Maintenance & cleanliness	★★★★
Facilities	★★★
Atmosphere & character	★★★★½
Security	★
Overall rating	★★★½

Sights
Birnam Institute
Beatrix Potter used to spend her childhood holidays in the Birnam area and this local arts centre is now home to an exhibition focusing on her work.
Station Road, Birnam
☎ *(01350) 727 674*
Website *www.birnaminstitute.com*
Admission *free*
Open *10am-5pm daily*

Dunkeld Cathedral
Dunkeld's cathedral has been around for around 1400 years and nowadays much of it remains in ruins, however there is a restored section that is still used as a church.
High Street, Dunkeld
Website *www.dunkeldcathedral.org.uk*
Admission *free*
Open *Jan-Mar Mon-Sat 9.30am-4pm, Sun 2pm-4pm; Apr-Sep Mon-Sat 9.30am-6.30pm, Sun 2pm-6.30pm; Oct-Dec Mon-Sat 9.30am-4pm, Sun 2pm-4pm*

Pitlochry
Many travellers stop at this small town en route to both the Grampians and the Highlands. Its attractions include two distilleries and the unique fish ladder. There are some good hiking trails around town and the Blair Castle is 11km north of here.

Practical Information
Tourist Information Centre
22 Atholl Road, Pitlochry
☎ *(01796) 472215*
Open *1 Jan-30 Mar Mon-Fri 9am-5pm, Sat 10am-2pm; 31 Mar-19 May Mon-Sat 9am-6pm, Sun 11am-5pm; 20 May-8 Sep Mon-Sat 9am-7pm, Sun 9am-6pm; 9 Sep-27 Oct Mon-Sat 9am-6pm, Sun 11am-5pm; 28 Oct-31 Dec Mon-Fri 9am-5pm, Sat 10am-2pm*

Coming & Going
Like Dunkeld and Birnam, Pitlochry lies on the main route between Edinburgh and Inverness, ensuring that there is frequent transport in and out of town. The train station in the town centre has regular trains to Inverness, Perth, Edinburgh and Glasgow and more frequent coaches ply the same route. The local Stagecoach buses go to Perth and Blair Athol (for Blair Castle).

Accommodation
Pitlochry Backpackers
Located right in the centre of town, this hostel has a huge lounge with a pool table and TV and plenty of seats by the big sash windows. The rooms are nicely maintained and the shower rooms are small but functional. The staff are very knowledgeable about the area and help create a cheery atmosphere about the place.
134 Atholl Road, Pitlochry
☎ *(01796) 470 044*
Website *www.scotlands-top-hostels.com*
Dorm bed *£11-12;* **double room** *£32-36;* **twin room** *£27-30*
Credit cards *Amex, MC, Visa*

Central Scotland – Aberdeen

Open *Easter-Oct; reception open 7am-11pm daily; curfew Mon-Thu 1am, Fri-Sat 2am, Sun 1am*

Maintenance & cleanliness	★★☆
Facilities	★★★☆
Atmosphere & character	★★★★
Security	★
Overall rating	★★★

Pitlochry SYHA

Just 15 minutes up the hill from the station, this old mansion is located in lovely grounds. The dorms are all en suite and are clean and tidy. There's a TV room and a quiet room and, if the weather is fine, places to sit outside. Guests get 50% off Pitlochry Festival Theatre tickets during the summer – a great bargain for one of Scotland's great theatres.

Knockard Road, Pitlochry
☎ *(01796) 472 308 or 0870 004 1145*
Website *www.syha.org.uk*
Dorm bed *£12.50-13.50 (£11.50-12.50 HI/SYHA)*
Credit cards *MC, Visa*
Open *Mar-Oct;* ***reception open*** *7.30am-10.30am & 4pm-11.45pm daily;* ***curfew*** *11.45pm*

Maintenance & cleanliness	★★★★
Facilities	★★★
Atmosphere & character	★★★
Security	★★☆
Overall rating	★★★★☆

Sights
Blair Castle

This stunning castle is home to the Atholl Highlanders, Britain's only private army, and the Dukes and Earls of Atholl. The castle features the usual collection of furniture and paintings as well as impressive gardens.

Blair Atholl
☎ *(01796) 481 207*
Website *www.blair-castle.co.uk*
Admission *£6.70 (£5.40 students); grounds only £2; joint ticket with entry to Scone Palace, Glamis Castle and Dewars World of Whisky £12*
Open *Jan-15 Mar Tue-Sat 9.30am-12.30pm; Apr-Oct 9.30am-4.30pm daily; Nov-Dec Tue-Sat 9.30am-12.30pm*

Fish ladder

The unique fish ladder allows salmon to swim upstream between the dammed River Tummel and Loch Faskally. It is located at the dam south of the train station.

Whisky distilleries

There are two distilleries in town and many travellers tour both. Bells Blair Athol distillery is the bigger of the two and it has well organised tours, while the tiny Edradour distillery is Scotland's smallest.

Bells Blair Athol Distillery*, Perth Road, Pitlochry*
☎ *(01796) 472003*
Admission *£3*
Open *Jan-Easter Mon-Fri 1pm-4pm; Easter-Sep Mon-Sat 9.30am-5pm, Sun noon-5pm; Oct Mon-Fri 10am-4pm; Nov-Dec Mon-Fri 1pm-4pm*

Edradour Distillery*, A924, Moulin (4km north of the town centre)*
☎ *(01796) 472095*
Website *www.edradour.co.uk*
Admission *free*
Open *Mar-Oct Mon-Sat 9.30am-5pm, Sun 10am-4pm; Nov to mid-Dec Mon-Sat 10am-4pm*

Aberdeen

Scotland's third largest city is a prosperous place that is the centre of Britain's oil industry. In addition to being the operations centre for the North Sea oilrigs, the Granite City has a strong student culture and some good pubs.

Practical Information
Tourist Information Centre

23 Union Street, Aberdeen
☎ *(01224) 288828*
Website *www.agtb.org*
Open *Jan-Jun Mon-Sat 9.30am-5pm; Jul-Aug Mon-Sat 9.30am-7pm, Sun 10am-4pm; Sep-Dec Mon-Sat 9.30am-5pm*

Coming & Going

Aberdeen has good transport connections to destinations throughout Scotland.

AIR
The busy airport (☎ (01244) 722 331; *website www.baa.co.uk/main/airports/aberdeen/*) has flights to many regional airports in the UK and International flights to Denmark, France, Faeroe Islands, Ireland and Norway. Bus 27 runs between the airport and the city centre.

BUS
Guild Street Coach Station has hourly buses to Edinburgh, Glasgow and Inverness and less frequent buses to most other Scottish destinations.

TRAIN
The train station is next to the coach terminal and there are hourly trains to Edinburgh and Glasgow as well as regular trains to Inverness and London.

Ferry
Aberdeen has a busy port with Northlink ferries *(website www.northlinkferries.co.uk)* sailing from here to the Orkney and Shetland Islands.

Local Transport
Aberdeen's public transport system, run by First Aberdeen (☎ (01224) 650 065; *website www.firstgroup.com*), is comprised of an extensive network of bus routes. Buses on major routes run every 15 minutes between 7am and 7pm.

Fares vary between 60p and £1.30 depending on the distance travelled. FirstDay is a day pass that costs £2.60, or £2.30 if purchased after 9.30am Mon-Fri and all day on weekends, and gives you one day of unlimited bus travel in the Aberdeen area (FirstDay isn't valid on night buses and park and ride services). Weekly and monthly tickets are also available.

Accommodation
King George VI Memorial Hostel
This lovely old granite townhouse is 15 minutes walk from the bus/train station and close to all amenities. It is kept very clean and tidy and, even when there are large groups in, a good nights sleep is on the cards. The lounge is rather functional but nice enough to chill out, read a book or watch some TV.
8 Queens Road, Aberdeen
☎ *(01224) 646 988 or 0870 155 3255*
Website www.syha.org.uk
Dorm bed £12.50-14.75 (£11.50-13.75 HI/SYHA)
Reception open 8am-11am & 4.30pm-11.45pm daily; **curfew** *2am*

TV **K** **L**

Maintenance & cleanliness	★★★★☆
Facilities	★★☆
Atmosphere & character	★★★
Security	★
Overall rating	★★★★☆

Eating & Drinking
Aberdeen is hardly a gastronomic paradise, but it does have some good budget eating options including the Ashvale fish and chip shop *(42 Great Western Road, Aberdeen;* ☎ *(01224) 596 981)*. The Safeway supermarket at 215 King Street is a good place to go if you want to stock up on picnic supplies or food to cook back at the hostel.

Sights
Aberdeen Art Gallery
Aberdeen's art gallery features a graceful marble interior and an art collection that includes the work of Impressionists and the Scottish Colourists.
Schoolhill, Aberdeen
☎ *(01224) 523 700.*
Website www.aagm.co.uk
Admission free
Open Mon-Sat 10am-5pm, Sun 2pm-5pm

Aberdeen Maritime Museum
This maritime museum chronicles the city's bond with the sea. Exhibits cover topics such as fishing, the North Sea oil industry, shipbuilding and the history of the port.
Shiprow, Aberdeen
☎ *(01224) 337700*
Website www.aagm.co.uk
Admission free
Open Mon-Sat 10am-5pm, Sun noon-3pm

Gordon Highlanders Museum
This museum focuses on the kilted soldiers of the British Army's Gordon Highlanders Regiment. In addition to the museum's historical collection there

are touch screen interactive displays and an audio-visual presentation.
St Lukes, Viewfield Road, Aberdeen
☎ *(01224) 319323*
Website *www.gordonhighlanders.com*
Admission £2.50
Open *Apr-Oct Tue-Sat 10.30am-4.30pm (last entry 4pm), Sun 1.30pm-4.30pm (last entry 4pm)*

Provost Skene's House

This 16th century mansion has been restored with an elegant 17th century interior and it also contains art and local history exhibits.
Guestrow, off Broad Street, Aberdeen
☎ *(01224) 523702*
Website *www.aagm.co.uk*
Admission *free*
Open *Mon-Sat 10am-5pm, Sun 1pm-4pm*

Satrosphere

This hands-on science museum has over 70 exhibits plus science demonstrations. Like most science museums, it is primarily a children's attraction.
179 Constitution Street, Aberdeen
☎ *(01224) 622 211*
Website *www.satrosphere.net*
Admission £5
Open *Mon-Sat 10am-5pm, Sun 11.30am-5pm*

Highland

This large region in northern Scotland is one of the country's most visited regions and most travellers that make it north of Edinburgh try to discover the real Scotland. The most popular areas in Highland include Loch Ness, the Cairngorms and the Isle of Skye.

Fort William & Ben Nevis

Fort William is a popular destination for hikers and skiers who come here because of its close proximity to Britain's highest mountain, Ben Nevis.

The town has a spectacular setting wedged between Ben Nevis and Loch Linnhe, but it is poorly planned and a busy dual carriageway cuts the town off from the waterfront.

Practical Information
INFORMATION CENTRES
Fort William Tourist Information Centre
Cameron Centre, Cameron Square, Fort William
☎ *(01397) 703 781*
Website *www.visit-fortwilliam.co.uk*
Open *Jan-Mar Mon-Sat 9am-5pm, Sun 10am-4pm; Apr-Jun Mon-Sat 9am-6pm, Sun 10am-4pm; Jul-Mon-Sat9am-7pm, Sun 10am-6pm; Aug Mon-Sat 9am-8.30pm, Sun 9am-6pm; Sep-Oct Mon-Sat 9am-6pm, Sun 10am-5.30pm; Nov-Dec Jan-Mar Mon-Sat 9am-5pm, Sun 10am-4pm*

Glen Nevis Visitor Centre
Glen Nevis, Fort William
☎ *(01397) 705 922*
Open *Easter to mid-May 9am-5pm daily; mid-May to Sep 9am-6pm daily; Oct 9am-5pm daily*

Coming & Going
There are several trains each day between Fort William and Glasgow's Queen Street Station and there is a daily train to London (Euston Station). Buses run from Fort William to Edinburgh, Glasgow, Oban and Inverness.

Local Transport
Highland Country Buses (☎ *(01397) 702 373; website www.rapsons.co.uk*) run Fort William's local bus service with buses around town as well as a country bus service that goes to Kinlochleven and Inverness.

The most useful routes for most travellers are buses 41 and 42 to Glen Nevis as well as buses to backpackers' accommodation in nearby towns like Corpach.

Accommodation
TOWN CENTRE
Bank Street Lodge
If you're stopping off in Fort William this is an ideal place to kip. The cool blue bedrooms with wooden bunks are clean and warm in winter. The kitchen is fairly well fitted out and there's a small lounge if you don't fancy sampling Fort William's heady nightlife!
Bank Street, Fort William
☎ *(01397) 700 070*
Website *www.accommodation-fortwilliam.com*
Dorm bed *£11*
Credit cards *Amex, MC, Visa*
Reception open *7am-11am & 5pm-11pm*

📺 🅺

Maintenance & cleanliness	★★★★
Facilities	★★
Atmosphere & character	★★★★
Security	★
Overall rating	★★★

Calluna
Calluna is perched above Fort William, with views over Loch Linnhe. It consists of self-catering apartments, which are used for groups as well as hostel accommodation. The rooms have combinations of bunks and single beds. Each apartment has a living room with TV.
Heathercroft, Fort William
☎ *(01397) 700 451*
Website *www.fortwilliamholiday.co.uk*
Dorm bed *£10.50-12*
Credit cards *MC, Visa*

🚗 📺 🅺 🅻

Maintenance & cleanliness	★★★★⯪
Facilities	★★
Atmosphere & character	★★
Security	★
Overall rating	★★★⯪

Fort William Backpackers
As popular in winter as it is in summer, this old mansion house is bright and welcoming. The lounge has window seats with great views and a roaring fire (sometimes even in summer). The kitchen is small and can get crowded but you're not far from restaurants and pubs if you'd rather eat out. It's mainly climbers and walkers who come here but there are 'indie' travellers too.
Alma Road, Fort William
☎ *(01397) 700 711*
Website *www.scotlands-top-hostels.com*
Dorm bed *£11-12*
Credit cards *MC, Visa*
Reception open *7am-11am & 5pm-11pm daily*
🚗 📺 🄺 🄻

Maintenance & cleanliness	★★★★
Facilities	★★★⯪
Atmosphere & character	★★★★★
Security	★
Overall rating	★★★★⯪

OUTSIDE THE TOWN CENTRE
There are several hostels outside the town centre, mostly in stunning natural settings, that cater mostly to outdoorsy-types.

Achintee Farm Bunkhouse
Right across the river from the Glen Nevis Visitor Centre, the hostel sites next to Achintee Farmhouse (B&B and self catering). It is suited to hill walkers and climbers with a fabulous drying room for your typically sodden clothes (this can be a very wet part of the country). There's also golf, mountain biking, canoeing, fishing and horse riding all nearby.
Glen Nevis, near Fort William
☎ *(01397) 702 240*
Website *www.glennevis.com*
Dorm bed *£10;* ***twin room*** *£24*
Credit cards *MC, Visa*
🚗 📺 🄺 🄻 🄽

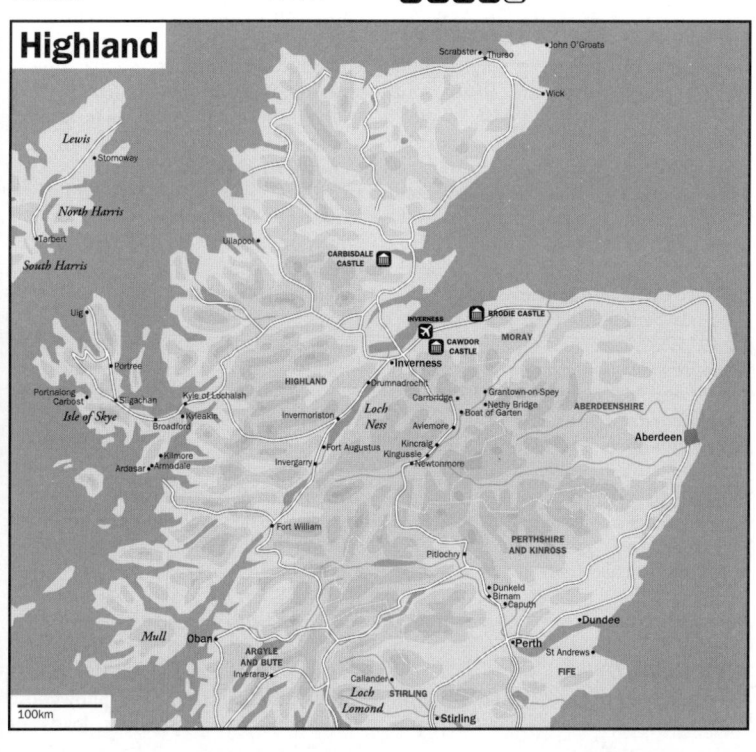

Ben Nevis Inn

Maintenance & cleanliness	★★★★
Facilities	★★½
Atmosphere & character	★★★★½
Security	★
Overall rating	★★★

This characterful bar and bunkhouse is a favourite of West Highland Way walkers and outdoorsy-types wishing to explore the nearby mountains. Live music, rustic interiors and great food make the Inn very popular. Bunkhouse accommodation is cramped yet adequate and there are basic kitchen and drying facilities.
Achintee, Glen Nevis, Fort William
☎ *(01397) 701 227*
Website *www.ben-nevis-inn.co.uk*
Dorm bed *£11-12*
Credit cards *MC, Visa*

Maintenance & cleanliness	★★★
Facilities	★★½
Atmosphere & character	★★★★½
Security	★
Overall rating	★★★

Farr Cottage Activity Centre

For those who are looking for more than just a place to sleep you'll find a lively, outgoing crowd here. The bar and TV lounge are excellent places to meet fellow travellers and make the most of your time here. The rooms are spotless and cosy and the kitchen is well stocked if you're cooking your dinner. However, if you can't be bothered or have no food, no worries they'll cater for every need, just give them a bit of warning.
Corpach, Fort William
☎ *(01397) 772 315*
Website *www.farrcottage.com*
Dorm bed *£11;* **twin room** *£30*
Credit cards *MC, Visa*
Reception open *7am-11am & 4pm-midnight*

Maintenance & cleanliness	★★★★★
Facilities	★★★
Atmosphere & character	★★★★½
Security	★
Overall rating	★★★★

Glen Nevis SYHA

For those wanting to ascend Britain's highest peak, Ben Nevis, via the popular tourist path this Norwegian-style hostel is perfect – the path begins just across the road. The hostel caters for outdoor enthusiasts and less active visitors with a large kitchen, lounge areas and drying room.
Glen Nevis, Fort William
☎ *(01397) 702 336 or 0870 553 255*
Website *www.syha.org.uk*
Dorm bed *£12.50-14.50 (£11.50-13.50 HI/SYHA)*
Credit cards *MC, Visa*
Reception open *7.30am-11am & 5pm-11.45pm daily*

Maintenance & cleanliness	★★★★½
Facilities	★★
Atmosphere & character	★★
Security	★
Overall rating	★★★

Loch Ossian SYHA

Something of a jewel in the SYHA crown, this place – and its location – has to be believed. Its use of renewable energy and 'green' water and waste systems means it makes the lowest possible impact on its dreamlike surroundings. The accommodation is suitably top-notch and the dry toilet system is almost pleasant! You can only get here by foot and you must bring your own sleeping bag (it cuts down on the washing!)
Corrour, By Fort William
☎ *(01397) 732 207 or 0870 004 1139*
Website *www.syha.org.uk*
Dorm bed *£12.50 (£11.50 HI/SYHA)*
Credit cards *MC, Visa*
Open *18 Mar-29 Oct*

Maintenance & cleanliness	★★★★★
Facilities	★★
Atmosphere & character	★★★★½
Security	★½
Overall rating	★★★★½

The Smiddy Bunkhouse

This stone and wooden alpine hut overlooking Loch Linnhe is 6.5km from Corpach. Inside the hostel the pine-clad walls create a cosy feel and it is furnished with robust yet comfy seating. The bunkrooms are alpine-style and very well looked after. The shower rooms are sparkling. The Snowgoose Mountain Centre provides loads of activities and courses, from winter survival to sailing and canoeing, so it's popular with university groups and outdoor types. There's a shop nearby for food supplies.

Station Road, Corpach, near Fort William
☎ *(01397) 772 467*
Website *www.highland-mountain-guides.co.uk*
Dorm bed *£10-15.60*
Credit cards *MC, Visa*

Maintenance & cleanliness	★★★★★
Facilities	★★★☆
Atmosphere & character	★★★★★
Security	★☆
Overall rating	★★★★

Hiking

The hike to the summit of Ben Nevis (15km; 5-7 hours) begins at the Glen Nevis Visitor Centre about 3km outside Fort William. During summer this is a very popular hike and the trail is busy with other hikers, but only experienced hikers tackle the summit during winter.

There are a lot of shorter walks around town including several walks in Glen Nevis.

Sights
West Highland Museum

This museum in the centre of Fort William is renowned for its Jacobite collections and it also has exhibits on archaeology, geology, natural and local history.

Cameron Square, Fort William
☎ *(01397) 702 169*
Website *www.fort-william.net/museum/*
Admission *£2*
Open *Jan-May Mon-Sat 10am-4pm; Jun Mon-Sat 10am-5pm; Jul-Aug Mon-Sat 10am-5pm, Sun 2pm-5pm; Sep Mon-Sat 10am-5pm; Oct-Dec Mon-Sat 10am-4pm*

Inverness & Loch Ness

The biggest city in the Highlands is a busy transport hub and a popular base for exploring nearby Loch Ness.

Inverness boasts a castle and a couple of minor museums, but the main draw card is Loch Ness, which is only 10km away.

Apart from trying to spot the illusive Loch Ness monster, the Loch's attractions include Kilravock Castle; Cawdor Castle, which was the setting for Shakespeare's Macbeth; as well as several small villages such as Beauly and Nairn.

Practical Information
Tourist Information Centre

Castle Wynd, Inverness
☎ *(01463) 234 353*
Open Jan to mid-Jun Mon-Sat 9am-5pm, Sun 10am-4pm; mid-Jun to Ag Mon-Sat 9am-7pm, Sun 9.30am-5pm; Sep-Dec Mon-Sat 9am-5pm, Sun 10am-4pm

American Express

Alba Travel, 43 Church Street, Inverness
☎ *(01463) 239 188*
Open *Mon-Fri 9am-5.30pm, Sat 9.30am-1pm*

Inverness Job Centre

River House, Young Street, Inverness
☎ *(01463) 888 100*
Website *www.inverness-online.com/jobcentre/*

Laundry

17 Young Street, Inverness
☎ *(01463) 242507*

Coming & Going

Inverness's airport *(website www.hial.co.uk/inverness-airport.html)* handles frequent flights, including budget airlines such as easyJet. The airport is located 16km east of Inverness and local buses run regularly between the airport and the city centre.

Coaches terminate at the coach station at Farraline Park. National Express coaches run to London and Scottish Citylink (☎ *0870 550 5050; website www.citylink.co.uk*) run coaches to destinations throughout Scotland with the most frequent services going to Edinburgh and Glasgow.

The train station on Station Square has trains to Aberdeen, Edinburgh, Glasgow, London and Thurso.

Local Transport

Highland Country buses (☎ *(01463) 222 244; website www.rapsons.co.uk*) run Inverness's public transport service; there are buses to destinations throughout the city and the surrounding countryside including much of the area around Loch Ness.

The Tourist Trail Rover ticket is a good deal if you want to do a lot of sightseeing by public transport. For £6, this travel pass gives you unlimited travel on Highland Country buses routes 11, 11C, 12, 12A and 13 which allow you to make a day trip from Inverness visiting Cawdor Castle, Culloden Battlefield and Loch Ness.

Accommodation

Bazpackers

This quiet, laid back hostel has a lovely garden and nice views with a homely feel to the living room and kitchen. This isn't a place you'd stay if you're looking for a wild time but is an ideal hostel for chilling and getting some shut eye.
4 Culduthel Road, Inverness
☎ *(01463) 717 663*
Dorm bed £9-11; **double/twin room** £24-28
Credit cards MC, Visa
Reception open 8am-11am & 5pm-11pm daily

Maintenance & cleanliness	★★★★☆
Facilities	★★★☆
Atmosphere & character	★★★★★
Security	★
Overall rating	★★★★☆

Eastgate Backpackers

Above the Zenabar restaurant (discount to guests) this colourful hostel is popular with young travellers. Warm in winter and busy in summer it has good facilities and a friendly atmosphere – perfect if you're on your own. The staff are well travelled and are on the ball so far as what their guests need.
38 Eastgate, Inverness
☎ *(01463) 718 756*
Website *www.eastgatebackpackers.com*
Dorm bed £9.50-12; **twin room** £26-30
Credit cards MC, Visa
Reception open 8am-11am & 4pm-11pm daily

Maintenance & cleanliness	★★★★
Facilities	★★
Atmosphere & character	★★★★★
Security	★
Overall rating	★★★★☆

Ho Ho Hostel

The huge living room with its windows that look over the street is the best thing about this hostel – bar the staff, who all seem to be travellers themselves. The kitchen is a fair size but struggles to cope if a rush on. The dorms and bathrooms are pretty basic.
23a High Street, Inverness
☎ *(01463) 221 225*
Website *www.hohohostel.force9.co.uk*
Dorm bed £9-10; **twin room** £24
Credit cards MC, Visa
Open Jan & Mar-Dec; **reception open** 8am-11am & 4pm-11pm daily

Maintenance & cleanliness	★★★
Facilities	★★
Atmosphere & character	★★★★
Security	★
Overall rating	★★★

Inverness Student Hostel

This affable hostel is tuned in to young backpackers who want something interesting, safe and homely. Its fireplace and window seats make for much lounging around, and there's a smoking area for those otherwise banished to doorways. If you don't like the colour pink, just keep your eyes closed.
8 Culduthel Road, Inverness
☎ *(01463) 236 556*
Website *www.scotlands-top-hostels.com*
Dorm bed £11-12
Credit cards MC, Visa
Reception open 7.30am-11am & 4pm-11pm daily; **curfew** 2.30am

Maintenance & cleanliness	★★★★
Facilities	★★★☆
Atmosphere & character	★★★★★☆
Security	★
Overall rating	★★★★☆

Inverness SYHA

This modern purpose-built youth hostel is popular with groups and can cater for big numbers. That aside it's clean

and fairly quiet with all the facilities you'd expect in a large hostel. There are a number of common areas and quiet rooms so you can find a place away from the kids. Good for an overnight stop.
Victoria Drive, Inverness
☎ *(01463) 231 771*
Website *www.syha.org.uk*
Dorm bed *£13-15 (£12-14 HI/SYHA)*
Credit cards *MC, Visa*
Curfew *2am*

Maintenance & cleanliness	★★★★
Facilities	★★★
Atmosphere & character	★★★★½
Security	★★★
Overall rating	★★★★½

The Long Lie In
An annex of the Ho Ho Hostel, this is a small self-contained unit with share room and kitchen but no lounge – you can use the Ho Ho's if you want to socialise, watch TV or chill out. It's pretty basic and a little unloved.
28 Ardconnel Street, Inverness
☎ *(01463) 713 517*
Website *www.longliein.force9.co.uk*
Dorm bed *£12*
Credit cards *MC, Visa*

Maintenance & cleanliness	★★
Facilities	★
Atmosphere & character	★★
Security	★★½
Overall rating	★★½

Eating & Drinking
The big Safeway supermarket on Millburn Road is the best spot to stock up on food. There is also the usual selection of fast food joints around town.

Sights
INVERNESS CITY
Inverness Castle
This castle dominates the city centre and its Drum Tower is open to visitors with an exhibition portraying the castle's history.
Between Castle Road & Castle Street, Inverness
☎ *(01463) 243 363*
Open *Easter-Nov 10.30am-5.30pm daily*

Inverness Museum & Art Gallery
This museum features mostly local history and the adjoining gallery plays host to a programme of art exhibitions.
Castle Wynd, Inverness
☎ *(01463) 237 114*
Admission *free*
Open Mon-Sat 9am-5pm

OUTSIDE INVERNESS CITY
Brodie Castle
This castle is located in Moray, 38km west of Inverness, so it is not technically in Highland but it is included in this chapter since it is close enough to Inverness to make a nice day trip. Brodie Castle dates from the 16th century and the interior features some nice art plus the usual collection of old furnishings and porcelain.
Brodie, Forres, Moray
☎ *(01309) 641 371*
Website *www.nts.org.uk*
Admission *£5 (£3.75 HI/SYHA)*
Open *Apr noon-4pm daily; May-Jun Mon-Thu & Sun noon-4pm; Jul-Aug noon-4pm daily; Sep Mon-Thu & Sun noon-4pm; grounds all year 9.30am-sunset daily*

Cawdor Castle
Located near Inverness Dalcross Airport, Cawdor Castle is one of Scotland's most famous as it was the setting for Shakespeare's *Macbeth*. The castle dates from the 14th century and its grounds boast some nice walks and golf course.
Website *www.cawdorcastle.com*
Admission *£6.50 (£5.50 students)*
Open 1 May-10 Oct 10am-5.30pm daily

Culloden Battlefield
This historic battlefield is the site of the last Jacobite uprising in 1746. Most of the battlefield including Leanach Cottage, which survived the battle, has been restored and there is an exhibition at the visitor centre that explains the history behind the battlefield.
B9006, Culloden Moor, Inverness
🚌 *12*
☎ *(01463) 790607*
Website *www.nts.org.uk*
Admission *£5 (£3.75 HI/SYHA)*

Open *Feb-Mar 11am-4pm daily; Apr-Jun 9am-6pm daily; Jul-Aug 9am-7pm daily; Sep-Oct 9am-6pm daily; Nov-Dec 11am-4pm daily*

Culrain & Carbisdale Castle

Although Culrain is no more than a small village a 45-minute drive north of Inverness, thousands of backpackers come here to stay at Carbisdale Castle – a youth hostel set inside a real Highland castle.

Accommodation
Carbisdale Castle SYHA
This must be the apogee of hostelling: a grand castle complete with a library, marble statues, sweeping staircases, stained glass windows, battlements and – they say – a ghost! There's heaps of space to spread out here and the grounds are worth a wander. It is clean, well cared for and certainly worth writing home about.
Culrain
🚌 *Macleod's Coaches Tain-Lairg bus to Invershin Hotel* 🚌 *Culrain*
☎ *(01549) 421 232 or 0870 004 1109*
Website *www.carbisdale.org*
Dorm bed *£14.50-15 (£13.50-14 HI/SYHA)*
Credit cards *MC, Visa*
Open *Mar-Oct; reception open 7am-11pm daily*

Maintenance & cleanliness	★★★★★
Facilities	★★★★☆
Atmosphere & character	★★★★☆
Security	★★
Overall rating	★★★★

Drumnadrochit

Only 20km south of Inverness, Drumnadrochit is one of the main tourist centres on Loch Ness. The town is home to two exhibition centres and the impressive Urquhart Castle.

Practical Information
Tourist Information Centre
The Car Park, Drumnadrochit
☎ *(01456) 459 076*

Coming and Going
Highland Country bus 17 goes to Inverness, which is only 30 minutes away, making Drumnadrochit close enough for a day trip.

Accommodation
Loch Ness Backpackers
If you're looking for a carefree, unhurried couple of days, this hostel takes some beating. There's a slight element of chaos and some of the furniture is a little bit worse for wear but the staff are very friendly and these little foibles just seem to add to its charm. There are dorms in the main farmhouse or in the converted barn (a bit like Butlin's chalets). Loch Ness and the floating log that folk think is the monster is 10 minutes away.
Coiltie Farmhouse, East Lewiston, Drumnadrochit
☎ *(01456) 450 807*
Website *www.lochness-backpackers.com*
Dorm bed *£11.50;* **twin room** *£26-27*
Credit cards *MC, Visa*

Maintenance & cleanliness	★★★★
Facilities	★★★☆
Atmosphere & character	★★★★★
Security	★
Overall rating	★★★☆

Sights
Official Loch Ness Exhibition
This is a museum about Loch Ness and the Loch Ness monster that attempts to provide a scientific and reasoned coverage of Nessie with information on the natural history and geology of the region and less emphasis on the stories and legends that surround the monster.
A82, Drumnadrochit
☎ *(01456) 450 573*
Website *www.loch-ness-scotland.com*
Admission *£5.95*
Open *Jan-Easter 10am-3.30pm daily; Easter-May 9.30am-5pm; Jun 9am-6pm; Jul-Aug 9am-8pm; Sep-Oct 9.30pm-5.30pm; Nov 10am-3.30pm*

Original Loch Ness Exhibition Centre
Like the Official Loch Ness Exhibition, this museum features exhibits on Loch Ness, the monster and various aspects

of Scottish history. It is a little more geared towards Nessie and the legends surrounding it.
Drumnadrochit
☎ *(01456) 450 342*
Website *www.lochness-centre.com*
Open *9am-8pm daily*

Urquhart Castle
Urquhart Castle is one of Scotland's largest and most important castles and it occupies a beautiful site, overlooking Loch Ness. The castle was built in the 1230s, but most of what you see today dates from the 14th and 15th centuries. There is a visitor centre at the castle with exhibits and an audio-visual presentation.
A82, 3.25km south of Drumnadrochit
☎ *(01456) 450 551*
Website *www.historic-scotland.gov.uk*
Admission *£6 (£4.50 students)*
Open *Jan-Mar 9.30am-4.30pm daily (last entry 3.45pm); Apr-Sep 9.30am-6.30pm daily (last entry 5.45pm); Oct-Dec 9.30am-4.30pm daily (last entry 3.45pm)*

Fort Augustus, Invermoriston & Invergarry

Fort Augustus, Invermoriston are at the southern end of Loch Ness. Invergarry is a little farther south on the bank of Loch Oich. All three villages offer a quieter alternative to staying in Drumnadrochit or Inverness.

Accommodation
FORT AUGUSTUS
Morag's Lodge
On a wooded hill overlooking the village of Fort Augustus lies this busy hostel. Catering for young adventurous climbers, canoeists and skiers, its bar is busy in the evenings with guests sharing – and boasting about – their sporting exploits. Evening meals are available.
Bunnoch Brae, Fort Augustus
☎ *(01320) 366 289*
Dorm bed *£12.50;* **twin room** *£30*
Credit cards *MC, Visa*

Maintenance & cleanliness	★★★★
Facilities	★★★★½
Atmosphere & character	★★★★★
Security	★
Overall rating	★★★★

INVERMORISTON
Loch Ness SYHA
This roadside and loch side hostel has a character all of its own. The myriad potted flowers make the Loch Ness SYHA almost Mediterranean and the private beach on the shore of Loch Ness hosts bonfires all year round. The big kitchen is a real bonus but its dining room/lounge with its wooden table and chairs and both a piano and Hammond organ that is the scene of much singing and joviality.
Glen Moriston, near Invermoriston
☎ *(01320) 351 274 or 0870 004 1138*
Website *www.syha.org.uk*
Dorm bed *£12-13 (£11-12 HI/SYHA)*
Credit cards *MC, Visa*
Open *Feb-Oct;* **reception open** *7.30am-11am & 4pm-11.45pm daily*

Maintenance & cleanliness	★★★
Facilities	★★★½
Atmosphere & character	★★★★½
Security	★
Overall rating	★★★

INVERGARRY
Invergarry Lodge
Just on the edge of a forest, this house is a bit of a tardis and can cater for 26 people. Clean and looked after, the rooms are bright and simply furnished. It's just 10 minutes away from a lovely country pub and delightful walks for spotters, bird watchers and tree huggers.
Mandally Road, Invergarry
☎ *(01809) 501412*
Website *www.invergarrylodge.co.uk*
Dorm bed *£11.50-12;* **twin room** *£26*
Credit cards *MC, Visa*

Maintenance & cleanliness	★★★★½
Facilities	★★★½
Atmosphere & character	★★★★½
Security	★★½
Overall rating	★★★

Strathspey & the Cairngorms

One of Scotland's most visited regions is the Cairngorm mountain range, Scotland's second highest, and the nearby towns on the River Spey.

The Cairngorms feature tundra and some good hiking trails including the 39km Lairig Ghru Trail. During winter there is a popular ski resort here.

Virtually all towns in the area straddle the River Spey, which is noted for its excellent salmon fishing.

All the towns in the region are ideal bases for exploring the Cairngorms. Most of them are small, quaint places but Aviemore, the region's largest town, has much less charm. Regardless of where you choose to stay, you should expect plenty of tourists, particularly during holiday periods.

Practical Information
Aviemore Tourist Information Centre
Grampian Road, Aviemore
☎ *(01479) 810 363*
Open *Jan-Jun Mon-Fri 9am-5pm, Sat 10am-4pm; Jul-mid Sep Mon-Sat 9am-6pm, Sun 10am-4pm; mid Sep-Dec Mon-Fri 9am-5pm, Sat 10am-4pm*

Grantown-on-Spey Tourist Information Centre
54 High Street, Grantown-on-Spey
☎ *(01479) 872 773*
Open *Easter-Oct 10am-5pm daily*

Kingussie Tourist Information Centre
Duke Street, Kingussie
☎ *(01540) 661 307*
Open *Apr-Aug Mon-Sat 9.30am-5.30pm; Sep-Oct Mon-Fri 9.30am-4.30pm*

Newtonmore Tourist Information Centre
Main Street, Newtonmore
☎ *(01540) 673912*
Website *www.newtonmore.com*
Open *Mon-Sat 9am-5pm*

Coming & Going
Aviemore is the best-connected town in the region and most travellers find it easiest to use this town as a transport hub while visiting the region. There are frequent trains and buses from here to Edinburgh, Glasgow and Inverness.

Local Transport
Highland Country (☎ *(01479) 811 211; website www.rapsons.co.uk*) operate bus services between Inverness and Newtonmore with stops at most towns in the Strathspey region, including Kingussie, Kincraig, Boat of Garten, Nethy Bridge, Grantown-on-Spey, Carrbridge and Aviemore. They also run a bus service between Aviemore and Cairngorm.

A funicular railway (*website www.cairngormmountain.com*) runs to the summit of Cairngorm, but there is no access to most hiking trails from the Ptarmigan Centre station at the top. The train runs every 15 minutes and costs £7.50 return.

Accommodation
AVIEMORE
Aviemore Bunkhouse
This spanking new hostel is next door to one of Aviemore's best pubs, which more than makes up for its lack of common area. It's got everything you could possibly need and the dorms and bathrooms are of the highest standard. Definitely for the backpacker who just wants somewhere clean and safe to crash.
Dalfaber Road, Aviemore
☎ *(01479) 811 181*
Website *www.aviemore-bunkhouse.com*
Dorm bed £12; **twin room** £29
Credit cards MC, Visa

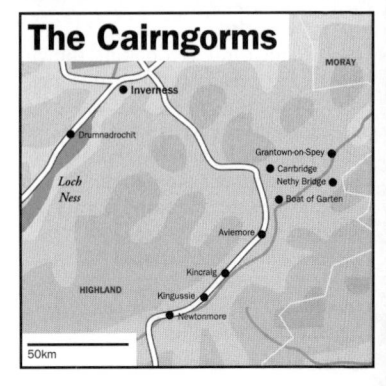

The Cairngorms

Maintenance & cleanliness	★★★★★
Facilities	★★
Atmosphere & character	★★★
Security	★★
Overall rating	★★★★½

Aviemore SYHA
This purpose-built hostel sits on wooded grounds and whilst big and modern, it still has a character and cheer all of its own. It's spotless – and you'll see staff constantly keeping it so – and very well maintained with an easy going atmosphere that makes everyone from travellers, outdoor types, groups and families, feel welcome.
25 Grampian Road, Aviemore
☎ *(01479) 810 345 or 0870 004 1104*
Website *www.syha.org.uk*
Dorm bed *£13-14 (£12-13 HI/SYHA)*
Credit cards *MC, Visa*
Reception open *7.30am-11am & 4pm-11.45pm daily;* **curfew** *2am*

🚗♿📺🅺🅻

Maintenance & cleanliness	★★★★★
Facilities	★★★
Atmosphere & character	★★★★
Security	★★½
Overall rating	★★★★

Cairngorm Lodge (Loch Morlich SYHA)
Now more geared to families, this hostel is still one of SYHA's flagships with enough common areas to ensure that backpackers and groups can chill out and spread out in almost luxurious surroundings. A base for the Norwegian government during WWII it has plenty of character on top of great facilities and, of course, an ideal location near Loch Morlich, 11km from Aviemore.
Loch Morlich, Glenmore Forest Park, 11km from Aviemore
☎ *(01479) 861 238 or 0870 004 1137*
Website *www.syha.org.uk*
Dorm bed *£12.50-13.50 (£11.50-12.50 HI/SYHA)*
Credit cards *MC, Visa*
Open *Christmas-Oct;* **reception open** *7.30am-11am & 4pm-11.45pm daily;* **curfew** *11.45pm*

♿📺🅺🅻

Maintenance & cleanliness	★★★★★
Facilities	★★★
Atmosphere & character	★★★
Security	★★½
Overall rating	★★★★½

BOAT OF GARTEN
Fraoch Lodge
This little hostel is right on the main road as you enter Boat of Garten. It is a homely and comfortable hostel that is a bit like staying at your posh aunt's. It is aimed at families and lovers of the hills, the owner can advise on the best routes or offer courses. Meals can be provided or you can cook in the outside kitchen/diner (it's better than it sounds).
Deshar Road, Boat of Garten
☎ *(01479) 831 331*
Website *www.scotmountain.co.uk*
Dorm bed *£10;* **twin room** *£28*
Credit cards *MC, Visa*

🚗📺🅺🅻

Maintenance & cleanliness	★★★★★
Facilities	★★★
Atmosphere & character	★★★★½
Security	★
Overall rating	★★★★

CARRBRIDGE
Carrbridge Bunkhouse
On the outskirts of this lovely village is this unrivalled cabin. Full of interesting things it must have taken years of thought and collecting to put together. It has a sauna, a glorious wooden 'sitootrie' (covered veranda) and the kind of rooms you've only ever seen in a spaghetti western. The outside fire can be enjoyed all year round and the area is midge free (a state-of-the-art contraption kills the blighters). Bring your own towels and sleeping bag (if you prefer).
Dalrachney House, Carrbridge
☎ *(01479) 841 250*
Website *www.carrbridge-bunkhouse.co.uk*
Dorm bed *£7*
Credit cards *MC, Visa*

🚗📺🅺🅻

Maintenance & cleanliness	★★★★★
Facilities	★★★★½
Atmosphere & character	★★★★★
Security	★
Overall rating	★★★★

GRANTOWN-ON-SPEY
Ardenbeg
On a street that lies parallel to the main trawl, this well designed and roomy

basement of a handsome granite house is a real find for families, small groups or individuals. The accommodation is top notch whilst the outdoor spaces such as the play park and the fire circle (for barbecues) are big enough to let different groups enjoy them. Guests can enjoy discounts in local restaurants and a free game of pool in the nearby pub.

Ardenbeg, Grant Road, Grantown-on-Spey
☎ *(01479) 872824*
Website *www.ardenbeg.co.uk*
Dorm bed *£11.50*
Credit cards *MC, Visa*
🚗 🅿 📺 🅺 🅻

Maintenance & cleanliness	★★★★★
Facilities	★★★
Atmosphere & character	★★★★★
Security	★★
Overall rating	★★★★

KINCRAIG
Glen Feshie Hostel

To find this charming country house follow the signs for Feshie Bridge and head past the gliding club. The accommodation is in a roomy loft and offers sturdy yet comfy beds. It has a kitchen, dining room and living room with a wood burning stove and heaps of character. There's free porridge in the mornings and meals can be prepared with notice. Fresh baked bread and fresh eggs are also available.

Balachroick House, Glen Feshie, near Kincraig
☎ *(01540) 651 323*
Dorm bed *£9*
🅿 🅺 🅻

Maintenance & cleanliness	★★★★★
Facilities	★★
Atmosphere & character	★★★★★
Security	★
Overall rating	★★★★

KINGUSSIE
Insh Hostel

This small country bungalow provides simple but quality accommodation. It is designed and kitted out with the hillwalker/outdoor sports person in mind and it is an ideal place to lay your head and recover from exertion. The dining kitchen is the common area and has a big enough table to fit everyone in.

Bothan Airigh Insh, by Kingussie
☎ *(01540) 661 051*
Dorm bed *£9;* **double/twin room** *£24*
🚗 🅺

Maintenance & cleanliness	★★★★★
Facilities	★★½
Atmosphere & character	★★★★
Security	★
Overall rating	★★★★½

The Laird's Bothy

This hostel is popular with groups who come to mountain bike, climb, ski and do a host of other outdoor sports. It's right next door to the rather good Tipsy Lord's restaurant and there are quite a few good eating and drinking places in the town itself. The accommodation is clean and the hostel has a great atmosphere, especially when it's busy.

High Street, Kingussie
☎ *(01540) 661 334*
Website *www.thetipsylaird.co.uk*
Dorm bed *£9*
Credit cards *MC, Visa*
Reception open *7am-10am & 4pm-10pm daily*
🚗 📺 🅺 🅻

Maintenance & cleanliness	★★★★½
Facilities	★★½
Atmosphere & character	★★★★★
Security	★
Overall rating	★★★★½

NETHY BRIDGE
Lazy Duck Hostel

On the edge of a forest and next to a duck pond is this fabulous bunkhouse. Designed to beguile even the most blasé backpacker, the accommodation is well laid out and has those little extras such as a secluded hammock and a red squirrel feeding point – that will make sure you wont forget it. The covered garden means you can sit out all year round.

Badanfhuarain, Nethy Bridge
☎ *(01479) 821 642*
Website *www.lazyduck.co.uk*
Dorm bed *£9.50*
Credit cards *MC, Visa*
🚗 ♿ 🅺 🅻

Maintenance & cleanliness	★★★★★
Facilities	★★★
Atmosphere & character	★★★★★
Security	★
Overall rating	★★★★

NEWTONMORE
Croftdhu Hostel
Take the road west at the Highlander Hotel and keep going up the single track until you see a modern slate-roofed bungalow. This purpose-built hostel is small but perfectly formed, providing three small cottages that each sleeps four. If you bring your own sleeping bag you can save £2.
Strane Road, Newtonmore
☎ *(01540) 673 504*
Website *www.croftholidays.co.uk*
Dorm bed *£12-14;* **double/twin room** *£28-32*
Credit cards *MC, Visa*

Maintenance & cleanliness	★★★★★
Facilities	★★★
Atmosphere & character	★★★★½
Security	★
Overall rating	★★★★

Newtonmore Hostel
Built to cater for walkers and climbers, this small hostel has got it all. From copious amounts of storage space to keep all your gear to a children's play area, the owners have thought of everything that adventurers and active families need to make their stay comfortable.
Craigelachie House, Main Street, Newtonmore
☎ *(01540) 673 360*
Website *www.highlandhostel.co.uk*
Dorm bed *£10;* **twin room** *£24*
Credit cards *MC, Visa*

Maintenance & cleanliness	★★★★★
Facilities	★★★
Atmosphere & character	★★★★★
Security	-
Overall rating	★★★★

Strathspey Mountain Hostel
On the main street in Newtonmore, this hostel is well placed for days on the hills and nights in the local pubs. Its welcoming kitchen/dining/living room is the hub of the hostel and it's well furnished and equipped. It is basic but cosy and it has an excellent drying room. If you arrive by public transport they'll knock 50p off the nightly rate.
Main Street, Newtonmore
☎ *(01540) 673 694*
Website *www.newtonmore.com/strathspey*
Dorm bed *£10*
Credit cards *MC, Visa*

Maintenance & cleanliness	★★★★★
Facilities	★★★½
Atmosphere & character	★★★★★
Security	★★
Overall rating	★★★★

Hiking
The main hiking trail in the Cairngorms is the Lairig Ghru trail (39km; 8 hours) which goes through the Cairngorms National Nature Reserve between Coylumbridge, near Aviemore, to Inverey, near Braemar.

Other hiking trails include the Northern Corries Path (7 hours), a challenging hike to the summit of Ben MacDui, which is Britain's second highest mountain.

The Windy Ridge Trail (3-4 hours) goes to the peak of Cairngorm.

Sights
Clan MacPherson Museum
This small museum features exhibits on the history of the MacPherson clan and the Highlands in general.
Main Street, Newtonmore
☎ *(01540) 673 332*
Website *www.clan-macpherson.org*
Admission *free*
Open *Apr-Oct 10am-5pm daily*

Highland Folk Museum
The exhibits at the Highland Folk Museum depict 400 years of Highland life in its two museums in Kingussie and Newtonmore.

The Kingussie museum features reconstructed houses that showcase the living and working conditions of bygone times. There are exhibits on farming and also an open-air section.
Kingussie
☎ *(01540) 661 307*
Website *www.highlandfolk.com*
Admission *£2*
Open *Apr-Aug Mon-Sat 9.30am-5.30pm; Sep-Oct Mon-Fri 9.30am-4.30pm*

The Newtonmore museum is an open-air museum set on 40 hectares. It features a

recreated Highland farm from the 1700s including buildings such as a croft house and a small township.
Newtonmore
☎ *(01540) 661 307*
Website www.highlandfolk.com
Admission £5
Open *Apr-Aug 10.30am-5.30pm daily; Sep 11am-4.30pm daily; Oct Mon-Fri 11am-4.30pm*

Highland Wildlife Park

This wildlife park near Kincraig allows you to see the animals that have roamed wild in the Scottish Highlands for hundred of years. The park is divided into different habitats ranging from forest and wetlands to woodlands and tundra.
☎ *(01540) 651 270*
Website www.highlandwildlifepark.org
Admission £8 (£5.50 students)
Open *10am-6pm daily (last entry 4pm)*

Loch Garten Osprey Centre

This nature reserve, run by the Royal Society for the Preservation of Birds (RSPB), is a great spot for spotting osprey as well as crested tits and Scottish crossbills.
Off the B970 between Aviemore and Nethybridge
☎ *(01479) 821 409*
Website www.rspb.org.uk/reserves/abernethyforest/
Admission £2.50
Open *Apr-Aug 10am-6pm daily*

Ruthven Barracks

The ruins of these infantry barracks date from 1719 and occupy an imposing position upon a hill, 1.6km south of Kingussie,
B970, 1.6km south of Kingussie
☎ *(01667) 460 232*
Admission *free*

Isle of Skye

This rugged and beautiful island is the most popular island with backpackers. It has a strong Gaelic influence and is touristy even though it doesn't have any major attractions.

The main towns on the Isle of Skye are Broadford and Portree, but Kyleakin is the island's backpacker hub.

Practical Information

Kyle of Lochalsh Tourist Information Centre
Car Park, Kyle of Lochalsh
☎ *(01599) 534 276*
Open May-Oct Mon-Sat 9am-5.30pm

Broadford Tourist Information Centre
The Car Park, Broadford, Isle of Skye
☎ *(01471) 822 713*
Open *Apr-Oct Mon-Sat 9.30am-5pm, Sun 10am-4pm*

Portree Tourist Information Centre
Bayfield House, Bayfield Road, Portree, Isle of Skye
☎ *(01478) 612 137*
Open *Jan-Mar Mon-Sat 9am-4pm; Apr-Jun Mon-Fri 9am-5pm, Sun 10am-4pm; Jul-Aug Mon-Sat 9am-7pm, Sun 10am-4pm; Sep-Oct Mon-Fri 9am-5pm, Sun 10am-4pm; Nov-Dec Mon-Sat 9am-4pm*

Uig Tourist Information Centre
Caledonian MacBrayne Ferry Terminal, Uig, Isle of Skye
Open *for ferry arrivals*

Coming & Going

The Skye Bridge connects the Isle of Skye to the mainland and Kyle of Lochalsh on the mainland side of the bridge is a major transport hub for travellers visiting the island.

Kyle of Lochalsh, which is often abbreviated to Kyle, has a train station with several trains a day from Inverness.

A shuttle bus (£1.70) crosses the bridge twice hourly, alternatively you can walk across the 3km bridge. The toll for cars is £5.70 each way.

Buses run to Fort William, Inverness and Glasgow.

Caledonian MacBrayne ferries sail from Uig on the island's north to Tarbert on the Isle of Harris and Lochmaddy on North Uist. There are also ferries between Mallaig and Armadale in southern Skye.

Local Transport

Highland Country buses (☎ *(01478) 61222; website* www.rapsons.co.uk) run bus services on the island and the nearby Lochalsh area, although many services are infrequent.

If you plan to rely on the island's bus service the Skye Rover ticket is a good deal. The Skye Rover costs £6 for a one-day ticket or £15 for a three-day ticket and it is valid on routes 50-59, 151, 152.

There are several short tours of the island that are aimed at backpackers. These include one, two and three day tours of the island that are run by Mac-Backpackers, in addition to their hop-on hop-off service that also serves the island.

Accommodation
KYLE OF LOCHALSH (MAINLAND)
Cuchulainns Backpackers Hostel
This small hostel is OK for a night stop. It has a reasonable kitchen and dining table, very sociable but a little cramped. There is no common room but a good bar next door with TV and Internet. The barman is the hostel manager. It is clean, but there are a few little niggles like the next-door restaurant's extractor fan, which is loud outside the dorm window well into the night. Smoking in bar only.
Station Road, Kyle of Lochalsh
☎ *(01599) 534 492*
Dorm bed £10; twin room £25
Credit cards MC, Visa (£2 surcharge)

Maintenance & cleanliness	★★★★
Facilities	★★☆
Atmosphere & character	★★
Security	★★
Overall rating	★★★☆

KYLEAKIN
Dun Caan
This lovely little hostel, run by an enthusiastic and friendly older couple, is well equipped for its size, with a good kitchen and eating area, a cosy common room with TV and games, and good dorms and bathrooms, tastefully decorated and very sociable. The view of the sea inlet, castle and hills is delightful and ever changing with the light.
Kyleakin, Isle of Skye
☎ *(01599) 534 087*
Website www.skyerover.co.uk
Dorm bed £11-12
Credit cards JCB, MC, Visa
Curfew 1am

Maintenance & cleanliness	★★★★★
Facilities	★★
Atmosphere & character	★★★★☆
Security	★★☆
Overall rating	★★★★☆

Kyleakin SYHA
This is a very well equipped modernised hostel, spanking clean with a very good kitchen and several good common areas including TV and Internet, all with excellent views. The spacious dorms have washbasins. Large groups are accommodated in a separate building. It is designed to cater for young backpackers and families.
Kyleakin, Isle of Skye
☎ *0870 004 1134*
Website www.syha.org.uk
Dorm bed £11.50-14 (£10.50-13 HI/SYHA)
Credit cards MC, Visa

Maintenance & cleanliness	★★★★★
Facilities	★★☆
Atmosphere & character	★★★★☆
Security	★★
Overall rating	★★★★☆

Skye Backpackers
This is a very sociable small hostel run by enthusiastic backpacker staff, having a small but practical kitchen and dining area, a cosy common room (smoking allowed) with guitars and no TV, and single-sex dorms. It has an adjacent

chalet with dorms and bathroom at a lower price. Groups from one of the tour companies are accommodated in a separate self-contained building.
Benmhor, Kyleakin, Isle of Skye
☎ (01599) 534 510
Website www.scotlands-top-hostels.com
Dorm bed £12; **double room** £28
Credit cards Amex, JCB, MC, Visa

Maintenance & cleanliness	★★★★
Facilities	★½
Atmosphere & character	★★★★½
Security	★
Overall rating	★★★

BROADFORD
Broadford SYHA
This is a very good hostel elevated above the shore of a bay 1km from Broadford with buses and shops. It has an excellent kitchen, a large dining room, a large common room with TV, a lawn with picnic table, and a great view. The staff is helpful. It caters for families and small groups as well as backpackers, and is well placed for walks, cycling and buses to all parts of the island and to the mainland.
Broadford, Isle of Skye
☎ 0870 004 1106
Website www.syha.org.uk
Dorm bed £12.25-13.50 (£11.25-12.50 HI/SYHA)
Credit cards Amex, Diners, JCB, MC, Visa
Open Mar-Oct; **reception open** 8am-10am & 2pm-late; **curfew** midnight

Maintenance & cleanliness	★★★★½
Facilities	★★
Atmosphere & character	★★★½
Security	★★
Overall rating	★★★★½

SLEAT PENINSULA
Armadale SYHA
This hostel is superbly situated overlooking the Sound of Sleat, and you can sometimes see whales from the hostel deck. It's clean and bright, with a very good kitchen and large dining area, and a comfy lounge with no TV. There are two large single-sex dorms with the women upstairs and men in the basement, but both bathrooms in the basement. It's ideal for walkers and cyclists and very sociable, but not for partying.
Ardvasar, Sleat, Isle of Skye
☎ 0870 004 1103
Website www.syha.org.uk
Dorm bed £12.25 (£11.25 HI/SYHA)
Credit cards MC, Visa
Open Apr-Sep; **lockout** 10.30am-5pm; **curfew** 11.45pm

Maintenance & cleanliness	★★★★½
Facilities	★★
Atmosphere & character	★★★
Security	★★
Overall rating	★★★★½

Flora MacDonald Hostel
This hostel is an old, plain building on a hillside with a tremendous view of the strait. It features a well equipped but plain kitchen and a long narrow dining/common room with a TV at one end, feeling not very homely. The single-sex dorms are cosier and the bathrooms are good. There is a self-contained annexe with a TV in the dorm, best for a family. The easy-going owner is a tour guide and a native of Skye, and he will pick you up from the ferry in Armadale. It's very quiet, not ideal if you are the only person there, but a group could have a lively time.
Kilmore, Sleat, Isle of Skye
☎ (01471) 844 440
Website www.isle-of-skye-tour-guide.co.uk
Dorm bed £11

Maintenance & cleanliness	★★★½
Facilities	★½
Atmosphere & character	★★★½
Security	★
Overall rating	★★★½

SLIGACHAN
Sligachan Bunkhouse
This bunkhouse lies among trees near a main road junction with a hotel amid desolate moor land, with an amazing view of the Cuillin Mountains (or clouds). There are no staff on site, you check in at the hotel. It is spacious, well equipped and maintained with a very good kitchen/eating area, a comfortable common room with coal fire and radio/CD player (no TV), and a good laundry

with drying rack. The dorms are good, but the bathrooms are substandard. It's an ideal base for fine hikes along marked trails or for climbing Britain's most rugged mountains. However it has a damp feel inside due to the climate and having to keep windows and doors shut against midges. It could feel very bleak in a rainy spell, though there is good heating available (extra charge).
Sligachan, Isle of Skye
☎ *(01478) 650 204*
Website *www.sligachan.co.uk*
Dorm bed £10-12
Credit cards *MC, Visa*
Open *Mar-Dec*

Maintenance & cleanliness	★★★★½
Facilities	★★½
Atmosphere & character	★★★★
Security	★★½
Overall rating	★★★★½

MINGINISH PENINSULA
Skyewalker Independent Hostel

This rather basic building is in a remote area of scattered cottages with lots of walks and views nearby. A former village school with simple decor, it is clean and well maintained by the friendly owners with a kitchen, a good common room (smoking allowed) with TV area, and cheap Internet. It has large grounds that feature an outdoor chess set. The bathrooms feel primitive but have large showers. There's a cafe and shop next door. It's in a very peaceful spot, and it makes a good base for walks on hills and coasts.
Old School, Portnalong, Isle of Skye
☎ *0800 027 7059*
Website *http://freespace.virgin.net/skyewalker.hostel/*
Dorm bed £8
Credit cards *Diners, JCB, MC, Visa*

Maintenance & cleanliness	★★★½
Facilities	★★★½
Atmosphere & character	★★★★½
Security	★½
Overall rating	★★★

Waterfront Bunkhouse

This bunkhouse overlooks a fjord with a spectacular view. It is superbly maintained, featuring a pleasant kitchen/dining room with a TV lounge area and a small deck. The kitchen is good, but rather small for the number of guests. The dorms and showers are very good. There is an adjacent bar and restaurant, but prices are not budget. If you want to visit a distillery, there's one just two minutes walk away!
The Old Inn, Carbost, Isle of Skye
☎ *(01478) 640 205*
Website *www.carbost.f9.co.uk*
Dorm bed £12-13
Credit cards *Diners, JCB, MC, Visa*

Maintenance & cleanliness	★★★★½
Facilities	★★★½
Atmosphere & character	★★★★½
Security	★½
Overall rating	★★★★½

PORTREE
Portree Independent Hostel

This is a good hostel well placed in the centre of the only town on Skye, close to all town activities and local walks and with bus access to most of Skye. Dorms and bathrooms are fairly spacious, but with some street noise. The giant well-equipped kitchen/dining room is fairly sociable, and there's a comfortable TV area in reception. The staff is helpful, and you can get a good breakfast for £1.50.
Old Post Office, The Green, Portree, Isle of Skye
☎ *(01478) 613 737*
Dorm bed £11-12
Credit cards *MC, Visa*

Maintenance & cleanliness	★★★★
Facilities	★★½
Atmosphere & character	★★★
Security	★★½
Overall rating	★★★

UIG & THE TROTTERNISH PENINSULA
Dun Flodigarry Hostel

This is an outstanding hostel with an excellent kitchen, a spectacular view across the sea to the mainland mountains (if not foggy), a large dining/sitting room that could be very sociable, a small lounge with piano and guitar, internet, no TV, outdoor tables (to use when there are no midges), a pub nearby (not cheap), and amazing mountain

walks from the hostel door. The owners are friendly and helpful.
Flodigarry, Staffin, Isle of Skye
☎ (01470) 552 212
Website *www.hostel-scotland.co.uk*
Dorm bed *£10;* **double room** *£30;* **twin room** *$22*

🚭 Ⓚ Ⓛ

Maintenance & cleanliness	★★★★½
Facilities	★★★
Atmosphere & character	★★★★
Security	★
Overall rating	★★★★½

Glenhinnisdal Bunkhouse

This tiny bunkhouse in a converted barn on a working farm has just six beds. It has a cosy common room with books and a coal fire, good dorms, and a good bathroom with a hot shower, but the kitchen is tiny and barely adequate. The owner is very helpful and can provide breakfast in the farmhouse. This hostel has a good atmosphere, and is a perfect starting point for walks to a fine ridge with stupendous cliffs and fantastic views.
1 Peinaha, Glenhinnisdal, Snizort, Isle of Skye
☎ (01470) 542 293
Website *www.skye.uk.com/glenhinnisdal*
Dorm bed *£6.50;* **twin room** *£15*

🚭 Ⓚ 🐾

Maintenance & cleanliness	★★★★½
Facilities	★★½
Atmosphere & character	★★★★★½
Security	½
Overall rating	★★★

Uig SHYA

Uig hostel has a stunning view over sea, bays, hills and headlands. Bright, cheerful and clean, it has a giant common/dining room, a lovely comfy lounge and a perfect kitchen, all with the same fabulous view. The manager is keen to help. It is near the ferry to the Western Isles, the intercity bus stops just by the hostel, and there are mountain walks from the hostel door. The curfew is waived if there is a music event in the village.
Uig, Isle of Skye
☎ 0870 004 1155
Website *www.syha.org.uk*
Dorm bed *£12-12.50 (£11-11.50 HI/SYHA)*
Credit cards *MC, Visa*

Open *Apr-Sep;* **lockout** *10.30am-2pm;* **curfew** *12.30am*

🚭 Ⓚ Ⓛ

Maintenance & cleanliness	★★★★½
Facilities	★★½
Atmosphere & character	★★★
Security	★★
Overall rating	★★★

Hiking

Skye boasts several excellent hiking trails, particularly in the impressive Cuillin Hills in central Skye. The Walks from Sligachan and Glen Brittle booklet (£1) details hikes in the area and is available from hostels and tourist information centres.

There are also some good hiking trails in the south including walks in the Sleat Peninsula.

Sights
Armadale Castle Gardens & Museum of the Isles

This castle in southern Skye features extensive gardens and a museum focusing on the Isle's clans, with an emphasis on the MacDonald clan.
Armadale, Isle of Skye
☎ (01471) 844 305
Website *www.clandonald.com*
Admission *£4.60*
Open *9.30am-5.30pm daily (last entry to gardens 5pm)*

Bright Water Visitor Centre

This visitor centre has displays about local history and the flora and fauna of Eilean Bàn.
The Pier, Kyleakin, Isle of Skye
☎ (01599) 530 040
Website *www.eileanban.org*
Admission *free*
Open *Apr-Oct Mon-Sat 9am-6pm; Sep-Oct Mon-Fri 10am-5pm*

Castle Moil

The ruins of this 15th century castle overlook Kyleakin Harbour.
Kyleakin, Isle of Skye
Admission *free*

Duntulm Castle

In the 1730s, the MacDonald clan abandoned this castle, 42km north of Portree in northern Skye, and it is now in ruins.

Kilmuir near Duntulm, Isle of Skye
Admission *free*

Dunvegan Castle
Located 35km west of Portree, this imposing castle dating from the ninth century is said to be the oldest inhabited castle in Scotland. The castle's interior has the usual collection of antiques and paintings along with a few historical relics.
Dunvegan Castle, Isle of Skye
🚌 *56*
☎ *(01478) 521 206*
Website *www.dunvegancastle.com*
Admission *£6*
Open *Jan-mid Mar 11am-4pm daily; mid Mar-Oct 10am-5pm daily; Nov-Dec 11am-4pm daily*

Ullapool

Ullapool is a busy transport hub with travellers coming here to catch the ferry to the Isle of Lewis.

Practical Information
Tourist Information Centre
Argyle Street, Ullapool
☎ *(01854) 612 135*
Open *Apr-Jun Mon-Sat 9am-5pm, Sun 10am-4pm; Jul-Aug Mon-Sat 9am-6pm, Sun 10am-5pm; Sep-Oct Mon-Sat 9am-5pm, Sun 10am-4pm*

Coming & Going
Scottish Citylink coaches from Inverness connect with Caledonian MacBryane (☎ *(01854) 612 358; **website** www.calmac.co.uk*) ferries to Stornoway on the Isle of Lewis.

Accommodation
TOWN CENTRE
Ullapool SYHA
Right on the picturesque shore, this youth hostel is one of Scotland's best-located hostels. Its cosy living room is perfect for a night in – but you're in Ullapool where there's whiskey and song to be experienced! Accommodation is in pretty basic – and standard – rooms.
Shore Street, Ullapool
☎ *(01854) 612 254 or 0870 004 1156*
Website *www.syha.org.uk*
Dorm bed *£12-13 (£11-12 HI/SYHA)*
Credit cards *MC, Visa*
Open *Mar-Oct;* **reception open** *7am-11am & 3pm-10.45pm daily;* **curfew** *11.45pm*

Maintenance & cleanliness	★★★★½
Facilities	★★½
Atmosphere & character	★★
Security	★
Overall rating	★★★½

West House
This hostel has a really nice feel to it and is close to all the action in Ullapool. Its big sprung, wooden bunks and huge shining bathrooms make the sharing part of hostelling a breeze. The kitchen and TV room, with the cheapest Internet in town, are well rigged out and the staff have an easygoing manner.
West Argyle Street, Ullapool
☎ *(01854) 613 126*
Website *www.scotpackers-hostels.co.uk*
Dorm bed *£11-12*
Credit cards *MC, Visa*

Maintenance & cleanliness	★★★★★
Facilities	★★★
Atmosphere & character	★★★★★
Security	★
Overall rating	★★★★

NEAR ULLAPOOL
Achininver SYHA
Achininver SYHA is a peach of a hostel located slap bang on one of Scotland's loveliest beaches. If you want to remove yourself from the hubbub of the tourist trail but still be able to experience highland hospitality you'll love this place. The facilities are pretty basic but they're clean and well kept. It's popular with walkers and cyclists.
Achiltibuie, Ullapool
☎ *(01854) 622 254 or 0870 004 1101*
Website *www.syha.org.uk*
Dorm bed *£11.75 (£10.75 HI/SYHA)*
Credit cards *MC, Visa*
Open *May-Sep*

Maintenance & cleanliness	★★★★★
Facilities	★★★½
Atmosphere & character	★★★★
Security	★
Overall rating	★★★★½

Sights
Ullapool Museum
This small museum features exhibits about local history dating back to Viking times.
7-8 West Argyle Street, Ullapool
☎ *(01854) 612 987*
Website *www.ullapool.co.uk/museum.html*
Admission *£2*
Open *Jan-Feb Wed-Thu & Sat 11am-3pm; Mar Mon-Sat 10am-3pm; Apr-Oct Mon-Sat 9.30am-5.30pm; Nov-Dec Wed-Thu & Sat 11am-3pm*

Thurso
Bustling Thurso is the major town on Scotland's north coast. There isn't a lot to see here, but it boasts a surprisingly good surf beach. Most travellers visit Thrust to catch a ferry to the Orkney Isles, which departs from nearby Scrabster.

Practical Information
Thurso Tourist Information Centre
Riverside Road, Thurso
☎ *(01847) 892 371*
Open *Apr-May Mon-Sat 10am-5pm; Jun-Sep Mon-Sat 10am-5pm, Sun 10am-4pm; Oct Mon-Sat 10am-5pm*

Coming & Going
Scottish Citylink and Highland Country buses (routes 58 and 958) operate coaches between Inverness and Thurso, via Wick.

Northlink Ferries (☎ *(01856) 851 144;* **website** *www.northlinkferries.co.uk*) depart Scrabster, 4km east of Thurso, for Stromness in the Orkney Islands.

Accommodation
Sandra's Backpackers
This expertly kitted out hostel is run by former backpackers who know a thing or two about making weary travellers feel contented and at ease. The clean pine alpine feel belies the fact that you're in a Scottish town, with everything feeling as if it's brand new. The common area is also the dining room but it works well.
24-26 Princes Street, Thurso
☎ *(01847) 894 575*
Website *www.sandras-backpackers.ukf.net*
Dorm bed *£10;* **double/twin room** *£28*
Credit cards *MC, Visa*

Maintenance & cleanliness		★★★★★
Facilities		★★★
Atmosphere & character		★★★★½
Security		★
Overall rating		★★★★

Thurso Youth Club Hostel
This absolute beauty of a converted watermill houses a smart hostel. It's extremely peaceful but still just minutes away from Thurso town centre. The quality of the renovation and the rooms makes for a very comfortable stay and it's popular with all types of travellers – well, the ones they get up here! Meals are available and are decently priced.
Old Mill, Millbanks Road, Thurso
☎ *(01847) 892 964*
Dorm bed *£8; price includes breakfast*
Credit cards *MC, Visa*
Open *Jul-Aug*

Maintenance & cleanliness		★★★★★
Facilities		★★★
Atmosphere & character		★★★★★
Security		★
Overall rating		★★★★

John O'Groats
If you're not into bird watching, Great Britain's most northerly point doesn't have a lot to offer. However it attracts lots of tourists – who also have Lands End (Cornwall) on their itinerary – who come here to say they've made it to the top of mainland Britain.

Coming & Going
Highland Country bus route 77 runs between Wick and Thurso, stopping en route at John O'Groats.

John O'Groats Ferries (☎ *(01955) 611 353;* **website** *www.jogferry.co.uk*) sail to Burwick in the Orkney Islands. A cheaper alternative is the ferry service run by Pentland Ferries (☎ *(01856) 831 226;* **website** *www.pentlandferries.co.uk*) that sails from Gills Bay, which is just a few kilometres west of John O'Groats.

Accommodation
John O'Groats SYHA

This white farmhouse has wonderful views over the Pentland Firth. The hostel itself is kept ship shape and has a cosy lounge if you want to batten down the hatches; otherwise there is a great wee pub nearby. If you're bird watching or just moodily staring out to sea this is just the right hostel for you.

Canisbay
☎ *(01955) 611 424 or 0870 004 1129*

Website *www.syha.org.uk*
Dorm bed *£12 (£11 HI/YHA)*
Credit cards *MC, Visa*
Open *Mar-Sep;* ***reception open*** *7.30am-11am & 4pm-11pm daily;* ***curfew*** *11.45pm*

🚗 📺 🇰 🇱

Maintenance & cleanliness	★★★★½
Facilities	★★½
Atmosphere & character	★★★★½
Security	★
Overall rating	★★★★½

Western Isles

Also known as the Outer Hebrides, this group of remote islands boasts a very traditional lifestyle with Scottish Gaelic speakers comprising 75% of the islands' population.

Lewis (Leodhas)

The majority of the Western Isles' population calls Lewis home, mostly living in fishing and crafting villages in the island's northwest and also in Stornoway on the east coast.

Lewis's main attractions are the Calanais Stones and the impressive Carloway Broch, dating from the Iron Age. Lewis also has some good surf beaches. Stornoway is the largest town on the islands and it has good transport connections making it a popular base for travellers.

Practical Information
Stornoway Tourist Information Centre
26 Cromwell Street, Stornoway
☎ *(01851) 703 088*
Open *Jan-Mar Mon-Fri 9am-5pm; Apr-Oct Mon-Sat 9am-6pm; Nov-Dec Mon-Fri 9am-5pm*

Coming & Going
Stornoway is the island's main transport hub with Caledonian MacBrayne ferries from Ullapool and an airport (☎ *(01851) 702 256; website www.hial.co.uk/stornoway-airport.html*) with flights from Edinburgh, Glasgow and Inverness on the Scottish mainland and inter island flights to Barra and Benbecula.

Local Transport
Buses depart from the terminal on Beach Street for destinations throughout the island.

Accommodation
STORNOWAY
Fairhaven Hostel
This hostel in the town centre is clean and well maintained. It has a well-equipped small kitchen, but the only eating area is in the lounge at low tables. That lounge has a TV and DVDs as well as a stereo. No smoking, no alcohol.
28 Francis Street, Stornoway, Isle of Lewis
☎ *(01851) 705 862*
Website *www.hebrideansurf.co.uk*
Dorm bed *£10;* **twin room** *£30*
[TV] [K] [N]

Maintenance & cleanliness	★★★★
Facilities	★★½
Atmosphere & character	½
Security	★
Overall rating	★★½

Laxdale Bunkhouse
This bunkhouse on a campsite is very clean and efficient with several thoughtful touches including an excellent sociable kitchen/dining area, and you can sit outside when weather and midges permit. It's a bit motel-like, with every room accessed from the veranda. The lounge is accessed with a key kept

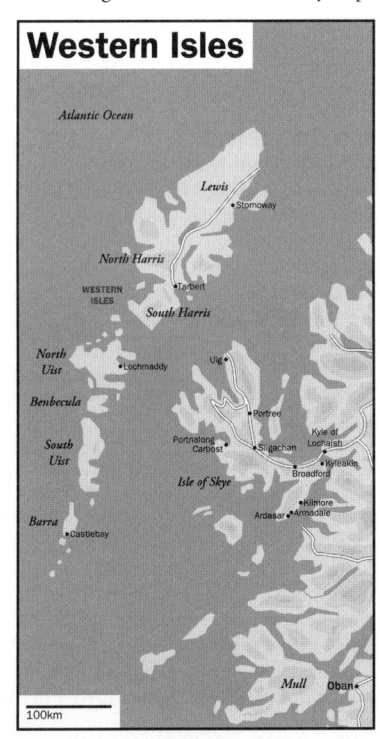

Western Isles

Atlantic Ocean

Lewis • Stornoway
North Harris • Tarbert
WESTERN ISLES
South Harris
North Uist • Lochmaddy • Uig
Benbecula • Portree
South Uist • Portnalong Carbost • Sligachan • Kyle of Lochalsh • Kyleakin
Isle of Skye • Broadford
Barra • Castlebay • Kilmore • Ardasar • Armadale
Mull • Oban
100km

in the kitchen, and is large and rather sterile with a big TV.
6 Laxdale Lane, Stornoway, Isle of Lewis
☎ *(01851) 706 966*
Website *www.laxdaleholidaypark.com*
Dorm bed *£10-11*
Credit cards *MC, Visa*

Maintenance & cleanliness	★★★★⯨
Facilities	★★⯨
Atmosphere & character	★★★⯨
Security	★★★★⯨
Overall rating	★★★

Stornoway Backpackers
This low-cost hostel (including free self-service breakfast) in the town centre looks a little run-down, but has a sociable easy-going atmosphere. The kitchen is OK with a dining table; the common room is simple and cosy without TV.
47 Keith Street, Stornoway, Isle of Lewis
☎ *(01851) 703 628*
Website *www.stornoway-hostel.co.uk*
Dorm bed *£9; price includes breakfast*

Maintenance & cleanliness	★★★
Facilities	★
Atmosphere & character	★★★
Security	★
Overall rating	★★⯨

AROUND LEWIS
Galson Farm Bunkhouse
This very small bunkhouse is well placed for people touring Lewis, especially cyclists. It has one bunkroom with six beds and sitting area, and a good kitchen. It's clean and well maintained.
Galson Farm, South Galson, Isle of Lewis
☎ *(01851) 850 492*
Website *www.galsonfarm.freeserve.co.uk*
Dorm bed *£10*

Maintenance & cleanliness	★★★⯨
Facilities	★
Atmosphere & character	★★★★⯨
Security	⯨
Overall rating	★★★⯨

Garenin SYHA
This basic but very sociable hostel is in an old thatched cottage that is part of a preserved old village. It has stone walls and open roof space. There's a good-sized common room/kitchen. Bring or hire a sheet sleeping bag. Guests keep the hostel clean. There's a café on the site, and lovely beach and cliff walks within metres.
Carloway, Isle of Lewis
Website *www.syha.org.uk*
Dorm bed *£8.50 (£7.50 HI/SYHA)*

Maintenance & cleanliness	★★★⯨
Facilities	⯨
Atmosphere & character	★★★★
Security	⯨
Overall rating	★★

Kershader SYHA
This always-open hostel is plain and functional, with a small kitchen, a room with dining table & chairs and a TV, good dorms and a great view. You need a sheet sleeping bag. There are good cheap laundry facilities, and a shop and café next door. It's a good base for touring the island or cycling amid the delightful local scenery.
Ravenspoint, Kershader, Isle of Lewis
☎ *(01851) 880 236*
Website *www.syha.org.uk*
Dorm bed *£9.75 (£8.75 HI/SYHA)*

Maintenance & cleanliness	★★★★⯨
Facilities	★★⯨
Atmosphere & character	★★
Security	⯨
Overall rating	★★★⯨

Sights
STORNOWAY
Lews Castle
This mock-Tudor style castle was built in the 19th century, but it is not open to visitors.

Museum nan Eilean
This museum has exhibits that document the history of the Western Isles.
Francis Street, Stornoway
☎ *(01851) 709 266*
Website *www.cne-siar.gov.uk/museum/museum.htm*
Admission *free*
Open *Jan-Mar Tue-Fri 10am-5pm, Sat 10am-1pm; Apr-Sep Mon-Sat 10am-5.30pm; Oct-Dec Tue-Fri 10am-5pm, Sat 10am-1pm*

AROUND LEWIS
Arnol Black House
This thatched cottage in the village of Arnol is a good example of a traditional Lewis house. It features an adjoining barn and a peat fire that burns with the smoke filtering through the roof.
42 Arnol, Barvas, Isle of Lewis
☎ *(01851) 710 395*
Website www.historic-scotland.gov.uk
Admission *£3*
Open *Jan-Mar Mon-Wed & Sat 9.30am-4.30pm, Sun 2pm-4.30pm; Apr-Sep 9.30am-6.30pm daily; Oct-Dec Mon-Wed & Sat 9.30am-4.30pm, Sun 2pm-4.30pm*

Calanais Stones
Dating from around 2900 BC, this cross-shaped stone formation, west of Stornoway, is a unique attraction that is complemented by an exhibition and video presentation that explains the site.
A858, 20km W of Stornoway, Isle of Lewis
☎ *(01851) 621 422*
Website www.historic-scotland.gov.uk
Open *Jan-Mar Mon-Sat 10am-4pm; Apr-Sep Mon-Sat 10am-7pm; Oct-Dec Mon-Sat 10am-4pm*

Dun Carloway
The ruins of this broch (fortification) date from the Iron Age and comprise a stone tower that is nine metres at its highest point. It is one of Scotland's best-preserved broch towers.
A858, 2½km south of Carloway, Lewis
Website www.historic-scotland.gov.uk
Admission *free*

Harris (Na Hearadh)
The southern portion of the island shared with Lewis is considerably more mountainous than its northern neighbour and it offers some good walking trails.

Tarbert (An Tairbeart) is the main settlement on Harris and it is here that most visitors choose to stay.

Practical Information
Tarbert Tourist Information Centre
Pier Road, Tarbert
☎ *(01859) 502 011*
Open *Apr-Oct Mon-Sat 9am-5pm*

Coming & Going
In addition to buses from Lewis, which stop near the tourist information centre; Caledonian MacBrayne ferries leave Tarbert for Uig on the Isle of Skye.

Accommodation
TARBERT
Rockview Bunkhouse
This hostel is on the main street of the village, which is quiet except when the ferry arrives. It is best to reserve in advance, because the door is locked, there are no staff on site and they may be hard to reach. Once inside you find a nice clean and bright hostel with a kitchen/eating area, a comfortable common room with TV, and good dorms (a large female dorm and a large mixed one) but with plastic mattress covers.
Main Street, Tarbert, Isle of Harris
☎ *(01859) 502 626*
Dorm bed *£10*
Credit cards *Amex, JCB, MC, Visa*
TV K L

Maintenance & cleanliness	★★★★
Facilities	★★
Atmosphere & character	★★★★½
Security	★
Overall rating	★★★

NORTH HARRIS
Rhenigidale SYHA
This traditional cottage in a tiny village on the seashore amid hills and fjords feels primitive but has all necessary facilities including a good shower and separate toilet, a well-equipped kitchen/dining room and a cosy common room with fire and books. Some visitors camp here and use the facilities. There's a great atmosphere, but you might have to keep windows shut against midges. Guests help to keep the hostel clean. Bring or hire a sheet sleeping bag.
Rhenigidale, Isle of Harris
Website www.syha.org.uk or www.gatliff.org.uk
Dorm bed *£9 (£8 HI/SYHA)*
K

Maintenance & cleanliness	★★★★½
Facilities	★
Atmosphere & character	★★★★½
Security	★½
Overall rating	★★★½

SOUTH HARRIS
Am Bothan
This hostel was designed and is run by the owner. The large common/dining room with well-equipped kitchen is unique and spacious, open to the roof, with a nautical flavour. It has a stereo and CDs; the owner removed the TV because it spoiled the atmosphere, but it's available on request, eg for football. There's also another small lounge. The dorms and bathrooms are top-class, and it's very clean. There's full central heating as well as a wood fire. Although Leverburgh is an uninspiring village, you have to pass through if you are touring the islands, and this hostel is not far from the ferry.
Ferry Road, Leverburgh, Isle of Harris
☎ *(01859) 520 251*
Website *www.ambothan.com*
Dorm bed *£13-14*
Credit cards *Amex, JCB, MC, Visa*

Maintenance & cleanliness	★★★★★
Facilities	★★★☆
Atmosphere & character	★★★★☆
Security	☆
Overall rating	★★★★

Drinishader Hostel
This hostel is a tiny cottage close to the seashore in a quiet, very scattered village. It has a cosy common room with fire, guitar and CD player, combined with a small well-equipped kitchen, and is very sociable. Dorms are spacious. The patio with a wonderful view is lovely. It's a bit too dark inside, and the one shower/toilet is inadequate if there are 12 hostel guests plus campers.
Golden Road, Drinishader, near Tarbert, Isle of Harris
Dorm bed *£8;* **twin room** *£18*
Open *Apr-Nov*

Maintenance & cleanliness	★★★★☆
Facilities	★★★☆
Atmosphere & character	★★★★☆
Security	☆
Overall rating	★★★★☆

The Uists (Uibhist)
This small archipelago is comprised of several flat islands including North Uist, South Uist and the small island of Benbecula, which lies between North and South Uist and is home to the islands' airport.

The islands features great salmon and trout fishing, but their remoteness is the major attraction with travellers trying to get away from the tourist trail.

Practical Information
Lochmaddy Tourist Information Centre
☎ *(01876) 500321*
Open *Easter-Oct Mon-Fri 9am-5pm, Sat 9.30am-1pm & 2pm-5.30pm*

Lochboisdale Tourist Information Centre
☎ *(01878) 700286*
Open *Easter-Oct Mon-Sat 9am-5pm*

Coming & Going
The airport (☎ *(01870) 602051;* website *www.hial.co.uk/benbecula-airport.html*) at Benbecula has direct flights to Glasgow, Barra and Stornoway.

Most budget travellers, however, will combine a visit to the Uists with Harris and Lewis and peraps Barra and will arrive by ferry from Harris or Barra.

Ferries sail from Lochmaddy in North Uist to Uig on the Isle of Skye and from Otternish in North Uist to Leverburgh in Harris.

From South Uist there are ferries from Lochboisdale to Oban and also a small ferry from Ludag to Eoligarry on Barra.

Local Transport
A causeway connects the Uist's three major islands and there is a bus service on the islands but it is not as frequent as some travellers would like. Public transport, even hitch-hiking, grinds to a halt on Sundays, as people on the islands are very religious.

Accommodation
NORTH UIST
Berneray SYHA
This rustic hostel comprises two small thatched cottages and also a camping area, in a stunning location on the beach of this small peaceful island. It has a combined kitchen/dining/common room with a wood stove, very

sociable but a bit limited if crowded. Guests keep the hostel clean. The bathrooms have no hot water, so don't plan on a shower here, but the dorms are spacious and heated and it's an amazing place to stay for a couple of nights.

Isle of Berneray, North Uist
Website *www.syha.org.uk*
Dorm bed £9 (£8 HI/SYHA)

Maintenance & cleanliness	★★★
Facilities	★
Atmosphere & character	★★★★★
Security	★
Overall rating	★★★★

My Grandfather's House (Taigh Mo Sheanair)

This family-run hostel is in an area of scattered houses 1.5 km from the main road. It is well-equipped and kept in perfect condition with a small kitchen, a lounge with computer and no TV, and great views from many rooms, even the shower room. Bring or hire a sheet sleeping bag. Being small, a group often books it, but you can camp here and use the facilities and it's very sociable.

Carnach, Claddach Baleshare, North Uist
☎ (01876) 580 246
Dorm bed £11

Maintenance & cleanliness	★★★★★
Facilities	★★
Atmosphere & character	★★★★
Security	★
Overall rating	★★★★

Uist Outdoor Centre

This bunkhouse is in a peaceful rural setting by a sea inlet. They run sea kayak courses, so there are often lots of activity going on. The hostel is well used but it's clean and spacious with a good kitchen, large lounge and dining area with a communal table. It's very sociable, and the staff are helpful.

Cearn Dusgaidh, Lochmaddy, North Uist
☎ (01876) 500 480
Website *www.uistoutdoorcentre.co.uk*
Dorm bed £9-11
Credit cards MC, Visa

Maintenance & cleanliness	★★★★
Facilities	★★
Atmosphere & character	★★★★
Security	★
Overall rating	★★★

BENBECULA
Ballivannich Bunkhouse

This small bunkhouse is conveniently located in the middle of the island chain, with no special scenery but a modest village and small airport nearby. It has a good kitchen, a comfy sitting room and dining area without TV, and power showers, everything in immaculate condition with beautiful decor. There's also an annexe with twin beds and kitchen. Being small, it's often booked up by a group.

22 Ballivannich, Benbecula
☎ (01764) 655 587
Dorm bed £11

Maintenance & cleanliness	★★★★★
Facilities	★
Atmosphere & character	★★★★
Security	★
Overall rating	★★★

SOUTH UIST
Howmore SYHA

This very basic hostel has a welcoming feel and should be very sociable. The kitchen and bathrooms are simple but have all you need, and there's a common area but without easy chairs. The guests keep the hostel clean. It is nicely located in open country not far from the main bus route and close to a long beach, and you can hike to the Uist Mountains from here.

Website *www.syha.org.uk*
Dorm bed £9 (£8 HI/SYHA)

Maintenance & cleanliness	★★★
Facilities	★
Atmosphere & character	★★★
Security	★
Overall rating	★★

Sights
NORTH UIST
Taigh Chearsabhagh Museum

This complex comprises several art galleries and a museum that has exhibits on local history although the displays

aren't that great compared to museums elsewhere in the country.
Lochmaddy, North Uist
☎ *(01876) 500 293*
Website *www.taigh-chearsabhagh.org*
Admission *£1*
Open *Mon-Sat 10am-5pm*

Trinity Temple (Teampull na Trionaid)

The ruins of this old church date from the 13th century (it is near the village of Clachan).
A865 Clachan, North Uist

RSPB Balranald Reserve

This nature reserve is a popular spot with birdwatchers that come here to observe the corncrake.
5km north of Bayhead, North Uist
☎ *(01870) 560 287*
Website *www.rspb.org.uk/reserves/balranald/*
Open *reserve always open; visitor centre Apr-Aug 9am-6pm daily*

SOUTH UIST
Kildonan Museum

This small museum houses a series of displays about the life and history of South Uist.
Kildonan, Lochboisdale, South Uist
☎ *(01878) 710 343*
Website *www.undiscoveredscotland.co.uk/southuist/kildonan/*
Open *Apr-Sep Mon-Sat 10am-5pm, Sun 2pm-5pm*

Barra (Barraigh)

The most southern of the Western Isles is a compact place with some good beaches. Castlebay, the island's major town, boasts a castle that overlooks the harbour.

Practical Information
Tourist Information Centre
☎ *(01871) 810 336*
Open *Easter-Oct Mon-Sat 9am-5pm, Sun 10am-11am*

Coming & Going

Barra's unique airport (☎ *(01878) 890 212; website www.hial.co.uk/barra-airport.html*) is the only airport in the world where scheduled commercial flights land on the beach. There are flights from Barra to Benbecula and Glasgow. A post bus to Castlebay meets all flights.

There's a small ferry that sails between Eoligarry at the island's north and Ludag in South Uist.

Caledonian MacBrayne (☎ *(01878) 700 288; website www.calmac.co.uk*) ferries sail between Castlebay and Oban. They also sail to Lochboisdale in South Uist.

Accommodation
Dunard Hostel

This small 16-bed hostel has the usual hostel facilities including a good kitchen and a cosy lounge with an open fire. It boasts lovely views of the castle and islands.
Castlebay, Isle of Barra
☎ *(01871) 810 443*
Website *www.isleofbarrahostel.com*
Dorm bed *£10; twin room £32*
K

Sights
"Dualchas" Barra Heritage & Cultural Centre

This excellent small museum features displays on local history as well as art exhibits.
Castlebay, Isle of Barra
☎ *(01871) 810 413*
Website *www.isleofbarra.com/heritage.html*
Admission *£2*
Open *Apr-Sep Mon-Sat 11am-4pm*

Kisimul Castle

The impressive Kisimul Castle in Castlebay harbour is the only surviving medieval castle in the Western Isles. It is the seat of the Clan Macneil and it boasts an 18m tower plus a dungeon and a great hall.
Castlebay Harbour, Castlebay, Barra
☎ *(01871) 810 313*
Website *www.historic-scotland.gov.uk*
Admission *£3.30*
Open *Apr-Sep 9.30am-6.30pm daily*

Orkney & Shetland

Orkney Islands

This archipelago of 70 islands is located just a short distance off Scotland's northern coast.

This islands feature a beautiful rugged coastline and a large number of prehistoric sites that include the breathtaking Ring of Brodgar and the Standing Stones of Stenness.

Orkney's main island, known as Mainland, is home to most Orcadians and is also where you'll find the islands' two major towns, Kirkwall and Stromness.

Apart from Mainland, other islands in the Orkneys that are worth visiting include Westray and Papa Westray. Westray is the largest of the outer islands and is home to some interesting prehistoric sites, but tiny nearby Papa Westray is perhaps a greater draw with Northern Europe's oldest house, dating from 3500 BC. Papa Westray is also popular with bird watchers as it is home to Europe's largest colony of Arctic Terns.

Orkney's main airport is located at Kirwall and has flights to Inverness, Glasgow, Edinburgh, Wick and Sumburgh in addition to flights connecting the various islands in the group. Kirkwall airport (☎ *(01856) 872 421; website www.hial.co.uk/kirkwall-airport. html*) is located around 4km outside the town centre and it is served by bus route 11, which meets most flights.

Three different ferry companies connect the Orkneys with the Scottish mainland. Northlink Ferries (☎ *(01856) 851 144; website www.northlinkferries.co.uk*) sail to Stromness from Scrabster, 4km east of Thurso. John O'Groats Ferries (☎ *(01955) 611 353; website www.jogferry.co.uk*) sail from John O'Groats to Burwick with a connecting bus to Kirkwall. The cheapest option is the ferry service provided by Pentland Ferries (☎ *(01856) 831 226; website www.pentlandferries.co.uk*) that sails to St Margaret's Hope on

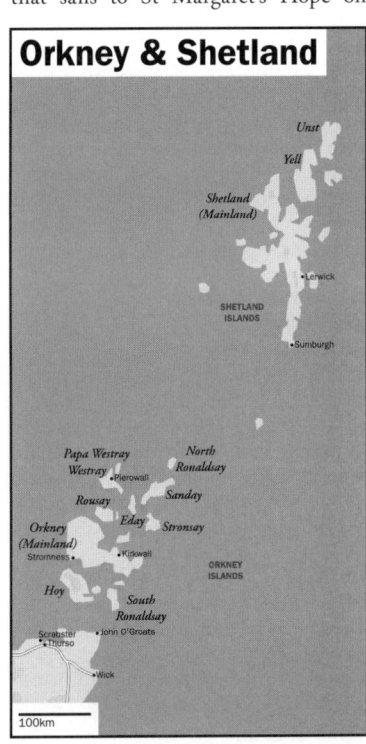

Practical Information
Kirkwall Tourist Information Centre
6 Broad Street, Kirkwall
☎ *(01856) 872 856*
Website *www.visitorkney.com*
Open *Jan-Mar Mon-Sat 1pm-3pm; Apr Mon-Sat 10am-4pm, Sun 10am-3pm; May-Aug Mon-Fri 8am-5pm, Sat-Sun 9am-4pm; Sep-Oct Mon-Sat 10am-4pm, Sun 10am-3pm; Nov-Dec Mon-Sat 1pm-3pm*

Stromness Tourist Information Centre
☎ *(01856) 850 716*
Website *www.visitorkney.com*
Open *Jan-Apr Mon-Fri 9am-5pm, Sat 10am-12.30pm & 1.30pm-4pm; May-Sep 8.30am-6pm daily; Oct-Dec Mon-Fri 9am-5pm, Sat 10am-12.30pm & 1.30pm-4pm*

Coming & Going
The Orkney Islands are served by both air and ferry services.

South Ronaldsay from Gill's Bay near John O'Groats, with bus connections to Kirkwall.

Local Transport

Public transport on the Orkney Islands is surprisingly good considering that a small population is spread across a relatively remote area.

There are bus services on Mainland that include an hourly bus between Kirkwall and Stromness (route 1) as well as several town services in Kirkwall. There are around five buses a day between Kirkwall and St Margaret's Hope on the island of South Ronaldsay, which is connected to Mainland, via a causeway that also crosses the small island of Burray. For £6 you can buy an Orkney Rover ticket that gives you a day's unlimited bus travel on the following Orkney Coaches routes: 1, 1A, 1C, 2, 2D, 3, 4, 4A, 5B, 6, 6B, 7, 8, 8A, 8B, 8C, 9A and 10.

There is a good network of ferry routes between the islands with departures for the outer islands departing from Kirkwall.

Kirkwall airport is the Orkney's air hub with flights to most islands operated by British Airways franchisee Loganair (☎ *(01856) 872 421; website* www.loganair.co.uk). There are also many short flights between the smaller islands including the short hop between Westray and Papa Westray, which at less than two minutes is the world's shortest scheduled commercial flight.

Accommodation

KIRKWALL
Kirkwall SYHA

This is a clean functional hostel – don't be put off by its unattractive exterior. In its favour, it's close to the main ferry terminals and everything you could possibly need (and get) in Kirkwall. The staff are a credit to the place and it is popular with backpackers.
Old Scapa Road, Kirkwall
☎ *(01856) 872 243 or 0871 330 8533*
Website www.syha.org.uk
Dorm bed £12-13 (£11-12 HI/SYHA)
Credit cards Amex, MC, Visa
Open Apr-Sep; **reception open** 7.30am-10.30am & 3pm-midnight daily

Maintenance & cleanliness	★★★★½
Facilities	★★★
Atmosphere & character	★★★
Security	★★
Overall rating	★★★

SOUTH RONALDSAY
Wheems Hostel

Located on an extensive organic farm, this hostel has great character. Its one dormitory, while basic, is extremely comfortable and clean. Cooking facilities are limited, although the bathrooms are almost palatial. The owners live on site and are able to give help with transport and other difficulties. It is beautifully situated and you can enjoy views over rural South Ronaldsay and the coastline. Camping is also available.
Eastside, South Ronaldsay
☎ *(01856) 831 357*
Dorm bed £6.50; **family room** (sleeps six) £30
Open Apr-Oct

Maintenance & cleanliness	★★★★
Facilities	★★½
Atmosphere & character	★★★★★
Security	★★
Overall rating	★★★★½

HOY
Rackwick Hostel

This is a clean and well maintained, if basic, hostel overlooking stunning sea, cliff and hill views. It has good facilities for backpackers with a well-equipped kitchen that's clean and stocked with condiments and spices. There's also a camping ground available.
☎ *(01856) 791 316*
Dorm bed £6.90-8
Open Mar-Sep

Maintenance & cleanliness	★★★★½
Facilities	★★
Atmosphere & character	★★★
Security	★
Overall rating	★★★

ROUSAY
Trumland Farm Hostel

This is a homely and well-equipped hostel in a particularly charming location that's rural but not remote. The rooms are small but not inhospitable and catering facilities are good with a fully equipped kitchen. There's a relaxed atmosphere here and the manager lives nearby and can offer assistance if required.

📍 *Rousay*
☎ *(01856) 821 252*
Dorm bed *£8-10;* **single room** *£11; linen extra £1*

🏠 📺 🍳 🅿️

Maintenance & cleanliness	★★★★
Facilities	★⯨
Atmosphere & character	★★★★★
Security	★★
Overall rating	★★★★⯨

EDAY
Eday Hostel
Local people run this hostel so whilst it may be basic it's welcoming. Overlooking sandy beaches and neighbouring islands, its remote location makes you feel safe and far far away from any hustle and bustle. The toilet and shower facilities are limited but spotless. Good value for money.

London Bay, Eday
☎ *(01867) 622 206*
Website *www.syha.org.uk*
Dorm bed *£7-8*
Open *Apr-Sep*

🏠 ♿ 🍳 🅿️

Maintenance & cleanliness	★★
Facilities	★
Atmosphere & character	★★⯨
Security	★
Overall rating	★★⯨

WESTRAY
The Barn
This is a converted barn in Westray's main village and is a superbly designed and maintained hostel with friendly local staff. The dorms are of various sizes but all are spacious and the kitchen is well stocked. Very near to the village shops and facilities, this hostel also provides a good base for exploring one of Orkney's most arresting islands.

Chalmersquoy, Westray
☎ *(01857) 677 214*
Website *www.thebarnwestray.com*
Dorm bed *£11.75*

🏠 ♿ 📺 🍳 🅿️

Maintenance & cleanliness	★★★★★
Facilities	★★★
Atmosphere & character	★★★★
Security	★★
Overall rating	★★★★

Bis Geos
This renovated traditional croft provides all mod cons and its use of local natural materials is stunning. There's a maritime theme throughout and under floor heating. The location is unrivalled with breathtaking views over Westray's cliffs. Everything is like new and the staff are flexible and helpful. There are two spacious social areas and a large kitchen, which makes for a good atmosphere.

Pierowall, Westray
📍 *Pierowall*
☎ *(01857) 677 420*
Website *www.bis-geos.co.uk*
Dorm bed *£11*
Credit cards *MC, Visa*
Open *May-Oct*

🏠 📺 🍳

Maintenance & cleanliness	★★★★★
Facilities	★★★
Atmosphere & character	★★★★★
Security	★★⯨
Overall rating	★★★★

PAPA WESTRAY
Papa Westray SYHA
This is a basic, no frills hostel that's well looked after. The dorms are comfortable and some rooms have en suite facilities. The common area and kitchen are both small but this hostel is fairly remote so it's unlikely to be too congested. There's also a guesthouse on site. If you want to explore this windswept island, you'll be ideally placed to do so.

Beltane House, Papa Westray
☎ *(01857) 644 267 or 0870 155 3255*
Website *www.syha.org.uk*
Dorm bed *£9-11 (£8-10 HI/SYHA)*

🏠 🍳 🅿️ 🚲

Maintenance & cleanliness	★★★★⯨
Facilities	★★★⯨
Atmosphere & character	★★★
Security	★★⯨
Overall rating	★★★

Sights
KIRKWALL
Bishop's & Earl's Palaces
The Bishop's Palace dates from the 12th century but the palace's round tower was added in the 16th century.

The adjoining Earl's Palace was built between 1600 and 1607 by Patrick Stewart, Earl of Orkney.
Palace Road, Kirkwall
☎ *(01856) 875 461*
Website *www.historic-scotland.gov.uk*
Admission *£2.20*
Open *Apr-Sep 9.30am-6.30pm daily*

Orkney Museum
This small museum has exhibits on 5000 years of local history.
Tankerness House, Broad Street, Kirkwall
☎ *(01856) 873 191*
Admission *free*
Open *Jan-Mar Mon-Sat 10.30am-12.30pm & 1.30pm-5pm; Apr Mon-Sat 10.30am-5pm; May-Sep Mon-Sat 10.30am-5pm, Sun 2pm-5pm; Oct-Dec Mon-Sat 10.30am-12.30pm & 1.30pm-5pm*

St Magnus Cathedral
Dating from 1137, Britain's most northern cathedral is documented in the *Orkneying Saga* and it contains the remains of St Magnus. This fine medieval cathedral is the only cathedral in Britain with its own dungeon.
Broad Street, Kirkwall
☎ *(01856) 874 894*
Admission *free*
Open *Jan-Mar Mon-Sat 9am-1pm & 2pm-5pm; Apr-Sep Mon-Sat 9am-7pm, Sun 2pm-6pm; Oct-Dec Mon-Sat 9am-1pm & 2pm-5pm*

STROMNESS
Stromness Museum
This museum details Orkney's seafaring tradition and the pioneering role of the Orcadians who sailed to Canada in the 18th and 19th centuries.
52 Alfred Street, Stromness
☎ *(01856) 850 025*
Admission *£2.50*
Open *Jan-Apr Mon-Sat 10am-5pm; May-Sep Sun 10.30am-12.30pm & 1.30pm-5pm; Oct-Dec Mon-Sat 10am-5pm*

AROUND MAINLAND
Broch of Gurness
This broch, dating from the first century, is surrounded by Iron Age structures and it contains artefacts from the Viking period.
Evie, Orkney
☎ *(01856) 751 414*
Website *www.historic-scotland.gov.uk*
Admission *£3*
Open *Apr-Sep 9.30am-6.30pm daily (last entry 6pm)*

Maeshowe Chambered Cairn
This Neolithic tomb dates before 2700 BC. It features a stone passageway leading to a burial chamber with Runic inscriptions.
A965, Stenness, 14.5km west of Kirkwall
☎ *(01856) 761 606*
Website *www.historic-scotland.gov.uk*
Admission *£3*
Tours depart *Jan-Mar 9.45am, 10.30am, 11.15am, noon, 12.45pm, 1.30pm, 2.15pm, 3pm, 3.45pm daily; Apr-Sep 9.45am, 10.30am, 11.15am, noon, 12.45pm, 1.30pm, 2.15pm, 3pm, 3.45pm, 4.30pm, 5.15pm daily; Oct-Dec 9.45am, 10.30am, 11.15am, noon, 12.45pm, 1.30pm, 2.15pm, 3pm, 3.45pm daily*

Ring of Brogar
This majestic stone circle dates from Neolithic times. It is a World Heritage site and it is located close to the Stones of Stenness.
B9055, 8km north east of Stromness
☎ *(01856) 841 815*
Website *www.historic-scotland.gov.uk*

Skara Brae Prehistoric Village
This well preserved collection of houses dates from the Stone Age. It was unearthed during a storm in 1850 and the houses feature stone furniture, painting a picture of life during Neolithic times.
B9056, Sandwick, 30km north west of Kirkwall
☎ *(01856) 841 815*
Website *www.historic-scotland.gov.uk*
Admission *Jan-Mar £4; Apr-Sep £5; Oct-Dec £4*
Open *Jan-Mar 9.30am-4.30pm daily (last entry 4pm); Apr-Sep 9.30am-6.30pm daily (last entry 6pm); Oct-Dec 9.30am-4.30pm daily (last entry 4pm)*

Stones of Stenness
This ancient stone circle features a circular earthen bank. It is close to the

Ring of Brogar and like Brogar, it is recognised by UNESCO as a World Heritage site.
B9055, 8km northeast of Stromness, Orkney
☎ *(01856) 841 815*
Website *www.historic-scotland.gov.uk*

PAPA WESTRAY
Knap of Howar
These two houses, dating from the Neolithic period, are believed to be the oldest houses in northwestern Europe.
400m west of Holland Farm, Papa Westray
☎ *(01856) 841 815*
Website *www.historic-scotland.gov.uk*

Shetland Islands

Backpackers seldom visit this remote island group, closer to Norway than to the Scottish mainland.

There is not a real lot to see here other than birds, sheep and the famous Shetland ponies, but some travellers visit the islands to make ferry connections to Norway, the Faeroe Islands and Iceland.

Like the Orkneys, the main island is known as Mainland.

Practical Information
Lerwick Tourist Information Centre
Market Cross, Lerwick
☎ *(01595) 693 434*
Open *Jan-Apr 9am-5pm daily; May-Sep Mon-Fri 8am-6pm, Sat 8am-4pm, Sun 10am-1pm; Oct-Dec 9am-5pm daily*

Coming & Going
Northlink Ferries (☎ *(01856) 851 144;* **website** *www.northlinkferries.co.uk*) operate ferries to Aberdeen and the Orkney Islands.

Smyril Line (**website** *www.smyril-line.com*) sails from the Shetlands to Bergen, Norway and Seydisfjördur, Iceland with a stop at Torshavn in the Faeroe Islands.

Sumburgh Airport (☎ *(01950) 460 654;* **website** *www.hial.co.uk/sumburgh-airport.html*) has flights to Kirkwall in the Orkneys; Aberdeen, Edinburgh, Glasgow, Inverness and Wick on mainland Scotland and Bergen and Oslo in Norway.

Local Transport
Public transport in the islands is infrequent but at least it's cheap with ferries between the islands charging no more than a couple of quid.

Accommodation
Lerwick SYHA
Overlooking one of Lerwick's beautiful parks, this lovely old mansion was built by a famous local herring merchant. Both inside and out, it is beautifully renovated and offers comfortable, quality accommodation. It's close to shops and pubs and right next door to the local theatre (the Garrison) and close to transport links that allow you to see all the island. There's a great café on site that serves giant platefuls of healthy fare.
Islesburgh House, King Harald Street, Lerwick
🚍 *Lerwick*
☎ *(01595) 692 114 or 0870 155 3255*
Website *www.islesburgh.org.uk*
Dorm bed *£13 (£12 HI/SYHA)*
Credit cards *MC, Visa*
Open *Apr-Sep;* **reception open** *8am-11am & 4.30pm-11.45pm daily;* **curfew** *11.45pm*

Maintenance & cleanliness	★★★★★
Facilities	★★★
Atmosphere & character	★★★★☆
Security	★★☆
Overall rating	★★★

Sights
LERWICK
Böd of Gremista
This restored 18th century booth previously functioned as a family home as well as a storehouse for the nearby fish-drying beach. It is also the birthplace of Arthur Anderson, the co-founder of P&O Ferries, and the museum features displays about his life.
Gemista, Lerwick
☎ *(01595) 695 057*
Website *www.shetland-museum.org.uk/bod/*

Admission free
Open *1 Jun-15 Sep Wed-Sun 10am-1pm & 2pm-5pm*

Clickimin Broch
This guard tower and adjoining buildings dates from the Iron Age. It is located around 1.6km southwest of the town centre.
A970, Lerwick
☎ *(01466) 793 191*
Admission free
Always open

The Shetland Museum
The largest museum in Shetland is located in the centre of Lerwick and its exhibits depict Shetland archaeology and culture and include a maritime section with a collection of boats.
Lower Hillhead, Lerwick
☎ *(01595) 695 057*
Website www.shetland-museum.org.uk
Admission free
Open *Mon 10am-7pm, Tue 10am-5pm, Wed 10am-7pm, Thu 10am-5pm, Fri 10am-7pm, Sat 10am-5pm*

SUMBURGH
Crofthouse Museum
This typical Shetland thatched cottage is a good example of a 19th century crofthouse.
5km north of Sumburgh
☎ *(01950) 460557*
Website www.shetland-museum.org.uk/crofthouse/
Admission free
Open *May-Sep 10am-1pm & 2pm-5pm*

Jarlshof Prehistoric & Norse Settlement
This ancient site comprises a Bronze Age village of oval stone houses as well as an Iron Age broch tower and a Viking settlement. There is also an exhibit in the adjoining visitors' centre that details the site's history.
A970, Sumburgh Head, Sumburgh
☎ *(01950) 460 112*
Website www.historic-scotland.gov.uk
Admission £3.30
Open *Apr-Sep 9.30am-6.30pm daily*

Northern Ireland

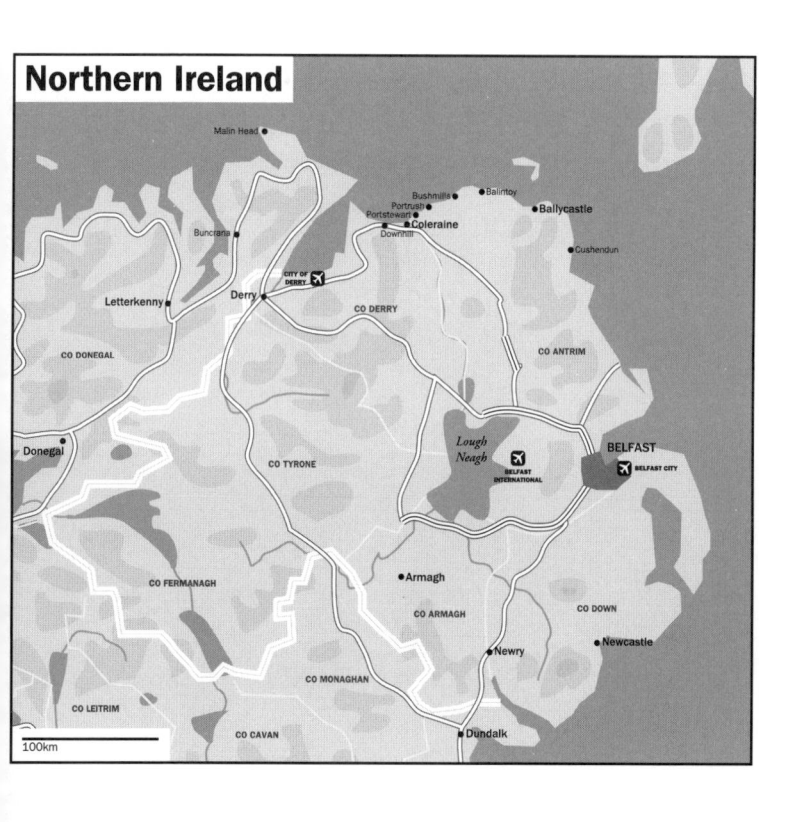

Northern Ireland

The much-publicised Troubles in Northern Ireland have put a lot of travellers off visiting Northern Ireland, which is a pity as it is a relatively safe destination with beautiful scenery and a unique culture.

County Derry

Derry (Londonderry; Doire Cholm Cille)

Derry (called Londonderry by the British) is Northern Ireland's second largest city and is Ireland's only remaining completely walled city. It is a pleasant city, particularly inside the walled old town. If you're travelling from Co Donegal in the Republic, Derry will be your first port-of-call in Northern Ireland.

Practical Information
Tourist Information Centre
44 Foyle Street, Derry
☎ *(028) 7126 7284*
Website www.derryvisitor.com
Open *Jan-mid Mar Mon-Fri 9am-5pm; mid Mar-Jun Mon-Fri 9am-5pm, Sat 10am-5pm; Jul-Sep Mon-Fri 9am-7pm, Sat 10am-6pm, Sun 10am-5pm; Oct Mon-Fri 9am-5pm, Sat 10am-5pm; Nov-Dec Mon-Fri 9am-5pm*

INTERNET ACCESS
bean-there.com
20 The Diamond, Derry
☎ *(028) 7128 1303*
Website www.bean-there.com
Open *Mon-Fri 8.30am-5.30pm, Sat 10am-5.30pm, Sun 10am-4pm*

Coming & Going
AIR
City of Derry Airport (☎ *(028) 7181 0784; website www.cityofderryairport.com*) has flights to Dublin, Glasgow, London (Stansted) and Manchester). The AIRporter bus (☎ *(028) 7126 9996*) runs between the airport and the city centre.

BUS
There are hourly bus services between Derry and Belfast as well as regular buses to Dublin. Buses stop on Foyle Street.

TRAIN
Derry's Waterside Station is across Craigavon Bridge on the western side of the River Foyle. Translink *(website www.translink.co.uk)* have direct trains to Belfast.

Accommodation
Derry City Independent Hostel
Derry City Independent Hostel is a nice hostel with a relaxed laidback atmosphere. It is decorated with souvenirs from the owners' own travels, which gives it an exotic feel. It boasts spacious dorms with high ceilings; a dining room with low tables and a cosy TV lounge with an open fire. The same people who own Steve's Backpackers run this hostel.
44 Great James Street, Derry
☎ *(028) 7137 7989*
Website www.derry-hostel.co.uk
Dorm bed £10; **double/twin room** £28; prices include breakfast

Maintenance & cleanliness	★★★
Facilities	★★☆
Atmosphere & character	★★★★★
Security	★
Overall rating	★★★

Steve's Backpackers
Steve's Backpackers is a small 18-bed hostel with a small sitting room downstairs and a cosy TV lounge on the top floor. It is run by the same people as Derry City Independent Hostel.
4 Asylum Road, Derry
☎ *(028) 7137 7989*
Website www.derry-hostel.co.uk
Dorm bed £10

Maintenance & cleanliness	★★★☆
Facilities	★★☆
Atmosphere & character	★★★★☆
Security	★
Overall rating	★★★☆

Sights
The Bogside Artists & Studio
This famous Catholic neighbourhood is best known for its murals, which depict the last 30 years of conflict in Derry. The Bogside Artists Studio offers the opportunity to meet the artists responsible for the murals and watch a one-hour slide presentation about them.
Unit 7, Meenan Square, Derry
☎ *(028) 7129 0371*
Website *www.bogsideartists.com*
Admission *£5*

City Walls
Derry's city walls date to the 17th century and have withstood several sieges including one that lasted for 105 days. You can walk the 1.5km circuit along the top of the walls, which offers views of the old city.

Free Derry Corner
A sign declaring, "You are now entering Free Derry", marks the entrance to the Bogside district. Nearby is a monument commemorating the 14 victims of the 1972 Bloody Sunday massacre.
Corner Fahan Street & Rossville Square, Derry

Guildhall
This neo-Gothic building boasts one of Ireland's largest collections of stained glass windows.
Guildhall Square, Derry
☎ *(028) 7137 7335*
Admission *free*
Open *Mon-Fri 9am-5pm*

Harbour Museum
This museum has exhibits about the city's maritime history.
Harbour Square, Derry
☎ *(028) 7137 7331*
Admission *free*
Open *Mon-Fri 10am-1pm & 2pm-4.30pm*

St Columb's Cathedral
Dating from 1633, St Columb's Cathedral is Derry's oldest building and it is also the oldest purpose-built Protestant cathedral in the British Isles.
London Street, Derry
☎ *(028) 7126 7313*
Website *www.stcolumbscathedral.org*
Admission *£1.30*
Open *summer Mon-Sat 9am-5pm; winter Mon-Sat 9am-1pm & 2pm-4pm*

Tower Museum
This museum has a variety of displays on local history including the Siege of Derry and the Troubles as well as the Spanish Armada.
Union Hall Place, Derry
☎ *(028) 7137 2411*
Admission *free*
Open *Jan-Jun Tue-Sat 10am-5pm; Jul-Aug Mon-Sat 10am-5pm, Sun 2pm-5pm; Sep-Dec Tue-Sat 10am-5pm*

Downhill
This tiny village near Coleraine has no shops but it has a lovely hostel by the sea.

Coming & Going
The closest train station is Castlerock on the Belfast-Derry line. Bus 134 connects Downhill with Coleraine and Limavady.

Accommodation
Downhill Hostel
Downhill Hostel is a big mansion right on the seafront that sleeps up to 26 travellers and two cats. It features a cosy lounge with an open fire and sea views, a dining room and a fully equipped kitchen with a big selection of herbs and spices. It has a great atmosphere and accommodation in spacious rooms with high ceilings.
12 Mussenden Road, Downhill
🚌 *134*
☎ *(028) 7084 9077*
Website *www.downhillhostel.com*
Dorm bed *£8;* **double/twin room** *£25*
Reception open *2pm-10pm daily*

Maintenance & cleanliness	★★★★
Facilities	★★
Atmosphere & character	★★★★★
Security	★★
Overall rating	★★★½

Sights
Downhill & Mussenden Temple
Fredrick Hervey, Bishop of Derry and Earl of Bristol built this large house perched upon the cliff top overlooking Downhill. Although the main house is

now in ruins the property is also home to the spectacular Mussenden Temple and a mausoleum to his brother.
Hezlett Farm, 107 Sea Road, Castlerock
☎ *134*
☎ *(028) 7084 8728*
Website www.ntni.org.uk
Admission free; parking £3.60
Open Mar-May Sat-Sun 11am-6pm; Jun 11am-6pm daily; Jul-Aug 11am-7.30pm daily; Sep 11am-6pm daily; Oct Sat-Sun 11am-5pm

Portstewart (Port Stíobaird)

This seaside town is a slightly classier alternative to neighbouring Portrush in County Antrim. It's main attraction is the 3.25km-long Portstewart Strand, which is one of Northern Ireland's top beaches.

Coming & Going

Portstewart is well served by buses with Ulsterbus *(website www.translink.co.uk)* buses 140 and 252 going to Coleraine and Portrush and bus 252 continuing along the coast to Larne, stopping en route at Bushmills, the Giant's Causeway and Ballycastle.

Accommodation
Rick's Causeway Coast Hostel

This small hostel has a friendly atmosphere. It has a basic kitchen plus a cosy common room with a TV and open fire. Some of the rooms have nice sea views.
4 Victoria Terrace (Atlantic Circle), Portstewart
☎ *(028) 7083 3789*
Dorm bed £8; double/twin room £20-24

TV K L

Maintenance & cleanliness	★★☆
Facilities	★★☆
Atmosphere & character	★★★★☆
Security	★
Overall rating	★★☆

Sights
Portstewart Strand & Barmouth

This 3.25km-long stretch of beach is backed by sand dunes that reach heights of up to 30 metres.

Website www.ntni.org.uk
Admission free, parking £4
Open Mar-Sep 10am-6pm daily; Oct Sat-Sun 10am-5pm

County Antrim

Northern Ireland's most visited county is home to the capital Belfast and the World Heritage-listed Giant's Causeway.

Portrush (Port Ruis)

This seaside resort is only 6km from Portstewart in County Derry and it is a town that is a popular family resort. Portrush has good transport connections making it a handy base for exploring the surrounding region.

Practical Information
Tourist Information Centre
Dunluce Centre, Sandhill Drive, Portrush
☎ *(028) 7082 3333*
Website www.colerainebe.gov.uk
Open Jun-Aug 9am-7pm daily

Coming & Going
BUS

Portrush is well served by buses with Ulsterbus *(website www.translink.co.uk)* buses 140 and 252 going to Coleraine and Portstewart and bus 252 continuing along the coast to Larne, stopping en route at Bushmills, the Giant's Causeway and Ballycastle.

TRAIN

The station on Eglington Street in the town centre has trains to Belfast and Derry.

Accommodation
Macools Portrush Independent Hostel

This small 18-bed hostel has a small kitchen, a cosy TV lounge and a dog named Guinness. The dorms are clean but cramped and there are sea views from the private rooms.
35 Causeway Street, Portrush
☎ *(028) 7082 4845*
Website www.portrush-hostel.com
Dorm bed £10; twin room £24

TV K

Maintenance & cleanliness	★★★
Facilities	★★☆
Atmosphere & character	★★★★☆
Security	★★☆
Overall rating	★★★☆

Bushmills & the Giant's Causeway

This historic village is home to the world's oldest licensed whiskey distillery and it is also the closest town to the Giant's Causeway, Northern Ireland's top visitor attraction, which makes it a popular stop for many backpackers.

Practical Information
Giant's Causeway Tourist Information Centre
44 Causeway Road, Bushmills
☎ *(028) 2073 1855*
Open *Jan-Feb 10am-4.30pm daily; Mar-Jun 10am-5pm daily; Jul-Aug 10am-6pm daily; Sep-Oct 10am-5pm daily; Nov-Dec 10am-4.30pm daily*

Coming & Going
Both bus 177 and 252 run to Portrush and the Giant's Causeway although bus 252 (the Antrim Coaster) continues along the coast as far as Larne, where you can transfer to a Belfast-bound train.

Accommodation
Mill Rest Bushmills Youth Hostel
The Bushmills Youth Hostel is a well-appointed place tucked in behind the main street of the village. The mezzanine-style rooms are well designed with en suite facilities and it is much more secure than the average small town hostel (with a locker for every bed). Facilities include a TV area with an open fire, Internet access, a good kitchen and a big dining room. However the dining room feels like a hospital cafeteria and the rest of the hostel feels equally sterile.
49 Main Street, Bushmills
🚌 *177, 252*
☎ *(028) 2073 1222*
Website *www.hini.org.uk*
Dorm bed *£11.50;* **twin room** *£30*
Credit cards *MC, Visa*
Reception open *Jan-Mar 8am-11am & 5pm-11pm daily; Apr-Sep 8am-11pm daily; Oct-Dec 8am-11am & 5pm-11pm daily*

Maintenance & cleanliness	★★★★★
Facilities	★★
Atmosphere & character	★
Security	★★★★☆
Overall rating	★★★

Sights
Giant's Causeway
The World Heritage-listed Giant's Causeway is Northern Ireland's top tourist attraction. It consists of around 40,000 basalt columns, each formed in a unique polygon shape, that were created 60 million years ago during a period of volcanic activity. Local folklore states that an Irish giant named Finn MacCool built the causeway so he could walk across the sea to Scotland to challenge a rival giant. Finn MacCool is also credited with creating Lough Neagh and the Isle of Man.
60 Causeway Road, Bushmills
🚌 *177, 252*
☎ *(028) 2073 1582*
Website *www.ntni.org.uk*
Admission *free; parking £5*
Always open

The Old Bushmills Distillery
This is the world's oldest licensed whiskey distillery, which was granted its licence by King James I in 1608. Tours of the distillery conclude with a sample of Bushmills whiskey.
2 Distillery Road, Bushmills
☎ *(028) 2073 1521*
Website *www.whiskeytours.ie*
Tours depart *Jan-Mar Mon-Fri 10.30am, 11.30am, 1.30pm, 2.30pm, 3.30pm, Sat-Sun 1.30pm, 2.30pm, 3.30pm; Apr-Oct Mon-Sat 9.30am-4pm, Sun noon-4pm; Nov-Dec Mon-Fri 10.30am, 11.30am, 1.30pm, 2.30pm, 3.30pm, Sat-Sun 1.30pm, 2.30pm, 3.30pm*

Ballintoy (Baile an Tuaighe)

This small village between Ballycastle and the Giant's Causeway has lovely coastal scenery and a couple of hostels that are a good base for exploring northern Antrim. Its main attractions are the two islands off the coast – Carrick-a-rede Island and Sheep Island. Sheep Island is a haven for birdlife including cormorants and puffins but the more popular of the two islands is the smaller Carrick-a-rede Island, accessible via a hair-raising rope bridge.

Coming and Going

The Antrim Coaster (bus 252) runs along the coast from Coleraine to Larne, stopping en route at Portstewart, Portrush, Bushmills and Ballycastle.

Accommodation
Sheep Island View Hostel

This clean and well-maintained hostel in the small village of Ballintoy has very good kitchen facilities with an adjoining dining room plus a TV lounge with an open fire.

42A Main Street, Ballintoy
☎ *(028) 2076 9391*
Website www.sheepislandview.com
Dorm bed £10
Credit cards MC, Visa

Maintenance & cleanliness	★★★★☆
Facilities	★★★☆
Atmosphere & character	★★★☆
Security	★★☆
Overall rating	★★★★☆

Whitepark Bay Youth Hostel

The Whitepark Bay Youth Hostel is a purpose-built hostel overlooking the sea, three miles from the Giant's Causeway. It is maintained to a high standard with new furnishings and accommodation in small dormitories. Facilities include a kitchen, a TV lounge and a lounge room with an open fire and ocean views.

157 Whitepark Road, 5km west of Ballintoy
☎ *(028) 2073 1745*
Website www.hini.org.uk
Dorm bed £11.50
Credit cards MC, Visa
Open 3 Jan-22 Dec; reception open Jan-Mar 8am-11am & 5pm-10pm daily; Apr-Sep 8am-10pm daily; Oct-Dec 8am-11am & 5pm-10pm daily

Maintenance & cleanliness	★★★★★
Facilities	★★
Atmosphere & character	★★☆
Security	★★★
Overall rating	★★★★☆

Sights
Carrick-a-rede Island & Rope Bridge

Fishermen have used a rope bridge to cross the 30m-deep chasm between the mainland and Carrick-a-rede Island for over 300 years. The original bridge consisted of a footrope and a single handrail, but in 2000 a new rope bridge was erected that has been load tested to more than 10 tonnes.

252
Website www.ntni.org.uk
Admission £3.50
Open 15 Mar-30 Jun 10am-6pm daily; 1 Jul-31 Aug 9.30am-7.30pm daily; 1-30 Sep 10am-6pm daily

Ballycastle (Baile an Chaisil)

This bustling seaside town is a popular base for travellers exploring the Causeway Coast.

Practical Information
Tourist Information Centre

Sheskburn House, 7 Mary Street, Ballycastle
☎ *(028) 2076 2024*
Website www.discovernorthernireland.com
Open Jan-Jun Mon-Fri 9.30am-5pm; Jul-Aug Mon-Fri 9.30am-7pm, Sat 10am-6pm, Sun 2pm-6pm; Sep-Dec Mon-Fri 9.30am-5pm

Coming & Going

Ulsterbus (*website* www.translink.co.uk) bus 252 stops at Ballycastle on the coastal route linking Coleraine and Larne, where you can transfer for a train to Belfast. Bus 131 offers a more direct route to Belfast.

Accommodation
Castle Hostel

The Castle Hostel is a good hostel with a small kitchen and a cosy TV lounge with an open fire.

62 Quay Road, Ballycastle
☎ (028) 2076 2337
Website www.castlehostel.com
Dorm bed £8; **double room** £20
Reception open 8am-11am & 5pm-10pm daily

📺 🍳 🄻

Maintenance & cleanliness	★★★
Facilities	★★
Atmosphere & character	★★★★
Security	★★
Overall rating	★★★

Cushendun (Bun Abhann Duinne)

This relatively remote village is reached by a breathtaking drive and it boasts a stunning seaside location.

Coming & Going

Cushendun is served by the Antrim Coaster bus (route 252), which runs along the coast between Larne and Coleraine.

Accommodation
Drumkeerin Camping Barn

This clean but basic hostel sleeps 14 in solid bunk beds. It has a small kitchen and TV lounge plus lovely sea views.
201A Torr Road, Cushendun
☎ (028) 2176 1554
Dorm bed £8

🍳 📺 🄺

Maintenance & cleanliness	★★★★
Facilities	★
Atmosphere & character	★★★
Security	★
Overall rating	★★★

Belfast (Béal Feirste)

Northern Ireland's largest city is a fascinating destination that is both a thriving cosmopolitan city and a window into Northern Ireland's troubled past.

Although much of the city centre is just like anywhere else in Britain & Ireland, many of Belfast's residential neighbourhoods are divided on sectarian lines with Catholic and Protestant areas displaying murals depicting each side's version of the Troubles that until recently dominated everyday life in Northern Ireland. You can get a taste of the division between Northern Ireland's two main religious groups by staying at the youth hostel in the staunchly Protestant Sandy Row area, although a much better idea is to take one of the highly recommended Black Taxi tours where a local cab driver takes you into the city's most divided areas giving a first-hand account of the Troubles.

Practical Information
Tourist Information Centre
47 Donegal Place, Belfast
☎ (028) 9024 5829
Website www.gotobelfast.com
Open Jan-May Mon-Sat 9am-5.30pm; Jun-Sep Mon-Sat 9am-7pm, Sun noon-5pm; Oct-Dec Mon-Sat 9am-5.30pm

Coming & Going
AIR
Belfast has two airports, Belfast City and Belfast International.

The busier of the two is Belfast International Airport (☎ *(028) 9448 4848; website www.bial.co.uk*) in Aldergrove, which has flights by Aer Lingus, British Airways, BMI and easyJet while the smaller – but more central – Belfast City Airport (☎ *(028) 9066 6630; website www.belfastcityairport.com*) handles FlyBE.com flights.

The Airbus (☎ *(028) 9066 6630; website www.translink.co.uk*) goes to Belfast International from Europa bus station running every half hour (£6 one-way). Take a train from Central Station to Sydenham Halt to get to Belfast City Airport (£1.50 one-way).

BUS
Bus Éireann (*website www.buseireann.ie*), Eurolines (*website www.eurolines.co.uk*) and Ulsterbus (*website www.translink.co.uk*) bus services depart from the Europa bus station on Great Victoria Street for destinations throughout Great Britain and Ireland.

Buses to the east coast in counties Antrim and Down leave from Laganside Bus Station off Donegall Quay.

FERRY
Seacat Ferries (☎ *0870 552 3523; website www.seacat.co.uk*) sail from Belfast to Troon near Glasgow in Scotland and

Belfast

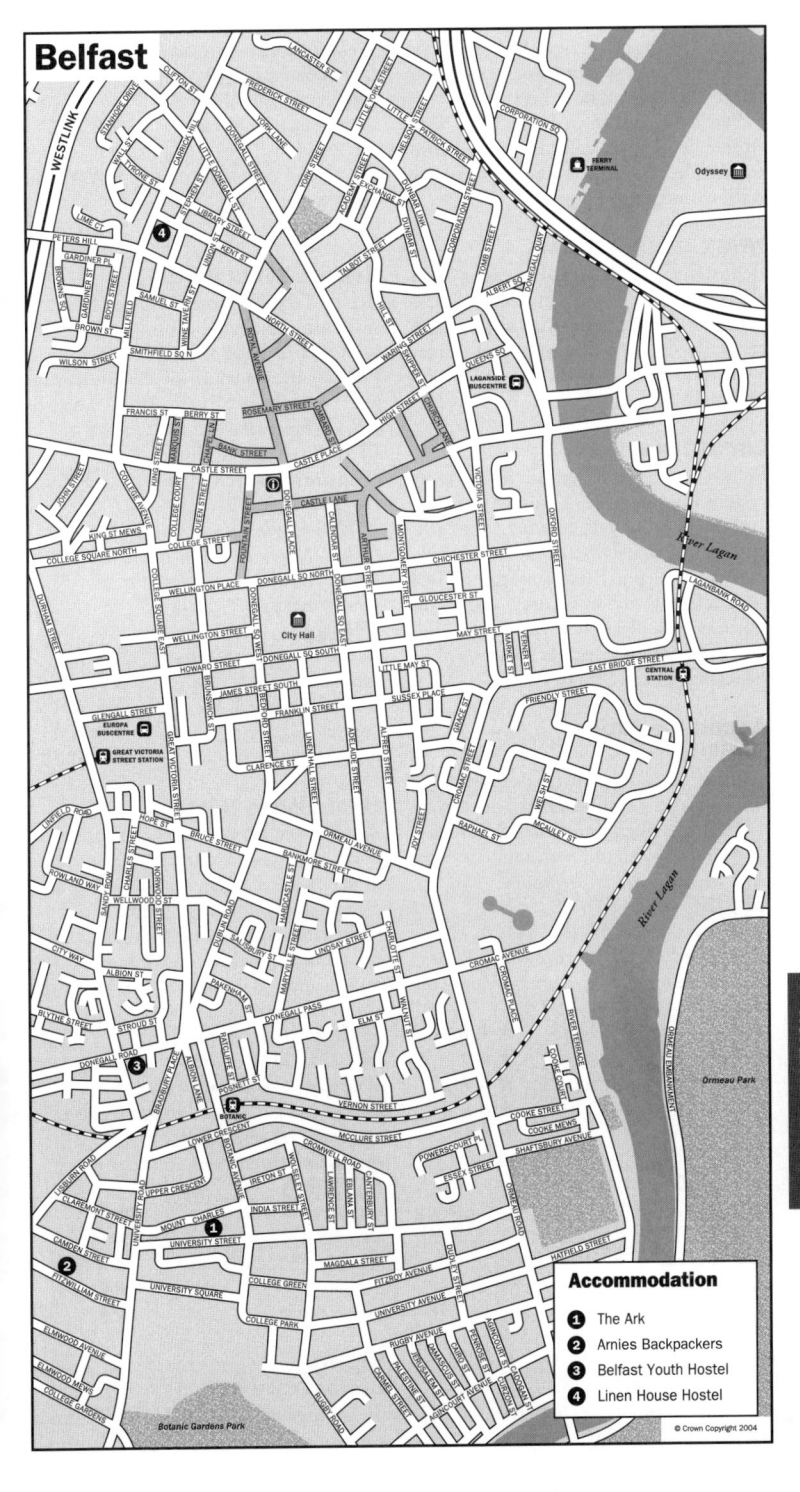

Accommodation

1. The Ark
2. Arnies Backpackers
3. Belfast Youth Hostel
4. Linen House Hostel

Norse Merchant Ferries (☎ 0870 242 4777; website www.norsemerchant.com) sail to Birkenhead near Liverpool.

Ferries depart from Donegall Quay, which is a five minute walk from Laganside Bus Station and a 15 minute walk from Central Station.

TRAIN
Belfast has several train stations with all trains terminating at Central Station. Some trains also stop at the more centrally located Botanic and Great Victoria Street stations. Trains go to Derry, Dublin and Larne.

Local Transport
Belfast's comprehensive public transport system is comprised of suburban trains and the Citybus bus network, both run by Translink (website www.translink.co.uk). The Centrelink bus (route 100) connects all the main bus and train stations as well as the Waterfront Hall and major shopping areas. One-way bus tickets cost from 90p to £1.10.

Accommodation
The Ark
This neat and tidy hostel near the university has a small kitchen and a cosy TV lounge. Accommodation is in clean dormitories with old bedding.
18 University Street, Belfast
☎ *(028) 9032 9626*
Website www.arkhostel.com
Dorm bed £9.50; *double room* £36
Reception open 8am-2am; *curfew* 2am

Maintenance & cleanliness	★★★
Facilities	★★☆
Atmosphere & character	★★★
Security	★★★☆
Overall rating	★★★☆

Arnie's Backpackers
This small 23-bed hostel is nothing fancy but it has a warm welcome. Facilities include a small kitchen, a small dining room with a fireplace and a cosy lounge with a piano and another fireplace. There's also a small barbecue area out the back. It has the best atmosphere of Belfast's hostels.
63 Fitzwilliam Street, Belfast
☎ *(028) 9024 2867*
Website www.arniesbackpackers.co.uk
Dorm bed £7-9.50

Maintenance & cleanliness	★★★☆
Facilities	★★☆
Atmosphere & character	★★★★★
Security	★
Overall rating	★★★☆

Belfast Youth Hostel
Belfast's HINI youth hostel has the standard kitchen, dining area, TV lounge and Internet access. It is in a Protestant area south of the city centre near Shaftsbury Square.
22-32 Donegall Road, Belfast
☎ *(028) 9031 5435*
Website www.hini.org.uk
Dorm bed £8.50-10.50 (£8-10 HI/HINI); *single room* £17-18 (£16-17 HI/HINI); *twin room* £26-28 (£24-26 HI/HINI)
Credit cards MC, Visa

Maintenance & cleanliness	★★★
Facilities	★★☆
Atmosphere & character	★★★
Security	★★★★
Overall rating	★★★☆

Linen House Hostel
This former linen factory, a short walk north of the city centre, is a cheap place to stay with a kitchen and dining area plus a basement lounge with a TV, pool table, table tennis, table football and old decaying sofas. It's good value and has quite a good atmosphere but it feels tired and could be in much better condition.
18-20 Kent Street, Belfast
☎ *(028) 9058 6400*
Website www.belfasthostel.com
Dorm bed £6.50-12; *single room* £15-20; *twin room* £24-30
Reception open 8am-midnight

Maintenance & cleanliness	★★☆
Facilities	★★☆
Atmosphere & character	★★★★☆
Security	★★☆
Overall rating	★★

Sights
Belfast City Hall
This imposing Classical Renaissance building features an ornate 53m-high

dome and an opulent Council Chamber that can be seen by taking a free tour.
Donegall Square, Belfast
☎ *Centrelink*
☎ *(028) 9027 0456*
Website *www.belfastcity.gov.uk*
Admission *free*
Tours *Jan-May Mon-Sat 2.30pm; Jun-Sep Mon-Fri 10.30am, 11.30am, 2.30pm, Sat 2.30pm; Oct-Dec Mon-Sat 2.30pm*

Black Taxi Tours
One of the most worthwhile things you can do in Belfast is take a Black Taxi Tour. These tours involve a local cab driver taking you into the areas most affected by the Troubles giving a firsthand account of the conflict. Tours generally include the murals in the Protestant Shankill Road and Catholic Falls Road, fortified police stations and the sites of various terrorist bombs. There are several companies offering these tours including the highly recommended Belfast Black Taxi Tours:
☎ *0800 052 3914 or (028) 9064 2264*
Website *www.belfasttours.com*
Tours cost *£20 for one or two passenger tour; £7.50 per person for larger group*
Tours depart *10am, noon, 2pm, 4pm, 6pm*

Odyssey
This huge complex by the docks features an IMAX theatre and an excellent science museum.
2 Queen's Quay, Belfast
☎ *(028) 9046 7700*
Admission *£5.50*
Open *Mon-Sat 10am-6pm, Sun noon-6pm*

Ulster Museum
This excellent museum has a varied collection including treasures recovered from the Spanish galleon Girona, which sank off the coast of Northern Ireland in 1588.
Stranmills Road, Belfast
☎ *69*
☎ *(028) 9038 3000*
Admission *free*
Open *Mon-Fri 10am-5pm, Sat 1pm-5pm, Sun 2pm-5pm*

Ulster Folk & Transport Museum
This open-air museum is set on 60 acres and features restored buildings depicting life in the early 1900s. It is about 12km from the city centre.
153 Bangor Road, Holywood
☎ *(028) 9042 8428*
Admission *£2-4*
Open *Jan-Feb Mon-Fri 10am-4pm, Sat 10am-5pm, Sun 11am-5pm; Mar-Jun Mon-Fri 10am-5pm, Sat 10am-6pm, Sun 11am-6pm; Jul-Sep Mon-Sat 10am-6pm, Sun 11am-6pm; Oct-Dec Mon-Fri 10am-4pm, Sat 10am-5pm, Sun 11am-5pm*

Counties Down & Armagh

Counties Down and Armagh cover the area between Belfast and the border with the Republic. The main attraction here is the Mourne Mountains, although this isn't a big draw for most backpackers.

Newcastle (An Caisleán Nua)

Newcastle is on the coast 50km south of Belfast. It doesn't offer much of interest, but some people stop here to break the journey between Belfast and Dublin.

Practical Information
Tourist Information Centre
Newcastle Centre, 10-14 Central Promenade, Newcastle
☎ *(028) 4372 2222*
Website *www.newcastletic.org*
Open *Jun Mon-Sat 10am-5pm, Sun 2pm-6pm; Jul-Aug Mon-Sat 9.30am-7pm, Sun 1pm-7pm; Sep Mon-Sat 10am-5pm, Sun 2pm-6pm*

Coming & Going
Ulsterbus *(website www.translink.co.uk)* have frequent buses to Belfast, Downpatrick, Newry and Dublin.

Accommodation
Newcastle Youth Hostel
Newcastle's youth hostel is conveniently located in the town centre. It has the usual facilities such as a kitchen, laundry

and a TV lounge but the rooms are a bit plain and it has an institutional feel.
30 Downs Road, Newcastle
☎ *(028) 4372 2133*
Website www.hini.org.uk
Dorm bed £11 (£10 HI)
Credit cards MC, Visa
Reception open 7.30am-10.30am & 5pm-11.30pm daily

Maintenance & cleanliness	★★½
Facilities	★½
Atmosphere & character	★½
Security	★★
Overall rating	★★

Armagh (Ard Macha)

Armagh bills itself as Ireland's Christian Capital and St Patrick is believed to have lived here in the 5th century. The city now has two St Patrick's Cathedrals, including one on the site where St Patrick built his original church in 445.

Practical Information
Tourist Information Centre
Old Bank Building, 40 English Street, Armagh
☎ *(028) 3752 1800*
Open Mon-Sat 9am-5pm, Sun 1pm-5pm

Coming & Going
Ulsterbus (*website www.translink.co.uk*) has buses to Armagh from Belfast, Dublin, Enniskillen and Portrush. Buses terminate at the bus station on Lonsdale Road.

Accommodation
Armagh City Youth Hostel
This neat and tidy hostel has good quality accommodation with en suite facilities in the rooms plus a good kitchen and lounge areas.
39 Abbey Street, Armagh
☎ *(028) 3751 1800*
Website www.hini.org.uk
Dorm bed £11.50
Credit cards MC, Visa
Reception open 8am-11am & 5pm-11pm daily

Sights
Armagh County Museum
This distinctive building houses an extensive collection with exhibits on natural history, railways, art and local history.
The Mall East, Armagh
☎ *(028) 3752 3070*
Website www.magni.org.uk
Admission free
Open Mon-Fri 10am-5pm, Sat 10am-1pm & 2pm-5pm

St Patrick's Church of Ireland Cathedral
Armagh's protestant cathedral is built on the site where St Patrick built his original church in 445. The Irish King Brian Ború is buried here and this medieval cathedral is also home to an eclectic collection of artefacts.
Cathedral Close, Armagh
☎ *(028) 3752 3142*
Admission free
Open Jan-Mar 10am-4pm daily; Apr-Oct 10am-5pm daily; Nov-Dec 10am-4pm daily; tours depart Jun-Aug Mon-Sat 11.30am & 2.30pm daily

St Patrick's Roman Catholic Cathedral
St Patrick's Roman Catholic Cathedral is a Gothic Revival-style cathedral that dates from 1873 and is noted for its intricate mosaics.
Cathedral Road, Armagh
☎ *(028) 3752 2802*
Website www.armagharchdiocese.org
Admission free
Open daily till dusk

St Patrick's Trian
St Patrick's Trian has a number of exhibits on the history of Armagh and St Patrick. It also features an exhibition on the *Gulliver's Travels* story.
40 English Street, Armagh
☎ *(028) 3752 1801*
Website www.saintpatrickstrian.com
Open Jan-Jun Mon-Sat 10am-5pm, Sun 2pm-5pm; Jul-Aug Mon-Sat 10am-5.30pm, Sun 2pm-6pm; Sep-Dec Mon-Sat 10am-5pm, Sun 2pm-5pm

Republic of Ireland

Leinster

This region encompasses the eastern portion of the Republic of Ireland and includes the capital Dublin and the Wicklow Mountains.

Co Dublin

Ireland's most-visited county comprises the capital, Dublin, and its suburbs.

Dublin (Baile Átha Cliath)

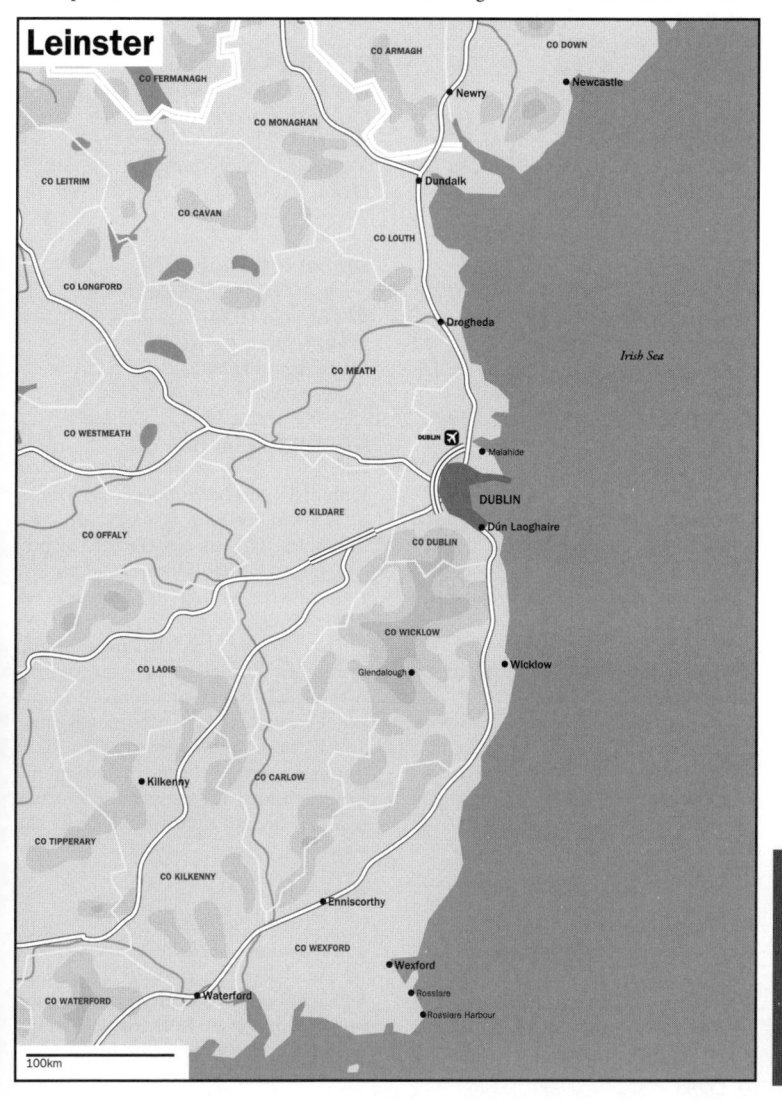

Although some parts of Dublin retain a drab and peculiarly quaint ambiance, the Irish capital has a new found reputation as a vibrant and youthful city. The River Liffey divides Dublin's split personality of the traditional working class neighbourhoods north of the river and the trendy shopping and nightlife areas south of the Liffey.

This youthful façade characterised by the Temple Bar area is set against a traditional backdrop of old Ireland that has enchanted travellers for years before the city became the latest weekend getaway for young Londoners and Parisians.

Practical Information
TOURIST INFORMATION CENTRES
Dublin Tourism
Information Centres
Suffolk Street, Dublin
☎ *1850 230 330 or (01) 605 7700*
Website *www.visitdublin.com*
Open *Jan-Jun Mon-Sat 9am-5.30am, Sun 10.30am-3pm; Jul-Aug Mon-Sat 9am-7pm, Sun 10.30am-3pm; Sep-Dec Mon-Sat 9am-5.30am, Sun 10.30am-3pm*

13 Upper O'Connell Street, Dublin
☎ *1850 230 330 or (01) 605 7700*
Website *www.visitdublin.com*
Open *Mon-Sat 9am-5pm*

Dublin Airport
☎ *1850 230 330 or (01) 605 7700*
Website *www.visitdublin.com*
Open *8am-10pm daily*

Northern Ireland Tourist Board
16 Nassau Street, Dublin
☎ *(01) 679 1977 or 1850 230 230*
Open *Mon-Fri 9.15am-5.30pm, Sat 10am-5pm*

EMBASSIES & CONSULATES
Australian Embassy
7th Floor, Fitzwilton House, Wilton Terrace, Dublin
☎ *(01) 664 5300; 24-hour information line (01) 664 5345*
Website *www.australianembassy.ie*
Open *Mon-Fri 8.30am-12.30pm & 1.30pm-4.30pm*

British Embassy
27 Merrion Road, Ballsbridge
☎ *(01) 205 3700*
Website *www.britishembassy.ie*
Open *Mon-Thu 9am-12.45pm & 2pm-5.15pm; Fri 9am-12.45pm & 2pm-5pm*

Canadian Embassy
4th Floor, 65 St Stephens Green South, Dublin
☎ *(01) 478 1988*
Website *www.dfait-maeci.gc.ca/ canadaeuropa/ireland/*
Open *Mon-Fri 8.30am-1pm & 2pm-5pm*

United States Embassy
42 Elgin Road, Ballsbridge
☎ *(01) 661 8777*
Website *http://dublin.usembassy.gov*
Open *Mon-Fri 8am-6.30pm*

INTERNET ACCESS
Central Cybercafe
6 Grafton Street, Dublin
☎ *(01) 677 8298*
Website *www.centralcafe.ie*
Open *Mon-Fri 9am-10pm, Sat-Sun 10am-9pm*

Global Internet Café
8 Lower O'Connell Street, Dublin
☎ *(01) 878 0295*
Website *www.globalcafe.ie*
Open *Mon-Fri 8am-11pm, Sat 9am-11pm, Sun 10am-10pm*

Coming & Going
AIR
Dublin Airport *(website www.aer-rianta.ie)* is 11km north of the city centre. Airlink buses (€5) run between the airport and Busáras, alternatively you can save your cash by taking the local bus 41, 41B, 41C (€1.75).

The airport has frequent flights throught Europe and the world. Although it is a busy airport, it is also small enough to be easily manageable, and is the base for several of Europe's fastest growing airlines including Aer Lingus and Ryanair with the usual facilities including fast food joints and a pub.

BUS
Bus Éirrean *(website www.buseireann.ie)*, Eurolines *(website www.eurolines.ie)* and Ulsterbus *(website www.ulsterbus.co.uk)* operate from Dublin's main bus station known as Busáras. This bus terminal is centrally located near Connolly Station.

TRAIN

Iarnród Éireann *(website www.irishrail.ie)* operates trains to most major destinations in Ireland with departures from Dublin's two main train stations, Connolly and Heuston.

Connolly Station is the more centrally located of the two and handles trains to Belfast and Derry in Northern Ireland as well as destinations in the north of the Republic such as Sligo.

Other routes including Dublin to Cork, Galway, Killarney, Waterford and Wexford operate out of Heuston station. Heuston station is located to the west of the centre near the Guinness Brewery.

There are frequent bus connections between the two stations.

FERRY

Dublin has two ferry ports. Sealink Ferries arrive at Dún Laoghaire which is easily accessible by DART trains from Connolly Station. B&I Ferries leave from Dublin Harbour which is connected to central Dublin by buses 53 and 53A.

HITCHHIKING

Ireland is one of the world's best countries to hitch in, however a lot of other people know this which means there is often a lot of competition on the roads. If you're heading north to Belfast, walk north along O'Connell Street to Drumcondra Road and wait there. If you don't fancy the 4km walk, take the airport bus and ask to be dropped off before the airport entrance.

Walk along Thomas Street, past the Guinness Brewery, and try your luck on Emmet Road for lifts to Cork, Killarney, Limerick or Waterford.

BUG Ride *(website http://europe.bugride.com)* is our own web-based ride sharing service, it allows travellers to both offer lifts and search for rides throughout Europe. This is a free service which links travellers to drivers – you contact the driver by email when you have found the ride you want.

Local Transport

Dublin has good public transport comprised of buses, trains and trams.

BUSES

Dublin Bus (☎ *(01) 873 4222; website www.dublinbus.ie)* operates Dublin's bus network, which has fairly frequent services with buses running at 10-20 minute intervals.

A round green sign indicates bus stops and you cannot board at bus stops marked Set Down Only.

A single bus trip costs from €0.90 to €1.85. Rambler tickets are valid for unlimited travel on Dublin Bus services including the Airlink bus, but not including night buses. These cost €5 for a one-day pass, €10 for a three-day pass, €15 for a five-day pass and €18 for a seven-day pass.

Night buses operate on Thursday, Friday and Saturday nights and charge a flat €4-6 fare.

DART & SUBURBAN TRAINS

Iarnród Éireann *(website www.irishrail.ie/dart/home/)* operates a network of suburban train lines including DART (Dublin Area Rapid Transport).

DART and the Northern, Western and Southeastern suburban services are served by Connolly, Tara and Pearce Stations in central Dublin. Southwestern suburban train services operate from Heuston Station.

The most useful of these are the DART services to Howth and the ferry terminal at Dún Laoghaire. A single trip between Dún Laoghaire and the city centre costs €1.80.

A Short-Hop ticket is a combined bus, DART and suburban train pass that costs €7.70 for a one-day pass, €15 for a three-day pass or €26 for a seven-day pass. A one-day pass valid only on DART and suburban train services costs €6.50.

LUAS

Dublin has a new tram network called Luas *(website www.luas.ie)*. There are two lines, the green line running from St Stephens Green to Sandyford and the more useful red line that connects Connolly and Heuston stations en route to Tallaght. One way tickets in the city centre cost €1.30, return tickets are €2.50, a one-day ticket costs €4.50 or €6 including bus travel.

Dublin

Accommodation

1. Abbey Court
2. Abraham House
3. Ashfield House
4. Avalon House
5. Barnacles Temple Bar
6. Brewery Hostel
7. Browns Hostel
8. Celts House
9. Citi Hostel
10. Cobblestones
11. Euro Hostel/City Manor
12. Four Courts
13. Globetrotters Tourist Hostel
14. Goin' My Way
15. International Youth Hostel (An Óige)
16. Issac's Hostel
17. Jacob's Inn
18. Kinlay House
19. Litton Lane Hostel
20. Marlborough Hostel
21. Mount Eccles Court
22. Oliver St John Gogarty
23. Paddy's Palace
24. Rainbow Hostel

Leinster – Dublin **367**

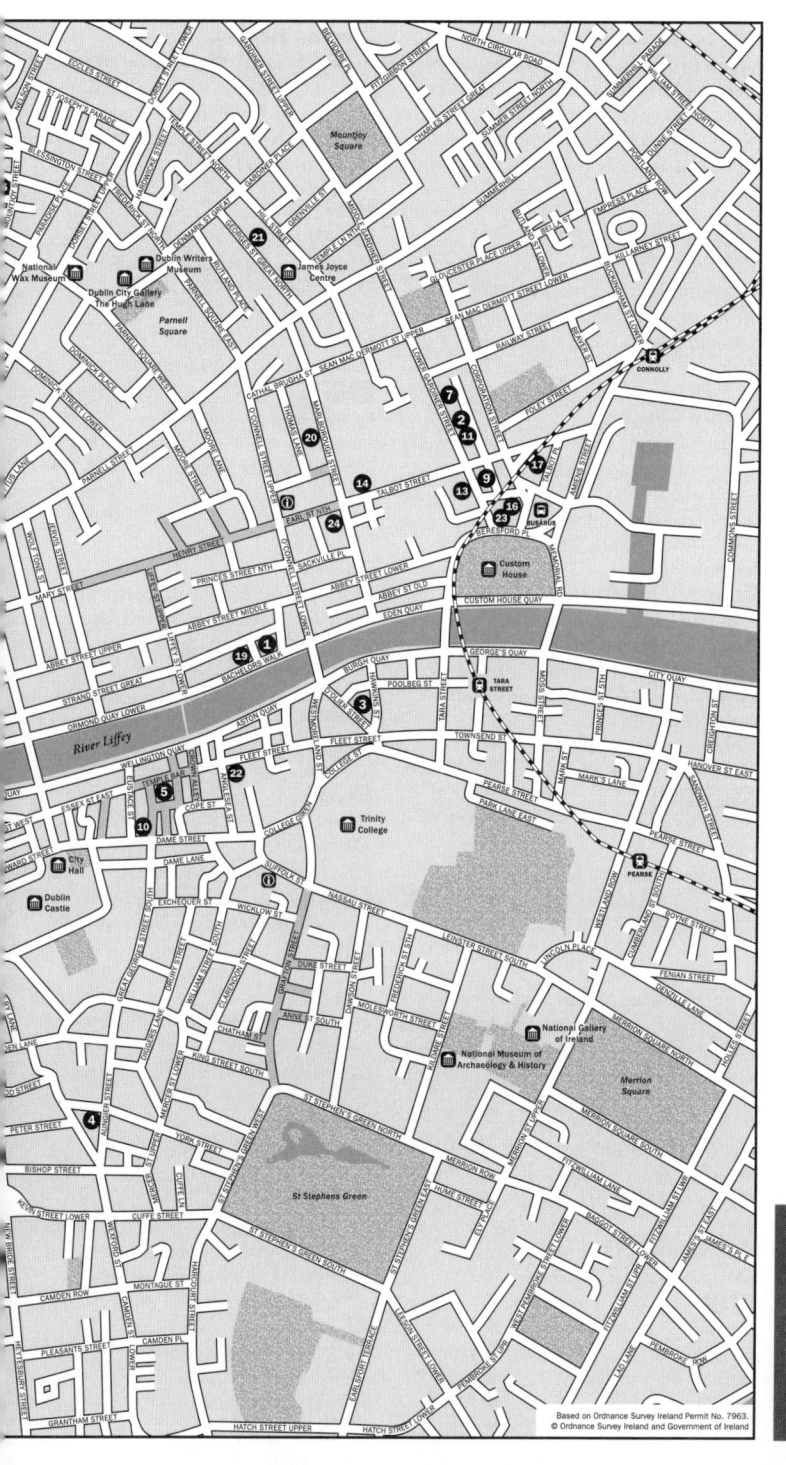

Accommodation

Compared with the rest of the country Dublin's hostels are overpriced and even more so in summer and long weekends when they jack their prices up to gouge every last euro from the unsuspecting traveller.

NORTH OF THE LIFFEY

This area is close to bus and train stations and the city centre but some parts of it are drab and depressing when compared with nicer areas south of the river.

Abbey Court

Abbey Court is a clean and well-maintained place with a big basement common area with two TV lounges, Internet access and a kitchen.
29 Bachelor's Walk, Dublin
🚌 *Abbey Street*
☎ *(01) 878 0700*
Website *www.abbey-court.com*
Bed in a four-bed dorm *€26-29;* **bed in a six-bed dorm** *€23-26;* **bed in a 12-bed dorm** *€18-21;* **double/twin room** *€76-88*
Credit cards *MC, Visa*
Reception open *24 hours*

Maintenance & cleanliness	★★★★☆
Facilities	★★☆
Atmosphere & character	★★☆
Security	★★★★★★
Overall rating	★★★☆

Abraham House

Abraham House has accommodation in tidy dorms with en suite bathrooms plus a quiet lounge area with Internet access, a kitchen and a dining room with TV.
82 Lower Gardiner Street, Dublin
☎ *(01) 855 0600*
Website *www.abraham-house.ie*
Dorm bed *€15-34;* **double room** *€96-120*
Credit cards *Amex, MC, Visa*
Reception open *24 hours*

Maintenance & cleanliness	★★★
Facilities	★★☆
Atmosphere & character	★★★☆
Security	★★★★☆
Overall rating	★★★☆

Browns Hostel

Browns Hostel offers clean accommodation and it features a vault-style common area that gives the hostel a good atmosphere. Shared facilities include a kitchen; a pool table and TV lounge.
89-90 Lower Gardiner Street, Dublin
🚌 *41, 90*
☎ *(01) 855 0034*
Website *www.brownshostelireland.com*
Dorm bed *€9.95-30; price includes breakfast*
Credit cards *Amex, MC, Visa*
Reception open *24 hours*

Maintenance & cleanliness	★★★
Facilities	★★
Atmosphere & character	★★★★★☆
Security	★★★★☆
Overall rating	★★★

Celts House

Celts House is a small hostel north of the city centre that is old but clean. Most accommodation is in private rooms and there are only three dormitories. It has a kitchen and dining room with a TV. It is a quiet hostel that doesn't have much atmosphere.
32 Blessington Street, Dublin
☎ *(01) 830 0657*
Website *www.celtshouse.com*
Dorm bed *€16-18.50;* **single room** *€32;* **double/twin room** *€51-64*
Credit cards *MC, Visa*
Reception open *9am-11pm daily*

Maintenance & cleanliness	★★★☆
Facilities	★
Atmosphere & character	★★
Security	★★★☆
Overall rating	★★

Citi Hostel

Citi Hostel offers basic accommodation at a bargain price but it could be better maintained. Although cramped, the dorms have high ceilings, which makes them feel spacious. Facilities include a kitchen and a small TV lounge.
61-62 Lower Gardiner Street, Dublin
🚌 *Busárus*
☎ *(01) 855 0035*
Dorm bed *€10-12*
Reception open *24 hours*

Maintenance & cleanliness	★★
Facilities	★
Atmosphere & character	★★★
Security	★★★☆
Overall rating	★★

Euro Hostel/City Manor

This basic hostel has the usual kitchen and TV lounge plus a small games room with a pool table.
80 Lower Gardiner Street, Dublin
🚇 *Busáras*
☎ *(01) 836 4900*
Dorm bed *€10-24;* **double room** *€50-80*
Reception open *24 hours*
📺🍴

Maintenance & cleanliness	★★★☆
Facilities	★
Atmosphere & character	★★
Security	★★★
Overall rating	★★

Globetrotter's Tourist Hostel

Globetrotter's is a brilliant hostel that is famous for its big Irish breakfasts. The building has loads of character with stained glass and features comfy furniture and bright, warm colours. Accommodation is in clean dormitories with solid custom-built bunk beds with thick inner spring mattresses and en suite bathrooms. Shared facilities include a good TV lounge, kitchen, a huge dining area and a nice courtyard.
46 Lower Gardiner Street, Dublin
🚇 *Busáras*
☎ *(01) 873 5893*
Website *www.globetrottersdublin.com*
Dorm bed *€21.50-25;* **double room** *€102-110; prices include breakfast*
Credit cards *Amex, MC, Visa*
Reception open *24 hours*
📺🍴

Maintenance & cleanliness	★★★★☆
Facilities	★★
Atmosphere & character	★★★★
Security	★★★
Overall rating	★★★

Goin' My Way

This small hostel is a good value place to stay with accommodation in tidy but simple rooms. It has a small but fully equipped kitchen, a dining room with a TV and a small garden at the back.
15 Talbot Street, Dublin
🚇 *Abbey Street*
☎ *(01) 878 8484 before 6am, (01) 874 1720 after 6pm*
Dorm bed *€15;* **twin room** *€44; prices include breakfast*
Reception open *9am-midnight;* **curfew** *midnight*
📺🍴

Maintenance & cleanliness	★★★☆
Facilities	★
Atmosphere & character	★★★
Security	★★
Overall rating	★★

International Youth Hostel (An Óige)

Dublin's An Óige hostel is an old building about a 10-minute walk north of the city centre. Accommodation is in clean rooms with new bunk beds. Common areas include a kitchen and dining room, a busy lounge near the reception, a games room with pool table and a TV lounge.
61 Mountjoy Street, Dublin
🚇 *10, 16, 16a, 19, 41*
☎ *(01) 830 1766*
Website *www.anoige.ie*
Dorm bed *€14-20 (€12-18 HI/An Óige)*
Credit cards *MC, Visa*
Reception open *24 hours*
🏠💼📺🍴📚

Maintenance & cleanliness	★★★
Facilities	★★☆
Atmosphere & character	★★☆
Security	★★★★★
Overall rating	★★★☆

Isaac's Hostel

Ireland's first independent travellers' hostel is hidden behind Busáras and it gets a bit of noise from the Dart train. It is a clean hostel that features a big reception/lounge area that usually has live music on Friday nights. It also has a good kitchen and a small courtyard area.
2-5 Frenchman's Lane, Dublin
🚇 *Busáras*
☎ *(01) 855 6215*
Website *www.isaacs.ie*
Dorm bed *€12.50-16.50; price includes breakfast*
Credit cards *MC, Visa*
Reception open *24 hours*
📺🍴

Maintenance & cleanliness	★★★
Facilities	★★☆
Atmosphere & character	★★★
Security	★★★★★★
Overall rating	★★★

Jacob's Inn

Jacob's Inn is a well-maintained hostel with accommodation in spacious dorms with high ceilings and en suite bathrooms. It has a common room with a pool table and TV, a restaurant and a mezzanine floor with Internet access and big screen video cinema.

21-28 Talbot Place, Dublin
🚌 *Busárus*
☎ *(01) 855 5660*
Website www.dublinbackpacker.com
Dorm bed €10-25
Credit cards MC, Visa
Reception open 24 hours
📺 🍳

Maintenance & cleanliness	★★★★
Facilities	★★☆
Atmosphere & character	★★★
Security	★★★★☆
Overall rating	★★★

Litton Lane Hostel

This hostel is housed in a former recording studio that once catered to the likes of U2 and Van Morrison and it tries to keep the building's heritage alive with Warhol-style murals depicting Irish musicians. It is a clean and well-maintained hostel with a bright TV lounge plus a kitchen and dining room with Internet access and table football.

2-4 Litton Lane, Dublin
🚌 *Abbey Street*
☎ *(01) 872 8389*
Website www.irish-hostel.com
Dorm bed €17-19; *price includes breakfast*
Credit cards Amex, MC, Visa
Reception open 24 hours
📺 🍳 💻

Maintenance & cleanliness	★★★☆
Facilities	★★☆
Atmosphere & character	★★★☆
Security	★★★☆
Overall rating	★★★

Marlborough Hostel

This is a fairly good hostel housed in a couple of restored Georgian buildings. It is clean and has a small courtyard with barbecue plus the usual TV lounge and kitchen.

81-82 Marlborough Street, Dublin
☎ *(01) 874 7629 or (01) 874 7812*
Website www.marlboroughhostel.com
Dorm bed €11.50-19; **twin room** €51; *prices include breakfast*
Credit cards MC, Visa
Reception open 24 hours
📺 🍳

Maintenance & cleanliness	★★★
Facilities	★★☆
Atmosphere & character	★★★☆
Security	★★★★
Overall rating	★★★☆

Mount Eccles Court

Mount Eccles Court is a clean and well-maintained hostel with common areas that include a lounge area, kitchen and dining room and a TV lounge.

42 Great George's Street, Dublin
☎ *(01) 873 0826*
Website www.eccleshostel.com
Dorm bed €11-27; **double/twin room** €74; *prices include breakfast*
Credit cards MC, Visa
Reception open 24 hours
📺 🍳 💻

Maintenance & cleanliness	★★★★☆
Facilities	★★☆
Atmosphere & character	★★☆
Security	★★★★☆
Overall rating	★★★☆

Paddy's Palace

Paddy's Palace is a relatively small hostel that has a small kitchen and dining area overlooking the Custom House plus a lounge with old sofas and a small TV.

5 Beresford Place (entrance on Lower Gardiner Street), Dublin
🚌 *Busárus*
☎ *(01) 888 1756*
Dorm bed €16-18; **twin room** €51; *prices include breakfast*
Credit cards Amex, MC, Visa
Reception open 24 hours
📺 🍳

Maintenance & cleanliness	★★★☆
Facilities	★
Atmosphere & character	★★★★☆
Security	★★★★☆
Overall rating	★★★☆

Rainbow Hostel
This small hostel offers clean but standard hostel accommodation with a first floor common area that includes a kitchen and a TV lounge with Internet access.
90-92 Marlborough Street, Dublin
🚇 *Abbey Street*
☎ *(01) 874 6233*
Dorm bed *€15.50-19.50*
Credit cards *MC, Visa*
Reception open *24 hours*
📺🄺

Maintenance & cleanliness	★★★
Facilities	★
Atmosphere & character	★★★
Security	★★★★
Overall rating	★★★½

SOUTH OF THE LIFFEY
Dublin's nicest areas are south of the River Liffey with the best-located hostels clustered around the Temple Bar area.

Ashfield House
This clean and well-maintained hostel has a spacious common area near the reception with Internet access, pool table and a TV. The hostel has a huge dining area but the kitchen is tiny. Accommodation is in nice rooms, all with en suite facilities.
19-20 D'Olier Street, Dublin
☎ *(01) 679 7734*
Website *www.ashfieldhouse.ie*
Bed in a four-bed dorm *€23-34;* **bed in a six-bed dorm** *€18-27;* **bed in a 14-bed dorm** *€13-19;* **single room** *€45-57;* **double/twin room** *€76-92; prices include breakfast*
Credit cards *MC, Visa*
Reception open *24 hours*
📺🄺🄻

Maintenance & cleanliness	★★★★
Facilities	★★
Atmosphere & character	★★★
Security	★★★★½
Overall rating	★★★

Avalon House
Avalon House is a very good hostel that has everything a city hostel needs including a TV lounge, a games room with pool table, Internet access, a large fully equipped kitchen and lots of sitting areas. It is well organised and manages to maintain a good atmosphere even though it has a no alcohol rule.
55 Aungier Street, Dublin
☎ *(01) 475 0001 or 1800 AVALON*
Website *www.avalon-house.ie*
Dorm bed *€13-27;* **single room** *€30-37;* **twin room** *€28-35*
Credit cards *MC, Visa*
Reception open *24 hours*
📺🄺🄻🄽

Maintenance & cleanliness	★★★½
Facilities	★★
Atmosphere & character	★★★★
Security	★★★★
Overall rating	★★★★½

Barnacles Temple Bar
This well located hostel provides quality accommodation with en suite facilities in all rooms. It has a fully equipped kitchen, dining room and a bright and airy common room with a fireplace and TV.
19 Temple Lane, Temple Bar, Dublin
☎ *(01) 671 6277*
Website *www.barnacles.ie*
Bed in a four-bed dorm *€24-27.50;* **bed in a six-bed dorm** *€20-25.50;* **bed in a 10-bed dorm** *€16.50-21.50;* **bed in an 11-bed dorm** *€14-17.50;* **double/twin room** *€65-78*
Credit cards *MC, Visa*
Reception open *24 hours*
🄱📺🄺🄽

Maintenance & cleanliness	★★★★½
Facilities	★★½
Atmosphere & character	★★★★½
Security	★★★★★
Overall rating	★★★★½

Brewery Hostel
This former library is just 100 metres from the Guinness Brewery. It has a big common room with a piano, fireplace and a TV, a small kitchen and dining room downstairs and an outdoor barbecue area. Accommodation is in tidy rooms, all with en suite facilities. The biggest dorm has 10 beds.
22-23 Thomas Street, Dublin
🚌 *123* 🚇 *James Street*
☎ *(01) 453 8600*
Dorm bed *€15-25;* **double/twin room** *€60-78; prices include breakfast*
Reception open *24 hours*
🄱🄺🄻

Maintenance & cleanliness	★★★½
Facilities	★★☆
Atmosphere & character	★★★★★½
Security	★★★½
Overall rating	★★★

Cobblestones
Budget Accommodation

This small hostel has clean, but crowded dorms and a small common room with a TV and very limited cooking facilities. It has a brilliant location in Temple Bar.
29 Eustace Street, Temple Bar, Dublin
☎ *(01) 677 5614*
Bed in a four-bed dorm €19-21; bed in a six-bed dorm €17.50-19.50; bed in an eight-bed dorm €16-18; double room €50-55; twin room €45-50
Credit cards MC, Visa
Reception open summer 24 hours; winter 8am-2am daily

📺 🍳

Maintenance & cleanliness	★★★★½
Facilities	★☆
Atmosphere & character	★★★½
Security	★★★
Overall rating	★★★½

Four Courts Hostel

The Four Courts is a big 230-bed hostel but it has a much better atmosphere than the average mega hostel. Accommodation is in spacious dorms with high ceilings and there are lots of common areas. Facilities include a kitchen and a big dining area with a TV plus a TV lounge with pool table downstairs.
15-17 Merchants Quay, Dublin
🚌 *53, 53A, 90, 748*
☎ *(01) 672 5839*
Website *www.fourcourtshostel.com*
Dorm bed €16.50-27; twin room €60-68; prices include breakfast
Credit cards MC, Visa
Reception open 24 hours

🅿 🍴 📺 🍳 🔒 ♿

Maintenance & cleanliness	★★★★
Facilities	★★☆
Atmosphere & character	★★★½
Security	★★★★★
Overall rating	★★★★½

Kinlay House

This big old building near Christ Church Cathedral has a fully equipped kitchen; a big dining room and a big TV lounge with Internet access. The biggest dorm has 24 beds.
2-12 Lord Edward Street, Dublin
☎ *(01) 679 6644*
Website *www.kinlayhouse.ie*
Bed in a four-bed dorm €22-28; bed in a six-bed dorm €20-26; bed in a 15-24 bed dorm €16-20; single room €44-56; twin room €54-70; prices include breakfast
Credit cards MC, Visa
Reception open 24 hours

📺 🍳 🔒

Maintenance & cleanliness	★★★
Facilities	★★☆
Atmosphere & character	★★★½
Security	★★★★½
Overall rating	★★★½

Oliver St John Gogarty

This hostel offers good quality accommodation above a cosy pub in the heart of Temple Bar. Facilities include a TV lounge plus kitchen and a big dining room.
18-21 Anglesea Street, Temple Bar, Dublin
☎ *(01) 671 1822*
Website *www.gogartys.ie*
Bed in a three-bed dorm €31-38; bed in a four-bed dorm €26-33; bed in a six-bed dorm €23-29; bed in an eight-bed dorm €20-26; bed in a 10-bed dorm €18-24
Credit cards MC, Visa

📺 🍳 🍴

Maintenance & cleanliness	★★★★
Facilities	★★☆
Atmosphere & character	★★★½
Security	★★★★
Overall rating	★★★

Eating & Drinking
EATING

The last twenty years have seen a dramatic improvement in Dublin's food scene. Although you can now get top-quality food in Dublin, pub meals and food at down-to-earth eateries like Bewley's Café and Beshoff's fish and chip shop are a more accurate representation of good value Dublin restaurants.

DRINKING

With around 1000 pubs, Dublin is one of the world's great drinking cities. There are pubs and bars to suit all tastes although the traditional Irish pub is what everyone comes here for. Although very touristy, the Temple Bar neighbourhood is a great spot to start a pub-crawl.

While you're in Dublin you should also make a point of visiting the Guinness brewery (see Sights below).

Sights
The Chimney Viewing Tower
An enclosed viewing platform has been added to the top of the 56m-high Jameson's Distillery chimney offering sweeping views of Dublin.
Smithfield Village, Dublin
🚌 *25, 25A, 67, 67A, 68, 69, 79, 90*
☎ *(01) 817 3800*
Website www.smithfieldvillage.com
Admission €5 (€3.50 students)
Open Mon-Sat 10am-5.30pm, Sun 11am-5.30pm

Christ Church Cathedral
Dating from 1030, Dublin's Christ Church Cathedral is one of the city's major landmarks and it houses a display of artefacts including gold, silverware and historic manuscripts.
Christchurch Place, Dublin
🚌 *49, 50, 51B, 54A, 56A, 65, 77, 77A, 78A, 90, 123* 🚌 *Four Courts*
☎ *(01) 677 8099*
Website www.cccdub.ie
Admission €5
Open Mon-Fri 9.45am-5pm, Sat-Sun 10am-5pm

Custom House
This striking building overlooks the Liffey and houses a visitor centre with displays on the building's history.
Custom House Quay, Dublin
🚌 *Busáras*
☎ *(01) 888 2538*
Admission €1 (students free)
Open Jan-mid Mar Wed-Fri 10am-12.30pm, Sun 2pm-5pm; mid Mar-Nov Mon-Fri 10am-12.30pm, Sat-Sun 2pm-5pm; Dec Wed-Fri 10am-12.30pm, Sun 2pm-5pm

Dublin Castle
Constructed on the foundations of a Viking fortress, Dublin Castle has undergone numerous renovations throughout the ages.
Dame Street, Dublin
🚌 *49, 56A, 77, 77A*
☎ *(01) 677 7129*
Website www.dublincastle.ie
Admission €4.50 (€3.50 students)
Open Mon-Fri 10am-5pm, Sat-Sun 2-5pm

Dublin City Gallery (The Hugh Lane)
The Hugh Lane is a gallery of modern art that has Ireland's largest collection of 20th-century art with Impressionist paintings by Degas, Monet and Renoir.
Charlemont House, Parnell Square North, Dublin
🚌 *3, 10, 11, 13, 16, 19*
☎ *(01) 874 1903*
Website www.hughlane.ie
Admission €7
Open Tue-Thu 9.30am-6pm, Fri-Sat 9.30am-5pm, Sun 1am-5pm

Dublin City Hall – The Story of the Capital
The Story of the Capital is an exhibition in the neo-Classical City Hall that shows how the city developed over the centuries. Exhibits include Civic Regalia such as the Great City Sword, the Great Mace and the Lord Mayor's chain.
Cork Hill, Dame Street, Dublin
🚌 *37, 39, 50, 50A, 54A, 56A, 77, 77A, 77B, 123*
☎ *(01) 672 2204*
Website www.dublincity.ie/cityhall
Admission €4 (€2 students)
Open Mon-Sat 10am-5.15pm, Sun 2pm-5pm

Dublin Writers' Museum
Dublin has a rich literary heritage and while there are museums focusing on individual writers like James Joyce or George Bernard Shaw, the Dublin Writers' Museum presents the best overview of all the city's major writers. It is housed in an 18th century mansion and contains memorabilia and rare manuscripts relating to the works of Beckett, Joyce, Shaw, Sheridan, Swift, Wilde, Yeats and other notable Dublin writers.

18 Parnell Square North, Dublin
🚌 *10, 11, 11B, 13, 13A, 16, 16A, 19, 19A*
☎ *(01) 872 2077*
Website *www.writersmuseum.com*
Admission *€6.25*
Open *Jan-May Mon-Sat 10am-5pm, Sun 11am-5pm; Jun-Aug Mon-Fri 10am-6pm, Sat 10am-5pm, Sun 11am-5pm; Sep-Dec Mon-Sat 10am-5pm, Sun 11am-5pm*

Dublinia

It's a bit of a tourist trap, although this multi-media depiction of Dublin's history does have its credits. Apart from the touristy waxworks, Dublinia offers an insight into the city's Viking heritage and life in Dublin during the 16th century.
St Michael's Hill, Christchurch, Dublin
🚌 *49, 50, 54A, 56A, 77*
Website *www.dublinia.ie*
Admission *€5.75 (€4.50 students)*
Open *Jan-Mar Mon-Sat 11am-4pm, Sun 10am-4.30pm; Apr-Sep 10am-5pm daily; Oct-Dec Mon-Sat 11am-4pm, Sun 10am-4.30pm*

GAA Museum & Croke Park Stadium

Croke Park is the home of the Gaelic Athletic Association (GAA) and Ireland's unique national sports: hurling and gaelic football. This museum provides an insight into this integral part of Irish culture with interactive exhibits and sporting memorabilia.
Croke Park, St Joseph's Avenue, Dublin
🚌 *3, 11, 11A, 16, 16A, 123*
☎ *(01) 819 2323*
Website *www.gaa.ie*
Admission *€5 (€3.50 students); including stadium tour €8.50 (€6 students)*
Open *Mon-Sat 9.30am-4.30pm, Sun noon-4.30pm; on match days the museum is only open to Cusack Stand ticket holders.*

Guinness Storehouse

Virtually every backpacker that makes it to Dublin makes a point of visiting the Guinness Storehouse. This new visitors' centre is housed in the original fermentation plant in the St James's Gate Brewery. Tours include an overview of the brewing process, an audio-visual presentation, a gallery of Guinness advertisements and a free pint of Guinness.
St James's Gate, Dublin
🚌 *51B, 78A, 90, 123* 🚆 *James Street*
☎ *(01) 408 4800*
Website *www.guinnessstorehouse.com*
Admission *€13.50 (€9 students)*
Open *Jan-Jun 9.30am-5pm daily; Jul-Aug 9.30am-9pm daily; Sep-Dec 9.30am-5pm daily*

Irish Museum of Modern Art

This museum, housed in a 17th century hospital, hosts a varied programme of temporary exhibitions of modern and contemporary art.
Royal Hospital, Military Road, Kilmainham, Dublin
🚌 *26, 51, 51B, 78A, 79, 90, 123*
🚆🚇 *Heuston*
☎ *(01) 612 9900*
Website *www.imma.ie*
Admission *free*
Open *Tue-Sat 10am-5.30pm, Sun noon-5.30pm*

James Joyce Centre

You can't visit Dublin without looking at least one monument dedicated to James Joyce. Even if you have never heard of James Joyce, you'll find the James Joyce Centre an interesting cultural centre that provides a fascinating insight into not just the great author, but also Dublin itself. It is a good idea to read *Ulysses* first to get more out of your visit to Dublin, since not just the museum but sites all over the city bear some relation to Joyce.
35 North Great George's Street, Dublin
🚆🚇 *Connolly* 🚌 *3, 10, 11, 13, 16, 19, 22, 123*
☎ *(01) 878 8547*
Website *www.jamesjoyce.ie*
Admission *€5 (€4 students)*
Open *Mon-Sat 9.30am-5pm, Sun 12.30pm-5pm*

National Gallery of Ireland

The National Gallery of Ireland displays a large collection of Irish and European art spanning all major European styles. The gallery features paintings by Brueghel, Caravaggio, El Greco and Rembrandt as well as works by Jack B Yeats.

Corner Clare Street & Merrion Square West, Dublin
🚌 5, 7, 7A, 44, 48A 🚆 Pearse
☎ (01) 661 5133
Website www.nationalgallery.ie
Admission free
Open Mon-Wed 9.30am-5.30pm, Thu 9.30am-8.30pm, Fri-Sat 9.30am-5.30pm, Sun noon-5.30pm

National Museum of Archaeology & History

The National Museum of Archaeology and History features a rich collection of artefacts dating thousands of years. Highlights of the museum include Celtic and medieval art that include the Ardagh Chalice, the Derrynaflan Hoard and the Tara Brooch.
Kildare Street, Dublin
🚌 7, 7A, 8, 10, 11, 13 🚆 Pearse
☎ (01) 677 7444
Website www.museum.ie
Admission free
Open Tue-Sat 10am-5pm, Sun 2pm-5pm

National Museum of Decorative Arts & History

Housed in the historic Collins Barracks, this museum displays decorative arts that chronicle Ireland's history. Exhibits include costume, furniture, weapons as well as ceramic, glass and silverware.
Collins Barracks, Benburb Street, Dublin
🚌 25, 25A, 66, 67, 90 🚆 Museum
☎ (01) 677 7444
Website www.museum.ie
Admission free
Open Tue-Sat 10am-5pm, Sun 2pm-5pm

National Museum of Natural History

Dublin's Natural History Museum has a huge collection that includes around two million dead animals including a dodo skeleton and countless insects.
Merrion Street, Dublin
🚌 7, 7A, 8 🚆 Pearse 🚆 St Stephens Green
☎ (01) 677 7444
Website www.museum.ie
Admission free
Open Tue-Sun 10am-5pm, Sun 2pm-5pm

National Wax Museum

Dublin's wax museum features prominent Irish literary and historical figures plus a life-size replica of Leonardo da Vinci's *Last Supper*.
Granby Row, Parnell Square, Dublin
🚌 11, 13, 16, 22, 22A
☎ (01) 872 6340
Admission €6 (€5 students)
Open Mon-Sat 10am-5.30pm, Sun noon-5.30pm

Old Jameson Distillery

The Old Jameson Distillery has been converted into a museum detailing the history, culture and science behind Irish whiskey. The tour of the museum concludes with a tasting of five types of whiskey.
Bow Street, Smithfield, Dublin
🚌 67, 67A, 68, 69, 79, 90
☎ (01) 807 2235
Website www.whiskeytours.ie
Admission €7.25 (€6.25 students)
Open 9.30am-5.30pm daily

The Shaw Birthplace

George Bernard Shaw was born in this house, which has been restored as an example of domestic life in Victorian Dublin.
33 Synge Street, Dublin
🚌 16, 16A, 19, 19A, 122
☎ (01) 475 0854
Admission €6.25
Open May-Sep Mon-Tue & Thu-Fri 10am-1pm & 2pm-5pm, Sat-Sun 2pm-5pm

St Patrick's Cathedral

The oldest Christian site in Dublin is built near the site where St Patrick used to hang out. Although the building dates from 1191, it has undergone extensive renovations during the 19th century.
Patrick's Close, Dublin
🚌 50, 54A, 56A
☎ (01) 475 4817
Website www.stpatrickscathedral.ie
Admission €4.20 (€3.20 students)
Open Jan-Feb Mon-Fri 9am-6pm, Sat 9am-5pm, Sun 10am-11am & 12.45pm-3pm; Mar-Oct Mon-Fri 9am-

6pm, Sat 9am-5pm, Sun 9am-11am & 12.45pm-3pm & 4.15pm-6pm

St Stephen's Green
St Stephen's Green is surrounded by many of Dublin's grandest Georgian buildings and is one Europe's great urban parks. Originally it was a fetid open space used for public hangings and burnings, however Sir Arthur Guinness tarted the square up adding ponds, gardens and a bandstand, making St Stephen's Green what it is today.
🚇 *St Stephens Green*

Trinity College Library
Ireland's most prestigious seat of learning is also one of Dublin's most important historical sites. Trinity College Dublin (TCD) is home to many of Dublin's finest buildings. It's good fun having a poke around the college grounds, but the Trinity College Library is definitely the highlight. The library's Long Room features the 19th-century *Book of Kells* plus several other historic manuscripts.
College Street, Dublin
🚇 *St Stephens Green* 🚇 *Pearce Street*
☎ *(01) 608 2320*
Website *www.tcd.ie/library/*
Admission *€7.50 (€6.50 students)*
Open *Jan-May Mon-Sat 9.30am-5pm, Sun noon-4.30pm; Jun-Sep Mon-Sat 9.30am-5pm, Sun 9.30am-4.30pm; Oct-Dec Mon-Sat 9.30am-5pm, Sun noon-4.30pm*

Waterways Visitor Centre
The Waterways Centre has an exhibition about Ireland's inland waterways including working models of engineering features.
Grand Canal Quay, Dublin
🚌 *2, 3* 🚇 *Grand Canal Dock*
☎ *(01) 677 7510*
Website *www.waterwaysireland.org*
Admission *€2.540 (€1.20 students)*
Open *Jan-May Wed-Sun 12.30pm-5pm; Jun-Sep 9.30am-5.30pm daily; Oct-Dec Wed-Sun 12.30pm-5pm*

Dún Laoghaire
This southern suburb is a busy port with ferries to England and the Isle of Man. It is also a pleasant spot and some people prefer staying here than in the city centre.

Practical Information
Dún Laoghaire Tourist Information Centre
Ferry Terminal, Dún Laoghaire
Website *www.visitdublin.com*
Open *Mon-Sat 10am-1pm & 2pm-6pm*

Coming & Going
Dún Laoghaire is easily accessible from the city centre by the DART train. Alternatively buses 7, 7A, 8 and 46A go into central Dublin.

Accommodation
Marina House
Marina House is a lovely stone building about a 10-minute walk from the centre of Dún Laoghaire. It features a small TV lounge, a nice courtyard/barbecue area and brilliant showers, however the kitchen could be better.
7 Old Dunleary Road, Dún Laoghaire
🚇 *Dún Laoghaire*
☎ *(01) 284 1524*
Website *www.marinahouse.com*
Dorm bed *€15-19*
Credit cards *MC, Visa*
📺 🍳

Maintenance & cleanliness	★★★★☆
Facilities	★★☆
Atmosphere & character	★★★★★☆
Security	★★
Overall rating	★★★

Sights
Joyce Museum & Tower
Jame's Joyce spent a week at the Martello Tower in 1904 and this tower in suburban Sandycove (about 1.5km north of Dún Laoghaire) has since been associated with this great author. The tower is the setting for the opening chapter in *Ulysees* and nowadays houses a collection of Joyce memorabilia.
Joyce Tower, Sandycove, Co. Dublin
🚇 *Sandycove*
☎ *(01) 280 9265*
Admission *€6.25*
Open *Feb-Oct Mon-Sat 10am-5pm, Sun 2pm-6pm*

Malahide (Mullach Íde)

This seaside town north of Dublin is best known for the 800-year-old Malahide Castle.

Coming & Going
The easiest way to get here is by the DART train from Dublin. Alternatively you can take bus 42 from the city.

Sights
Malahide Castle
Malahide Castle was home to the Talbot family from 1185 right up to 1973 and it is furnished with antiques and features a large collection of Irish portrait paintings.
Malahide, Co Dublin
🚌 *42* 🚊 *Malahide*
☎ *(01) 846 2184*
Website *www.malahidecastle.com*
Admission *€6.25; joint ticket to Fry Model Railway €10.50*
Open *Jan-Mar Mon-Sat 10am-5pm, Sun 11am-5pm; Apr-Oct Mon-Sat 10am-5pm, Sun 11am-6pm; Nov-Dec Mon-Sat 10am-5pm, Sun 11am-5pm*

Tara's Palace
Tara's Palace is an impressive doll's house built at 1:12 scale, taking over 10 years to build.
Malahide Castle Demense, Malahide
🚌 *42* 🚊 *Malahide*
☎ *(01) 846 3779*
Admission *€2 donation*
Open *Apr-Sep Mon-Sat 10am-1pm & 2pm-5pm, Sun 2pm-6pm*

Fry Model Railway
The impressive Fry Model Railway was originally built in the 1920s and 1930s.
Malahide Castle Demense, Malahide
🚌 *42* 🚊 *Malahide*
☎ *(01) 846 3779*
Admission *€6.25; joint ticket to Malahide Castle €10.50*
Open *Apr-Sep Mon-Sat 10am-1pm & 2pm-5pm, Sun 2pm-6pm*

County Louth

Most travellers see County Louth from the window of a bus while travelling between Dublin and Northern Ireland. However it is worth stopping to visit Drogheda.

Drogheda (Droichead Átha)

Founded by the Normans in the 12th century, this bustling town on the River Boyne was an important centre during medieval times but now is just another stop on the N1 highway linking Dublin and Belfast.

Practical Information
Drogheda Tourist Information Centre
Bus station, Donore Road, Drogheda
☎ *(041) 983 7070*
Website *www.eastcoastmidlands.ie*
Open *Mon-Sat 9.30am-5.30pm, Sun noon-5pm*

Coming & Going
Buses and trains go to Belfast and Dublin with the most frequent being the half-hourly bus service to Dublin. Buses stop at the corner of Donore Road and John Street and the train station is east of the town centre.

Accommodation
Green Door Lodge
This is a modern well-maintained hostel with a dining room/TV lounge, a kitchen, a reading room and also an outdoor area with a barbecue and river views.
47 John Street, Drogheda
☎ *(041) 983 4422*
Website *www.greendoor.hostel.com*
Dorm bed *€15-20;* ***double/twin room*** *€50-60*
Credit cards *MC, Visa*
Reception open *9am-11pm daily*

Maintenance & cleanliness	★★★★
Facilities	★★
Atmosphere & character	★★★½
Security	★★
Overall rating	★★★

Sights
Millmount Museum
Housed in a former military barracks, the Millmount Museum displays artefacts pertaining to local history including an

exceptional collection of guild and trade banners.
Millmount, Drogheda
☎ *(041) 983 3097*
Website www.millmount.net
Admission €5.50 (€4 students)
Open Mon-Sat 10am-5.30pm, Sun 2.30pm-5.30pm

Monasterboice High Crosses & Round Tower
St Buite founded this early Christian monastic site in the 6th century. Monasterboice is noted for its ornate high crosses, which are said to be among Ireland's best examples. Unfortunately it is difficult to get to without your own car.
Monasterboice, near Drogheda
☎ *(041) 982 2813*

Old Mellifont Abbey
The ruins of Ireland's first Cistercian monastery date from 1142. The abbey's visitor centre has an exhibition of artefacts from the site. Like Monasterboice, the Old Mellifont Abbey is difficult to get to by public transport.
Tullyallen, Drogheda
☎ *(041) 982 6053*
Website www.heritageireland.ie
Admission €2 (€1.25 students)
Open May-Sep 10am-6pm daily

County Wicklow

The county immediately south of Dublin is known as the garden of Ireland and it's a popular weekend getaway for Dubliners. Much of the county is taken up by the rolling Wicklow Mountains, which the energetic can traverse on the Wicklow Way hiking trail.

Wicklow (Cill Mhantáin)

This seaside town is a pleasant spot to break the drive south from Dublin. Some travellers use the town as a base for visiting the Wicklow Mountains.

Practical Information
Tourist Information Centre
Fitzwilliam Square, Wicklow
☎ *(0404) 69117*
Website www.wicklow.ie/tourism
Open Jan-May Mon-Fri 9.30am-1pm & 2pm-5.30pm; Jun-Sep Mon-Fri 9am-6pm, Sat 9.30am-6.30pm; Oct-Dec Mon-Fri 9.30am-1pm & 2pm-5.30pm

Coming & Going
BUS
Bus Éireann (*website* www.buseireann.ie) buses connect Wicklow with Dublin, Waterford and Wexford with buses departing from the Grand Hotel.

TRAIN
Wicklow is on the train line linking Dublin with Wexford and Rosslare Harbour. The station is on Church Street, a 15-minute walk from the town centre.

Accommodation
Wicklow Bay Hostel
The Wicklow Bay Hostel is a big solid building dating from 1842. It features tall ceilings, which make the rooms feel very spacious. Facilities include a fully equipped kitchen and a big dining room.
Marine House, The Murrough, Wicklow
☎ *(0404) 69213*
Website www.wicklowbayhostel.com
Dorm bed €14-16
Credit cards MC, Visa

Maintenance & cleanliness	★★★★½
Facilities	★
Atmosphere & character	★★★★
Security	★★
Overall rating	★★★

Sights
Wicklow's Historic Gaol
This historic prison is run as a museum showing how prisoners were treated in the 18th century.
Kilmantin Hill, Wicklow
☎ *(0404) 61599*
Website www.wicklowshistoricgaol.com
Admission €6.50 (€4.50 students)
Open Apr-Oct 10am-5pm daily

Wicklow Mountains National Park

This picturesque area of low mountains and rolling countryside contains the Wicklow Way, a hiking trail that passes by several An Óige youth hostels.

Picturesque Glendalough is the most visited spot in the park. This valley has a couple of lakes and the monastery established by St Kevin in the 6th century.

Practical Information
Glendalough National Park Information Centre
☎ *(0404) 45425*
Website www.heritageireland.ie
Open *Apr Sat-Sun 10am-6pm; May-Aug 10am-6pm daily; Sep Sat-Sun 10am-6pm*

Glendalough Tourist Information Centre
☎ *(0404) 45688*
Website www.wicklow.ie/tourism
Open *Jun-Sep Mon-Sat 10am-1pm & 2pm-6pm*

Coming & Going
Bus Éireann *(website www.buseireann.ie)* and St Kevin's Bus Service *(☎ (01) 281 8119)* run buses from Dublin to Glendalough and the Wicklow Mountains.

Accommodation
Glendalough Youth Hostel
This big flash hostel is a clean and functional place with top quality amenities that include the usual kitchen; laundry and a small TV lounge. Accommodation is in dormitories with en suite bathrooms and good quality beds.
Glendalough
☎ *(0404) 45342*
Website www.anoige.ie
Dorm bed *€17-19.50 (€15-17.50 HI/An Óige)*
Credit cards *MC, Visa*
Reception open *8am-11pm daily*

Maintenance & cleanliness		★★★★★
Facilities		★★
Atmosphere & character		★★
Security		★★★
Overall rating		★★★★☆

Knockree Youth Hostel
This basic youth hostel consists of several farm buildings with views of the surrounding countryside.
Knockree, near Enniskerry
☎ *(01) 286 4036*
Website www.anoige.ie
Dorm bed *€11-12 (€9-10 HI/An Óige)*
Reception open *high season 5pm-10pm daily; low season 5pm-9pm daily; **lockout** 10am-5pm daily*

Tiglin Youth Hostel
The Tiglin Youth Hostel is a big stone building built around a large courtyard. Facilities are basic and include limited kitchen facilities with accommodation in dorms with old metal bunks.
R 763, Devil's Glen (near Ashford)
☎ *(0404) 49049*
Website www.anoige.ie
Dorm bed *€11-12 (€910 HI/An Óige)*
Open *Feb-Nov; **reception open** 10am-5pm daily*

Maintenance & cleanliness		★★★☆
Facilities		-
Atmosphere & character		★★☆
Security		★★☆
Overall rating		★★☆

Sights
Glendalough Visitor Centre
Set on a monastic site founded by St Kevin in the 6th century, the Glendalough Visitor Centre has an exhibition about the site and also shows an audio-visual presentation.
Glendalough, Co Wicklow
☎ *(0404) 45352*
Website www.heritageireland.ie
Admission *€2.75 (€1.25 students)*
Open *Jan-mid Mar 9.30am-5pm daily; mid Mar-mid Oct 9.30am-6pm daily; mid-Oct-Dec 9.30am-5pm daily*

County Wexford
This county at the southeastern corner of Ireland is the gateway for many travellers arriving at Rosslare Harbour by ferry from Great Britain and France.

Enniscorthy (Inis Coirthaidth)
This appealing town north of Wexford played an important role in Irish history when it was the scene of fierce resistance during the Rebellion of 1798. It

is dominated by a Norman castle that dates from 1205.

Practical Information
Enniscorthy Tourist Information Centre
Castle Hill, Enniscorthy
☎ *(054) 34699*
Website *www.southeastireland.com*
Open *Mon-Sat 10am-6pm, Sun 2pm-5.30pm*

Coming & Going
Enniscorthy lies on the train line between Dublin and Rosslare. Buses to Dublin, Waterford and Wexford stop on Templeshannon Quay.

Accommodation
Enniscorthy Holiday Hostel
This clean and well-maintained hostel as good facilities that include a TV lounge, pool table, free Internet access and a kitchen. It has spacious rooms with comfortable beds and en suite bathrooms.
Platform 1, Railway Square, Enniscorthy
☎ *(054) 37766*
Dorm bed €16; **double room** €40; **twin room** €35
Credit cards *MC, Visa*
Reception open *10am-9pm daily*

Maintenance & cleanliness	★★★★★
Facilities	★★
Atmosphere & character	★★☆
Security	★★★☆
Overall rating	★★★

Sights
National 1798 Visitor Centre
This centre portrays the events of the 1798 Rebellion using interactive displays and audio-visual presentations.
Millpark Road, Enniscorthy
☎ *(054) 37596*
Website *www.1798centre.com*
Admission €6 (€4 students)
Open *Mon-Sat 9.30am-6.30pm, Sun 11am-6.30pm*

Wexford (Lough Garman)

This historic town has a fascinating history dating to the 2nd century. It was settled by the Vikings in the 9th century and conquered by the Normans in 1169. Its growth depended on its role as a port and it still has a maritime feel to it even though its shipping business has been lost to nearby Waterford and Rosslare.

Practical Information
Wexford Tourist Information Centre
Crescent Quay, Wexford
☎ *(053) 23111*
Website *www.southeastireland.com*
Open *Jan-Mar Mon-Fri 9.30am-5.30pm; Apr-Sep Mon-Sat 9am-6pm; Nov-Dec Mon-Fri 9.30am-5.30pm*

Coming & Going
Both buses and trains stop here en route between Dublin and Rosslare and buses also go to Limerick.

Trains and buses stop at the station on Redmond Square.

Accommodation
Kirwan House Tourist Hostel
This small hostel near Wexford town centre has a warm and cosy atmosphere and it features a good TV lounge, a small kitchen and a small barbecue area.
Friary Church View, 3 Mary Street, Wexford
☎ *(053) 21208*
Dorm bed €14-17; **double room** €40
Reception open *8am-10pm daily*

Maintenance & cleanliness	★★★
Facilities	★★☆
Atmosphere & character	★★★★
Security	★★
Overall rating	★★★☆

Sights
Irish National Heritage Park
This 35-acre open-air museum tries to cover 9000 years of history with displays on the Stone Age, Bronze Age, Celtic and early Christian times and the times of Viking and early Norman settlement. It is 5km north west of the town centre.
N11, Ferrycarrig, Co Wexford
☎ *(053) 20733*
Website *www.inhp.com*
Admission €7 (€5.50 students)
Open *9.30am-5pm daily*

Selskar Abbey
Selskare Abbey dates to the 13th century, although it replaces an earlier temple dedicated to the Norse god Odin.

West Gate Tower
This 13th century tower comprises part of Wexford's town walls. It is now home to a craft gallery and there is also an audio-visual presentation here about the development of Wexford.
West Gate, Wexford
☎ *(053) 46506*
Open *summer Mon-Sat 10am-6pm, Sun noon-6pm; winter Tue-Sat 10am-5pm, Sun noon-6pm*

Rosslare Harbour (Ros Láir)
Rosslare is Ireland's second-largest ferry port with ferries to France and Wales. However there is not much to do in town and travellers only come here to make transport connections.

Coming & Going
Rosslare is an important transport hub with buses and trains meeting ferries from France and Wales.

BUS
Bus Éireann *(website www.buseireann.ie)* has buses to Cork, Dublin, Galway, Limerick, Waterford and Wexford. Buses terminate at the ferry terminal.

TRAIN
There are trains from Rosslare to Dublin and Limerick via Waterford and Wexford. Trains depart from the station at the ferry terminal.

FERRY
Irish Ferries *(website www.irishferries.com)* sail from Rosslare Harbour to Cherbourg and Roscoff in France and Pembroke in Wales. Stena ferries *(website www.stenaline.co.uk)* sail between Rosslare and Fishguard in Wales.

Accommodation
Rosslare Harbour Youth Hostel
This hostel is in an old house that is kept neat and tidy and there is additional accommodation in a newer annex. It has a nice common room with a log fire, TV and Internet access and there is also a small kitchen.
Goulding Street, Rosslare Harbour
☎ *(053) 33399*
Website *www.anoige.ie*
Dorm bed *€12.50-14.50 (€10.50-12.50 HI/An Óige)*
Credit cards *Amex, MC, Visa*
📺 🅺

Maintenance & cleanliness	★★★
Facilities	★★
Atmosphere & character	★★★
Security	★
Overall rating	★★

County Kilkenny
County Kilkenny is wedged between Counties Carlow, Laois, Tipperary, Waterford and Wexford and the county town, Kilkenny is the star attraction drawing travellers from around the world for its castle and medieval streetscape.

Kilkenny (Cill Chainnigh)
Kilkenny is one of the most visited towns in southeast Ireland. It is a charming town with narrow streets dating from Norman and medieval times plus a big castle and a world-famous brewery.

Practical Information
Kilkenny Tourist Information Centre
Rose Inn Street, Kilkenny
☎ *(056) 51500*
Website *www.kilkennytourism.ie*
Open *Jan-Mar Mon-Sat 9am-5pm; Apr-Jun Mon-Sat 9am-6pm, Sun 11am-1pm & 2pm-5pm; Jul-Aug Mon-Sat 9am-7pm, Sun 11am-1pm & 2pm-5pm; Sep Mon-Sat 9am-6pm, Sun 11am-1pm & 2pm-5pm; Oct-Dec Mon-Sat 9am-5pm; Apr-Jun Mon-Sat 9am-6pm, Sun 11am-1pm & 2pm-5pm*

Coming & Going
Both buses and trains leave from the station on Dublin Road, which is accessible by walking across the river and up John Street. Buses go to Cork,

Dublin, Galway, Limerick, Rosslare and Waterford and trains stop in Kilkenny en route between Dublin and Waterford.

Accommodation
Kilkenny Tourist Hostel
This centrally located hostel has a great atmosphere with a cosy sitting room with and open fire plus a good dining room and a fully equipped kitchen.
35 Parliament Street, Kilkenny
☎ *(056) 63541*
Website *http://homepage.eircom.net/~kilkennyhostel/*
Dorm bed *€14-17;* **twin room** *€36-38*
Reception open *9am-11pm daily*
K L

Maintenance & cleanliness	★★★½
Facilities	★★½
Atmosphere & character	★★★★★
Security	★★
Overall rating	★★★½

Sights
Black Abbey
The Holy Trinity Church (known as the Black Abbey) was founded in the 13th century by the Dominican Order. This beautiful church is noted for its intricate stained glass windows.
Abbey Street, Kilkenny

Kilkenny Castle
This 12th century castle was home to the wealthy Butler family from 1391 to 1935 and was extensively remodeled during Victorian times. It features a 45m-long portrait gallery with fine paintings and tapestries, plus rooms decorated in the style of the 1830s. Admission is by guided tour only.
The Parade, Kilkenny
☎ *(056) 772 1450*
Website *www.heritageireland.ie*
Tours cost *€5 (€2 students)*
Open *Jan-Mar 10.30am-12.45pm & 2pm-5pm daily; Apr-May 10.30am-5pm daily; Jun-Aug 9.30am-7pm daily; Sep-Dec 10.30am-12.45pm & 2pm-5pm daily*

Rothe House
Merchant Prince John Rothe built this Tudor town house in 1594. The house contains a heritage centre with exhibits relating the town's history.
Parliament Street, Kilkenny
☎ *(056) 77 2893*
Website *www.kilkennyarchaeologicalsociety.ie*
Admission *€3 (€2 students)*
Open *Jan-Feb Mon-Sat 1pm-5pm; Mar-Oct Mon-Sat 10.30am-5pm, Sun 3pm-5pm; Nov-Dec Mon-Sat 1pm-5pm*

Smithwick's Brewery
Ireland's oldest brewery produces Budwiser, Kilkenny and Smithwick's beer at this large brewery near St Francis Abbey on Parliament Street. During summer you can take a tour, which concludes with a couple of free pints.
Parliament Street, Kilkenny
☎ *(056) 21014*
Admission *free, but you need to get a ticket in advance*
Tours *Jul-Aug Mon-Fri 3pm*

St Canice's Cathedral
This Anglican cathedral is Ireland's second-longest medieval cathedral. Most of the building dates from the 13th century and it is noted for the 30.5m-high 9th-century Round Tower where monks once took refuge. Nowadays the brave can climb the tower for breathtaking views of the city.
Irishtown, Kilkenny
☎ *(056) 776 4971*
Admission *Round Tower €2 (€1.50 students)*
Open *Jan-Easter Mon-Sat 10am-1pm & 2pm-4pm, Sun 2pm-4pm; Easter-Oct Mon-Sat 9am-1pm & 2pm-6pm, Sun 2pm-6pm; Oct-Dec Mon-Sat 10am-1pm & 2pm-4pm, Sun 2pm-4pm*

Munster

This region in southwest Ireland encompasses Counties Clare, Cork, Kerry, Limerick, Tipperary and Waterford.

County Tipperary

The Rock of Cashel is the main attraction in Munster's only land-locked county.

Tipperary (Thiobriad Árann)

Tipperary's county town was made famous by the song; *It's a Long Way to Tipperary*, which was written by an English man who had never visited the town. Although it's a pleasant-enough place, Tipperary doesn't hold enough to interest the average traveller.

Practical Information
Tourist Information Centre
Excel Centre, Mitchell Street, Tipperary
☎ *(062) 51457*
Website www.tipperary.ie
Open Mon-Sat 9.30am-5.30pm

Coming & Going
BUS

Bus Éireann *(website www.buseireann.ie)* buses stop in Tipperary en route between Limerick and Waterford and Bernard Kavanagh Coaches *(website www.bkavcoaches.com)* operate a service between Tipperary and Dublin stopping at Cashel.

TRAIN

Tipperary is on the Ennis to Rosslare line, which also stops in Limerick and Waterford, and Limerick Junction station is only 3km from the town centre and has direct trains to Cork, Dublin and Tralee.

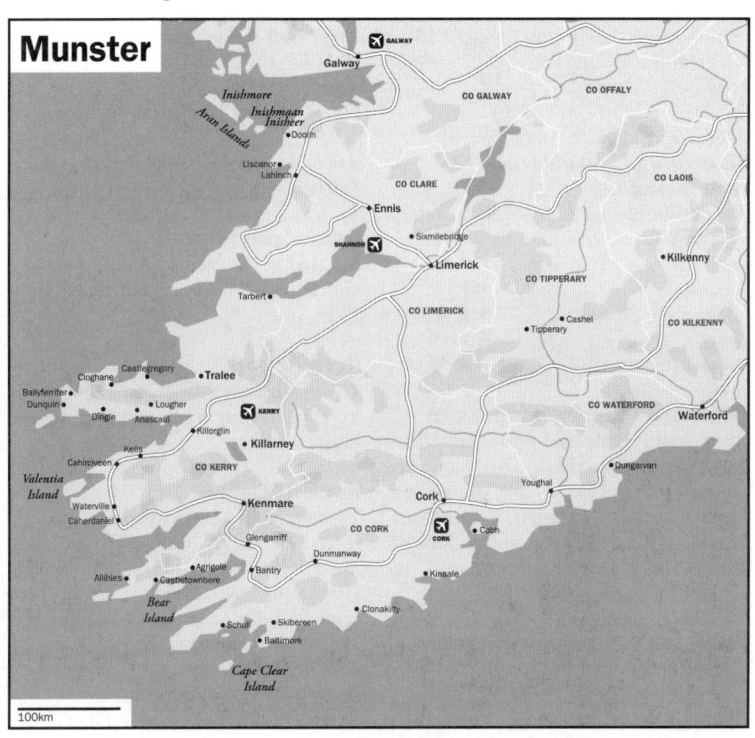

Cashel
(Caiseal Mumhan)

Cashel has a rich history and was the seat of the Kings of Munster. Its main attraction is the Rock of Cashel (pictured on the cover of this book) where Irish kings have been crowned and where St Patrick is believed to have preached.

Practical Information
Tourist Information Centre
City Hall, Main Street, Cashel
☎ *(062) 61333*
Open *Apr-Sep Mon-Sat 9.15am-6pm*

Coming & Going
Cashel lies on the N8 highway linking Dublin and Cork, which ensures that there are frequent buses in both directions. There are also buses to Limerick.

Accommodation
Cashel Holiday Hostel
This centrally located hostel is in a 250-year-old Georgian house with lots of character. It has a kitchen with a big dining room plus a cosy lounge with a TV, piano and a log fire.
John Street, Cashel
☎ *(062) 62330*
Website *www.cashelhostel.com*
Dorm bed *€15;* **double room** *€44;* **twin room** *€40*
Reception open *8.15am-9.30pm daily*

Maintenance & cleanliness	★★★
Facilities	★★
Atmosphere & character	★★★★½
Security	★★
Overall rating	★★★

O'Brien's Farm House Hostel
This lovely hostel is in a well-maintained stone farmhouse that boasts comfortable rooms plus a cosy TV lounge and kitchen. It has a pleasant location just outside town with views of the Rock of Cashel and Hore Abbey.
Dundrum Road, Cashel
☎ *(062) 61003*
Dorm bed *€15;* **double/twin room** *€45-50*
Open *15 Jan-20 Dec*

Maintenance & cleanliness	★★★★★
Facilities	★★
Atmosphere & character	★★★★★
Security	★★½
Overall rating	★★★★

Sights
Brú Ború Cultural Centre
Located next to the Rock, this cultural centre presents traditional Irish music and dance performances.
☎ *(062) 61122*
Website *www.comhaltas.com*
Admission *€5 (€3 students);* **theatre show** *€15*
Open *Jan-mid Jun Mon-Fri 9am-5pm; mid Jun-mid Sep Mon 9am-5pm, Tue-Sat 9am-9pm; mid Sep-Dec Mon-Fri 9am-5pm*

Cashel Heritage Centre
Located in the same building as the tourist information centre, the Cashel Heritage Centre makes an excellent introduction to Irish history with particular emphasis on Cashel. You will get more out of your visit to the Rock if you visit the Heritage Centre first.
Town Hall, Main Street, Cashel
☎ *(062) 62511*
Admission *free*
Open *Jan-Feb Mon-Fri 9.30am-5.30pm; Mar-Oct 9.30am-5.30pm daily; Nov-Dec Mon-Fri 9.30am-5.30pm*

Dominican Friary
Located at the base of the Rock is this Dominican Friary, which dates from 1243.

Hore Abbey
This 13-century Cistercian abbey sits in a field near O'Brien's Farmhouse Hostel.

Rock of Cashel
The striking Rock of Cashel encompasses several medieval buildings including the High Cross, Romanesque Chapel and round tower dating from the 12th century, a 13th century cathedral and a 15th century castle.
☎ *(062) 61437*
Admission *€5 (€2 students)*
Open *Jan-mid Mar 9am-3.45pm daily;*

mid Mar-mid Jun 9am-4.45pm daily;
mid Jun-mid Sep 9am-6.15pm daily;
mid Sep-Dec 9am-3.45pm daily

County Waterford

Waterford (Port Láirge)

Waterford is Ireland's oldest city boasting over 1000 years of history. It was founded by Vikings in 853 and later became an important centre for the Normans and in the 18th century it developed on the wealth of its glass industry.

Nowadays Waterford is a busy port and commercial centre that is famous for producing crystal.

Practical Information
Waterford Tourist Office
41 The Quay, Waterford
☎ *(051) 875 823*
Website www.discoverwaterford.com
Open Jan-Mar Mon-Sat 9am-5pm;
Apr-Jun Mon-Sat 9am-6pm; Jul-Aug
Mon-Sat 9am-6pm, Sun 11am-5pm;
Sep-Oct Mon-Sat 9am-6pm; Nov-Dec
Mon-Sat 9am-5pm

Coming & Going
AIR
Waterford's South East Regional Airport *(website www.flywaterford.com)* is served by Aer Arann *(website www.aerarann.com)* with flights to Lorient, France and to London and Manchester. The airport is 6km south of the city centre.

BUS
Bus Éireann *(website www.buseireann.ie)* buses go to Cork, Dublin, Galway and Limerick. Buses stop opposite the tourist information centre on the Quay.

TRAIN
Waterford's train station is on the northern side of the River Suir. Trains go to Dublin, Kilkenny, Limerick and Rosslare.

Accommodation
Unfortunately there are no hostels in Waterford so you won't be able to stay overnight unless you have the money to blow on a hotel or B&B.

Sights
Reginalds Tower
This round tower dates from the 12th century and has been used as a military store, mint and a prison. It is Ireland's oldest urban monument.
The Quay, Waterford
☎ *(051) 304220*
Website www.heritageireland.ie
Admission €2 (€1 students)
Open Easter-May 10am-5pm daily;
Jun-Sep 9.30am-6.30pm daily; Oct
10am-5pm daily

Waterford Crystal Visitors Centre
The visitors centre displays the world's largest collection of Waterford Crystal and you can also take a tour of the factory to see crystal being produced.
Cork Road, Kilbarry
☎ *(051) 332 500*
Website www.waterfordvisitorcentre.com
Admission €7.50
Open Jan-Feb 9am-5pm daily; Mar-Oct 8.30am-4.15pm daily; Nov-Dec 9am-5pm daily

Waterford Museum of Treasures
This excellent museum at the Granary on Merchant's Quay displays a collection of artefacts and audio-visual presentations that illustrates 1,000 years of Waterford's history.
The Granary, Merchants Quay, Waterford
☎ *(051) 304 500*
Website www.waterfordtreasures.com
Admission €4 (€3 students)
Open Jan-Mar 10am-5pm daily;
Apr-May 9.30am-6pm daily; Jun-Aug
9.30am-9pm daily; Sep 9.30am-6pm
daily; Oct-Dec 10am-5pm daily

County Cork

Located in southwest Ireland, County Cork is home to the country's second-largest city plus a scenic coastal area that includes much of the Beara Peninsula.

Youghal (Eochaill)

Youghal (pronounced yarl) is a pleasant seaside town between Waterford and Cork. Medieval town walls still stand at the western edge of the town centre.

Coming & Going
Some Bus Éireann *(website www.buseireann.ie)* buses stop in Youghal en route between Waterford and Cork.

Accommodation
Evergreen House
This nice hostel is in a newly renovated building near the sea. Accommodation is in small rooms with good quality beds and en suite bathrooms. Shared facilities include a small but fully equipped kitchen and a nice TV lounge.
The Strand, Youghal
☎ *(024) 92877*
Dorm bed** €14-16;* ***double/twin room *€38-42*
📺 🅚

Maintenance & cleanliness	★★★★½
Facilities	★★
Atmosphere & character	★★★
Security	★★
Overall rating	★★★

Cork (Corcaigh)

The Republic of Ireland's second-largest city has only 160,000 people and is the main commercial centre of southwestern Ireland. Although the city centre has a few attractive buildings Cork generally isn't considered a nice place in comparison with other Irish towns.

Most people use Cork as a base for visiting the Blarney Castle, 8km north of the city centre.

Practical Information
Cork Tourist Information Office
Áras Fáilte, Grand Parade, Cork
☎ *(021) 425 5100*
Website *www.corkkerry.ie*
Open *Jan-May Mon-Sat 9.15am-5.30pm; Jun-Aug Mon-Fri 9am-6pm, Sat 9am-5.30pm; Sep-Dec Mon-Sat 9.15am-5.30pm*

LAUNDRY
Western Road Laundrette
Opposite College Gate, Western Road, Cork
☎ *(021) 427 9937*
Open *Mon-Fri 9am-9pm, Sat 9am-6pm*

Coming & Going
AIR
Cork Airport *(website www.cork-airport.com)* has flights to destinations throughout Ireland, Great Britain and Europe. It is 8km from the city centre and is served by a frequent bus service into the city centre (€3.40 one-way).

BUS
Cork's bus terminal is at the corner of Merchant's Quay and Parnell Place with Bus Éireann *(website www.buseireann.ie)* running buses to most major towns and cities.

TRAIN
There are direct trains between Cork and Dublin, which depart from the station east of the city centre on Lower Glanmire Road.

Accommodation
Campus House
This small hostel west of the city centre is in an old house that could be better maintained. Although a bit worn, it has a cosy TV lounge and a relatively good kitchen.
3 Woodland View, Western Road, Cork
☎ *(021) 434 3531*
Dorm bed *€13*
📺 🅚

Maintenance & cleanliness	★★
Facilities	★
Atmosphere & character	★★★★½
Security	★★½
Overall rating	★★

Cork International Youth Hostel
Cork's An Óige youth hostel is in a big house with an impressive exterior, but inside it looks institutional. Facilities include a TV lounge and a tiny kitchen.
1 Redclyffe, Western Road, Cork
☎ *(021) 454 3289*
Website *www.anoige.ie*
Dorm bed *€12-15 (€10-13 HI/An Óige)*
Credit cards *Amex, MC, Visa*
Reception open *8am-midnight*
🚗 📺 🅚

Maintenance & cleanliness	★★★
Facilities	★★☆
Atmosphere & character	★★
Security	★★★
Overall rating	★★★☆

Kelly's Hostel

Kelly's Hostel is a small hostel in a residential area south of the city centre that has a cosy common room plus accommodation in literary-themed rooms with murals and poetry painted on the walls.
25 Summerhill South, Cork
☎ *(021) 431 5612*
Website *www.kellyshostel.com*
Dorm bed €14-18; **double room** €46
Credit cards MC, Visa

📺 K

Maintenance & cleanliness	★★★☆
Facilities	★
Atmosphere & character	★★★★
Security	★★
Overall rating	★★★☆

Kinlay House

This big hostel offers clean and functional accommodation in a modern building down a laneway behind St Anne's church. It has the usual kitchen and laundry facilities plus a big TV lounge.
Bob & Joan Walk, Shandon, Cork
☎ *(021) 450 8966*
Website *www.kinlayhouse.ie*
Dorm bed €13-18; **single room** €25-30; **double/twin room** €40-50; *prices include breakfast*
Credit cards Amex, JCB, MC, Visa
Reception open 24 hours

📺 K L

Maintenance & cleanliness	★★★
Facilities	★★☆
Atmosphere & character	★★★☆
Security	★★★★
Overall rating	★★★☆

Sheila's Hostel

Sheila's is a very good hostel that is converted from two Victorian houses. It features two kitchens, two dining rooms, a TV lounge, sauna and a small outdoor terrace.
4 Belgrave Place, Wellington Road, Cork
☎ *(021) 450 5562*
Website *www.sheilashostel.ie*

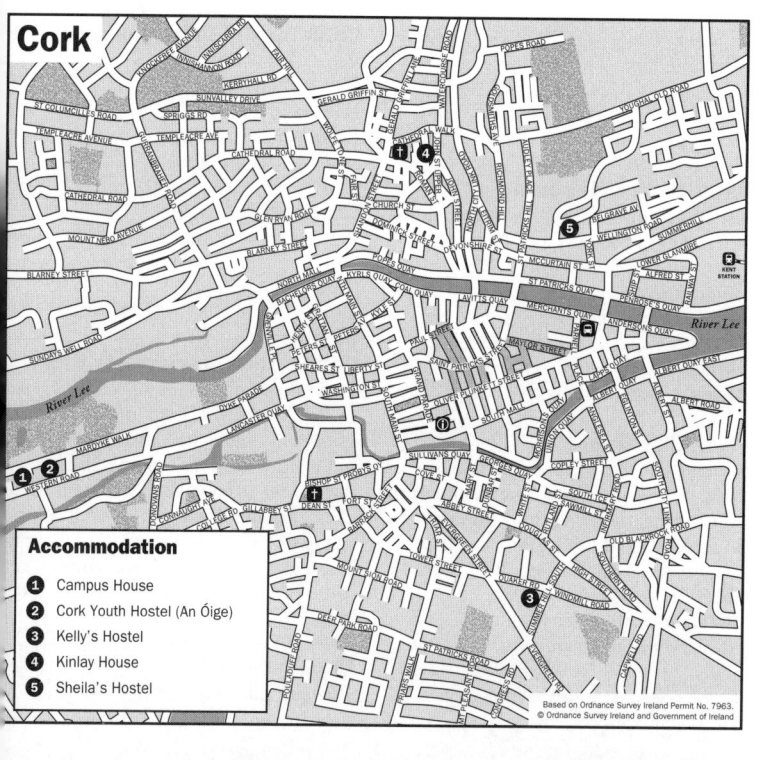

Accommodation
1. Campus House
2. Cork Youth Hostel (An Óige)
3. Kelly's Hostel
4. Kinlay House
5. Sheila's Hostel

Dorm bed €12-16; double/twin room €44-50
Credit cards MC, Visa
Reception open 24 hours

Maintenance & cleanliness	★★★★
Facilities	★★
Atmosphere & character	★★★★½
Security	★★★★½
Overall rating	★★★★½

Sights
Blarney Castle
The Blarney Castle is one of Ireland's biggest attractions. Built as a fortress in 1446, it is one of the country's oldest castles and one of Munster's strongest fortresses. Its main drawcard is the Stone of Eloquence, or the Blarney Stone. Legend says that those who kiss the Blarney Stone are bestowed with the gift of eloquence.
Blarney, 8km northwest of Cork
☎ *(021) 438 5252*
Website www.blarneycastle.ie
Admission €7
Open Jan-Apr Mon-Sat 9am-sunset, Sun 9.30am-sunset; May Mon-Sat 9am-6.30pm, Sun 9.30am-5.30pm; Jun-Aug Mon-Sat 9am-7pm, Sun 9.30am-5.30pm; Sep Mon-Sat 9am-6.30pm, Sun 9.30am-5.30pm; Oct-Dec Mon-Sat 9am-sunset, Sun 9.30am-sunset

Cork Butter Museum
This museum focusses on the butter industry and its impact on Cork's economy.
The Tony O'Reilly Centre, O'Connell Square, Shandon, Cork
☎ *(021) 430 0600*
Website www.corkbutter.museum
Admission €3 (€2.50 students)
Open Mar-Oct 10am-5pm daily

Cork City Gaol
One of Cork's major attractions is this former prison that is now a museum illustrating the crime and punishment in the 19th and early 20th century.
Convent Avenue, Sundays Well, Cork
☎ *(021) 430 5022*
Website www.corkcitygaol.com
Admission €6 (€5 students)
Open Jan-Feb 10am-5pm daily; Mar-Oct 9.30am-6pm daily; Nov-Dec 10am-5pm daily

St Fin Barre's Cathedral
This cathedral is one of Ireland's most beautiful, featuring over 1260 sculptures, marble mosaics and stained glass windows. It was built in the late 19th century on the site where St Fin Barre established a school in the 7th century.
Dean Street, Cork
☎ *(021) 496 3387*
Website www.cathedral.cork.anglican.org
Admission €3 (€1.50 students)
Open Jan-Mar 10am-12.45pm & 2pm-5pm daily; Apr-Sep 10am-5.30pm daily; Oct-Dec 10am-12.45pm & 2pm-5pm daily

Cobh (An Cobh)
Cobh (pronounced cove) is built on an island in Cork Harbour. It started off as a seaside resort in the 17th century but later became a major port with 2½-million emigrants sailing from here. Cobh was also the last port of call for the ill-fated *Titanic*.

Practical Information
Cobh Tourist Information Office
Royal Cork Yacht Club
☎ *(021) 481 3301*
Website www.cobhharbourchamber.ie
Open Mon-Fri 9.30am-5.30pm, Sat-Sun 11.30am-5.30pm

Coming & Going
The easiest way to get here is by train with frequent services running between Cork and Cobh.

Sights
Cobh – the Queenstown Story
This exhibition in Cobh's restored train station traces the steps of 2½ million Irish emigrants who sailed from Cobh. It includes exhibits on the sinking of the *Titanic* (Cobh was her last port of call) and the *Lusitania*, as well as the story of Annie Moore who sailed from Cobh and was the first ever immigrant to be processed at Ellis Island in New York.
Cobh Heritage Centre, Cobh
☎ *(021) 481 3591*
Website www.cobhheritage.com
Admission €5 (€4 students)

***Open** Jan-May 9.30am-4pm daily; May-Nov 9.30am-5pm daily; Nov-Dec 9.30am-4pm daily*

Kinsale (Cionn tSáile)

This elegant town is one of County Cork's most attractive. It is situated on a harbour, which is guarded by two fortresses.

Practical Information
Tourist Information Centre
Pier Road, Kinsale
☎ *(021) 477 2234*
***Website** www.corkkerry.ie*
***Open** Mar-Jun Mon-Sat 9am-6pm; Jul-Aug 9am-6pm daily; Sep-Nov Mon-Sat 9am-6pm*

Accommodation
Dempsey's Hostel

Dempsey's is a small hostel tucked behind a Texaco service station on the road to Cork. It is a simple hostel with a cosy TV lounge and a basic kitchen. Accommodation is in clean but plain rooms.

Eastern Road, Kinsale
☎ *(021) 477 2124*
***Dorm bed** €13-16;* ***double room** €34-40*

Maintenance & cleanliness	★★★☆
Facilities	★★☆
Atmosphere & character	★★★
Security	★
Overall rating	★★

Guardwell Lodge

This excellent hostel is a purpose-built place with a sunny atrium; a brilliant kitchen and a TV lounge. Accommodation is in nice rooms with en suite bathrooms and top quality mattresses. It is right in the heart of the town centre, making it the best located of Kinsale's hostels.

Guardwell Street, Kinsale
☎ *(021) 477 4686*
***Website** www.guardwelllodge.com*
***Dorm bed** €15-18;* ***single room** €27;* ***double/twin room** €50-54*
***Credit cards** Amex, MC, Visa*
***Reception open** 24 hours*

Maintenance & cleanliness	★★★★★
Facilities	★★
Atmosphere & character	★★☆
Security	★★★★
Overall rating	★★★★☆

Sights
Charles Fort

The large star-shaped fortress was built between 1678 and 1682 and was a British naval base until 1922. It offers impressive views of Kinsale Harbour.

Summer Cove, Kinsale
☎ *(021) 477 2263*
***Website** www.heritageireland.ie*
***Admission** €3.50 (€1.25 students)*
***Open** Jan-mid Mar 10am-5pm daily; mid Mar-Oct 10am-6pm daily; Nov-Dec 10am-5pm daily*

Desmond Castle & Wine Museum

Originally built as a customhouse around 500 years ago, Desmond Castle has been used as an ordnance store, prison and workhouse and it now houses the International Museum of Wine. The museum's displays show how Kinsale was an important port for the wine trade.

Cork Street, Kinsale
☎ *(021) 477 4855*
***Website** www.desmondcastle.ie*
***Admission** €2.75 (€1.25 students)*
***Open** mid Apr-Oct 10am-6pm daily*

Dunmanway (Dún Mánmhai)

This 17th century town is built around two triangular town squares and is surrounded by mountains. The main reason that most travellers visit is to stay at the tranquil Shiplake Mountain Hostel, 5km outside town.

Accommodation
Shiplake Mountain Hostel

This small hostel is in a peaceful rural location in the hills 5km from Dunmanway. It consists of a house with a kitchen and a cosy common room with a wood heater and accommodation is in simple but tidy rooms. However most people prefer to stay in the cute barrel-top caravans. The hostel offers free pick

up from Dunmanway but if you're driving you should follow the signs from the KCK TV and Electrical store on the market square.
Shiplake, 5km from Dunmanway
☎ *(023) 45750*
Website *www.shiplakemountainhostel.com*
Dorm bed *€11-12;* **double/twin room** *€25-32;* **camping** *€7 per person*

Maintenance & cleanliness	★★★★
Facilities	★★☆
Atmosphere & character	★★★★★
Security	☆
Overall rating	★★★

Clonakilty (Cloch na Coillte)

This attractive town is best known as the home of Irish hero Michael Collins, who is commemorated at the Michael Collins Centre.

Practical Information
Tourist Information Centre
Ashe Street, Clonakilty
☎ *(023) 332 226*
Website *www.corkkerry.ie*
Open *Mar-May Mon-Sat 9.30am-5.30pm; Jun Mon-Sat 9am-6pm; Jul-Aug Mon-Sat 9am-7pm; Sep-Nov Mon-Sat 9.30am-5.30pm*

Accommodation
Old Brewery Hostel
This is a nice purpose-built hostel with very good kitchen facilities.
Emmet Square, Clonakilty
☎ *(023) 33525*
Dorm bed *€12;* **double room** *€30*
Reception open *2pm-8pm daily*

Maintenance & cleanliness	★★★★☆
Facilities	★
Atmosphere & character	★★★
Security	★★☆
Overall rating	★★★☆

Sights
Michael Collins Centre & Arigideen Heritage Park
The Centre has exhibits relating to Michael Collins and it features a short video presentation about the life of the military leader and Irish hero.
Castleview, Clonakilty
☎ *(023) 46107*
Website *www.reachireland.com*
Admission *€5 (€3 students)*
Open *Mon-Sat 10.30am-6pm*

Skibbereen (Sciobairín)

Skibbereen was one of Ireland's worst affected towns hit by the Irish Famine of the 1840s. The Skibbereen Heritage Centre is a moving tribute to the thousands who lost their lives.

Practical Information
Tourist Information Centre
Town Hall, North Street, Skibbereen
☎ *(028) 21766*
Website *www.corkkerry.ie*
Open *Jan-May Mon-Fri 9.15am-5.30pm; Jun Mon-Sat 9am-6pm; Jul-Aug 9am-7pm daily; Sep-Dec Mon-Fri 9.15am-5.30pm*

Accommodation
Russagh Mill Hostel
This hostel is a stone building that was originally a corn mill. Accommodation is in basic dorms and a lot of groups stay here. It is around 3km outside the town centre; at the roundabout turn onto the R596 (signposted Tragumna).
R596, Russagh, Skibbereen
☎ *(028) 22451*
Website *www.russaghmillhostel.com*
Dorm bed *€11-12*
Open *16 Apr-30 Oct*

Sights
Skibbereen Heritage Centre
The Heritage Centre houses two exhibitions including the moving Great Famine Exhibition, which commemorates this tragic period of Irish history that changed the country forever.
Old Gasworks Building, Upper Bridge Street, Skibbereen
☎ *(028) 40900*
Website *www.skibbheritage.com*
Admission *€4.50 (€3.50 students)*
Open *10 Apr-24 May Tue-Sat 10am-6pm; 27 May-20 Sep 10am-6pm daily; 23 Sep-31 Oct Tue-Sat 10am-6pm*

Baltimore

Baltimore has a yacht harbour and ferries sail from here to Cape Clear Island.

Coming & Going

Between June and August West Cork Coastal Cruises *(website www.westcorkcoastalcruises.com)* run daytrips from Baltimore to Cape Clear Island, departing Baltimore at 11.30am and arriving back at 5.30pm allowing two hours on the island. You can often see whales and dolphins from the boat.

Accommodation
Rolf's Holidays

Rolf's Holidays is a very nice hostel that is comprised of several stone buildings. Accommodation is in spotless rooms and shared facilities include a small kitchen and dining room and an outdoor seating area. The hostel also features a classy restaurant, café and wine bar.

Baltimore Hill, Baltimore
☎ *(028) 20289*
Website www.rolfsholidays.ie
Dorm bed €13-15; **double/twin room** €40
Credit cards MC, Visa
Reception open 8am-10pm daily

Maintenance & cleanliness	★★★★★
Facilities	★½
Atmosphere & character	★★★½
Security	★
Overall rating	★★★½

Cape Clear Island (Oileán Chléire)

Irish-speaking Cape Clear Island is located off the southwest coast and the island is a popular retreat for many backpackers intent on discovering the 'real Ireland'.

Coming & Going

Between June and September Karycraft Ferries (☎ *(028) 28278)* sail daily between Schull and Cape Clear Island. Between June and August West Cork Coastal Cruises *(website www.westcorkcoastalcruises.com)* run daytrips from Baltimore to Cape Clear Island, departing Baltimore at 11.30am and arriving back at 5.30pm allowing two hours on the island. You can often see whales and dolphins from the boat.

Accommodation
Cape Clear Island Youth Hostel

This An Óige youth hostel is in an old coast guard station with lovely sea views.

Old Coast Guard Station, South Harbour, Cape Clear Island
☎ *(028) 41968*
Website www.anoige.ie
Dorm bed €14-15 (€12-13 HI/An Óige)

Schull

During summer this seaside town is a popular base for visiting Cape Clear Island.

Coming & Going

Between June and September Karycraft Ferries (☎ *(028) 28278)* sail daily between Schull and Cape Clear Island.

Accommodation
Schull Backpackers Lodge

Schull Backpackers Lodge is a brilliant purpose-built hostel that features the usual kitchen, laundry and TV lounge plus a cosy common room with an open fire and a sunny garden barbecue area.

Culla Road, Schull
☎ *(028) 28681*
Website www.schullbackpackers.com
Dorm bed €15; **single room** €20; **double room** €44
Reception open 9am-9pm daily

Maintenance & cleanliness	★★★★★
Facilities	★★½
Atmosphere & character	★★★★
Security	★★
Overall rating	★★★★

Bantry (Beanntrai)

The French invaded this important coastal town twice – in 1689 and 1796. The town's main attraction is Bantry House, but this isn't a big draw for most backpackers.

Accommodation
Bantry Harbour View Independent Hostel
This basic hostel by the harbour has old furnishings, which make it feel a bit tired and worn although it has a more homely feel than Bantry's other hostel. Facilities include the usual TV lounge and kitchen.
Harbour View, Bantry
☎ *(027) 51140*
Dorm bed *€10*

Maintenance & cleanliness	★★
Facilities	★
Atmosphere & character	★★★½
Security	★
Overall rating	★★

Bantry Independent Hostel
This hostel offers basic accommodation with shared facilities that include a TV lounge and a small kitchen and dining area. It is near O'Mahoney's Quickpick Food Store about a 10-minute walk from the town centre.
Reenrour East, Bantry
☎ *(027) 51050*
Dorm bed *€11*
Credit cards *MC, Visa*

Maintenance & cleanliness	★★
Facilities	½
Atmosphere & character	★★
Security	★
Overall rating	★½

Sights
Bantry House & Gardens
This large manor house was built around 1740 and houses a collection of fine tapestries, furniture and objets d'art. There is also an exhibition on the French Armada.
☎ *(027) 50047*
Website *www.bantryhouse.ie*
Admission *house, gardens & French Armada exhibition €10 (€8 students); gardens & French Armada exhibition only €4*
Open *Mar-Oct 9am-6pm daily*

Beara Peninsula

This rugged peninsula is a good alternative to the Ring of Kerry or the Dingle Peninsula while providing similar rugged coastal scenery. Like the Ring of Kerry the Beara Peninsula has a good choice of budget accommodation, however very few tourists come here so it is a much more authentic experience.

Accommodation
ADRIGOLE
This locality refers to the rural area about halfway between Glengarriff and Castletownbere.

Hungry Hill Lodge
This nice purpose-built hostel features a cosy TV lounge with an open fire plus a big fully equipped kitchen. It is very clean and the amenities are of a high standard. The hostel is next to the pub on the R572 in Adrigole.
R572, Adrigole (check in at the pub next door)
☎ *(027) 60228*
Website *www.hungryhilllodge.com*
Dorm bed *€15;* **single room** *€22;* **double room** *€30-40;* **camping** *€7 per person*
Credit cards *MC, Visa*
Reception open *8.30am-10pm daily*

Maintenance & cleanliness	★★★★★
Facilities	★★½
Atmosphere & character	★★★★½
Security	★★
Overall rating	★★★★½

ALLIHIES (NA HAILICNI)
Allihies is a pretty spot near the western end of the Beara Peninsula that offers lovely ocean views.

Allihies Youth Hostel
This An Óige youth hostel is in a house overlooking the sea about 1.5km from the centre of the village.
R 575, Allihies, Beara Peninsula
☎ *(027) 73014*
Dorm bed *€14.50 (€12.50 HI/An Óige)*
Open *Jun-Sep; lockout 10am-5pm*

CASTLETOWNBERE
Castletownbere is the peninsula's major settlement and one of the country's largest fishing ports.

Garranes Hostel
Garranes Hostel is part of the Dzogchen Beara Buddhist Retreat. It provides good quality backpackers' accommodation that features a cosy common room with a fireplace and good kitchen facilities. It is in a rural location about 8km from Castletownbere.
☎ *(027) 73032*
Website *www.dzogchenbeara.ie*
Dorm bed *€12;* ***family room*** *€30*

Maintenance & cleanliness	★★★½
Facilities	★★½
Atmosphere & character	★★★★½
Security	½
Overall rating	★★★

Ocean View Lodge
This brand new purpose-built hostel has a central position in the heart of Castletownbere. There is no star rating because it wasn't completed when BUG visited to research this book.
☎ *(027) 71693*
Website *www.bearahostel.com*
Dorm bed *€15*

GLENGARRIFF
This tiny village lies at the southeastern corner of the Beara Peninsula, where the N71 meets the R572.

Murphy's Village Hostel
This excellent hostel in the centre of Glengarriff village is a clean and well-maintained hostel with facilities that include a cosy common room with an open fireplace and a good kitchen.
N71, Glengarriff
☎ *(027) 63555*
Dorm bed *€13-15*
Credit cards *MC, Visa*

Maintenance & cleanliness	★★★★½
Facilities	★★½
Atmosphere & character	★★★★
Security	★★
Overall rating	★★★★½

County Kerry
County Kerry is one of Ireland's most visited counties. Its scenic coastline includes the popular Ring of Kerry and the Dingle Peninsula and it also includes the towns of Kenmare, Killarney and Tralee.

Kenmare (Neidín)
Located between the Beara Peninsula and the Ring of Kerry, Kenmare is a quiet town that makes a good base for visiting either peninsula. Although its location ensures that plenty of tourists pass through town, it still retains a more authentic Irish feel than many of the other major towns in County Kerry.

Practical Information
Tourist Information Centre
The Square, Kenmare
☎ *(064) 41233*
Website *www.corkkerry.ie*
Open *May-Jun Mon-Sat 9am-1pm & 2pm-5.30pm; Jul-Oct Mon-Sat 9am-6pm, Sun 10am-5pm*

Coming & Going
Kenmare isn't as well connected by public transport as nearby Killarney and is best suited to people travelling by car.

Bus Éireann *(website www.buseireann.ie)* has buses to Cork, Killarney and Tralee.

Accommodation
Fáilte Hostel
Fáilte Hostel is a tidy hostel in the town centre that has the usual TV lounge and a fully equipped kitchen with an Aga cooker.
Corner Henry & Shelbourne Streets, Kenmare
☎ *(064) 42333*
Website *www.neidin.net*
Dorm bed *€13;* ***double room*** *€34*
Open *Apr-Oct*

Kenmare Lodge Hostel
Kenmare Lodge Hostel is a simple hostel that has the usual kitchen and laundry facilities.
27 Main Street, Kenmare
☎ *(064) 40662*
Dorm bed *€14*

Sights
Kenmare Heritage Centre
The Kenmare Heritage Centre has exhibits on various aspects of local history.
The Square, Kenmare
☎ *(064) 41233*
Website *www.corkkerry.ie/kenmare heritagecentre*
Admission *free*
Open *May-Jun Mon-Sat 9am-1pm & 2pm-5.30pm; Jul-Oct Mon-Sat 9am-6pm, Sun 10am-5pm*

Killarney (Cill Airne)

This busy tourist town at the eastern end of the Ring of Kerry is an attractive place despite being packed with souvenir shops. It has good transport connections, which make it a convenient place for independent travellers to use as a base for exploring the Ring of Kerry and the nearby Killarney National Park.

Practical Information
Tourist Information Centre
Beech Street, Killarney
☎ *(064) 31633*
Website *www.corkkerry.ie/killarneytio*
Open *Jan-May Mon-Sat 9.15am-1pm & 2.15pm-5.30pm; Jun Mon-Sat 9am-6pm, Sun 10am-1pm & 2.15pm-6pm; Jul-Aug Mon-Sat 9am-8pm, Sun 10am-1pm & 2.15pm-6pm; Sep Mon-Sat 9am-6pm, Sun 10am-1pm & 2.15pm-6pm; Oct-Dec Mon-Sat 9.15am-1pm & 2.15pm-5.30pm*

Coming & Going
AIR
Aer Arann *(website www.aerarann.com)* flies to Dublin and Manchester and Ryanair *(website www.ryanair.com)* flies to Frankfurt Hahn and London Stansted from Kerry Airport *(website www.kerryairport.ie)*, which is about halfway between Killarney and Tralee.

A shuttle bus (€6) meets flights from Frankfurt Hahn, but passengers from all other destinations will need to take a taxi to the nearby village of Farranfore, where you can make bus and train connections to Killarney and other destinations.

BUS
Killarney has good bus connections with Bus Éireann *(website www.buseireann.ie)* services going to Cork, Kenmare, Limerick, Tralee and the Ring of Kerry. Buses depart from the train station on Park Road.

TRAIN
Killarney is on the train line that runs from Tralee to Dublin. The station is on Park Road east of the town centre.

Accommodation
Killarney International Youth Hostel
This big youth hostel, 5km outside Killarney, has extensive common areas that include a kitchen with a big dining room, a TV lounge with Internet access plus a quiet common room with books and games. The dorms are crammed with metal bunk beds but the four-bed dorms are more spacious. To get here take the Killorglin bus to the Golden Nugget Pub (Fossa Cross).
Aghadoe House, Fossa, Killarney
☎ *(064) 31240*
Website *www.anoige.ie*
Dorm bed *€14-17 (€12-15 HI/An Óige)*
Credit cards *MC, Visa*
Reception open *8am-midnight*
📺🅺🅻

Maintenance & cleanliness	★★★
Facilities	★★★☆
Atmosphere & character	★★★☆
Security	★★★☆
Overall rating	★★★

Neptune's Killarney Town Hostel
Neptune's is a big centrally located hostel in the centre of Killarney. Some rooms, such as the doubles, are of a very high standard but the regular dorms are nothing special. Facilities include a small TV lounge, free Internet access and a basic kitchen (no oven) and the atmosphere feels a little institutional.
New Street, Killarney
☎ *(064) 35255*
Website *www.neptuneshostel.com*
Dorm bed *€12-17.50;* **single room** *€23-35;* **double room** *€33-40*
Credit cards *MC, Visa*
Reception open *7.30am-11.30pm daily*
📺🅺🅻

Maintenance & cleanliness	★★★☆
Facilities	★★
Atmosphere & character	★★☆
Security	★★
Overall rating	★★★☆

The Súgán
This small central hostel has the best atmosphere of Killarney's hostels. Although a bit cramped, it has loads of character and includes a small kitchen and a common room with an open fire.
Michael Collins Place, Lewis Rd, Killarney
☎ *(064) 33104*
Website *www.killarneysuganhostel.com*
Dorm bed *€12-13*
🅚

Maintenance & cleanliness	★★★
Facilities	★
Atmosphere & character	★★★★★
Security	★
Overall rating	★★★☆

Sights
Coolwood Wildlife Sanctuary
This wildlife park and sanctuary near Killarney town is home to the Red Squirrel and the rare Golden Eagle.
Coolcaslagh, Killarney
☎ *(064) 36288*
Open *Apr-Oct 11am-6pm daily*

Killarney National Park
Located south of Killarney town, this 10,000 hectare national park is noted for is lake and mountain scenery. The park is home to red deer and it encompasses several attractions including Ross Castle, Muckross Friary and the majestic Muckross House.

Practical Information
Killarney National Park Information Centre
Muckross House, N71, Killarney National Park, 6.5km from Killarney
☎ *(064) 35960*
Website *www.heritageireland.ie*
Open *mid Mar-Jun 9am-6pm daily; Jul-Aug 9am-7pm daily; Sep-Oct 9am-6pm daily*

There is also an information point at Torc Waterfall
Open *end Jun-mid Sep 9.30am-6.30pm*

Accommodation
Black Valley Youth Hostel
This very basic hostel has limited kitchen facilities plus a common room with a small TV. It looks nice from the outside but inside it feels a bit dated although it is kept neat and tidy. It has a very remote location near the Gap of Dunloe.
☎ *(064) 34712*
Website *www.anoige.ie*
Dorm bed *€14-15 (€12-13 HI/An Óige)*
Open *Mar-Nov*
🅟 📺 🅚

Maintenance & cleanliness	★★★☆
Facilities	★
Atmosphere & character	★★★☆
Security	☆
Overall rating	★★

Sights
Muckross Friary
Dating from the 15th century, this well-preserved Franciscan Friary features Ireland's only Franciscan tower that is as wide as its church.
Muckross Estate, N71, 4km from Killarney
☎ *(064) 31440*
Website *www.heritageireland.ie*
Admission *free*
Open *mid Jun-early Sep 10am-5pm (last entry 4.15pm) daily*

Muckross House & Gardens
One of Ireland's most prominent stately homes, this Victorian mansion is surrounded by gardens and is furnished to portray the aristocratic lifestyles of those who lived in the house.
N71, Muckross, Killarney National Park, 6.5km from Killarney
☎ *(064) 31440*
Website *www.heritageireland.ie*
Admission *€5.50 (€2.25 students)*
Open *Jan-mid Mar 9am-5.30pm daily (last entry 4.45pm); mid Mar-Jun 9am-6pm daily (last entry 5.15pm); Jul-Aug 9am-7pm daily (last entry 6.15pm); Sep-Oct 9am-6pm daily (last entry 5.15pm); Nov-Dec 9am-5.30pm daily (last entry 4.45pm)*

Muckross Traditional Farms
This open-air museum is comprised of three working farms that feature

machinery and farm animals including traditional Kerry cows.
N71, 6.5km from Killarney
☎ *(054) 31440*
Website *www.heritageireland.ie*
Admission *€5 (€2 students)*
Open *mid Mar-Apr Sat-Sun 1pm-6pm; May 1pm-6pm daily; Jun-Sep 10am-7pm daily; Oct Sat-Sun 1pm-6pm*

Ross Castle

This fortress is believed to have been built in the last 15th century by one of the Donoghue Ross chieftains. The castle has been restored and is decked out with period furniture from the 16th and 17th centuries.
Ross Road, Killarney
☎ *(064) 35851*
Website *www.heritageireland.ie*
Admission *€5 (€2 students)*
Open *Apr 10am-5pm daily; May 10am-6pm daily; Jun-Aug 9am-6.30pm daily; Sep 10am-6pm daily; Oct Tue-Sun 10am-5pm*

Ring of Kerry (Iveragh Peninsula)

The Ring of Kerry refers to the popular route taken by tour buses along the N70, which follows the coast around the Iveragh Peninsula. It offers lovely scenery and has a good choice of hostels but both the Beara and Dingle Peninsulas offer a similar experience with fewer tourists.

Getting Around

Transport connections are part of the reason why the Ring of Kerry is so popular in comparison with the Beara and Dingle Peninsulas, however renting a car is still the best way to explore the region.

If you're not driving the best option is to avoid the tour buses that clog the road out of Killarney and take the Bus Éireann (website www.buseireann.ie) bus that runs around the Ring of Kerry during the summer months.

Accommodation
KELLS
Caitins Hostel

Caitins is a small hostel above a pub facing the ocean and all the rooms boast spectacular sea views. Kitchen facilities and other common areas are very limited but you'll probably want to spend most of your time in the pub anyway.
N70, Kells
☎ *(066) 947 7614*
Website *www.patscraftshop.com*
Dorm bed *€13*
Credit cards *Amex, MC, Visa*

Maintenance & cleanliness	★★★
Facilities	★
Atmosphere & character	★★
Security	★
Overall rating	★★

CAHERSIVEEN (CATHAIR SAIDHTHIN)
Sive Hostel

Sive Hostel is a small hostel in Cahersiveen that offers comfortable accommodation with facilities that include a fully equipped kitchen and a cosy sitting room with cable TV and an open fire.
15 East End, Cahersiveen
☎ *(066) 947 2717*
Dorm bed *€12.50;* **double/twin room** *€30-33*

Maintenance & cleanliness	★★★★½
Facilities	★★
Atmosphere & character	★★★½
Security	★
Overall rating	★★★½

WATERVILLE (AN COIREÁN)
Peter's Place

This colourful hostel is a bit worn around the edges but it has a good location opposite the beach.
N70, Waterville
☎ *(066) 947 4608*
Dorm bed *€10;* **double room** *€25*

CAHERDANIEL (CATHAIR DONAL)
Travellers Rest Hostel

Travellers Rest Hostel is a small hostel that has comfortable rooms and common areas that include a kitchen, a cosy TV lounge and a dining room with country-style décor.
N70, Caherdaniel
☎ *(066) 947 5175*
Dorm bed *€12.50-16*

Sights
Derrynane House National Historic Park
The Irish statesman, Daniel O'Connell lived in this house, which contains artefacts relating to his life.
N70, 3.5km from Caherdaniel
☎ *(066) 947 5113*
Website *www.heritageireland.ie*
Admission *€2.75 (€1.25 students)*
Open *Jan-Mar Sat-Sun 1pm-5pm; Apr Tue-Sun 1pm-5pm; May-Sep Mon-Sat 9am-6pm, Sun 11am-7pm; Oct Tue-Sun 1pm-5pm; Nov-Dec Sat-Sun 1pm-5pm*

Killorglin (Cill Orglan)
This town at the north eastern end of the Ring of Kerry is best known for the annual Puck Fair festival *(website www.puckfair.ie)*, which offers a variety of events centred around a goat being crowned King Puck for the three days of the festival. The 2005 Puck Fair will be held on 10-12 August.

Accommodation
Laune Valley Farm Hostel
The farm hostel is 2km from the town centre and
Banshagh, N70, Killorglin
☎ *(066) 976 1488*
Dorm bed *€13-15;* **double/twin room** *€40-50*
🚗 🅺 🅻

Tralee (Trá Lí)
County Kerry's most important town is a useful transport hub and a good base for exploring the Dingle Peninsula.

Each August Tralee hosts the Rose of Tralee *(website www.roseoftralee.ie)*, one of the world's longest running beauty pageants.

Practical Information
Tourist Information Centre
Ashe Memorial Hall, Denny Street, Tralee
☎ *(066) 712 1288*
Website *www.shannonregiontourism.ie*
Open *Jan-Apr Mon-Fri 9am-5pm; May-Jun Mon-Sat 9am-6pm; Jul-Aug Mon-Sat 9am-7pm, Sun 9am-6pm; Oct Mon-Sat 9am-6pm; Nov-Dec Mon-Fri 9am-5pm*

Coming & Going
AIR
Aer Arann *(website aerarann.com)* flies to Dublin and Manchester and Ryanair *(website www.ryanair.com)* flies to Frankfurt Hahn and London Stansted from Kerry Airport *(website www.kerryairport.ie)*, which is about halfway between Killarney and Tralee. Coming from the airport you will need to take a taxi to the village of Farranfore, where you can make bus and train connections to Tralee and other destinations.

BUS
Bus Éireann *(website www.buseireann.ie)* has buses from Tralee to Cork, Dingle, Killarney, Limerick and the Ring of Kerry. Buses depart from the train station north of the town centre.

TRAIN
The train station on Oakpark Road north of the town centre has direct trains to Dublin. Change at Mallow for connecting trains to Cork.

Accommodation
Finnegan's Hostel
This centrally located hostel is well appointed with en suite bathrooms, comfy beds, a fully equipped kitchen and an opulent lounge with a piano, big leather sofas, a TV and an open fireplace.
17 Denny Street, Tralee
☎ *(066) 712 7610*
Website *www.finneganshostel.com*
Dorm bed *€16;* **double room** *€40*
📺 🅺 🅻

Maintenance & cleanliness	★★★★
Facilities	★★★☆
Atmosphere & character	★★★★★
Security	★★
Overall rating	★★★★☆

Westward Court
Westward Court is a clean hostel with good amenities that include quality beds in small dorms (the largest dormitory has four beds), all with en suite. Shared facilities aren't very extensive though, and it doesn't have much of a

social atmosphere.
Mary Street, Tralee
☎ *(066) 718 0081*
Website *www.iol.ie/kerry-insight/westward*
Dorm bed €17-18; **single room** €25; **double/twin room** €46; *prices include breakfast*
Reception open *8am-3pm;* **curfew** *3am*

🚗 📺 K L

Maintenance & cleanliness	★★★★
Facilities	★★½
Atmosphere & character	★★½
Security	★★
Overall rating	★★★½

Sights
Kerry County Museum
Ireland's second-largest museum displays artefacts dating from prehistoric times to the present day.
Ashe Memorial Hall, Denny Street, Tralee
☎ *(066) 712 7777*
Website *www.kerrymuseum.ie*
Admission €8
Open *Jan-Mar Tue-Fri 10am-4.30pm; Apr-May Tue-Sat 9.30am-5.30pm; Jun-Aug 9.30am-5.30pm daily; Sep-Dec Tue-Sat 9.30am-5pm*

Dingle Peninsula

The Dingle Peninsula provides a slightly less touristy alternative to the Ring of Kerry. It features stunning coastal scenery and has a good selection of backpackers' hostels.

Dingle is the only real town on the peninsula and many backpackers spend a night here but the small villages are what most people come to visit the Dingle Peninsula.

Coming & Going & Local Transport
Although driving is the best way to see the peninsula, Bus Éireann *(website www.buseireann.ie)* run buses to Tralee and also to Dunquin at the far end of the peninsula.

Anascaul & Lougher
The N86 Dingle-Tralee Road passes through this rural region en route to Dingle. Although there are a couple of hostels here, most travellers shoot straight through to Dingle before looking for a bed for the night.

Accommodation
Bog View Hostel
The Bog View is a basic hostel with views of the surrounding countryside, although power lines obscure much of the view.
N86, Lougher
☎ *(066) 915 8125*
Dorm bed €9.50-12
Open *Jun-Aug*

🚗

Maintenance & cleanliness	★★★½
Facilities	★
Atmosphere & character	★★
Security	★
Overall rating	★★½

Fuchsia Lodge
Fuchsia Lodge is a large concrete block building with basic facilities that include the usual TV lounge, laundry and a small kitchen.
N86, Anascaul
☎ *(066) 915 7150*
Dorm bed €13-14; **double/twin room** €32-36

🚗 ♿ 📺 K L

Maintenance & cleanliness	★★
Facilities	★★½
Atmosphere & character	★★½
Security	★
Overall rating	★★½

Dingle Town (An Daigean)
Dingle Town is the biggest town on the peninsula although it can get very crowded with tourists during summer it has a good selection of pubs and a lot of backpackers spend a night here.

Practical Information
Tourist Information Centre
The Quay, Dingle
☎ *(066) 915 1188*
Website *www.corkkerry.ie/dingletio*
Open *mid Mar-Jun Mon-Sat 9.30am-6pm, Sun 9.30am-6pm; Jul-Aug Mon-Sat 9am-7pm, Sun 10am-5pm; Sep-Oct Mon-Sat 9.30am-6pm, Sun 9.30am-5pm*

Accommodation
Ballintaggart House
This big 300-year-old concrete house offers views to the sea and was originally built as a hunting lodge and served as a soup kitchen during the Potato Famine. It is on the Dingle-Tralee road about a 20-minute walk to the town centre.
Racecourse Road, Dingle
☎ *(066) 915 1454*
Website www.dingleaccommodation.com
Dorm bed €15-22; single room €28-70; double/twin room €56-70
Open 16 Mar-31 Oct

Grapevine Hostel
This small 26-bed hostel in the town centre has a great atmosphere. It features a cosy lounge with an open fire plus a small kitchen and dining room. All the rooms have en suite facilities.
Dykegate Street, Dingle
☎ *(066) 915 1434*
Website www.grapevinedingle.com
Dorm bed €13-16

Maintenance & cleanliness	★★★
Facilities	★★☆
Atmosphere & character	★★★★☆
Security	★★☆
Overall rating	★★★

Rainbow Hostel
This excellent hostel just outside Dingle is in a big farmhouse that is clean and well maintained with shiny polished floors, a nice big kitchen and a dining room with a piano.
Milltown, Dingle
☎ *(066) 915 1044*
Website www.net-rainbow.com
Dorm bed €13; double/twin room €32
Reception open low season 9am-10pm daily; high season 8am-11.30pm daily

Maintenance & cleanliness	★★★★★
Facilities	★★
Atmosphere & character	★★★★☆
Security	★★☆
Overall rating	★★★★☆

Sights
Celtic & Prehistoric Museum
This museum has ancient artefacts dating from the Jurassic era and also including the Stone and Bronze Ages and the Celtic, Viking and Saxon eras. It is home to Ireland's only fossil Woolly Mammoth and dinosaur egg nest.
Kilvicadowning, Ventry
☎ *(066) 915 9191*
Admission €5
Open 10am-5.30pm daily

Dingle Oceanworld Aquarium
Dingle's aquarium has the usual assortment of tropical fish, sharks complete with a walk-through underwater tunnel.
The Wood, Dingle
☎ *(066) 915 2111*
Admission €8.50 (€6.50 students)
Open 10am-6pm daily

Dunquin (Dún Chaoin)
This seaside village has lovely views to the Blasket Islands. The Blasket Centre is the main attraction in town.

Accommodation
Dún Chaoin Youth Hostel
This small hostel has lovely sea views and facilities that include a small kitchen, common room and conservatory.
R559, Dunquin
☎ *(066) 915 6121*
Website www.anoige.ie
Dorm bed €13.50-14 (€11.50-12 HI/An Óige)
Lockout 10am-5pm daily

Maintenance & cleanliness	★★★☆
Facilities	★★☆
Atmosphere & character	★★★
Security	★
Overall rating	★★

Sights
The Blasket Centre
This museum/interpretive centre in Dunquin at the tip of the Dingle Peninsula has displays honouring the people who once lived on the Great Blasket Island. The island once had a vibrant community that is noted for its unique literary achievements, however Great Blasket was abandoned in 1953 as its population had dwindled to the point where it could no longer support itself.
R559, Dunquin

☎ *(066) 915 6444*
Website *www.heritageireland.ie*
Admission *€3.50 (€1.25 students)*
Open *Easter-Jun 10am-6pm daily; Jul-Aug 10am-7pm daily; Sep-Oct 10am-6pm daily*

Ballyferriter (Baile an Fheirtéaraigh)

This small village in the Gaeltacht area north east of Dunquin has a small hostel. The main attraction here is the visitor centre at nearby Gallarus Oratory.

Accommodation
Black Cat Hostel

This small eight-bed hostel is above a shop and has a small common room/kitchen.
R559, Ballyferriter
☎ *(066) 915 6286*
Dorm bed *€12*

Maintenance & cleanliness	★★☆
Facilities	★
Atmosphere & character	★★☆
Security	★
Overall rating	★★

Sights
Gallarus Visitor Centre

Dating from the 8th century, this historic church is a stunning example of a dry stone building that is still waterproof after more than 1000 years.
Gallarus Oratory, R559 between Ballyferriter and Feohanagh
☎ *(066) 915 5333*
Open *Jan-Mar 9am-5pm daily; Apr-Sep 9am-9pm daily; Oct-Dec 9am-5pm daily*

Cloghane (An Clochán) & Mount Brandon

Cloghane is a tiny village wedged between 953m-high Mount Brandon and Brandon Bay.

Accommodation
Mount Brandon Hostel

This brilliant hostel is perhaps the nicest building in Cloghane. The stone hostel is very well equipped with en suite facilities in all rooms, a cosy TV lounge with an open fire, a small – but fully equipped – kitchen and a waterfront dining area with lovely views.
Cloghane
☎ *(066) 713 8299*
Website *www.mountbrandonhostel.com*
Dorm bed *€16;* **single room** *€25;* **twin room** *€36*

Maintenance & cleanliness	★★★★★
Facilities	★★★☆
Atmosphere & character	★★★★★
Security	★★
Overall rating	★★★★

Stradbally (Straid Baile) & Castlegregory (Caislean Chriare)

These two villages on the north coast of the Dingle Peninsula are situated 10km apart. Castlegregory is a popular windsurfing destination with a beach facing onto Tralee Bay.

Accommodation
Conor Pass Hostel

This small eight-bed hostel offers basic accommodation with a small kitchen/common area. Check in at Tomásin's Bar across the road.
Stradbally, Castlegregory
☎ *(066) 713 9179*
Dorm bed *€13-14*
Credit cards *MC, Visa*
Open *15 Mar-31 Oct*

Maintenance & cleanliness	★★★☆
Facilities	★
Atmosphere & character	★★
Security	★
Overall rating	★★

Fitzgerald's Euro Hostel

This small hostel above a pub and general store has recently been renovated with new floors and a fresh coat of paint. It provides basic accommodation with a good kitchen. Because of renovations that were underway we were not able to see all the facilities and have not given a star rating.

Strand Street, Castlegregory
☎ *(066) 713 9133*
***Dorm bed** €14*
***Credit cards** MC, Visa*

Tarbert (Tairbeart)

Many travellers pass through Tarbert to take the Tarbert-Killimer Car Ferry, which is a handy shortcut to County Clare. Otherwise the main draw for travellers is the 300-year-old Tarbert House.

Coming & Going

Bus Éireann *(website www.buseireann.ie)* runs buses to Ballybunnion, Listowel and Tralee and to Galway via the Cliffs of Moher.

If you're driving you may want to take the 20-minute journey across the Mouth of the Shannon on the Tarbert-Killimer Car Ferry, which cuts 137km off your journey. The ferry departs hourly on the half hour.

Accommodation
Ferry House Hostel

This stone building in the town centre is a clean and well-maintained hostel with a small TV lounge and a good kitchen.

The Square, Tarbert
☎ *(068) 36555*
***Dorm bed** €10; **double/twin room** €34-40*
***Credit cards** MC, Visa*
***Open** 7 Jan-19 Dec*

📺 🇰 🇱

Maintenance & cleanliness	★★★★
Facilities	★
Atmosphere & character	★★★
Security	★★
Overall rating	★★★

Sights
Tarbert House

Dating from 1690, this elegant residence has hosted many notable historical figures including Charlotte Brontë, Winston Churchill, Daniel O'Connor, Benjamin Franklin and Lord Kitchener.

☎ *(068) 36198*
***Admission** €2*
***Open** 10am-noon & 2pm-4pm daily*

County Limerick

Limerick (Luimneach)

This important city boasts an impressive castle and plenty of attractive 18th century Georgian buildings, however its reputation is of a grimy industrial city and it attracts very few visitors.

Practical Information
Tourist Information Centre

Arthurs Quay, Limerick
☎ *(061) 317 522*
Website *www.shannonregiontourism.ie*
***Open** Jan-Apr Mon-Fri 9.30am-5.30pm, Sat 9.30am-1pm; May-Jun Mon-Sat 9.30am-5.30pm; Jul-Aug Mon-Fri 9am-6.30pm, Sat-Sun 9am-6pm; Sep-Oct Mon-Sat 9.30am-5.30pm; Nov-Dec Mon-Fri 9.30am-5.30pm, Sat 9.30am-1pm*

Coming & Going

Limerick is an important transport hub with a busy international airport as well as trains and buses.

AIR

Shannon Airport *(website www.shannonairport.com)* is in Co Clare, about 20 minutes from Limerick city centre. It has direct flights to North America as well as many European destinations.

BusÉireann *(website www.buseireann.ie)* runs direct bus services between Limerick and Shannon Airport.

BUS

Bus Éireann *(website www.buseireann.ie)* has direct bus services to most towns and cities in Ireland including Cork, Dublin, Galway and Waterford.

TRAIN

There are direct trains from Limerick to Ennis and Rosslare Harbour. Change at Limerick Junction for trains to Cork, Dublin and Tralee.

Accommodation

Limerick no longer has a hostel. The closest backpackers' accommodation is at the Jamaica Inn in Sixmilebridge, Co Clare.

Jamaica Inn

This excellent purpose-built hostel is built around a courtyard and designed so the sleeping areas are separated from the noisy common areas. Facilities include a small kitchen and dining area, a restaurant and a cosy common room with a TV, table football and a fireplace. There are also two friendly dogs named Bob and Marley.
Sixmilebridge
☎ *(061) 369 220*
Website www.jamaicainn.ie
***Dorm bed** €15-20;* ***single room** €30-32;* ***double/twin room** €48-50*
***Credit cards** MC, Visa*
***Reception open** 8.30am-10pm daily*

Maintenance & cleanliness	★★★★★
Facilities	★★★☆
Atmosphere & character	★★★★
Security	★★
Overall rating	★★★★

Sights
CITY CENTRE
Hunt Museum

An 18th century customs house houses one of the largest art and antiquity collections in Ireland. The collection includes the Mary Queen of Scots cross, the Leonardo da Vinci horse as well as works by Gauguin, Picasso, Renoir and Yeats.
The Custom House, Rutland Street, Limerick
☎ *(061) 312 833*
Website www.huntmuseum.com
***Admission** €6.50 (€5.25 students)*
***Open** Mon-Sat 10am-5pm; Sun 2pm-5pm*

King John's Castle

This impressive Anglo-Norman castle was built between 1200 and 1210. It offers sweeping views of Limerick and the surrounding countryside and there is also an exhibition with historical exhibits and an audio-visual presentation.
Nicholas Street, Kings Island, Limerick
☎ *(061) 360 788*
Website www.shannonheritage.com/KJC.htm
***Admission** €7.50*
***Open** Jan-Mar 10.30am-4.30pm daily (last entry 3.30pm); Apr-Oct 10am-5.30pm daily (last entry 4.30pm); Nov-Dec 10.30am-4.30pm daily (last entry 3.30pm)*

St Mary's Cathedral

This 12th century cathedral near St John's Castle is noted for its intricate carvings.
Nicholas Street, Kings Island, Limerick
☎ *(061) 416 238*
***Admission** free*
***Open** 9.15am-5pm daily*

NEAR LIMERICK
Bunratty Castle & Folk Park

Bunratty Castle & Folk Park is in Co Clare between Limerick and Shannon Airport. Bunratty was originally a Viking trading camp. Four castles have been built on this site and the present castle was built around 1425 replacing an earlier Norman castle. The castle was extensively renovated during the 1950s and it is now considered Ireland's most authentically complete furnished castle. The adjoining Folk Park is an open-air museum that features elegant Bunratty House as well as a collection of smaller farmhouses, a pub and church that have been set up to depict village life in 19th century Ireland.
Bunratty, Co Clare (13km from Limerick city centre)
☎ *(061) 360 788*
Website www.shannonheritage.com
***Admission** €7.95-10.50*
***Open** Jan-May 9.30am-5.30pm daily (last entry to castle 4pm, last entry to Folk Park 4.45pm); Jun-Aug 9am-6pm daily (last entry to castle 4pm, last entry to Folk Park 4.45pm); Sep-Dec 9.30am-5.30pm daily (last entry to castle 4pm, last entry to Folk Park 4.45pm)*

County Clare

County Clare encompasses much of the area between Galway and Limerick. The county's main attraction is the spectacular Cliffs of Moher.

Ennis (Inis)

County Clare's biggest town is a lovely place that is overlooked by most tourists. It is a bustling town built on the banks of the River Fergus.

Practical Information
Tourist Information Centre
Arthur's Row, Ennis
☎ *(065) 28366*
Website www.shannonregiontourism.ie
Open Jan-Mar Mon-Fri 9.30am-1pm & 2pm-6pm; Apr-Jun Mon-Sat 9.30am-1pm & 2pm-6pm; Jul-Sep 9am-1pm & 2pm-6pm daily; Oct Mon-Sat 9.30am-1pm & 2pm-6pm; Nov-Dec Mon-Fri 9.30am-1pm & 2pm-6pm

INTERNET ACCESS
Pc eireann
37E Lower Market Street, Ennis
☎ *(065) 684 8411*
Open Mon-Sat 9am-7pm

Coming & Going
AIR
Shannon Airport (*website www.shannonairport.com*) is about 20 minutes from Ennis. It has direct flights to North America as well as many European destinations.

Bus Éireann (*website www.buseireann.ie*) runs direct bus services between Ennis and Shannon Airport.

BUS
Bus Éireann (*website www.buseireann.ie*) has direct bus services Limerick and Galway.

TRAIN
There are direct trains from Ennis to Limerick and Rosslare Harbour. Change at Limerick Junction for trains to Cork, Dublin and Tralee.

Accommodation
Abbey Tourist Hostel
This hostel is a little worn around the edges while still offering relatively clean accommodation. It has a big kitchen/dining room and a TV lounge with a piano. It has strange rules such as set times that you can use the kitchen or TV lounge and you can only use the laundry under supervision.
Club Bridge, Harmony Row, Ennis
☎ *(065) 682 2620*
Website www.abbeytourishostel.com
Dorm bed €14-16; single room €25; double room €40
Credit cards MC, Visa
Reception open 7.30am-1.30am; curfew Mon-Wed 1.30am, Thu-Sat 3.30am, Sun 1.30am

TV K L

Maintenance & cleanliness	★★★☆
Facilities	★★☆
Atmosphere & character	★★
Security	★★☆
Overall rating	★★

Lios Rua Hostel
This lovely small hostel is in a farmhouse in the countryside 15km from Ennis. The outside looks a little tired but it is nicely renovated inside. It has a fully equipped kitchen, a cosy TV lounge and nice bathrooms. The location is only really convenient if you're driving.
Lisroe, Kilmaley, Ennis
☎ *(065) 683 9109*
Website www.liosruahostel.com
Dorm bed €12-13; double/twin room €28-30
Open Feb-Oct

🅿 TV K L

Maintenance & cleanliness	★★★★
Facilities	★
Atmosphere & character	★★★★
Security	★
Overall rating	★★★

Sights
Clare Museum
This museum displays artefacts depicting 6000 years of history in County Clare.
Arthur's Row, Ennis
☎ *(065) 682 3382*
Website www.clarelibrary.ie/eolas/claremuseum/
Admission €3.50
Open Jan-May Tue-Sat 9.30am-1pm & 2pm-5.30pm; Jun-Sep 9.30am-5.30pm daily; Oct-Dec Tue-Sat 9.30am-1pm & 2pm-5.30pm

Dromore Wood & Visitor Centre
Dromore Wood is a 400-hectare nature reserve with archaeological and historical relics that include the 17th century O'Brien Castle, plus two ring forts and the sites of Cahermacrea Castle and Killakee Church.

Ruan, Ennis
☎ *(065) 683 7166*
Website *www.heritageireland.ie*
Admission *free*
Dromore Wood open *during daylight hours;* **Visitor Centre open** *mid Jun-mid Sep Mon-Fri 10am-6pm (last entry 5.15pm)*

Ennis Friary
This 13th century Franciscan Friary boasts several sculptures from the 15th and 16th centuries.
Abbey Street, Ennis
☎ *(065) 682 9100*
Website *www.heritageireland.ie*
Admission *€1.50 (75c students)*
Open *Apr-May Tue-Sun 10am-5pm (last entry 4.15pm); Jun-mid Sep 10am-6pm daily (last entry 5.15pm); mid Sep-Oct Tue-Sun 10am-5pm (last entry 4.15pm)*

Lahinch (Leacht Uí Chonchubhair)

In the late 19th century Lahinch developed as a seaside resort and it is now popular with surfers and travellers that use it as a base for visiting the nearby Cliffs of Moher.

Practical Information
Tourist Information Centre
Main Street, Lahinch
☎ *(065) 708 2082*
Open *9am-6pm daily*

Accommodation
Lahinch Hostel
This hostel catering to travellers and surfers has accommodation in clean and comfortable rooms plus a small kitchen and TV lounge.
Main Street, Lahinch
☎ *(065) 708 1040*
Website *www.visitlahinch.com*
Dorm bed *€15;* **double room** *€35*
Reception open *9am-10pm daily*

Maintenance & cleanliness	★★★
Facilities	★★☆
Atmosphere & character	★★★
Security	★★★☆
Overall rating	★★★☆

Liscanor (Lios Ceannúir) & the Cliffs of Moher

The Cliffs of Moher are one of Ireland's most visited sites and Liscanor is one of the closest villages and many travellers stay here. Liscanor's attractions include a ruined castle and O'Brien's Monument, 3km north of town.

Accommodation
Liscanor Village Hostel
The Liscanor Village Hostel is one of Ireland's longest established hostels. Although relatively clean, this hostel shows its age but it has everything you need including a big kitchen and small TV lounge. The friendly owner is a good source of information on the local area.
R478, Liscanor
☎ *(065) 708 1550*
Dorm bed *€12-13;* **double room** *€30-32*
Reception open *8am-1pm & 5pm-midnight*

Maintenance & cleanliness	★★★☆
Facilities	★★☆
Atmosphere & character	★★★★☆
Security	-
Overall rating	★★

Sights
Cliffs of Moher & O'Brien's Tower
Western Ireland's top attraction is the 214m-high Cliffs of Moher, which stretch along 8km of County Clare's coastline with its highest and most impressive point 3km north of Liscanor. O'Brien's Tower, built in 1857 by Cornelius O'Brien, is the best vantage point of the Cliffs affording spectacular views to the Aran Islands and Galway Bay. The Cliffs of Moher is an important bird watching site with over 30,000 breeding pairs of seabirds.
R478, 3km north of Liscanor
☎ *(061) 360 788*
Website *www.shannonheritage.com*
Admission *€1.50 (students free)*
O'Brien's Tower open *Mar-May 9.30am-6pm daily; Jul-Aug 9.30am-8pm daily; Sep-Oct 9.30am-6pm daily;* **visitor centre open** *Jan-May 9.30am-6pm daily; Jun-Aug 9am-6.30pm daily; Sep-Dec 9.30am-6pm daily*

Doolin (Dubh Linn)

This tiny village north of the Cliffs of Moher is world famous for the traditional Irish music that is played in its three pubs. It is a popular destination with backpackers boasting several excellent hostels.

Coming & Going

Buses connect Doolin with the Cliffs of Moher, Dublin, Ennis, Galway and Limerick.

Accommodation
Aille River Hostel

This lovely hostel has a quiet location with a sunny deck with views of the river. There's a small kitchen, a cosy living area with a turf fire and the laundry has free washing machines.

Doolin
☎ *(065) 707 4260*
***Dorm bed** €12-12.50;* ***double room** €28-31;* ***camping** €6*

Maintenance & cleanliness	★★★★½
Facilities	★★½
Atmosphere & character	★★★★★
Security	★
Overall rating	★★★★½

Flanagan's Village Hostel

This hostel on the edge of the village has accommodation in neat and tidy rooms plus a cosy lounge with a turf fire.
☎ *(065) 707 7464*
***Dorm bed** €12.50;* ***double room** €30-33*

Maintenance & cleanliness	★★★★½
Facilities	★★½
Atmosphere & character	★★★★½
Security	★
Overall rating	★★★½

Rainbow Hostel

Rainbow Hostel is a lovingly restored traditional-style house with a small kitchen, a nice dining room and a cosy common room with a turf stove. It is a good place to stay to explore the region as Mattie gives a slide show and free guided walks.

Roadford, Doolin
☎ *(065) 707 4415*
***Website** www.rainbowhostel.com*
***Dorm bed** €12-12.50*
***Credit cards** MC, Visa*

Maintenance & cleanliness	★★★★★
Facilities	★★½
Atmosphere & character	★★★★½
Security	★
Overall rating	★★★★½

Paddy's Doolin Hostel

Paddy's Doolin Hostel is a big place that offers basic accommodation with shared facilities that include a big kitchen and TV lounge. The décor feels a little tired and the no alcohol rule combines to dampen the atmosphere. Some accommodation is in the building across the road, which has en suites in all rooms and the extra building makes it possible to separate groups from independent travellers.

Fisher Street, Doolin
☎ *(065) 707 4421*
***Website** www.kingsway.ie/doolinhostel/*
***Dorm bed** €12.50-16;* ***double room** €36*
***Credit cards** MC, Visa*
***Reception open** 8am-9pm daily*

Maintenance & cleanliness	★★★
Facilities	★★½
Atmosphere & character	★★½
Security	★★
Overall rating	★★

Connaught

The Connaught region in western Ireland includes the much-visited city of Galway as well as County Galway's Connemara region, the historic village of Cong, the lively towns of Westport and Sligo and several outlying islands including the Aran Islands.

County Galway

This large county offers a variety of attractions, which include vibrant Galway City, the scenic Connemara region and the Aran Islands.

Galway (Gaillimh)

Galway is the republic's third largest city and one of Europe's fastest growing cities.

It is a lively place with a charming old centre and a good selection of pubs, clubs and live music venues.

Practical Information
Galway Tourist Information Centre
Forster Street, Galway
☎ *(091) 537 7000*
Open *Jan-Apr Mon-Fri 9am-5.45pm, Sat 9am-12.45pm, Sun 9am-5.45pm; May-Jun 9am-5.45pm daily; Jul-Aug 9.30am-7.45pm daily; Sep 9am-5.45pm daily; Oct-Dec Mon-Fri 9am-5.45pm, Sat 9am-12.45pm, Sun 9am-5.45pm*

Salthill Tourist Information Centre
Seapoint Promenade, Salthill
☎ *(091) 520 500*
Open *May-Sep 9am-5.45pm daily*

LAUNDRY
Prospect Hill Launderette
Prospect Hill, Galway
Open *Jan-May Mon-Sat 8.30am-6pm; Jun-Aug Mon-Fri 8.30am-8.30pm; Sep-Dec Mon-Sat 8.30am-6pm*

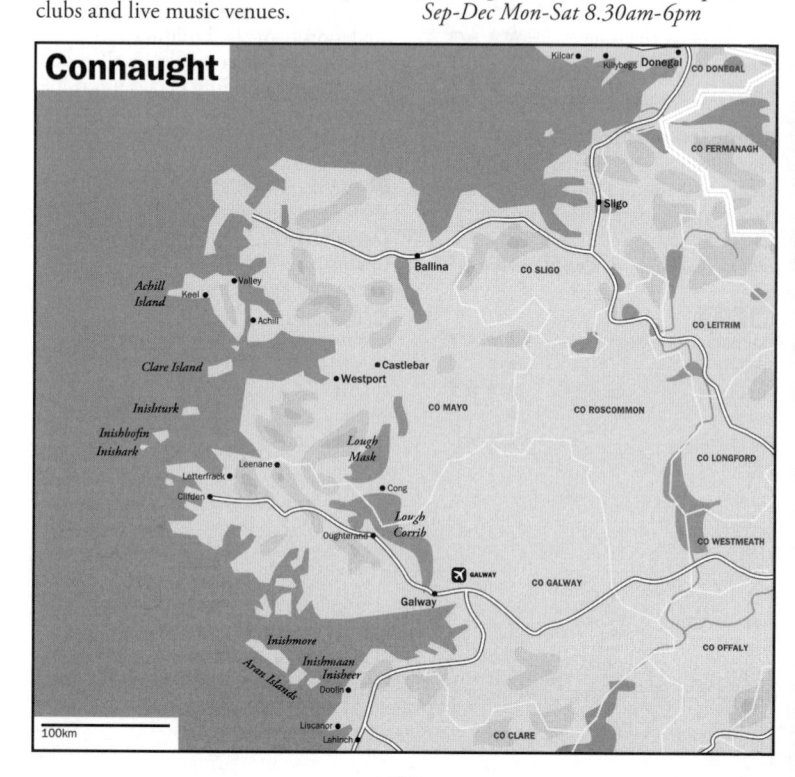

Coming & Going
AIR
Galway Airport *(website www.galwayairport.com)* is in Carnmore, 6km from the city centre. Aer Arann *(website www.aerarann.ie)* and British Airways *(website www.ba.com)* have flights from Galway to Birmingham, Dublin, Edinburgh, Glasgow, London, Lorient and Manchester.

Aer Arann Islands *(website www.aerarannislands.ie)* flies to the Aran Islands from Connemara Regional Airport, which is about a 50 minute drive from Galway. An airport shuttle bus runs to Connemara Airport from Galway city centre, departing from Kinlay House Hostel on the corner of Merchant's Road and Victoria Place.

Citylink (☎ *(091) 564 163; website www.citylink.ie)* run four daily bus services between Galway and Shannon Airport near Limerick.

BUS
Bus Éireann *(website www.buseireann.ie)* runs buses to most destinations throughout Ireland.

Citylink (☎ *(091) 564 163; website www.citylink.ie)* operates an express bus service between Galway and Dublin with one-way tickets costing €12. BusNestor (☎ *(091) 797 484 or 1800 42 42 48)* is another bus company running buses between Galway and Dublin. Both BusNestor and Citylink buses have stops at Dublin's city centre and Dublin Airport.

Michael Nee Coaches (☎ *(095) 34682)* runs buses between Galway and Connemara. Buses leave from Forster Street near the train station and tourist information centre and cost €9 one-way or €12 return.

TRAIN
Galway's train station is near Eyre Square with direct trains to Dublin. The train journey from Galway to Dublin takes around three hours.

Accommodation
Archview Hostel
Archview is surprisingly disappointing compared to the high standard set by Galway's other hostels. It has limited kitchen facilities and a TV lounge with old ratty sofas and was dirty and in need of maintenance when we visited. However it is the cheapest place in town and is centrally located, making it a great value place to stay if you don't mind sleeping in squalor.
1 Upper Dominick Street, Galway
☎ *(091) 586 661*
Dorm bed *€10*
📺 🅚 🅛

Maintenance & cleanliness	★
Facilities	★
Atmosphere & character	★★
Security	★½
Overall rating	★½

Barnacles
Barnacles has an unbeatable location on a pedestrian mall in the city centre. It's a very good hostel and all the rooms have en suite bathrooms and it also features a fully equipped kitchen and a nice TV lounge with an open fire.
Quay Street House, 10 Quay Street, Galway
☎ *(091) 568 644*
Website *www.barnacles.ie*
Dorm bed *€12-24 (€10.80-21.60 ISIC, VIP);* **double/twin room** *€49-57 (€44.10-51.30 ISIC, VIP); prices include breakfast*
Credit cards *MC, Visa*
Reception open *8am-11.30pm daily; 24 hour check in available*
📺 🅚 🅛

Maintenance & cleanliness	★★★★
Facilities	★★
Atmosphere & character	★★★
Security	★★★★
Overall rating	★★★★½

Eyre Square Hostel
This hostel offers simple accommodation with a common area that includes a small kitchen and TV lounge. It is in the city centre above a sandwich bar and pet shop.
35 Eyre Street, Galway
☎ *(091) 568 432*
Website *www.eyresquarehostel.com*
Dorm bed *€13-17*
Credit cards *MC, Visa*

Maintenance & cleanliness	★★★½
Facilities	★★½
Atmosphere & character	★★★
Security	★★
Overall rating	★★★½

Galway Hostel

This hostel near the train/bus station has a good atmosphere and the usual facilities such as a small kitchen and a TV lounge with Internet access. The dorms are simple but clean and there are lots of historic photos of Galway on the walls.
Station Road, Galway
☎ *(091) 566 959*
Dorm bed *€13-15; price includes breakfast*
Reception open *24 hours*
📺 🇰

Maintenance & cleanliness	★★★½
Facilities	★
Atmosphere & character	★★★★½
Security	★★★
Overall rating	★★★

Kinlay House

This big hostel near Eyre Square and the bus/train station has extensive common areas that include a TV lounge, two small kitchens, a dining area with a medieval mural and an area with Internet access and table football. The biggest dorm has eight beds and around half the rooms have en suite bathrooms.
Corner Merchant's Road & Victoria Place, Galway
☎ *(091) 565 244*
Website *www.kinlayhouse.ie*
Dorm bed *€15-25;* **double/twin room** *€46-54; price includes breakfast*
Credit cards *MC, Visa*
Reception open *24 hours*
📺 🇰

Maintenance & cleanliness	★★★½
Facilities	★★½
Atmosphere & character	★★★★½
Security	★★★★½
Overall rating	★★★

Salmon Weir Hostel

This small hostel has the best social atmosphere of Galway's hostels but facilities are limited to the standard TV lounge, Internet access and kitchen and it's not quite as well maintained as some of the city's flashier hostels.
3 St Vincent Avenue, Galway
☎ *(091) 561 133*
Website *www.salmonweirhostel.com*

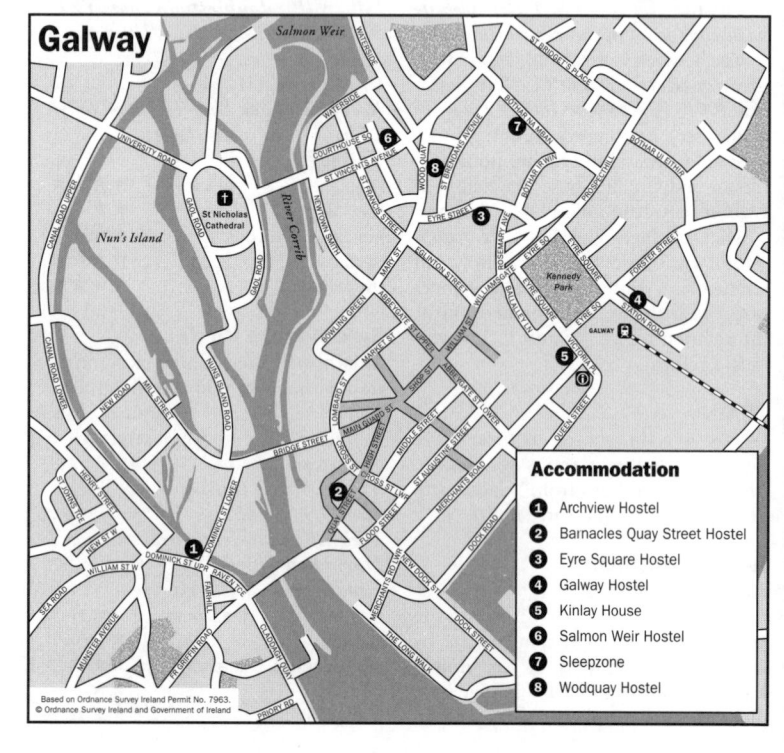

Accommodation

1. Archview Hostel
2. Barnacles Quay Street Hostel
3. Eyre Square Hostel
4. Galway Hostel
5. Kinlay House
6. Salmon Weir Hostel
7. Sleepzone
8. Wodquay Hostel

Dorm bed** €11-16;* ***double/twin room *€36-40*
Reception open** 8am-3am;* ***curfew *3am*
📺 🅺

Maintenance & cleanliness	★★★☆
Facilities	★
Atmosphere & character	★★★★
Security	★★☆
Overall rating	★★★☆

Sleepzone

Sleepzone is a large hostel with top quality fittings. Accommodation is in clean dorms with en suites in most rooms. Other facilities include a good TV lounge, a quiet reading room, an outdoor terrace and brilliant Internet access including free WiFi access. The corporate style ambience coupled with the no alcohol rule may not suit some people but if you're looking for somewhere clean and secure then Sleepzone is a good choice.

Bóthar na mBan, Woodquay, Galway
☎ *(091) 566 999*
Website *www.sleepzone.ie*
Bed in an eight-bed dorm *€13-18;* ***bed in a six-bed dorm*** *€15-20;* ***bed in a four-bed dorm*** *€18-22;* ***single room*** *€30-50;* ***double/twin room*** *€45-60; prices include breakfast*
Credit cards *MC, Visa*
Reception open *24 hours*
🏠 📺 🅺 🅻 🅽

Maintenance & cleanliness	★★★★★
Facilities	★★
Atmosphere & character	★
Security	★★★★☆
Overall rating	★★★★☆

Woodquay Hostel

Woodquay is a nice clean hostel with accommodation in tidy rooms with new bunk beds and new mattresses. Common areas include a TV lounge and a kitchen with a good dining room.

23-24 Woodquay, Galway
☎ *(091) 562 2618*
Dorm bed *€15-20*
Reception open *8am-11pm daily;* ***curfew*** *3am*
📺 🅺 🅽

Maintenance & cleanliness	★★★★
Facilities	★
Atmosphere & character	-
Security	★★
Overall rating	★★

Sights

Cathedral of Our Lady Assumed into Heaven

This relatively new cathedral dates from 1965 and was built on the site of a notorious prison. The cathedral features a large copper domed roof and was constructed mostly from local materials. Recitals are held in the cathedral during summer.

Gaol Road, Galway
Website *www.galwaycathedral.org*
Concerts *€8*
Open *Mon-Fri 9am-6pm*

Galway Altantaquaria

Ireland's largest aquarium is home to a large variety of marine life including salmon, stingrays and the angel shark.

The Promenade, Toft Park, Salthill
☎ *(091) 585 100*
Website *http://gofree.indigo.ie/~mbjg/*
Admission *€7 (€5 students)*
Open *10am-6pm daily*

Galway City Museum

This museum features exhibits relating to Galway's history including displays about Galway's fishing industry as well as exhibits about Galway's medieval heritage. The museum is housed within the Spanish Arch, which was built in 1584 as an extension of Galway's city walls.

Fishmarket, Spanish Arch, Galway
Admission *€2 (€1 students)*
Open *10am-1pm & 2pm-5pm daily*

Lynch's Castle

Lynch's Castle is regarded as one of Ireland's best examples of a town castle, which were elegant mansions built for wealthy merchants during the 15th and 16th centuries. Although it now houses a branch of the AIB Bank, the building dating from 1320 was originally home to the powerful Lynch family that ruled Galway between the 13th and 18th centuries. There is a small exhibition at the front of the building.

Corner Abbeygate & Shop Streets, Galway
☎ *(091) 567041*
Admission *free*
Open *Mon-Wed 10am-4pm, Thu 10am-5pm, Fri 10am-4pm*

Nora Barnacle House
James Joyce's wife, Nora Barnacle was the inspiration for the character Molly Bloom in Joyce's famous novel *Ulysees*. Nora Barnacle's House in Galway's Bowling Green neighbourhood has now been turned into a small museum.
8 Bowling Green, Galway
☎ *(091) 564 743*
Admission *€2.50*
Open *mid May-mid Sep Wed-Fri 10am-1pm & 2pm-5pm*

St Nicholas Church
St Nicholas Church was originally built by the Lynch family in 1320 but has been rebuilt several times over the last 600 years. The church is noted for its intricate medieval detail that includes carved gargoyles and mermaids and it is believed that Christopher Columbus visited the church before setting sail for America in 1492.
Market Street, Galway
Admission *free*
Open *9am-5.45pm daily*

Aran Islands (Oileán Árann)

The three Aran Islands in Galway Bay are home to a rugged landscape and several important Celtic archaeological sites. Due to the islands' isolation, traditional Irish language and culture has been preserved and for many travellers this is the main reason for visiting the Aran Islands.

Coming & Going
AIR
Aer Arann *(website www.aerarann islands.ie)* offers the quickest way of getting to the Aran Islands with flights from Connemara Regional Airport in Inveran, west of Galway, to all three islands taking less than 10 minutes. The return airfare to any island from Connemara Airport is €44 (€37 students). The airfare includes the cost of the airport shuttle bus from Galway city centre, which departs from Kinlay House Hostel on the corner of Merchant's Road and Victoria Place.

FERRY
There are three ferry companies that sail to the Aran Islands from either Doolin or Rossaveal on the mainland.
   Aran Islands Fast Ferries *(☎ (065) 707 4550; website www.aranislands fastferries.com)* sails between Doolin and Inishere. The return fare is €20.
   Island Ferries *(☎ (091) 568 903; website www.aranislandferries.com)* sails to all three islands from Rossaveal. The return fare is €19 return (€15 students).
   The Queen of Aran II *(☎ (091) 566 535; website www.queenofaran2.com)* sails between Rossaveal and Inishmore. The return fare is €19 (€14 students).
   Aran Islands Fast Ferries and Island Ferries also operate ferry services that connect the three islands with one-way fares costing around €10.
   Rossaveal is about a 45-minute drive from Galway and most ferry companies operate shuttle buses. The ferry trip between Rossaveal and Inishmore takes around 30-40 minutes.

Inishere (Inis Oirr)

Inishere is the smaller of the three Aran Islands and at only 8km from Doolin, it is the closest island to the mainland. O'Brien's Castle is the main attraction on Inishere.

Accommodation
Bru Radharc Na Mara Hostel
This small hostel near the ferry jetty offers lovely views.
West Village, Inishere
☎ *(099) 75024*
Dorm bed *€13*
Open *Mar-Oct*
L

Inishmaan (Inis Meáin)

The middle island is a rugged place that has been immortalised in John M Synge's *Riders to the Sea* and Robert Flaherty's film, *Man of Aran*.

Inishmore (Inish Mór)

Inishmore's attractions include Dún Aonghasa and Ionad Árainn – Aran Heritage Centre.

Accommodation
Mainistir House
This popular hostel offers great sea views from its cosy lounge room.
Main Road, Inishmore
☎ *(099) 61169*
***Dorm bed** €12;* ***single room** €20*

Sights
Dún Aonghasa
This large stone fort perched on a cliff overlooking the ocean dates from prehistoric times.
Kilmurvey, Inishmore
☎ *(099) 61008*
***Website** www.heritageireland.ie*
***Admission** €2 (€1 students)*
***Open** Jan-Feb 10am-4pm daily; Mar-Oct 10am-6pm daily; Nov-Dec 10am-4pm daily*

Ionad Árainn – Aran Heritage Centre
The Aran Heritage Centre depicts over 2000 years of history on the Aran Islands through displays of photographs, maps and charts. Robert Flaherty's 1934 film, *Man of Aran* is shown here daily.
Kilronan, Inishmore
☎ *(099) 61355*
***Website** www.visitaranislands.com*
***Admission** centre only €3.50 (€3 students); centre & film €5.50 (€5 students)*
***Open** Apr-May 11am-5pm daily; Jun-Aug 10am-7pm daily; Sep-Oct 11am-5pm daily*

Clifden (An Clochán)
This attractive small town is considered the main hub of the sparsely populated Connemara region.

Practical Information
Tourist Information Centre
Galway Road, Clifden
☎ *(095) 21163*
***Website** www.connemara-tourism.org*
***Open** Jun Mon-Sat 10am-6pm daily; Jul-Aug Mon-Sat 9am-6pm, Sun noon-4pm*

Coming & Going
Bus Éireann *(website www.buseireann.ie)* runs buses to Galway and during summer also has buses to Leenane and Westport. Bus Éireann buses stop next to the library on Market Street.

Michael Nee Coaches *(☎ (095) 34682)* runs buses between Galway and Clifden. Buses leave from the courthouse and the trip to Galway costs €9 one-way or €12 return.

Accommodation
Brookside Hostel
This concrete building, a couple of minutes walk to the town centre, has clean accommodation but it feels dated with old lino floors and old furnishings and it could be spruced up a bit. Facilities include a kitchen and dining area with a TV. Richard, the manager, has a lot of knowledge about the Connemara region.
Fairgreen, Clifden
☎ *(095) 21812*
***Dorm bed** €11.50;* ***double room** €30*
***Open** Mar-Oct*
🛏 📺 Ⓚ Ⓛ

Maintenance & cleanliness	★★★½
Facilities	★★½
Atmosphere & character	★★
Security	★★½
Overall rating	★★

Clifden Town Hostel
Clifden Town Hostel is a wonderful hostel with a nice cosy lounge area and two small kitchens. It is a clean and comfortable place to stay and there are lovely river views from some rooms. They sometimes close in winter so it's best to call ahead if you're travelling between November and March.
Market Street, Clifden
☎ *(095) 21076*
***Website** www.clifdentownhostel.com*
***Dorm bed** €13-15;* ***double/twin room** €32-34*
***Reception open** 8am-midnight*
Ⓚ

Maintenance & cleanliness	★★★★½
Facilities	★
Atmosphere & character	★★★★½
Security	★★½
Overall rating	★★★

Inishbofin (Inish Bó Finne)
This small island 11km off the Connemara coast has lovely coastal scenery.

Coming & Going
The Inishboffin ferry *(website www.inishbofinferry.com)* sails between Inishbofin and Cleggan (about 16km northwest of Clifden). The return fare costs €15.

Accommodation
Inishbofin Island Hostel
This former farmhouse features a large conservatory with lovely views of the Connemara coastline plus a cosy common room and a small kitchen.
Inishbofin
☎ *(095) 45855*
Website *www.inishbofin-hostel.ie*
Dorm bed *€10-12;* **double/twin room** *€30-36*
Open *Apr-Sep*
♿ 🇰 🇱

Letterfrack (Leitir Fraic)
This small village was established by a Quaker couple from Yorkshire who came to Connemara to contribute to post-famine relief. There is little to do here other than drink in the local pubs but many people come here for the local hostel and its welcoming atmosphere.

Coming & Going
Bus Éireann *(website www.buseireann.ie)* runs buses to Clifden and Galway and during summer also has buses to Leenane and Westport.

Accommodation
Old Monastery House
The Old Monastery is in a big old stone house with loads of character that is cluttered with various bits of artwork and other nik naks. When we visited it was undergoing extensive renovation, which should see an improvement, but it is still not the sort of place that would suit everyone. Facilities include a kitchen and several lounges with open fires.
Letterfrack
☎ *(095) 41132*
Dorm bed *€12-13;* **double/twin room** *€30-32; prices include breakfast*
Credit cards *MC, Visa*
🚗 ♿ 🇰 🇱 ✈

Maintenance & cleanliness	★★
Facilities	★
Atmosphere & character	★★★★★
Security	-
Overall rating	★★

Connemara National Park
This 2000-hectare national park near Letterfrack is noted for its mountains, bogs, and heaths and it is home to Connemara ponies and red deer.

The park's visitor centre features exhibitions and an audio-visual presentation.

Leenane (An Líonán)
There's not much to Leenane, but it does enjoy a lovely setting on Killary Harbour and Killary Fjord – Ireland's only fjord – is nearby.

Coming & Going
During summer Bus Éireann *(website www.buseireann.ie)* runs buses to Clifden and Galway and Westport.

Accommodation
K2 – the Killary Centre
K2 – the Killary Centre is a big purpose-built centre that caters to a lot of groups that come for adventure activities that are run from here. It has nice rooms with en suite facilities and there's a good TV lounge with an open fire and a café with a picturesque view of Killary Harbour. It is about a four-minute drive west of Leenane village.
N59, Leenane
☎ *(095) 43411*
Website *www.killary.com*
Dorm bed *€16-22;* **single room** *€28;* **double/twin room** *€56; prices include breakfast*
Credit cards *MC, Visa*
Reception open *Mon-Fri 9am-11pm, Sat 8am-9pm, Sun 8am-5pm*
🚗 📺

Maintenance & cleanliness	★★★★★
Facilities	★★
Atmosphere & character	★★
Security	★★½
Overall rating	★★★

Activities
The Killary Centre (☎ *(095) 43411; website www.killary.com*) runs a variety of adventure activities that include rock climbing, kayaking, mountain biking, sailing and windsurfing.

County Mayo
Largely composed of rolling hills, boggy plains and the odd mountain, County Mayo is known for its rugged coastline and vibrant towns like Westport. However the most famous attraction is Croagh Patrick, the mountain where St Patrick is believed to have fasted in 441.

Cong (Conga)
This small village is set on an island on the Cong River that runs between Lough Corrib and Lough Mask.

The classic film *the Quiet Man*, starring John Wayne and Maureen O'Hara, was shot here in 1951 and ever since it has attracted movie buffs that come here to visit scenes from the film. However Cong is surrounded by historic and prehistoric monuments, which indicate that it has a lot more to offer than a few film locations.

The village centre features the medieval Cong Abbey and the ruins of the 12th century Monks Fishing House. Attractions in the surrounding countryside include Ashford Castle as well as Neolithic tombs and stone circles.

Practical Information
Tourist Information Centre
Abbey Street, Cong
☎ *(092) 46542*
Website *www.visitmayo.com*
Open *Mar-Nov 10am-1pm & 2pm-6pm daily*

Accommodation
Cong Youth Hostel
Cong's youth hostel is a big place that also incorporates a caravan park. It has nice accommodation in neat and tidy rooms, many of which have en suite bathrooms (nicer than the shared bathrooms). Although the rooms are quite nice, the common areas feel institutional with the sort of furniture you would expect to find in a school. Facilities include a kitchen and large dining area, a huge barbecue area and an impressive mini cinema with a big screen that shows *the Quiet Man* every night at 11pm. The helpful and enthusiastic owners have extensive local knowledge.
Lisloughrey, Quay Road, Cong
☎ *(092) (094) 954 6089*
Website *www.quietman-cong.com*
Dorm bed *€15 (€13 HI/An Óige); double room €32*
Credit cards *MC, Visa*
Reception open *8.30am-8.30pm daily*

Maintenance & cleanliness	★★★½
Facilities	★★
Atmosphere & character	★★★
Security	★★
Overall rating	★★★

Courtyard Hostel
This rustic farm hostel has very basic accommodation and needs a lot of maintenance to bring it up to the standard of other hostels, but there are some travellers who love this sort of place. It is in Cross, several kilometres east of Cong.
Garracloon Lodge, Cross
☎ *(092) 46203*
Dorm bed *€10*

Maintenance & cleanliness	★★
Facilities	★
Atmosphere & character	★★★
Security	★
Overall rating	★★

Quiet Man Hostel
The Quiet Man is right in the town centre and has accommodation in small dormitories with TVs in all rooms and en suite bathrooms in most rooms. The hostel has an institutional feel to it and the TVs in the rooms keep people from mingling in the common area and it appears that there are many long-term guests who aren't backpackers, which doesn't help either the atmosphere or the security in this hostel.
Abbey Street, Cong
☎ *(094) 954 6511*
Website *www.quietman-cong.com*
Dorm bed *€14*

*Reception open 7am-11.30am &
6.30pm-midnight*

🚗 📺 🅺

Maintenance & cleanliness	★★★☆
Facilities	★
Atmosphere & character	★☆
Security	★
Overall rating	★★☆

Sights
Ashford Castle
Between 1852 and 1939 Ashford Castle was home to the heirs of the Guinness empire however it is now a luxury hotel and the most backpackers can see is its exterior while strolling around its gardens.

Cong Abbey
This important early Christian monument dates from the 12th century and during its turbulent history the Vikings, Normans and English have ransacked it.
Abbey Street, Cong
Admission *free*
Always open

Monks Fishing House
The ruins of this 12th century structure sit over the river and feature a hole in the floor where monks would sit and fish.
Admission *free*
Always open

Quiet Man Cottage Museum
This museum recreates the film set of *the Quiet Man* with the ground floor of the cottage designed as a replica of the "White-o-Mornin" cottage.
Circular Road, Cong
☎ *(094) 954 6089*
Website *www.quietman-cong.com/museum.htm*
Admission *€3.75*
Open *10am-5pm daily*

Westport (Cathair na Mart)

This small, but bustling, town is home to some good pubs but most people visit for easy access to Croagh Patrick, which is only 8km from here.

Practical Information
Tourist Information Centre
James Street, Westport
☎ *(098) 25711*
Website *www.irelandwest.ie*
Open *Apr-Jun Mon-Sat 9am-5.45pm;
Jul-Aug Mon-Sat 9am-6.45pm, Sun 10am-6pm; Sep-Oct Mon-Sat 9am-5.45pm*

Coming & Going
BUS
Bus Éireann *(website www.buseireann.ie)* has buses to Achill Island, Ballina, Dublin and Galway. Buses leave from Mill Street.

TRAIN
There is a direct train service between Westport and Dublin. The train station is on Altamont Street.

Accommodation
Abbeywood House
This small hostel behind a school opposite the Maxol service station on Newport Road has a small kitchen with an open fire and a TV lounge with Internet access. The biggest dorm has 10 beds but most are smaller. The beds and mattresses are new but other furnishings are much older.
Newport Road, Wesport
☎ *(098) 25496*
Website *www.abbeywoodhouse.com*
Dorm bed *€16-20;* ***double/twin room*** *€48; prices include breakfast*
Credit cards *MC, Visa*
Reception open *7.30am-11.30pm daily*

🚗 📺 🅺 🅻

Maintenance & cleanliness	★★★★☆
Facilities	★★
Atmosphere & character	★★★
Security	★★☆
Overall rating	★★★

The Old Mill
The Old Mill is a good hostel in a former whiskey distillery next to the tourist information centre. The old stone building has a common area that comprises a kitchen and lounge and upstairs is accommodation in big 18-bed dorms. Apart from the big dormitories, this is an excellent hostel that is clean and well maintained.

James Street, Westport
☎ *(098) 27045*
Website *www.oldmill-hostel.com*
Dorm bed *€14-15*
Credit cards *Amex, MC, Visa*
♿ 🄺 🄻

Maintenance & cleanliness	★★★★⯪
Facilities	★⯪
Atmosphere & character	★★★★
Security	★
Overall rating	★★★

Sights
Clew Bay Heritage Centre
This 19th century stone building features displays about the history of Westport.
The Quay, Westport
☎ *(098) 26852*
Website *www.museumsofmayo.com/clewbay.htm*
Admission *€3*
Open *Apr-May Mon-Fri 10am-2pm; Jun Mon-Fri 10am-5pm; Jul-Aug Mon-Fri 10am-5pm, Sun 3pm-5pm; Sep Mon-Fri 10am-5pm; Oct Mon-Fri 10am-2pm*

Croagh Patrick
Located 8km from Westport, this 765m high mountain – known as the Reek – is closely linked to St Patrick. Many believe that in 441 St Patrick fasted on the mountain for forty days and each year on Reek Sunday (the last Sunday in July) over 25,000 pilgrims visit the Reek.

Many travellers climb to the summit for spectacular views of the surrounding countryside. It takes two hours to climb to the top and another one and a half hours to come back down.

Croagh Patrick Information Centre
This information centre at the foot of Croagh Patrick has exhibits about the mountain and its historical and cultural significance. Anyone contemplating climbing Croagh Patrick is advised to visit the centre first.
Teach na Miasa, Murrisk
☎ *(098) 64114*
Website *www.croagh-patrick.com*
Admission *free*
Open *17 Mar-May 10am-6pm daily; Jun-Aug 10am-7pm daily; Sep-Oct 11am-5pm daily*

Westport Heritage Centre
The Westport Heritage Centre is located inside the tourist information centre and features exhibits relating to Croagh Patrick and the history of Westport.
James Street, Westport
☎ *(098) 25711*

Achill Island
(Acaill Oileán)

Achill Island is a relatively accessible place as a bridge connects it with the Corraun Peninsula. The island has some nice scenery but the settlements on the island feel a little drab.

Practical Information
Achill Tourist Information Centre
R319, Cashel, Achill Island
☎ *(098) 47353*
Website *www.visitchill.com*
Open *Mon-Fri 10am-5pm*

Coming & Going
Bus Éireann *(**website** www.buseireann.ie)* runs buses to Achill Island from Westport and Galway, however services aren't very frequent and many travellers rely mostly on hitching.

Accommodation
Railway Hostel
This hostel is in a former train station on the mainland across the bridge from Achill Island. It has the usual kitchen and laundry plus a common room with an open fire.
Polrany, Achill Sound
☎ *(098) 45187*
Dorm bed *€10*
🄺 🄻

Rich View Hostel
Rich View Hostel is a small 16-bed hostel that has basic accommodation in small dorms plus a small lounge with an open fire and a kitchen that is limited to a couple of hobs, a microwave and a toaster.
R319, Upper Keel, Achill Island
☎ *(098) 43462*
Dorm bed *€10;* ***double/twin room*** *€26*
🅿 🄺 🐾

Maintenance & cleanliness	★★
Facilities	★
Atmosphere & character	★★★
Security	-
Overall rating	★★½

The Valley House Hostel
The Valley House is a big old mansion that features a comfortable sitting room with a TV, Internet access and an open fire; a big dining room with a grand piano and another fireplace; a small fully equipped kitchen and a courtyard with barbecues and a cosy pub with a pool table and a good craic. The dorms are simple but neat and tidy with new mattresses and the biggest dorms have 10 beds. The hostel has an atmosphere of faded elegance.
The Valley, Achill Island
☎ *(098) 47204*
Website *www.valley-house.com*
Dorm bed *€13;* ***double/twin room*** *€32*
Credit cards MC, Visa

Maintenance & cleanliness	★★★½
Facilities	★★½
Atmosphere & character	★★★★
Security	★
Overall rating	★★★½

Ballina (Béal an Átha)
Mayo's largest town is a vibrant place with some excellent pubs. It is renowned throughout Ireland for its fishing but the town doesn't attract many backpackers.

Practical Information
Tourist Information Centre
Cathedral Road, Ballina
☎ *(096) 70848*
Website *www.ballina.ie*
Open *May Mon-Sat 10am-1pm & 2pm-5.30pm; Jun-Aug 10am-5.30pm daily; Sep Mon-Sat 10am-1pm & 2pm-5.30pm*

Coming & Going
BUS
Bus Éireann *(website www.buseireann.ie)* has buses to Donegal, Dublin, Sligo and Donegal. Buses stop on Kevin Barry Street near the train station.

TRAIN
Ballina lies at the end of the train line linking it with Dublin. Change at Manulla Junction for trains to Westport.

Accommodation
Blind Brook Hostel
The small hostel, 3km outside Ballina, features a cosy TV lounge with an open fire, plus extensive facilities that include a tennis court, football pitch, a driving range and a golf course.
Sligo Road, Ballina
☎ *(096) 72939*
Website *www.blindbrook.net*
Dorm bed *€13-16*

County Sligo
County Sligo offers a varied landscape that includes mountains, lakes and coastline and it is synonymous with YB Yeats. Most travellers visit only one place in the county – Sligo Town.

Sligo (Sligeach)
The largest town in northwest Ireland is a busy commercial centre with a good pub scene.

Practical Information
Tourist Information Centre
Aras Reddan, Temple Street, Sligo
☎ *(071) 916 1201*
Website *www.irelandnorthwest.ie*
Open *Jan-May Mon-Fri 9am-5pm; Jun-Aug Mon-Sat 9am-7pm, Sun 10am-6pm; Oct-Dec Mon-Fri 9am-5pm*

INTERNET ACCESS
Cygo Internet Café
19 O'Connell Street, Sligo
☎ *(071) 40082*
Open *Mon-Thu 10am-10pm, Fri-Sat 10am-7pm*

Coming & Going
AIR
Sligo Airport *(website www.sligoairport.com)* is on Strandhill Road, 8km from the town centre. Aer Arann *(website www.aerarann.com)* operates flights between Sligo and Dublin.

BUS
Bus Éireann *(website www.buseireann.ie)* has buses from Sligo to Derry, Donegal, Dublin, Galway and Letterkenny. Buses stop outside the train station on Lord Edward Street.

TRAIN
There are direct trains to Dublin from the station on Lord Edward Street.

Accommodation
Eden Hill Hostel
This hostel is near the Esso service station on Pearse Road about a 20-minute walk south of the town centre. It is a big Victorian house with a cosy TV lounge, a fully equipped kitchen and a nice dining area with a fireplace. The biggest dorm has 10 beds.
Ashbrooke, Pearce Road, Marymount, Sligo
☎ *(071) 914 3204*
***Dorm bed** €14; **double/twin room** €37*
***Credit cards** MC, Visa*
***Reception open** 8am-10pm daily*

Maintenance & cleanliness	★★★
Facilities	★★
Atmosphere & character	★★★★
Security	★★
Overall rating	★★★

Harbour House
Harbour House was built in the 1880s for Sligo's harbour master. It is a clean and well-appointed hostel that has a sitting room, dining area and a small but fully equipped kitchen. All the rooms have en suite amenities and most have TVs. The hostel has a brilliant bed to shower/toilet ratio of 3:1.
Finisklin Road, Sligo
☎ *(071) 917 1547*
Website *www.harbourhousehostel.com*
***Dorm bed** €18; **single room** €25;*
***double/twin room** €40-44*
***Credit cards** Diners, MC, Visa*
***Reception open** 8.30am-10.30pm daily; late check in with prior arrangement*

Maintenance & cleanliness	★★★★
Facilities	★★
Atmosphere & character	★★
Security	★★★
Overall rating	★★★

Strandhill Lodge & Hostel
Strandhill Lodge and Hostel is near the beach in Strandhill, 5km from the centre of Sligo and close to Sligo Airport. It is a neat and tidy place that is popular with surfers. It has a small kitchen and dining room and a cosy TV lounge. It is a good option if you are driving or if you like to fall asleep to the sound of the surf.
Shore Road, Strandhill, Sligo
☎ *(071) 68313*
Website *www.strandhillaccommodation.com/hostel.htm*
***Dorm bed** €15; **double/twin room** €30-40*

Maintenance & cleanliness	★★★★
Facilities	★★
Atmosphere & character	★★
Security	★★
Overall rating	★★★

White House Hostel
The White House Hostel is comprised of two houses (a white one and a brown one) with around 40 beds between the two. Each house has a small but fully equipped kitchen and a cosy lounge and accommodation in clean but simple dorms. The biggest dorm has eight beds.
Markievicz Road, Sligo
☎ *(071) 914 5160*
***Dorm bed** €12.50*
***Reception open** 8am-10pm daily*

Maintenance & cleanliness	★★★
Facilities	★
Atmosphere & character	★★★★
Security	★
Overall rating	★★

Sights
Carrowmore Megalithic Cemetary
Featuring over 60 tombs, Carrowmore Megalithic Cemetary (5km from Sligo) is one of Europe's most important megalithic sites.
N59, Carrowmore
☎ *(071) 916 1534*
Website *www.heritageireland.ie*
***Admission** €2*
***Open** Easter-Oct 10am-5.15pm daily (last entry 4.30pm)*

Model Arts & Niland Gallery
This art museum displays an excellent collection of Irish art including works by Paul Henry, Estella Solomons as well as John and Jack B Yeats.
The Mall, Sligo
☎ *(071) 914 1405*
Admission *free*
Open *Tue-Sat 10am-5.30pm, Sun 11am-4pm*

Sligo Abbey
The Abbey was built in 1252 as a Dominican Friary but was burnt down in 1414 and destroyed again during the 1641 rebellion. It is noted for its carved Gothic and Renaissance tomb sculpture and its sculptured 15th century high altar.
Abbey Street, Sligo
☎ *(071) 914 6406*
Website *www.heritageireland.ie*
Admission *€2*
Open *10am-6pm daily*

Sligo County Museum
This museum has exhibits relating to local history including a collection of Yeats artefacts and memorabilia.
Sligo County Library, Stephen Street, Sligo
☎ *(071) 914 1623*
Admission *free*
Open *Jan-May Tue-Sat 2pm-4.50pm; Jun-Sep Tue-Sat 10am-noon & 2pm-4.50pm; Oct-Dec Tue-Sat 2pm-4.50pm*

Yeats Memorial Building
This 19th century brick building is home to the Yeats Society and it contains an art gallery and an exhibition about the life of WB Yeats.
Hyde Bridge, Sligo
☎ *(071) 914 2693*
Website *www.yeats-sligo.com*
Admission *free*
Open *Mon-Wed 10am-4pm, Thu-Fri 10am-2pm*

County Donegal

Ireland's most northwestern county is Ireland at its most authentic. Its rugged coastline includes the towering cliffs of the Slieve League Peninsula plus there are plenty of picturesque towns and villages and large swathes of Gaelic-speaking gaeltacht area.

Donegal Town (Dún na nGall)

This quaint town on the River Eske has a compact town centre and plenty of welcoming pubs. Coming from Sligo, many travellers stop here for a day or two before heading to the Slieve League Peninsula.

Practical Information
Tourist Information Centre
The Quay, Donegal
☎ *(074) 972 1148*
Website *www.irelandnorthwest.ie*
Open *Apr-Jun Mon-Fri 9am-5pm, Sat 10am-2pm; Jul-Aug Mon-Sat 9am-6pm, Sun noon-4pm; Sep-Oct Mon-Fri 9am-5pm, Sat 10am-2pm*

Coming & Going
Bus Éireann *(website www.buseireann.ie)* and McGeehan Coaches *(website www.mcgeehancoaches.com)* have direct buses from Donegal Town to Derry, Dublin, Glencolumbcille, Killybegs, Letterkenny and Sligo.

Accommodation
Ball Hill Youth Hostel
The Ball Hill Youth Hostel is housed in an old coast guard station that was built in the 1860s. It has a good atmosphere with lots of local information posted on the walls. Facilities are limited and include a basic kitchen, a cosy common room with a fireplace and a balcony with spectacular sea views. The hostel is by the waterfront 5km from the centre of Donegal Town and the location is only convenient if you're driving.
Ball Hill, Donegal
☎ *(074) 972 1174*
Website *www.anoige.ie*
Dorm bed *€13-14.50*
Open *Apr-Sep*

Maintenance & cleanliness		★★☆
Facilities		★★☆
Atmosphere & character		★★★★★
Security		★☆
Overall rating		★★

Donegal Town Independent Hostel
Donegal Town Independent Hostel is a good place to stay about a 10-minute walk outside the town centre. It has the usual facilities such as a kitchen and a cosy TV lounge with a fireplace.
Killybegs Road, Donegal Town
☎ *(074) 972 2805*
Dorm bed *€12; double room €28*

Maintenance & cleanliness		★★★
Facilities		★★☆
Atmosphere & character		★★★
Security		★★☆
Overall rating		★★★☆

Sights
Donegal Abbey
The ruins of Donegal Abbey date from 1474. The Abbey is noted as the site where Franciscans compiled the Annals of the Four Masters, an epic chronicle of Irish history.

Donegal Castle
This 15th century castle in the town centre features extensive 17th century additions. It is furnished with French

tapestries and Persian rugs and there are informative displays about the castle's former owners.
Bridge Street, Donegal
☎ *(073) 22405*
Website *www.heritageireland.ie*
Admission *€3.50 (€1.25 students)*
Open *mid Mar-Oct 10am-6pm daily (last entry 5.15pm)*

Donegal Railway Heritage Centre

Although County Donegal no longer has any train service, it once was well served by narrow gauge railways. The Donegal Railway Heritage Centre has artefacts and displays on the county's railway heritage.
Tirconnaill Street, Donegal
☎ *(074) 972 2655*
Website *www.countydonegalrailway.com*
Admission *€3.50*
Open *Apr-May Mon-Fri 10am-5pm; Jun-Sep Mon-Fri 10am-5pm, Sat 11am-5pm, Sun 2pm-5pm*

Slieve League Peninsula

The Slieve League Peninsula's rocky coastline is renown for its cliffs, which reach heights of 610m making them Europe's highest.

Coming & Going & Local Transport

Although Bus Éireann *(website www.buseireann.ie)* and McGeehan Coaches *(website www.mcgeehancoaches.com)* run buses from Donegal Town to Killybegs and Glencolumbcille, buses are infrequent and many travellers without a car find hitchhiking the most practical way to get around.

Accommodation
DUNKINELLY

Dunkinelly is a small village on the coast road between Donegal Town and Killybegs.

Blue Moon Hostel & Camping

This small hostel is above an accountant's office in Dunkineely (between Donegal Town and Killybegs). It is clean but basic with a small common area with a TV and limited kitchen facilities. Accommodation is in six-bed dorms with three-tier bunks.
R 263, Dunkinelly
☎ *(074) 973 7264*
Dorm bed *€10;* **camping** *€5 per person*

Maintenance & cleanliness	★★✫
Facilities	★
Atmosphere & character	★★★
Security	-
Overall rating	★★

Gallagher's Farm Hostel

This small 18-bed hostel is in a stone farmhouse that has two very basic kitchens, a small common room with a fireplace and a games room with table tennis. Accommodation is in simple dormitories with old plastic coated mattresses. It is just outside the village of Bruckless near Dunkineely.
Darney, Bruckless
☎ *(074) 973 7057*
Website *http://homepage.eircom.net/-farmhostel/*
Dorm bed *€12.50;* **camping** *€7.50 per person*

Maintenance & cleanliness	★★★
Facilities	★
Atmosphere & character	★★★★✫
Security	✫
Overall rating	★★★✫

CARRICK, KILCAR AND TEELIN

The area around the villages of Carrick, Kilcar and Teelin is the closest point to the Slieve League cliffs. To get to the cliffs, at Carrick take the road to Teelin and keep driving to the lookout at the end of the road. Derrylahan Hostel is the closest hostel to the cliffs but you need a car to get to both the hostel and the cliffs.

Derrylahan Independent Hostel

This farm hostel is comprised of several buildings that sleep 38 people in total. The main building has most of the common areas including the kitchen and two lounges – one with a fireplace and one with a TV. Most accommodation is in six bed dorms and there's a newer

building with en suite facilities and a separate building that is used for groups.
Coast Road, Derrylahan, Kilcar
☎ *(074) 973 8079*
Website http://homepage.eircom.net/-derrylahan
Dorm bed €12

Maintenance & cleanliness	★★★½
Facilities	★★
Atmosphere & character	★★★
Security	½
Overall rating	★★★½

MALINBEG & GLENCOLMCILLE

The western end of the peninsula boasts spectacular scenery and great coastal views, but as Mary at the Dooey Hostel points out, "there's feck all to do here".

Dooey Hostel

This unique place is perched on a rocky outcrop overlooking the sea. The building has a maze of narrow corridors and the low ceilings give it plenty of character. It has basic facilities that include several small kitchens and a TV lounge with spectacular ocean views, but it's not the sort of place that will appeal to everyone.
Glencolmcille
☎ *(074) 30130*
Website www.dooeyhostel.com
Dorm bed €11.50; double room €24

Maintenance & cleanliness	★★½
Facilities	★
Atmosphere & character	★★★★
Security	½
Overall rating	★★

Malinbeg Hostel

This new purpose-built hostel overlooking the sea at Malinbeg has good quality accommodation and facilities that include a cosy lounge with an open fire, a small but fully equipped kitchen and a small dining room.
Malinbeg, Glencolmcille
☎ *(074) 973 0006*
Dorm bed €12; double room €28-30

Maintenance & cleanliness	★★★★★
Facilities	★★½
Atmosphere & character	★★★
Security	-
Overall rating	★★★

Letterkenny (Leitir Ceannain)

Bustling Letterkenny is Co Donegal's largest town and many travellers pass through while making transport connections to Derry in Northern Ireland.

Practical Information
Tourist Information Centre
Neil T Blaney Road, Letterkenny
☎ *(074) 912 1160*
Website www.irelandnorthwest.ie
Open Jan-Jun Mon-Fri 9am-5pm; Jul-Aug Mon-Sat 9am-8pm, Sun 10am-2pm; Sep-Dec Mon-Fri 9am-5pm

Coming & Going

Buses to Derry, Dublin and destinations throughout Co Donegal depart from the bus station at the corner of Port and Pearce Roads.

Accommodation
Port Hostel

Port Hostel is in a quiet laneway just off busy Port Road. It offers comfortable accommodation with all the usual hostel facilities.
Orchard Crest, Letterkenny
☎ *(074) 25315*
Dorm bed €12-18
Credit cards MC, Visa
Reception open Jan-Mar 10am-10pm daily; Apr-Sep 10am-11pm daily; Oct-Dec 10am-10pm daily; curfew 1.30am

Sights
Donegal County Museum

This museum is housed in an old workhouse and it contains local history exhibits dating back to the Stone Age.
High Road, Letterkenny
☎ *(074) 912 4613*
Admission free
Open Mon-Fri 10am-12.30pm & 1pm-4pm, Sat 1pm-4.30pm

Inishowen Peninsula

The Inishowen Peninsula is a beautiful spot that is a popular weekend holiday destination with people from Letterkenny and Derry. Although there are no must see attractions, most people visiting the peninsula make it up to

Malin Head, Ireland's northern-most point, as well as the towns of Buncrana and Carndonagh.

Practical Information
Buncrana Tourist Information Centre
Railway Road, Buncrana, Inishowen
☎ *(074) 936 2600*
Website *www.irelandnorthwest.ie*
Open *May-Sep Mon-Fri 9am-5pm, Sat 10am-2pm, Sun noon-3pm*

Accommodation
Malin Head Hostel
This clean and well-appointed hostel has a cosy lounge with an open fire and spectacular sea views.
Malin Head, Inishowen Peninsula
☎ *(074) 937 0309*
Website *http://homepage.eircom. net/~malinheadhostel/*
Dorm bed *€12.50*
Open *Mar-Oct*

Sandrock Holiday Hostel
This purpose-built hostel provides comfortable accommodation for 20 guests in two dormitories. Common areas include a fully equipped kitchen plus a dining area and lounge room.
Port Ronan Pier, Malin Head, Inishowen Peninsula
☎ *(074) 937 0289*
Website *www.carndonagh.com/sandrock*
Dorm bed *€10*

Index

A
Aberdeen (Aberdeen, Scotland) 313-15
Abergavenny (Monmouthshire, Wales) 264
Abergwaun; see Fishguard (Pembrokeshire, Wales)
Aberhonddu; see Brecon (Powys, Wales)
Abertawe; see Swansea (Swansea, Wales)
Aberystwyth (Ceredigion, Wales) 265-66
Acaill Oileán; see Achill Island (Co Mayo)
Achill Island (Co Mayo) 415-16
Adrigole (Co Cork, Ireland) 392
Aer Arann 29
Aer Lingus 29
airlines
  Aer Arann 29
  Aer Lingus 29
  BMI 29
  bmi baby 29
  British Airways 29
  easyJet 29
  Flybe 29
  Jet2 29-30
  MyTravelLite 30
  Ryanair 30
  Thomson Fly 30
air travel 29-30
Allihies (Co Cork, Ireland) 392
Alloway (South Ayrshire, Scotland) 300-01
Alnwick (Northumberland, England) 247
Alstonefield (Staffordshire, England) 190
Ambleside (Cumbria, England) 208
Anascaul (Co Kerry, Ireland) 398
Anglesey, Isle of (Isle of Anglesey, Wales) 272-273
An Caisleán Nua; see Newcastle (Co Down, Northern Ireland)
An Clochán; see Cloghane (Co Kerry, Ireland)
An Cobh; see Cobh (Co Cork, Ireland)
An Coireán; see Waterville (Co Kerry, Ireland)
An Daigean; see Dingle Town (Co Kerry, Ireland)
An Líonán; see Leenane (Co Galway, Ireland)
An Óige 26
An Tairbeart; see Tarbert (Western Isles, Scotland)
Aran Islands (Co Galway, Ireland) 410-11
Ard Macha; see Armagh (Co Armagh, Northern Ireland)
Argyll and Bute 303-306
Armadale (Highland, Scotland) 330-32
Armagh (Co Armagh, Northern Ireland) 360
Arran, Isle of (North Ayrshire, Scotland) 301-02
Arundel (West Sussex, England) 119
ATM cards 23
Avebury (Wiltshire, England) 130-131
Aviemore (Highland, Scotland) 324-25
Ayr (South Ayrshire, Scotland) 300-01

B
backpackers' hostels 25-28
Baile an Chaisil; see Ballycastle (Co Antrim, Northern Ireland)
Baile an Fheirtéaraigh; see Ballyferriter (Co Kerry, Ireland)
Baile an Tuaighe; see Ballintoy (Co Antrim, Northern Ireland)
Baile Átha Cliath; see Dublin (Co Dublin, Ireland)
Bakewell (Derbyshire, England) 187-88
Ballina (Co Mayo) 416
Ballintoy (Co Antrim, Northern Ireland) 354-55
Ballycastle (Co Antrim, Northern Ireland) 355-56
Ballyferriter (Co Kerry, Ireland) 400
Baltimore (Co Cork, Ireland) 391
Bangor (Gwynedd, Wales) 272
bank accounts
  Ireland 24
  UK 23
Bannockburn (Stirling, Scotland) 307
Bantry (Co Cork, Ireland) 391-92
Barnard Castle (County Durham, England) 240
Barraigh; see Barra (Western Isles, Scotland)
Barra (Western Isles, Scotland) 342
Bath (Somerset, England) 139-43
Battle (East Sussex, England) 114-15
Béal an Átha; see Ballina (Co Mayo)
Béal Feirste; see Belfast (Co Antrim, Northern Ireland)
Beamish (County Durham, England) 241-42
Beanntraí; see Bantry (Co Cork, Ireland)

Beara Peninsula (Co Cork, Ireland) 392-93
bed bugs 27
Belfast (Co Antrim, Northern Ireland) 356-59
Bellingham (Northumberland, England) 250
Benbecula (Western Isles, Scotland) 341
Ben Nevis (Highland, Scotland) 316-19
Berkshire 158-59
Berwick-upon-Tweed (Northumberland, England) 247-48
Betws-y-Coed (Conwy, Wales) 266-67
Beverley (East Riding of Yorkshire, England) 224-25
Birkenhead (Merseyside, England) 202
Birmingham (West Midlands, England) 169-75
Birnam (Perthsire & Kinross, Scotland) 311-12
Blackpool (Lancashire, England) 205-06
Blaenau Ffestiniog (Gwynedd, Wales) 266
Blaenavon (Torfaen, Wales) 264-65
BMI 29
bmi baby 29
Boat of Garten (Highland, Scotland) 325
Borrowdale (Cumbria, England) 209
Bournemouth (Dorset, England) 131-32
Bradford (West Yorkshire, England) 217-18
Brecon (Powys, Wales) 263
Brecon Beacons National Park (Monmouthshire & Powys, Wales) 262-63
Brighton (East Sussex, England) 115-19
Bristol (Somerset, England) 143-46
British Airways 29
British bank accounts 23
BritRail 43-44
Brit Xplorer pass 31-32
Brixham (Devon, England) 134-36
Broadford (Highland, Scotland) 330
Broadstairs (Kent, England) 110
Broad Haven (Pembrokeshire, Wales) 257-58
Broch of Gurness (Orkney Islands, Scotland) 346
Bude (Cornwall, England) 157
Buncrana (Co Donegal, Ireland) 422
Bun Abhann Duinne; see Cushendun (Co Antrim, Northern Ireland)
Burnham Deepdale (Norfolk, England) 102
Bushmills (Co Antrim, Northern Ireland) 354
bus travel 30-35
   Arriva 30-31
   Brit Xplorer pass 31-32
   Bus Éireann 34
   easyBus 32-33
   First 31
   MacBackpackers 33
   Megabus 33
   National Express 31-32, 33
   Paddywagon 35
   Road Trip 33-34
   Scottish Citylink 32, 33
   Shaggy Sheep 34
   Stagecoach 32
Buttermere (Cumbria, England) 209
Buxton (Derbyshire, England) 188
Byrness (Northumberland, England) 250

C

Caerdydd; see Cardiff (Cardiff, Wales)
Caernarfon (Gwynedd, Wales) 270-71
Caherdaniel (Co Kerry, Ireland) 396-97
Cahersiveen (Co Kerry, Ireland) 396
Cairngorms, the (Highland, Scotland) 324-28
Caiseal Mumhan; see Cashel (Co Tipperary, Ireland)
Caislean Chriare; see Castlegregory (Co Kerry, Ireland)
Callander (Stirling, Scotland) 308-09
Cambridgeshire 97-100
Cambridge (Cambridgeshire, England) 97-99
Canterbury (Kent, England) 107-09
Capel Curig (Conwy, Wales) 267
Cape Clear Island (Co Cork, Ireland) 391
Caputh (Perthshire & Kinross, Scotland) 312
Carbost (Highland, Scotland) 331
Cardiff (Cardiff, Wales) 253-56
Carlisle (Cumbria, England) 213-14
Carrbridge (Highland, Scotland) 325
Carrick (Co Donegal, Ireland) 420-21
car travel
   Ireland 45-46
   UK 46-48
Cas-gwent; see Chepstow (Monmouthshire, Wales)
Cashel (Co Tipperary, Ireland) 384-85

Castlebay (Western Isles, Scotland) 342
Castlegregory (Co Kerry, Ireland) 400-01
castles
- Alnwick Castle (Northumberland, England) 247
- Arundel Castle (West Sussex, England) 119
- Ashford Castle (Co Mayo) 414
- Barnard Castle (County Durham, England) 240
- Berwick Castle (Northumberland, England) 247-48
- Blair Castle (Perthsire & Kinross, Scotland) 313
- Blarney Castle (Co Cork, Ireland) 388
- Blenheim Palace (Oxfordshire, England) 163
- Brodick Castle (North Ayrshire, Scotland) 302
- Brodie Castle (Moray, Scotland) 321
- Bunratty Castle (Co Clare, Ireland) 402
- Caernarfon Castle (Gwynedd, Wales) 270
- Caerphilly Castle (Caerphilly, Wales) 256
- Camber Castle (East Sussex, England) 112-13
- Carbisdale Castle (Highland, Scotland) 322
- Cardiff Castle (Cardiff, Wales) 255
- Carlisle Castle (Cumbria, England) 213
- Castle Acre Castle (Norfolk, England) 101
- Castle Keep (Tyne and Wear, England) 245
- Castle Moil (Highland, Scotland) 332
- Cawdor Castle (Highland, Scotland) 321
- Chepstow Castle (Monmouthshire, Wales) 262
- Conwy Castle (Conwy, Wales) 271-72
- Culzean Castle (South Ayrshire, Scotland) 301
- Deal Castle (Kent, England) 111-12
- Donegal Castle (Co Donegal, Ireland) 419-20
- Dover Castle (Kent, England) 111
- Dunollie Castle (Argyll & Bute, Scotland) 306
- Duntulm Castle (Highland, Scotland) 332-33
- Dunvegan Castle (Highland, Scotland) 333
- Edinburgh Castle (Midlothian, Scotland) 287
- Harlech Castle (Gwynedd, Wales) 270
- Hastings Castle (East Sussex, England) 114
- Helmsley Castle (North Yorkshire, England) 230
- Herstmonceux Castle (East Sussex, England) 115
- Inveraray Castle (Argyll & Bute, Scotland) 305
- Inverness Castle (Highland, Scotland) 321
- Kilkenny Castle (Co Kilkenny, Ireland) 382
- King John's Castle (Co Limerick, Ireland) 402
- Kisimul Castle (Western Isles, Scotland) 342
- Leeds Castle (Kent, England) 106-07
- Lews Castle (Western Isles, Scotland) 338
- Lincoln Castle (Lincolnshire, England) 183
- Malahide Castle (Co Dublin, Ireland) 376
- Norwich Castle (Norfolk, England) 104
- Old Sarum Castle (Wiltshire, England) 130
- Pembroke Castle (Pembrokeshire, Wales) 260
- Peveril Castle (Derbyshire, England) 189
- Restormel Castle (Cornwall, England) 149
- Richmond Castle (North Yorkshire, England) 236
- Rock of Cashel (Co Tipperary, Ireland) 384
- Ross Castle (Co Kerry, Ireland) 396
- Royal Citadel (Devon, England) 138
- Scarborough Castle (North Yorkshire, England) 234
- Scone Palace (Perthsire & Kinross, Scotland) 311
- Skipton Castle (North Yorkshire, England) 234
- Southsea Castle (Hampshire, England) 124
- Stirling Castle (Stirling, Scotland) 308

St Andrews Castle (Fife, Scotland) 310
St Brivel's Castle (Gloucestershire, England) 262
Tintagel Castle (Cornwall, England) 157
Tower of London (London, England) 86-87
Urquhart Castle (Highland, Scotland) 323
Walmer Castle (Kent, England) 112
Warwick Castle (Warwickshire, England) 168
Windsor Castle (Berkshire, England) 159
Castleton (Derbyshire, England) 188-89
Castletownbere (Co Cork, Ireland) 392-93
Castle Acre (Norfolk, England) 101
Cathair na Mart; see Westport (Co Mayo)
Cathair Saidhthin; see Cahersiveen (Co Kerry, Ireland)
Cheddar (Somerset, England) 148
Cheltenham (Gloucestershire, England) 163-64
Chepstow (Monmouthshire, Wales) 261-62
Cheshire 203-05
Chester (Cheshire, England) 203-04
Chichester (West Sussex, England) 119-20
Cill Airne; see Killarney (Co Kerry, Ireland)
Cill Chainnigh; see Kilkenny (Co Kilkenny, Ireland)
Cill Mhantáin; see Wicklow (Co Wicklow, Ireland)
Cill Orglan; see Killorglin (Co Kerry, Ireland)
Cionn tSáile; see Kinsale (Co Cork, Ireland)
Clifden (Co Galway, Ireland) 411
Cliffs of Moher (Co Clare, Ireland) 404
Cloch na Coillte; see Clonakilty (Co Cork, Ireland)
Cloghane (Co Kerry, Ireland) 400
Clonakilty (Co Cork, Ireland) 390
coach travel; see bus travel
Cobh (Co Cork, Ireland) 388-89
Conga; see Cong (Co Mayo)
Cong (Co Mayo) 413-14
Coniston (Cumbria, England) 209
Connaught 406-18
Connemara (Co Galway, Ireland) 411-13
Connemara National Park (Co Galway, Ireland) 412
Conwy (Conwy, Wales) 271-72
Corbridge Roman Site (Northumberland, England) 249
Corcaigh; see Cork (Co Cork, Ireland)
Cork (Co Cork, Ireland) 386-88
Cornwall 148-57
Corpach (Highland, Scotland) 318
Corris (Gwynedd, Wales) 267
County Antrim 353-59
County Clare 402-05
County Cork 385-93
County Derry 351-53
County Donegal 419-22
County Down 359-60
County Dublin 363-77
County Durham 240-42
County Galway 406-13
County Kerry 393-401
County Kilkenny 381-82
County Limerick 401-02
County Louth 377-78
County Mayo 413-16
County Sligo 416-18
County Tipperary 383-85
County Waterford 385
County Wexford 379-81
County Wicklow 378-79
Coventry (West Midlands, England) 175-76
credit cards 23
Criccieth (Gwynedd, Wales) 269
Croagh Patrick (Co Mayo) 415
Culloden Battlefield (Highland, Scotland) 321-22
Culrain (Highland, Scotland) 322
Cumbria 207-14
Cushendun (Co Antrim, Northern Ireland) 356
Cymru; see Wales

D

Deal (Kent, England) 111-12
Dentdale (Cumbria, England) 214
Derbyshire 186-92
Derby (Derbyshire, England) 186-87
Derry (Co Derry, Northern Ireland) 351-52
Derwentwater (Cumbria, England) 211
Devon 132-39
Dingle Peninsula (Co Kerry, Ireland) 398-401
Dingle Town (Co Kerry, Ireland) 398-99
Doire Cholm Cille; see Derry (Co Derry, Northern Ireland)

Dolgellau (Gwynedd, Wales) 267
Donegal Town (Co Donegal, Ireland) 419-20
Doolin (Co Clare, Ireland) 405
Dorset 131-32
Dover (Kent, England) 110-11
Downhill (Co Derry, Northern Ireland) 352-53
Drinshader (Western Isles, Scotland) 340
driving; see car travel
Drogheda (Co Louth, Ireland) 377-78
Droichead Átha; see Drogheda (Co Louth, Ireland)
Drumnadrochit (Highland, Scotland) 322-23
Dubh Linn; see Doolin (Co Clare, Ireland)
Dublin (Co Dublin, Ireland) 363-76
Dunkeld (Perthsire & Kinross, Scotland) 311-12
Dunkinelly (Co Donegal, Ireland) 420
Dunmanway (Co Cork, Ireland) 389-90
Dunquin (Co Kerry, Ireland) 399-400
Dún Chaoin; see Dunquin (Co Kerry, Ireland)
Dún Laoghaire (Co Dublin, Ireland) 376
Dún Mánmhai; see Dunmanway (Co Cork, Ireland)
Dún na nGall; see Donegal Town (Co Donegal, Ireland)
Durham (County Durham, England) 240-41

E

East Anglia 97-105
East Riding of Yorkshire 223-25
East Sussex 112-19
easyJet 29
Edale (Derbyshire, England) 191
Eday (Orkney Islands, Scotland) 345
Eden Project (Cornwall, England) 149
Edinburgh (Midlothian, Scotland) 279-90
Edwinstowe (Nottinghamshire, England) 185-86
Ellesmere Port (Cheshire, England) 205
Ely (Cambridgeshire, England) 99-100
employment agencies 20-21
Enniscorthy (Co Wexford, Ireland) 379-80
Ennis (Co Clare, Ireland) 402-04
Eochaill; see Youghal (Co Cork, Ireland)
Eton (Berkshire, England) 158-59
Exeter (Devon, England) 132-34

F

Falmouth (Cornwall, England) 149-50
festivals & events
  Edinburgh Festival Fringe 286
  Edinburgh International Festival 286
  Edinburgh Military Tattoo 286
  Henley Royal Regatta 159
  Hogmanay 286-87
  Puck Fair festival 397
Ffestiniog Railway 270
Fife 309-10
Fishbourne Roman Palace (West Sussex, England) 120
Fishguard (Pembrokeshire, Wales) 261
Flybe 29
Fort Augustus (Highland, Scotland) 323
Fort William (Highland, Scotland) 316-19
Fountains Abbey (North Yorkshire, England) 229
Fowey (Cornwall, England) 148-49

G

Gaillimh; see Galway (Co Galway, Ireland)
Galway (Co Galway, Ireland) 406-410
Gateshead (Tyne and Wear, England) 242, 244-45
Giant's Causeway (Co Antrim, Northern Ireland) 354
Glasgow (Strathclyde, Scotland) 291-300
Glastonbury (Somerset, England) 146-47
Glencolmcille (Co Donegal, Ireland) 421
Glendalough (Co Wicklow, Ireland) 378-79
Glengarriff (Co Cork, Ireland) 393
Glen Feshie (Highland, Scotland) 326
Glen Nevis (Highland, Scotland) 317-19
Gloucestershire 163-65
Gloucester (Gloucestershire, England) 164-65
Gosport (Hampshire, England) 124-25
Grantown-on-Spey (Highland, Scotland) 325-26
Grasmere (Cumbria, England) 210
Great Yarmouth (Norfolk, England) 104-05

H

Hadrian's Wall (Northumberland, England) 248-49
Hadrian's Wall (Tyne and Wear, England) 246
Hampshire 120-127

Harlech (Gwynedd, Wales) 270
Harris (Western Isles, Scotland) 339-40
Harrogate (North Yorkshire, England) 228-29
Hartlepool (Tees Valley, England) 239-40
Hastings (East Sussex, England) 113-14
Hathersage (Derbyshire, England) 189-90, 222
Hawes (North Yorkshire, England) 236-37
Haworth (West Yorkshire, England) 219
Hay-on-Wye (Monmouthshire, Wales) 262
health cover
 Ireland 21-22
 UK 22
Helmsley (North Yorkshire, England) 230-31
Henley-on-Thames (Oxfordshire, England) 159-60
Herstmonceux (East Sussex, England) 115
Hexham (Northumberland, England) 248
Highland 316-35
hiking
 Ben Nevis (Highland, Scotland) 319
 Cairngorms, the (Highland, Scotland) 327
 Croagh Patrick (Co Mayo) 415
 Lairig Ghru trail (Highland, Scotland) 327
 Northern Corries Path (Highland, Scotland) 327
 Windy Ridge Trail (Highland, Scotland) 327
HINI 26
hitchhiking 48-49
Hostelling International (HI) 26-27
Hostelling International Northern Ireland (HINI) 26
hostels 25-28
hostel cards 25
Housesteads (Northumberland, England) 249
Hoy (Orkney Islands, Scotland) 344
Hull (East Riding of Yorkshire, England) 223-24
Hunstanton (Norfolk, England) 102

I

Ilfracombe (Devon, England) 138-39
Independent Backpackers Hostels Scotland (IBHS) 27
Independent Holiday Hostels of Ireland (IHH) 27-28
Independent Hostel Owners (IHO) 28
Ingleton (North Yorkshire, England) 236
Inis; see Ennis (Co Clare, Ireland)
Inishbofin (Co Galway, Ireland) 411-12
Inishere (Co Galway, Ireland) 410
Inishmaan (Co Galway, Ireland) 410
Inishmore (Co Galway, Ireland) 410-11
Inishowen Peninsula (Co Donegal, Ireland) 421-22
Inish Bó Finne; see Inishbofin (Co Galway, Ireland)
Inish Mór; see Inishmore (Co Galway, Ireland)
Inis Coirthaidth; see Enniscorthy (Co Wexford, Ireland)
Inis Meáin; see Inishmaan (Co Galway, Ireland)
Inis Oirr; see Inishere (Co Galway, Ireland)
Inveraray (Argyll & Bute, Scotland) 304-05
Invergarry (Highland, Scotland) 323
Invermoriston (Highland, Scotland) 323
Inverness (Highland, Scotland) 319-22
Irish bank accounts 24
Ironbridge Gorge (Shropshire, England) 177-79
Isle of Skye (Highland, Scotland) 328-33
Iveragh Peninsula (Co Kerry, Ireland) 396-97

J

Jarrow (Tyne and Wear, England) 244
Jedburgh (Scottish Borders, Scotland) 277-78
Jet2 29-30
John O'Groats (Highland, Scotland) 334-35

K

Keel (Co Mayo) 415
Kells (Co Kerry, Ireland) 396
Kendal (Cumbria, England) 207-08
Kenilworth (Warwickshire, England) 168
Kenmare (Co Kerry, Ireland) 393
Kent 106-12
Keswick (Cumbria, England) 210-11
Kielder (Northumberland, England) 250
Kilcar (Co Donegal, Ireland) 420-421
Kilkenny (Co Kilkenny, Ireland) 381-82
Killarney (Co Kerry, Ireland) 394-95

Killarney National Park (Co Kerry, Ireland) 395-96
Killorglin (Co Kerry, Ireland) 397
Kilmore (Highland, Scotland) 330
Kincraig (Highland, Scotland) 326
Kingston-upon-Hull (East Riding of Yorkshire, England) 223
Kings Lynn (Norfolk, England) 100-01
Kingussie (Highland, Scotland) 326
Kinsale (Co Cork, Ireland) 389
Kirkwall (Orkney Islands, Scotland) 344-46
Knaresborough (North Yorkshire, England) 228-29
Kyleakin (Highland, Scotland) 329-30
Kyle of Lochalsh (Highland, Scotland) 329

L

Lahinch (Co Clare, Ireland) 404
Lake District National Park (Cumbria, England) 208-13
Lancashire 205-07
Lancaster (Lancashire, England) 206-07
Lands End (Cornwall, England) 152-53
Leacht Uí Chonchubhair; see Lahinch (Co Clare, Ireland)
Leeds (West Yorkshire, England) 215-17
Leeds Castle (Kent, England) 106-07
Leenane (Co Galway, Ireland) 412-13
Legoland (Berkshire, England) 159
Leicestershire 181-82
Leicester (Leicestershire, England) 181-82
Leinster 363-82
Leitir Ceannain; see Letterkenny (Co Donegal, Ireland)
Leitir Fraic; see Letterfrack (Co Galway, Ireland)
Leodhas; see Lewis (Western Isles, Scotland)
Lerwick (Shetland Islands, Scotland) 347-48
Letterfrack (Co Galway, Ireland) 412
Letterkenny (Co Donegal, Ireland) 421
Leverburgh (Western Isles, Scotland) 340
Lewis (Western Isles, Scotland) 337-39
Lichfield (Staffordshire, England) 180-81
Limerick (Co Limerick, Ireland) 401-02
Lincolnshire 182-183
Lincoln (Lincolnshire, England) 182-83

Lios Ceannúir; see Liscanor (Co Clare, Ireland)
Liscanor (Co Clare, Ireland) 404
Liverpool (Merseyside, England) 199-203
Llanberis (Gwynedd, Wales) 266-69
Llandudno (Conwy, Wales) 271-72
Llanfairpwllgwyngyllgogerychwyrndrobwllllantysiliogogogoch (Isle of Anglesea, Wales) 272-73
Llangollen (Denbighshire, Wales) 272
Loch Lomond (Argyll & Bute, Scotland) 303-04
Loch Ness (Highland, Scotland) 319-22
London 53-96
Londonderry; see Derry (Co Derry, Northern Ireland)
Lougher (Co Kerry, Ireland) 398
Lough Garman; see Wexford (Co Wexford, Ireland)
Ludlow (Shropshire, England) 176-77
Luimneach; see Limerick (Co Limerick, Ireland)

M

MacBackpackers 33
Maeshowe (Orkney Islands, Scotland) 346
Maidstone (Kent, England) 106-07
Malahide (Co Dublin, Ireland) 377
Malham (North Yorkshire, England) 235-36
Malham Tarn (North Yorkshire, England) 236
Malinbeg (Co Donegal, Ireland) 421
Malin Head (Co Donegal, Ireland) 422
Manchester (Greater Manchester, England) 193-99
Margate (Kent, England) 109-10
Matlock (Derbyshire, England) 190
Matlock Bath (Derbyshire, England) 190
Melrose (Scottish Borders, Scotland) 278
Merseyside 199-203
Middlesbrough (Tees Valley, England) 238-39
Minginish Peninsula (Highland, Scotland) 331
Mount Brandon (Co Kerry, Ireland) 400
Mullach Íde; see Malahide (Co Dublin, Ireland)
Munster 383-405
MyTravelLite 30

N

Nant Gwynant (Gwynedd, Wales) 268-69
national parks
    Brecon Beacons National Park (Monmouthshire & Powys, Wales) 262
    Connemara National Park (Co Galway, Ireland) 412
    Killarney National Park (Co Kerry, Ireland) 395
    Lake District National Park (Cumbria, England) 208-13
    Northumberland National Park (Northumberland, England) 249-50
    North York Moors National Park (North Yorkshire, England) 230
    Peak District National Park (Derbyshire, England) 187-92
    Pembrokeshire Coast National Park (Pembrokeshire, Wales) 257-59
    Snowdonia National Park (Conwy & Gwynedd, Wales) 266
    Wicklow Mountains National Park (Co Wicklow, Ireland) 378-79
    Yorkshire Dales National Park (North Yorkshire, England) 234-37
    Yorkshire Dales National Park (Cumbria, England) 214
Na Hearadh; see Harris (Western Isles, Scotland)
Neidín; see Kenmare (Co Kerry, Ireland)
Nether Wastwater (Cumbria, England) 212
Nethy Bridge (Highland, Scotland) 326
Newcastle-upon-Tyne (Tyne and Wear, England) 242-46
Newcastle (Co Down, Northern Ireland) 359-60
Newquay (Cornwall, England) 154-56
Newtonmore (Highland, Scotland) 327
New Lanark (South Lanarkshire, Scotland) 300
Norfolk 100-05
Northern Ireland 351-60
Northumberland 246-50
Northumberland National Park (Northumberland, England) 249-50
Northumbria 238-50
North Uist (Western Isles, Scotland) 340-42
North Yorkshire 225-37
North Yorkshire Moors Railway 231
North York Moors National Park (North Yorkshire, England) 230
Norwich (Norfolk, England) 103-04
Nottinghamshire 183-86
Nottingham (Nottinghamshire, England) 183-85

O

Oakamoor (Staffordshire, England) 191
Oban (Argyll & Bute, Scotland) 305-06
Oileán Árann; see Aran Islands (Co Galway, Ireland)
Oileán Chléire; see Cape Clear Island (Co Cork, Ireland)
Once Brewed (Northumberland, England) 248-49
Orkney Islands 343-47
Outer Hebrides; see Western Isles
Oxfordshire 159-63
Oxford (Oxfordshire, England) 160-62

P

Paddywagon 35
Paignton (Devon, England) 134-36
Papa Westray (Orkney Islands, Scotland) 345, 347
Parc Cenedlaethol Eryri; see Snowdonia National Park (Conwy & Gwynedd, Wales)
Parc Cenedlarthol Bannau Brycheiniog; see Brecon Beacons National Park (Monmouthshire & Powys, Wales)
passports 14-15
Patterdale (Cumbria, England) 211-12
Peak District National Park (Derbyshire, England) 187-92
Pembrokeshire Coast National Park (Pembrokeshire, Wales) 257-59
Pembroke (Pembrokeshire, Wales) 259-60
Penfro; see Pembroke (Pembrokeshire, Wales)
Penwith Peninsula (Cornwall, England) 152-53
Penzance (Cornwall, England) 150-52
Perthshire and Kinross 310-13
Perth (Perthsire & Kinross, Scotland) 310-11
Pevensey (East Sussex, England) 115
Pickering (North Yorkshire, England) 231
Pitlochry (Perthsire & Kinross, Scotland) 312-13
Plymouth (Devon, England) 136-38
Poole (Dorset, England) 131-32
Porthmadog (Gwynedd, Wales) 269-70
Portree (Highland, Scotland) 331

Portrush (Co Antrim, Northern Ireland) 353-54
Portsmouth (Hampshire, England) 120-25
Portstewart (Co Derry, Northern Ireland) 353
Port Eynon (Swansea, Wales) 257
Port Láirge; see Waterford (Co Waterford, Ireland)
Port Stíobaird; see Portstewart (Co Derry, Northern Ireland)

R

rail travel; see train travel
rambling; see hiking
Retail Export Scheme 24
Rhenigidale (Western Isles, Scotland) 339
Richmond (North Yorkshire, England) 236
Rievaulx Abbey (North Yorkshire, England) 230-31
Ring of Brogar (Orkney Islands, Scotland) 346
Ring of Kerry (Co Kerry, Ireland) 396-97
Ripon (North Yorkshire, England) 229-30
Road Trip 33-34
Robin Hoods Bay (North Yorkshire, England) 232-33
Rosslare Harbour (Co Wexford, Ireland) 381
Ros Láir; see Rosslare Harbour (Co Wexford, Ireland)
Rousay (Orkney Islands, Scotland) 344-45
Rugby (Warwickshire, England) 169
Ryanair 30
Rye (East Sussex, England) 112-13

S

Salisbury (Wiltshire, England) 128-30
Saltaire (West Yorkshire, England) 218-19
Sandwich (Kent, England) 112
Scarborough (North Yorkshire, England) 233-34
Schull (Co Cork, Ireland) 391
Sciobairín; see Skibbereen (Co Cork, Ireland)
Scottish Borders 277-78
Scottish Youth Hostel Association (SYHA) 27
Segedunum Roman Fort (Tyne and Wear, England) 246
Settle (North Yorkshire, England) 235
Shaggy Sheep 34
Sheffield (South Yorkshire, England) 220-23
Sheringham (Norfolk, England) 103
Sherwood Forest (Nottinghamshire, England) 185-86
Shetland Islands 347-348
Shrewsbury (Shropshire, England) 177
Shropshire 176-79
Skara Brae (Orkney Islands, Scotland) 346
Skibbereen (Co Cork, Ireland) 390
Skipton (North Yorkshire, England) 234
Skye, Isle of (Highland, Scotland) 328-33
Sleat Peninsula (Highland, Scotland) 330
Slieve League Peninsula (Co Donegal, Ireland) 420-21
Sligachan (Highland, Scotland) 330-31
Sligeach; see Sligo Town (Co Sligo, Ireland)
Sligo Town (Co Sligo, Ireland) 416-18
Snowdonia National Park (Conwy & Gwynedd, Wales) 266-69
Somerset 139-48
Southampton (Hampshire, England) 125-26
Southsea (Hampshire, England) 120-25
South Ronaldsay (Orkney Islands, Scotland) 344
South Shields (Tyne and Wear, England) 246
South Uist (Western Isles, Scotland) 341
South Yorkshire 220-23
Staffordshire 179-81
star ratings 12-13
Stirling 306-09
Stirling (Stirling, Scotland) 306-08
Stockton-on-Tees (Tees Valley, England) 238-39
Stoke-on-Trent (Staffordshire, England) 179-80
Stonehenge (Wiltshire, England) 130
Stones of Stenness (Orkney Islands, Scotland) 346-47
Stornoway (Western Isles, Scotland) 337-38
Stow-on-the-Wold (Gloucestershire, England) 163
Stradbally (Co Kerry, Ireland) 400-01
Straid Baile; see Stradbally (Co Kerry, Ireland)

Stratford-upon-Avon (Warwickshire, England) 165-67
Strathspey (Highland, Scotland) 324-28
Stromness (Orkney Islands, Scotland) 346
student cards 24-25
Student Work Abroad Programme
  Ireland 18
  UK 19
St Andrews (Fife, Scotland) 309-13
St Davids (Wales) 260-61
St Ives (Cornwall, England) 153-54
St Just (Cornwall, England) 152
St Michael's Mount (Cornwall, England) 152
Sumburgh (Shetland Islands, Scotland) 348
Sunderland (Tyne and Wear, England) 245
surfing
  Newquay (Cornwall, England) 156
  Sennen (Cornwall, England) 153
Swansea (Wales) 256-57
SYHA 27

T

Tairbeart; see Tarbert (Co Kerry, Ireland)
Tarbert (Co Kerry, Ireland) 401
Tarbert (Western Isles, Scotland) 339-40
tax
  Ireland 19-20
  UK 20
  Value Added Tax (VAT) 24
Teelin (Co Donegal, Ireland) 420-21
Teeside; see Tees Valley
Tees Valley 238-40
The Valley (Co Mayo) 416
Thiobraid Árann; see Tipperary (Co Tipperary, Ireland)
Thomson Fly 30
Thurso (Highland, Scotland) 334
Tintagel (Cornwall, England) 157
Tintern (Monmouthshire, Wales) 261-62
Tintern Abbey (Monmouthshire, Wales) 262
Tipperary (Co Tipperary, Ireland) 383
tipping 24
Torbay (Devon, England) 134-36
Torquay (Devon, England) 134-36
tourism offices 14
tourist visas 15
train companies

Arriva Trains Northern 35
Arriva Trains Wales 35
c2c 35
Central Trains 35
Chiltern Railways 35
Eurostar 35
First Great Western 35
First Great Western Link 35
First North Western 35-36
First ScotRail 36
Gatwick Express 36
Great North Eastern Railway (GNER) 36
Heathrow Express 36
Hull Trains 36
Merseyrail 36
Midland Mainline 36
One 36
Silverlink 36
Southern 36
South Eastern Trains 36
South West Trains 36
Thameslink 36
TransPennine Express 36-37
Virgin Trains 37
WAGN 37
Wessex Trains 37
train travel 35-44
  BritRail 43-44
  Great Britain 35-44
  Ireland 44
  travel passes 37-45
Tralee (Co Kerry, Ireland) 397-98
travellers' cheques 22
Trá Lí; see Tralee (Co Kerry, Ireland)
Tremadog (Gwynedd, Wales) 269-70
Trossachs, the (Stirling, Scotland) 308-09
Trotternish Peninsula (Highland, Scotland) 331-33
Tyddewi; see St Davids (Pembrokeshire, Wales)
Tynemouth (Tyne and Wear, England) 244

U

Uibhist; see Uists, the (Western Isles, Scotland)
Uig (Highland, Scotland) 332
Uists, the (Western Isles, Scotland) 340-42
Ullapool (Highland, Scotland) 333-34

V

Value Added Tax (VAT) 24
  Retail Export Scheme 24

Vindolanda (Northumberland, England) 249

W

Wales 253-273
walking; see hiking
Wallsend (Tyne and Wear, England) 246
Warwickshire 165-169
Warwick (Warwickshire, England) 167-68
Wastwater (Cumbria, England) 212
Waterford (Co Waterford, Ireland) 385
Waterville (Co Kerry, Ireland) 396
Wells-next-the-Sea (Norfolk, England) 102-03
Wells (Somerset, England) 147-48
Wensleydale (North Yorkshire, England) 236-37
Western Isles 337-342
Westport (Co Mayo) 414-15
Westray (Orkney Islands, Scotland) 345
West Midlands 169-76
West Sussex 119-20
West Yorkshire 215-19
Wexford (Co Wexford, Ireland) 380
Whitby (North Yorkshire, England) 231-32
Wicklow (Co Wicklow, Ireland) 378
Wicklow Mountains National Park (Co Wicklow, Ireland) 378-79
Wiltshire 128-31
Winchester (Hampshire, England) 126-27
Windermere (Cumbria, England) 212-13
Windsor (Berkshire, England) 158-59
Woodstock (Oxfordshire, England) 162-63
Wooler (Northumberland, England) 250
working 18-21
  Ireland 18
  UK 18-19
working holidaymaker programme
  Ireland 18
  UK 19
Wye Valley (Monmouthshire, Wales) 261-62

Y

YHA 26-27
Ynys Môn; see Anglesey, Isle of (Isle of Anglesey, Wales)
Yorkshire 215-37
Yorkshire Dales National Park (North Yorkshire, England) 234-37
York (North Yorkshire, England) 225-28
Youghal (Co Cork, Ireland) 386
Youlgreave (Derbyshire, England) 192
youth hostels 25-28
Youth Hostel Association (YHA) 26-27
Ystradgynlais (Swansea, Wales) 257
Y Fenni; see Abergavenny (Monmouthshire, Wales)
Y Gelli; see Hay-on-Wye (Monmouthshire, Wales)

Z

Zennor (Cornwall, England) 152

Map Index

B

Bath 140
Belfast 357
Birmingham 170
   Birmingham Transport 172
Brighton 116
Bristol 144
British Isles 8

C

Cairngorms 324
Canterbury 108
Cardiff 254
Central Scotland 303
Cork 387

D

Dublin 366

E

Edinburgh 280
England 51
Exeter 133

G

Glasgow 294
   Glasgow Transport 296

H

Heart of England 158
Highland 317

I

Isle of Skye 329

L

Leeds 216
Leinster 363
Liverpool 199
London
   Bayswater & Paddington 72
   Camden Town & Kings Cross 76
   The City & Southwark 82
   Earls Court & Kensington 74
   London Underground 60
   Victoria & Westminster 80
   West End 78

M

Manchester 194
   Metrolink tram network 196
Munster 383

N

Newcastle-upon-Tyne 243
North West England 193
Northern Ireland 349
Northumbria 238

O

Orkney & Shetland Islands 343
Oxford 161

P

Penzance 151
Plymouth 137
Portsmouth 121

R

Republic of Ireland 361

S

Salisbury 129
Scotland 275
Scottish Borders 277
Sheffield 221
South East England 106
South West England 128

W

Wales 251
Western Isles 337

Y

York 226
Yorkshire 215

Map Credits

Maps are created by BUG Backpackers Guide using data and base maps supplied by the following organisations: Ordnance Survey (Great Britain), Ordnance Survey of Northern Ireland, Ordnance Survey Ireland and Graphi-Ogre/Geo-Atlas. Public transport maps are supplied by CENTRO, GMPTE, SPT and Transport for London. Full map acknowledgements are as follows:

The following maps are reproduced from Ordnance Survey mapping on behalf of Her Majesty's Stationery Office © Crown Copyright 100043535 2004: Bayswater & Paddington (London), Camden Town & Kings Cross (London), The City & Southwark (London), Earls Court & Kensington (London), Victoria & Westminster (London), West End (London), Brighton, Canterbury, Portsmouth, Bath, Bristol, Exeter, Penzance, Plymouth, Salisbury, Birmingham, Oxford, Liverpool, Manchester, Leeds, Sheffield, York, Newcastle-upon-Tyne, Cardiff, Edinburgh, Glasgow.

The Belfast map is reproduced from the 2000 Ordnance Survey of Northern Ireland 1:12000 Belfast Street Map with the permission of the Controller of Her Majesty's Stationery Office, © Crown Copyright 2000.

The following maps are based on Ordnance Survey Ireland Permit No. 7963.
© Ordnance Survey Ireland and Government of Ireland: Dublin, Cork, Galway.

The following maps were produced using base mapping from the Geo-Atlas Europe Vector royalty-free CDROM: British Isles, England, East Anglia, South East England, South West England, Heart of England, North West England, Yorkshire, Northumbria, Wales, Scotland, Scottish Borders, Central Scotland, The Cairngorms, Highland, Isle of Skye, Western Isles, Orkney & Shetland Islands, Northern Ireland, Republic of Ireland, Leinster, Munster, Connaught, County Donegal.

Transport maps are supplied by the following organisations: Transport for London (London Underground); CENTRO (Birmingham rail network); Strathclyde Passenger Transport (Glasgow rail and subway network); GMPTE (Manchester Metrolink tram network).

The London Underground rondel symbol is used with permission of Transport for London.

Visiting Australia?

you need a copy of
BUG Australia

3rd edition

Available from bookshops or online at **www.bugbooks.com**

BUG Australia is a completely updated and revised travel guide with accurate and comprehensive information for independent budget travellers visiting Australia. It is written specifically for backpackers and has more relevant information than any other guidebook. BUG's hostel reviews feature our exclusive star rating system that makes it easy to find a great hostel at a glance.

Other 'budget' travel guides cater to everyone and include information on motels, hotels and five-star resorts, which results in a big fat guidebook with very little information for genuine budget travellers. Because we focus on information for backpackers we can give you more detailed reviews of more hostels than any other guidebook.

bugaustralia.com

the backpackers' ultimate guide

Visiting New Zealand?

you need a copy of
BUG New Zealand
2nd edition

Available from
bookshops or online
at **www.bugbooks.com**

BUG New Zealand is a completely updated and revised travel guide with accurate and comprehensive information for independent budget travellers visiting New Zealand. It is written specifically for backpackers and has more relevant information than any other guidebook. BUG's hostel reviews feature our exclusive star rating system that makes it easy to find a great hostel at a glance.

Other 'budget' travel guides cater to everyone and include information on motels, hotels and five-star resorts, which results in a big fat guidebook with very little information for genuine budget travellers. Because we focus on information for backpackers we can give you more detailed reviews of more hostels than any other guidebook.

bugpacific.com

the backpackers' ultimate guide

Visit us online

BUG's extensive network of websites is an excellent resource when planning your trip. It includes comprehensive destination specific sites for Australia *(bugaustralia.com)*, Europe *(bugeurope.com)* plus New Zealand and the Pacific *(www.bugpacific.com)* and during 2005 BUG will launch websites for Africa, Asia and the Americas.

BUG was one of the first websites to offer online hostel reviews and it is still the most useful hostel resource on the web.

BUG constantly strives to be the most comprehensive hostel guide around. BUG's online hostel reviews are better because:

- BUG is independent (it isn't affiliated with any hostel organisation; hostels can't advertise in BUG and BUG doesn't allow hostels to submit their own hostel description);

- BUG has hostel reviewers on the road checking and updating information and also writing their own reviews (which feature BUG's exclusive BUG star ratings);

- BUG only lists and reviews hostels – no hotels, B&Bs, apartments or resorts – just hostels.

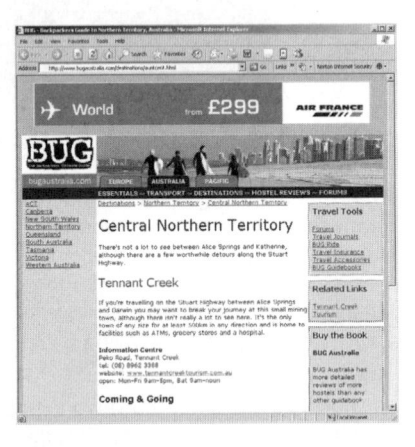

"...if you're going to backpack it, there's one site that is absolutely fantastic for all your travel needs – the Backpackers' Ultimate Guide, at www.bug.co.uk."
The Globe & Mail (Canada)

bug.co.uk

the backpackers' ultimate guide